The
New International
Lesson Annual
2004-2005

September–August

The
New International
Lesson Annual

2004–2005

September–August

Abingdon Press
Nashville

PREFACE

The 2004–2005 edition of *The New International Lesson Annual* is both firmly rooted in the tradition of the International Lesson Series *and* on the cutting edge of twenty-first-century Sunday school curriculum designed for a life-changing relationship with God through Jesus Christ. Each weekly session is designed to give you and your students the knowledge you need to integrate the truth of the scripture lesson into your own heart and life.

The lessons in this book are based on the work of the Committee on the Uniform Series of the National Council of Churches, a representative ecumenical group of writers, editors, pastors, and Christian educators who work together to develop a framework around which each session is built. Although the International Lesson Series predated the National Council of Churches by decades, this series has always been designed ecumenically by church leaders and teachers who are passionate about their own relationship with God and about sharing God's good news with others.

Although adult learners often use *The New International Lesson Annual*, it is mainly designed for teachers of adults who want a solid biblical basis for each session and a teaching plan that will help them lead their classes. The following features are especially valuable for busy teachers who want to provide in-depth Bible study experiences for their students. Each lesson includes the follow sections:

Previewing the Lesson highlights the background and lesson scripture, focus of the lesson, three goals for the learners, and supplies you will need to teach. New this year is a pronunciation guide in lessons where you may find unfamiliar words or names.

Reading the Scripture includes the scripture lesson printed in both the *New Revised Standard Version* and the *New International Version*. By printing these two highly respected translations in parallel columns, you can easily compare them for in-depth study. If your own Bible is another version, you will then have three translations to explore as you prepare each lesson.

Understanding the Scripture closely analyzes the background scripture by looking at each verse. Here you will find help in understanding concepts, ideas, places, and persons pertinent to each week's lesson.

Interpreting the Scripture looks at the lesson scripture and relates it to contemporary life.

Sharing the Scripture provides you with a detailed teaching plan. It is divided into two major sections: *Preparing to Teach* and *Leading the Class*.

In the *Preparing to Teach* section you will find a devotional reading related to the lesson for your own spiritual enrichment and a "to-do list" to prepare your mind and classroom for the session.

The *Leading the Class* portion begins with "Gather to Learn" activities to welcome the students and draw them into the lesson. Here, the students' stories and experiences are highlighted as preparation for the Bible story. The next three headings of *Leading the Class* are the three main "Goals for the Learners." The first goal always focuses on the Bible story itself. The second goal relates the Bible story to the lives of the adults in your class. The third goal prompts the students to take action on what they have learned. You will find a variety of activities under each of these goals to help the learners fulfill them. The activities are diverse in nature: listening, reading, writing, speaking, singing, drawing, interacting with others, and meditating. The lesson ends with "Continue the Journey," where you will find closing activities, preparation for the following week, and ideas for students to commit themselves to action during the week, based on what they have learned.

In addition to these weekly features, you will find:

Teacher helps, which in this volume include an article entitled "Preparing a Meaningful Sunday School Lesson," which is an overview to help you plan for your class session, and "Suggested Reference Books," which is an annotated list of specific books in several categories that will aid your own study and research.

Background articles for each quarter are designed to give you a broader scope of the materials to be covered than is possible in each weekly lesson.

Introductions to each quarter provide you a quick survey of each lesson to be studied in the quarter.

Index of Background Scriptures is offered for those of you who keep back copies of *The New International Lesson Annual* so that you can easily locate scripture passages from previous years.

Evaluation Form is located at the end of the book. Please take a few minutes at the end of the Sunday school year in August to return it to me. Your ideas are important to us, and many changes that are made occur because readers have written to suggest them.

I love to hear from our readers! If you ever have any questions or comments, please write to me and include your e-mail address and/or phone number. I will respond as soon as your message reaches my home office in Maryland.

Dr. Nan Duerling
Abingdon Press
P.O. Box 801
Nashville, TN 37202

We thank you for choosing *The New International Lesson Annual* and pray that God will work through this material, as you are guided by the Holy Spirit, to lead your students to the life-changing discipleship that Jesus yearns for in each of us. God's grace and peace be with you.

Nan Duerling, Ph.D.
Editor

CONTENTS

SECOND QUARTER

Called to Be God's People
December 5, 2004–February 27, 2005

UNIT 1: GOD CALLS A PEOPLE
(December 5-26)

UNIT 2: THE CALL OF JESUS AND HIS FOLLOWERS
(January 2-30)

UNIT 3: "WHOSOEVER WILL—COME!"
(February 6-27)

THIRD QUARTER

God's Project: Effective Christians
March 6–May 29, 2005

UNIT 1: SAVED BY GOD
(March 6-27)

UNIT 2: THE CHRISTIAN LIFE
(April 3-24)

UNIT 3: SET FREE
(May 1-29)

FOURTH QUARTER

Jesus' Life, Teachings, and Ministry
June 5–August 28, 2005

UNIT 1: JESUS' LIFE
(June 5-26)

UNIT 2: JESUS' MINISTRY OF TEACHING
(July 3-31)

UNIT 3: JESUS' MINISTRY OF COMPASSION
(August 7-28)

FIRST QUARTER
The God of Continuing Creation

SEPTEMBER 5, 2004–NOVEMBER 28, 2004

As we begin this new Sunday school year, we will explore God's creation of a people set apart for a divine purpose, God's ongoing acts of re-creation within the community of faith, and the new creation God offers in Jesus Christ. As a result of this study we will be able to recognize that God is indeed a God of continuing creation.

Unit 1, "Created for a Purpose," includes four sessions based on Genesis, Exodus, and Deuteronomy. "Discovering Our Value in God's Creation," the lesson for September 5, examines the familiar story of the creation of humanity as told in Genesis 2. In the lesson for September 12, "Beginning Again," we will look at the second chances God gives, as illustrated in the story of Noah and the Flood, found in Genesis 6:5–9:17. On September 19, we turn to the story of Moses' call in Exodus 3–4 as we study "Power for Deliverance." Deuteronomy 29:1-29 is the basis for the session on September 26 entitled "Becoming God's People," which considers God's covenantal relationship with the Israelites.

In Unit 2, "God's Creativity Continues," we will spend five weeks investigating acts of re-creation that God accomplished on behalf of Israel. These lessons are rooted in the books of 2 Samuel, the prophets Isaiah, Jeremiah, and Ezekiel, and the Psalms. On October 3, 2 Samuel 7 is the background for the lesson "Leaving a Legacy," which explores God's creation of a new dynasty through David. Isaiah 43, which we will consider on October 10 in the lesson "Re-creating Community," examines God's continuing care for the covenant community exiled in Babylon. "Creating a New Covenant," the lesson for October 17, delves into Jeremiah 29:1-14 and 31:31-34 to hear about God's promise of a new covenant. On October 24, we move in "Looking for Hope" to the familiar story of the valley of the dry bones, recorded in Ezekiel 37. Psalm 73 is the foundation for "Creating a Renewed Trust," the lesson for October 31. Here we will learn from the psalmist's experience how our trust in God can be renewed through worship.

In Unit 3, "A New Creation," we will study the Sermon on the Mount in Matthew, and Paul's teachings in 1 and 2 Corinthians and Ephesians. The unit begins on November 7 with "Living by New Rules," a study on Christian integrity grounded in Matthew 5. The theme of creation continues as we consider resurrection and the new body that Paul writes about in 1 Corinthians 15, which is our lesson for November 14, "Counting on Resurrection." "New Beginnings," the session for November 21, proclaims the good news of 2 Corinthians 5:11-21 that those who are "in Christ" are new creations. The fall quarter ends on November 28 with a study of Ephesians 2:11-21, which teaches how we as Christians are "Becoming One Family."

MEET OUR WRITER

DR. REBECCA ABTS WRIGHT

Rebecca Abts Wright is a United Methodist minister and the daughter, sister, and great niece (twice) of ministers. She received her master of divinity degree from Wesley Theological Seminary in Washington, D.C., and served parishes in West Virginia and Maryland before returning to school for a doctorate degree in Old Testament from Yale University. While in Connecticut, she was co-pastor for a five-point and then a two-point charge. She is now associate professor of Old Testament at the School of Theology, the University of the South, Sewanee, Tennessee, which is a seminary of the Episcopal Church. She delights in returning to Wesley Seminary every summer to teach in the Course of Study School. She has two daughters, Helen Kate and Anna Miriam, and one dog. Her current hobby is gardening, which seems to mean mostly trying to salvage a few vegetables from the deer and some fruit from the birds.

God's Continuing Creation

One afternoon several years ago I struck up a conversation with the young daughter of a seminary student as we were walking into the classroom building. As adults often do, I asked her how she was enjoying school. "Third grade is hard," she replied, "because we have to answer all the questions. Next year will be better, because fourth grade is mostly math and no more questions."

I wasn't sure where she had gotten such information, but I am fairly sure that by now she has realized that "all the questions" were not disposed of in third grade. She was indeed right in one respect however: sometimes dealing with questions can be hard—even harder than math!

Some issues are basic to human life and have a way of returning again and again, both within individuals and for communities and even whole populations. Who am I? Who are we? Who is God? How can we know God? What does God want for us and from us? What is life for? What are good ways of living our lives? Given the sort of world we find ourselves in, how are we supposed to relate to God and to each other?

Answers to these questions may often seem elusive. We can come to provisional conclusions at times, yet each answer frequently appears to raise a dozen more questions. It is no surprise to you that the people of God have asked these and many other similar questions over the centuries. The Bible is full of stories of questions and solutions, of humans' seeking to discern God's will and of God's yearning to be in relationship with people.

The lessons this quarter range throughout much of the Bible, giving examples of a number of ways the community of faith has dealt with some very big issues. The lessons do not avoid the deeply difficult matters of human sin and our yearning to reestablish relationships, of longing for second chances when we make a wreck of all around us. By the end of the quarter, the biblical witness and the shared conversations within the class will have suggested a variety of paths, if not to final resolutions, at least to workable directions to take.

The quarter itself is divided into three units, each devoted to a different facet of creation. These may be summarized as purpose, continuity, and renewal. Each of the lessons within the quarter is built around one of these very large questions. The biblical material is used in biblical order—that is, lesson 1 has a text from Genesis, lesson 3 from Exodus, and so on. Yet this arrangement is not meant to imply that the issues discussed in Genesis are solved before we arrive at Exodus, or that Paul's correspondence with the early Christian congregations in Corinth and Ephesus was on subjects far beyond what King David or any of the Old Testament prophets could have imagined.

We begin with creation and in a sense we never leave that subject. Unit 1, September 5 through September 26, is "Created for a Purpose." As we see in lesson 1, "Discovering Our Value in God's Creation," Genesis is absolutely clear that God is the creator, and that God created a good world out of love for that creation. As part of creation, we are valued by God. Even when people sin God never abandons creation. Time and time again humans have found it necessary to start over again. All that we need for such new beginnings is provided by God. Lesson 2, September 12, "Beginning Again," uses the story of Noah to remind us that our Lord is a God of second, and even third and fourth, chances.

There are other times when we are in bad situations that are not of our own making. Can God help then? Will God come to our aid? Lesson 3, "Power for Deliverance," on September 19 uses Exodus 3 as the starting point to discuss these matters. God knows our physical conditions. Even more does our Lord provide for those needs we have that are so much deeper than physical existence or physical deliverance. Human beings need companionship and a genuine sense of belonging. Deuteronomy 29 is discussed on September 26 in a lesson titled "Becoming God's People." One of the ways we are enabled to meet our belonging needs is by being part of the covenant community. Within the community we are both accepted and held accountable.

Although the individual weekly lessons can stand alone, they also yield a trajectory that moves from our being valued within creation to the acknowledgment of sin and God's provisions for deliverance, to the formation of community as the people of God. Because these big issues are not answered once and for all, we loop through them again in Unit 2: "God's Creativity Continues." Lesson 5 on October 3 is "Leaving a Legacy," built upon 2 Samuel 7. There is a basic human need to be needed, to be involved in a purpose greater than mere existence. We can find God's grace and purpose in our own lives, even without being King David. It is one of the paradoxes of the faith, that by losing ourselves in God's will we are enabled to find our truer selves than if we put our focus on building up our own names and legacies.

One of the familiar and disheartening threads in adult lives, in both individuals and communities, is sin. Sin may be experienced as personal failure or as disruption of our common life together. Disruptions may also be the result of forces well beyond our control. There are countless settings in which "Re-creating Community" is a goal deeply needed and deeply yearned for. On October 10, Isaiah 43 is the basis for discussion of God's joining with us in such a project. Jeremiah 29 and 31 provide the starting place for lesson 7, "Creating a New Covenant," on October 17. For all our attempts at recreating community and living into the new covenant our Lord offers us, we may yet find ourselves in situations of despair, circumstances of seeming hopelessness. "Looking for Hope" is no small matter. This is the subject of lesson 8 on October 24, grounded in Ezekiel 37.

This second unit, exploring the continuity of God's creativity, concludes on October 31 with lesson 9, "Creating a Renewed Trust." Psalm 73 is the foundation of this lesson, reminding us that praise and worship can assist us in reestablishing our relationship with God and with the rest of the community of faith. Sin is real. The negative effects of sin fall not only on the sinner, but can cut a wide swath through a community. It is not necessary to focus only on sin and its toll. Even in the midst of our lives in this fallen world worship is possible and can be life-giving.

Unit 3, "A New Creation," begins on November 7 with lesson 10, "Living by New Rules." This lesson is based on Matthew 5, a chapter that contains the first portion of Jesus' Sermon on the Mount. In the sermon Jesus makes clear both that what is new in the Incarnation does not cancel out or negate the Old Testament and that the Christian life is lived on the basis of strong personal integrity. These "new rules" stand in continuity with the "old rules" God gave to Israel.

Lesson 11, "Counting on Resurrection," on November 14 explores our understandings of human life past earthly death, based upon the apostle Paul's discussion of resurrection in 1 Corinthians 15. Lesson 12, November 21, is called "New Beginnings" and is based on Paul's discussion of reconciliation in 2 Corinthians 5. The final lesson of this quarter is on November 28, "Becoming One Family," based on Ephesians 2. These three lessons take the theme of God's creation far beyond what people can do on their own. Clearly we cannot raise ourselves from the dead and must trust God as the source of our life in the world to come. And many of us have experienced being outsiders, even outcasts, in situations where reconciliation and wholeness seem as impossible as raising the dead. God's creative spirit and activity can bring life out of seemingly dead situations in this world as well as in the next.

It may seem to you that there is a bit of repetition this quarter. For example, lesson 2 is "Beginning Again" and lesson 12 is called "New Beginnings." Yet these different lessons with similar focuses all make some important points. The biggest issues we humans face are never answered once and for all. We return to them in new circumstances and at later stages in our lives. The matters of belonging, of forgiveness, of community, of communion with our Lord remain with us through all our ages and stages. Not surprisingly at all, these are the same issues the people who inhabit the Bible faced, and by the grace and inspiration of the Holy Spirit they left some of their stories for us. The repetition, the revisiting of similar issues, is not circular however. It is not merely covering the same old ground over and over again. Rather it can be thought of as a spiral. Each time we reach the same east/west point, we are at a different elevation. You might think of this as climbing a spiral staircase toward higher understandings. Or perhaps it is like the drill bit of an oil well, churning around and around into the depths of knowledge.

Regardless of the figure of speech we might use, the affirmation of the Bible from start to finish is that the creator God has built into this good creation provision for community, both with each other and with God. Because sin, both individual and corporate, is also a feature of the world, as we know it, our gracious God has made provision for forgiveness, for reconciliation, for the reestablishment of ruptured relationships.

These can be abstract notions, hard to discuss in theoretical terms. Thankfully the Bible is anything but aridly theoretical. It is, rather, full of stories of people who seem to be an awful lot like us and like our neighbors. Nor does the Bible contain only good examples and people who always make only the right decisions. We can learn from some of the "dead ends" and other mistakes biblical people make, although we often seem determined to make our own mistakes instead of learning from those of others. When we read the stories we have a responsibility to discern the messages they have for us today—in our own vastly different time and circumstances.

All of which brings up another important issue: just how is the Bible to be used responsibly by the Body of Christ and by individual Christians? I must admit there have been times when I would prefer to have a simple answer book, one to which I could turn with every question and find a clear verse that would tell me exactly what to do in any given situation. But, we believe, this is not how the Bible functions within the church. We need to interpret what we read, praying for the guidance of the Holy Spirit, and testing our interpretations within the group. We need to listen for God in one another and encourage one another in the venture.

In a time of shifting cultural values I know that I often long for absolutes. But the church is clear in its witness that there is only one absolute and that is God. Nothing else—not church doctrine, not even an interpretation of the Bible itself—is absolute. For everything we know is filtered through our finite human consciousness and thus everything we know is subject to error, to misinterpretation, even to willful blindness. Part of the wondrous grace of God shows itself in the reality that God deals with us where we are and as we are. Our recurring issues elicit recurring input from God.

I believe that God speaks to us in all our wild diversity and particularity. And when one faith community (ancient Israel, for example, or the early church) is inspired to write of their encounters with God, and people of a faith community in a vastly different time and place (us) are inspired to read of those encounters with God, some "translation" will be necessary. By this I mean not only the move from Hebrew in the Old Testament and Greek in the New to English. I also mean matters such as cultural assumptions held then but no longer.

Take, for instance, the matter of "sunrise" and "sunset." We know, as the ancient people did not, that the sun does not actually rise up from under the earth in the morning, travel across the sky, and then go down under the earth at night. We know, as our ancestors did not, that the earth is round and rotates on its axis, which merely gives the appearance of sunrise and sunset. And yet we continue to use the words "sunrise" and "sunset" to describe what appears to our eyes to be the case, although our minds understand differently. That the biblical writers were wrong in some of what they believed to be factual does not detract in the least from the truths they proclaimed. (And as a matter of humility, we would do well to remember that generations after us will discover many of our closely held viewpoints to be wrong.)

Ancient peoples believed that slavery was acceptable; we do not. I believe God always starts with us where we are and then patiently prods and calls and pushes and cajoles and invites us to deeper understandings and more abundant life. No human community will ever get it totally right; we always have more to learn from God. Such learning can be painful when it means we have to give up one idea for another. But such learning can also be freeing and exciting as we move closer to the life we were created for, the fuller life within the Body of Christ.

A final reminder: we are not saved by our knowledge, nor by our respect for the Bible. We are saved by God's grace, made known to us most fully in the life, death, resurrection, and ascension of Jesus Christ. The creative and creating power of God manifested in the Holy Spirit inspired the biblical writers. That same creative and creating power is still at work, inspiring us as we read and study and interpret God's Word. Thanks be to God for the marvelous gift of Scripture.

SEPTEMBER 5

UNIT 1: CREATED FOR A PURPOSE

DISCOVERING OUR VALUE IN GOD'S CREATION

PREVIEWING THE LESSON

Lesson Scripture: Genesis 2:4*b*-7, 15-24
Background Scripture: Genesis 2
Key Verse: Genesis 2:7

Focus of the Lesson:
People want to feel worthwhile and special. Where can we look to validate our existence? Genesis says God created humankind out of love, and the text implies we are the pinnacle of God's creation.

Goals for the Learners:
(1) to explore an account of creation that spotlights God's care for humankind.
(2) to consider what believing that they are God's unique creation means to them.
(3) to give thanks for their relationship with the God of all creation.

Supplies:
Bibles, pictures of famous and ordinary people that you have gathered, newsprint and marker, paper and pencils, hymnals

---

READING THE SCRIPTURE

NRSV
Genesis 2:4*b*-7, 15-24

In the day that the LORD God made the earth and the heavens, 5 when no plant of the field was yet in the earth and no herb of the field had yet sprung up—for the LORD God had not caused it to rain upon the earth, and there was no one to till the ground; 6 but a stream would rise from the earth, and water the whole face of the ground—

NIV
Genesis 2:4*b*-7, 15-24

When the LORD God made the earth and the heavens—5and no shrub of the field had yet appeared on the earth and no plant of the field had yet sprung up, for the LORD God had not sent rain on the earth and there was no man to work the ground, 6but streams came up from the earth and watered the whole surface of the ground—

7 then the LORD God formed man from the dust of the ground, and breathed into his nostrils the breath of life; and the man became a living being.

15 The LORD God took the man and put him in the garden of Eden to till it and keep it. 16 And the LORD God commanded the man, "You may freely eat of every tree of the garden; 17 but of the tree of the knowledge of good and evil you shall not eat, for in the day that you eat of it you shall die."

18 Then the LORD God said, "It is not good that the man should be alone; I will make him a helper as his partner." 19 So out of the ground the LORD God formed every animal of the field and every bird of the air, and brought them to the man to see what he would call them; and whatever the man called every living creature, that was its name. 20 The man gave names to all cattle, and to the birds of the air, and to every animal of the field; but for the man there was not found a helper as his partner. 21 So the LORD God caused a deep sleep to fall upon the man, and he slept; then he took one of his ribs and closed up its place with flesh. 22 And the rib that the LORD God had taken from the man he made into a woman and brought her to the man. 23 Then the man said,

"This at last is bone of my bones
  and flesh of my flesh;
this one shall be called Woman,
  for out of Man this one was taken."
24 Therefore a man leaves his father and his mother and clings to his wife, and they become one flesh.

7the LORD God formed the man from the dust of the ground and breathed into his nostrils the breath of life, and the man became a living being.

15The LORD God took the man and put him in the Garden of Eden to work it and take care of it. 16And the LORD God commanded the man, "You are free to eat from any tree in the garden; 17but you must not eat from the tree of the knowledge of good and evil, for when you eat of it you will surely die."

18The LORD God said, "It is not good for the man to be alone. I will make a helper suitable for him."

19Now the LORD God had formed out of the ground all the beasts of the field and all the birds of the air. He brought them to the man to see what he would name them; and whatever the man called each living creature, that was its name. 20So the man gave names to all the livestock, the birds of the air and all the beasts of the field.

But for Adam no suitable helper was found. 21So the LORD God caused the man to fall into a deep sleep; and while he was sleeping, he took one of the man's ribs and closed up the place with flesh. 22Then the LORD God made a woman from the rib he had taken out of the man, and he brought her to the man.

23The man said,

"This is now bone of my bones
  and flesh of my flesh;
she shall be called 'woman,'
  for she was taken out of man."
24For this reason a man will leave his father and mother and be united to his wife, and they will become one flesh.

UNDERSTANDING THE SCRIPTURE

Introduction. Of all the familiar stories in the Bible, surely this is one of the most well known. It is also, potentially, one of the most troublesome. One reason we have dif-ficulty with it is that we read too fast; we already know what it says, so we pay scant attention to the details that are within as we read or listen to it. We also tend to bring all sorts of other things to mind when reading it, including Sunday school lessons from the past. One other main cause of trouble is that the Bible was not written originally in English and that no translation from any language into any other language can ever be completely exact. Thus, we have three tasks to keep in mind:

• read what is there.
• do not read what is not there.
• learn some of the changes that are made when translating into English.

Genesis 2:1-4a. The idea of Sabbath rest, so important to the Priestly writers, comes at the end of the creation story in chapter 1. God's rest on the seventh day serves as the model for human rest on that same day.

Genesis 2:4b-7. At the beginning of this creation account, we have a dry and dusty earth without any living things. Why? According to verse 5 there are two reasons: there is no rain and there is no farmer. Without rain plants cannot live; without a gardener a garden cannot thrive.

Hebrew has two words that are both routinely translated into English as "man." One of them means "individual male human being." The other one means "human being without specifying gender" or "human beings in general, without regard for gender." If English had a simple word for this second concept, we could eliminate a good bit of confusion, not only in this biblical text, but also in the rest of the Bible and in much of our life!

What God creates in verse 7 is a generalized human being, *ha'adam*. The writer makes a wordplay that is typical of Hebrew. We might translate the intent by saying, "the LORD God formed Dusty from the dust of the ground," or even "the LORD God picked up a clod of clay and formed Clod." It must not have been important to the writer to specify that the creature was male. (At the end of our passage, "male" and "female" do come in, using different Hebrew words.)

Shaping the creature is not enough. God also breathes "the breath of life" into its nostrils so that it becomes alive. What an intimate picture this is. God is not merely manipulating stuff, not sitting at a cosmic computer keyboard, but touching, forming, being close enough to breathe God's breath, God's spirit, into *ha'adam*.

Genesis 2:8-14. God immediately places *ha'adam* in a fertile garden, through which four rivers flow. These rivers are named Pishon (possibly located in the Arabian Peninsula), Gihon (supposedly the source of water for Jerusalem, though its connection with Arabia or Ethiopia is unclear), Tigris, and Euphrates (the latter two being well-known rivers in the Mesopotamian river valley). These four rivers supposedly feed an underground spring from which a stream arises to water the earth (2:6).

Genesis 2:15-17. Now that there is a farmer, God can have a farm. Work is specified in verse 15 and it is a gift from God to the farmer. The farmer may also eat whatever is produced, with the exception of the fruit of one tree. This tree is called "the tree of the knowledge of good and evil" in English. It would be closer to the Hebrew idiom to term it "the tree of infinite knowledge." That is, it is not a tree of moral knowledge alone, or a tree of knowing all about bad things. It is, rather, a tree of knowing *everything*. This is why the serpent in chapter 3 says that eating it will make people "like God" (3:5).

Genesis 2:18-20. Work to do and food to eat are necessary to life, and God has provided them. But God sees that that is not enough for the sort of life God wants the humans to experience. In order to avoid isolation and loneliness, God decides to make for *ha'adam* a "suitable partner" or "appropriate helper." Lest the word "helper" seem to indicate a lesser status, it is good to remember that this word is used in other books, including the Psalms, and it refers there to God—scarcely an "assistant human being."

God forms the world's menagerie and

brings the animals, one at a time, to let the first creature name them. Naming in the ancient Mediterranean world was of greater symbolic importance than it usually is for us. The one who gave a name to someone or something was thought to have power over that individual. By letting humans name the other animals, God is shown to be giving them dominion over the other creatures. Thus we are responsible for the rest of the natural order, including all plants and animals.

Genesis 2:21-24. There are many "helpful" animals but the basic problem of human loneliness has not yet been solved. So God puts *ha'adam* to sleep and takes a "side," closing up the place where it was removed. In Hebrew this is more than a "rib," closer to a "side" of beef. From this piece, God forms another creature.

Upon awakening *ha'adam* gives a joyous cry of recognition. "This is it! This one is like me! This is 'woman' because she came out of 'man.'" And now, at last, we have in verse 23 the words for individual male human being and individual female human being. It is interesting also that the man does not "name" the woman in the same way that the animals are named. That is, there is not the same sort of dominion-conferring here as with the animals—and as there will be at the end of chapter 3, when she is given the name Eve after the two of them have sinned.

But that is getting ahead of the story, for the final verse of the chapter shows us a picture of harmony and mutuality. The two of them "were both naked and were not ashamed" of each other (2:25). The appropriate "partner," the suitable "helper" has been found. There is productive work to do and plenty of food to eat. There is human society and a close relationship with God. This is the intention with which our loving Creator began.

INTERPRETING THE SCRIPTURE

Admitting the Problems Up Front

Creation stories may seem quaint and not quite respectable for twenty-first century adults to believe in. We sometimes feel awkward when challenged by a neighbor or co-worker who puts the issue in stark either/or terms: either you believe everything in the Bible just the way it is written, or you cannot believe any of it at all.

For the Bible's authors, and for the community of faith throughout generations and centuries, however, the more important issue is how to relate the content of the Scriptures to our own lives. The Bible is much more "practical" than "theoretical." It does not begin with a proof of the existence of God; it assumes God. There is nothing wrong with philosophical speculation and arguments, with asking hard questions and raising issues, as long as such activities do not take the place of our own faithful living.

If we are willing to admit that we do not have all the answers and to go on from that point, we are more likely to be open to what we do find within Scripture. Such will be the approach throughout this quarter's lessons.

The "Why?" Questions

Often the most compelling questions are those that ask "Why?" Alas, they are also often the most difficult to answer. Why was I born? Why did God create the world at all? Genesis 2 suggests two different sorts of answers to those questions. First, humans were created to take care of the world. Second, people were made in order to provide companionship for each other. Implied in the account is that in some way we were also created to provide companionship for God.

Some of the origin accounts of other ancient peoples tell of the creation of human beings by the gods specifically to be slaves, or at least servants. They were made to do the work the gods did not want to do themselves. Such is emphatically not the case in Genesis.

At some level, we must admit that we do not know why God chose to create our world. We can only affirm that God did choose to create it. That is, God was under no compulsion. We believe that the world was created by a good God and for good.

Freedom and Power

Part of the good news of this creation account is that we have been given responsibilities from the very beginning. Our place on earth is neither useless nor merely decorative. What we do *does* matter. When the power of naming the animals was given to *ha'adam*, it carried with it implicit power over them. What we do in the world does make a difference to the world. God has trusted us with this power.

The difficulty comes in when we realize that not every use of our God-given freedom and power to make a difference results in a positive difference. Many animal and plant species have become extinct in the past one hundred years because of the carelessness or greed of people. At the same time, many animal and plant species are being preserved by the actions of caring people.

Our freedom is not without boundaries. This limitation of our freedom is pointed to in the Genesis account by the prohibition against eating the fruit of one tree in the original garden. Only God can know everything. Only God is absolute.

Freedom, Power, and Love

God has given us freedom. Compared with the divine freedom, ours seems puny.

Nonetheless, we are not created as robots or puppets, incapable of independent thoughts and actions. Along with this freedom comes a certain amount of power. Again, compared with the divine power it may not seem like much. A look at the history of our last century, or just the past decade, shows that we have the power to do terrible damage both to each other and to the home God made for us. Our freedom and power are gifts of God's love and must be tempered by our own love.

"Love" is a tricky word because in English it usually refers to an emotion, but in the Bible its meaning is somewhat different. A better translation, when you see the word "love" in the Bible, would usually be "be loyal" for verb forms and "loyalty" for nouns. If we are loyal to God and to each other, we will not use our freedom and power for the exploitation of either the earth or any of its inhabitants.

God shows great loyalty to humans by, for instance, making the sun rise "on the righteous and on the unrighteous" (Matthew 5:45). That is, we do not have to be good enough to deserve the sunrise. God shows great love and loyalty to humans by entrusting the world to us.

Jesus often used the figure of speech comparing God to a parent. Parents know that infants have to be protected and cared for all the time. Human babies are not able to fend for themselves. But human parents know that babies, as they grow, need to take responsibility for more and more of their own life. It would be much less messy for the mother to feed the child, never relinquishing the spoon to those unsteady hands. But the short-term gain of a cleaner table would be offset by the long-term crippling of the child's ability to eat independently.

Similarly, the parents of growing children know that combination of pride and heart-in-the-mouth anxiety on the first day of school, the first week at summer camp, the first time taking the car for a solo drive. We set limits for our children, but we make them shifting boundaries as the children mature and learn. We both set limits and grant freedom to our children to help them grow into healthy and responsible adults.

Is it not the same way with God? God has created us for relationship and encourages us, cheering us on as we grow into our freedom and as we learn to be good stewards of our power. The ancient writers expressed this with the story of the good garden with its gardener. The human story is told not as a tale of a numberless throng, but with individuals.

SHARING THE SCRIPTURE

PREPARING TO TEACH

Preparing Our Hearts

This week's devotional reading is found in Psalm 150. Here the psalmist summons all of creation to offer joyous praise to God. Offer your own praise to God. Perhaps you will do so with music, as in this psalm. Or perhaps you will use art, motions, or words to praise God. However you choose to do so, praise God for "mighty deeds" and "surpassing greatness" as Creator, Sustainer, and Ruler.

Pray that you and your students will set aside regular times to praise God.

Preparing Our Minds

Study the background, which encompasses all of Genesis 2, and lesson scripture, which focuses on verses 2:4*b*-7 and 15-24.

Write on newsprint:

information for next week's lesson, found under "Continue the Journey."

Plan the suggested talk for "Explore an Account of Creation That Spotlights God's Care for Humankind" if you choose to lecture rather than lead a class discussion.

LEADING THE CLASS

(1) Gather to Learn

❖ Welcome the class members and introduce any guests.

❖ Pray that all who have come today will recognize that they are unique and valuable because God has created them.

❖ Show pictures of famous and ordinary people that you have collected from magazines, websites, or perhaps your own album. If the person is well known, ask the students to comment on what they have experienced of this individual's unique skills and talents. If this person is known only to you, talk about how he or she is a unique individual.

❖ Discuss with the class why they believe that God would choose to create each of us as a unique individual.

❖ Read aloud today's focus statement: **People want to feel worthwhile and special. Where can we look to validate our existence? Genesis says God created humankind out of love, and the text implies we are the pinnacle of God's creation.**

(2) Explore an Account of Creation That Spotlights God's Care for Humankind

❖ Choose a volunteer to read Genesis 2:4*b*-7 and someone else to read verses 15-24.

❖ Discuss these questions with the class, or answer them yourself in a lecture. You will find information to help with the discussion or lecture in the Understanding the Scripture portion for these verses.

(1) The writer makes clear that God had made the heavens and the earth but

had not yet caused any vegetation to come to life. Why had the vegetation not yet "sprung up"? (See verses 4b-5.)

(2) **What do we know about the creature that was formed from the dust?** (See verse 7. Note that the Hebrew *ha'adam* can be used to refer to humanity in general.)

(3) **Just as God used the dust of the ground to form *ha'adam*, so God created other animals from the dust. What conclusions would you draw from God's willingness to allow *ha'adam* to name the other animals?** (See verses 18-20.)

(4) **How are we to understand God's intentions for the relationship between *ha'adam* and a "partner" or "helper"?** (See verses 18-20. Be sure to note that the same word refers to God as a "helper" in several books, especially the Psalms. Hence, "helper" cannot be understood as one who is subservient or of lesser value.)

❖ Invite several pairs of students to role-play a conversation between the Man (the Hebrew word is *'ish*) and the Woman (the Hebrew word is *'ishshah*) as they meet one another for the first time.

❖ Brainstorm a list of provisions that God has made for *ha'adam*. The class might include ideas such as: *food, work, boundaries (command not to eat of the tree of the knowledge of good and evil), the privilege of naming the animals, and a companion who was bone of bone and flesh of flesh.* List the students' ideas on newsprint.

(3) Consider What Believing That the Learners Are God's Unique Creation Means to Them

❖ Distribute paper and pencils. Ask the students to draw a picture of themselves. Artistic ability is not important, but if that is a stumbling block for some students, suggest that they draw a symbol of a talent, personal trait, or gift they value in themselves.

❖ Suggest that the students talk with a partner or small group about what they have identified as an important characteristic. Encourage them to say how they use this characteristic for the benefit of others. Note that the students have the option of whether they will show their picture to others.

❖ Conclude this portion of the session by asking each student to affirm everyone in the group by saying, **"[Name], I affirm your (characteristic, gift, or talent) and give thanks to God for you as a unique individual."**

(4) Give Thanks for the Learners' Relationship with the God of All Creation

❖ Guide the group in writing a litany to thank God for their relationship with creation and the Creator.

■ Ask each person to name a person or part of God's creation for which they are thankful. List these ideas on newsprint.

■ Help the class to develop a response that they will read in unison, such as "We give you thanks, O God, for the diverse creation you have freely given us."

■ Assign different individuals or small groups to write a sentence about one or more items that the class has listed. Be sure each group has paper and pencils.

■ Put the litany together by asking each group to read their sentence(s) and the class to respond with the response that you have written together.

❖ Close this portion of the lesson with a time for quiet meditation. Invite the students to offer their individual prayers of praise and thanksgiving both for being God's unique creation and for being able to enjoy the diversity of all creation.

(5) Continue the Journey

❖ Pray that the class members will continue to give thanks to God, who has created them as unique individuals.

❖ Read aloud this preparation for next week's lesson. You may also want to post it on newsprint for the students to copy. Prepare for next week's session, entitled "Beginning Again," by reading Genesis 6:5–9:17. This is a lengthy passage but the story of Noah and the Flood is quite familiar. Look especially at 6:5-8; 7:1-5, 17, 23; 8:14-16; and 9:1, 16. Keep these ideas in mind as you study the lesson: When faced with the consequences of wrongdoing, most people long for a second chance. What reassurance do we have that God will let us try again? The flood story shows God's grace toward human beings and all creation.

❖ Read aloud the following three ideas. Challenge the students to commit themselves to use these activities as a springboard to spiritual growth.

(1) Take action this week to show someone else that you value him or her. A phone call to say "hello," a compliment for a job well done, an e-mail, or an invitation for lunch are just a few ways that you can let others know how important they are.

(2) Ponder the diversity of creation. Think about the numerous varieties of plants, animals, and other species. Think about several people you truly enjoy knowing. What makes each of these friends or family members unique? Give thanks to God in prayer for the great diversity that exists among all creation, especially the human family.

(3) Note that ha'adam's job, according to verse 15, is to cultivate and care for the garden. This work seems natural in an agricultural setting. What might God be saying to you about your job and its purpose? What does God's assignment of work to ha'adam suggest about the value of work?

❖ Sing or read aloud "All Creatures of Our God and King."

❖ Ask the students to echo this benediction from 2 Corinthians 13:11-14 as you read it phrase by phrase: Finally, brothers and sisters, farewell. Put things in order . . . agree with one another, live in peace; and the God of love and peace will be with you. . . . The grace of the Lord Jesus Christ, the love of God, and the communion of the Holy Spirit be with all of you. Amen.

Beginning Again

PREVIEWING THE LESSON

Lesson Scripture: Genesis 6:5-8; 7:1-5, 17, 23; 8:14-16; 9:1
Background Scripture: Genesis 6:5–9:17
Key Verse: Genesis 9:16

Focus of the Lesson:
When faced with the consequences of wrongdoing, most people long for a second chance. What reassurance do we have that God will let us try again? The flood story shows God's grace toward human beings and all creation.

Goals for the Learners:
(1) to examine the flood story and consider how the element of God's saving grace is present.
(2) to identify second chances that they have been given.
(3) to develop and implement a plan to give second chances to others.

Supplies:
Bibles, newsprint and marker, paper and pencils, hymnals

READING THE SCRIPTURE

NRSV
Genesis 6:5-8

The LORD saw that the wickedness of humankind was great in the earth, and that every inclination of the thoughts of their hearts was only evil continually. 6 And the LORD was sorry that he had made humankind on the earth, and it grieved him to his heart. 7 So the LORD said, "I will blot out from the earth the human beings I have created—people together with animals and creeping things and birds of the air, for I am sorry that I have made them." 8 But Noah found favor in the sight of the LORD.

NIV
Genesis 6:5-8

⁵The LORD saw how great man's wickedness on the earth had become, and that every inclination of the thoughts of his heart was only evil all the time. ⁶The LORD was grieved that he had made man on the earth, and his heart was filled with pain. ⁷So the LORD said, "I will wipe mankind, whom I have created, from the face of the earth—men and animals, and creatures that move along the ground, and birds of the air—for I am grieved that I have made them." ⁸But Noah found favor in the eyes of the LORD.

Genesis 7:1-5, 17, 23

Then the LORD said to Noah, "Go into the ark, you and all your household, for I have seen that you alone are righteous before me in this generation. 2 Take with you seven pairs of all clean animals, the male and its mate; and a pair of the animals that are not clean, the male and its mate; 3 and seven pairs of the birds of the air also, male and female, to keep their kind alive on the face of all the earth. 4 For in seven days I will send rain on the earth for forty days and forty nights; and every living thing that I have made I will blot out from the face of the ground." 5 And Noah did all that the LORD had commanded him.

17 The flood continued forty days on the earth; and the waters increased, and bore up the ark, and it rose high above the earth. . . . 23 He blotted out every living thing that was on the face of the ground, human beings and animals and creeping things and birds of the air; they were blotted out from the earth. Only Noah was left, and those that were with him in the ark.

Genesis 8:14-16

14 In the second month, on the twenty-seventh day of the month, the earth was dry. 15 Then God said to Noah, 16 "Go out of the ark, you and your wife, and your sons and your sons' wives with you."

Genesis 9:1, 16

God blessed Noah and his sons, and said to them, "Be fruitful and multiply, and fill the earth. . . .

16 When the bow is in the clouds, I will see it and remember the everlasting covenant between God and every living creature of all flesh that is on the earth."

Genesis 7:1-5, 17, 23

[1]The LORD then said to Noah, "Go into the ark, you and your whole family, because I have found you righteous in this generation. [2]Take with you seven of every kind of clean animal, a male and its mate, and two of every kind of unclean animal, a male and its mate, [3]and also seven of every kind of bird, male and female, to keep their various kinds alive throughout the earth. [4]Seven days from now I will send rain on the earth for forty days and forty nights, and I will wipe from the face of the earth every living creature I have made."

[5]And Noah did all that the LORD commanded him.

[17]For forty days the flood kept coming on the earth, and as the waters increased they lifted the ark high above the earth. . . . [23]Every living thing on the face of the earth was wiped out; men and animals and the creatures that move along the ground and the birds of the air were wiped from the earth. Only Noah was left, and those with him in the ark.

Genesis 8:14-16

[14]By the twenty-seventh day of the second month the earth was completely dry. [15]Then God said to Noah, [16]"Come out of the ark, you and your wife and your sons and their wives."

Genesis 9:1, 16

Then God blessed Noah and his sons, saying to them, "Be fruitful and increase in number and fill the earth. . . .

[16]Whenever the rainbow appears in the clouds, I will see it and remember the everlasting covenant between God and all living creatures of every kind on the earth."

UNDERSTANDING THE SCRIPTURE

Genesis 6:5-13. The story of Noah and the Ark is really a story for adults. It is probably because of that lovely animal parade, all the species marching two by two up the ramp, and because of the rainbow placed in the sky afterwards, that we think of it as primarily for children. Violence has increased on the earth since creation and God is distraught. The good creation is not turning out the way the Lord had hoped. Rather, the humans are spoiling what God had intended with their evil, and grieving the very heart of God. Killing each other began with Cain and Abel in Genesis 4. Soon people were reveling in vengeance, gloating about killing someone for a mere bruise and being avenged seventy-seven fold, as Lamech boasted to his wives (Genesis 4:23-24).

God determined to stop the cycle of violence by wiping out the humans along with the rest of the animals. But one man, Noah, "found favor in the sight of the LORD." Why? The text is absolutely silent on that point. We know nothing about Noah until God says that he is the only righteous man of his generation. After God has made the choice of Noah, we see that he follows God's instructions and prepares for the flood to come. Is that why he was chosen, because he followed God? That cannot be the answer because God chooses him before we see him obey in any way. And after the flood, past the bounds of today's text, Noah plants a vineyard, makes wine, and gets drunk (9:20-21). He is not a "perfect" human being in every respect. So why does God choose Noah? We are not told. All we can say is that the choice of Noah is a matter of grace, and nothing that we can figure out ourselves.

Genesis 6:14–7:24. The Lord's destruction of creation was not to be utterly complete. God saved Noah, his wife, his sons, and their wives, and along with them a representative sample of every kind of animal and bird and creeping thing. The inhabitants of the ark would repopulate the earth after God had wiped it clean.

Some of the language used in these chapters makes clear that we are to see the story of Noah in light of the creation accounts. What God does through the flood is described not just as destruction, but also as "uncreation." The Lord undoes what had been done at the beginning. The "floodgates" and the "windows of the heavens" (Genesis 7:11) that are opened represent the release of the original chaos waters from their bounds as God had fixed them in Genesis 1:9.

God's instructions to Noah are thorough and specific so that Noah, his family, and the animals could survive the coming disaster. Then, after the flood the world could be repopulated. Several times the text reports that "Noah did all that God commanded him" (Genesis 6:22, 7:5, 9, 16). We see in this the faithfulness of God and the obedience of Noah. In that cooperation was made possible a new beginning, a second chance for all of creation.

Genesis 8:1–9:7. When the ark has come to rest on dry ground after the flood, God repeats the blessing and the instructions that had been given to the animals and humans in creation: "Be fruitful and multiply, and fill the earth" (9:1; see also 9:7; 8:17; 1:28). God also goes to "Plan B" for what may be eaten. In Genesis 1 the living creatures were given all the fruits and vegetables of creation for food. Now God says that it is permissible to eat meat, as long as the blood is carefully removed first. This is because the blood represents the life, and life belongs only to God.

In biblical times "blood" is a symbol of life much more than of death. When Jesus gives the cup to his disciples at the Last Supper, and says that his blood is shed for them, he is of course alluding to his impending death. At the same time he is giving them the most powerful symbol of his *life* to them and to all of the disciples who follow after, including us.

Genesis 9:8-17. The Lord made a covenant with the whole of creation on that day, promising never again to destroy all living things from the earth. As a sign of that covenant, a reminder and promise, God put "his bow" in the sky. The reminder is for both sides of the covenant, for creation and for God. We look at the bow and remember that the Lord has promised second chances. God looks at the bow and remembers that the earth is not to be subject to divine destruction again.

Yes, the bow is what we call a rainbow, but the word has a much deeper significance. In the time this story was put together as part of the Bible, the most advanced weapons the people knew were bows and arrows. With these new weapons, one no longer had to be within arm's reach of the enemy; injuries could be inflicted from a safer distance. This is the kind of "bow" that the Hebrew word represents. This is the kind of "bow" that God puts in the sky. It is a sign of divine disarmament. God is now weaponless, the rainbow says, and will give the whole creation another chance.

The covenant God makes with Noah and with creation is unconditional. That is, the Lord does not say, "I will keep my part of the covenant as long as you are faithful to your part." In fact, there is no second part to the agreement, nothing that people have to promise to do in order for God to maintain the divine part of the agreement. Nor is the covenant only between God and humans. It is "between God and every living creature of all flesh that is on the earth" (Genesis 9:16, key verse).

INTERPRETING THE SCRIPTURE

Warnings

It has been a long day, a very long day. Nothing went right at work. You have a headache. The children are bickering in the living room as you try to prepare supper. "I'm warning you," you call out. "Behave yourselves or there's going to be trouble." The spaghetti boils over, the telephone rings, and the dog chases the cat through the kitchen. Then you hear a crash from the living room, followed by a loud wail. For a split second you think this must be what is was like for God just before the flood.

Many cultures have stories of great floods. Many religions have tales of angry gods destroying whole populations. Is the story of Noah and the Ark just another ancient folktale? Not really. God speaks to us, I believe, in ways that we can understand, because God is passionately interested in genuine communication with us. Thus, if a particular population is familiar with flood stories, God can use the framework of the flood story to teach us. The Bible has many instances of such "cultural borrowing" and in every case while the form may be similar to what is found elsewhere, the biblical content is always special.

One of the things we learn about God from this story is that the Lord does not act without giving us warnings—lots and lots of warnings. Another way to express it is that God gives us many chances. Not until virtually the whole human population had run amok did God send the deluge.

Plans

God warns Noah of the impending flood. But a warning by itself would not have been enough unless there were also instructions for what Noah was supposed to do about it. The detailed instructions God gives Noah can be seen as a sign of grace, of another chance offered to the human race through him.

How do we as a society deal with grave difficulties and with the possibility of second chances? Too often we seem to be able to give warnings and even make promises, but we omit the middle step of plans. A few years ago there was an anti-drug campaign built around the slogan "Just Say No." Now saying no to drugs—or to any other destructive habit—is a good thing. And some people may be able to maintain that "No" by warnings and threats of what will happen to them and their families if they yield or succumb. But that will not be enough for everyone. Saying no to one way of life must be accompanied by a better life to which one can say yes. There must be something positive, a goal toward which to move, as well as leaving the negative, the forbidden behind.

And for those people who are already caught by the scourge of drugs, there needs also to be a clear and possible plan for getting out once they have made that decision. It is a scandal that so many people who want to be released from their addictions have nowhere to go. Drug and alcohol treatment facilities are woefully underfunded and short-staffed, to say nothing of most of them being financially out of reach for the great majority of addicts who want to leave their addictions behind. The situation is as if God had said to Noah "You must stop your ordinary life because you need to prepare for the flood" but said nothing else. Only because God tells Noah how and what to prepare, by building the ark, can Noah and his family truly be said to have a second chance. A second chance by itself, with no help or guidance, will likely not have a different outcome from the first chance.

Promises

God promises to look at the rainbow and remember the covenant made with the whole of creation. There is a major difference between God's promises and our promises: we are not always able to keep ours. And one of the dangers of thinking of humans as being made in God's image is that we sometimes mentally reverse that, and think of God as being in our image. God is bigger and better and stronger and smarter than people are, we think, but we tend to think of God as having some of our flaws too. Since we do not always keep our promises, even when we want to, how can we be sure that God won't sometimes go back on a covenant? The hard answer is that we cannot *prove* that God's promises are unbreakable the same way we can prove that we have a quarter in our pocket or that Interstate 24 goes between Nashville and Chattanooga in Tennessee.

Proving that God keeps promises is more like proving that a triangle has three sides. The three-sidedness of triangles is not something that has to be proved, because it is part of the very definition of triangles. If there are more or fewer than three sides, the figure cannot be a triangle. Similarly, if a covenant is broken or a promise not kept, then our covenant partner is not the one, true, living God of the Bible who is involved. It is part of God's very being to offer saving grace and second chances. Part of our lives as children of God, created in the image of God, is to offer second chances to those around us, and to be willing to use those second chances we need from others.

But What If?

There's a line in a familiar song that says, "It won't be water, but fire next time." Some people read the account of Noah and agree that the Bible says the Lord will not overwhelm the world with water again. But, they say, since Genesis 9 does not say anything about any other means of destruction, God is perfectly able to send fire or anything else, just so long as it is not another flood. I don't think that God participates in this sort of legalism. I once had a parishioner who, when his wife died, was sure that it was his fault. As he explained it to me, every night he had prayed that God would keep their three grown children safe. But since he and his wife lived together and did nearly everything together, he never thought to pray that God would keep her safe. If only he had prayed daily for her too, he was sure, she would not have died.

But it really was not his fault. God's promises do not depend on us. A scary part of all this is that God's promises do not control human behavior. The Lord will not destroy the world again. This is not the same thing as saying that God will intervene to make sure we do not destroy ourselves, whether by war, pollution, global

warming, or some as yet unimagined folly.

The flood does not signal God's ultimate giving up on creation. Despite the destruction, the un-creation that is in the forecast, God makes plans to start over again. Once again the Lord is willing to give humans partial responsibility for the outcome. This is great good news and simultaneously great responsibility.

The harried parent we began with may suggest the children take the dog out for a walk before supper so that by the time the meal is ready the whole family can sit down together in restored peace. It is by giving and receiving new chances in our life together that we are enabled to live out God's gracious covenant love.

SHARING THE SCRIPTURE

PREPARING TO TEACH

Preparing Our Hearts

This week's devotional reading is found in Genesis 9:8-17, which is part of today's background scripture. What do you think about when you see a rainbow? Is it for you a sign of God's continuing grace and covenant? Notice that God makes the covenant not only with humankind but also with "every living creature of all flesh that is on the earth" (9:16). What does this covenant and its sign, the rainbow, tell you about God? What do you believe about a possible destruction of the earth in the future? Do you believe that is God's will? What understanding of the nature of God informs your response?

Pray that you and your students will recognize God's gracious willingness to allow us to begin again when we have fallen short of the mark.

Preparing Our Minds

· Study the background passage from Genesis 6:5–9:17, and lesson scripture from

Genesis 6:5-8; 7:1-5, 17, 23; 8:14-16; 9:1. Genesis 9:16 is the key verse. Be sure to allot sufficient time to read and explore this long passage. Try to read this familiar story with "fresh eyes," looking for new insights.

Write on newsprint:
    information for next week's lesson, found under "Continue the Journey."

Plan to talk in the Gather to Learn portion about an individual who has been given a second chance. You may need to do some research on the Internet or media to find a suitable example.

Practice reading aloud today's scripture lesson. You may want to mark your Bible so as to move seamlessly from one portion of the passage to another.

LEADING THE CLASS

(1) Gather to Learn

❖ Welcome the class members and introduce any guests.
❖ Pray that the students will listen to

and appreciate God's message for them this day.

❖ Tell the story of someone who has been given a second chance, perhaps after an arrest, indiscretion, life-threatening illness, or divorce. Do not use an example that members of the class would likely know, unless it is a public figure. What happened? Why was this person given a second chance? How did he or she use that chance?

❖ Read aloud today's focus statement: **When faced with the consequences of wrongdoing, most people long for a second chance. What reassurance do we have that God will let us try again? The flood story shows God's grace toward human beings and all creation.**

(2) Examine the Flood Story and Consider How the Element of God's Saving Grace Is Present

❖ Invite the class to retell the story of Noah and the Flood as they remember it. Encourage volunteers to each add one or two points to the story.

❖ Read aloud Genesis chapter 6, verses 5-8; chapter 7, verses 1-5, 17, and 23; chapter 8, verses 14-16; and chapter 9, verses 1 and 16 (key verse) to focus on the particular parts of the story we will be exploring.

❖ Discuss the following questions.

(1) **What does this story say to you about humankind?**

(2) **What does this story say to you about the nature of God?**

(3) **Where do you perceive God's grace in this story?**

❖ Distribute paper and pencils. Ask the students to imagine themselves as Noah as the rain begins to beat down. What would you want to say to God?

❖ Choose several volunteers to read or tell their ideas.

(3) Identify Second Chances That the Learners Have Been Given

❖ Encourage the students to tell a small

group about an incident from childhood or adolescence that enraged a parent or other significant adult in their life. What happened? How did the significant adult react? What prompted the adult to give them a second chance?

❖ Ask the class to state words or phrases that describe how it feels to be given a second chance. List these ideas on newsprint.

❖ Provide quiet time for the adults to reflect on second chances that God has given them. Suggest that they close their eyes and experience the same kinds of feelings that they recall from childhood when a significant adult offered a second chance.

❖ Ask the learners to continue their reflection by asking God to give them a second chance they need now in their lives.

❖ Conclude this portion of the lesson with these words: **O Lord, hear our prayers.**

(4) Develop and Implement a Plan to Give Second Chances to Others

❖ Read aloud this case study and ask the students to respond as if they were the pastor: **Margie had been a hardworking volunteer in the church for decades. She heard through the grapevine that a committee coworker, Ellen, had been complaining to others that Margie had been slacking off and doing a poor job. Margie was furious. She told the pastor that she was quitting her job on the evangelism committee and was unwilling to work on any other committees. Suppose you had been Margie's pastor. What would you say to her about offering Ellen a second chance? What would you as the pastor say to Ellen?**

❖ Distribute paper and pencils, if the students do not already have them. Ask them to follow these steps to develop and implement a plan to give a second chance to someone. Read the steps aloud, pausing after each one to allow the students to write.

■ **Step 1: Write the name of someone who needs a second chance from you.**

- Step 2: Write the reason for this need.
- Step 3: Write whatever you would be willing to do to give this person a second chance in order to mend a broken relationship.
- Step 4: Write this statement: I commit myself, with God's help, to take this action by next Sunday. I will reach out, but I realize I have no control over how the other person responds. I pray that God will open [Name's] heart to me so that we may begin anew together.

(5) Continue the Journey

❖ Pray that the class members will use the plans they have created to reach out to others and give them an opportunity to begin anew.

❖ Read aloud this preparation for next week's lesson. You may also want to post it on newsprint for the students to copy. **Prepare for next week's session entitled "Power for Deliverance" by reading background scripture from Exodus 3–4 and focusing on Exodus 3:1-12, which is the familiar passage of God's call to Moses. As you study the lesson, consider these ideas: Everyone likes to get out of a bad situation. What can we do when such escapes seem beyond our power? The Exodus story** shows that God can and will deliver those who cannot save themselves.

❖ Read aloud the following three ideas. Challenge the students to commit themselves to use these activities as a springboard to spiritual growth.

(1) Pray silently, or write a prayer in your spiritual journal, thanking God for a second chance you have recently been given.
(2) Offer someone else a second chance.
(3) Ponder this question: Are there any circumstances under which you could not offer someone else a second chance? Are there any circumstances under which God will not offer someone a second chance? If there is a disparity between what God is willing to offer and what you are willing to do, what changes do you need to make?

❖ Sing or read aloud "This Is a Day of New Beginnings."

❖ Ask the students to echo this benediction from 2 Corinthians 13:11-14 as you read it phrase by phrase: **Finally, brothers and sisters, farewell. Put things in order . . . agree with one another, live in peace; and the God of love and peace will be with you. . . . The grace of the Lord Jesus Christ, the love of God, and the communion of the Holy Spirit be with all of you. Amen.**

POWER FOR DELIVERANCE

PREVIEWING THE LESSON

Lesson Scripture: Exodus 3:1-12
Background Scripture: Exodus 3–4
Key Verse: Exodus 3:10

Focus of the Lesson:
Everyone likes to get out of a bad situation. What can we do when such escapes seem beyond our power? The Exodus story shows that God can and will deliver those who cannot save themselves.

Goals for the Learners:
(1) to explore God's call to Moses to deliver the Hebrews from slavery in Egypt.
(2) to recall and give thanks for God's deliverance of them from difficult circumstances.
(3) to identify and implement ways to act as God's deliverers for others.

Pronunciation Guide:

Amorites	(am' uh ryts)	Jebusites	(jeb' yoo syts)
Canaanites	(kay' nuh nyts)	Jethro	(jeth' roh)
Hittites	(hit' tyts)	Midian	(mid' ee uhn)
Hivites	(hiv' yts)	Perizzites	(per' i zyts)
Horeb	(hor' eb)	theophany	(thee of' un nee)

(Note: Where you see a "y" in the last syllable, think of "i" sound, as in "sky.")

Supplies:
Bibles, newsprint and marker, paper and pencils, hymnals

READING THE SCRIPTURE

NRSV
Exodus 3:1-12

Moses was keeping the flock of his father-in-law Jethro, the priest of Midian; he led his flock beyond the wilderness, and came to Horeb, the mountain of God. 2 There the angel of the LORD appeared to him in a flame

NIV
Exodus 3:1-12

Now Moses was tending the flock of Jethro his father-in-law, the priest of Midian, and he led the flock to the far side of the desert and came to Horeb, the mountain of God. ²There the angel of the LORD appeared of fire out of a bush; he looked, and the bush was blazing, yet it was not consumed. 3 Then Moses said, "I must turn aside and look at this great sight, and see why the bush is not burned up." 4 When the LORD saw that he had turned aside to see, God called to him out of the bush, "Moses, Moses!" And he said, "Here I am." 5 Then he said, "Come no closer! Remove the sandals from your feet, for the place on which you are standing is holy ground." 6 He said further, "I am the God of your father, the God of Abraham, the God of Isaac, and the God of Jacob." And Moses hid his face, for he was afraid to look at God.

7 Then the LORD said, "I have observed the misery of my people who are in Egypt; I have heard their cry on account of their taskmasters. Indeed, I know their sufferings, 8 and I have come down to deliver them from the Egyptians, and to bring them up out of that land to a good and broad land, a land flowing with milk and honey, to the country of the Canaanites, the Hittites, the Amorites, the Perizzites, the Hivites, and the Jebusites. 9 The cry of the Israelites has now come to me; I have also seen how the Egyptians oppress them. **10 So come, I will send you to Pharaoh to bring my people, the Israelites, out of Egypt."** 11 But Moses said to God, "Who am I that I should go to Pharaoh, and bring the Israelites out of Egypt?" 12 He said, "I will be with you; and this shall be the sign for you that it is I who sent you: when you have brought the people out of Egypt, you shall worship God on this mountain."

to him in flames of fire from within a bush. Moses saw that though the bush was on fire it did not burn up. ³So Moses thought, "I will go over and see this strange sight—why the bush does not burn up."

⁴When the LORD saw that he had gone over to look, God called to him from within the bush, "Moses! Moses!"

And Moses said, "Here I am."

⁵"Do not come any closer," God said. "Take off your sandals, for the place where you are standing is holy ground." ⁶Then he said, "I am the God of your father, the God of Abraham, the God of Isaac and the God of Jacob." At this, Moses hid his face, because he was afraid to look at God.

⁷The LORD said, "I have indeed seen the misery of my people in Egypt. I have heard them crying out because of their slave drivers, and I am concerned about their suffering. ⁸So I have come down to rescue them from the hand of the Egyptians and to bring them up out of that land into a good and spacious land, a land flowing with milk and honey—the home of the Canaanites, Hittites, Amorites, Perizzites, Hivites and Jebusites. ⁹And now the cry of the Israelites has reached me, and I have seen the way the Egyptians are oppressing them. **¹⁰So now, go. I am sending you to Pharaoh to bring my people the Israelites out of Egypt."**

¹¹But Moses said to God, "Who am I, that I should go to Pharaoh and bring the Israelites out of Egypt?"

¹²And God said, "I will be with you. And this will be the sign to you that it is I who have sent you: When you have brought the people out of Egypt, you will worship God on this mountain."

UNDERSTANDING THE SCRIPTURE

Introduction. Today's Scripture text is the call of Moses. It follows a form biblical scholars have named the "prophetic call narrative." Just as we think "fairy tale," when we hear a story that starts out "Once upon a time," early readers and hearers of this account would automatically recognize that Moses was being called by God to be a prophet. In biblical terms, a prophet is *not* someone who gazes into a crystal ball and predicts the future. Rather, a prophet is an individual called by God for a specific purpose. Most of the prophets we are familiar with were called to speak for God to the community, to remind the people of God's presence and care, and of the community's responsibilities to each other and to the Lord.

This literary form, the prophetic call narrative, has five parts, which will be discussed in relation to this story:

- setting
- theophany
- task
- objection
- answer

Exodus 3:1-4. The *setting* is usually brief, just a statement of the conditions into which God will speak. In our case here the setting includes the last two and a half verses of Exodus 2: "The Israelites were groaning under their bondage and cried out; and their cry for help from their slavery rose up to God. God heard their moaning and God remembered his covenant with Abraham, Isaac, and Jacob; God saw the Israelites and God knew" (author's translation). When God is the subject of the verbs "to hear," "to remember," "to see," or "to know," early Bible readers expected God to act very soon. And yet the next verse turns to Moses who is tending sheep, "out in the middle of nowhere." Once again it seems that God chooses to act not independently, but alongside human beings.

The next portion of the literary form is the *theophany*. A theophany is a manifestation, an appearance of God or some sort of messenger of God. In this case that role is filled by the burning bush. The sight was unusual and caught Moses' attention. How could a bush be on fire and yet not be burning up? Notice too that as soon as the bush has Moses' attention, it drops out of the story. The point of this account is not the miracle of a nonconsumed bush, but rather

the conversation between Moses and God. It does not matter that one verse says the angel of the Lord appeared and another speaks of both God and the Lord. When trying to describe a unique experience, our words will always fail at least to some extent.

Exodus 3:5-12. God's first command is that Moses must remove his sandals because the ground is holy. Surely Moses' sandals will not get the ground dirty, will they? Hardly. The point here is a cultural matter that is opaque to us, because our culture is different from that of the Bible. In that time and place slaves went barefooted and free people wore sandals. By standing barefoot on that ground, Moses is acknowledging that in God's presence he is not in charge. Moses is not more than a servant or slave to God. (Another example of this may be seen in Jesus' parable in Luke 15: when the wandering son comes home, ready to be a servant in his father's household, the father calls for sandals for his son's feet. Everyone who sees the returned boy will know that he has been received back as a free member of the family and not as a slave.)

God then tells Moses that the plight of the Israelites in their Egyptian bondage has been observed. God has come down to free them. This sounds like wonderful news, until verse 10: "I will send you to Pharaoh to bring my people, the Israelites, out of Egypt." This is the *task* to which Moses is being called.

Moses *objects* immediately. It might sound as if he is merely being polite. "Oh, no, I'm not good enough for this job." Or maybe he responds in a voice of panic: "Why me?" Remember that Moses is in Midian precisely because he had run away from Egypt: Pharaoh wanted to kill him for striking, and killing, an Egyptian overseer.

God then answers Moses with the first and greatest promise: "I will be with you." There is no easy assurance: "Don't worry. I will make sure you have a simple time of it;

it will not be hard at all. All the Israelites will work together and the Egyptians will cooperate too and send you on your way. You will be universally revered and followed." No, the promise of God is that of the Lord's presence, nothing more—and nothing less either.

Exodus 3:3–4:17. For the rest of chapter 3 and into Exodus 4 Moses raises more *objections*. He really, really doesn't want to accept this job! God is patient, listens to each complaint, and continues to assure Moses of the divine presence. The job will not be easy; Moses certainly cannot do it on his own. But Moses does not have to do it alone. God will be with him, and with all Israel.

God makes some important assertions in these verses. First, what happens on earth does not go unnoticed or uncared for. The Israelites are enslaved in Egypt. There is no way they can get themselves out of their bondage. All they can do is cry out, and God hears and responds to their cries. Second,

God assures Moses that there is continuity with the past: this is no new God, but the God of Abraham, Isaac, and Jacob. God will do new things, will act in new situations, but is always the same God. Finally, even in those situations that seem hopeless to us, God asks for our participation. The parts that are impossible for us, the Lord will indeed do. But God does not act in a vacuum; God asks for our cooperation. Once again we see how much God trusts us and believes in us, that we are given a portion of responsibility to act in accordance with the divine will.

Exodus 4:18-31. Moses' actions indicate that he has *answered* his prophetic call. He gathers up his wife and sons and returns to Egypt, meeting Aaron along the way. They take the news of God's call and promise to the Israelites. Upon being told that God is going to save them, all the people worship the Lord.

INTERPRETING THE SCRIPTURE

What a Mess!

It seems so easy to get in over our heads. There may be someone in your group who is old enough to remember Laurel and Hardy movies and the refrain Ollie would say—often while bopping Stan over the head—"Well, this is another fine mess you've gotten us into." We can watch old slapstick comedies for entertainment because we know that regardless of how much trouble the players get themselves into, there will always be a way out by the end of the movie.

"Real life" doesn't always feel that way. We ask ourselves how did we get here? And more to the point: Is there any way out? Sometimes our predicament is of our own making. Other times we do everything as we are supposed to and still have troubles.

Our car has been reliable for many years now. Still, when driving my older daughter to college one August the engine suddenly stopped. We were on an eight-lane Interstate highway at the time; it was terrifying to be in traffic and all of a sudden lose all power. Not even the hazard lights would blink. We sat there in the second lane with a feeling of utter and complete helplessness.

What a Surprise!

God knows our plight. God cares about our plight.

Because there had been an accident up ahead of us, the traffic on the highway was moving only about 30 miles an hour instead of the usual 70 when our car stopped. I got out and raised the hood. Before much time had passed a tow truck driver, who had been called for the nearby accident, came along and pushed us to the shoulder of the road. We were safe. Was that man an angel? No, he was a man doing his job who was also willing to help out in a situation that was not his job. About an hour later a highway patrol officer gave us a jumpstart and we made it to a nearby service station where the problem was diagnosed as a dead alternator. I had not paid much attention to the erratic speedometer that afternoon, but learned that it can be a symptom of alternator trouble.

This is a mundane example. But it may illustrate some points. I am a careful driver and I try to take good care of my car. Still, I was suddenly in a dangerous situation that I did not know how to fix by myself. Help came, though not all at once. A great deal of time and some extra expense were required before the episode was at an end. But at the end, all was well.

Looking around at the horrors of the world it may appear that God is nowhere to be found. But looking with different eyes may give us some hope as we observe ordinary people helping each other in routine matters. With the eyes of faith we may recognize God's presence in such neighbors, just as Moses was made aware of God in a most personal way while tending sheep.

What a Job!

We are not always eager to hear that God wants our cooperation. It would be so much easier just to sit back and let God take care of everything. We would be happy to sit on the sidelines and cheer God on, of course, but we would rather not be in the middle of the struggle. Yet here is another way in which God honors us, in that we do have actual freedom and responsibility. God works with us, but at the same time depends on us to do the things that we are capable of doing. God even expects us to learn from our mistakes. And so, when the speedometer needle began jumping wildly

a few days after my return home, I took the car immediately to the mechanic instead of continuing on my errands. And thus I was not stranded—or worse—when it turned out that the new alternator was faulty. (I promise: you will not have to read any more about my car!)

The first time people cut down all the trees from a hillside and experienced a flood the following spring, it could be said to have been an honest mistake. But once we see that clear-cut hillsides tend to lead to flooding then we, not the Lord, are responsible if we keep on cutting all the trees. God will do the "God parts" to deliver us; God does not do our parts for us.

Few people are called by God to be Moses figures. Most of us live on a smaller, less grand, scale. This in no way means that we are not also called to play our part in deliverances, whether large or small. Mentoring a child through Big Brothers/Big Sisters or driving one day each week for Meals on Wheels takes more effort than writing a check to those organizations, just as going back to Egypt was harder for Moses than continuing to tend sheep in Midian. Many kinds of deliverance need human participation. The Meals on Wheels program, for instance, delivers much more than nourishing food: for many of the clients it also delivers them from spirit-bruising loneliness and lack of companionship.

We may be more comfortable seeing ourselves primarily in the "Moses" position, as cooperating with God to help someone else's plight. Can we also see ourselves in the "Israelite" position, being in deep trouble from which we can see no immediate way out?

Yes Moses heard and followed God's call. But note carefully what went before: the enslaved Israelites called out to God from their bondage. They had not given up all hope; they were willing to cry out to the Lord. What stops us from admitting our fears and needs to God?

Deliverance has two sides and we may be surprised to discover that as we do what seems our puny effort for a large cause, God is simultaneously delivering us from our own private bondages. How often do people return from mission trips, for example, proclaiming that they received so much more than they gave!

What a Promise!

God's initial promise to called individuals and God's eternal promise to all of creation is that of presence. God will be with us. This was the promise to the Patriarchs (Genesis 26:3, 24; 28:15; 31:3), to Moses and Joshua (Exodus 3:12; 4:12, 15, Deuteronomy 31:23; Joshua 1:5; 3:7), to King Solomon (1 Kings 11:38), and through prophets to all Israel (Isaiah 41:10; 43:2, 5; Jeremiah 30:11; 42:11; 46:28; Haggai 1:13). This is the same word of promise that Jesus speaks at the end of Matthew's Gospel (28:20). Life may be full of troubles, but God will never abandon us. In the Lord's presence and with the Lord's guidance *we* have the possibility of overcoming every burden and bondage.

SHARING THE SCRIPTURE

PREPARING TO TEACH

Preparing Our Hearts

This week's devotional reading is found in Exodus 3:13-17, which is part of our background reading and immediately follows today's lesson scripture. Here is the familiar story of God, in response to Moses' question, telling him the divine name: YHWH. This name appears as "Lord" in the NRSV and other translations. Notice that this name is a verb: "I am" or "I will be who I am." Although the name tells us nothing about the essence of God, it does prompt us to ask what God will be. As we continue to read the story of God's interaction with humankind, we learn that God is a liberator, healer, and covenant maker, among many other things.

Pray that you and your students will recognize and give thanks for God's presence and power to deliver them from different situations.

Preparing Our Minds

Study the background from chapters 3 and 4 of Exodus, and the lesson scripture from Exodus 3:1-12. Again this week we have a familiar passage. Try to read with "fresh eyes" to see what new revelations God has for you.

Write on newsprint:

this sentence stem, which will be used in the portion entitled "Identify and Implement Ways to Act As God's Deliverers for Others": To answer God's call to deliver the oppressed, I commit myself to. . . .

information for next week's lesson, found under "Continue the Journey."

Plan a lecture as suggested in "Explore God's Call to Moses to Deliver the Hebrews from Slavery in Egypt."

Check with your pastor and/or the chair of your missions/outreach committee to see what your church is doing to assist oppressed peoples around the world.

LEADING THE CLASS

(1) Gather to Learn

❖ Welcome the class members and introduce any guests.

❖ Pray that the students will open their hearts to the possibility that God is calling them to act as a liberator for someone in a difficult or oppressive situation.

❖ Encourage the students to name historical characters who have acted as liberators. Perhaps several students know the stories well enough to talk about one or more of these persons. If you prefer to lecture, select at least one such person and give a brief synopsis of his or her work and the changes that came about as a result of it. Here are some persons to consider: *Mahatma Gandhi, Martin Luther King, Jr., Cyrus the Great, Mother Teresa*, and *Deborah* (Judges 4–5).

❖ Read aloud today's focus statement: **Everyone likes to get out of a bad situation. What can we do when such escapes seem beyond our power? The Exodus story shows that God can and will deliver those who cannot save themselves.**

(2) Explore God's Call to Moses to Deliver the Hebrews from Slavery in Egypt

❖ Give an introductory lecture in which you use the Understanding the Scripture portion to explain the parts of the prophetic call narrative. These five parts are included in the background scripture, but note that the students will not see all of them in today's lesson scripture.

❖ Choose volunteers to read Exodus 3:1-12 as a drama. Assign students to read the parts to a narrator, Moses, and God. Ask the entire class to read "Moses, Moses!" in verse 4.

❖ Ask several pairs of students to role-play a conversation between Moses and God, beginning with God's call from the burning bush. Since the story continues with Moses finding many excuses for not wanting to answer this call, suggest that the "Moses" actor(s) create their own contemporary excuses.

❖ Conclude this portion of the lesson by discussing ways in which we try to avoid God's call and reasons we agree (sometimes after long haggling!) to obey God.

(3) Recall and Give Thanks for God's Deliverance of the Learners from Difficult Circumstances

❖ Point out that although most people in the class likely have not been oppressed as

the Hebrews were, we all face situations that prompt us to cry out to God to save, rescue, liberate, or deliver us. The Bible promises us that God will be with us. (If time permits, you may want to look at some of the passages noted in "What a Promise!" in the Interpreting the Scripture section.)

❖ Distribute paper and pencils. Ask the students to write a psalm of praise to God for delivering them from difficult circumstances. Some students may prefer to write a letter of thanks to God. Students who are in the midst of difficult circumstances may want to write a psalm or letter seeking God's help.

❖ Invite volunteers to read their psalm or letter to the class.

(4) Identify and Implement Ways to Act As God's Deliverers for Others

❖ Encourage the students to name groups of people who are oppressed in the world today. List these groups on newsprint. Invite students to state: *who these groups are, where they live,* and *why they are oppressed.*

❖ Review the list. Encourage the students to suggest ways that they as individual Christians, and as part of your congregation, could reach out to these people. List their ideas on newsprint. Add any ideas that your pastor or mission/outreach committee chairperson shared with you as to how your church is aiding those who are oppressed. Here are some ideas you might want to explore:

- Support a Christian missionary in an oppressed region.
- Send financial aid through a church agency, such as UMCOR (United Methodist Committee on Relief), or a reputable nonprofit organization.
- Learn how the policies of your country are affecting these people. Write to government officials to raise your concerns and push for public policy that will assist those who are oppressed.

- Pray for people in the group(s) you have identified.
- See if there are ways you can provide hands-on support. Perhaps your church or denomination has a missions organization (such as Volunteers in Mission) through which you could use your skills to assist others.

❖ Help the class make a commitment to act.

- Suggest that everyone study the list and select at least one item for action, or choose another item that is not listed. (Be certain that "pray" is an option on the list, since all Christians, regardless of their skills or economic circumstances, can offer intercessory prayer.)
- Form a circle, or several circles if the group is large.
- Post newsprint on which you have written words of commitment. Tell the group that you will go around the circle clockwise and give each person an opportunity to state what he or she is willing to do.
- Say these words of commitment **"To answer God's call to deliver the oppressed, I commit myself to. . ."** and complete the sentence with whatever you are willing to do.

(5) Continue the Journey

❖ Remain in the circle and pray that the class members will trust in God to deliver all people from difficult situations.

❖ Read aloud this preparation for next week's lesson. You may also want to post it on newsprint for the students to copy. **Prepare for next week's session entitled**

"Becoming God's People" by reading Deuteronomy 29:1-29. Look especially at verses 2-15. As you study, consider these ideas: Most people want to be part of a community. Where can we find the relationships that we seek? The passage shows that God calls us into covenant community, giving us both acceptance and responsibility.

❖ Read aloud the following three ideas. Challenge the students to commit themselves to use these activities as a springboard to spiritual growth.

(1) Ponder this question: From what difficult situations do you need deliverance? Pour your heart out to God in prayer. Keep in mind that although God acts on your behalf, God's solution to the problem and the divine timetable for solving it may bear no resemblance to your solution or time frame.

(2) Offer prayers, financial support, political advocacy, or whatever action you can take to help free the world's oppressed people.

(3) Talk with someone who is in a difficult situation about God's power to liberate. Assist that person in whatever ways are appropriate.

❖ Sing or read aloud "Go Down, Moses."

❖ Ask the students to echo this benediction from 2 Corinthians 13:11-14 as you read it phrase by phrase: **Finally, brothers and sisters, farewell. Put things in order . . . agree with one another, live in peace; and the God of love and peace will be with you. . . . The grace of the Lord Jesus Christ, the love of God, and the communion of the Holy Spirit be with all of you. Amen.**

BECOMING GOD'S PEOPLE

PREVIEWING THE LESSON

Lesson Scripture: Deuteronomy 29:2-15
Background Scripture: Deuteronomy 29:1-29
Key Verses: Deuteronomy 29:12a-13a

Focus of the Lesson:
Most people want to be part of a community. Where can we find the relationships that we seek? The passage shows that God calls us into covenant community, giving us both acceptance and responsibility.

Goals for the Learners:
(1) to investigate ways that God's grace was revealed to the Israelites.
(2) to consider the impact that membership in God's covenant community has on their lives.
(3) to invite others to experience the Christian community.

Pronunciation Guide:

Bashan	(bay' shun)	Og	(og)
Gadites	(gad' yts)	Reubenites	(roo' bi nyts)
Heshbon	(hesh'bon)	Sihon	(sy' hon)
Manasseh	(muh nas' uh)		

(Note that "y" sounds as an "i," such as in "sky.")

Supplies:
Bibles, newsprint and marker, paper and pencils, hymnals

READING THE SCRIPTURE

NRSV
Deuteronomy 29:2-15

2 Moses summoned all Israel and said to them: You have seen all that the LORD did before your eyes in the land of Egypt, to Pharaoh and to all his servants and to all his land, 3 the great trials that your eyes saw, the signs, and those great wonders. 4 But to this

NIV
Deuteronomy 29:2-15

²Moses summoned all the Israelites and said to them:

Your eyes have seen all that the LORD did in Egypt to Pharaoh, to all his officials and to all his land. ³With your own eyes you saw those great trials, those miraculous signs day the LORD has not given you a mind to understand, or eyes to see, or ears to hear. 5 I have led you forty years in the wilderness. The clothes on your back have not worn out, and the sandals on your feet have not worn out; 6 you have not eaten bread, and you have not drunk wine or strong drink—so that you may know that I am the LORD your God. 7 When you came to this place, King Sihon of Heshbon and King Og of Bashan came out against us for battle, but we defeated them. 8 We took their land and gave it as an inheritance to the Reubenites, the Gadites, and the half-tribe of Manasseh. 9 Therefore diligently observe the words of this covenant, in order that you may succeed in everything that you do.

10 You stand assembled today, all of you, before the LORD your God—the leaders of your tribes, your elders, and your officials, all the men of Israel, 11 your children, your women, and the aliens who are in your camp, both those who cut your wood and those who draw your water—**12 to enter into the covenant of the LORD your God,** sworn by an oath, which the LORD your God is making with you today; **13 in order that he may establish you today as his people,** and that he may be your God, as he promised you and as he swore to your ancestors, to Abraham, to Isaac, and to Jacob. 14 I am making this covenant, sworn by an oath, not only with you who stand here with us today before the LORD our God, 15 but also with those who are not here with us today.

and great wonders. [4]But to this day the LORD has not given you a mind that understands or eyes that see or ears that hear. [5]During the forty years that I led you through the desert, your clothes did not wear out, nor did the sandals on your feet. [6]You ate no bread and drank no wine or other fermented drink. I did this so that you might know that I am the LORD your God.

[7]When you reached this place, Sihon king of Heshbon and Og king of Bashan came out to fight against us, but we defeated them. [8]We took their land and gave it as an inheritance to the Reubenites, the Gadites and the half-tribe of Manasseh.

[9]Carefully follow the terms of this covenant, so that you may prosper in everything you do. [10]All of you are standing today in the presence of the LORD your God—your leaders and chief men, your elders and officials, and all the other men of Israel, [11]together with your children and your wives, and the aliens living in your camps who chop your wood and carry your water. [12]**You are standing here in order to enter into a covenant with the LORD your God,** a covenant the LORD is making with you this day and sealing with an oath, [13]**to confirm you this day as his people,** that he may be your God as he promised you and as he swore to your fathers, Abraham, Isaac and Jacob. [14]I am making this covenant, with its oath, not only with you [15]who are standing here with us today in the presence of the LORD our God but also with those who are not here today.

UNDERSTANDING THE SCRIPTURE

Introduction. "Covenant" is a word with numerous meanings. In church settings we often use it to mean some sort of agreement that is stronger than ordinary. It also may have negative connotations, as in "restrictive covenants" in some real estate transactions. In biblical terms, covenant is used most often for special agreements between God and the people. For the form of these agreements, Israel borrowed from a treaty form that was in use in surrounding cultures. But it was only the *form* that Israel borrowed; the *content* was substantially different in several important ways.

In secular covenants, the weaker party had to make promises to the stronger. There were two basic promises. First was a pledge of absolute loyalty. The weaker party, typically after losing in battle to the one requiring the covenant, had to promise neither to give nor to seek military aid with any other people. Second, the payment of tribute was required, whether in the form of grain and other foods, slaves, or money. These covenants, or treaties, often began with the recital of the great deeds of the conquering party and ended with the threat that if all the stipulations were not carried out in their entirety, the conquerors would return and totally annihilate those who broke the covenant.

The majority of the book of Deuteronomy is presented as a sort of farewell sermon by Moses to all Israel, shortly before his death. These are not the same people who were adults when they were freed from Egypt, but rather the next generation. You may remember that the first generation had not been willing to heed God's commands and so were forced to wander in the wilderness for forty years until that generation died out. Now it is almost time to enter into the promised land, and Moses recites their history to them, reminding them of all God has done on their behalf and reminding them also of what they have promised to God.

Deuteronomy 29:1-13. Some of the parallels between the Canaanite treaties and what we find in Deuteronomy are easy to see. Moses reminds the Israelites of God's mighty acts on their behalf, beginning forty years ago in the land of Egypt. When Israel was enslaved to Pharoah, God acted to free them from their bondage. What Israel could not do for themselves, God did for them. Since having left Egypt, and for all the years in the wilderness, God has continued to provide for them. Not only has the Lord given them manna to eat, even their clothing and shoes have not worn out. When other tribes came out against them for war, God saved Israel.

Just as at Mount Sinai (referred to as Horeb in verse 1) when God spoke to all the people and offered them a covenant, so now also are all the people included. The Lord does not limit important matters to the priests or the elders. Rather, all the men and the women and the children and even the foreigners are to be included. God also makes it clear that it is not the current generation alone, but all who are to follow after, who are to be considered among the people of the covenant.

Deuteronomy 29:14-29. The major requirement on Israel's part is absolute loyalty. They are to serve the Lord and only the Lord. There is no argument presented as to whether or not any other gods actually exist. Regardless of their existence, for Israel there is to be only one God, only one recipient of worship and ultimate loyalty. Moses reminds the people that they have indeed seen idols worshiped by other nations. Some have been made of wood or stone; others are magnificent creations of silver and gold. Nevertheless, the command is absolute: Israel is to worship the Lord and no other gods.

Moses warns against trying to have it both ways: trying to remain within the covenant while secretly turning to other gods. That is a sure path to ruin and destruction he asserts. If Israel thinks that they can add any gods, they will find themselves under the curses enumerated earlier, in Deuteronomy 27, among other texts.

The parents of those standing before Moses had entered into the covenant with the Lord at Mount Sinai (Mount Horeb). God has fed them daily with manna, reminding them day in and day out of the divine faithfulness and care. They must now decide for themselves whether or not they will accept their places within the covenant community. It is not gender or age, bloodlines or place of birth that makes one a member of the community. What is required is the choice, the decision, to accept what God is offering to them. God's faithfulness has been apparent.

Alas, the faithlessness of the people has also been apparent. But the Lord has not given up on them. As long as the people will follow God, God will be delighted to maintain relationship with them. Even when they have turned aside, worshiping a golden calf while still at Mount Sinai (see Exodus 32) or being tempted to enter in to some of the religious practices of other cultures they have come in contact with during their wilderness wanderings, God has punished them. But God has never abandoned them.

Today Moses puts the choice before them once again. Choose God and life within the covenant community. Or turn to other gods, who are not really gods at all, and live under the Lord's anger and curse.

INTERPRETING THE SCRIPTURE

Where We Were

Memory is important to people both as individuals and as members of groups. Memory and identity are closely tied together. For the community of faith, memory and identity are rooted in our remembrance of what God has done for us. Within Israel this memory always looks back to the time of slavery in Egypt and the glorious freedom God granted them under the leadership of Moses. The Christian church continues the theme of memory every time the Lord's Supper is celebrated and we hear the minister repeat Jesus' instructions to his disciples: "Do this in remembrance of me" (Luke 22:19; 1 Corinthians 11:24-25).

This healthy memory is neither a yearning for the "good old days" for those whose memories are happy nor a wallowing in self-pity for those whose remembrances are painful. The focus of our remembering is not so much on us as on what the Lord has done for us, and thus it helps us keep in mind who is God and who is not God. That is, memory helps us not to forget that it is by God's grace and not our own skill or power or cleverness that we are now who we are.

Some of us have come from terrible situations. Some grew up in abusive households. Others have emigrated from war ravaged or deeply impoverished lands. Still others may have spent time sunk far down into addictions or catastrophic illness. Much of our character may have been formed by events that happened to us and by people whom we did not choose. We feel damaged, left out, and perhaps not worthy of a place in the community of God's people.

On the other hand, there are many folks who grew up with cheerful childhoods, attentive parents, and robust church families. We have vigorous health and each day unfolds before us as a new joy. We can empathize with people who have come through troubled pasts, but we have not experienced such hardships ourselves. As others did not choose their difficult situations, neither are we to congratulate ourselves for having arranged to live through relatively easier circumstances.

As with individuals, so it is with congregations. Some have been beset by struggles for sufficient funds or enough people in areas of declining population. Others have known the disruption of squabbles or worse among the membership. Many, of course, are vibrant congregations of all sizes that celebrate being part of the Body of Christ.

Where We Are

Whether difficult or serene, our past has had much to do with the people and groups we are now. Most of us can place ourselves in imagination on the plains of Moab with

Moses and the freed Israelites. We are between: we have been redeemed by God's grace from our past and are looking ahead to a closer future with our Lord.

Community is one of the great gifts God offers us. We are truly not created to live in complete isolation (Genesis 2:18). One of the most spectacular aspects of the living God is that the Lord wants to be in communion with us, both with the entire community and with each of us as individuals. It is the gracious activity of God that offers us the possibility of living in community.

Such community life needs a certain structure, a certain number of rules and regulations if we humans are to live up to our created capabilities. If everyone wants to be on the cleanup crew and no one is willing to cook, the dinner is in trouble. The tricky part is not to substitute the rules for the true undergirding of the community, which is God's grace. We do not "earn" our way in; we accept our way in. Moses reminds the people over and over again what they have witnessed God doing for them. God has acted; now it is their turn to act, by pledging themselves to fidelity to this gracious God and by renouncing all other gods. It is a decision that has to be made numerous times, for some of us even daily or more often. It is a decision which we, as members of the community, can assist and support others in making.

Warnings of Where We Might Be

God's promises do not come without warnings. The blessings for living as part of the covenant are coupled with curses for turning one's back on God and the community.

We are no different from Israel in that we are tempted by what we see around us. We have no plans to give up God; we simply want to add some of what we observe around us. If I worship God on Sunday, what is so bad about chasing material success on other days? After all, I have to live in

the real world, don't I? Part of the Christian message, going back to its roots within the Jewish faith community, is that God is Lord of the entire world. Try as we might to split life into a "sacred" and a "secular" dimension God is still God of all. Our membership within this group means that nothing in our lives is outside the reach of God's concern and care. It means also that no person is ever totally excluded; all have the option of being members, if they choose to accept the offered grace of God.

Where We Can Be

Religious people are sometimes scoffed at for being unrealistic or utopian in their outlook. As long as religion is private, some say, it is all right, but religious beliefs and ideas should not be taken into the public arena. And yet, Moses never tells the people that the instructions he has received from God are a matter of their private lives only. Quite the contrary. The blessings offered to the community are corporate as well as individual.

Notice the inclusiveness of not only verse 2 and its reference to "all Israel," but the spelling out of those assembled in verses 10 and 11: "the leaders . . . elders . . . officials . . . children . . . women and . . . the aliens." This is the community from God's vantage point in that it is inclusive of everyone who is physically present. The point is not that all are automatically members whether they are interested or not, but that all are given the opportunity to choose for themselves whether or not they wish to join.

This radical inclusiveness, this radical hospitality, is another way of describing what Jesus called the "kingdom of God" or "kingdom of heaven." It is the goal toward which God both invites us and pushes us. When we have experienced the unbounded acceptance of God as it is lived out with our fellow pilgrims we take on the responsibility of inviting others into the group with us. In hearing others' stories and reciting our own we catch glimpses of the remarkable diversity of God's grace.

God's people are not those who are perfect, nor those who are better than everyone else. God's people are those who remember what God has done for them and who want others to join them in that same gracious freedom.

SHARING THE SCRIPTURE

PREPARING TO TEACH

Preparing Our Hearts

This week's devotional reading is found in Deuteronomy 30:15-20. In this sermon attributed to Moses, he calls upon the people to choose between several opposites:
- obeying or disobeying God.
- prosperity or adversity.
- life or death.
- blessings or curses.

Moses is adamant in admonishing the people not to worship the gods of other cultures. To disobey God by failing to worship God alone results in adversity, death, and curses.

We can easily step back from Moses' warning, assuming that we do not worship idols made of stone or wood or precious metals. But do we worship the gods of money, or power, or status? If so, Moses would tell us that we are disobeying God just as surely as the Hebrew people who might worship idols in the promised land. We do have a choice, however. God has set the boundaries, given us clear choices, and warned us of the consequences. Life-giving obedience to God or death-dealing disobedience: which do you choose?

Pray that you and your students will choose to obey God, despite the obstacles our society places in our path.

Preparing Our Minds

Study the background, Deuteronomy 29:1-29, and lesson scripture, Deuteronomy 29:2-15.

Write on newsprint:
information for next week's lesson, found under "Continue the Journey."

Locate your denomination's membership vows. You will likely find them in your church hymnal. If you are uncertain, ask your pastor in advance for this information. If these vows are not in the hymnal you use in class, be sure to write them on newsprint.

Plan a lecture for "Investigate Ways That God's Grace Was Revealed to the Israelites" if you do not choose to do a discussion.

LEADING THE CLASS

(1) Gather to Learn

❖ Welcome the class members and introduce any guests.

❖ Pray that the students will be receptive to God's word for them today.

❖ Brainstorm responses to this question: **Why do people long to be part of a group or community?** Write the students' ideas on newsprint.

❖ Ask the group to discern which of these reasons express a universal human need (for example, the need to belong and be accepted), and which point toward specific motivations to join a certain organization (for example, the need to be with the "right" group of people).

❖ Read aloud today's focus statement: **Most people want to be part of a community. Where can we find the relationships that we seek? The passage shows that God calls us into covenant community, giving us both acceptance and responsibility.**

(2) Investigate Ways That God's Grace Was Revealed to the Israelites

❖ Read Deuteronomy 29:2-15 yourself as if you are Moses speaking to the people.

❖ Discuss these investigative questions with the group, or plan a lecture that answers them.

(1) Who was present?

(2) What was the occasion?

(3) Where is this scene set?

(4) When is the action occurring?

(5) How has God treated the people, according to Moses?

(6) Why is Moses reviewing and renewing the covenant?

❖ Distribute paper and pencils. Ask the students to work in small teams to write about what God has done for and with their community of faith. How has God been gracious to this church? (See Deuteronomy 29:2-9 for ideas as to how God was gracious to the Israelites.)

❖ Invite the groups to report on their ideas.

(3) Consider the Impact That Membership in God's Covenant Community Has on the Learners' Lives

❖ Distribute hymnals or post newsprint on which you have written your denomination's membership vows. (If you are United Methodist, you will find these vows on pages 45-49, in *The United Methodist Hymnal.* Note especially the top of page 48.)

❖ Point out the context for reception into the church. This service may be connected to baptism, for it is in baptism that we become part of the covenantal Christian community of faith. It may also be connected to confirmation, for in that ritual we likely make our first public profession of faith in Jesus Christ.

❖ Read aloud the actual vows that members profess when they join your church.

❖ Do this silent meditation with the class.

■ Try to imagine yourself saying these vows for the first time. What did they mean to you then? (pause)

■ How have you tried to live out these vows as a faithful member of Christ's holy church? (pause)

■ Which of these vows do you feel you need help in fulfilling? Ask God now to give you power and guidance to remain faithful to this covenant. (pause)

■ How has your membership in God's covenant community had an impact on your life? Perhaps you can more easily answer that question if you also consider what your life might be like without Christ's church. (pause)

■ Open your eyes when you are ready.

❖ Invite volunteers to talk about any insights they gleaned during the silent meditation.

❖ Conclude this portion of the lesson by asking the students to read in unison the membership vows. Suggest that they consider this reading a renewal of their covenant vows.

(4) Invite Others to Experience the Christian Community

❖ Read again Deuteronomy 29:14-15.

❖ Note that since "all Israel" had been summoned, according to verse 2, this covenant renewal ceremony includes not only the present generation but also the past and future ones. Clearly, God intends for others to be invited into the faith community.

❖ Talk about why the students have chosen to be part of this community of faith by asking these questions and writing answers on newsprint.

(1) What attracted you to join or visit this congregation?

(2) Which of those attractions still exist for you?

(3) What new attractions have been added?

(4) What most excites you about this congregation right now?

❖ Divide the class into groups of four each. Ask that one of the students role-play a scene inviting a second student to experience the community of faith within your specific congregation. The "Christian" should speak about Christ and how he can be found in the people and programs of your congregation. The one being invited should feel free to ask questions and make comments. The other two students in each group are to act as silent observers. After the role-play, the observers will comment on the effectiveness of the exchange between the "Christian" and one being invited. The two observers should become the actors, and the actors now assume the role of the observers.

❖ Suggest that the students use the skills they have just sharpened to invite at least one person to join them in worship and Sunday school next week.

(5) Continue the Journey

❖ Pray that all who bear the name of Christ will live as God's obedient people.

❖ Read aloud this preparation for next week's lesson. You may also want to post it on newsprint for the students to copy. **Prepare for next week's session entitled "Leaving a Legacy" by reading 2 Samuel 7. Our lesson will explore verses 18-29. As you read, keep these ideas in mind: Most people would like to do something important enough that they will be remembered. What role does God's grace and purpose have in what we accomplish? In David's case, God promised to establish his heirs and throne forever.**

❖ Read aloud the following three ideas. Challenge the students to commit themselves to use these activities as a springboard to spiritual growth.

(1) Ponder all the "communities" you belong to: your church, neighborhood, work, clubs, and family. Why do you choose to belong? What kinds of ties bind you to these groups? What covenants—written or unwritten—do you have with the people in each group?

(2) Create a timeline on which you write words or draw symbols that call to mind something that God has done for you. Start with birth (you may have been baptized when you were just a few weeks old) and recall rituals or occasions when you felt especially close to God.

(3) Review the vows you made when you joined a church. What promises did you make? How faithful have you been to those promises? What help do you need to ask for from God to live more faithfully in accordance with these covenantal promises?

❖ Sing or read aloud "Blest Be the Tie That Binds."

❖ Ask the students to echo this benediction from 2 Corinthians 13:11-14 as you read it phrase by phrase: **Finally, brothers and sisters, farewell. Put things in order . . . agree with one another, live in peace; and the God of love and peace will be with you. . . . The grace of the Lord Jesus Christ, the love of God, and the communion of the Holy Spirit be with all of you. Amen.**

UNIT 2: GOD'S CREATIVITY CONTINUES
LEAVING A LEGACY

PREVIEWING THE LESSON

Lesson Scripture: 2 Samuel 7:18-29
Background Scripture: 2 Samuel 7
Key Verse: 2 Samuel 7:16

Focus of the Lesson:
Most people would like to do something important enough that they will be remembered. What role does God's grace and purpose have in what we accomplish? In David's case, God promised to establish his heirs and throne forever.

Goals for the Learners:
(1) to explore God's covenant with David and its significance for both Israelites and Christians.
(2) to claim ways that God has worked through them to build up the covenant community.
(3) to identify and take at least one action to leave a legacy for the faith community.

Pronunciation Guide:
Davidic   (duh vid' ik)

Supplies:
Bibles, newsprint and marker, paper and pencils, hymnals

READING THE SCRIPTURE

NRSV
2 Samuel 7:16, 18-29

16 Your house and your kingdom shall be made sure forever before me; your throne shall be established forever.

¹⁸ Then King David went in and sat before the LORD, and said, "Who am I, O Lord GOD, and what is my house, that you have brought me thus far? 19 And yet this was a small thing in your eyes, O Lord GOD; you have

NIV
2 Samuel 7:16, 18-29

¹⁶'Your house and your kingdom will endure forever before me; your throne will be established forever.'"

¹⁸Then King David went in and sat before the LORD, and he said:

"Who am I, O Sovereign LORD, and what is my family, that you have brought me this far? ¹⁹And as if this were not enough in your spoken also of your servant's house for a great while to come. May this be instruction for the people, O Lord GOD! 20 And what more can David say to you? For you know your servant, O Lord GOD! 21 Because of your promise, and according to your own heart, you have wrought all this greatness, so that your servant may know it. 22 Therefore you are great, O LORD God; for there is no one like you, and there is no God besides you, according to all that we have heard with our ears. 23 Who is like your people, like Israel? Is there another nation on earth whose God went to redeem it as a people, and to make a name for himself, doing great and awesome things for them, by driving out before his people nations and their gods? 24 And you established your people Israel for yourself to be your people forever; and you, O LORD, became their God. 25 And now, O LORD God, as for the word that you have spoken concerning your servant and concerning his house, confirm it forever; do as you have promised. 26 Thus your name will be magnified forever in the saying, 'The LORD of hosts is God over Israel'; and the house of your servant David will be established before you. 27 For you, O LORD of hosts, the God of Israel, have made this revelation to your servant, saying, 'I will build you a house'; therefore your servant has found courage to pray this prayer to you. 28 And now, O Lord GOD, you are God, and your words are true, and you have promised this good thing to your servant; 29 now therefore may it please you to bless the house of your servant, so that it may continue forever before you; for you, O Lord GOD, have spoken, and with your blessing shall the house of your servant be blessed forever."

sight, O Sovereign LORD, you have also spoken about the future of the house of your servant. Is this your usual way of dealing with man, O Sovereign LORD?

[20]"What more can David say to you? For you know your servant, O Sovereign LORD. [21]For the sake of your word and according to your will, you have done this great thing and made it known to your servant.

[22]"How great you are, O Sovereign LORD! There is no one like you, and there is no God but you, as we have heard with our own ears. [23]And who is like your people Israel—the one nation on earth that God went out to redeem as a people for himself, and to make a name for himself, and to perform great and awesome wonders by driving out nations and their gods from before your people, whom you redeemed from Egypt? [24]You have established your people Israel as your very own forever, and you, O LORD, have become their God.

[25]"And now, LORD God, keep forever the promise you have made concerning your servant and his house. Do as you promised, [26]so that your name will be great forever. Then men will say, 'The LORD Almighty is God over Israel!' And the house of your servant David will be established before you.

[27]"O LORD Almighty, God of Israel, you have revealed this to your servant, saying, 'I will build a house for you.' So your servant has found courage to offer you this prayer. [28]O Sovereign LORD, you are God! Your words are trustworthy, and you have promised these good things to your servant. [29]Now be pleased to bless the house of your servant, that it may continue forever in your sight; for you, O Sovereign LORD, have spoken, and with your blessing the house of your servant will be blessed forever."

UNDERSTANDING THE SCRIPTURE

Introduction. Much has happened since Israel entered the promised land. As with other groups of human beings, there have been times of faithfulness and times of sin. God has kept all the promises made to their ancestors Abraham, Isaac, and Jacob. They have become a great nation and have their own land. They have been ruled by judges, who are individuals raised up by God in times of crisis. They have not had a continuing centralized government, but rely on God to provide the kind of leader they need at the time they need it.

Even when the Israelites decided they wanted to be like all the other nations and have a human king, instead of having only the Lord as king, God was willing to give them what they asked. The first experiment with human kingship did not seem to work very well with the reluctant Saul. God tries again, however, with David and the experiment appears to be going much better.

2 Samuel 7:1-3. David has won many military victories. The city of Jerusalem has been captured and has become Israel's capital city. David decides one day to build a temple for the Lord. Until now the Ark of the Covenant, which serves as the visual reminder of the presence of God, has been kept in the tent of meeting. At first the prophet Nathan gives David the go-ahead for this project.

2 Samuel 7:4-17. Then God speaks to Nathan in a dream and sends a different message for the king. Basically, the Lord says that a fancy house for God is not necessary. Then, in a play-on-words, God says that instead of David's building a house for the Lord, the Lord will build a house for David. The "House of David" will be an everlasting succession of descendants, one of whom will always be on the throne in Jerusalem. As an apparent concession to the human need to have visible symbols, however, God agrees that David's son after him will be allowed to build a temple.

2 Samuel 7:18-29. King David responds with a psalm of praise and thanksgiving to God. He repeats some of the basic history of Israel and of God's gracious dealings with the people and with David himself. Then David asks for God's blessing on his house. Which house: the temple or the succession of his descendants on the throne? I think that just as God made a play on the word "house," so does David. The king is asking both that the temple to be built by Solomon will last and that David's memory and lineage will be blessed forever.

In the subsequent history of Israel, David is remembered as the greatest of all their kings. Under King David, the country reached its greatest geographical size. Under King David, the country enjoyed relative prosperity and relative security from border skirmishes by would-be encroaching neighbors. Taxation of the general population was also relatively low, since the royal upkeep could be met by King David's conquest of new territories and new peoples. It would not have been surprising for the people to look back, from times of troubles, to a "Golden Age" under David, even if there had not been the Davidic covenant.

But there was a Davidic covenant. For many generations the Davidic dynasty continued on the throne in Jerusalem. When, after the death of King Solomon, the northern ten tribes split and formed the nation of Israel, the two remaining tribes comprising the Southern Kingdom of Judah kept the Davidic dynasty going. For close to four hundred years, a descendant of David ruled in Jerusalem. There was never such an unbroken continuity in the Northern Kingdom. The nation of Judah took all this to mean that God was being faithful to the covenant made with David.

However, as we will see in subsequent lessons, the religious and political situations in Judah did change. For one thing, many of the religious leaders came to see the Davidic covenant as a one-sided guarantee from the Lord that required nothing on their part. "Because God made a promise to King David," they seemed to say, "it does not matter how we live. God is faithful. God will always protect us." Of course God is faithful. But God desires a faithful relationship with the entire community, not lip service combined with selfishness and greed and with exploitation of the weaker members of society for the benefit of the strongest.

Despite repeated calls to repentance from a succession of prophets, despite warnings that putting reliance in military might and military alliances with the "super power" nations was inevitably leading them toward disaster, Judah increasingly turned away from God. And finally the disaster arrived, in the form of the Babylonian army. From 586 B.C. there was no Jewish state, no independent political entity descended from Israel and Judah. During the Exile in Babylon, the people yearned to go back home, to be gathered together again under a king who was a descendant of David.

Never again was Israel or Judah a nation as they had been. Even when King Cyrus of Persia allowed the exiles to begin returning home in 538 B.C., it was not the sort of kingdom it had been in David's day. The longing for a new Davidic king was strong and continuing. This longing gathered other meanings as well. The people asked God to send them someone who could take away their distress, who could restore them to their former glory. Remembering David, they prayed for a "son of David." Such a title meant more than biological descent. In their idiom, "son of X" can also mean someone who has characteristics of X. Thus, the people were not interested only or even primarily in the family tree of their new leader. They wanted someone who would be *like* David.

Since kings were traditionally anointed, people began to speak of their hope in terms of an "Anointed One." Taking the Hebrew word "anointed" and putting it into our alphabet gives us "messiah." When Christians speak of Jesus as the Messiah, we are calling upon a millennia-long hope for one sent by God to lead us back to the ways of God. Both titles Christians use for Jesus, "Son of David" and "Messiah," reflect this ancient memory of God's relationship with King David and the promises made to him and his descendants.

INTERPRETING THE SCRIPTURE

Pride and Humility

Our culture has an ambivalent relationship with pride. We have heard the saying that "Pride goes before a fall," and still we react to our child's success with "I'm so proud of you!" Is it a bad thing to take pride in our accomplishments or to want to be remembered?

Eighty-some years ago a man was born in a rural area. He grew up and moved away and made both a name for himself and a great fortune. He decided to "give back" something to his home county so he bought some hilltop land, overlooking the little town in the valley in which he was born. He had a large library built on the bluff and named it after himself. It is lit by floodlights after dark and can be seen from miles around. This library is a most imposing structure. The major road from the library on the bluff to his hometown has been renamed in his honor. The building was intended to be a research library, but it stands empty of books because the plan is that they will not be installed until after his death. There is a statue of the man in front of the building.

The local citizens also know that this man changed his citizenship to a foreign country so that he would not have to pay income taxes in the United States. The construction of his library building employed many local folks for a few years. But now those jobs are gone. His name lives on, but not in as helpful a way as it might have done.

Humility is as problematic for us as pride. When I hear of humility I think of the character Uriah Heep in Charles Dickens' novel *David Copperfield*. He is an oily character, flattering in the extreme, and not the sort I enjoy being around. He is certainly not someone I want to take as a role model.

How do we find the appropriate balance of proper pride and genuine humility? Much comes, I believe, from remembering all God has done for us that we could not possibly have done for ourselves. I do not believe it is wrong to be happy about—to take pride in—things we do, especially if we view our accomplishments as a cooperative venture of several kinds. That is, most of what we do involves our own efforts and also grows out of what has gone before us. Even if we work by ourselves, countless "anonymous" people in our community support us (those who keep the electricity and the water flowing, for instance), and all of us are upheld by God's grace.

Memory

No one wants to be forgotten. Oh, I'd be pleased for some of the mistakes I have made, some of the sins I have committed, to be wiped from everyone's memory. But I do not want everyone who has known me to forget me as soon as I have died. It is within memory that I find the sort of legacy I would like to leave. I remember both of my grandmothers, for example. They were exceedingly different women—at least as I remember them—and yet I want to be like them both. In a way I use them, and other

people I have known, as templates for my own life.

Similarly, when Israel looked for an example of what they needed, they asked God for a king who resembled their memory of David. When Jesus instituted the Lord's Supper, he said that our eating and drinking should be done in memory of him. This kind of memory involves putting ourselves into the story from the past and using it as guide for our present and future.

Immortality

A quip is attributed to the comedian and filmmaker Woody Allen: I do not want to achieve immortality through my work; I want to achieve immortality by not dying. Part of the Christian hope is that God provides a new life for us—in some entirely unknown and unexplainable way—when our life on earth is over. Still, we want to believe that our life is not without meaning and purpose here. For the Christian, I believe, the sort of immortality that comes with having one's name on a bridge or a stadium, a park or a school, is not wrong but neither is it necessary.

Legacy

Like it or not, some of my genes will live on after me in my daughters, and in any children they have, and their descendants, and on and on as long as the lines continue. But bits of biological data are not what I think of when I consider my legacy. What of my words? As long as any copy of this *New International Lesson Annual* still exists, then I suppose my words live on. But this is not quite what I have in mind either.

Both of my grandmothers, like the majority of women of their generation, did all sorts of needlework. They sewed clothes and made quilts; they did embroidery and hooked rugs. My mother is a sewer and a quilter and she saved remnants from baby clothes she made for me to make into a quilt for my first daughter's birth. When my daughters both wanted to knit scarves this past winter, I was delighted to think that some of their great-grandmothers' legacy was being reanimated in yet another generation.

I had an elderly parishioner once who told me, eyes twinkling all the while, that she used to wish people would say, "Here comes Mary. Now we'll get a lot of work done." Instead, she reported they said, "Here comes Mary. Now we'll have lots of fun." That wasn't such a bad thing to be known for, she decided, because the fun made the work go more easily.

David was a king and so his legacy would be kingly. Public people have public lives and leave public remembrances. Those of us who are nonfamous and nonpublic leave things behind us that are just as

enduring. The work God gives us to do, the people with whom we share our lives, the memories of those who have gone before us, are the raw materials with which we construct what we leave.

David's legacy was, in part, his sons and their sons and their sons throughout the generations. This should not lead us to think, however, that descendants are the primary way to be remembered. After all, Jesus has no legacy of that sort since he did not have children. And yet, in part because of the grace of God in the lives of ordinary people, we are able to be part of the church.

Where do you sense God's grace and purpose at work in your life? Look at the members of your Sunday school group, and don't forget to include yourself. Being together for each other is a good starting place for exploring that question.

SHARING THE SCRIPTURE

PREPARING TO TEACH

Preparing Our Hearts

This week's devotional reading is found in 2 Samuel 7:10-17, which immediately precedes our lesson scripture. Here the prophet Nathan speaks to David about the covenant that God is making with him to establish "a house," meaning here "a dynasty." David's descendants will sit on the throne forever. From the Bible we learn that after the fall of Jerusalem in 586 B.C. no Israelite king ruled in Jerusalem. However, Christians believe the promise of this covenant has been fulfilled in Jesus—the Messiah, Son of David—who reigns forever and ever. How do you understand the connection between Jesus and David?

Pray that you and your students will listen for the voice of God speaking to you, perhaps through a prophet, prayer, meditation, sermon, or another way.

Preparing Our Minds

Study the background scripture for today, 2 Samuel 7, and lesson scripture, 2 Samuel 7:18-29.

You may also want to read Matthew 1:1-17 to see the emphasis Matthew puts on Jesus' relationship with David in the birth story. Luke 2:1-14 also accents this relationship. Matthew 22:41-46 shows Jesus talking with the Pharisees about David's Son.

Write on newsprint:

information for next week's lesson, found under "Continue the Journey."

Plan any lectures that you will use.

LEADING THE CLASS

(1) Gather to Learn

❖ Welcome the class members and introduce any guests.

❖ Pray that the students will consider

the legacy they are leaving, even as they consider the legacy that King David left.

❖ Invite the students to tell stories of legacies they have received from a loved one. Such legacies may include a cherished possession, but they are also likely to include skills that have been learned from the loved one, memories of time spent together, mannerisms, favorite sayings, or other intangible things for which the individual may want to be remembered.

❖ Read aloud today's focus statement: **Most people would like to do something important enough that they will be remembered. What role does God's grace and purpose have in what we accomplish? In David's case, God promised to establish his heirs and throne forever.**

(2) Explore God's Covenant with David and Its Significance for Both Israelites and Christians

❖ Note that according to our background scripture in 2 Samuel 7:1-17, God created a covenant with David. Through the prophet Nathan, God promises David that there will be a place for the people of Israel, that enemies shall not afflict them, and that David's descendants will rule on his throne forever.

❖ Select a volunteer to read 2 Samuel 7:18-29, which is the prayer David offers in response to the announcement of God's covenant.

❖ Label three sheets of newsprint, using one heading for each: *David, God, God's Relationship with the Israelites.* Ask these three questions and fill in the students' responses on the appropriate sheet.

(1) **What does this prayer tell you about David?**

(2) **What does this prayer tell you about God?**

(3) **What does this prayer say about God's relationship with the Israelites?**

❖ Read, retell, or create a lecture from the information under "2 Samuel 7:18-29" in

Understanding the Scripture to help the students understand why God's covenant with David is significant for both Israelites and Christians.

❖ Explore David's legacy by assigning three teams to read (1) Matthew 1:1-17, (2) Luke 2:1-14, and (3) Matthew 22:41-46 and answer this question for their assigned passage: **What does this passage tell you about the relationship between David and Jesus?**

❖ Ask the teams to report their findings to the class.

(3) Claim Ways God Has Worked Through the Learners to Build Up the Covenant Community

❖ Point out that in today's passage we see God working through David, and promising to work through his descendants, in order to build up the covenant community. As Christians, we believe this promise was ultimately fulfilled in Jesus, who came ushering in the reign of God.

❖ Choose one of the following options to help the adults identify ways they too are building up the community.

■ **Option 1:** Ask the learners to recall people who are pillars of their current or a previous congregation. Such people show in word and deed that they are devoted to God. Discuss these questions:

(1) **How has this special person built up the faith community?**

(2) **How would you describe the legacy that you have inherited from this person?**

(3) **How has this special person's legacy empowered you to build up the faith community?**

■ **Option 2:** Invite each student to tell the class (or partner or small group if the class is large) one thing he or she has done to help build up the church. The answers may include a specific project or committee the person is involved in, action the person takes outside of the church to invite others in, prayers for the church, efforts to make others feel welcomed. Close this activity by thanking the students for claiming their contributions to the covenant community.

(4) Identify and Take at Least One Action to Leave a Legacy for the Faith Community

❖ Distribute paper and pencils. Encourage the students to write a brief obituary, or epitaph that they would want to be remembered by on their tombstone. Ask the students to think about whether or not they are doing what they need to do, or being who they need to be, in order for this obituary or epitaph to be an accurate reflection of their lives.

❖ Invite the students to tell the class or a small group what they have written. Students may be able to affirm each other's desire to be remembered. Simply saying "That really sounds like you," or "How wonderful! I didn't realize you did such and such" are ways of offering affirmation.

❖ Conclude this section by asking the students to think about one step they can take this week to live up to the way they hope to be remembered. Suggest that they write this commitment for action on their paper.

(5) Continue the Journey

❖ Pray that the students will find ways to leave a spiritual legacy to future generations.

❖ Read aloud this preparation for next week's lesson. You may also want to post it on newsprint for the students to copy. **Prepare for next week's session entitled "Re-creating Community" by reading Isaiah 43. Our lesson will examine verses 1-2, 10-13, and 18-19. As you get ready for this lesson, keep these ideas in mind: People often long for a sense of security and hope. Where can we find this? Isaiah says that God continues to reclaim and establish the covenant community.**

❖ Read aloud the following three ideas. Challenge the students to commit themselves to use these activities as a springboard to spiritual growth.

(1) **Collect some pictures and write information about yourself when you were a child, teenager, and younger adult. Share this information with a child or grandchild as a way of leaving a legacy.**

(2) **Write a prayer expressing thanks for God's goodness and your hope for future generations.**

(3) **Ponder the kind of legacy you are leaving to your church family. Have you set an example of love? Have you used your God-given gifts to build up the Body of Christ? Have you remembered your church in your will? What do you hope people will say about you when you are deceased? What additions or changes do you want to make to your legacy?**

❖ Sing or read aloud the first and fifth verses of "All Glory, Laud, and Honor."

❖ Ask the students to echo this benediction from 2 Corinthians 13:11-14 as you read it phrase by phrase: **Finally, brothers and sisters, farewell. Put things in order . . . agree with one another, live in peace; and the God of love and peace will be with you. Greet one another with a holy kiss. . . The grace of the Lord Jesus Christ, the love of God, and the communion of the Holy Spirit be with all of you. Amen.**

RE-CREATING COMMUNITY

PREVIEWING THE LESSON

Lesson Scripture: Isaiah 43:1-2, 10-13, 18-19
Background Scripture: Isaiah 43
Key Verse: Isaiah 43:1

Focus of the Lesson:
People often long for a sense of security and hope. Where can we find this? Isaiah says that God continues to reclaim and establish the covenant community.

Goals for the Learners:
(1) to unpack the promises God makes to the exiles in Babylon.
(2) to affirm the security and hope they experience because God has called, redeemed, and named them.
(3) to bear witness to God the redeemer.

Pronunciation Guide:
lectio divina   (lek'tee oh dee ve' nuh)

Supplies:
Bibles, newsprint and marker, paper and pencils, optional materials for a collage (pictures, construction paper, scissors, glue), hymnals

---

READING THE SCRIPTURE

NRSV
Isaiah 43:1-2, 10-13, 18-19
But now thus says the LORD,
he who created you, O Jacob,
he who formed you, O Israel:
Do not fear, for I have redeemed you;
I have called you by name, you are mine.
2 When you pass through the waters, I will
be with you;
and through the rivers, they shall not
overwhelm you;

NIV
Isaiah 43:1-2, 10-13, 18-19
But now, this is what the LORD says—
he who created you, O Jacob,
he who formed you, O Israel:
"Fear not, for I have redeemed you;
I have summoned you by name; you
are mine.
2 When you pass through the waters,
I will be with you;
and when you pass through the rivers,
they will not sweep over you.

when you walk through fire you shall not
  be burned,
and the flame shall not consume you.
10 You are my witnesses, says the LORD,
  and my servant whom I have chosen,
so that you may know and believe me
  and understand that I am he.
Before me no god was formed,
  nor shall there be any after me.
11 I, I am the LORD,
  and besides me there is no savior.
12 I declared and saved and proclaimed,
  when there was no strange god among
    you;
  and you are my witnesses, says the
    LORD.
13 I am God, and also henceforth I am He;
  there is no one who can deliver from my
    hand;
  I work and who can hinder it?
18 Do not remember the former things,
  or consider the things of old.
19 I am about to do a new thing;
  now it springs forth, do you not
    perceive it?
I will make a way in the wilderness
  and rivers in the desert.

When you walk through the fire,
  you will not be burned;
  the flames will not set you ablaze.
10 "You are my witnesses," declares the
    LORD,
  "and my servant whom I have chosen,
so that you may know and believe me
  and understand that I am he.
Before me no god was formed,
  nor will there be one after me.
11 I, even I, am the LORD,
  and apart from me there is no savior.
12 I have revealed and saved and
    proclaimed—
  I, and not some foreign god among you.
You are my witnesses," declares the LORD,
  "that I am God.
13 Yes, and from ancient days I am he.
  No one can deliver out of my hand.
  When I act, who can reverse it?"
18 "Forget the former things;
  do not dwell on the past.
19 See, I am doing a new thing!
  Now it springs up; do you not perceive
    it?
I am making a way in the desert
  and streams in the wasteland."

UNDERSTANDING THE SCRIPTURE

Introduction. It was only three weeks ago that our lesson was about God's deliverance of Israel from bondage in Egypt. We saw that God did for the people what they could not do for themselves by freeing them from slavery, making a covenant with the entire community, and ultimately leading them into a new land. Now they are in bondage again, although this time in Babylon.

Israel and Judah found it hard to be different from their neighbors. God had listened to their request and granted them a king so they could be like their neighbors round about (1 Samuel 8:5, 20). But as they had become more and more like their neighbors they also became less a holy people of God. Not only did they have a human king instead of relying on God to be their monarch, but also much of their community life was not all that different from what could be seen in the surrounding cultures. The rich were exploiting the poor and the strong taking advantage of the weak. New gods were being worshiped.

It does not appear that Israel ever entirely abandoned the Lord, but they did not remain faithful; they added several of the gods their Canaanite neighbors served. We can read in the prophets Amos and Hosea God's plea for the people to repent and return to the covenant ratified so many centuries before at Mount Sinai.

There was another besetting sin that got Israel and Judah into great trouble, and eventually led to the destruction of both nations. They wanted to be military powers. They wanted to have a standing army and to fight wars. They wanted to make alliances with bigger powers and fight more wars. In fact, the request for a king so that they could be like everyone else was also so that the "king may govern us and go out before us and fight our battles" (1 Samuel 8:20).

Israel and Judah even went to war *against each other*. When Assyria was the region's superpower Israel and Syria thought it would be a good idea to team up with Judah and together go against Assyria. When Judah refused to join the alliance, Israel and Syria attacked Judah. This is what scholars call the Syro-Ephraimite War. (Ephraim is another name for the Northern Kingdom of Israel.) In 722 B.C. Assyria conquered Israel. They took as captives the people who had any particular skills that the Assyrians wanted—as was the custom of any conquering nation. The Assyrians went one step further. They also mixed up the conquered populations. That is, they moved some people from Israel to Syria and some from Syria to Israel, as well as combining people from wherever else they were victorious. This was done largely to prevent conquered populations from overthrowing the Assyrian yoke. If the people in any given area did not speak the same language they would not be able to cooperate to the point of ridding themselves of Assyrian domination.

In the course of the next century and a half, Assyria waned as a regional superpower and Babylon's strength grew. By 596 B.C. Babylon had conquered most of the Southern Kingdom of Judah and made it a vassal state. The prophet Jeremiah told the people that their punishment from God was to serve the king of Babylon for a time and that they should not try to rebel. Naturally, that was not a popular message. (Can you imagine what might happen to a preacher who said the United States should serve Russia or Cuba or Afghanistan or Iraq—or anyone else at all—for a few years?) For ten years Babylon tried to make Judah behave as a relatively free vassal state and pay the required taxes. The powerful people in Judah, however, were unwilling to heed Jeremiah's words and continued to try to get another nation to come fight Babylon for them. Finally King Nebuchadrezzar got tired of Judah's nonsubmissive behavior. In 586 B.C., the Babylonian army overran Jerusalem, destroyed the Temple and much of the rest of the city, and carried off a portion of the population into captivity.

Isaiah 43:1-7. Into this situation of captivity God speaks a new word through the prophet many people call "Second Isaiah." God's first word is to remind the people that the one speaking to them is the one who created them. The Lord then assures them that they need not fear: they have been redeemed.

One of the most remarkable verses in the entire Bible is the final portion of Isaiah 43:1. God has called us by name; we belong to God. That is, God knows us individually and particularly. We are more than just statistics, more than anonymous, interchangeable parts. And even after all these generations of Israel's turning aside toward more enticing "gods," God still claims a personal relationship with the community.

As we have seen before as in the call of Moses (Exodus 3–4), God does not promise a trouble-free life. What the Lord promises is that God will never abandon us. The text does not imply "*If* you have troubles I will be with you," but rather, "*When* you are in difficulties I will be there too."

Isaiah 43:8-13. We who have seen God's gracious hand at work in the past are God's witnesses. Again we see what an important part memory plays in our identity.

Isaiah 43:14-21. The hand of the Lord will deliver once more. Verse 18*a* may seem strange in the midst of all the talk of memory. But the message is that we need not dwell on the past to the point that it blinds us to what God is doing now and is about to do in the future.

Isaiah 43:22-28. In the final section of the passage, God through Isaiah reminds the people of how they got into their predicament in the first place and warns them not to repeat the sin. What was this sin that landed them in exile except the abandonment of God? What God asks for, what God demands, is loyalty. The Lord will not have patience with our worship of anything as a rival to God.

INTERPRETING THE SCRIPTURE

Security: An Impossible Dream?

A few days after my younger daughter Anna's fifteenth birthday we drove down to the Motor Vehicle Department's regional office for her to take the test to get her learner's permit. She had studied the test preparation booklet. She had her passport and birth certificate in hand. I had my driver's license and photo identification card from work. We were well prepared. But she did not get to take the test that day because we had not known that we also needed "proof of address" in the form of a piece of official mail, postmarked within the past thirty days, with our address on it. "But we do not have home delivery," I told the officer. "I get some mail at work and we have a post office box for family mail." He was unmoved. As I was trying to figure out how we could obtain this additional paper, I asked him the reason for the new requirement. "It's for national security," he replied.

Certainly many Americans have begun to think differently about national security since September 11, 2001. Some of the freedoms we had long taken for granted are being curtailed, at least temporarily. There is a new cabinet level Department of Homeland Security. Traveling by air now often requires not only walking through a metal detector but also taking off one's shoes and socks for an inspector and having one's luggage gone through by hand. The public schools in our county require that children's backpacks be made of transparent materials. And there have been too many unfortunate incidents of authorities being called because someone "looked like a terrorist" or was "behaving in a suspicious manner."

There is less openness, less trusting of other people. And we may well be more secure as a result. But there is no way to guarantee that nothing bad will ever happen to an American citizen. Some people are wondering where the "break even" point is, where we should limit public spending on "security" in order to use the money for other things the nation needs. We have locks on the exterior doors of our house because we do not want a stranger to walk in and steal anything. At the same time we know that locks or our barking dog would not stop a determined burglar. We try to be prudent, but we do not want to live in unending fearfulness.

Security: An End in Itself?

In some ways the word "security" is like the word "freedom" in that it can be thought of in terms of "security *from* something" or "security *for* something." The word God speaks through the prophet in Isaiah 43:1 is marvelous: "Do not fear, for I have redeemed you." "Do not fear," says God. But this is not the security of never having to face difficult situations. It is, rather, the security of knowing that God is with us and that God will never abandon us. For the very next verse does not say, "If you pass through the waters" or other distresses, but rather, "*When*" these things happen to you.

The notion that God is with us no matter what happens can free us from timidity. In the security of God's loving presence, we can live as children of God.

All right. That sounds good, or at least like something one would be expected to hear at church. But what does it mean?

God calls us by name as individuals. We are secure to be who we are and not worry that we are not as athletic as Lee, or as musical as Will, or as good a cook as Terry. We still belong to God and to Jesus Christ. We are still members of the Body of Christ, the church, in all our individuality.

Security: Corporate or Individual?

Today's passage from Isaiah is addressed to the faith community as a whole. What does that do for the individual? God may pay attention to the whole church, but can/does God actually care for me personally? Put another way, do I have to belong to the group for God to care about me? The simple answer is no. God cares for both the group and the individuals who compose it, as well as for people who are outside the group. Part of our difficulty is encapsulated in the heading of this section.

Maybe you have heard the quip that people can be divided into two categories—those who divide everything into two categories and those who do not. God's word is much more "both/and" than "either/or." The Lord does not have to choose between being attentive to individuals on the one hand, or caring for the whole of creation on the other. In imitation of God, neither do we. Indeed, looking at both sides and refusing to be caught up in either/or choices is one way that we have of living out God's statement in verse 12 that we are the Lord's witnesses.

Are people like us within God's care? Of course! Are people different from us also within God's care? This is where our notions of God may carry us into uncomfortable places. The biblical witness is clear that God is the God of all creation, of the whole world and all who inhabit it. This does not mean that God approves of everything "they" do—any more than God approves of what we do when it is sinful. But being sinful does not cast us out of the Lord's presence, nor away from God's care.

Security: Old or New?

Some people find their security in the comfortable routine of the way things have always been done. Being in familiar places with people they have known as long as they can remember is reassuring. For them, innovation can be very painfully unpleasant. For them verses such as Isaiah 43:18-19*a* can be upsetting.

It may be helpful to remember that the new things God does are rooted securely in what God has done in the past. The new grows out of the old. It may well be surprising at first, but it is not ever a denial of what has gone before.

The downside to security comes when we worship safety instead of worshiping God. Following God sometimes feels risky even for people with a strong and vital faith. God does not promise to make sure that everything is always the same as it was before, that once we learn a routine, we would never be jolted out of it.

The security that Christians find is that in our following our Lord, even in those routine, jolting times, God never abandons us. We may be far from home. We may be in grave danger. We may even die. Still the message of the Bible is clear: God will never abandon us, either in this life or the next.

SHARING THE SCRIPTURE

PREPARING TO TEACH

Preparing Our Hearts

This week's devotional reading is found in Isaiah 42:5-13. Here we are reminded that the Creator God has called people and entered into a covenant with them. The ideas in verses 6-7 are echoed (though not quoted) in Luke 4:18-19 as Jesus announces his mission. As Simeon lifts up the newborn Jesus in the Temple, he paraphrases Isaiah 42:6 (see Luke 2:32). In Isaiah, God announces that something new is springing forth. What would it mean in your life for God to do "new things"?

Pray that you and your students will be open to the new things that our creative God is doing.

Preparing Our Minds

Study the background, which is Isaiah 43, and lesson scripture, found in verses 1-2, 10-13, and 18-19.

Write on newsprint:

information for next week's lesson, found under "Continue the Journey."

Gather pictures (magazines are a good source), scissors, glue, and large construction paper if you plan to do the collage suggested in "Affirm the Security and Hope the Learners Experience Because God Has Called, Redeemed, and Named Them."

Prepare the optional lectures suggested in "Unpack the Promises God Makes to the Exiles in Babylon" and "Bear Witness to God the Redeemer."

LEADING THE CLASS

(1) Gather to Learn

❖ Welcome the class members and introduce any guests.

❖ Pray that the students will find peace and security within this community of faith that God has created.

❖ Invite the class to think back to a day when they felt that their security as a nation was being threatened. Discuss these questions.

(1) **What happened to cause you to feel threatened?**

(2) **How did your government react?**

(3) **What words of promise did you want to hear when security was threatened?**

(4) **How did faith in God help you in this time of crisis?**

(5) **What kind of witness were you able to make for God as a result of this threat?**

❖ Read aloud today's focus statement: **People often long for a sense of security and hope. Where can we find this? Isaiah says that God continues to reclaim and establish the covenant community.**

(2) Unpack the Promises God Makes to the Exiles in Babylon

❖ Use an ancient method of reading the Scriptures known by the Latin words *lectio divina*. We will use a group study approach to this method by following these ten steps, as adapted from an outline by Father Luke Dysinger. Although the oral reading may be done for the entire class, sharing of ideas should be done in small groups.

■ **Step 1:** Read aloud Isaiah 43:1-2, 10-13, 18-19 twice. Ask the students to listen each time for a word or phrase that they find meaningful.

■ **Step 2:** Allow a minute or two for the adults to think about and silently repeat the chosen word or phrase.

■ **Step 3:** Ask each person to state the word or phrase that attracted him or her, but without discussing why.

- **Step 4:** Choose another person to read the same passage.
- **Step 5:** Provide time for the students to reflect silently on how or where this passage intersects with their own life.
- **Step 6:** Invite each person to state how Christ is speaking to them by saying, "I hear" or "I see. . . ."
- **Step 7:** Select another volunteer to read the same passage a third time.
- **Step 8:** Encourage the students to reflect silently on this question: **What does this passage suggest that God wants me to do this week?**
- **Step 9:** Tell the adults to share whatever insights they have gleaned.
- **Step 10:** Ask the adults to pray aloud or silently for the student on their right.

❖ Ask the students to look in their Bibles at this passage from Isaiah and call out any promises that God makes to the exiles in Babylon. Or, if you prefer, locate these promises yourself and create a brief lecture on them.

❖ Invite the students to consider how these promises may affect their own lives millennia after Isaiah recorded them.

(3) Affirm the Security and Hope the Learners Experience Because God Has Called, Redeemed, and Named Them

❖ Determine ways that society offers security. List these ideas, or create a collage using symbols of security.

❖ Discuss these questions in relation to the collages or list.
　(1) How much security do the pictured/named items *really* offer you?
　(2) How do our efforts to insulate ourselves from danger affect the way we live together in community?
　(3) What more reliable security measures might you take?

❖ Post a sheet of newsprint. Invite the students to list ways that the Creator God has called, redeemed, and named them.

❖ Close this section of the lesson by asking the students to ponder how the realization of God's care for them makes them feel secure in a very insecure world.

(4) Bear Witness to God the Redeemer

❖ Distribute hymnals. Ask the students to page through to find hymns that speak to them about God (or Jesus) as the redeemer. Invite the students to discuss these questions. You may want to give them paper and pencils to record their ideas. Or, locate the hymns yourself and answer these questions in a lecture that you have prepared.
　(1) What does the selected hymn say to you about how and why God offers redemption?
　(2) What promises for the community of faith do you find in the selected hymn?
　(3) What security and hope does this hymn offer to you?

❖ If time permits and if there is a class member who can play these hymns without rehearsal, sing at least one verse of each selected hymn.

❖ Note that just as the hymn writers bear witness to God, so too we bear witness, each in our own way. Post a sheet of newsprint. Give the students no more than three minutes to brainstorm as many ways that they can be witnesses as possible.

❖ Remind the class that God intends to "do a new thing" (43:19). Continue the brainstorming by asking the students to think creatively about new ways that they can try to bear witness to God. List their ideas.

❖ Encourage them to select one of these new ideas and commit themselves to trying it this week.

(5) Continue the Journey

❖ Pray that the adults will find security and hope as they continue to place their faith in God, who holds the future.

❖ Read aloud this preparation for next week's lesson. You may also want to post it on newsprint for the students to copy. **Prepare for next week's session entitled "Creating a New Covenant" by reading Jeremiah 29:1-14 and 31:31-34. The session will focus on 29:10-14 and 31:31-34. Consider these ideas as you study: Most people want their life to have spiritual meaning. How might this be achieved? Jeremiah says that God will write a new covenant on the heart that will establish a deep and genuine relationship with God.**

❖ Read aloud the following three ideas. Challenge the students to commit themselves to use these activities as a springboard to spiritual growth.

(1) **Write answers to these questions in your spiritual journal: Where, or from whom, do I seek security and stability? Have acts of terrorism redefined my ideas of security? If so, how? What message of hope does Isaiah 43 have for me in my daily life?**

(2) **Reread Isaiah 43:8-10. How are you a witness and servant for God? Identify at least one person or group to whom you could offer witness and service this week.**

(3) **Consider the ways in which the covenant community of faith offers stability and hope for the future. List as many words or phrases as you can in your journal to describe this stability and hope.**

❖ Sing or read aloud "You Are Mine," found on page 2218 of *The Faith We Sing*.

❖ Ask the students to echo this benediction from 2 Corinthians 13:11-14 as you read it phrase by phrase: **Finally, brothers and sisters, farewell. Put things in order . . . agree with one another, live in peace; and the God of love and peace will be with you. . . . The grace of the Lord Jesus Christ, the love of God, and the communion of the Holy Spirit be with all of you. Amen.**

CREATING A NEW COVENANT

PREVIEWING THE LESSON

Lesson Scripture: Jeremiah 29:10-14; 31:31-34
Background Scripture: Jeremiah 29:1-14; 31:31-34
Key Verse: Jeremiah 31:33

Focus of the Lesson:
Most people want their life to have spiritual meaning. How might this be achieved? Jeremiah says that God will write a new covenant on the heart that will establish a deep and genuine relationship with God.

Goals of the Lesson:
(1) to explore what Jeremiah means by a new covenant of the heart.
(2) to reflect on broken and restored relationships in their own lives.
(3) to reaffirm their covenant with God.

Pronunciation Guide:
Nebuchadnezzer   (neb' uh kuhd nez'uhr)
Torah   (toh' ruh)

Supplies:
Bibles, old piece of ceramic ware or pottery, hammer (optional), newsprint and marker, paper and pencils, hymnals

---

READING THE SCRIPTURE

NRSV
Jeremiah 29:10-14

10 For thus says the LORD: Only when Babylon's seventy years are completed will I visit you, and I will fulfill to you my promise and bring you back to this place. 11 For surely I know the plans I have for you, says the LORD, plans for your welfare and not for harm, to give you a future with hope. 12 Then when you call upon me and come and pray to me, I will hear you. 13 When you search

NIV
Jeremiah 29:10-14

[10]This is what the LORD says: "When seventy years are completed for Babylon, I will come to you and fulfill my gracious promise to bring you back to this place. [11]For I know the plans I have for you," declares the LORD, "plans to prosper you and not to harm you, plans to give you hope and a future. [12]Then you will call upon me and come and pray to me, and I will listen to you. [13]You will seek

for me, you will find me; if you seek me with all your heart, 14 I will let you find me, says the Lord, and I will restore your fortunes and gather you from all the nations and all the places where I have driven you, says the Lord, and I will bring you back to the place from which I sent you into exile.

Jeremiah 31:31-34

31 The days are surely coming, says the Lord, when I will make a new covenant with the house of Israel and the house of Judah. 32 It will not be like the covenant that I made with their ancestors when I took them by the hand to bring them out of the land of Egypt—a covenant that they broke, though I was their husband, says the Lord. **33 But this is the covenant that I will make with the house of Israel after those days, says the Lord: I will put my law within them, and I will write it on their hearts; and I will be their God, and they shall be my people.** 34 No longer shall they teach one another, or say to each other, "Know the Lord," for they shall all know me, from the least of them to the greatest, says the Lord; for I will forgive their iniquity, and remember their sin no more.

me and find me when you seek me with all your heart. ¹⁴I will be found by you," declares the Lord, "and will bring you back from captivity. I will gather you from all the nations and places where I have banished you," declares the Lord, "and will bring you back to the place from which I carried you into exile."

Jeremiah 31:31-34

³¹ "The time is coming," declares the Lord,
　　"when I will make a new covenant
　with the house of Israel
　　and with the house of Judah.
³² It will not be like the covenant
　　I made with their forefathers
　when I took them by the hand
　　to lead them out of Egypt,
　because they broke my covenant,
　　though I was a husband to them,"
　　　　　　　　declares the Lord.
³³ **"This is the covenant I will make with**
　　the house of Israel
　　after that time," declares the Lord.
"I will put my law in their minds
　　and write it on their hearts.
I will be their God,
　　and they will be my people.
³⁴ No longer will a man teach his neighbor,
　　or a man his brother, saying, 'Know the
　　Lord,'
　because they will all know me,
　　from the least of them to the greatest,"
　　　　　　　　declares the Lord.
　"For I will forgive their wickedness
　　and will remember their sins no more."

UNDERSTANDING THE SCRIPTURE

Jeremiah 29:1-4. Before the Babylonians conquered Judah, razing the Temple and taking much of the population off into exile, they made Judah a vassal state. In 597 B.C. they plundered the Temple and took as captives people who had particular skills they wanted in Babylon. As long as Judah paid monetary tribute to Babylon and refrained from making political or military alliances with any other nation, King Nebuchadnezzar of Babylon would allow the people of Judah to remain as they were, in relative freedom. It is to the first group of captives that the prophet Jeremiah sent a letter.

Jeremiah 29:5-9. Through Jeremiah, God tells the people that their fate and the fate of the nation in which they are now living are bound up together. Instead of fighting against their punishment, God instructs the people to settle down and establish themselves in Babylon. God specifically warns them that if any prophets come along with different advice, the people are not to listen to them or follow them because such prophets are not proclaiming the word of the Lord.

Jeremiah 29:10-14. God says that the time of exile will end. After the specified seventy years, the people will be brought back to their own land. The return will be far better than merely a change of address for the people. There will be a restoration of a close relationship between God and the people. Their turning away from God has led them to this place of exile, but God has not abandoned them.

Jeremiah 31:31-34. Once again the people will be bound to the Lord with a covenant. Verse 31 calls it a "new" covenant, but we need to be careful how we think of that adjective. The covenant will be new in the same sense that every month there is a "new moon" in the sky. The new moon does not mean a different physical object from what was there last month. Rather, it refers to the fact that for a night or two the moon was not visible, and now it can be seen again. Similarly, the people have abandoned their side of the covenant and their actions brought disastrous consequences down upon their heads. But God is willing to try again with them, to restore the covenant as it was initiated with the entire Israelite community at Mount Sinai.

This renewed covenant will be with more than just the exiles in Babylon, for God speaks of both the house of Israel and the house of Judah. God intends to include within the covenant community descendants of those who had split apart centuries before.

This covenant will be different in some matters from the Sinai covenant. One of the major differences is that this covenant is going to be in the heart and mind of every single member of the community. It will not be something only on tablets of stone; it will not be something that the leaders are to take care of. It will be an agreement between the Lord and every last person who chooses to join.

There are two important words in verse 33 that have more than one meaning. If we are not careful, we may seriously misunderstand what Jeremiah's message here is. First is the word "law." For many of us, "law" is the opposite of "grace." It sounds rather grim and foreboding to think of having the whole law of God written on our hearts, doesn't it? But the word translated into English as "law" is the Hebrew word "torah." "Torah" can refer to the entire first five books of the Bible. It can indicate a specific law. But its more general meaning is very close to what Christians usually mean when using the phrase "the word of the Lord." God's word includes laws, of course, and also accounts of grace. What Jeremiah says is going to be written on the heart would be better described as the "instruction" of God rather than any sort of legalistic compilation of laws piled upon more laws.

The other word whose use here we may misunderstand is "heart." For most English-speaking people the heart is the seat of the emotions. It is different in Hebrew. For the people to whom Jeremiah was writing, the heart was the place where they thought and made decisions. The heart was the seat of the will and the intellect. The NIV translation comes closer to this understanding by using the parallel lines: "I will put my law in their minds/ and write it on their hearts."

We also see once again that God's goal is more than the careful keeping of individual laws, but rather the establishment and living out of a relationship. God's goal is to have this relationship with each individual within the community and not with people "in general." When verse 34 says that no one will have to teach another, it is not talking about the abolishing of Sunday school classes! Rather, what is to be done away with, what is no longer necessary, is a hierarchy in which some people are totally dependent on others for knowledge of the Lord. "From the least of them to the greatest," everyone will be able to have a personal, individual, direct relationship with God.

What has stood in the way of this relationship is sin. God does not say that sin suddenly does not matter any more, but rather that our sin is forgiven. God refuses to keep holding it over our heads, to allow it to continue as a barrier to relationship. This is something that we need to take into our minds (or in the Hebrew idiom, "hearts") because we find it so hard to believe. People sometimes think it a mark of great piety to say, "I'll never forgive myself." God is saying here that God forgives our sin in order that we not be estranged from God. How sad for anyone to refuse this renewal of the covenant relationship for which we were created.

INTERPRETING THE SCRIPTURE

After the Last Straw

What child has never tested the limits of a parent's patience? What teenager has never pushed at the boundaries of getting chores done or coming home at the appointed hour? And when, after a number of warnings from the parents, the punishment finally comes after one last "test," what child does not feel aggrieved? "What did I do to deserve this punishment?" is the wailed response. The child may shower the parent with apologies and earnest promises never to disobey again, but it is too late. The limit has been reached and crossed and the punishment—the time out, the grounding, the loss of some privileges—has actually arrived.

Testing limits and eventually getting caught is not limited to children of course. One too many times sliding through a stop sign or drifting above the speed limit may result in a ticket. Showing up late for work one time too many may even lead to being fired. The punishment rarely feels appropriate to the individual infraction. We tend not to remember the weight of accumulated misdeeds, but to think only of the current one.

So it happened with the biblical nations as we see in today's text. Neither Israel nor Judah took God seriously. Too many of the people believed either that God didn't pay much attention to what was going on outside the bounds of the Temple, or that even if the Lord did notice, nothing much would happen. And then, finally, there was a portion of the Babylonian army carting off treasures from the Temple, and people from the palace.

We know in our own lives that there does sometimes come that "last straw" moment when one incident, seemingly small in itself, can set off a whole chain of bad reactions. We would give anything to take back the hasty words, to un-say the insensitive joke. But what has happened cannot be undone.

What Now?

We see in today's biblical text that God does not abandon the people, even when they are in far-off exile. In fact, God sends word to them, by way of the letter from the prophet Jeremiah. What is surprising is that the letter does not exhort them just to tough it out, to take their punishment and meditate on their sins. Nor is the message one of gloating, of singing endless choruses of "I told you so." Rather, the Lord tells the captives to make lives for themselves in Babylon. How is that possible? "How could we sing the LORD's song in a foreign land?" they wonder (Psalm 137:4).

In a sense the message to the exiles is that they must simply take their punishment. This means not spending all their energies trying to figure out a way around it, nor wallowing the entire time in despair. God is still with them, even in Babylon. God wants the best for them, even as they are in exile. They are to live as full a life as possible in their present situation, trusting in God that things will be better in the future. They are not to put their lives "on hold" until that better future arrives.

It is not just when our lives have gone seriously off track that we may neglect living in the present. The nursery-school child wants to be "big" and go to kindergarten. The elementary student can hardly wait for junior high. The young teenager longs for a driver's license. The high school student looks forward to college and living independently of family. The graduate wants a first job, and then a better job, and then just one more promotion. The worker waits for retirement when it will be possible to do all those things that a job interferes with.

There is nothing wrong with a positive anticipation of the future, of course. What is not good is for the anticipation to blind us to all the opportunities and good things in our lives at this present moment. The other side of the present's being short-changed in favor of anticipation is the belief that we are not able, for whatever reasons, to live as we would like in the present. In terms of spiritual life, time and "goodness" seem to be the usual stumbling blocks. "If only I had enough time, I could have the sort of spiritual life I want," may be a common lament. Far more serious to one's spiritual side is the belief that "If I were good enough, God would seem closer to me."

God Can't Be Serious!

There are innumerable hints and helps easily available for people looking to find time for their prayer life. Far more serious is the situation for people who believe themselves unworthy of a closer life with God. This was a major part of what was facing the exiles to whom Jeremiah sent God's word of condolence and instruction. They were living in physical exile in large part because of sin. For many, their immediate plight was due to the sin of others; for some it was their own sin that had landed them in Babylon. Regardless of where they pointed their accusing fingers, the reality of the terrible effects of sin had landed them in what many considered a hopeless situation.

God does not scold them again. God astounds them by saying that the covenant, which they have broken over and over again, is going to be renewed. And everything that they believe stands between them and God—the legacy of generations of sin—is going to be removed by the Lord. The news is almost too good to believe. God understands the human difficulty in taking seriously such a message. This is why Jeremiah phrases it in terms of the covenant's being written on the "heart." If Jeremiah were to send his message today, into our culture and in our idioms, he might say God will get the message "into our thick skulls" and "keep it on our minds."

Making ourselves *feel* a particular way is not the point, even if it were possible. God wants us to know, to understand, that a closer spiritual walk is possible. We do not have to turn away or give up because of anything at all that is in our past. Whatever the sins of the past are, God is eager to forgive them. It certainly is not the way most of us experience human relationships. But then, God is not human! God will allow us our independence to turn away, to refuse to believe such good news, to continue to assert it is too good to be true. Still, God removes every impediment that we are willing to relinquish.

What Future?

Our future does, to a certain degree, grow out of our past. But between past and future is God's present. In God's present is found forgiveness and the offer of a renewed covenant relationship with every single individual person. We need not wait for "the leaders" to do something. We do not have to wait until we are better people or living in a better situation. In seeking the welfare of the community in which we find ourselves at this moment, we find our own welfare.

SHARING THE SCRIPTURE

PREPARING TO TEACH

Preparing Our Hearts

This week's devotional reading is found in Jeremiah 30:18-22. Here the prophet writes of a day when the conditions of the people's current reality will be reversed. Their "fortunes" will be restored and they will rejoice and give thanks. The covenant will be renewed between God and the people. Do you long for a restored relationship with God? What is your present relationship? How would you like to see that changed?

Pray that God will empower you and your class members to accept the restored relationship that God wants you to experience.

Preparing Our Minds

Read the background from Jeremiah 29:1-14 and 3:31-34. Study the lesson scripture, Jeremiah 29:10-14 and 31:31-34.

Write on newsprint:

information for next week's lesson, found under "Continue the Journey."

Bring a broken plate, flowerpot, or other ceramic piece. Or, bring an old ceramic piece and a hammer.

Plan a brief lecture to introduce Jeremiah's letter to the exiles who are living in Babylon.

LEADING THE CLASS

(1) Gather to Learn

❖ Welcome the class members and introduce any guests.

❖ Pray that the students will be open to renewing their covenantal relationship with God.

❖ Write on newsprint the word "covenant." Ask the students to call out words or phrases that define that word. Then invite them to list different types of covenants that people enter into, such as marriage, promises to uphold a property covenant, or covenant with God.

❖ Read aloud today's focus statement: **Most people want their life to have spiritual meaning. How might this be achieved? Jeremiah says that God will write a new covenant on the heart that will establish a deep and genuine relationship with God.**

(2) Explore What Was Happening in Israel's Life When Jeremiah Spoke These Words

❖ Study Jeremiah 29:10-14.

■ Prepare a brief lecture using the information from verses 1-9 of Jeremiah 29 in the Understanding the Scripture portion, and "What Now?" in the Interpreting the Scripture section to set the stage for today's lesson. Explain that the prophet Jeremiah has written a letter to the Israelite exiles who are living in Babylon.

■ Enlist a volunteer to read Jeremiah 29:10-14. Ask the students to imagine themselves as the exiles in Babylon to whom this letter is addressed. Point out that at the time Jeremiah was writing this letter, God's people had sinned by worshiping the gods of their neighbors and treating marginalized members of the society unjustly.

- Consider these questions in a discussion. Or, write your own answers to them and present them as a short lecture.

    (1) **What does this passage say to you about God?**

    (2) **What does this passage suggest about the kinds of behaviors God expects of us?**

    (3) **Had you been in exile, what response might this letter evoke for you?**

❖ Delve into the new covenant as recorded in Jeremiah 31:31-34.

- Ask a different volunteer to read Jeremiah 31:31-34.

- Encourage the students to talk about their understandings of the new covenant by discussing these three questions.

    (1) **How would you describe the new covenant about which Jeremiah writes?**

    (2) **Who can participate in this new covenant?** (Be certain to point out that Jeremiah is writing these words to Jewish people. Although Christians understand this phrase to refer to the new covenant that we have through the body and blood of Christ, it also had meaning for the exiles as they looked ahead to the future. Ezekiel, another exilic prophet, also wrote about a new heart and new spirit. See Ezekiel 11:19-20; 18:31; 36:26.)

    (3) **What does it mean to say that this covenant is written "on the heart"?**

- Read the information from Jeremiah 31:31-34 in the Understanding the Scripture portion.

- Invite the students to react to these ideas by questioning, affirming, or disagreeing with them.

(3) Reflect on Broken and Restored Relationships in the Learners' Lives

❖ Hold up the old piece of ceramic ware or pottery that you brought. If it is not already broken, use the hammer to break it into several pieces. Place the broken pieces on the worship table or other space where everyone may see them.

❖ Invite the students to meditate for several minutes on how this broken pottery (or an imagined piece if you had none to bring) may symbolize a broken relationship with another person or with God. Suggest that they think about how the relationship was broken, how it might be mended/restored, and how the new relationship may be different from the old one.

❖ Encourage the students to talk about how relationships can be restored.

❖ Distribute paper and pencils. Ask them to write a letter to God in which they describe how they feel they have not been faithful to their covenant and outlining changes that they want to make in their relationship with God.

(4) Invite the Learners to Commit to Living in a Close Relationship with God

❖ Invite the class members to read in unison today's key verse, Jeremiah 31:33.

❖ Discuss these questions:

    (1) **What does it mean to say that God is your God?**

    (2) **What does it mean to say that you are God's people?**

    (3) **What are some of the marks or distinguishing characters of the people of God?**

❖ Ask the students to close their eyes and focus their attention on this guided imagery exercise.

- **Envision yourself in the presence of God, however that might look and feel to you.** (Pause)

- **Listen as God tells you how you have been living faithfully. How do**

God's words make you feel? (Pause)

- Listen again as God speaks to you about areas of your life that you have tried to keep distant from God. (Pause)
- Ask God to help you make changes so as to be living in a deeply personal and close relationship with God through Christ Jesus. (Pause)
- Close the guided imagery with this prayer: Gracious God, I give you thanks and praise for the covenant you have with me through Jesus Christ, our Lord and Savior. By your Holy Spirit, empower me to see you more clearly and love you more dearly so that I might always live in an intimate relationship with you. Amen.

(5) Continue the Journey

❖ Read aloud this preparation for next week's lesson. You may also want to post it on newsprint for the students to copy. **Prepare for next week's session entitled "Looking for Hope" by reading Ezekiel 37. In class we will concentrate on verses 1-14, the familiar story of the valley of the dry bones. Keep this focus in mind as you** read: **People in depression and despair are often incapable of hope. What is the source of our hope when all is bleak? Ezekiel affirms that God can bring new life and restoration to the direst of circumstances.**

❖ Read aloud the following three ideas. Challenge the students to commit themselves to use these activities as a springboard to spiritual growth.

(1) Write a poem or psalm of praise concerning the feelings associated with a restored relationship with God.

(2) Take at least one step to act on the commitment you made in class to deepen your relationship with God.

(3) Do whatever is in your power to restore and renew a broken relationship with a family member, friend, neighbor, or colleague.

❖ Sing or read aloud "Living for Jesus," found on page 2149 in *The Faith We Sing.*

❖ Ask the students to echo this benediction from 2 Corinthians 13:11-14 as you read it phrase by phrase: **Finally, brothers and sisters, farewell. Put things in order . . . agree with one another, live in peace; and the God of love and peace will be with you. . . . The grace of the Lord Jesus Christ, the love of God, and the communion of the Holy Spirit be with all of you. Amen.**

LOOKING FOR HOPE

PREVIEWING THE LESSON

Lesson Scripture: Ezekiel 37:1-14
Background Scripture: Ezekiel 37
Key Verse: Ezekiel 37:14

Focus of the Lesson:
People in depression and despair are often incapable of hope. What is the source of our hope when all is bleak? Ezekiel affirms that God can bring new life and restoration to the direst of circumstances.

Goals of the Lesson:
(1) to study the restoration God promised to the exiles in Babylon.
(2) to affirm God's power to renew their lives.
(3) to give thanks for the hope God offers them.

Supplies:
Bibles, newsprint and marker, paper and pencils, hymnals

READING THE SCRIPTURE

NRSV
Ezekiel 37:1-14

The hand of the LORD came upon me, and he brought me out by the spirit of the LORD and set me down in the middle of a valley; it was full of bones. 2 He led me all around them; there were very many lying in the valley, and they were very dry. 3 He said to me, "Mortal, can these bones live?" I answered, "O Lord GOD, you know." 4 Then he said to me, "Prophesy to these bones, and say to them: O dry bones, hear the word of the LORD. 5 Thus says the Lord GOD to these bones: I will cause breath to enter you, and you shall live. 6 I will lay sinews on you, and will cause flesh to come upon you, and cover

NIV
Ezekiel 37:1-14

[1]The hand of the LORD was upon me, and he brought me out by the Spirit of the LORD and set me in the middle of a valley; it was full of bones. [2]He led me back and forth among them, and I saw a great many bones on the floor of the valley, bones that were very dry. [3]He asked me, "Son of man, can these bones live?"

I said, "O Sovereign LORD, you alone know."

[4]Then he said to me, "Prophesy to these bones and say to them, 'Dry bones, hear the word of the LORD! [5]This is what the Sovereign LORD says to these bones: I will

you with skin, and put breath in you, and you shall live; and you shall know that I am the LORD."

7 So I prophesied as I had been commanded; and as I prophesied, suddenly there was a noise, a rattling, and the bones came together, bone to its bone. 8 I looked, and there were sinews on them, and flesh had come upon them, and skin had covered them; but there was no breath in them. 9 Then he said to me, "Prophesy to the breath, prophesy, mortal, and say to the breath: Thus says the Lord GOD: Come from the four winds, O breath, and breathe upon these slain, that they may live." 10 I prophesied as he commanded me, and the breath came into them, and they lived, and stood on their feet, a vast multitude.

11 Then he said to me, "Mortal, these bones are the whole house of Israel. They say, 'Our bones are dried up, and our hope is lost; we are cut off completely.' 12 Therefore prophesy, and say to them, Thus says the Lord GOD: I am going to open your graves, and bring you up from your graves, O my people; and I will bring you back to the land of Israel. 13 And you shall know that I am the LORD, when I open your graves, and bring you up from your graves, O my people. **14 I will put my spirit within you, and you shall live, and I will place you on your own soil; then you shall know that I, the LORD, have spoken and will act, says the LORD."**

make breath enter you, and you will come to life. [6]I will attach tendons to you and make flesh come upon you and cover you with skin; I will put breath in you, and you will come to life. Then you will know that I am the LORD.'"

[7]So I prophesied as I was commanded. And as I was prophesying, there was a noise, a rattling sound, and the bones came together, bone to bone. [8]I looked, and tendons and flesh appeared on them and skin covered them, but there was no breath in them.

[9]Then he said to me, "Prophesy to the breath; prophesy, son of man, and say to it, 'This is what the Sovereign LORD says: Come from the four winds, O breath, and breathe into these slain, that they may live.'" [10]So I prophesied as he commanded me, and breath entered them; they came to life and stood up on their feet—a vast army.

[11]Then he said to me: "Son of man, these bones are the whole house of Israel. They say, 'Our bones are dried up and our hope is gone; we are cut off.' [12]Therefore prophesy and say to them: 'This is what the Sovereign LORD says: O my people, I am going to open your graves and bring you up from them; I will bring you back to the land of Israel. [13]Then you, my people, will know that I am the LORD, when I open your graves and bring you up from them. **[14]I will put my Spirit in you and you will live, and I will settle you in your own land. Then you will know that I the LORD have spoken, and I have done it, declares the LORD.' "**

UNDERSTANDING THE SCRIPTURE

Introduction. The Exile was not a short event in the life of Israel. Perhaps at first it was not hard for the people to keep up their hopes that God would restore them to their own land. But as years became decades and they were still not released, despair began to replace hope. Finally, it had been too long

for them to believe there was any promise in their future; they could not see that anything positive was happening. They gave up and considered themselves as good as dead. It is in these circumstances that the prophet had a vision.

Ezekiel 37:1-3. Ezekiel recorded many

visions, some of them strange and hard for us to connect with our own lives (see Ezekiel 1, for an example). The vision in chapter 37, however, seems straightforward. Israel is in exile. The people have just about given up hope. Their expectation for a better future is as alive as a valley full of dry and disconnected bones. When God asks Ezekiel whether or not the bones can live, the prophet gives a careful reply: "O Lord GOD, you know."

We do not have any tone of voice recorded with any statements in the Bible. Perhaps Ezekiel said this with robust confidence. "Oh God, you know that you can do all things. If you want these bones to live then of course they will." Or Ezekiel may have uttered only a tired whisper. "Oh God, I don't know anything anymore. Everything is bleak. Do you not see how bad off we are? But if anyone knows, you do."

Ezekiel 37:4-10. God tells Ezekiel to prophesy to the dry bones. Why does God make such a request? Could not the Lord have revived those bones without Ezekiel's help? Well, yes and no. I think there are two related reasons, or one reason in two parts, for God's order to the prophet. First, God desires a cooperative relationship with human beings. This relational nature seems to be so much a part of the definition of God that an aloof or separated "God" would be as impossible for biblical prophets to conceive as a notion of dry rain or cold heat. Of course the sovereign God could act alone, but God chooses instead to act with human beings.

Second, the order God gives Ezekiel is not a random command; nor does it seem to have anything to do with the task at hand. God does not tell Ezekiel to gather the bones or sort them into skeletons. Rather, the command fits who Ezekiel is as an individual. If Ezekiel had been a singer, I think God would have said, "Sing to the bones." Had he been a baker the order would have been, "Bake for the bones." God tells him to prophesy because Ezekiel is a prophet. That

is, God is not asking him to do something outside his nature or something he is unable to do. Notice that the Lord even helps Ezekiel along by giving him the message to proclaim.

Ezekiel does not argue. He does not ask, "What good can that do?" Ezekiel obeys and the bones start connecting. The restoration does not end with bare skeletons, but rather sinews and flesh and skin are added. Bodies are formed. They look like people, but are not alive because "there was no breath in them" (37:8). Has Ezekiel stopped too soon? Might he be thinking, "What is the point of putting flesh and skin on bones? They are still just dead bodies." So God gives further orders that Ezekiel "prophesy to the breath" (37:9). The bodies then come alive and stand on their feet.

Ezekiel 37:11-14. God then explains to the prophet the meaning of the vision. The exiles are saying, "We might as well be dead because we have no future; there is no hope for us." God proclaims that they do indeed have a future because God will revive them and even return them to their homeland. God's spirit will be in them (37:14) and they will know the Lord.

There is a wordplay here in the Hebrew that is not possible to capture in a simple English translation. The Hebrew word for "breath" also means "wind" and "spirit." In verses 8, 9, 10, and 14 the same word is translated these three ways. One meaning that can be conveyed this way is that merely having "breath" does not make one alive. It is the "spirit" which gives true life. The breath is necessary, of course, but it is not all that is necessary.

God then gives Ezekiel a similar message to prophesy to the people in exile, who think they might as well be dead, that they are living in graves because they are not in their own land. God promises that they will be restored to their land and that they will be alive again. The culmination of the promise is not only that they will be able to return home, but also that they will know "that I, the LORD, have spoken and will act" (37:14). The source of their hope is not in their own abilities. It is not even in their prophet. The source of their hope is in the God who has not abandoned them, who is with them even in exile.

Ezekiel 37:15-22. Then God tells Ezekiel to show the people a "sign act," a "visual parable." The prophet takes two sticks, one signifying Judah and the other for Israel. God is promising to reunite these divided nations into one whole. Since Israel had

been overrun by Assyria in 722 B.C., this may be an even greater miracle than the restoration of Judah from being dry bones.

Ezekiel 37:23-28. Not only will God restore the people, they will be saved from idolatry, the major sin that led to the destruction of each nation in the first place. God will dwell with them in an eternal covenant of "shalom," a word meaning not only peace, but also health, wholeness, and integrity.

INTERPRETING THE SCRIPTURE

Many Dry Bones

A young woman from Korea lives in this country because her husband was offered a university position that was precisely suited to his training and aspirations. But she is lonely. Her family and friends are thousands of miles away. The people at the church she attends are friendly, she reports, "but all the English is faster than in books." The food in Tennessee is different from what she has always known. Many of the things she does automatically, such as bowing when greeting or leaving someone, are considered strange by those she meets and her well-intentioned actions seem to separate her from potential friends. "I am happy for my husband," she says, "but inside myself I feel like the scattered bones Ezekiel saw."

Have you ever attended church in a huge sanctuary with only a few people present? Have you been a member of a church that felt itself burdened by a large building and a declining congregation? I have. And I remember what a choir member, Charles, said at one meeting, "When I look out over the empty pews on Sunday morning, with just the faithful few scattered around, I think it must be how Ezekiel felt looking at that valley of dry bones. How can this church live?"

In each of these cases there is no decision actually to give up. We may have some notion of what would make the situation better, but we feel powerless to effect any substantial changes. We may know full well what we would like the situation to be, but have no idea how to get from where we are to where and how we yearn to live. Still, we feel a kinship, a responsibility. We may be seeing dry bones, but at least they are *our* dry bones. For whatever reasons, we cannot simply turn and walk away. And yet, if the question were asked candidly, "Can you live in this alien culture?" or "Can this congregation live in this place?" the answer might come out like Ezekiel's: "Oh God, you know."

From Bones to Bodies

Ezekiel follows God's instructions and the bones do indeed come together. They are reconstituted as skeletons and those skeletons are enfleshed, covered with skin. The prophet certainly could not have done this himself. But, however miraculous the change in that valley, it is not enough.

This brings us to the question: What is life? We know that it is intended to be more than mere physical existence. There are end-of-life issues that the church needs to be facing clearly and carefully. Is it a good thing to prolong physical life endlessly if the person is in an irreversible coma? Is physical life with unrelenting severe pain better than death? These are questions I raise not to discuss here, but because I think the church should continue to talk about them in other venues.

What I want to raise in this section of this chapter is the difficult one of whether "bodies" equal "health" or "success." Of course the bodies in the pews are just about the simplest thing to count. And do not misunderstand please: I think having people in church is *a good thing*. But just as Ezekiel was not satisfied with spirit-less bodies, we should not be either. Ezekiel continues to listen to God's instructions and continues to follow. Only after this second round of prophesying are those bodies infused with the life-giving Spirit of God. How tragic it is if we listen only long enough to have the first appearance of a better situation instead of continuing to be open to God's promptings.

Prophets Who Prophesy

As I wrote in the Understanding the Scripture section, I believe that God told Ezekiel to prophesy simply because Ezekiel was a prophet. God used Ezekiel's gifts. From the prophet's point of view it may have seemed a silly thing to do. What is the point of prophesying if there is no one to hear? But by being faithful both to his identity and to the call of God, Ezekiel is the catalyst for the reviving of those bones.

Genesis 1:26-27 tells us that we are created in the image of God. We are not created in the image of each other. The apostle Paul tells us we are the Body of Christ and goes on to remind his hearers that bodies are made up of different parts with different functions (1 Corinthians 12:12-31). In times of discouragement we may well feel that our own abilities are not the right kind or

not the right amount to make the situation any better.

In such circumstances Ezekiel can be very instructive. To follow his pattern is to do three simple-sounding things, remembering that "simple" and "simplistic" are not the same. First, Ezekiel saw the circumstances of the people as they really were. He did not look at that valley of bones in his vision and say, "Oh, it's not all that bad really. Everyone will feel better tomorrow." Second, he was willing to listen for God and listen to God. When God told him to prophesy to the bones, the prophet did not tell God that it wouldn't help. He didn't say he wasn't up to the job. And finally, whether or not Ezekiel thought it would make any difference in the reality of his world, he did what he heard God ask. What God required of him was none other than to be his own true self and to use what was his own true gift.

The Goal and the Source

Believing that I can do nothing helpful or that my group has no positive future is a recipe for deep depression. Combining Ezekiel's vision with Paul's figure of speech about the body may help us out of such times. The "eyes" in the group can help make sure the situation is being observed accurately. The "ears" in the group can be on the alert for God's word. Each member of the group can assist all the others in being their true selves, and in bringing their gifts to the fore.

The starting place for the church or for individuals is not "how can we do everything that must be done?" but rather "what am I able to do?" I believe that if each individual's gifts are celebrated and used, we will have positive results past anything we could imagine at the beginning. In order for this to happen, however, we must be clear about the goal we have in mind. The church is not supposed to be an incubator of get-rich-quick schemes nor a dispenser of simple sayings to individual members. It is, however, to proclaim Jesus Christ and the reign of God in such a way that we can begin to live that life in this world, here and now.

The goal is to live more nearly as people created in the image of God. The source of both our help and our hope is that same Creator God. It is in remembering this congruence between our goal and the source of our hope that we can help each other. The solutions may not turn out to be as we had envisioned them, for the God we serve is the one who says, "See, I am doing a new thing" (Isaiah 43:19 NIV).

SHARING THE SCRIPTURE

PREPARING TO TEACH

Preparing Our Hearts

This week's devotional reading is found in Ezekiel 37:24-28, which is part of today's background scripture. Imagine hearing these words of hope as an exile in the land that had conquered your own country. Envision yourself returning home where God will live among you and establish a covenant of peace. These words sound incredible, for you feel that God has abandoned you, left you in a strange place. Yet, the prophet brings words of hope. What words of hope do you need to hear in your own life right now? What expectations do you have that God can enable your hope to be fulfilled?

Pray that you and the students will open yourselves to receive new hope from God, especially in those areas of your life where you feel in despair and depressed.

Preparing Our Minds

Study Ezekiel 37, the background, and the lesson scripture from verses 1-14.

Write on newsprint:

information for next week's lesson, found under "Continue the Journey."

LEADING THE CLASS

(1) Gather to Learn

❖ Welcome the class members and introduce any guests.

❖ Pray that all who are present will open their hearts and minds to hear the word that God has for them this day.

❖ Invite the students to suggest world, national, or local situations where hope is needed. List these ideas on newsprint. Some possibilities include: *countries where war and hatred are perennial problems; communities that have a large number of AIDS patients; cities torn by violence and poverty.*

❖ Encourage the students to suggest changes that need to come about in each situation in order for the people to have hope. Add these ideas to the newsprint.

❖ Read aloud today's focus statement: **People in depression and despair are often incapable of hope. What is the source of our hope when all is bleak? Ezekiel affirms that God can bring new life and restoration to the direst of circumstances.**

(2) Study the Restoration God Promised to Exiles in Babylon

❖ Choose two volunteers to read today's passage from Ezekiel 37:1-14. One person will read the words of Ezekiel, and another, the words of God.

❖ Encourage the students to imagine

themselves as exiles in Babylon hearing Ezekiel's vision of bones coming to life in the valley. Ask these questions.

(1) **What might you assume about the setting described in verses 1 and 2?** (This valley could remind the exiles of a battlefield strewn with Israelites who died at the hands of the conquering Babylonian army.)

(2) **What is the importance of "breath" in this vision?** (See Understanding the Scripture, Ezekiel 37:11-14, second paragraph.)

(3) **What hope would you have after hearing Ezekiel's vision?** (See verses 11-14 in Understanding the Scripture.)

❖ Point out that this vision is addressed to a group of people who feel cut off from the living. The vision is not about resurrection, as Christians understand that term. Rather, it is about transformation.

❖ Discuss with the group how this vision is relevant to the Christian church. Are we in need of revitalization? If so, why? What promises do we need to hear from God?

(3) Affirm God's Power to Renew the Learners' Lives

❖ Distribute paper and pencils. Invite the students to write about a situation in their own lives that seems hopeless. This situation may affect them individually or it may have an impact on the community at large. Assure the students that what they write will remain confidential. Here are some ideas:

- Perhaps a devastating illness has struck them or a loved one.
- Maybe a major plant closing in their town has left a gaping hole in the local economy.
- Possibly they feel powerless to stop development or redevelopment that will change the character of their community.

❖ Share this thought attributed to Viktor Frankl, a well-known concentration camp survivor, author, and psychiatrist who believed that we are not shaped so much by what happens to us, but rather by how we respond to those events.

❖ Suggest that the students try to write a scenario of how they could respond to whatever event has created a sense of hopelessness within them. As an alternative, some students may want to imagine themselves as Israelites in Babylon and write about how they might respond to the life-changing event of exile.

❖ Conclude this activity by inviting volunteers to affirm their belief that God does have the power to bring about renewal and hope.

(4) Give Thanks for the Hope God Offers

❖ Suggest that the learners look again at Ezekiel 37:1-14 to find reasons that the exiles had to have hope in God. List these reasons on newsprint.

❖ Use another sheet of newsprint. Help the students to write a litany of thanksgiving to God based on the list they have made. If the class is large, you may prefer to divide into groups to write the litany. Remember to write a refrain, such as, **"We give thanks to you, O God of hope."**

❖ Read the litany together.

❖ Think about individuals or groups of people who need to hear these words of hope. Consider ways that you might share this good news in word and deed with those who are in despair, lonely, or anxious about a future that seems bleak. Covenant together to tell at least one person about how God brings hope to those who seemingly have no hope.

(5) Continue the Journey

❖ Pray that each one who is present will feel God's Spirit stirring within, recognize that God can touch their lives with hope and new life, and share this good news with others.

❖ Read aloud this preparation for next week's lesson. You may also want to post it on newsprint for the students to copy. **Prepare for next week's session entitled "Creating a Renewed Trust" by reading Psalm 73, noting especially verses 1-3, 12-13, 16-18, and 21-26. Keep this focus in mind as your study this lesson: Many people get discouraged over injustices in the world. What can we do to regain our perspective? The Psalms show how trust in God was renewed through worship and how God deserves our thanks.**

❖ Read aloud the following three ideas. Challenge the students to commit themselves to use these activities as a springboard to spiritual growth.

(1) **Record in your spiritual journal those situations in your own life that cause you despair or anxiety. Pray that God will bring about hope and new life in those areas.**

(2) **Offer words of hope to someone who is in the valley of despair. Let that person know that God can make all things new. Share the prophet's experience in Ezekiel 37.**

(3) **Make a list of hopes that you have for yourself, your loved ones, and your church. Pray about each one. Review the list periodically and check off hopes that have come to fruition.**

❖ Sing or read aloud "Spirit of God, Descend upon My Heart." As an alternative, if your students know the gospel tune "Dem Bones," you may prefer to sing that.

❖ Ask the students to echo this benediction from 2 Corinthians 13:11-14 as you read it phrase by phrase: **Finally, brothers and sisters, farewell. Put things in order . . . agree with one another, live in peace; and the God of love and peace will be with you. . . .The grace of the Lord Jesus Christ, the love of God, and the communion of the Holy Spirit be with all of you. Amen.**

CREATING A RENEWED TRUST

PREVIEWING THE LESSON

Lesson Scripture: Psalm 73:1-3, 12-13, 16-18, 21-26
Background Scripture: Psalm 73
Key Verse: Psalm 73:26

Focus of the Lesson:
Many people get discouraged over injustices in the world. What can we do to regain our perspective? The psalms show how trust in God was renewed through worship and how God deserves our thanks.

Goals for the Learners:
(1) to delve into the meaning of Psalm 73.
(2) to explore their willingness to trust God in unfair situations.
(3) to identify some unfair situations in the world today and commit themselves to fight for God's justice.

Pronunciation Guide:
antithetic parallelism	(an ti thet' ik par' al lel ism)
synonymous parallelism	(syn on' y mus par' al lel ism)
synthetic parallelism	(sin thet' ik par' al lel ism)

Supplies:
Bibles, newsprint and marker, paper and pencils, hymnals

READING THE SCRIPTURE

NRSV
Psalm 73:1-3, 12-13, 16-18, 21-26
  Truly God is good to the upright,
    to those who are pure in heart.
2 But as for me, my feet had almost
      stumbled;
    my steps had nearly slipped.
3 For I was envious of the arrogant;
    I saw the prosperity of the wicked.

NIV
Psalm 73:1-3, 12-13, 16-18, 21-26
¹ Surely God is good to Israel,
    to those who are pure in heart.
² But as for me, my feet had almost slipped;
    I had nearly lost my foothold.
³ For I envied the arrogant
    when I saw the prosperity of the
      wicked.

12 Such are the wicked;
    always at ease, they increase in riches.
13 All in vain I have kept my heart clean
    and washed my hands in innocence.
16 But when I thought how to understand
    this,
    it seemed to me a wearisome task,
17 until I went into the sanctuary of God;
    then I perceived their end.
18 Truly you set them in slippery places;
    you make them fall to ruin.
21 When my soul was embittered,
    when I was pricked in heart,
22 I was stupid and ignorant;
    I was like a brute beast toward you.
23 Nevertheless I am continually with you;
    you hold my right hand.
24 You guide me with your counsel,
    and afterward you will receive me with
    honor.
25 Whom have I in heaven but you?
    And there is nothing on earth that I
    desire other than you.
26 My flesh and my heart may fail,
    but God is the strength of my heart and
    my portion forever.

[12] This is what the wicked are like—
    always carefree, they increase in wealth.
[13] Surely in vain have I kept my heart pure;
    in vain have I washed my hands in
    innocence.
[16] When I tried to understand all this,
    it was oppressive to me
[17] till I entered the sanctuary of God;
    then I understood their final destiny.
[18] Surely you place them on slippery ground;
    you cast them down to ruin.
[21] When my heart was grieved
    and my spirit embittered,
[22] I was senseless and ignorant;
    I was a brute beast before you.
[23] Yet I am always with you;
    you hold me by my right hand.
[24] You guide me with your counsel,
    and afterward you will take me into
    glory.
[25] Whom have I in heaven but you?
    And earth has nothing I desire besides
    you.
[26] **My flesh and my heart may fail,**
    but God is the strength of my heart
    and my portion forever.

UNDERSTANDING THE SCRIPTURE

Introduction. The book of Psalms is a collection of poetry containing diverse hymns, songs, prayers, and meditations. Hebrew poetry differs in several ways from English poetry. It does not work on the basis of rhyme or strict metric patterns. Instead, Hebrew poetry is organized by what is called parallelism. Two, or sometimes three, consecutive lines are related to each other such that the second line echoes or "seconds" the first and adds another layer of meaning to it. For example, "Today is bright/The sun is shining" is an example of what is called synonymous parallelism. "Today is bright/It is not raining" is antithetic parallelism, so called because one line is stated positively and the other in the neg-

ative. It is not the meaning of the two lines that is opposite, but only the way the meaning is expressed.

"Today is bright/It is Sunday" exemplifies the final major category, called synthethic parallelism. Basically, any relationship that is neither synonymous nor antithethic is synthetic. Synthetic parallelism cannot be just any random two lines, however. "Today is bright/Our dog's name is Gailor" would not qualify because there is nothing in either of those lines that connects with anything in the other line.

Psalm 73:1 is synonymous, in which "the upright" in line one is further defined as "pure in heart" in the second. An antithetic pair can be seen in verse 4. The arrogant "have no pain" and they are "healthy and sleek."

Knowing one more common feature of Hebrew poetry will make it easier to understand. In many psalm verses the verb is stated in the first line and assumed without being restated in the second. Thus verse 1 could be spelled out more completely as "Truly God is good to the upright/[truly God is good] to those who are pure in heart." As is the case with poetry in many languages, Hebrew poetry is often very compact and spare rather than spelling out every nuance. Additionally, it is not uncommon to find rare words and unusual phrasing in poetry.

One more introductory comment seems necessary. We do not know who wrote many of the prayers and hymns that make up the Psalter. There is no reason to believe that none of the composers could have been women, but it is likely that most were men. Thus, for ease of expression instead of saying "he or she" when referring to the author, I will use the masculine pronoun.

Psalm 73:1-9. This psalm begins with praise of God and affirmation of God's gracious attention but then turns quickly to something else. The psalmist recounts a "close call" which could have resulted in his separation from God. For the author of this psalm looks at the world as it is and not only as it ought to be, and he is also honest about himself. This psalm describes one side of a major issue that has to be faced by all people who believe in a benevolent God. If God is good, why is there so much evil in the world? Why do the wicked prosper? And why do good people suffer?

The shortest truthful answer to these questions is that we do not know. The negative effects of human sin do not fall only upon the one who has committed that particular instance of sin. These verses recognize a fact everyone has come up against: from what we can see, there are bad people who "are not in trouble as others are" (73:5).

And it seems highly unfair of God to allow the world to be this way.

This poet, however, goes a level deeper and recognizes his own envy in verse 3. He lays his complaint about the wicked before God in some detail, but he is not thereby intending to hold himself up as an example of perfect virtue. He recognizes and confesses the danger to his own spirit of being envious of others.

Psalm 73:10-12. While these verses continue the complaint, they contain a specific element I want to underline. Verse 11 describes the attitude of the "practical atheist." There is no denial of God's existence here. But there is no recognition that God has anything to do with our lives on earth. It is a matter of believing in God as an abstract concept and at the same time assuming that God has little or nothing to do with one's regular everyday life.

Psalm 73:13-17. The poet reflects on what appears to him to be the unfairness of his situation. Why has he bothered to try to live according to God's will? He is a good person; where is his reward? Once again, he brings himself up short, realizing that his feelings of being mistreated by God are not reflective of the truth of God's dealings with the world in general or with him in particular. When the task of trying to figure it all out becomes too much, he goes to worship.

Psalm 73:18-20. Within the context of worship comes the realization that the wicked are not as enduring as God is. They may seem to be in charge at the present moment, but the time will come when they will be seen to be as insubstantial as a dream. While the dream is going on it often seems to the dreamer to be reality. When the dreamer wakes, however, the details of what had seemed so real—even frightening—fade quickly.

Psalm 73:21-28. The psalmist makes another confession as he realizes that in his challenging of the way he observes and experiences the world, he was acting ignorantly toward God. He awakens to his experience of the presence of God and that in God's presence, nothing material matters ultimately. God is faithful and the faithful presence of God is better than anything else. "There is nothing on earth that I desire other than you," he finally exclaims (73:25b).

INTERPRETING THE SCRIPTURE

First, Be Honest

The first rule of prayer is simple: be honest. God already knows what is in our heart and on our mind. If we try to fool God, or if we think that prayer must be a matter of a limited number of topics or emotions, then God may have trouble answering us in ways we can hear. One of the treasures of the book of Psalms is the plain honesty found throughout the book. How often would you be willing to pray out loud in your Sunday school group and say, "God, it looks as if you are not being fair to me. I try to live a good life and yet I face daily troubles. It looks to me as if the scoundrels who think nothing of you and who cheat and steal are living lives of ease."

The psalmist is discouraged because he looks at the world around him and sees it as it is. Admitting his discouragement is not a bad thing. God would have a harder time communicating with him and answering his prayers if he were not willing to tell the Lord just what is on his mind.

Somewhere the notion has arisen that people of true and deep faith are never discouraged and that if they have any troubles at all they never complain about them. "Just have faith and everything will turn out just fine," is neither helpful nor true much of the time.

Look at Yourself

The honesty of the psalmist is not limited to his views of other people and reactions to the outside world. There is also an unblinking scan of the individual's interior life and relations to others. Tell God what you really want. Get all those negative emotions out of your system so that they do not fester, or come out in destructive ways.

Admit the troubles but do not then wallow in them, nor fuss and complain endlessly to everyone within earshot. Feel free to tell God that you want your enemies destroyed, but do not use prayer as a way to "psych" yourself and your group into charging out against those enemies as soon as worship is over. For in issuing orders to God about how to take care of your enemies, you will probably realize that you have your not-so-nice sides too.

Look at God

What is worship for? Does God need our praise? Worship is, among other things, the gracious reaching out to us by our heavenly Father. Worship is emphatically not a "spectator sport." It is not entertainment, something performed by the pastor and choir and organist for which the congregation participates primarily as audience. No, worship is the work of the whole congregation, even though different people take different parts. It is one way in which we as the community of faith praise God and confess our sins to God, and also a time in which we have glimpses of God.

You have probably heard the quip, "I can worship God just as well on the golf course as in church." And, of course, that is true: it is possible to worship God anywhere at all. The pinch comes, though, when one asks, "Do you worship God when you're on the golf course, or at the beach, or wherever it is you choose to be instead of at church?"

One Modern Example

"I was so upset and angry most of the time it was hard to go to church," Lorena admitted to her Sunday school class. "There were all my brothers and sisters in Christ smiling and looking good. And I'd smile back, of course, but it felt fake. I was sure they could see through me."

The class was discussing how our understandings of God had changed since we were children, and what had brought about those changes. Lorena had volunteered to tell part of her story, though she warned us, "It's not very exciting."

Lorena was raising two children, living as a single mother. She was married to their father, but he was in the Army and stationed overseas. Her extended family was halfway across the country from where she and the children lived near the base that was Jamal's Stateside posting. Their firstborn was a healthy and very active eight-year-old boy. Their daughter was six and was mildly mentally retarded. She suffered from a baffling array of mild to moderate physical ailments that the doctors could never quite pin down. The local public school had difficulty providing an appropriate learning environment for Keesha. Some days the school principal would telephone Lorena at work and tell her she must pick up Keesha immediately because she was sick. Keesha, however, often would cry when her mother arrived and beg to be allowed to stay at school, saying she felt fine.

"Some days I'd just feel so weary," Lorena told us. "Johnnie was doing fine, but then kids would tease him because of Keesha. You know how kids can be . . ." she trailed off. "And I was just so full of bitter questions. Jamal and I loved each other so much. Why couldn't he get a job outside the Army so we could live together as a family? How come so many people who didn't even like each other much got to be together? And why didn't the school fulfill its responsibility for Keesha? Why did that principal keep calling me so I had to take off work and come get her when she was really okay to be in school? And why couldn't the doctor find out what the problem with her was so they could fix it? Was it something I had done that made her that way? I'd see all those other people who never gave God a second thought, getting along just fine. And I'd start to wonder why didn't God ever seem to listen or to help us? But I tried not to dwell on that part, because the last thing in the world we needed was for God to be mad at us!

"Then one day in church I really listened to the Psalms. The psalmist was just going on and on about how he had done everything right but wasn't getting anywhere. And that he could see his enemies living just fine and it just didn't seem fair to him. And something just sort of clicked with me. I just poured out everything to God. All my disappointments about Jamal and me being so far apart. And how scared I was for Keesha. And how I was afraid I wasn't spending enough time with Johnnie. I think I'd always been afraid to talk to God like that before. But once I started paying attention, I saw that lots and lots of the psalms were like that. And a feeling came over me that I can't rightly describe. But like God was really listening to me and *wanted* to listen to me.

"It didn't change anything about the outward parts of my life, but it started to change me inside. Worship for me now is different too. It's not that I can't talk to God anywhere and any time I want to, but somehow being together with all of you and all the rest of the people and talking with God . . . well . . . it's just good. And I'm so glad God wants to listen to us."

SHARING THE SCRIPTURE

PREPARING TO TEACH

Preparing Our Hearts

This week's devotional reading is found in Psalm 91:1-10. The psalmist writes with amazing confidence in God's willingness and ability to offer protection and guidance. Do you trust God to the extent that the psalmist does? What evidence supports your answer?

Pray that you and the adults in your class will "fear not," for God is able to protect you.

Preparing Our Minds

Study the background scripture, Psalm 73, and lesson scripture, Psalm 73:1-3, 12-13, 16-18, and 21-26.

Write on newsprint:

information for next week's lesson, found under "Continue the Journey."

Plan a brief lecture for "Delve into the Meaning of Psalm 73."

LEADING THE CLASS

(1) Gather to Learn

❖ Welcome the class members and introduce any guests.

❖ Pray that God's Spirit will overshadow all who are present so that the word of the Lord may be plainly heard and understood.

❖ Encourage the students to describe some current unfair situations that they see locally, nationally, and globally. Write their ideas on newsprint.

❖ Discuss these questions.

(1) **How do you feel when you hear, for example, that some highly paid executive whose actions have caused the downfall of a company and loss of jobs and pensions goes unpunished?** (You may wish to create specific questions based on examples that the class brainstormed.)

(2) **How does an apparently unfair situation such as this affect your trust in God?**

❖ Read aloud today's focus statement: **Many people get discouraged over injustices in the world. What can we do to regain our perspective? The Psalms show how trust in God was renewed through worship and how God deserves our thanks.**

(2) Delve into the Meaning of Psalm 73

❖ Choose four readers and assign each volunteer one of these passages: Psalm 73:1-3, 12-13, 16-18, or 21-26. All readers need not use the same translation of the Bible.

❖ Note these points in a brief lecture. If you choose, you may want to add information from the introduction in Understanding the Scripture to help the students learn more about how to read the poetry of the Psalms.

■ God is always present and always good.

■ Evildoers seem to "live the good life," but that prosperity does not last.

■ It is tempting to follow prosperous evildoers, for we may be envious of them.

■ Those who want to be near to God renew their trust in God as they worship in the sanctuary. Through worship, we realize the folly of evildoers and choose to be close to God.

❖ Invite the students to respond to the psalmist by evaluating and discussing these ideas, either with the entire class, or with a partner, or in a small group:

■ how realistic they believe the writer's ideas are in our world.

- why they believe (or do not believe) that evildoers "fall to ruin" as the psalmist claims in verse 18.
- how their experience of God in worship is similar to or different from that of the psalmist.

(3) Explore the Learners' Willingness to Trust God in Unfair Situations

❖ Read aloud "One Modern Example," found in the Interpreting the Scripture portion. Ask the students to listen for ideas that resonate with them.

❖ Invite the class members to use this example as a springboard for discussion of unfair situations they have seen or experienced in their own family. *A word of caution here:* Do not let individuals get bogged down in the details of their own difficult situations.

❖ Reread a portion of the next to last paragraph of "One Modern Example," beginning with "Then one day in church," and ending with, "everything to God."

❖ Distribute paper and pencils. Encourage the students to write a few words about an experience that helped them to recognize that they could trust God, no matter what the circumstances.

❖ Encourage volunteers to read their ideas.

(4) Identify Unfair Situations in the World Today and Commit to Fight for God's Justice

❖ Look again at the list of unfair situations that the students brainstormed at the beginning of the session. Provide an opportunity for them to add ideas.

❖ Ask them to look at the list to see which of these situations they might be able to address. Put an asterisk next to possibilities. Note that there are many ways to work in such situations:

- advocacy (such as writing letters to elected officials or speaking on behalf of those who have been unfairly treated).

- financial/resource support (pledging money or goods to a group that works on behalf of the affected persons).
- hands-on support (working as a volunteer to assist those who are unfairly treated).

❖ Try to agree on one item for action, or choose several and divide the class into groups based on interest in the identified situations.

❖ Develop a plan of action as to how the class could go about tackling this unfair situation. Each individual will need to act according to his or her talents, abilities, interests, and time constraints. Help the group discern what they will do, when they will do it, the resources needed to accomplish this task, and the criteria by which they will evaluate how well they have done what they set out to do.

❖ Provide a way for the students to commit themselves to act on the plan they have developed to fight against injustice. One way to do this would be for the class to create a covenant, such as *"Trusting in God to guide my actions, I commit myself to work for justice for the homeless people in our community."* You could write the covenant on newsprint and have each person sign it, or simply read the covenant aloud together.

(5) Continue the Journey

❖ Pray that all who have participated in today's gathering will feel free to pour their hearts out to God, knowing that God is with them even in unjust situations.

❖ Read aloud this preparation for next week's lesson. You may also want to post it on newsprint for the students to copy. **Prepare for next week's session entitled "Living by New Rules" by reading Matthew 5. We will look particularly at verses 17-18, 21-22, 27-28, 31-35, 38-39, 43-44. As you study this first portion of the Sermon on the Mount, keep this focus in mind: Many people have a strong personal** sense of integrity. What guides our integrity as Christians? Jesus taught that both attitude and action are important.

❖ Read aloud the following three ideas. Challenge the students to commit themselves to use these activities as a springboard to spiritual growth.

(1) Keep an eye out for stories in the media that demonstrate unfair situations in today's world. Pray about these situations. Ask God to show you where you might be able to make a difference in these unfair conditions.

(2) Make a list of circumstances in your own life that seem unfair to you. Read Psalm 73 with your own situations in mind.

(3) Attend worship this week. As you do, notice how your trust in God is renewed as you participate in the worship experience.

❖ Sing or read aloud "O God, Our Help in Ages Past."

❖ Ask the students to echo this benediction from 2 Corinthians 13:11-14 as you read it phrase by phrase: **Finally, brothers and sisters, farewell. Put things in order . . . agree with one another, live in peace; and the God of love and peace will be with you. . . . The grace of the Lord Jesus Christ, the love of God, and the communion of the Holy Spirit be with all of you. Amen.**

UNIT 3: A NEW CREATION

LIVING BY NEW RULES

PREVIEWING THE LESSON

Lesson Scripture: Matthew 5:17-18, 21-22, 27-28, 31-35, 38-39, 43-44
Background Scripture: Matthew 5
Key Verse: Matthew 5:17

Focus of the Lesson:
Many people have a strong personal sense of integrity. What guides our integrity as Christians? Jesus taught that both attitude and action are important.

Goals for the Learners:
(1) to explore the connections Jesus makes between attitude and action.
(2) to evaluate the connection between attitude and action in their lives.
(3) to articulate several important guidelines for Christian living and commit to abide by them.

Supplies:
Bibles, newsprint and marker, paper and pencils, optional commentaries, hymnals

READING THE SCRIPTURE

NRSV
Matthew 5:17-18, 21-22, 27-28, 31-35, 38-39, 43-44

17 "Do not think that I have come to abolish the law or the prophets; I have come not to abolish but to fulfill. 18 For truly I tell you, until heaven and earth pass away, not one letter, not one stroke of a letter, will pass from the law until all is accomplished.

21 "You have heard that it was said to those of ancient times, 'You shall not murder'; and 'whoever murders shall be liable to judgment.' 22 But I say to you that if you are angry with a brother or sister, you will be liable to judgment; and

NIV
Matthew 5:17-18, 21-22, 27-28, 31-35, 38-39, 43-44

17"Do not think that I have come to abolish the Law or the Prophets; I have not come to abolish them but to fulfill them. 18I tell you the truth, until heaven and earth disappear, not the smallest letter, not the least stroke of a pen, will by any means disappear from the Law until everything is accomplished.

21"You have heard that it was said to the people long ago, 'Do not murder, and anyone who murders will be subject to judgment.' 22But I tell you that anyone who is angry with his brother will be subject to if you insult a brother or sister, you will be liable to the council; and if you say, 'You fool,' you will be liable to the hell of fire.

27 "You have heard that it was said, 'You shall not commit adultery.' 28 But I say to you that everyone who looks at a woman with lust has already committed adultery with her in his heart.

31 "It was also said, 'Whoever divorces his wife, let him give her a certificate of divorce.' 32 But I say to you that anyone who divorces his wife, except on the ground of unchastity, causes her to commit adultery; and whoever marries a divorced woman commits adultery.

33 "Again, you have heard that it was said to those of ancient times, 'You shall not swear falsely, but carry out the vows you have made to the Lord.' 34 But I say to you, Do not swear at all, either by heaven, for it is the throne of God, 35 or by the earth, for it is his footstool, or by Jerusalem, for it is the city of the great King.

38 "You have heard that it was said, 'An eye for an eye and a tooth for a tooth.' 39 But I say to you, Do not resist an evildoer. But if anyone strikes you on the right cheek, turn the other also.

43 "You have heard that it was said, 'You shall love your neighbor and hate your enemy.' 44 But I say to you, Love your enemies and pray for those who persecute you."

judgment. Again, anyone who says to his brother, 'Raca,' is answerable to the Sanhedrin. But anyone who says, 'You fool!' will be in danger of the fire of hell.

27"You have heard that it was said, 'Do not commit adultery.' 28But I tell you that anyone who looks at a woman lustfully has already committed adultery with her in his heart.

31"It has been said, 'Anyone who divorces his wife must give her a certificate of divorce.' 32But I tell you that anyone who divorces his wife, except for marital unfaithfulness, causes her to become an adulteress, and anyone who marries the divorced woman commits adultery.

33"Again, you have heard that it was said to the people long ago, 'Do not break your oath, but keep the oaths you have made to the Lord.' 34But I tell you, Do not swear at all: either by heaven, for it is God's throne; 35or by the earth, for it is his footstool; or by Jerusalem, for it is the city of the Great King.

38"You have heard that it was said, 'Eye for eye, and tooth for tooth.' 39But I tell you, Do not resist an evil person. If someone strikes you on the right cheek, turn to him the other also.

43"You have heard that it was said, 'Love your neighbor and hate your enemy.' 44But I tell you: Love your enemies and pray for those who persecute you."

UNDERSTANDING THE SCRIPTURE

Matthew 5:1-12. Matthew uses some "shorthand" in his Gospel. He does not need to begin his account by saying Jesus spoke with authority or that he was going to talk about God's law. All this, and more, was conveyed to Matthew's audience by saying Jesus "went up the mountain, and . . . sat down" (5:1). In Jesus' day, authori-

tative words were proclaimed by seated speakers (see Luke 4:20, for example). The truth of Jesus' claims is clearly based on his authority.

This first portion of the Sermon on the Mount is usually called The Beatitudes, from the Latin for the first word in verses 3-11. The usual translation in English is blessed," or, in some newer translations, "happy," though these words do not convey the full meaning. In our vocabulary happiness is associated with a feeling. The blessings of the Beatitudes, however, are based on God's actions, not our feelings. Moreover, the Beatitudes point to the future, to a time when God's kingdom will come. They show the blessings that God bestows on those who live as authentic Christians. In response, Christians are to act in accordance with the new rules of God's coming kingdom.

Matthew 5:13-16. Next come some familiar sayings. By using common figures of speech, Jesus tells his followers to be who they are, who they are created and called to be, for the good of the whole world.

Matthew 5:17-20. Jesus emphasizes here that he is not bringing a new message, or intending to do away with what God has said before to Israel. The phrase "the law and the prophets" was one way of referring to the Bible of Jesus' day, what Christians now call the Old Testament. Just as God tells Moses at the burning bush, "I am the God of your father, the God of Abraham, the God of Isaac, and the God of Jacob" (Exodus 3:6), Jesus is telling his listeners that he is sent by the very same God whom they have known all along.

In saying that he has come to "fulfill" the law, Jesus is saying that the law is not impossible. It is, as Moses reported in Deuteronomy 30:11-14, neither too hard nor too far away, but is very near to us. Among other things, Jesus will teach and live out the spirit of the ancient law in righteousness. "Righteousness" is a word we rarely use outside the church. We can substitute "right relationships" and be accurate. So we might paraphrase verse 20, "Unless you live in right relationship with God and with other people more than the leaders do, you will never begin to experience the life of the kingdom of God here on earth." The concepts of righteousness and justice are closely intertwined.

Matthew 5:21-47. These verses begin a section of the Sermon on the Mount commonly referred to as the "antitheses" or opposites. And Jesus does say several times "You have heard . . . but I say to you. . . ." However, he is not saying that what the people have heard in the past is wrong (with one exception in verse 43), but rather that they have not taken what they have heard far enough. In the first example, Jesus says that we should not be angry and insult brothers and sisters or call them fool (5:22). Is an insult really as bad as *murder?* In terms of its effects on the other person, of course not. But in terms of its corroding effects on our own soul, then, yes it is as bad to call someone a name as to hit him, as evil to hate as to kill.

Reconciliation—the way to that right relationship the church calls righteousness—is even more important than the formal public worship of God! If we remember, when offering our gift in church, that someone has something against us, we are to go make it up to that person. Then we return to church and make our offering. It is not a matter of *either* worship God *or* be reconciled. We are to do both, starting with reconciliation.

Verses 29-30 are easy to misunderstand because we do not divide the body figuratively the same way Jesus' first audience did. In ancient Palestine the eyes and ears stand for how the world affects us. The mouth and the hands stand for how we affect the world. So what Jesus is saying is that if there is something in the world that is causing us to sin, we should get away from it. Or if we are doing something that is causing us to sin, we should stop doing it. That is, it is better to do without some pastime or some habit than to lose salvation because we cannot give up those things.

Throughout this section, Jesus is trying to get the people to look beyond the surface of their words and actions and the words of the law. We need to understand what the law is pointing toward, what it is trying to accomplish, and then to work toward that goal, rather than being slavish in following the letter of the law. For example, instead of being concerned what we swear on, whether heaven or earth or "cross my heart," Jesus is urging us to tell the simple truth and stop there.

Especially in the verses about going a second mile or turning the cheek to one who strikes us, it is exceedingly important to remember that Jesus was speaking these words first to his disciples and then to the rest of the crowds who were there and that he was talking about situations of choice.

Jesus is *not* telling a battered wife or an abused child that they should simply accept their mistreatment. Jesus is speaking to people in situations where they have the possibility of striking back and saying that it is more likely to defuse a situation to refrain from striking back.

Matthew 5:48. This final verse seems totally impossible. The difficulty stems from our different understanding of the word translated "perfect." The Greek word also means "complete." We might say, "Be completely what you were created to be, as God is completely God."

INTERPRETING THE SCRIPTURE

By Whose Measure?

A major stumbling block to Christians earnestly trying to follow Jesus' teachings is that we sometimes forget what has changed in the last two thousand years. It is not easy always to be on the lookout for cultural differences between biblical texts and our own language and lives, especially when the biblical words seem altogether straightforward. But such care is necessary if we are not to misunderstand Jesus in significant ways. Jesus' main theme in this chapter is teaching how to live life on earth as we should. One result of such living is that we begin to experience the kingdom of God (or "kingdom of heaven" as it is called in Matthew's Gospel) in this life, before we die.

In some ways, Jesus' teaching could be considered countercultural, both in his day and in ours. Much of what he said went against some of the popular and accepted ways people behaved. And much of what he said is different from what we hear all around us today. The question in this week's Focus of the Lesson is so significant in part because it can be so difficult to live: "What guides our integrity as Christians?"

The population of Palestine in the first century had a hard time being faithful to God *and* not getting on the wrong side of the occupying Romans at the same time. Could the Jews of Jesus' day be both religious and patriotic? And where was their ultimate loyalty? What if the claims of Caesar and of God came into conflict? These are our questions too.

Our nation's Bicentennial, July 4, 1976, fell on a Sunday. Some of the people in one of my churches wanted me to cancel the worship service so that they could go to the celebration in the county seat. I told them they were free to go to the parade, of course, but there would still be a worship service at church. Their parting comment was, "God is all right in his place, but this is *America!*"

I was probably being too stubborn, too legalistic, about not canceling a worship service. But their statement has haunted me ever since. What guides our integrity as Christians? Certainly not a rigid adherence to laws we make about church attendance. But if our attention to God can happen only when we don't have something more interesting to do, then I think our Christianity is pretty shallow. If we say we are Christians, there should be some evidence in our lives that we are attempting to follow Jesus.

Legal Is Right?

It is legal for U.S. companies to set the price for their product at whatever level they choose. And if our major goal in life is to get as much money as possible—and to keep as much of what we earn as possible—then it is reasonable to expect prices to be high and equally reasonable to expect that consumers will try to find lower prices. Increasing numbers of people are attempting to buy prescription drugs over the Internet. Those who live close enough to the border cross over into Canada to have their prescriptions filled. Why? Because many drugs are vastly more expensive in the United States. Several of the large pharmaceutical companies are trying to make both practices illegal. This one example reminds us that if our ultimate loyalty is to God, then we may ask what level of profit is "enough" for corporations, when their products can be a literal matter of life and death to their consumers.

The town I live in has a small hospital that is over one hundred years old. A few years ago a large hospital management corporation acquired it. The community has recently found out that the management company wants to close our hospital because it isn't making enough money. There is nothing illegal about their plans. But this is the closest emergency room for a great many people living in this area. The facility has always operated in the black, but apparently a small profit is not enough. How much is enough?

These are big questions. If something is legal, does that guarantee that it is also right? Is being right the same thing as being Christian?

But That's Not Fair!

One of the hardest aspects of the Christian message to communicate adequately is the notion of grace. From earliest childhood we are admonished to "play fair"

and to take turns. Our language is full of sayings such as "You get what you pay for" and "There's no such thing as a free lunch." We have little trouble remembering that the Bible says "an eye for an eye, a tooth for a tooth" even though we may not realize that that was radical in its own day. In a time of massive retaliation, "an eye for an eye" was considered unfair!

Jesus, however, is talking about integrity measured against a very different scale. When our personal "bottom line" is the kingdom of heaven, we are free to make our actions fit our beliefs, even if those beliefs are not the ones followed by our neighbors.

When one of my daughters was a toddler, she would sometimes become so upset that she would scream and kick and hit. At such times, I would gather her onto my lap and sit in the rocking chair, rocking and humming to her with my arms wrapped snugly around her. At first she would continue to kick, but gradually she would calm. Then I would try to find out what had gone wrong. On the literal level, it was not "fair" that she kicked me, because not only had I not done anything to her, I loved her and told her so. But because I was the adult, I was free to absorb her hits and kicks until she calmed down. I also wanted her to know that I loved her regardless of her actions toward me. She was too young to understand all those words, but I wanted her to understand that message by the way I treated her. When we love someone, when we have that person's ultimate best interests at heart, then a strict calculus of what is "fair" does not enter into our minds.

An Impossible Possibility

Trying to make our words and actions match, trying to put our neighbor's welfare above our own even when that is not "fair"—these may seem to be nearly impossible tasks. The final saying of Jesus in today's lesson seems an even more unattainable goal. How can we be "perfect" as God is perfect? As the Understanding the Scripture section points out, the Greek word translated "perfect" also means "whole" and "complete." We can strive to be whole, complete human beings created in the image of God.

Still, such a goal does not appear within the realm of possibility most of the time, does it? But God's grace is available to assist us. And Jesus' teachings, as in Matthew 5, provide a guide for us. Each time we do as we say, each time we act on the outside the way we believe on the inside, we get closer to that goal. There is a line from an ancient prayer I find helpful, praying God "that we may show forth your praise not only with our lips, but in our lives." By God's grace, which we are able to see most clearly in Jesus Christ, we can indeed live in that direction.

SHARING THE SCRIPTURE

PREPARING TO TEACH

Preparing Our Hearts

This week's devotional reading is found in Matthew 5:1-12. This familiar listing of the Beatitudes is part of today's background scripture. Try rewriting the ending of each of the Beatitudes the way most humans would. For example, "Blessed are the meek, *for they shall be used as doormats by everyone.*" Compare the typical human view with what God says about the blessings that those who are living in anticipation of the fullness of the reign of God can expect. Consider how these blessings from God affect your life now and in the future.

Pray that you and your students will practice the behaviors that the Sermon on the Mount sets forth.

Preparing Our Minds

Study the background, which is all of Matthew 5. Pay particular attention to the verses of the scripture lesson: 17-18, 21-22, 27-28, 31-35, 38-39, and 43-44.

Write on newsprint:
ideas for group discussion in the portion entitled "Evaluate the Connection Between Attitude and Action in the Learners' Lives."

information for next week's lesson, found under "Continue the Journey."

Plan a lecture if you prefer that format to the suggested group work in the "Explore the Connections Jesus Makes Between Attitude and Action" section.

LEADING THE CLASS

(1) Gather to Learn

❖ Welcome the class members and introduce any guests.

❖ Pray that the students will recognize that their attitudes and actions are important components of their Christian discipleship.

❖ Brainstorm with the class answers to this question: **What are the marks of a person who lives with integrity?** List their ideas on newsprint.

❖ Distribute paper and pencils. Encourage the students to choose a few of the marks and write examples of how they fulfill each one. Tell them that they will not be asked to share their responses.

❖ Read aloud today's focus statement: **Many people have a strong personal sense of integrity. What guides our integrity as Christians? Jesus taught that both attitude and action are important.**

(2) Explore the Connections Jesus Makes Between Attitude and Action

❖ Set the stage for today's lesson by noting that:

- Matthew 5 is the beginning of the collection of teachings in chapters 5 through 7 known as the Sermon on the Mount.
- in verse 1 that we learn that Jesus teaches with authority because he "sat down" as a respected rabbi would.
- Jesus speaks from the mountain, a place associated with revelation from God.
- hearing Jesus speak with authority from the mountain would remind his Jewish listeners of Moses.

❖ Select six volunteers and assign each of them to read one of the following passages: Matthew 5:17-18, 21-22, 27-28, 31-35, 38-39, and 43-44.

❖ Divide the class into six groups and assign each one a passage. If possible, provide each group with at least one commentary. Participants will also need paper and pencils. Ask the groups to work together to discern the meaning of the passage in light of the cultural context in which Jesus spoke. Challenge them to think about how their assigned passage applies to them today.

❖ Provide time for each group to tell the class what they have discerned from their reading and discussion.

❖ As an alternative if you prefer to use a lecture format, do the work for each group prior to class and give your findings in a brief talk.

(3) Evaluate the Connection Between Attitude and Action in the Learners' Lives

❖ Post newsprint with the following information on it and ask the students to discuss their responses among their assigned groups.

How would you react if:

- you claimed the idea of oneness and

equality in Christ but were with a group where racial or ethnic slurs and jokes were being tossed about?
- you claimed to love your enemy but had an opportunity to spread gossip about him or her?
- you claimed fidelity to your spouse but met a coworker who really appealed to you?
- you were wronged and had a chance to get even with the person who caused you harm?

❖ Provide a few moments of quiet reflection time. Ask each student to consider these questions: **Are my actions congruent with my attitudes? Or, in popular parlance, does my walk match my talk? If not, what changes do I need God to help me make?**

❖ Invite volunteers to make any observations about insights they have gleaned from this activity.

(4) Articulate Several Important Guidelines for Christian Living and Commit to Abide by Them

❖ Ask the students to look again at the verses for today's lesson with an eye to discerning guidelines for contemporary Christian living.

❖ List ideas for these guidelines on newsprint. Continue to refine the wording until the class agrees by consensus. You will probably have time to develop three to five statements.

❖ Talk about the kinds of attitudes one would need to hold and the actions one would need to exhibit in order to live according to these guidelines.

❖ Encourage the students to make an oral commitment to live by these guidelines. You might do this by beginning, **"In order to live more faithfully as Christ's disciples, we the members of the (name of your Sunday school class) agree to abide by these guidelines for living."** Then, have them read in unison each of the guidelines they have agreed to follow.

(5) Continue the Journey

❖ Pray that those who have participated in today's session will live so that their attitudes and their actions reflect the teaching and example of Christ.

❖ Read aloud this preparation for next week's lesson. You may also want to post it on newsprint for the students to copy. **Prepare for next week's session entitled "Counting on Resurrection" by reading 1 Corinthians 15. Our lesson will look specifically at verses 42-57. Keep this focus in mind as you read: Most people wonder about life after death. What are we to believe? Paul wrote about the new body and our assurance of resurrection in Christ.**

❖ Read aloud the following three ideas. Challenge the students to commit themselves to use these activities as a springboard to spiritual growth.

(1) **Evaluate some of your recent actions. Do you believe that they reflect your stated attitudes, or are you aware of a "disconnect" between the two? What do you need to do to bring your actions into line with your attitudes?**

(2) **Look for examples of people who have, in your opinion, not lived with integrity. What aspects of their behavior do you find particularly troublesome? Why? Jot down your thoughts in a spiritual journal. The purpose here is not to be judgmental but rather to note behaviors that you find problematic.**

(3) **Recall an incident in which your integrity may have been questioned. What happened to raise this question? How was the matter resolved? What changes did you make in your behavior?**

❖ Sing or read aloud "Dear Lord, Lead Me Day by Day."

❖ Ask the students to echo this benediction from 2 Corinthians 13:11-14 as you read it phrase by phrase: **Finally, brothers and sisters, farewell. Put things in order . . . agree with one another, live in peace; and the God of love and peace will be with you. . . . The grace of the Lord Jesus Christ, the love of God, and the communion of the Holy Spirit be with all of you. Amen.**

COUNTING ON RESURRECTION

PREVIEWING THE LESSON

Lesson Scripture: 1 Corinthians 15:42-57
Background Scripture: 1 Corinthians 15
Key Verse: 1 Corinthians 15:55

Focus of the Lesson:
Most people wonder about life after death. What are we to believe? Paul wrote about the new body and our assurance of resurrection in Christ.

Goals for the Learners:
(1) to examine Paul's understanding of the resurrection.
(2) to explore what Jesus' resurrection means for them.
(3) to take at least one step to prepare for their own death.

Pronunciation Guide:
imperishability   (im per' ish abil i ty)

You will need these supplies:
Bibles, newsprint and marker, paper and pencils, optional recording of Handel's *Messiah* that includes the selections listed in "Examine Paul's Understanding of the Resurrection," compact disc or tape player and extension cord or batteries, hymnals

---

READING THE SCRIPTURE

NRSV
1 Corinthians 15:42-57

42 So it is with the resurrection of the dead. What is sown is perishable, what is raised is imperishable. 43 It is sown in dishonor, it is raised in glory. It is sown in weakness, it is raised in power. 44 It is sown a physical body, it is raised a spiritual body. If there is a physical body, there is also a spiritual body. 45 Thus it is written, "The first man, Adam, became a living being"; the

NIV
1 Corinthians 15:42-57

[42]So will it be with the resurrection of the dead. The body that is sown is perishable, it is raised imperishable; [43]it is sown in dishonor, it is raised in glory; it is sown in weakness, it is raised in power; [44]it is sown a natural body, it is raised a spiritual body.

If there is a natural body, there is also a spiritual body. [45]So it is written: "The first man Adam became a living being"; the last

last Adam became a life-giving spirit. 46 But it is not the spiritual that is first, but the physical, and then the spiritual. 47 The first man was from the earth, a man of dust; the second man is from heaven. 48 As was the man of dust, so are those who are of the dust; and as is the man of heaven, so are those who are of heaven. 49 Just as we have borne the image of the man of dust, we will also bear the image of the man of heaven.

50 What I am saying, brothers and sisters, is this: flesh and blood cannot inherit the kingdom of God, nor does the perishable inherit the imperishable. 51 Listen, I will tell you a mystery! We will not all die, but we will all be changed, 52 in a moment, in the twinkling of an eye, at the last trumpet. For the trumpet will sound, and the dead will be raised imperishable, and we will be changed. 53 For this perishable body must put on imperishability, and this mortal body must put on immortality. 54 When this perishable body puts on imperishability, and this mortal body puts on immortality, then the saying that is written will be fulfilled:

"Death has been swallowed up in victory."
55 "Where, O death, is your victory?
Where, O death, is your sting?"
56 The sting of death is sin, and the power of sin is the law. 57 But thanks be to God, who gives us the victory through our Lord Jesus Christ.

Adam, a life-giving spirit. 46 The spiritual did not come first, but the natural, and after that the spiritual. 47 The first man was of the dust of the earth, the second man from heaven. 48 As was the earthly man, so are those who are of the earth; and as is the man from heaven, so also are those who are of heaven. 49 And just as we have borne the likeness of the earthly man, so shall we bear the likeness of the man from heaven.

50 I declare to you, brothers, that flesh and blood cannot inherit the kingdom of God, nor does the perishable inherit the imperishable. 51 Listen, I tell you a mystery: We will not all sleep, but we will all be changed— 52 in a flash, in the twinkling of an eye, at the last trumpet. For the trumpet will sound, the dead will be raised imperishable, and we will be changed. 53 For the perishable must clothe itself with the imperishable, and the mortal with immortality. 54 When the perishable has been clothed with the imperishable, and the mortal with immortality, then the saying that is written will come true: "Death has been swallowed up in victory."
55 "Where, O death, is your victory?
Where, O death, is your sting?"
56 The sting of death is sin, and the power of sin is the law. 57 But thanks be to God! He gives us the victory through our Lord Jesus Christ.

UNDERSTANDING THE SCRIPTURE

1 Corinthians 15:1-11. In all our discussion of this chapter from Paul's letter, we need to hold in front of us what he says in verse 51: "Listen, I will tell you a mystery." It is certainly not inappropriate to think, speculate, and try to figure out what Jesus' resurrection means, as long as we are willing to allow that ultimately it is more than we can comprehend within our mortal minds.

Paul begins this chapter by reminding the Corinthians of the heart of the gospel message he preached to them: Jesus died, was buried, and was raised from the dead. The resurrected Christ appeared to many people and in different ways. Paul's experience, coming as it did after the ascension, was not the same as that of Cephas and James and the other apostles. Even so, Paul does not consider that he has not seen the risen Christ. Indeed, Paul's experience of Christ can be strengthening to other

Christians since Paul began as a persecutor of the church. That is, there is no sin that can disqualify someone ultimately from belief in Christ and a saving relationship through that belief.

1 Corinthians 15:12-34. Now, apparently, there are some members of the church in Corinth who are disputing the resurrection of the dead. Paul, using a form of argumentation with which they would have been more familiar than we are, argues in an "all or nothing" manner. If they are denying any resurrection, then Christ has not been raised, faith is worthless, and those who are putting their belief and hope in Christ are merely to be pitied. This is emphatically not the case, however, Paul asserts. Christ *has* been raised and they are living in a middle time, between the first evidence of resurrection and the final subjugation of all things to Christ and through Christ to God.

If this is not the case, then we might as well live as if there is no tomorrow for, in an ultimate sense, there is none. "Live it up now, because when you're dead you're dead" would be an acceptable philosophy for those who do not know God. Paul says the Corinthians should be ashamed of such an attitude because they know better.

1 Corinthians 15:35-50. A deeper question for some of the Corinthians is that they believe in a body/spirit division that says everything physical is inherently bad and that the good can be only spiritual. Thus, they are offended by the notion of a resurrected body. (In fact, the phrase "resurrection of the dead" could just as well be translated "raising of the corpses.") So they ask what seem obvious questions: *How* are the dead raised? And *what kind of body* do they have? Paul begins with the analogy of gardening. A seed is changed when it sprouts and grows into a plant. It is impossible to tell, by looking at seeds alone, what kind of plants they will become. We can add analogies to his. A tadpole becomes a frog; a caterpillar changes into a butterfly. If we saw tadpoles and frogs together, or caterpil-

lars and butterflies, but did not know their relationship, it certainly would not be apparent to our eyes. Just as God gives a physical body to each creature—whether seed or plant, butterfly or tadpole—God is in charge of the resurrected body. Paul asserts that we can know a few things about it: the earthly body is perishable; the raised body is imperishable.

In verse 44 Paul speaks of a "spiritual body." In human terms this is something of an impossibility, like saying an "in out" or an "up down." We are all earthly now, made of dust and perishable, as was Jesus in his earthly life. But as Jesus has been raised from this life to another sort of life, so will we be. Paul cannot define the life to come in any more concrete terms, but returns again to faith in Christ.

1 Corinthians 15:51-58. It is a mystery, something that humans cannot explain or comprehend, something that belongs entirely in the realm of God. In verse 54 Paul paraphrases one line of a great vision of life in the kingdom of God from the prophet Isaiah: "[the LORD] will swallow up death forever" (Isaiah 25:8; see also Isaiah 25:6-9). For the greatest enemy we see in this life is death. In the life to come, in the fullness of the kingdom of God, we will be able to sing the taunting song: "Where, O death, is your victory? Where, O death, is your sting?" (1 Corinthians 15:55, today's key verse).

For now, in this life and on this side of our own death, sin makes us afraid of death and the law makes us afraid of sin's power. That is, we know we are sinners, try as we might to overcome sin. One of the things that grinds our sinfulness into our consciousness is the realization that we cannot keep all the law. It is simply beyond us. And so, rather than letting the law lead us to the grace of God we see most clearly in Jesus Christ, we tend to let the law focus us on our failings, on sin and death.

Paul concludes this section by breaking into a hymn of praise and thanksgiving to God, the God who through Jesus Christ frees us from the endless downward tangle of sin and death. Because of the grace and victory granted us by God, Paul exhorts the Corinthians to be unwavering in their labor for the Lord, knowing that they do not labor in vain.

Notice carefully the order of these final two verses. Paul emphatically does not tell his readers to work hard in order to be granted the victory. Yes, I know that in other places this seems to be what Paul is saying, as in chapter 9 (especially verses 24-27) of this same letter. The order of Paul's entire argument is very significant: because God has raised Jesus from the dead, we too can be raised. Because God has given us this hope and this victory in Jesus Christ, we can "be steadfast, immovable, always excelling in the work of the Lord" (15:58a).

INTERPRETING THE SCRIPTURE

Don't Be a Sucker

The couple sat in my living room, seeming a bit nervous. Gregory had been a church member all his life; Marta had stopped going after confirmation because, as she said, "I just couldn't believe it anymore." When their dating started getting serious, Gregory asked Marta to try church again, at least for a little while. Before attending worship, Marta wanted to "check out" the pastor. I was impressed with her evident love for Gregory that she would attempt something that was so hard for her.

I asked Marta if she would mind telling me more about not being able to believe. "Well," she began, "our parents always made a big deal with us kids about Santa Claus at Christmas, that Santa is really real and that a lot of our presents came from him. And at Easter there was the Easter Bunny and all the candy he'd bring us. Of course, as we got older each of us discovered that neither Santa nor the Easter Bunny is real. They might be nice for children, but they're really lies grown-ups tell children. They're just a fairy tale, a way to get kids to be good, at least when it's close to Christmas or Easter. So I figured that Jesus was probably just another lie, a way for leaders to make their followers be good." Her voice dropped to a whisper. "And I did not want to be disappointed again."

In a culture awash with advertising, with unsolicited mail in both physical and virtual mailboxes, we do well to remember the old saying, "If it seems too good to be true, it probably is." Does this warning apply also to Christianity? There have been myriads of people who think so, from today's "professional" atheists all the way back to some members of Paul's congregation in Corinth. We do not want to be disappointed. We do not want to be considered "suckers" or to be seen as childish. And so, in a culture that prides itself on its scientific reason and technological prowess, many hesitate to claim a belief in something that lies outside the realm of our everyday experience.

Doubt and questions are never condemned in the Bible, especially when admitted to in good faith. Never does Jesus criticize someone for asking him an honest question or raising difficult issues. Remember so-called "Doubting Thomas" who wanted the same experience of the risen Christ as the rest of the disciples had had (John 20:24-29). Jesus also tells the disciples that there are some things they cannot yet understand and other questions that even Jesus himself cannot answer. (See, for example, Matthew 24:36.)

So we can start out by admitting to questions, by admitting to not wanting to look foolish, and also by admitting that we may not find answers to all of our questions.

Too Future Oriented?

There is another issue in ruminating about life after death that needs to be taken seriously, and that is that we not take the issue so seriously as to diminish our life before death. You have probably known people who are so frightened of God and of the possibility of being sent to Hell for some infraction that they live without joy. Life for them is a series of endless regulations, of minute rules about everything. This is the sort of living under the law that Paul meant in verse 56: "The sting of death is sin and the power of sin is the law." There is no place for grace in such a calculus. This fear-based living is one of the things from which Christ's resurrection frees us.

On the other hand there are people, also represented by some in the Corinthian church to whom Paul is arguing, who believe the only thing worthwhile in God's creation is the spiritual side. Some of them may be described in the quip about the woman who was "so heavenly minded she was no earthly use." Physical life, the physical world, is of little interest. In fact, they are believed to be detrimental to one's spiritual health. Thus, "worldly enjoyments" are to be shunned. Paul tries to say to the Corinthians that precisely because there was a bodily resurrection, God through Christ has redeemed the whole of creation. This world, this fallen and sinful world, also is redeemed. From the very beginning, Creation was intended by its Creator for good. People who try to set aside physical life may shush children's laughter in the church as not being sufficiently reverent. They may argue against church-sponsored parties. There is an important point that Christians not be frivolous, but joy and enjoyment of the good gifts of God are not to be despised.

This attitude may also get in the way of the church's mission activities in terms of trying to improve people's lives on earth. According to some people, housing and medical care, education and community sanitation are of this world and, therefore, not the church's proper concern. I disagree and think Paul is clear in this chapter, too. It is not necessary for the present to be wretched in order for the future to be glorious. We do not "earn" pleasures in heaven by enduring sufferings on earth.

Maybe, But So What?

Most of us have to find a balance point between knowing and not knowing. We cannot wait until we have incontrovertible proof of life after death before we decide how we are going to live our lives, simply because such proof is not available to us in this life. Many find reassurances in reports of "near death experiences" related by some people. Perhaps you have felt the presence of a loved one who has died—a presence you could not explain but could not explain away either.

How would you want to live, and how would you want others to live, if there were no life after death? Would the world not be a better place in *this* life if we all followed the teachings of Jesus in *this* life, regardless of what may be in the future?

Trust and Grace

Part of God's gift of human freedom is our ability either to trust or to refuse to trust. God is worthy of our trust, but does not compel either belief or particular actions. The Bible is full of evidence of God's grace and yet we sometimes think it is too good to be true. We find ourselves back in the place that Marta described: we do not want to be disappointed. And so we come together and share ourselves, share what we have experienced, in part to shore up each other's trust in God's goodness and grace.

A curious thing may happen. As we live within a community of faith, working together and sharing both doubts and certainties with each other honestly, we may experience glimpses of life in the kingdom of God. For, as Jesus told his disciples, the kingdom of God or kingdom of heaven is not reserved for life after death, but can begin in this life if we will but let it (Luke 17:21). What we can experience here is a foretaste, a tiny glimpse, of what God can do. It is grace. We do not need to earn it; indeed, we cannot earn it. We need only to accept it with gratitude and joy.

SHARING THE SCRIPTURE

PREPARING TO TEACH

Preparing Our Hearts

This week's devotional reading is found in 1 Corinthians 15:1-11, which is part of our background scripture. Here Paul writes specifically about the resurrection of Christ. Paul's discussion touches on why Christ died, his resurrection, and his post-resurrection appearances. Contemporary Christians certainly have differing views on the resurrection. Was it physical and/or spiritual? What is your belief? Suppose you could learn with absolute certainty what happened. How might that knowledge change your faith—or would it?

Pray that you and your students will view mortality through the lens of the promise of resurrection.

Preparing Our Minds

Study 1 Corinthians 15, which is this week's background scripture, and our lesson from 1 Corinthians 15:42-57.

Write on newsprint:

information for next week's lesson, found under "Continue the Journey."

Secure a copy of Handel's *Messiah* that includes the selections listed in the "Examine Paul's Understanding of the Resurrection" section. Your church or public library will probably have a copy. Be sure to bring a compact disc or tape player, plus extension cord and plug adapter or batteries.

LEADING THE CLASS

(1) Gather to Learn

❖ Welcome the class members and introduce any guests.

❖ Pray that the students will approach today's lesson with open hearts, open minds, and a willingness to ask questions so as to grow in their beliefs.

❖ Distribute paper (preferably unlined) and pencils. Ask students who enjoy drawing to sketch themselves as they would like to be. Suggest that the other students draw a circle in the center of their page and write the words "my body" in it. Then have them draw spokes off of that circle and write words or phrases to describe how they would like their body to appear.

❖ Point out that no matter what they have drawn or written, our current bodies will be made imperishable, immortal, at the time of our resurrection.

❖ Read aloud today's focus statement: **Most people wonder about life after death. What are we to believe? Paul wrote about the new body and our assurance of resurrection in Christ.**

(2) Examine Paul's Understanding of the Resurrection

❖ Begin today's Bible study by reading 1 Corinthians 15:42-50, immediately followed by selections from Handel's *Messiah* that are based on our lesson scripture. Likely, many of the class members will know Paul's writing in 1 Corinthians 15 from Handel's musical setting.

- Recitative, "Behold, I tell you a mystery," 1 Corinthians 15:51, 52.
- Song, "The trumpet shall sound," 1 Corinthians 15:52, 53.
- Recitative, "Then shall be brought to pass the saying," 1 Corinthians 15:54, 55.
- Duet, "O Death, where is thy sting?" 1 Corinthians 15:55, 56.
- Chorus, "But thanks be to God," 1 Corinthians 15, 57.

❖ Invite the students to discuss the feelings the music evoked in them. Give them an opportunity to relate how this music did—or did not—convey Paul's message concerning resurrection and the new body that we will receive.

(3) Explore What Jesus' Resurrection Means for the Learners

❖ Distribute paper and pencils. Encourage the students to answer this question:

(1) What do I believe about Jesus' resurrection?

(2) What do I believe Jesus' resurrection means for me?

❖ Collect the papers and shuffle them. Read several of the answers and invite the class to respond. (Be sure to set a tone that allows for open discussion, skepticism, even disbelief, if that is where the students are in their spiritual life. You can hold fast to your own belief without insisting that everyone hold these same beliefs. Remind the group that we are all in different places in our faith journeys and, therefore, will have divergent beliefs, all of which need to be respected.)

❖ Conduct an informal debate in which students argue both sides of this proposition: **Belief in the resurrection of Jesus and in our own resurrection is fundamental to Christianity. It is the cornerstone for all else we believe.** Even if all students accept

this premise, see if a few devil's advocates will argue the negative side.

❖ Distribute hymnals. Ask the students to turn to the section where the hymns concerning Jesus' resurrection are located. Choose at least one (or more, if you want to work in groups) and consider what the words say about the writer's beliefs concerning the resurrection. Provide an opportunity for the students to probe and question the ideas expressed in the hymns, in light of their own beliefs and Paul's teachings in 1 Corinthians 15.

(4) Take at Least One Step to Prepare for Death

❖ Encourage the students to think about their own mortality and death by asking these questions. Pause after each one so that the adults may meditate on them silently.

(1) What do you expect will happen when you die?

(2) Who do you expect to see when you die?

(3) How do you think heaven will appear?

(4) What do you expect your imperishable body to be like?

❖ Challenge the students to think of ways that they can prepare for their own death. Create a checklist of things that can be done and list them on newsprint. Here are some ideas to spark discussion: *prepare a will; sign advance directives; plan a funeral or memorial service; decide how your body is to be disposed of after death; live in a close relationship with God.*

❖ Ask for a show of hands to see how many people have actually completed each item.

❖ Conclude this portion of the lesson by inviting the students to commit themselves to take at least one step in the next three weeks to prepare for their transition from this life to the next.

(5) Continue the Journey

❖ Pray that the participants will give careful consideration to their beliefs about Jesus' resurrection and their own.

❖ Read aloud this preparation for next week's lesson. You may also want to post it on newsprint for the students to copy. **Prepare for next week's session entitled "New Beginnings" by reading 2 Corinthians 5:11-21, which is both our background and lesson scripture. This focus statement will help to guide your reading and study: People often long for a fresh start, where the past is no longer a factor. Where can we find such renewal? Paul writes of the new creation we have become in Christ and the possibilities this raises for reconciliation in broken relationships with God and others.**

❖ Read aloud the following three ideas. Challenge the students to commit themselves to use these activities as a springboard to spiritual growth.

(1) **Write in your spiritual journal about how your views concerning the resurrection of Jesus and your own resurrection have changed over the years. What faith issues and experiences have helped to shape these views?**

(2) **Imagine what resurrection will be like. Are you looking forward to being reunited with loved ones? Picture them in their resurrected, imperishable bodies.**

(3) **Comfort someone who is mourning. If an opportunity arises, share what you believe about resurrection and life after death.**

❖ Sing or read aloud "Hymn of Promise."

❖ Ask the students to echo this benediction from 2 Corinthians 13:11-14 as you read it phrase by phrase: **Finally, brothers and sisters, farewell. Put things in order . . . agree with one another, live in peace; and the God of love and peace will be with you. . . . The grace of the Lord Jesus Christ, the love of God, and the communion of the Holy Spirit be with all of you. Amen.**

NEW BEGINNINGS

PREVIEWING THE LESSON

Lesson Scripture: 2 Corinthians 5:11-21
Background Scripture: 2 Corinthians 5:11-21
Key Verse: 2 Corinthians 5:17

Focus of the Lesson:
People often long for a fresh start, where the past is no longer a factor. Where can we find such renewal? Paul writes of the new creation we have become in Christ and the possibilities this raises for reconciliation in broken relationships with God and others.

Goals for the Learners:
(1) to discover what Paul teaches about the "new start" available in Christ.
(2) to demonstrate what "new start" means for them.
(3) to discern and engage in the ministry of reconciliation.

Shirley

Supplies:
Bibles, newsprint and marker, paper and pencils, optional commentaries, hymnals

---

READING THE SCRIPTURE

NRSV
2 Corinthians 5:11-21

11 Therefore, knowing the fear of the Lord, we try to persuade others; but we ourselves are well known to God, and I hope that we are also well known to your consciences. 12 We are not commending ourselves to you again, but giving you an opportunity to boast about us, so that you may be able to answer those who boast in outward appearance and not in the heart. 13 For if we are beside ourselves, it is for God; if we are in our right mind, it is for you. 14 For the love of Christ urges us on, because we are convinced that one has died for all;

NIV
2 Corinthians 5:11-21

[11]Since, then, we know what it is to fear the Lord, we try to persuade men. What we are is plain to God, and I hope it is also plain to your conscience. [12]We are not trying to commend ourselves to you again, but are giving you an opportunity to take pride in us, so that you can answer those who take pride in what is seen rather than in what is in the heart. [13]If we are out of our mind, it is for the sake of God; if we are in our right mind, it is for you. [14]For Christ's love compels us, because we are convinced that one died for all, and therefore all died. [15]And he

therefore all have died. 15 And he died for all, so that those who live might live no longer for themselves, but for him who died and was raised for them.

16 From now on, therefore, we regard no one from a human point of view; even though we once knew Christ from a human point of view, we know him no longer in that way. **17 So if anyone is in Christ, there is a new creation: everything old has passed away; see, everything has become new!** 18 All this is from God, who reconciled us to himself through Christ, and has given us the ministry of reconciliation; 19 that is, in Christ God was reconciling the world to himself, not counting their trespasses against them, and entrusting the message of reconciliation to us. 20 So we are ambassadors for Christ, since God is making his appeal through us; we entreat you on behalf of Christ, be reconciled to God. 21 For our sake he made him to be sin who knew no sin, so that in him we might become the righteousness of God.

died for all, that those who live should no longer live for themselves but for him who died for them and was raised again.

[16]So from now on we regard no one from a worldly point of view. Though we once regarded Christ in this way, we do so no longer. **[17]Therefore, if anyone is in Christ, he is a new creation; the old has gone, the new has come!** [18]All this is from God, who reconciled us to himself through Christ and gave us the ministry of reconciliation: [19]that God was reconciling the world to himself in Christ, not counting men's sins against them. And he has committed to us the message of reconciliation. [20]We are therefore Christ's ambassadors, as though God were making his appeal through us. We implore you on Christ's behalf: Be reconciled to God. [21]God made him who had no sin to be sin for us, so that in him we might become the righteousness of God.

UNDERSTANDING THE SCRIPTURE

2 Corinthians 5:11-15. Have you noticed how often the sessions in this quarter have talked about starting over? One reason for this is that we human beings need new beginnings and second chances. We need these on several levels—as individuals, as groups within churches, as congregations, even as whole nations.

Even with only this brief piece from Paul's Corinthian correspondence, it is not difficult to read between the lines and sense some of the very real human conflict he experienced in his ongoing relationship with these people. The apostle has had some fractious times with this congregation, and on a purely human level he has been hurt by it. Yet he is trying to live by the words he commends to them. "If we are out of our mind," he says in verse 13 (NIV) as if

in answer to some who have accused him of just that, "If we are out of our mind, it is God's business."

How does Paul manage to continue being in relationship with these people? He manages by seeing that everything is changed by his experience of the love of Christ (5:14a). Paul is motivated, is "urged on," by his realization of Christ's love for him and for all humanity.

Paul's arithmetic may seem odd at first. What does he mean "one has died for all; therefore all have died" (5:14b)? This is certainly not the way we experience death. But consider representative government for instance. When the two Tennessee senators vote for a bill, it is as if all of Tennessee has voted in its favor. We do not all travel to Washington, D.C. to cast our ballots, but send two individuals to do that on our behalf. Similarly, Christ has done all that is necessary on our behalf. We can live this fuller life, this life of reconciliation, before we go through our own individual deaths.

It may seem to those who have not experienced this radical love that Paul is indeed out of his mind to continue to support and love his detractors. But Christ's death for us, he asserts, means that we are freed to live for God and for each other. We are therefore also freed from being guided by what others think of us.

2 Corinthians 5:16-17. Understanding what God through Christ has done for us changes our whole outlook. We are enabled to see people more nearly as God sees them, rather than from our stunted, and most likely selfish, points of view. As he often does, Paul takes himself as the prime example. He once knew Christ from the limitations of a strictly human view—and he persecuted the church with great enthusiasm and vigor. When Christ and his unsearchable love for Paul confronted him, Paul was changed. And the change was not limited to his opinions about Christ. No, his entire outlook was so different that he could use no other language than to say he had become a "new creation."

I believe in inclusive language. But there are times when we have to admit that English is limited. What Paul says in verse 17 is much stronger and more personal than "there is a new creation." For anyone in Christ, "he is a new creation" and "she is a new creation." This is an exceedingly individual and particular matter, not adequately encompassed by the impersonal "there is a new creation."

This phrase "new creation" is similar to the "new covenant" in Jeremiah 31 discussed on October 17. Paul feels himself so changed that he refers to himself as a new creation, but that does not mean that there is no continuity with who Paul was before his conversion. Paul is not killed and a different human being put in his place. Rather, all the best parts of him, all the characteristics that reflect the image of God in which he was created,

come to the fore. His attitude changes; his outlook on himself and on everyone else is altered. He leaves behind his old ways as he embraces his new life in Christ.

2 Corinthians 5:18-21. How was Paul able to make such a radical change? His point in verse 18 is that he, Paul, did not do it but that the change, the new creation, is a gift from God. Having received this grace he is called to spread it to others. This is his ministry, to be a reconciler among people and between humans and God. This ministry is not something Paul could ever do on his own; but rather, in imitation of what God has already done through Christ, he finds his motivation and strength for the task.

What does Paul mean by reconciliation? "Being reconciled" to something is often thought of in terms of making the best of a not very good situation. "In order to keep her diabetes under control, she reconciled herself to the necessity of insulin shots for the rest of her life." "He reconciled himself to a long commute to work because he loved both his job and the community he lived in." It would sound strange to hear people say that they were reconciled to their delightful family life.

Clearly Paul does not have this negative sense in mind, nor just the bookkeeper's notion of getting everything in balance or making everything come out even. Reconciliation is another way of saying that God has done for us what we are unable to do on our own or for ourselves. God has removed the barriers, the obstacles, to our living in harmonious and joyful relationship with each other and with God. Another word for this "all relationships set right" is "righteousness," as Paul uses the word in verse 21.

Paul knows God's love of him through Christ. Paul knows what a dramatic difference that has made in his life. And now he devotes his life to the spreading of this message, to those who do not seem particularly grateful to receive it as well as to all who support him in his work.

INTERPRETING THE SCRIPTURE

Amazing Grace

One of the best-known Christian hymns, at least in the English-speaking world, is "Amazing Grace." It is used in churches of vast denominational range, children sing it at camp, and bagpipers play it at state funerals. These familiar words echo what Paul is saying yet again to the Corinthian church.

Has this hymn become so familiar that we no longer pay attention to its words? Has it lost its power to move us? Has life, even life within the Christian community, become such a routine that we think nothing new is possible? Or are there some who believe they are so broken, so scarred by their past, that mending shattered relationships with other people or even with God are utterly impossible? Today's lesson from Paul can give us courage and hope that God's grace and Christ's love are not in short supply, nor are they of limited power.

I Was a Wretch and Blind

The world has been privileged to witness a startling example of new life and reconciliation this past decade in South Africa. It would have been so easy for the entire country to descend into a protracted civil war, with endless reprisals and paybacks on all sides for generations of brutality and mistreatment. There was some fighting, some killing, and some reprisals. But they did not reach anything near the level that many analysts were expecting. In part, the nation was spared more violence because of the Truth and Reconciliation Commission and its patient detailed work over the course of years. Note carefully the order of nouns in that name: Truth and Reconciliation. Before the nation could move forward into new ways of living together, the truth had to be told, horrifical-

ly painful as it must have been for many of the participants, both for those speaking and for those listening.

Conversion and reconciliation are difficult in part because they require such honesty on our part. For me to allow myself to be made new, I first must admit that the old me needs to be changed. After that difficult step, I then have to be willing to give up my favorite bad habits. That too is hard.

Have you ever been hurt by something a close friend said or did? You have led a highly unusual life if this has never happened to you! How did you react when that friend came to apologize? We tend to do one of two things, neither of which is conducive to a restoration of the relationship. We may make light of the error or pretend we were not hurt, and thus not allow the one who has wronged us to express true regret and ask for our forgiveness. Or we may let our friend offer an apology and say we accept it, but continue to carry that hurt and resentment deep inside us.

Each of these reactions keeps our own self at the center of our private universe. When we realize, as Paul did, what Christ's action on our behalf has done, it becomes possible to rearrange our ways of looking at things and to reestablish God at the center. Or, to put it more nearly as it happens, it is possible to let God through Christ do the necessary rearranging.

What If They Are Still Wretches?

Sometimes we seem to get stuck half way through the process of being made new. We see ourselves in a new light, but are not yet willing to extend that to others, especially to those we feel have hurt us. It is almost as if we say, "I am a Christian and will be willing to have a relationship with you if you are a Christian—and if you act in the ways that I think Christians should act." As long as we cling to this attitude, we are still regarding others from "a human point of view" (5:16). Sometimes "being human" is used as an excuse, as a cop-out even. "Maybe God can forgive her, but I'm only human. I cannot forgive what she did to me."

The death penalty is a subject on which few people are neutral. Yet more and more people in our country, speaking from the perspective of religious conviction, are saying that it is wrong. I have to admit to myself that if the mother of a murdered child can, through Christ, find the ability to forgive a murderer, how can I say that one who has insulted or otherwise hurt me is undeserving of my forgiveness? And there is part of the point: we are ALL undeserving of forgiveness, if forgiving is to be calculated on that basis.

Humans killed God's own Son. God forgives us. This is the completely illogical set of circumstances Paul tries to come to grips with in this passage. God's forgiveness is not just "in general" but for all the specific bits of mean-spiritedness, or disinterest, with which I can, and all too often do, afflict my neighbors. Yes, they may very well actually *be* wretches. Measured against Jesus, so am I. And in the light of Jesus' death and resurrection, we are all still loved by God and invited into renewed relationships.

When Almost All Is Made New

I heard a sermon illustration once, relating a children's Sunday school lesson on the story of Jesus' raising Lazarus from the dead. "What do you think Lazarus's first words were when he came out of the tomb?" the teacher asked. "I know! I know! He said, 'Ta da!'" offered one eager student with a flourish as a magician gives at the end of a particularly spectacular trick. Here is the exuberant joy that can accompany a fresh start.

Such Lazarus moments are available to us all. And yet, the Lazarus who walked out of that tomb was still a human being living with other human beings. He had to learn in his new perspective on life how to get along with them.

Roberto tells his own story with a rueful laugh. "My wife didn't like it when I didn't go to church. And then I went and got saved and she didn't like it even more. 'Cause once I got saved I was always trying to tell everyone else I was better than they were and being real careful to point out all their bad spots to them. I was hardest on her. But she stuck by me, I don't know how." He pauses, reaches for his wife's hand, gives it a squeeze. "She was patient. She kept praying for me. Then one Sunday our oldest boy said he wasn't going to church anymore. I got mad of course and asked him why not. He said he was afraid if he got saved like I did he'd lose all his friends by telling them how bad they were and he'd rather just forgive them and keep being friends." Roberto stops for a long moment. "That really got to me. I didn't learn my lesson all at once, but I began to see that if Jesus forgave me and died for me it was partly so I could forgive other people too. It's been real hard because I said some hateful things to people. But most of them have forgiven me when I told them how sorry I was for the way I behaved and that I didn't want them to think Jesus made me act so hateful." Roberto had come to understand what a new beginning in Christ really meant. We too have a fresh start in Christ and are called to live as his new creatures.

SHARING THE SCRIPTURE

PREPARING TO TEACH

Preparing Our Hearts

This week's devotional reading is found in 2 Corinthians 4:16–5:5. Paul uses two images—tenting and clothing—to describe how we Christians live by faith. We live now in an earthly tent, but one day we will be "clothed with our heavenly dwelling" (5:2). Things now are temporary—even challenging problems and setbacks. We live by faith, however, because we know that we are being prepared for a glorious eternal future. In what areas of your life do you need to rely on faith?

Pray that you and your students will live by faith in this life so as to be prepared to live eternally with God.

Preparing Our Minds

Study the background and lesson scripture, both of which are found in 2 Corinthians 5:11-21.

Write on newsprint:

information for next week's lesson, found under "Continue the Journey."

LEADING THE CLASS

(1) Gather to Learn

❖ Welcome the class members and introduce any guests.

❖ Pray that the students will be open to Paul's teachings about new beginnings, and willing to make such beginnings themselves.

❖ Brainstorm with the class a generic list of "new beginnings" that many adults experience. Here are some ideas to add to your list on newsprint: *marriage, divorce, birth of a child, empty nest, retirement, a new residence.*

❖ Discuss how people might experience a fresh start in each of the situations you have brainstormed. Invite the class members to tell how they made new beginnings in these situations.

❖ Read aloud today's focus statement: **People often long for a fresh start, where the past is no longer a factor. Where can we find such renewal? Paul writes of the new creation we have become in Christ and the possibilities this raises for reconciliation in broken relationships with God and others.**

(2) Discover What Paul Teaches About the "New Start" Available in Christ

❖ Choose one reader for 2 Corinthians 5:11-15.

❖ Use one of these three options to discern what this passage reveals about Paul.

- **Option 1:** Divide the students into groups. Ask them to use different translations and commentaries (if available) to determine what Paul is saying about himself and his ministry. Invite the groups to report to the entire class.

- **Option 2:** Create a lecture based on various translations, commentaries, and the Understanding the Scripture portion. Focus on what Paul is saying about himself and his ministry.

- **Option 3:** Distribute paper and pencils. Ask the class members to work with partners to rewrite the information in these five verses as if they were reporters covering Paul's defense of his ministry. Provide an opportunity for several pairs to read what they have written.

❖ Select a volunteer to read 2 Corinthians 5:16-21.

- Ask the students to explain their understanding of these ideas: *new creation, ministry of reconciliation, in Christ,* and *ambassadors for Christ.*

- Develop a portrait of the Christian, based on understandings of the word list just discussed. List on newsprint the traits of this person, this "new creature."
- Provide time for the students to reflect silently on this question: **How closely do I conform to this portrait?**

(3) Demonstrate What the "New Start" Means for the Learners

❖ Read aloud the following scenarios and ask class members to role-play how they might respond so as to give the other person a "new start." You will need two characters for each scenario.

- **Scenario 1: Your 17 year old son or grandson returns home with the front fender hanging from your car and an empty tank of gas. He had taken the vehicle without your permission.**
- **Scenario 2: Your best friend blabbed personal information that you had shared in confidence. This betrayal got back to you through a mutual friend.**
- **Scenario 3: A neighbor with whom you have strained relations through the years is seriously ill and needs help in the yard and around the house.**

❖ Discuss how the three role-plays demonstrated a "new start." Consider how the actions of the players were, or were not, in keeping with Paul's teachings. Invite the class to suggest other ways that a "new start" could have been offered in each situation.

(4) Discern and Engage in the Ministry of Reconciliation

❖ Read the first paragraph under "I Was a Wretch and Blind" in the Interpreting the Scripture portion. Some students familiar with the Truth and Reconciliation Commission may wish to comment further on its work.

❖ Point out that a ministry of reconciliation may restore two or more individuals or, as with the Truth and Reconciliation Commission in South Africa, may affect entire societies.

❖ Read the following quotation by theologian John Howard Yoder (1927–1997): **"The church must be a sample of the kind of humanity within which . . . economic and racial differences are surmounted. Only then will she have anything to say to the society that surrounds her about how those differences must be dealt with. Otherwise her preaching to the world a standard of reconciliation which is not her own experience will be neither honest nor effective."**

❖ Discuss these questions in light of the Yoder quotation.
(1) In what situations is the contemporary church challenged to act as ministers of reconciliation?
(2) In what specific arenas are your congregation and/or denomination working to bring about reconciliation?
(3) How effective would you say that the church's ministry of reconciliation is?
(4) What roles can you as individuals and members of this class play in bringing about reconciliation? (You may wish to list on newsprint any ideas that the group identifies.)

❖ Invite the students to make a commitment to engage as ambassadors of Christ in the ministry of reconciliation. Distribute paper and pencils and ask them to list one or more steps they will take this week to fulfill their ministry of reconciliation. Do not ask the students to share their plans aloud, but do ask them to initial their papers as a sign of their commitment to do what they intend.

(5) Continue the Journey

❖ Pray that all who have come today will recognize that they are new creatures in

Christ and as such can experience reconciliation and renewed relationships with others and with God. Moreover, as Christ's ambassadors they are called to engage in a ministry of reconciliation.

❖ Read aloud this preparation for next week's lesson. You may also want to post it on newsprint for the students to copy. **Prepare for next week's session entitled "Becoming One Family" by reading Ephesians 2:11-21, which is both our background and lesson scripture. Think about this focus for the lesson: People who feel like outsiders often yearn to be brought into community. How do we achieve this? The passage says we are "made one" through the unity we have in Christ.**

❖ Read aloud the following three ideas. Challenge the students to commit themselves to use these activities as a springboard to spiritual growth.

(1) **Identify at least one way that you can engage in "the ministry of reconciliation" and do whatever you can to fulfill this ministry.**

(2) **Pray that God will enable you to be reconciled with someone from whom you have been estranged.**

(3) **Look through the eyes of God at someone you find challenging to get along with and like. How would Jesus treat this person? What positive changes can you make, with God's help, to relate to this person in a more Christlike way?**

❖ Sing or read aloud "Come and Dwell in Me," which is based in part on 2 Corinthians 5:17, today's key verse.

❖ Ask the students to echo this benediction from 2 Corinthians 13:11-14 as you read it phrase by phrase: **Finally, brothers and sisters, farewell. Put things in order . . . agree with one another, live in peace; and the God of love and peace will be with you. . . . The grace of the Lord Jesus Christ, the love of God, and the communion of the Holy Spirit be with all of you. Amen.**

BECOMING ONE FAMILY

PREVIEWING THE LESSON

Lesson Scripture: Ephesians 2:11-21
Background Scripture: Ephesians 2:11-21
Key Verse: Ephesians 2:19

Focus of the Lesson:
People who feel like outsiders often yearn to be brought into community. How do we achieve this? The passage says we are "made one" through the unity we have in Christ.

Goals for the Learners:
(1) to understand what the passage says about how Christians are to relate to one another.
(2) to become aware of reasons they might erect barriers.
(3) to identify and make a commitment to tear down barriers.

Supplies:
Bibles, newsprint and marker, paper and pencils, hymnals

READING THE SCRIPTURE

NRSV
Ephesians 2:11-21

11 So then, remember that at one time you Gentiles by birth, called "the uncircumcision" by those who are called "the circumcision"—a physical circumcision made in the flesh by human hands—12 remember that you were at that time without Christ, being aliens from the commonwealth of Israel, and strangers to the covenants of promise, having no hope and without God in the world. 13 But now in Christ Jesus you who once were far off have been brought near by the blood of Christ. 14 For he is our peace; in his flesh he has made both groups into one and

NIV
Ephesians 2:11-21

¹¹Therefore, remember that formerly you who are Gentiles by birth and called "uncircumcised" by those who call themselves "the circumcision" (that done in the body by the hands of men)—¹²remember that at that time you were separate from Christ, excluded from citizenship in Israel and foreigners to the covenants of the promise, without hope and without God in the world. ¹³But now in Christ Jesus you who once were far away have been brought near through the blood of Christ.

¹⁴For he himself is our peace, who has

has broken down the dividing wall, that is, the hostility between us. 15 He has abolished the law with its commandments and ordinances, that he might create in himself one new humanity in place of the two, thus making peace, 16 and might reconcile both groups to God in one body through the cross, thus putting to death that hostility through it. 17 So he came and proclaimed peace to you who were far off and peace to those who were near; 18 for through him both of us have access in one Spirit to the Father. **19 So then you are no longer strangers and aliens, but you are citizens with the saints and also members of the household of God,** 20 built upon the foundation of the apostles and prophets, with Christ Jesus himself as the cornerstone. 21 In him the whole structure is joined together and grows into a holy temple in the Lord.

made the two one and has destroyed the barrier, the dividing wall of hostility, [15]by abolishing in his flesh the law with its commandments and regulations. His purpose was to create in himself one new man out of the two, thus making peace, [16]and in this one body to reconcile both of them to God through the cross, by which he put to death their hostility. [17]He came and preached peace to you who were far away and peace to those who were near. [18]For through him we both have access to the Father by one Spirit.

[19]**Consequently, you are no longer foreigners and aliens, but fellow citizens with God's people and members of God's household,** [20]built on the foundation of apostles and prophets, with Christ Jesus himself as the chief cornerstone. [21]In him the whole building is joined together and rises to become a holy temple in the Lord.

UNDERSTANDING THE SCRIPTURE

Introduction. Although it is traditional to ascribe the letter to the Ephesians to the apostle Paul, scholars question whether he wrote it himself. Many commentators believe that it was more probably written by a disciple of Paul, after the apostle's own lifetime. Having said this, it is important to note that the issues are similar to what we have seen in excerpts from Paul's correspondence with the Corinthian church, and they are resolved in similar ways. We can certainly affirm that it is "Pauline" regardless of who may actually have written it.

Why would someone write a letter and put another person's name on it? We need to remember that at that time there were not copyright laws nor book tours nor any of the trappings of celebrity authorship sometimes seen today. Ancient letters were sometimes memorized by a messenger and delivered orally. If the messenger knew the recipients particularly well, there might be personal

flourishes delivered within the recitation. Whoever wrote this piece was more concerned that the message be spread than that the author get credit and public acclaim.

Ephesians 2:11-12. First in our passage there is the reminder of what the recipients of the letter were by birth, what they were before their conversion to being followers of Christ. They were "the uncircumcised," aliens, strangers, without hope, and without God. This collection of descriptors is about as bleak and dismal as one can get.

Ephesians 2:13-17. In stark contrast to the previous situation of the Ephesians described in the last two verses, they now belong. The previous hostility between the groups has been overcome by Christ and specifically by "the blood of Christ" (2:13). In our culture we most often associate blood with violence, with crime, and death. And this is part of what is meant here, in reference to Jesus' death on the cross. But "blood" in the Bible also stands for something quite different. Remember the discussion of blood in connection with God's covenant with Noah in the session for September 12. There we said that blood is a symbol of life much more than of death. When Jesus gives the cup to his disciples at the Last Supper, saying, "This is my blood, shed for you" he is of course alluding to his impending death. At the same time he is giving them the most powerful symbol of his *life* to them and to all of the disciples who follow after, including us.

Thus, both Jesus' death and his life have enabled the end of hostility and enmity between the two groups. The "dividing wall" (2:14) is gone. This detail may refer to the wall in the Jerusalem Temple that separated the court where Gentiles were allowed from the space of the Jews. The "commandments and ordinances" (2:15) are abolished. Does this mean now that "anything goes"? Hardly. As we saw on November 7, the deeper level of the Law and its intention for our good is maintained in Christ. But the picky little rules and regulations with which we vex each other are done away with. Christ freed us to live by the law of love. And this law of love, of mutual loyalty, creates one humanity, instead of two warring factions. The message to both groups, "to you who were far off and . . . to those who were near" (2:17) is the same message. The goal is reconciliation to God and to the rest of creation, including all the fractious people within it.

Ephesians 2:18-21. The author uses several images in these verses, from architecture and government and household management. As literature we would say it is a wildly mixed metaphor. But in trying to describe this new creation, he cannot use just one image for such a radically new reality. Precisely because there is only one God and one Spirit, there is only one citizenship, one household. All the divisions enumerated in verses 11 and 12—divisions that from a human perspective were very nearly insurmountable—are now done away with.

Even more, the newcomers are not brought in as visitors or as second-class citizens but as full members of the family, "members of the household of God" (2:19). In a day when citizenship was not just a matter of birth, but was limited primarily to those with wealth or the proper family connections, it was a radically freeing notion that *all* could be citizens in God's household. These are not "hyphenated citizens" but full and equal members of the community. No more is there an "in group" and an "out group." No more are people divided into "us" and "them."

What binds this new structure together, what keeps it together, is Christ Jesus. But not Christ Jesus in a vacuum. The "apostles and prophets" are also mentioned as being the foundation. That is, even though there is a "new" covenant, the "old" covenant is the foundation upon which it is built. Gentiles are being brought into what was formerly a Jewish group without having to become Jews themselves. And Jews in this new group do not have to give up their former relationship to God.

In another lovely mixed metaphor, the author concludes this section of his letter by asserting that in Christ the structure "grows" into a temple. The Romans had destroyed the Temple in Jerusalem in the year A.D. 70. Both the Gospel of John (2:19-21) and Paul's first letter to the Corinthians (6:19) use the figure of speech of an individual's body being a temple. But here it is the communion of saints, the faith community, the collective group that is being compared to a temple. Although the author does not continue with the description of the temple to remind the people that it has diverse parts, as Paul does with his magnificent "body" metaphor in 1 Corinthians 12:12-27, the fact remains. As the body is not composed of identical organs, neither is the temple a collection of identical bricks in one undifferentiated wall. As members of the household of God we celebrate our diversity of creation alongside our unity in Christ.

INTERPRETING THE SCRIPTURE

Aliens and Strangers

Our world knows a lot about aliens and strangers. There are more refugees in the world today than there have ever been before. In some parts of the world there are even "permanent refugee camps" in which generations come and go with little realistic hope of ever leaving or gaining a home of their own. The big cities of the United States have large, and largely invisible, populations of people without permanent homes. And suburbia is not exempt from this human tragedy. Statistics do not confirm our stereotypical views of homeless people either. Do you know what the average age of a homeless person in the United States was in the fall of 2002? Nine years old.

Now that foreign terrorism has come to our shores, and we have experienced first-hand the fear and uncertainty that many other countries have had to live with for decades, we are even less likely to be welcoming to strangers, especially those who look different from us. All of this is real and tragic and of interest to God and therefore also to us as Christians.

There is, however, another type of alien with which we are also familiar. These are people who live on the other side of town, right next door, or even in our own families. They are not foreigners, but they are still people who feel left out. I dare say nearly every one in your group has felt like an outsider at one time or another. It is especially tragic to have people within the community of faith who feel as if they do not belong.

Recognizing Walls

Walls, even in the church, come in a myriad of sizes and shapes. Many people cannot see me as their sister in Christ because I am ordained. My gender creates a wall in their minds that separates me from some ways of serving our Lord. The first Hispanic family in an Anglo church knows what walls feel like. The Koreans in formerly all–African American neighborhoods recognize barriers. Homosexuals, adults who cannot read, people who are blind, people who are poor—all manner of people experience the deep pain of separation even within the church.

We may try to make ourselves feel better by looking the other way, by pretending not to notice, when someone trips over part of a wall. We say the homeless should stop being lazy and at the very least take a bath before coming to our church. We congratulate the blind man for being able to get around, but do not bother to tell him about coffee hour because we might then be responsible for directing him to the fellowship hall. In countless subtle, and not so subtle, ways we call those not like us "uncircumcised."

Then there are the dilemmas that occur within the congregation. Little irritations not tended to and resolved can fester and become ugly. Small disagreements papered over instead of being solved can spread. I have become convinced that most congregations have some members from "central casting." There will be a crusty curmudgeonly type with a heart of gold. At least one person is constitutionally unable to agree with any new idea. Another individual will never think there is enough money available to undertake any new project. Some will rejoice in the sounds of young children in the sanctuary during worship; others will fret over the very same sounds.

Worst of all may be when Christians use theological labels to categorize each other negatively. One whose experience of Jesus is different may be called "liberal" or "fundamentalist," depending on the position of the one casting aspersions.

The Wall Came Tumbling Down

I am old enough to remember clearly when the Berlin Wall went up and also when it began to come down. The latter time, of course, was much more fun. Once the youths realized that they were not going to be shot at on the Wall, some began dancing on top of it while others tore out big chunks. There was an all too brief moment of nearly worldwide euphoria as that monument of the Cold War was reduced to rubble. Eventually the partying ended and the hard work of cobbling together one country out of two enemies began. The result has been mixed.

That particular concrete and wire construction was not the only thing that was dismantled. The former Soviet Union dissolved into independent republics. Fighting broke out and old tribal hatreds flared up in the Balkans, sections of Africa, the Philippines—the list is sadly a long one.

As Christians we may look at such events in recent history and bemoan the sad state of affairs. But that is far from our only option. We can put our reliance on God and continue to live as faithfully as we are able, instead of expecting that we can set all things right by ourselves. False hopes and cheap grace can stop up our ears to the message we read in Ephesians.

How Far Down?

Relationships. Starting over. Second chances. Forgiveness. Reconciliation. Grace. These are some of the big issues covered in this quarter's biblical texts from both the Old and New Testaments. The core message of Christianity is so simple and at the same time it is far from simplistic. God created a good world, including all the people in it. God loves us and wants us to live full and joy-filled lives within the good creation. In part because we humans are stubborn and slow to get the message, God became incarnate and lived a human life as Jesus of Nazareth. Jesus taught that we could begin to live life with each other in God's realm here on earth. One of the ways we do that is by living with integrity, by matching our deeds to our words. All that we could not do for ourselves in terms of salvation and reconciliation, God through Christ has done for us out of boundless divine love and loyalty.

As Pheme Perkins writes in her commentary on Ephesians in volume XI of *The New Interpreter's Bible*, "We may form close, personal relationships with people of very different racial, ethnic, socioeconomic, or educational backgrounds in the church community. But do such experiences translate into what happens at work, on the street, in school? Not always. When it does not, can we honestly say that Christ bridges the gap of our hostilities and differences?"

God is interested in us as individuals. God is interested in us as members of the community of faith. God is interested in every single human being on earth. When we begin to understand God's great love for us, we are enabled to reach out to others who are near us and like us. Finally we may be able to grow in Christ to the point of helping to break down barriers, not only in the church but in the rest of the world as well.

SHARING THE SCRIPTURE

PREPARING TO TEACH

Preparing Our Hearts

This week's devotional reading is found in Ephesians 2:4-10, which immediately precedes today's scripture lesson. Here Paul reminds us of what we were like before we were saved by the grace of God. Our salvation is God's gift to us, not anything that we could work to earn or merit. What response will you make to God's gracious salvation today?

Pray that you and your students will give thanks for God's graciousness in making you part of one family in Christ.

Preparing Our Minds

Study the background and lesson scripture, both of which are found in Ephesians 2:11-21.

Write on newsprint:

true and false statements in the "Become Aware of Reasons the Learners Might Erect Barriers" portion.

information for next week's lesson, found under "Continue the Journey."

LEADING THE CLASS

(1) Gather to Learn

❖ Welcome the class members and introduce any guests.

❖ Pray that each person will feel welcomed into this group, which is part of the Body of Christ.

❖ Encourage students to recall incidences from childhood and adolescence when they felt as if they were outsiders. Maybe they were often the last person picked for a team, or the wallflower at a dance. Perhaps they never felt like part of the "in" crowd. Possibly their race, ethnic origin, or gender made them feel separate from others. Discuss these questions, either as a class or in smaller groups.

(1) What kinds of attitudes or behaviors made you, or others you know, feel excluded?

(2) What are some ways that people who feel excluded can be brought into a group and made to feel included?

❖ Read aloud today's focus statement: **People who feel like outsiders often yearn to be brought into community. How do we achieve this? The passage says we are "made one" through the unity we have in Christ.**

(2) Understand What the Passage Says About How Christians Are to Relate to One Another

❖ Choose someone to read Ephesians 2:11-21. Ask the students to be aware of words or phrases that "jump out" at them.

❖ List on newsprint the words that the students identified. Discuss with the students why these words in particular were relevant to them.

❖ Encourage the students to summarize this passage in one or two sentences. If the class is large, you may want to work in groups to do this.

❖ Ask the adults to read Paul's words through the eyes of the modern church-goer.

(1) What are the walls that divide us within the church at-large today? (Think here of denominational issues, such as who can be ordained, who can receive communion, one church claiming a corner on the market to Truth, and so on.)

(2) Paul writes that we "are no longer strangers and aliens, but . . . members of the household of God" (2:19). Do you think that all

Christians feel as if they are equal members of the household? If not, who is alienated? Why?

(3) **What steps need to be taken within the church universal to break down the barriers that divide us from one another?**

❖ Divide the class into groups and give each group paper and pencils. Ask them to write what Paul would have to say about being one in Christ, based on the discussion and study they have just completed.

❖ Invite a spokesperson from each group to read the group's ideas to the whole class.

(3) Become Aware of Reasons the Learners Might Erect Barriers

❖ Note that we have talked about barriers in the church universal. Now turn attention to our beliefs, attitudes, and behaviors as individual Christians.

❖ Distribute paper and pencils to each student. Post the following statements, which you will write on newsprint prior to class. Ask the students to mark each item *True* or *False*.

(1) **I sometimes erect a barrier when I meet someone who is unlike me in terms of race, ethnic group, socio-economic status, age, or for some other reason.**

(2) **I may put up walls because I am afraid of people whose ways are unknown to me.**

(3) **I do not like to associate with people whose beliefs are different from mine, even if they are Christian.**

(4) **I prefer to associate with people who are socially and economically my equal.**

(5) **I do not like people who challenge my ideas.**

❖ Provide quiet time for the adults to review their answers and consider these questions: **Do my answers reflect the oneness in Christ to which I am called to live?**

If not, what changes do I need to make in my personal beliefs, attitudes, and behaviors?

❖ Invite the students to note any ideas they have gleaned from this activity, or questions that come to mind.

(4) Identify and Make a Commitment to Tear Down Barriers

❖ Note that barriers come in many forms. They may be physical, emotional, intellectual, or spiritual. Work with the class to identify barriers in your own church that need to be torn down, either figuratively or literally. Encourage the students to name as many barriers as possible, and list them on newsprint. Here are some possibilities.

- Building lacks handicap accessibility, thus sending the message that those who have difficulty maneuvering are not welcome.
- Participation on church committees is closed to all but the most long-standing members of the church.
- Sermons and Sunday school materials do not reach people of differing educational levels.
- People who are not wearing the "right" clothes or who do not live in the "right" neighborhood are not welcomed.
- People whose theological point of view differs from most other members feel as if their ideas and beliefs are not valued.

❖ Agree together on a few of these barriers that the class members would be willing to tackle. They may not be able to solve the entire problem, but they could become a catalyst for change in the congregation.

❖ Determine what needs to be done to begin the process of dismantling the barriers you have identified. Consider who will do what, when, with whom, how much the task might cost, and how long it might be before real results are apparent.

❖ Invite the students to stand, if able,

and recite today's key verse, Ephesians 2:19, as a sign of their commitment to work to tear down barriers so that all who come to your church will be welcomed as a member of God's household.

(5) Continue the Journey

❖ Pray that all who have participated this day will reach out to others and help them feel and act as an integral part of the family of God.

❖ Read aloud this preparation for next week's lesson. You may also want to post it on newsprint for the students to copy. **Prepare for next week's session entitled "The Call to Follow God" by reading Genesis 11:27–12:9, which is both the background and lesson scripture for this lesson. Consider this focus as you study the lesson: People decide who or what to follow, and this involves trust. How do we respond when we feel God's call? By the way they followed God into an unknown future, Abram and Sarai model the trust we are to have in God.**

❖ Read aloud the following three ideas. Challenge the students to commit themselves to use these activities as a springboard to spiritual growth.

(1) Look around your church, community, and workplace. Who seems alienated or alone? Find at least one way you can help bring this person into your circle of friends.

(2) Attend an ecumenical service, or a service of a denomination other than you own. What features could you find in this service that are similar to your own way of worshiping? What do these common features suggest about the oneness of the Christ's church?

(3) Read about some ecumenical dialogues going on between various Christian groups. What issues separate groups from one another? How do you think these issues could be resolved?

❖ Sing or read aloud "Help Us Accept Each Other."

❖ Ask the students to echo this benediction from 2 Corinthians 13:11-14 as you read it phrase by phrase: **Finally, brothers and sisters, farewell. Put things in order . . . agree with one another, live in peace; and the God of love and peace will be with you. . . . The grace of the Lord Jesus Christ, the love of God, and the communion of the Holy Spirit be with all of you. Amen.**

SECOND QUARTER
Called to Be God's People

DECEMBER 5, 2004–FEBRUARY 27, 2005

During the winter quarter we will survey the Bible from Genesis to the Gospel of John by exploring the theme of *call*. This study will help us examine the variety of ways in which God calls the community of faith to live out the purpose for which we were created.

Unit 1, "God Calls a People" begins on December 5 with God's call to Abram and Sarai to leave their country and go to a place where God will show them. This first lesson, "The Call to Follow God," delves into Genesis 11:27–12:9. The session for December 12, "Leadership Qualities," considers God's selection of David as Israel's second king, as described in 1 Samuel 16:1-4*b*, 6-13, and 2 Samuel 7:8-16. "When the Unexpected Happens," the lesson for December 19, revisits the angel's message to the sleeping Joseph, as recorded in Matthew 1:17-25. This unit ends on December 26 with the story in Luke 2:22-38 of Simeon and Anna, two faithful people who had long-awaited the arrival of the Messiah, as they meet the newborn in the Temple.

Unit 2, "The Call of Jesus and His Followers," which is a study of the Gospel of Mark, begins on January 2, 2005. In Mark 1:14-28, we see Jesus begin his ministry of "Spreading the Good News" by calling fishermen as the first disciples. The session for January 9, "Sharing God's Hospitality," reviews Mark 2:13-17 to illustrate that Jesus is building an inclusive community that can even include a tax collector named Levi (Matthew). "Preparing for the Job," the January 16 session from Mark 6:6*b*-13 and 3:13-19, explores how Jesus equipped and sent out the Twelve for ministry. Mark 8:27-38 is the basis for the lesson on January 23, "Giving Your All." Here, Jesus talks about the need to deny oneself, take up the cross, and follow him. This unit ends on January 30 with "Moving Toward Greatness," rooted in Mark 10:13-45. In this passage, Jesus tells his followers that if they wish to become great, they must serve others.

The final unit for this quarter, "Whosoever Will—Come!" which begins on February 6, 2005, focuses on overcoming. The first session, "Overcoming Grief," taken from Ruth 1, portrays the widowed Ruth as she steadfastly stands by her widowed mother-in-law, Naomi. "Overcoming Pride," the session for February 13, examines 2 Kings 5 where we find the story of Naaman, an Aramean military leader who was stricken with leprosy. "Overcoming Uncertainty," the session for February 20, looks at the beloved passage from John 3:1-21. As Jesus and the Pharisee, Nicodemus, talk about an appropriate relationship between oneself and God, Nicodemus learns that he must be born again, from above. This unit and the winter quarter conclude with "Overcoming Prejudice," another familiar story from John's Gospel, John 4:1-42. Jesus' willingness to talk with a woman—and a Samaritan woman at that—indicates that God's reign is open to all who will come.

MEET OUR WRITER

DR. CHARLES D. YOOST

Charles D. Yoost has served as the senior pastor of the Church of the Saviour in Cleveland Heights, Ohio, since 1998. Worship services of his United Methodist congregation are broadcast locally on radio and television, and internationally by way of the Internet at www.wclv.com.

From 1992 to 1998, Yoost served as the Mansfield, Ohio district superintendent. Prior to that, he had been appointed to Church Hill United Methodist Church and Northampton United Methodist Church, both in Ohio.

Yoost earned his bachelor of arts degree from the University of Akron. He received a master of theology and doctor of ministry degrees from Boston University School of Theology.

He chaired the Legislation and Evaluation Committee, General Board of Discipleship of The United Methodist Church, 2001–2004 quadrennium. He also chairs the Board of Congregational Development for the East Ohio Annual Conference, and is a member of the Steering Committee of the United Methodist Youth Ministry Organization. Yoost serves as a trustee of Ohio Northern University and the Ohio East Area Foundation of the United Methodist Church. He has also been a delegate to the United Methodist General Conference in 1996 and 2000, and a delegate to the World Methodist Conference in 1996.

This is the second time Yoost has written for the *New International Lesson Annual*. He is also the author of five *Daily Bible Study* publications. He has written Sunday school lessons and daily devotions for *Mature Years* magazine, and for *Circuit Rider* magazine, a United Methodist publication for clergy.

Yoost is married and has two adult sons. His wife, Barbara, is a nursing instructor at Kent State University in Kent, Ohio. Son, Timothy and his wife, Jennie, are students at the University of Louisville Medical School in Louisville, Kentucky. Son Stephen is a student at Ohio State University Moritz College of Law.

In his leisure time, Yoost enjoys playing the organ and the piano.

CALLED TO BE GOD'S PEOPLE

I have a clergy friend who gives the following counsel to persons who are contemplating the ordained or professional ministry as an occupation: "Don't become a pastor unless you can't do anything else!" Most people are taken aback by this statement, which on the surface may appear cynical and sarcastic. Then my friend explains that one should only become a pastor if the call of God upon one's heart and life is so strong that the person feels convicted that he or she must pursue the ministry as a career choice.

Such counsel is thoroughly biblical and gets at the root of the lessons for the winter quarter. The Bible is more than a historical record. It is the record of people who were encountered by God and who felt compelled to follow where God led. Some report that the heavens opened and they heard audible voices. Others saw God's hand at work in much more natural and less obvious ways. All the people we will study experienced the claim of God upon their lives and felt compelled to act.

When one responds to the need for pastoral leadership in our day, typically a certifying committee will meet with the candidate. Among the first issues the committee will raise is this: "Share with us the story of your call." Pastors are not selected because of their aptitude for certain tasks, although certain gifts are desirable for pastoral work. They are not chosen because of the need. Pastoral leaders are commissioned and ordained because they have felt the call of God upon their lives, and they have chosen to follow the path on which they feel God is leading them. In like manner, when discouraged, disillusioned, or experiencing spiritual dryness, pastors are encouraged to remember the experience of their call. They are encouraged to seek to recapture the feelings and insights surrounding that experience. Pastors, I repeat, are not simply trained, educated, and taught certain skills. No one has any business in pastoral ministry if he or she has not experienced the call of God upon one's heart and life.

It is my conviction that God calls not only pastors, but God calls all people. Of course, some have experienced God's call more overtly and have responded more completely. But I believe that God has a purpose for every person. As a little boy once said, "God don't make no junk!" Each of us is on this earth for a reason. God created us, and God has a purpose for our lives.

It is a basic Judeo-Christian principle that we are not on this earth by accident, but rather by the purposeful design of Almighty God. Abram was a prosperous shepherd and landowner living in the city of Haran. Suddenly God appeared to Abram and called him to leave his country, his clan, and his home, and journey to a land that God promised to reveal to him. God's word came as a clear summons to break with the past and to set out on a new venture of faith, trusting in God alone.

The Genesis narrative makes it clear that God's intentions for the world are being mediated in and through Abram and his descendants, although later writings will demonstrate that God's blessing does not come through this family alone. The exact nature of "chosen people" status will need to be interpreted time and again in the centuries to follow. However, God's choice of Abram will lead to blessings for all the families of the earth. What initially seems to be an exclusive action has inclusiveness as its ultimate goal. Those who are chosen by God always have a mission to fulfill. Being chosen is not only a blessing, but carries a responsibility as well. Abram responds positively to God's call. Genesis 12:4 states simply, "So Abram went, as the LORD had told him."

Throughout the Bible, stories of God's call will be shared. Moses, Joshua, Deborah, Gideon, to name a few, all heard the call of God and sought to follow the leading of God's Spirit. When the fledgling nation desired to have a king, the prophet Samuel, responding to a call from God, anointed Saul. When Saul faltered in his leadership, God had Samuel anoint someone else. God's choice of David as king illustrates another of the basic themes of the Bible: God often goes to the most unexpected places and uses the most unlikely people to fulfill God's purposes. From a common family God chose David, the shepherd. The eighth son of Jesse became the greatest king Israel had ever known. In the years that followed, when the people dreamed of the promised Messiah, they hoped that he would be like David.

When the unexpected happens, special qualities are demanded from those whom God calls. For Christians, the story of God's call reaches a pinnacle in the story of the birth of Jesus, who was called to be the Savior of the world. From a human standpoint, Joseph was confronted with starling news. Mary, his betrothed, was pregnant, and Joseph was not the father! How would the couple deal with this news? We learn a great deal about the character of both Joseph and Mary by their response. Even though she was undoubtedly the subject of rumor and gossip, Mary remained calm. Joseph was "a righteous man and unwilling to expose her to public disgrace" (Matthew 1:19). Responding to the words of an angel who appeared to him in a dream, Joseph took Mary as his wife. His obedience allowed Jesus to be adopted as a true son of David. Joseph and Mary's response shows us how to cope in a positive way when the unexpected happens to us in life.

Oftentimes I have observed that some of the most visionary people are those who are advanced in years. Probably nobody in the Bible saw God's hand at work more clearly than did Simeon or Anna. The aging process had not blurred their vision. Simeon and Anna were looking forward to seeing the Messiah. They knew that with the birth of every child God gives the world yet another chance. With the birth of every baby comes a fresh perspective and a renewed sense of hope. Simeon and Anna did not know when the Messiah would appear, but they were ready to embrace every child in the hope that God might use that baby to usher in the messianic age.

As every parent knows, babies grow up! As he matured, Jesus responded to the claim of God upon his life and began to fulfill God's purposes for him. Besides preaching the good news that the time of salvation as foretold by John the Baptist had begun, Jesus continued the biblical tradition of the call by inviting persons to follow him. From the outset, Jesus called people to share in his ministry of preaching, teaching, and healing. Again, Jesus demonstrated that the call of God comes to ordinary people as they go about their daily tasks. There is no hint that the fishermen whom Jesus called did anything unusual to attract his attention. Jesus simply saw in them qualities that God could use in spreading the message of salvation to all people.

One of the people who responded to Jesus' call was Levi or Matthew. Fellow Jews despised Levi because he was a tax collector. We do not know whether Levi had cheated his fellow Jews and therefore "deserved" to be ostracized from polite society. All we know is that Jesus accepted this tax collector, forgave his past, and opened to him a new life of love and service in God's kingdom. The story of Levi's call makes it clear that no one is beyond the love and concern of Almighty God. Every person can be used in the service and the building of God's kingdom. Jesus calls us to an inclusive community where all are made to feel welcome. The invitation to each of us is the same: "Follow me."

It is clear from the earliest tradition that while the call comes to all of us, Jesus chose twelve disciples as the nucleus of the Christian community. The number twelve reminds us of the twelve tribes, and indicates that Jesus has come to restore Israel. The disciples are to be an extension of Jesus' ministry, and as such they are full participants in Jesus' mission. Like Jesus, they speak and act with authority.

From the outset, Jesus called individuals to be part of a movement, rather than to be isolated followers. The Christian faith is meant to be lived in fellowship with other people. It is also true that from the outset the Christian church has been a diverse fellowship. Matthew or Levi was a tax collector, and therefore an outcast. Simon was one of the band of fiery and violent nationalists who were pledged to rid the country of its foreign yoke. There were unlettered fishermen in the group, as well as Judas Iscariot, a traitor. All of these persons lived and worked together as followers of Jesus. All these were called by Jesus, equipped for the tasks of ministry, and sent out. God was able to use this motley band of twelve to change the world!

When we hear the call of Christ, we must not assume that following Jesus will be easy. In fact, in some situations it may not be clear what the faithful response should be. The first disciples were continually missing the point of Jesus' teaching. In spite of numerous explanations of his purpose and his calling, the disciples continued to expect Jesus to be a political messiah who would physically overthrow Rome, rather than a suffering servant who would change the hearts and lives of his followers. It was difficult for the disciples to hear that Jesus would suffer and die. It is hard for us to hear the hard words of Jesus today!

Although the disciples left everything to follow Jesus, they continued struggling to understand Jesus' way of life. They were forever slipping back into the old way of thinking. Jesus reminded them time and again that discipleship is not a matter of power and prestige, but a matter of service. Still today we need to be reminded that as long as we measure our successes and failures by the standards of the world, we will fail to grasp the essence of Jesus' teaching. Following Jesus means allowing God to change our value system, reorder our priorities, and use our lives in faithful service.

If we are going to follow God faithfully as Jesus beckons, then we are going to have to deal with the obstacles that life often places in our way. The sadness of grief and loss can paralyze us. Social scientists tell us that clinical depression is rampant in our society today. While biblical people did not have the advantage of modern diagnostic tools, they coped with grief and loss on a daily basis.

When her husband and both of her sons died in the land of Moab where they had gone to seek a better life, Naomi understandably became bitter. When she chose to return to her native Bethlehem, her daughter-in-law, Ruth, decided to go with her. "Where you go, I will go; where you lodge, I will lodge; your people shall be my people, and your God my God" (Ruth 1:16b). These beautiful words, often shared at weddings, tell of Ruth's love and loyalty to her mother-in-law. Ruth was helped to work through her grief by ministering to Naomi. By accepting Ruth's care, Naomi was able to experience God's healing power in her life as well.

Naaman, a Syrian general, was afflicted with the dreaded disease of leprosy. Upon learning that he might find help in Israel, Naaman took an extravagant load of gifts to Elisha, the prophet. Elisha did not have an audience with Naaman, but through a messenger gave him simple instructions to wash in the Jordan River. Naaman was offended, but listened to his servants who encouraged their master to follow Elisha's instructions. When Naaman complied, he was healed, and became a believer in the God of Israel. Once Naaman was able to swallow his pride, God acted in Naaman's life, and his health was restored.

Some folks get to the point in life where they understand that there are many things that they have taken for granted, but upon reflection realize they are not sure about. Jesus' talk about the new life intrigued Nicodemus, but this respected member of the Jewish Sanhedrin did not fully understand what Jesus meant. When Jesus described the life of faith as being born again, Nicodemus took Jesus literally! Jesus carefully explained to Nicodemus that the process of coming to faith is to undergo such a radical change in life that it is analogous to the birth experience itself. It can only be described as starting all over again. There is no indication that Nicodemus's initial encounter with Jesus caused him to come to faith. The scholarly debate apparently did not produce a disciple. In the final analysis, one must take a leap of faith to become a believer. The claims of the gospel cannot be proved scientifically. Instead, we are challenged to put our faith and trust in God.

Of all the barriers to following God's call, perhaps none is more problematic than that of prejudice. When Jesus met the woman at the well, he was in Samaritan territory. There was plenty of reason to be put off, for Jews had no dealings with Samaritans. Furthermore, Jewish men did not initiate conversation with unknown women, and Jewish teachers never engaged in public conversation with women. However, Jesus ignored all these barriers and initiated a conversation with the Samaritan woman. To her credit, the woman also refused to be inhibited by social convention. Instead, she willingly talked with Jesus. Their discussion focused on living water. Like Nicodemus, the woman was initially confused by Jesus' analogy. Unlike Nicodemus, she not only came to faith but also went back to the village to tell her friends about a man who "told me everything I have ever done" (John 4:39). Thus, the anonymous Samaritan woman became the first Christian evangelist!

These are just a few examples of God's call from the pages of the Bible. The point is clear: the God who called Abram, David, Joseph, Simeon, Anna, the first twelve disciples, Levi, Ruth, Naaman, Nicodemus, and the Samaritan woman is also calling people in our day. Only those who refuse to listen are rejected. God has a purpose and a mission for each of us to accomplish. There is a reason why we were born.

A contemporary song that is gaining in popularity is John Bell's "The Summons" (*The Faith We Sing*, Nashville: Abingdon Press, 2000, no. 2130). The words, which ask if we will follow if God calls our name, clearly help us to hear the biblical call in our day. May we hear God's call and heed the summons now!

UNIT 1: GOD CALLS A PEOPLE
THE CALL TO FOLLOW GOD

PREVIEWING THE LESSON

Lesson Scripture: Genesis 11:27–12:9
Background Scripture: Genesis 11:27–12:9
Key Verse: Genesis 12:1

Focus of the Lesson:
People decide who or what to follow, and this involves trust. How do we respond when we feel God's call? By the way they followed God into an unknown future, Abram and Sarai model the trust we are to have in God.

Goals for the Learners:
(1) to explore the story of Abram and Sarai, particularly highlighting the challenge, risk, and uncertainty they faced in responding to God's call.
(2) to recognize and affirm that God has a plan for their lives even though they might not yet understand what it is.
(3) to identify ways that God may be calling them today.

Pronunciation Guide:

Ai	(i)	Chaldea	(kal dee' uh)
Babylonia	(bab uh loh' nee uh)	Haran	(hair' uhn)
Shechem	(shek' uhm)	Ur	(oor)

Supplies:
Bibles, newsprint and marker, paper and pencils, objects for a worship center, optional commentaries, map showing Chaldea, hymnals

---

READING THE SCRIPTURE

NRSV
Genesis 11:27-32

27 Now these are the descendants of Terah. Terah was the father of Abram, Nahor, and Haran; and Haran was the father of Lot. 28 Haran died before his father Terah in the land of his birth, in Ur of the Chaldeans.

NIV
Genesis 11:27-32

27This is the account of Terah.

Terah became the father of Abram, Nahor and Haran. And Haran became the father of Lot. 28While his father Terah was still alive, Haran died in Ur of the Chaldeans, in the land of his

29 Abram and Nahor took wives; the name of Abram's wife was Sarai, and the name of Nahor's wife was Milcah. She was the daughter of Haran the father of Milcah and Iscah. 30 Now Sarai was barren; she had no child.

31 Terah took his son Abram and his grandson Lot son of Haran, and his daughter-in-law Sarai, his son Abram's wife, and they went out together from Ur of the Chaldeans to go into the land of Canaan; but when they came to Haran, they settled there. 32 The days of Terah were two hundred five years; and Terah died in Haran.

Genesis 12:1-9

Now the LORD said to Abram, "Go from your country and your kindred and your father's house to the land that I will show you. 2 I will make of you a great nation, and I will bless you, and make your name great, so that you will be a blessing. 3 I will bless those who bless you, and the one who curses you I will curse; and in you all the families of the earth shall be blessed."

4 So Abram went, as the LORD had told him; and Lot went with him. Abram was seventy-five years old when he departed from Haran. 5 Abram took his wife Sarai and his brother's son Lot, and all the possessions that they had gathered, and the persons whom they had acquired in Haran; and they set forth to go to the land of Canaan. When they had come to the land of Canaan, 6 Abram passed through the land to the place at Shechem, to the oak of Moreh. At that time the Canaanites were in the land. 7 Then the LORD appeared to Abram, and said, "To your offspring I will give this land." So he built there an altar to the LORD, who had appeared to him. 8 From there he moved on to the hill country on the east of Bethel, and pitched his tent, with Bethel on the west and Ai on the east; and there he built an altar to the LORD and invoked the name of the LORD. 9 And Abram journeyed on by stages toward the Negeb.

birth. 29Abram and Nahor both married. The name of Abram's wife was Sarai, and the name of Nahor's wife was Milcah; she was the daughter of Haran, the father of both Milcah and Iscah. 30Now Sarai was barren; she had no children.

31Terah took his son Abram, his grandson Lot son of Haran, and his daughter-in-law Sarai, the wife of his son Abram, and together they set out from Ur of the Chaldeans to go to Canaan. But when they came to Haran, they settled there.

32 Terah lived 205 years, and he died in Haran.

Genesis 12:1-9

The LORD had said to Abram, "Leave your country, your people and your father's household and go to the land I will show you.
2"I will make you into a great nation
  and I will bless you;
I will make your name great,
  and you will be a blessing.
3I will bless those who bless you,
  and whoever curses you I will curse;
and all peoples on earth
  will be blessed through you."

4So Abram left, as the LORD had told him; and Lot went with him. Abram was seventy-five years old when he set out from Haran. 5He took his wife Sarai, his nephew Lot, all the possessions they had accumulated and the people they had acquired in Haran, and they set out for the land of Canaan, and they arrived there.

6Abram traveled through the land as far as the site of the great tree of Moreh at Shechem. At that time the Canaanites were in the land. 7The LORD appeared to Abram and said, "To your offspring I will give this land." So he built an altar there to the LORD, who had appeared to him.

8From there he went on toward the hills east of Bethel and pitched his tent, with Bethel on the west and Ai on the east. There he built an altar to the LORD and called on the name of the LORD. 9Then Abram set out and continued toward the Negev.

UNDERSTANDING THE SCRIPTURE

Genesis 11:27-29. The genealogy of Abram's father helps to put the story of Abram and Sarai in context. Weaving together stories from different traditions, the author wishes to show the connection between Abram and "all the families of the earth" (12:3).

Genesis 11:30. Within the context of the genealogical history of this family, the author notes that Sarai, whose name means "princess," is barren. This fact is especially noteworthy in light of the promise that God will soon make with her husband. Indeed, Sarai's infertility will become a central theme as the story unfolds.

Genesis 11:31-32. Chaldea was another name for Babylonia, and helps to link the Abram narrative with the story of the Tower of Babel (11:1-9). Ur was a center of one of the earliest great civilizations on Earth, and in Abram's time was still a city of notable wealth and culture. Although they were migrating toward the land of Canaan, Terah and his family had gotten stalled along the way, settling in Haran, which is located in what is today southeastern Turkey, on a tributary of the Euphrates River.

Genesis 12:1. The early chapters of Genesis (1–11) provide the story of human origins, which many scholars believe are largely more poetic than historical. These narratives provide the background and context for the story of God's relationship with the Hebrew people. Beginning with Genesis 12, much more of the material has been verified by archaeology, and is therefore considered by modern definition more historical.

Although the biblical writer has made it clear that Abram and his family have not appeared out of the blue, a new chapter in the story of God's relationship with humankind begins with God's call to Abram (and by implication, to Sarai as well). God's word comes as a clear summons to break with the past, and to set out on a new venture of faith, trusting in God alone. We are to assume that the God who is calling Abram is a God who is already known by Abram and his family, for God is not introduced to the reader. From the context we can surmise that this is the God who created the world and who has been engaged with the peoples of the world from the very beginning. God appears suddenly, without introduction, and calls Abram to leave his country, his clan, and his home, and to journey to a land that God promises to reveal to him.

Genesis 12:2-3. God's promise is not only that Abram will have land but also that his descendants will become "a great nation." Trusting in this promise, of course, requires great faith, given the reality of Sarai's infertility.

Through much of the narrative that follows, the theme of blessing and promise will be emphasized. A blessing is God's gift, and signifies goodness and well-being in life. It involves every aspect of one's existence, including both spiritual and physical dimensions. In the Old Testament, God's blessing is most apparent in fertility and in the multiplication of life. It implies prosperity in every realm of one's existence, from flocks and herds, to healthy children, to a peaceful life with one's neighbors, to general success in whatever ventures one undertakes.

The Genesis narrative makes it clear that God's intentions for the world are being mediated in and through Abram's family. Later writings will demonstrate that God's blessing does not come through this family alone. Yet this passage makes it abundantly clear that Abram and his descendants enjoy a special relationship with God. The exact nature of this "chosen people" status will need to be interpreted time and again through the centuries to follow.

We should note that the promise of "blessing those who bless you" brings

Abram into relationship with those outside the chosen community. Those who treat the descendants of Abram in life-sustaining ways will receive a blessing from God; but God will punish those who treat Abram's descendants with contempt.

The final phrase of verse 3 tells us that God's choice of Abram will lead to blessings for all the families of the earth. What initially seems to be an exclusive action has inclusiveness as its ultimate goal. Those who are chosen by God always have a mission to fulfill. Being chosen is not only a blessing but also a responsibility. Through God's action all the families of the earth will be blessed. Christians see this action of God culminating in Jesus, a descendant of Abram who came to bring salvation to the whole world.

These verses also seem to imply that all who respond to God's call as Abram did will be blessed as Abram was blessed. Those who refuse to respond to the divine initiative will have to suffer the consequences.

Genesis 12:4-5. God's promises imply a future and a hope. The narrative understates Abram's great leap of faith, saying simply, "So Abram went, as the LORD had told him." The author also notes that Abram was 75 years old when he began the journey. Here is not a rebellious teenager leaving home to seek his fortune, but a mature man and his wife who had to pack "all the possessions that they had gathered." Thus, the themes of faith and trust are subtly underscored as Abram and his nephew Lot and their families set out on the journey toward Canaan.

Genesis 12:6-9. When the entourage reaches Canaan, God informs Abram that he is now standing in the land promised to Abram's descendants. Abram moves through the land, from Shechem, a Canaanite city located about 40 miles north of Jerusalem, south to Bethel, a Canaanite sanctuary to the god "El." The Negeb is a dry highland area in the far south of Palestine.

Worship is obviously an integral part of Abram's life. At each spot, he builds an altar marked by trees or stones. These altars function as a continuing reminder to the people of God's presence with them and God's promise to them.

INTERPRETING THE SCRIPTURE

God's Call and Promise to Abram and Sarai

One summer Sunday morning following worship a woman came into my office. A longtime member of the congregation I pastor, she had come to say "good-bye." That next week she would be moving from her home in Cleveland, Ohio, to live with family members in Maryland. It was a bittersweet moment. Jean had been our church librarian for several years, following a long career as a beloved public librarian. She had given of herself tirelessly to the children, youth, and adults of our community. She was grateful for the invitation from her niece and family to make her home with them, as her health had begun to fail. Moving was a big step for Jean. She would be far from her friends and familiar surroundings and places she loved. Yet she also told me she knew this was the best decision for her. We had prayer, wiped a few tears, and she departed.

Jean is not the only person to make a brave decision that involves moving halfway across the country. Frequently we are confronted with situations that mean being uprooted from the familiar and comfortable places in our lives. Job changes, changes in our family situation, health problems, economic upheavals, and many other transitions confront twenty-first century people. Can we see the hand of God at work in these situations?

Abram and Sarai believed that it was not only life's circumstances but the call of God that was leading them to move from their country, their clan, and their extended family to go to an unknown land that God was promising to them. Can we hear the voice of God as we are called to make changes in our lives and respond to new circumstances?

God's instruction to Abram and Sarai was clear. It was the simple word "go." We recall the words of the resurrected Christ as he gave the Great Commission to his followers: "Go therefore and make disciples of all nations" (Matthew 28:19). In preaching on this passage, our bishop asked the pastors, "What part of the word 'go' don't you understand?" Responding to God's call implies movement. God leads; we are expected to follow.

God had a plan for Abram and Sarai. They were to be the parents of a great nation, and God would provide the land that they would need in order to prosper. Their job was to trust the promises of God and to follow where they felt that God was leading them.

Jews and Christians believe that God calls all of us, that every person that God created has a purpose and a reason for being on this earth. God has a plan for your life and mine. We can give ourselves to no higher purpose than to seek to discern that call and to follow where God leads.

Abram and Sarai Are Obedient

"Obedience" is not a popular word in our culture today. To obey means to comply with a command, and we don't want anyone telling us what to do. Yet if we are going to be faithful to the message of the Bible, we are going to need to follow the instructions of God.

Genesis 12:4 tells us simply, "Abram went, as the LORD had told him." Sarai and Abram had enough faith to believe that God

would take care of them on the journey. They had no evidence that the land where God was taking them was any better than their current residence. Yet they went forth in faith and in trust.

How hard it is to take risks in this life, especially as we get older. Most of us would rather settle for what is known than to take a chance on the unfamiliar. The story is told of a medieval feudal lord who offered two choices to those who were convicted of high crimes: the gallows or the red door. The criminals almost always chose the gallows. One day one of the guards asked the lord what form of death was behind the red door. "There is no torture behind the red door," replied the lord. "The red door leads to freedom." Yet fear of the unknown kept most criminals from choosing that door. Will we say "yes" to God and venture into an unknown future as Abram and Sarai were willing to do?

Abram and Sarai Face Many Challenges on the Way

I have already alluded to the fact that Abram and Sarai had to leave the comforts of their home to respond to God's call. Not all of us are called literally to pack our belongings and move to a different location. However, discerning and following God's purposes may often mean personal inconvenience and putting other's needs before our own. Our congregation has been involved in the Interfaith Hospitality Network for the past four years. Every few weeks we host up to fourteen homeless people for seven nights. Volunteers cook meals, help care for their children, and sleep at the church alongside those who have no other place to stay. There are continuing challenges associated with this ministry. However, the intangible rewards cause a significant number of volunteers to serve God and our fellow human beings in this way.

I have often said that God has no retirement plan! Abram and Sarai were well past retirement age when God called them. God promised they would become a great nation, yet the writer has told us that Sarai was barren. Does God have a cruel sense of humor? No, God is challenging Abram and Sarai to be faithful and to put their trust in God alone. Only God can bring a great nation from the womb of barren Sarai! Only God can safely lead this elderly couple through the desert to a new land. What will you accomplish this coming week that is so far-fetched that you will succeed only if God is with you?

Faith Sustains Us on the Journey

If it was not clear previously that Abram and Sarai were persons of faith, it becomes obvious as they journey into Canaan, for at Shechem and at Bethel, Abram builds an altar to the Lord. When they moved to a foreign land, Abram and Sarai took their faith with them. They did not hesitate to continue the practice of regular worship in their new location. I remember visiting with a couple that is new to our community and our church. The woman said, "My grand-mother used to tell me that the first thing to do when you move is to look for a church!" This young couple has already learned that their faith will help sustain them in a strange and unfamiliar place. When we move, God goes with us. God is always by our side.

Abram and Sarai's faith is an inspiration to us. How can we encourage and support those who are asked to take new and challenging responsibilities? How can we reach out to those on the journey? Certainly some of the most meaningful ministries of the church occur when we are in transition times in our lives. Members of our congregation take casseroles to families following the birth of a child. Many expressions of love surround those who are hospitalized. Some of our folks open their homes to the family members of those who come to our local hospitals from a great distance. A listening ear and an understanding heart go a long way to ease the burden when we are in unfamiliar surroundings. May God help each of us to hear the call, to follow where God leads, and to support others on their journey.

SHARING THE SCRIPTURE

PREPARING TO TEACH

Preparing Our Hearts

This week's devotional reading is found in Jeremiah 1:4-10. What does God call Jeremiah to do? How does Jeremiah react? Had you been Jeremiah, what assurance would you have had that God was truly calling you? How has God called you? How have you responded to God?

Pray that you and your students will be open to the call of God on your lives and ready to answer that call by trusting God to lead you into an unknown future.

Preparing Our Minds

Study the background and lesson scripture, which are both from Genesis 11:27–12:9.

Write on newsprint:
activities 1-3 under "Explore the Story of Abram and Sarai" on newsprint.
questions specified for "Identify Ways God Calls Us Today."
information for next week's lesson, found under "Continue the Journey."

Plan to set up a worship center, or provide items that a group can use during the session to create the center. You will need a small table, Bible, candle, and matches. You may also want to place flowers and an offering basket on the table. Consider adding an object that will remind the students of God's call on their lives. A telephone may be a readily understood symbol for "call."

LEADING THE CLASS

(1) Gather to Learn

❖ Welcome each of the students and introduce any newcomers.

❖ Pray for you and the students to be open to God's call and willing to follow wherever God may lead you.

❖ Read aloud the story of Jean, found in the first two paragraphs in "God's Call and Promise to Abram and Sarai."

❖ Invite participants to tell stories of experiences they have had when their immediate future was uncertain and they had to trust God to lead them into the unknown.

❖ Link these stories to today's Bible lesson by noting that God commanded Abram and Sarai to leave their home and trust God to take them to a new land. They obeyed and walked with God into an uncertain future that would later prove to be filled with amazing blessings.

❖ Read aloud today's focus statement: **People decide who or what to follow, and this involves trust. How do we respond when we feel God's call? By the way they followed God into an unknown future, Abram and Sarai model the trust we are to have in God.**

(2) Explore the Story of Abram and Sarai

❖ Choose a volunteer to read Genesis 11:27-32.

❖ Use information from Understanding the Scripture to present the following information (a) as a lecture, (b) as a discussion, or (c) as student research from commentaries.

(1) Find Chaldea, which is another name for Babylonia and the city of

Ur on a map. About how far did Abram's family have to travel to reach Haran, located in what is now southeastern Turkey?

(2) What do you learn from these six verses about Abram's family?

(3) What point is made here about Sarai that will run as a continuing thread through this story?

❖ Select two persons to read Genesis 12:1-9, one to be the voice of the narrator and one to be the voice of God.

(1) What command does God give Abram?

(2) What blessings does God promise to Abram and, by implication, to Sarai?

(3) How does Abram respond to God? Pantomime Abram's actions.

❖ Use a lecture or brainstorming session to present what is known or can be inferred about Abram and Sarai from the biblical account.

Point 1: They were an elderly couple.

Point 2: They had no children.

Point 3: They willingly obeyed God.

Point 4: They trusted God's promises, even though all of them had yet to be fulfilled.

Point 5: They sensed that God had a plan for their lives.

Point 6: They expressed their gratitude to God through worship.

Point 7: Abram and Sarai have been revered as models of faith.

❖ Invite the students to do at least one of the following three activities. You may want to divide into groups and let each group do a different activity. If you do divide, allow time for the groups to come together to share insights from their work. Either read this information aloud, or post it on newsprint.

Activity 1: Assume that you are Abram or Sarai. Write a letter to a friend explaining your call from God, your response, and the risks and challenges you are facing.

Activity 2: Encourage the students to role-play a conversation between Abram and Sarai after Abram builds an altar to God at Shechem.

Activity 3: Offer the students an opportunity to create a worship center or altar for today's class session.

*(3) Recognize and Affirm God's
Plan for Our Lives*

❖ Read aloud the last two paragraphs under "God's Call and Promise to Sarai and Abraham."

❖ Distribute paper and pencils. Ask the students to draw a timeline on which they label events that they believe illustrate milestones of God's plan for their life. Ask them to consider this question: **What response have you made to each of these milestones?**

(4) Identify Ways God Calls Us Today

❖ Read or retell the information concerning the Interfaith Hospitality Network, found in the first paragraph of "Abram and Sarai Face Many Challenges on the Way."

❖ Make a list on newsprint of ways that your congregation is answering God's call to serve others in need.

❖ Brainstorm ideas that your congregation, either by itself or in partnership with other congregations, could implement that would broaden or deepen its ministry to those in need. Record these ideas on newsprint. Make a tentative plan of action to show how you might get started in making these visions a reality.

❖ Distribute paper and pencils, but give students the option of quiet reflection if they choose not to write. Post these directions where everyone can see them.

Write about a call on your life that you know came from God. What was this call? How did you act on it? What blessings came to you and/or others as a result of this call? If you have not yet acted on this call, what commitment will you make to explore this call and begin to make a response?

(5) Continue the Journey

❖ Light a candle on the worship center that you, or one of the groups earlier in the session, have set up.

❖ Pray that class members have heard God's call for this leg of their faith journey and will commit themselves to following God's direction for their lives.

❖ Read aloud this preparation for next week's lesson. You may also want to post it on newsprint for the students to copy. **Prepare for next week's session by reading 1 Samuel 16:1-4b, 6-13, and 2 Samuel 7:8-16. Focus on 1 Samuel 16:1-4b, 6-13 for our lesson entitled "Leadership Qualities." Keep this focus in mind as you prepare: People choose leaders for a variety of reasons. What makes a leader faithful? The story of David shows that God calls leaders based on inward qualities, not external ones.**

❖ Read aloud the following three ideas. Challenge the students to commit themselves to use these activities as a springboard to spiritual growth.

(1) **Continue to identify ways that God is calling you. Look for opportunities to serve God by serving others.**

(2) **Reflect on how Abram and Sarai may be models of faith for your life. God may not be asking you to pack up everything and leave your familiar surroundings, though that is possible. Consider what God may be asking you to leave behind as you press ahead to become a more faithful disciple.**

(3) **Pray about what you can do to assist people who are transient. For example, could you volunteer at an airport or other center of public transportation where you could offer hospitality to travelers? Or could you be an advocate for migrant workers who are always on the move.**

❖ Sing or read aloud "Where He Leads Me."

❖ Ask the students to echo this benediction as you read it phrase by phrase: **Grant, O Lord, that what has been said with our lips we may believe in our hearts, and that what we believe in our hearts we may practice in our lives; through Jesus Christ our Lord. Amen.**

LEADERSHIP QUALITIES

PREVIEWING THE LESSON

Lesson Scripture: 1 Samuel 16:1-4*b*, 6-13
Background Scripture: 1 Samuel 16:1-4*b*, 6-13; 2 Samuel 7:8-16
Key Verse: 1 Samuel 16:7

Focus of the Lesson:
People choose leaders for a variety of reason. What makes a leader faithful? The story of David shows that God calls leaders based on inward qualities, not external ones.

Goals for the Learners:
(1) to examine the story of David's anointing.
(2) to explore the inner qualities that God considers more important than external factors.
(3) to help one another identify these inner qualities in themselves.

Pronunciation Guide:

Abinadab	(uh bin' uh dab)	Jesse	(jes'ee)
Eliab	(i li' uhb)	Shammah	(sham' uh)

Supplies:
Bibles, newsprint and marker, paper and pencils, hymnals

READING THE SCRIPTURE

NRSV
1 Samuel 16:1-4*b*, 6-13

The LORD said to Samuel, "How long will you grieve over Saul? I have rejected him from being king over Israel. Fill your horn with oil and set out; I will send you to Jesse the Bethlehemite, for I have provided for myself a king among his sons." 2 Samuel said, "How can I go? If Saul hears of it, he will kill me." And the LORD said, "Take a heifer with you, and say, 'I have come to sacrifice to the LORD.' 3 Invite Jesse to the sacrifice,

NIV
1 Samuel 16:1-4*b*, 6-13

The LORD said to Samuel, "How long will you mourn for Saul, since I have rejected him as king over Israel? Fill your horn with oil and be on your way; I am sending you to Jesse of Bethlehem. I have chosen one of his sons to be king."

²But Samuel said, "How can I go? Saul will hear about it and kill me."

The LORD said, "Take a heifer with you and say, 'I have come to sacrifice to the and I will show you what you shall do; and you shall anoint for me the one whom I name to you." 4 Samuel did what the LORD commanded, and came to Bethlehem. The elders of the city came to meet him. . . .

6 When they came, he looked on Eliab and thought, "Surely the LORD's anointed is now before the LORD." 7 But the LORD said to Samuel, "Do not look on his appearance or on the height of his stature, because I have rejected him; **for the LORD does not see as mortals see; they look on the outward appearance, but the LORD looks on the heart."** 8 Then Jesse called Abinadab, and made him pass before Samuel. He said, "Neither has the LORD chosen this one." 9 Then Jesse made Shammah pass by. And he said, "Neither has the LORD chosen this one." 10 Jesse made seven of his sons pass before Samuel, and Samuel said to Jesse, "The LORD has not chosen any of these." 11 Samuel said to Jesse, "Are all your sons here?" And he said, "There remains yet the youngest, but he is keeping the sheep." And Samuel said to Jesse, "Send and bring him; for we will not sit down until he comes here." 12 He sent and brought him in. Now he was ruddy, and had beautiful eyes, and was handsome. The LORD said, "Rise and anoint him; for this is the one." 13 Then Samuel took the horn of oil, and anointed him in the presence of his brothers; and the spirit of the LORD came mightily upon David from that day forward. Samuel then set out and went to Ramah.

LORD.' ³Invite Jesse to the sacrifice, and I will show you what to do. You are to anoint for me the one I indicate."

⁴Samuel did what the LORD said. When he arrived at Bethlehem, the elders of the town trembled when they met him.

⁶When they arrived, Samuel saw Eliab and thought, "Surely the LORD's anointed stands here before the LORD."

⁷But the LORD said to Samuel, "Do not consider his appearance or his height, for I have rejected him. **The LORD does not look at the things man looks at. Man looks at the outward appearance, but the LORD looks at the heart."**

⁸Then Jesse called Abinadab and had him pass in front of Samuel. But Samuel said, "The LORD has not chosen this one either." ⁹Jesse then had Shammah pass by, but Samuel said, "Nor has the LORD chosen this one." ¹⁰Jesse had seven of his sons pass before Samuel, but Samuel said to him, "The LORD has not chosen these." ¹¹So he asked Jesse, "Are these all the sons you have?"

"There is still the youngest," Jesse answered, "but he is tending the sheep."

Samuel said, "Send for him; we will not sit down until he arrives."

¹²So he sent and had him brought in. He was ruddy, with a fine appearance and handsome features.

Then the LORD said, "Rise and anoint him; he is the one."

¹³So Samuel took the horn of oil and anointed him in the presence of his brothers, and from that day on the Spirit of the LORD came upon David in power. Samuel then went to Ramah.

UNDERSTANDING THE SCRIPTURE

1 Samuel 16:1. Samuel had acted on the Lord's behalf in anointing Saul to be Israel's first king. Eventually, God tells Samuel that Saul, "has turned back from following me, and has not carried out my commands" (1 Samuel 15:10). Samuel is grief-stricken over Saul's actions. But God calls Samuel out of this immobilized state to move on. God has rejected Saul as king, and has chosen another. As God's agent, it is the role of the prophet to anoint the person whom God has chosen. God does not reveal who the new king will be, but simply instructs Samuel to fill his horn with oil and go to the house of Jesse the Bethlehemite.

One of the basic themes of the Bible is that God often finds possibilities in the most unexpected places and uses the most unlikely people to fulfill God's purposes. Jesse is not described as a person of wealth or power. His family tree is not distinguished. Jesse's grandmother was Ruth, an immigrant Moabite woman (Ruth 4:17). His grandfather was Boaz, whose ancestors included Tamar, an adulteress (Genesis 38); and Rahab, a prostitute (Joshua 2). Yet from this unlikely family, God has chosen a king.

1 Samuel 16:2-4b. Even though he has had difficult assignments in the past as a prophet of the Lord, Samuel is afraid. If Samuel anoints another king while Saul occupies the throne, he will be guilty of treason. Therefore, God provides a plan. Saul is to take an animal with him and offer a sacrifice to the Lord in Bethlehem. Is God helping Samuel to be deceitful? No, for an animal sacrifice and a ritual meal would have been part of the ceremony of anointing a king. Rather, God appears to be pointing out practicalities that Samuel seems unable to figure out in his immobilized state of grief and fear.

Samuel does as God commands. He reassures the frightened elders in Bethlehem that he has come in peace to offer a sacrifice.

1 Samuel 16:6-7. When Samuel saw Jesse's sons, he assumed that Eliab would be God's chosen one, for he was the eldest (17:13), and seemed a logical choice. After all, Eliab was apparently tall and good looking (as was Saul according to 1 Samuel 9:2). But God rebukes Samuel for moving toward a hasty judgment. The point of the story is that God is guiding the process, not Samuel. Samuel is looking for God's chosen one, but not really seeing. He has not been able to discern the qualities that God desires in a leader. God sees differently from mortals, who often settle for outward appearances. "The LORD looks on the heart," the will and character of a person. So God rejects Eliab.

1 Samuel 16:8-10. One after another seven of Jesse's sons are paraded in front of Samuel, and God rejects them all!

1 Samuel 16:11. Finally, as the drama heightens, Samuel asks Jesse if he has any other sons. Jesse has omitted his youngest, who is tending the sheep.

1 Samuel 16:12. It is almost as if God is saying, "You'll know him when you see him," for as soon as David appears, Samuel recognizes that he is the one. Since God has rebuked Samuel for looking at outward appearances, it is ironic that the narrator seems eager to describe the shepherd boy as physically attractive. We soon learn that he is ruddy, handsome and has beautiful eyes, no less! While he has the heart to be anointed by God, David is good-looking as well!

1 Samuel 16:13. In his prophetic role, Samuel anoints David in the presence of Jesse's whole family, and "the spirit of the LORD came mightily upon David from that day forward." God's spirit will enable David to rule when the time comes. However, we should note that while David has officially been anointed as king of Israel, knowledge of Samuel's actions would not become public for some time.

2 Samuel 7:8-11a. This passage focuses on God's covenant with David. One Bible commentator calls chapter 7 the most important theological text in the books of Samuel. Again, God speaks through the words of a prophet, this time through the mouth of the prophet Nathan. First of all, there is a review of God's favorable history with David: "I took you . . . I have been with you . . . I have cut off all your enemies." God has been with David through thick and thin. Now God promises (1) to make David a great name; (2) to give Israel a place among the nations; and (3) to give David and his people rest from all their enemies.

2 Samuel 7:11b. With the kingdom secure and his own palace built, David has proposed that he build a temple for the Lord. By the use of a play on words God reverses

David's proposal by saying, "I will make you a house."

2 Samuel 7:12. Unlike what Israel experienced with Saul's leadership, which God has rejected, a son will be allowed to succeed David on the throne. David's family will establish a dynasty, a new concept for the people of Israel.

2 Samuel 7:13. Although God will not permit David to build a temple, his son will be allowed to build "a house for my name." The son, of course, will be Solomon. Note that the promise of David's house extends well beyond Solomon, for the throne of the kingdom will be established by God and made secure "forever."

2 Samuel 7:14-15. God's relationship with David and his descendants will be an intimate one. It will be as that of a loving father with his son. Further, unconditional grace is promised. God may chastise the king for disobeying God's covenant commands, and God will take appropriate disciplinary action. But even this will not cause God to cease in steadfast love toward David and his descendants, as had happened with Saul.

2 Samuel 7:16. God promises never to give up on David and David's lineage! Again God reassures David that his throne will be established forever. These promises of an enduring line for David became part of the foundation of the messianic hope in later Judaism. In difficult days the people held to the promises that God had made and looked for God to bring a new David in every situation. In future times, God's presence would not be dependent upon a temple, but upon God's unconditional and everlasting promise to the lineage of David. The message is clear: God will not abandon God's people. God's kingdom will endure from age to age.

INTERPRETING THE SCRIPTURE

God Rejects Saul and Chooses a New King

The people of Israel had placed their hope in Saul, who was their first king. It was obviously a great disappointment that Saul faltered in his leadership. Even though he repented of his sinful actions, God determined that Saul was no longer capable of leading the fledgling nation, and chose a new king to replace him.

As the one who had anointed Saul "to reign over the people of the LORD" (1 Samuel 10:1), Samuel had a difficult time with the news. After all, he had been with Saul from the beginning of Saul's tenure. We can relate to Samuel's feelings of grief. How many times in the past few years have our leaders disappointed us? Scandals in government abound. Mismanagement and shortsightedness seem to be the order of the day. In business, greed, the desire for personal gain, and preoccupation with the bottom line often overshadow more altruistic concerns. The church can hardly afford to point an accusing finger at corruption in government and mismanagement in the corporate world, for problems with leadership have emerged and continue to surface within the Body of Christ in every denomination. None of us is perfect, and we must not hold our leaders to unrealistic expectations. Yet moral and ethical failures on the part of leadership take a tremendous toll on the Body of Christ, and there comes a time when we must say, "Enough." Painful though it was, Samuel became convinced that a change of leadership was needed. Once again the prophet put himself at God's disposal in the process of anointing a new king.

"The Lord Looks on the Heart"

Modern media reinforces the fact that we are an image-conscious society where appearances are all-important. Even in ancient Israel it seems that good looks played a role in the selection of leaders, for we read that when Saul was chosen, "There was not a man among the people of Israel more handsome than he." Furthermore, "he stood head and shoulders above everyone else" (1 Samuel 9:2). When it came time to choose a new king, it seemed logical that Samuel would again look for someone tall and good-looking. But God had different criteria in mind!

What are the inner qualities needed for leadership? In recent years, there has been much discussion in the church concerning vision. Certainly those who would help us to move forward should have the gift of extraordinary vision to help us to perceive possibilities that are fully known only to God. God is calling us to move beyond the externals and the superficialities to ask those who would lead us to be selfless in their focus, putting the needs of the community ahead of their own personal concerns.

God chose a shepherd to be the king of Israel. Shepherds are persons whose livelihood is spent caring for the needs of others. They must be comfortable being alone for long periods of time. Is there anyone who is more alone than the CEO of a company or the head of a nation? David was the eighth child of a common family, so he was obviously used to sharing and to negotiation. What qualities of leadership did God see in David? Obviously, God saw in that shepherd boy the makings of Israel's greatest king!

Samuel Anoints David to Be King

When pastors are introduced to congregations, typically the conversation begins with the new pastor sharing the story of his or her call. What does it mean to be called by God? Who is called? How does God choose people to perform the various tasks of ministry in and for the world?

There must be as many call stories as there are Christians, for I believe that not only pastors, but also *every* person that God created, are called to ministry. I remember a woman in my first parish who told me every Sunday on her way out of church, "Pastor, I pray for you every day." Hers was a ministry of prayer. Is there a more significant ministry in the life of a congregation than the ministry of intercessory prayer?

God also calls and designates persons for professional roles within the community. In the Old Testament, the fact that kings were anointed meant not only that they were expected to be leaders of the people, but also to follow God's will and purpose in the performance of their tasks.

While not many of us will be chosen for such a high-profile position as David was, many times we are called to perform tasks for which we feel unqualified and ill-equipped. Many folks shy away from leadership, especially when the demands seem heavy and the support system unclear. Will we consider the fact that when we are asked to take more responsibility and assume greater leadership it may be the hand of God working in our midst? To what specific ministry is God calling you? God may see qualities in you that you do not recognize within yourself. God may be speaking to you through the voice of people in your church and in your community, just as God used Samuel to speak to David.

Because Samuel felt that God had chosen David, Samuel anointed David to be king. The text does not record any conversation about this action. Samuel simply did what God asked him to do, and David responded in humble faith. Will we?

God's Spirit Comes Upon David

Those whom God chooses, God equips for the task. God does not leave anyone to sink or swim. The Bible tells us that after he was anointed, "The spirit of the LORD came mightily upon David" (16:13). In other words, David was empowered for the work that God asked him to perform.

One of the joys of pastoral ministry is the opportunity to see folks grow and change. I have seen insecure youth mature and become leaders in the church. I have seen women who described themselves as "just housewives" make a significant impact in their communities on behalf of justice issues. I have seen retired people build houses for the poor, minister with the homeless, tutor at-risk children, and bring comfort and encouragement to the sick in hospitals and nursing-care facilities. When the

Spirit of the Lord comes upon a person, there is no telling what may happen! One thing is crystal clear: life will never be the same for those who allow the Spirit of God to work in their hearts! Their churches will not be the same, nor will their communities!

People respond to leadership. When folks recognize the grace of God at work in someone's life in a mighty way, they instinctively desire to become part of what God is doing. David became Israel's greatest king. He was able to capture the imagination and unify the spirit of the people of Israel in a way that was unparalleled in the history of their nation. May each of us allow God to use us in the service and building of God's kingdom in our day. Only God knows what the results will be!

SHARING THE SCRIPTURE

PREPARING TO TEACH

Preparing Our Hearts

This week's devotional reading is found in 2 Samuel 7:18-29. After hearing the prophet Nathan's words concerning God's covenant promise, David responds with humble thanks and praise. Remember times when God has called you. How did you respond? What qualities, such as the ability to lead, did God equip you with to fulfill this call?

Pray that you and your students will offer thanks and praise to God not only for your personal call but also for the call of all persons who are able to exert strong leadership on behalf of God's domain.

Preparing Our Minds

Study the background scripture in 1 Samuel 16:1-4b, 6-13, and 2 Samuel 7:8-16. Note that the session focuses only on the passages from 1 Samuel.

Prepare a five-minute lecture concerning Saul in which you highlight: (a) why he was

chosen to be Israel's first king (1 Samuel 9:1–10:16); (b) how he proves himself to be a worthy leader (1 Samuel 11:1-15); and (c) why God rejected Saul (1 Samuel 13:7b-15a and another account in 15:1-35).

Write on newsprint:

information for next week's lesson, found under Continue the Journey.

LEADING THE CLASS

(1) Gather to Learn

❖ Welcome the class members and introduce any guests.

❖ Pray that the students will appreciate leadership qualities that they can identify in themselves and others.

❖ Invite the students to brainstorm answers to this question: **What traits do you want to see in an effective leader?** Record ideas on newsprint. Encourage the students to think of the word "leader" in a broad sense to include heads of state, corporations, and the church.

❖ Build a bridge between this activity and

today's lesson by pointing out that in 1020 B.C., God had instructed Samuel to anoint Israel's first leader, Saul. Unfortunately, Saul did not have the leadership qualities God's people needed, so God commanded the prophet Samuel to anoint David, a young shepherd, to rule over the Israelites.

❖ Read aloud today's focus statement: **People choose leaders for a variety of reason. What makes a leader faithful? The story of David shows that God calls leaders based on inward qualities, not external ones.**

(2) Examine the Story of David's Anointing

❖ Set the stage for today's lesson by sharing the five-minute lecture outlined in Preparing Our Minds concerning why Saul was anointed and then rejected.

❖ Present today's scripture passage in one of these two ways.

Option 1: Invite four students to come to the front of the class and read 1 Samuel 16:1-4*b* and 6-13 as a drama. One adult will be the voice of the narrator, one of Samuel, one of Jesse, and one of God.

Option 2: Ask selected class members, or the whole group if the class is small, to pantomime the story of David's selection as you read aloud 1 Samuel 16:1-4*b* and 6-13.

❖ Lead a discussion of the following questions, or address them in a lecture. The information in Understanding the Scripture will provide some clues.

(1) **What do we know about Jesse's ancestors?**

(2) **What does the fact that Jesse's ancestors were a varied lot of undistinguished people suggest about how God selects leaders?**

(3) **Why is Samuel afraid to follow God's directions?**

(4) **What criteria caused Samuel to assume that Eliab was God's choice? What did Samuel learn when God told him that Eliab was not to be king?**

(5) **Why is the description of David so ironic in this situation?**

(6) **What do we learn about what God will do for those whom God has chosen to lead?**

(3) Explore the Inner Qualities God Considers Important

❖ Based on what they know about why Saul was rejected and David accepted, challenge the students to brainstorm a list of characteristics that God seeks in a faithful leader. Record these ideas on newsprint.

❖ Compare this list with the qualities of a good leader that they identified in "Gather to Learn." Note similarities and differences.

❖ Divide the class into two groups (or multiples of two if you have a large attendance). Ask each group to work on one question. Distribute paper and pencils to at least one person in each group who will jot down ideas that are expressed. At a time you specify, ask each group to report back to the gathered class.

Group 1: If heads of business were to embody the leadership characteristics that God considers important, what changes would you expect to see in the way businesses are run?

Group 2: If church leaders were to embody the leadership characteristics that God considers important, what changes would you expect to see in the way churches operate?

(4) Help One Another Identify Important Inner Qualities in Themselves

❖ Distribute paper and pencils to each student. Ask the students to tear the paper in half horizontally.

❖ Divide the students into groups of three to identify some inner qualities they embody that make for an effective leader.

Option 1: Ask the students to work independently to write some inner qualities that they recognize in the two classmates in their group. On each half of the paper, list characteristics for one of the students for that person to keep. This option will work well if class members know each other well and/or if many people enjoy thinking quietly. There may be some discussion after everyone has passed on a sheet to the other two students.

Option 2: Ask each of the three students in the group to state the characteristics they believe they have to engage in faithful leadership. The other two students should affirm these qualities, if possible. This option will work if class members do not know each other well and/or if many people enjoy social interaction rather than quiet contemplation. People need to feel free to speak about themselves without fear of judgment or ridicule.

❖ Wrap up this activity by inviting each person to state within his or her group how he or she will try to use these God-given leadership traits in the week and months to come.

(5) Continue the Journey

❖ Pray that the students will commit themselves to leading faithfully as God has called them. Give thanks for the leadership characteristics that have been identified in each class member. Ask God to embolden each student to use wisely the traits he or she has been given.

❖ Read aloud this preparation for next week's lesson. You may also want to post it on newsprint for the students to copy. **Prepare for next week's session by reading Matthew 1, focusing especially on verses 17-25. In keeping with our theme of "call"** this session will show how Joseph responds "When the Unexpected Happens." Ponder this focus as you read: **People are often confronted by unexpected circumstances. How do we respond in these cases? What can we learn from Mary and Joseph, who responded to God's call by trusting God?**

❖ Read aloud the following three ideas. Challenge the students to commit themselves to use these activities as a springboard to spiritual growth.

(1) **Be alert for news stories that indicate that a leader is—or is not—living up to his or her responsibilities. Pray that God will empower this person with the inner qualities of a Christlike leader.**

(2) **Think back to a recent political election or other opportunity that you had to select a leader. What criteria were important to you in determining who would be the best leader?**

(3) **Recall a leader in business, politics, or the church who you believe failed his or her constituents. Why do you think this person stumbled? How might you have been able to encourage this person? What did you do to help?**

❖ Sing or read aloud "A Charge to Keep I Have."

❖ Ask the students to echo this benediction as you read it phrase by phrase: **Grant, O Lord, that what has been said with our lips we may believe in our hearts, and that what we believe in our hearts we may practice in our lives; through Jesus Christ our Lord. Amen.**

WHEN THE UNEXPECTED HAPPENS

PREVIEWING THE LESSON

Lesson Scripture: Matthew 1:17-25
Background Scripture: Matthew 1
Key Verse: Matthew 1:24

Focus of the Lesson:
People are often confronted by unexpected circumstances. How do we respond in these cases? What can we learn from Mary and Joseph, who responded to God's call by trusting God?

Goals for the Learners:
(1) to analyze the challenge faced by Mary and Joseph, according to Matthew's account.
(2) to consider how unusual and unexpected circumstances often present a possibility for responding to God in trust and faithfulness.
(3) to develop a plan for how they will listen to God when the unexpected happens.

Supplies:
Bibles, newsprint and marker, paper and pencils, hymnals

READING THE SCRIPTURE

NRSV
Matthew 1:17-25

17 So all the generations from Abraham to David are fourteen generations; and from David to the deportation to Babylon, fourteen generations; and from the deportation to Babylon to the Messiah, fourteen generations.

18 Now the birth of Jesus the Messiah took place in this way. When his mother Mary had been engaged to Joseph, but before they lived together, she was found to be with child from the Holy Spirit. 19 Her

NIV
Matthew 1:17-25

[17]Thus there were fourteen generations in all from Abraham to David, fourteen from David to the exile to Babylon, and fourteen from the exile to the Christ.

[18]This is how the birth of Jesus Christ came about: His mother Mary was pledged to be married to Joseph, but before they came together, she was found to be with child through the Holy Spirit. [19]Because Joseph her husband was a righteous man and did not want to expose her to public

husband Joseph, being a righteous man and unwilling to expose her to public disgrace, planned to dismiss her quietly. 20 But just when he had resolved to do this, an angel of the Lord appeared to him in a dream and said, "Joseph, son of David, do not be afraid to take Mary as your wife, for the child conceived in her is from the Holy Spirit. 21 She will bear a son, and you are to name him Jesus, for he will save his people from their sins." 22 All this took place to fulfill what had been spoken by the Lord through the prophet:
23 "Look, the virgin shall conceive and bear a son,
   and they shall name him Emmanuel,"
which means, "God is with us." **24 When Joseph awoke from sleep, he did as the angel of the Lord commanded him; he took her as his wife,** 25 but had no marital relations with her until she had borne a son; and he named him Jesus.

disgrace, he had in mind to divorce her quietly.
²⁰But after he had considered this, an angel of the Lord appeared to him in a dream and said, "Joseph son of David, do not be afraid to take Mary home as your wife, because what is conceived in her is from the Holy Spirit. ²¹She will give birth to a son, and you are to give him the name Jesus, because he will save his people from their sins."
²²All this took place to fulfill what the Lord had said through the prophet: ²³"The virgin will be with child and will give birth to a son, and they will call him Immanuel"— which means, "God with us."
²⁴When Joseph woke up, he did what the angel of the Lord had commanded him and took Mary home as his wife. ²⁵But he had no union with her until she gave birth to a son. And he gave him the name Jesus.

UNDERSTANDING THE SCRIPTURE

Matthew 1:1. Matthew begins his Gospel with a genealogy designed to stress the continuity between the Old Testament and the new work that God will begin in Jesus Christ. Names are important. "Jesus" comes from the same Greek word as Joshua. Just as Joshua was the successor to Moses' authority, so Jesus will fulfill Moses' role in a new way. "Christ" is not part of Jesus' name. "Christ" is the Greek and "messiah" the Hebrew for the English word "anointed." Jesus is the "son of Abraham," which refers not only to Jesus' ancestry, but also to the fact that Jesus is the authentic heir to the promises God made to this patriarch. In like manner, "son of David" is a messianic title, indicating that Jesus is the heir to the royal throne.

Matthew 1:2. The purpose of the list of names is not to give an accurate historical record of Jesus' ancestry, but to place the story of Jesus in the context of the activity that culminates in the coming of God's kingdom. By beginning with Abraham, Matthew wants us to know that Jesus is a direct descendant of the one through whom God promised to bless all nations (Genesis 12:1-3).

Matthew 1:3-4. Rarely were women mentioned in Jewish genealogies. Thus the mention of Tamar is unusual. It is even more surprising to find her listed in light of the fact that she was the Canaanite wife of Judah's eldest son, Er. When Er died prematurely, Judah refused Tamar the normal consideration of remarriage. So Tamar tricked Judah into fathering a son with her, who became part of the messianic line (Genesis 38). Thus we find questionable ethics as well as Gentiles in the ancestry of Jesus.

Matthew 1:5. As the genealogy continues, we find mention of another Gentile woman,

Rahab. Rahab was a prostitute, who protected the spies who were sent to Jericho. For her help, she and her family were spared during the later destruction of the city by the Israelites. Next we find the Gentile woman Ruth, a Moabite, for whom a book of the Bible is named. Moabites were specifically excluded from the Israelite community, even after ten generations (Deuteronomy 23:3).

Matthew 1:6-11. It is important for Matthew to lift up Jesus' relationship to David, this great king through whom God's promises to Abraham seemed destined to be fulfilled. David stands at the apex of Israel's story. Yet David did not bring in God's kingdom, for both the nation and King David broke the covenant. After David's reign the story of Israel began a sharp decline, resulting in the destruction of Jerusalem and the exile of God's people to a foreign land.

Another woman appears in the story, as Matthew notes that "the wife of Uriah" was Solomon's mother. Uriah's wife was, of course, the beautiful Bathsheba, for whom David lusted. On a dark day in history, David sent Uriah to the front lines where he was killed. David subsequently married Bathsheba, and Solomon was the result of that union.

Matthew 1:12-15. The deportation to Babylon was a low point in Israel's history. Reference to the Exile reminds us of the nation's failings and its hope for a brighter future.

Matthew 1:16. The last of the five women to be named is Mary, the mother of Jesus. Matthew's genealogy begins the Gospel story on an inclusive note. One of the Gospel's primary themes is that all are included in God's plan: men and women, Jews and Gentiles, saints and sinners.

Matthew 1:17. Matthew has arranged his list in groups of fourteen. In the days before printed materials were readily available, his style would have made it easier for people to memorize.

Matthew 1:18. Jewish weddings involved three steps. The engagement was often made through the parents or by a professional matchmaker when the couple were only children. Marriage was deemed to be far too serious a step to be left to the dictates of human passion and the human heart. Betrothal was absolutely binding and lasted for one year. During that time the couple were already legally considered husband and wife, and unfaithfulness was considered adultery. Betrothal could be dissolved only by death or divorce. At the end of the year of betrothal, the marriage took place.

Matthew 1:19. Joseph has become aware of Mary's pregnancy, but does not know its divine source. The Law of Moses required capital punishment in such cases (Deuteronomy 22:23-27), although by Matthew's time the punishment, while still severe and humiliating, had been mitigated by rabbinic practice. The only thing we learn about Joseph's character is that he is a righteous man. Before he knew the whole story, Joseph had already decided not to go by the letter of the law. Out of consideration for Mary, he would divorce her quietly.

Matthew 1:20-21. The focus turns to the actions of God, who through an angel speaks to Joseph in a dream. The angel counsels Joseph not to be afraid, then says in effect, "Do not hesitate to take Mary as your wife." The angel explains Mary's pregnancy, announcing the divine act that has already occurred. Joseph is to name the child, thus accepting the baby as his own, and adopting him into the Davidic line as an authentic "son of David." The name "Jesus" literally means "he shall save." In the Old Testament the name referred to God's deliverance of the people from their enemies and the establishment of God's kingdom. By adding the words, "save his people from their sins," Matthew depicts Jesus as the one through whom forgiveness is announced.

Matthew 1:22-23. While the Isaiah passage refers neither to a virginal conception nor an event in the long-range future, through his citing of Isaiah 7:14 Matthew seeks to demonstrate that prophecy is being fulfilled. The word translated as "virgin" in the Greek could mean "young woman" in the Hebrew. Because Jesus' virgin birth is not mentioned again in the Gospel of Matthew, it seems the conviction that Jesus is "Emmanuel—God with us," is more significant than the circumstances of his birth.

Matthew 1:24-25. Joseph obeys the instructions of the angel by his treatment of Mary and by his giving to Jesus the name revealed by the angel. Joseph does more than the angel commands by having no sexual relations with Mary until the child is born. Thus Matthew underscores the fact that Joseph is not the biological father of Jesus.

INTERPRETING THE SCRIPTURE

Joseph and Mary Are Confronted with Surprising News

A woman called the church one morning. She had gone to the doctor for what she anticipated would be a routine visit. She soon discovered she needs to have surgery. A man commented on his way out of church Sunday, "Your sermon was very meaningful to me. I found out Friday that I am going to lose my job." Another man came home to hear his wife say, "I don't love you anymore. I want a divorce." As our nation has enjoyed prosperity, more and more people have invested in the stock market. These days a downturn in the economy has a dramatic affect on a majority of the population, especially those whose retirement income depends heavily on dividend checks. For years we took matters of safety and security for granted in this country. September 11, 2001, changed that attitude forever. Now long lines at airports are typical, and the news of terrorist threats and the possibility of terrorist activity gets our attention quickly and continues to be high on our list of concerns.

I have not forgotten a quote a friend once shared with me, "Life is what happens while you are busy making other plans." That has been true for me through the years. Does it ring true in your life? Occasionally I will visit with someone who seems to have everything organized, and who lives an ordered life with few interruptions and surprises. Most people's story is just the opposite! "I was planning to go to college when the war came, and I was drafted." "We were getting ready to buy a house when my husband was transferred to a city halfway across the country." "We planned to stay in our own home, but my wife's health failed."

Matthew's Gospel begins with some surprising news. During the year-long betrothal period in their relationship, Mary "was found to be with child from the Holy Spirit" (Matthew 1:18). Although Luke goes into great detail concerning the announcement of this event to Mary, Joseph receives no advance warning. In fact, he learns what has happened after the fact.

Joseph and Mary Respond

To be sure, Mary was not the first girl to become pregnant out of wedlock. However, while the law of Moses that called for death by stoning was generally not practiced in the Jewish culture of that time, shame and humiliation would have caused a great deal of embarrassment both for Mary's and for Joseph's families.

We are given a great deal of insight into the character of Mary and Joseph by their response to the pregnancy. Even though she would certainly have been the subject of rumor and gossip, Mary remains calm. Joseph, we learn, is "a righteous man and unwilling to expose her to public disgrace" (1:19).

The Chinese character for "crisis" is the combination of the characters for danger and opportunity. There is always the danger that we will lose our focus and go to pieces when crisis comes. Yet every crisis is also a possibility for growth and an opportunity to become stronger. How do we handle the crises of life? Young Mary and Joseph can serve as role models for us. They kept cool heads when confronted with news that was destined to change the rest of their lives. How will we cope with the unexpected?

An Angel Intervenes

While Joseph has been busy figuring out a solution to his problem, he suddenly learns that God has a different solution. The Bible tells us that an angel of the Lord appeared to Joseph in a dream and encouraged him not to be afraid to take Mary as his wife. God's plans are always bigger than our plans! God desires to use us for bigger purposes than we ever dreamed.

Has an angel ever intervened in your life? God may speak to you by a dream, as God spoke to Joseph. God's messengers may come to us in a different way. A friend may say, "You have a gift for teaching. Have you ever considered volunteering to tutor at the middle school?" "You have a nice voice. You should sing in the choir!" "When they talk about helping people, you seem to come alive. And you are such a good listener. Do you know how much our shut-ins would appreciate a visit?" It is a fundamental Judeo-Christian belief that God may use any person to further God's work. We are called to pay attention to one another, for we do not know through whom God will speak.

God also uses situations and circumstances to intervene in people's lives. "I didn't hear the voice of God. I simply saw the need and I responded," someone says. Yet who gave them the eyes to see and the

ability to respond? I believe that God is always calling us to deeper levels of commitment and greater avenues of service. Are we as open to God's voice as Joseph was? What is God trying to say to us today?

Joseph and Mary Trust God and Obey

If Joseph doubted that the voice he heard was the voice of God speaking through an angel, there is no mention of it in Matthew's Gospel. Instead, the text tells us, "when Joseph awoke from sleep, he did as the angel of the Lord commanded him" (Matthew 1:24). He went ahead with the marriage, and when the baby was born, Joseph adopted the child as his very own, and named him "Jesus" as the angel had told him to do.

Sports hopefuls are told to "check their egos at the door" when they become part of a professional team. How much faith it must have taken for Joseph to put aside his ego and to accept the fact that he would not be the biological father of Mary's son. Don't you imagine that on dark days Joseph questioned what he had been told and wondered whether he had made the right decision? Don't you suppose humble Mary often asked herself why God had chosen her for the honor of birthing God's own son, while at the same time making her a topic of town gossip for the rest of her life? Don't you think there were days when Mary would have much preferred that God would have chosen somebody else upon which to focus the eternal spotlight?

How much difference it makes when we are willing to respond positively to unusual and unexpected circumstances! Others are blessed when we are able to use the raw material of life in a creative way! How much our families and friends and business acquaintances suffer when we are not able to rise to the occasion and see the hand of God at work in the midst of difficult situations.

By trusting God's guidance, Joseph

accepted the seemingly impossible as possible. He was able to see God's hand at work in spite of all the evidence to the contrary. Because he was willing to obey the angel's instruction, Joseph became a blessing to others and made a significant contribution to salvation history. Through her obedience, Mary played an essential role in the drama of salvation as well. Joseph's obedience allowed Jesus to be adopted as a true son of David. Because of Mary's obedience, Jesus was born the Son of God. Both are role models for the life of faith. Both show us how to cope in a positive way when the unexpected happens.

SHARING THE SCRIPTURE

PREPARING TO TEACH

Preparing Our Hearts

This week's devotional reading is found in Luke 1:26-32. As you read this familiar passage of the angel Gabriel's annunciation to Mary of the coming birth of Jesus, look for new ideas or "angles" that you have not explored before. Think especially about how the unexpectedness of this news must have upset Mary's plans for a quiet marriage and normal family life. Mary agreed to be God's servant (1:38). How do you respond when God's call creates life-changing surprises?

Pray that you and your students will be open to God's unexpected surprises, since such events can lead to spiritual growth that cannot occur any other way.

Preparing Our Minds

Study the background and lesson scripture, found in Matthew 1 and 1:17-25, respectively.

Write on newsprint:

the directions for preparing for next week's lesson.

clues under "Analyze the Challenge Faced by Mary and Joseph."

Prepare any lectures that you plan to give.

LEADING THE CLASS

(1) Gather to Learn

❖ Welcome the class members and introduce any guests.

❖ Pray that the students will be open to trusting God in all situations, including those unexpected ones that create major changes in one's life.

❖ Help the class identify some surprises that require major life changes.

Option 1: Invite the students to talk with a partner, a small group, or the entire class about some news that had a major impact on their life plans. At the time, this impact may have seemed positive or negative. In retrospect, what impact did this event really have on their lives? What clues indicated that God was present? How did the event serve as a catalyst for spiritual growth?

Option 2: Use the first and second paragraphs under "Mary and Joseph Are Confronted with Surprising News" in Interpreting the Scripture to create a lecture that demonstrates how our own lives can be changed by unexpected news.

❖ Segue into today's lesson by noting that Joseph and Mary had plans for a wedding and normal family life that were interrupted by Gabriel's announcement to Mary. Joseph subsequently had to make major decisions about what to do with his seemingly adulterous wife.

❖ Read aloud today's focus statement: **People are often confronted by unexpected circumstances. How do we respond in these cases? We can learn from Mary and Joseph, who responded to God's call by trusting God.**

(2) Analyze the Challenge Faced by Mary and Joseph

❖ Choose two volunteers, one to read the part of the angel and one to read the part of the narrator in Matthew 1:17-25.

❖ Suggest that the students listen and look for clues about the following people and situations, which you may want to write on newsprint. Discuss their ideas and add information from the Understanding the Scripture portion. Or, if you use a lecture format, create a short lecture based on these ideas, which you can use after the scripture passage is read.

- **clues about marriage in the first century.** (See information in Matthew 1:18.)
- **clues about Joseph.** (See Matthew 1:19.)
- **clues about Jesus, as revealed by the angel.** (See Matthew 1:20-21 and 22-23.)
- **clues about how Joseph and Mary respond to this life-changing news.** (See Matthew 1:24-25.)

❖ Brainstorm with the students some ways that Mary and Joseph can be role models for us as we are called by God into unfamiliar territory. (Focus especially here on the ideas of faithfulness and trust in God.) List ideas on newsprint.

(3) Consider Possibilities for Responding to God in Trust

❖ Set up a role-play between "Joseph" and a friend of his. Have Joseph tell the friend how he feels about (1) the extraordinary news of Mary's pregnancy, (2) the angel's appearance to him, and (3) the trust that he is willing to place in God.

❖ Challenge the class members to identify other biblical figures whose call from God greatly changed their lives. Noah, Abraham, Gideon, Ruth, David, and the Twelve are but a few among many who were called and had to decide how they would respond. Encourage the adults to talk about these persons and their way of coping with unexpected change. If you choose to do a lecture, talk about these biblical figures yourself.

❖ Identify ways that persons the students know—or know about—have responded to challenging circumstances. How did any of these people recognize God's call in the midst of these circumstances?

(4) Develop a Plan for Listening to God

❖ Encourage the students to brainstorm ideas for ways in which they listen for God's direction, especially when they are confronted with unexpected circumstances. List these ideas on newsprint. Here are some suggestions: pray, meditate, read the Bible, look for opportunities that God provides, counsel with the pastor and believing friends.

❖ Distribute paper and pencils. Invite the students to write down an unexpected event in their lives that currently confronts them. Examples might include: dealing with aging parents who need increasing care, helping a child who has behavioral problems, caring for an ill spouse, battling an illness of their own, being laid off from a job, living in new surroundings, or being forced into an early retirement.

❖ Suggest that the students create a personal plan of action for dealing with a situation they have identified. Encourage them to make the plan as specific as possible. For example, instead of saying, "I will pray," say, "I will pray for fifteen minutes in the morning and twenty minutes after dinner, asking God to guide me as I make decisions for my grandmother who is no longer able to care for herself."

❖ Provide quiet time so that the students can listen for God's guidance to deal with the unexpected situation they are facing.

❖ Invite volunteers to share their action plans, but do not press anyone to share information he or she would prefer not to discuss.

(5) Continue the Journey

❖ Pray that when the students are confronted by unexpected events they will trust God completely to care for them and wisely direct their actions.

❖ Read aloud this preparation for next week's lesson. You may also want to post it on newsprint for the students to copy. **Prepare for next week's session by reading Luke 2:22-38, which is both the background and lesson scripture for the session "Searching for Hope in the Right Places." Here we will see the response of Simeon and Anna to the baby Jesus. Keep this focus statement in mind as you read: People need a sense of hope. Where do**

they find it? According to Simeon and Anna, hope lies in the Christ child.

❖ Read aloud the following three ideas. Challenge the students to commit themselves to use these activities as a springboard to spiritual growth.

(1) **Implement the plan of action you have created for listening to God as you confront an unexpected situation.**

(2) **When an unusual event occurs this week, respond with faith and trust in God. Write about this event and your response to it in your spiritual journal.**

(3) **Keep Joseph's obedient trust in mind, especially when family members or friends disappoint you in this holiday season.**

❖ Sing or read aloud "Emmanuel, Emmanuel."

❖ Ask the students to echo this benediction as you read it phrase by phrase: **Grant, O Lord, that what has been said with our lips we may believe in our hearts, and that what we believe in our hearts we may practice in our lives; through Jesus Christ our Lord. Amen.**

Searching for Hope in the Right Places

PREVIEWING THE LESSON

Lesson Scripture: Luke 2:22-38
Background Scripture: Luke 2:22-38
Key Verses: Luke 2:30-31

Focus of the Lesson:
People need a sense of hope. Where do they find it? According to Simeon and Anna, hope lies in the Christ child.

Goals for the Learners:
(1) to explore the story of Simeon and Anna.
(2) to affirm and celebrate the hope that Christ's birth brings to the world.
(3) to identify ways they can be bearers of hope to others.

Pronunciation Guide:

Asher	(ash' uhr)	Phanuel	(fuh nyoo' uhl)
Nunc Dimmittis	(noonk' di mit' is)	Simeon	(sim' ee uhn)

Supplies:
Bibles, newsprint and marker, paper and pencils, hymnals

READING THE SCRIPTURE

NRSV
Luke 2:22-38

22 When the time came for their purification according to the law of Moses, they brought him up to Jerusalem to present him to the Lord 23 (as it is written in the law of the Lord, "Every firstborn male shall be designated as holy to the Lord"), 24 and they offered a sacrifice according to what is stated in the law of the Lord, "a pair of turtledoves or two young pigeons."

NIV
Luke 2:22-38

²²When the time of their purification according to the Law of Moses had been completed, Joseph and Mary took him to Jerusalem to present him to the Lord ²³(as it is written in the Law of the Lord, "Every firstborn male is to be consecrated to the Lord"), ²⁴and to offer a sacrifice in keeping with what is said in the Law of the Lord: "a pair of doves or two young pigeons."

25 Now there was a man in Jerusalem whose name was Simeon; this man was righteous and devout, looking forward to the consolation of Israel, and the Holy Spirit rested on him. 26 It had been revealed to him by the Holy Spirit that he would not see death before he had seen the Lord's Messiah. 27 Guided by the Spirit, Simeon came into the temple; and when the parents brought in the child Jesus, to do for him what was customary under the law, 28 Simeon took him in his arms and praised God, saying,

29 "Master, now you are dismissing your
    servant in peace,
    according to your word;
30 for my eyes have seen your salvation,
31 which you have prepared in the
      presence of all peoples,
32 a light for revelation to the Gentiles
and for glory to your people Israel."

33 And the child's father and mother were amazed at what was being said about him. 34 Then Simeon blessed them and said to his mother Mary, "This child is destined for the falling and the rising of many in Israel, and to be a sign that will be opposed 35 so that the inner thoughts of many will be revealed—and a sword will pierce your own soul too."

36 There was also a prophet, Anna the daughter of Phanuel, of the tribe of Asher. She was of a great age, having lived with her husband seven years after her marriage, 37 then as a widow to the age of eighty-four. She never left the temple but worshiped there with fasting and prayer night and day. 38 At that moment she came, and began to praise God and to speak about the child to all who were looking for the redemption of Jerusalem.

[25]Now there was a man in Jerusalem called Simeon, who was righteous and devout. He was waiting for the consolation of Israel, and the Holy Spirit was upon him. [26]It had been revealed to him by the Holy Spirit that he would not die before he had seen the Lord's Christ. [27]Moved by the Spirit, he went into the temple courts. When the parents brought in the child Jesus to do for him what the custom of the Law required, [28]Simeon took him in his arms and praised God, saying:

[29]"Sovereign Lord, as you have promised,
    you now dismiss your servant in peace.
[30] For my eyes have seen your salvation,
[31] which you have prepared in the sight of
      all people,
[32]a light for revelation to the Gentiles
    and for glory to your people Israel."

[33]The child's father and mother marveled at what was said about him. [34]Then Simeon blessed them and said to Mary, his mother: "This child is destined to cause the falling and rising of many in Israel, and to be a sign that will be spoken against, [35]so that the thoughts of many hearts will be revealed. And a sword will pierce your own soul too."

[36]There was also a prophetess, Anna, the daughter of Phanuel, of the tribe of Asher. She was very old; she had lived with her husband seven years after her marriage, [37]and then was a widow until she was eighty-four. She never left the temple but worshiped night and day, fasting and praying. [38]Coming up to them at that very moment, she gave thanks to God and spoke about the child to all who were looking forward to the redemption of Jerusalem.

UNDERSTANDING THE SCRIPTURE

Luke 2:22. Following his circumcision on the eighth day after his birth, according to the ancient custom, and his official naming (2:21), Jesus is taken to the Temple for two further acts: the redemption of the firstborn, and the purification of the mother.

Luke 2:23. As a reminder of the Exodus, the firstborn child was consecrated to the Lord (Exodus 13:2). The firstborn male was to be redeemed, or "bought back" from God at a price of five shekels of silver (Numbers 18:15-16).

Luke 2:24. After the birth of a male child, the mother was considered ceremonially unclean for seven days and underwent purification for thirty-three days (the period was twice as long for a female child) according to Leviticus 12:1-5. At the end of that time, forty (or eighty) days from the child's birth, the mother was to offer a lamb and a pigeon or a turtledove. If she could not afford a lamb, she could offer instead two turtledoves or pigeons (Leviticus 12:6-8). The offering of two pigeons instead of the lamb and the pigeon was technically called, "the offering of the poor." It was the offering of the poor that Mary brought, reminding us that it was into an ordinary home that Jesus was born, a home where the family members knew all about the difficulties of making a living and the haunting insecurity of life.

Luke 2:25. Luke introduces Simeon by noting his piety and his spirit of hope in looking forward to the "consolation of Israel." In other words, Simeon has been looking for and forward to the messianic age. Just as the Spirit had come upon John, Mary, Elizabeth, and Zechariah (see Luke 1), so now Simeon is identified as one in whom the Spirit rests.

Luke 2:26. For Simeon, the birth of Jesus fulfilled Israel's hope for a royal Messiah. Under the inspiration of the Holy Spirit he has been informed that he will not die before the Messiah comes.

Luke 2:27. The meeting in the Temple is no accident. Simeon is guided there by the Holy Spirit. The Spirit inspires him to go to the Temple at just the moment when the parents of Jesus are performing their ritual duties. What is about to happen is God's doing.

Luke 2:28. It is clear to Simeon that in Jesus, Simeon's hopes are fulfilled. The birth of a child, the fulfillment of God's promises, the consolation of Israel, and the coming of the Messiah are all occasions for praising God.

Luke 2:29-32. Taking the child in his arms, Simeon pronounces a prophetic hymn that in traditional liturgy is called the "Nunc Dimittis," so named from the opening words in Latin. The main point of the poem is that salvation has now come and that this salvation is for all people. Not only will there be glory to Israel, but there will also be "a light for the revelation to the Gentiles." Simeon has been watching for the coming of the Lord's anointed, and now as a faithful watchman, he is dismissed from his post by his master. Simeon can depart because he has seen the coming of the one who will bring salvation. Simeon's blessing relates the birth of Jesus to the fulfillment of the promise of salvation found in the Scriptures of Israel and looks ahead to the inclusion of Gentiles as well as Jews in the purposes of God. "Peace" occurs twelve times in Luke, where it is both the goal and the result of God's redemptive work in Jesus. Simeon saw God's salvation not because he was at the right place at the right time, but because his continuing devotion to the things of the Spirit led him to see that God's hand was at work in Jesus' birth.

Luke 2:33-35. Mary and Joseph marvel at what has been said. Then Simeon offers a special blessing to Jesus' mother. Simeon's words remind us that the coming of the Messiah brings decision making and judgment. The fact that many will fall foreshadows that Jesus' own people will reject him. Jesus will also be the cause whereby many will rise out of the old life and into the new. Simeon's image of the sword reveals that the coming of the Messiah will also bring suffering. The suffering pierces the soul of the mother of Jesus, a prediction of his passion.

Luke 2:36-37. Luke now introduces Anna as a female parallel witness to

Simeon. Anna's advanced age is emphasized. She evidently married quite young and was widowed seven years after her marriage. As a widow, she had known sorrow, yet she had not grown bitter. Sorrow had caused Anna to grow deeper in faith and closer to God, rather than to make her resentful against God. Even though she was by the standards of the ancient world quite elderly, Anna had never ceased to hope. William Barclay notes: "Age can take away the bloom and the strength of our bodies, but age can do worse—the years can take away the life of our hearts until the hopes that we once cherished die and we become dully contented and grimly resigned to things as they are." Anna found the source of encouragement and strength in her participation in the life of the Temple. She spent her time in God's house with God's people.

Luke 2:38. Like Simeon, Anna arrives at that very hour when Jesus is dedicated. She gives thanks to God and also indicates that the hope of redemption is fulfilled in the child. Those who have been waiting for the Messiah must wait no longer. A new age has begun! Anna praises God and tells others about the child, bearing witness to what she has seen and heard.

Thus Simeon and Anna declare that Jesus is the one who will bring salvation to Israel, but not all will receive this salvation. Jesus will be rejected, and many in Israel will reject the gospel. But the coming of Jesus also signals "a light for revelation to the Gentiles" (2:32). Hope will be offered to all people!

INTERPRETING THE SCRIPTURE

Mary and Joseph Bring Jesus to the Temple

Although the person and work of Jesus are the central focus of Christianity, a careful reading of the Scriptures reminds us that there are many significant players in the Gospel story. The influence of Jesus' parents on his upbringing cannot be overemphasized. Throughout the story of Jesus' birth and early years, we see evidence that Mary and Joseph were devout Jews who valued the rituals of the faith. Eight days after Jesus' birth, Mary and Joseph presented him for circumcision and gave him the name announced by the angel Gabriel.

A couple once said to their pastor, "Our son is seven years old. When should we start taking him to church?" The pastor replied, "Well, you've already missed the best seven years of his life." Modern theories on education reinforce the practices of ancient Judaism. Children should be included as part of the faith community from the moment of birth. The early years are forma-tive, as faith is more "caught" than "taught."

Meet Simeon, Who Lived in Hope!

In every church there seem to be parishioners who show interest in and give special attention to children. When I was a denominational executive and was not able to attend worship regularly with my wife and young teenage sons due to my travel and speaking engagements, there were several older men in the congregation who took our sons under their wing. Every Sunday these gentlemen would go out of their way to find out how things were going in school, and generally get a pulse on my sons' lives. Sometimes these conversations would lead to plans for a milkshake or a hamburger later in the week. My wife observed that she could see our sons growing and blossoming as they shared in conversation with these men, who were old enough to be their grandfathers.

Don't you suppose Simeon was like that? Do you think that Jesus was the first child Simeon "took in his arms"? I'll bet Simeon was there to support and encourage every young family who brought their children to the Temple for the rites of passage. The Bible tells us that Simeon lived in hope. He had a reason to keep living, for he had been told he would see the Messiah before he died. Simeon stayed alert and hopeful, for he did not know which child God would choose.

Thomas Pettepiece has observed, "there are people who have curled up and died in a corner for no other reason than they lost hope. . . . Without hope we give up—we lose our will to fight, to trust, to live. There are too many people in this world today who have begun to lose hope—those who hunger for life's basic needs but see no relief; those who see too many problems and cannot find a solution."

Television advertising is loaded with the promises of false hope. If we take a certain pill, drive a certain car, exercise using a certain machine—then we will have a happy and satisfying life. Those who place their hopes in these products are always disappointed.

Simeon knew that in the birth of every child God gives the world yet another chance. Simeon lived in expectation of the new day foretold by the prophets and promised by God. He did not know when the Messiah would appear, but he was ready to embrace every child in the hope that God might use that baby to usher in the messianic age.

What are we communicating to the children and youth of our communities? Teenagers are committing suicide at an alarming rate. Many believe a nuclear war is inevitable and see no hope for tomorrow. Let us reach out to them, confident that in so doing God will enliven their hope for a brighter tomorrow and renew our sense of hope as well.

Simeon Recognizes the Messiah

I have said that the birth of every child brings new hope and promise to the world, yet I would not want to suggest that Jesus was just another baby. The church has always understood that in Jesus the fullness of God dwelled uniquely, and that Jesus' life, death, and resurrection have changed the course of history. Simeon was looking not for just any child, but for a certain child who was "destined for the falling and the rising of many in Israel, and to be a sign that will be opposed so that the inner thoughts of many will be revealed" (2:34-35).

The coming of Jesus forces each of us to make a decision. Is he the one? Is he the Messiah? A young man in our membership class shared that he had studied many religions and discovered that there is no proof for any of them. It finally comes down to taking a leap of faith: acting on what we know, and trusting that God will continue to guide us into a fuller understanding as we follow where we believe God is leading.

Simeon was confronted with a child he trusted was God's Messiah. Perhaps he did not live long enough to hear the Sermon on the Mount, to witness the Crucifixion, or to encounter the risen Christ. But based on what he knew, he was confident that he had seen God's Messiah, the one who would save Israel and usher in God's kingdom.

Anna Recognizes the Messiah and Tells Others About Him

If Luke holds Simeon in high esteem, no less a place of honor is given to Anna, who also followed the leading of the Holy Spirit and was present for the dedication of Jesus in the Temple. We joke about people who are so involved they seem to live at the church! Anna was one who "never left the temple." She worshiped "with fasting and prayer night and day" (2:37).

Where do we find God? Not only in the church or temple, to be sure. But someone has said, "If you were looking for someone who lived in Chicago, you wouldn't go to Los Angeles on the off chance that he or she was there on business or vacation." Anna was able to discern the presence of the Messiah because she was attuned to the things of the Spirit.

When she recognized Jesus as God's promised Messiah, Anna praised God. She couldn't keep her joy to herself! The Bible tells us that she began "to speak about the child to all who were looking for the redemption of Jerusalem" (2:38). People were yearning for a better life in Anna's day. The Jews found Roman rule to be oppressive. Many believed that an intervention by

God was their only hope. Into this climate came Anna, with news that God had acted, that the Messiah had come. He probably wasn't what they were expecting, however. For he was a tiny baby, only eight days old!

What do you suppose was the reaction to Anna's news? It was probably nearly identical to the reaction we will receive if we share the good news about Jesus during this Christmastide. It will sound crazy to some, but "to us who are being saved it is the power of God" (1 Corinthians 1:18). Anna took the leap of faith. She believed that Jesus was the Messiah she had hoped for and long awaited, and shared that good news with others. Will we?

SHARING THE SCRIPTURE

PREPARING TO TEACH

Preparing Our Hearts

This week's devotional reading is found in Psalm 71:1-8. Here an elderly worshiper seeks salvation in the form of deliverance from his enemies. The author of this psalm was clear that his hope had always been—and continues to be—in God, his "rock" and "fortress." Where do you look for hope? If your hope is not in God, who or what are you relying on to aid you? The psalmist teaches us that we can trust God in all the situations of our lives.

Pray that you and your students will bring the good news of Jesus to those who are seeking hope.

Preparing Our Minds

Study the background and lesson scripture, both of which are in Luke 2:22-28.

Write on newsprint:

the questions for both groups under Gather to Learn.

next week's assignment under "Continue the Journey."

Plan for the size group you think you will have today. Some families may be out of town, but others may have guests whom they will bring to class with them. Be sure you have enough supplies on hand. You may want to check with some class members about providing special refreshments.

Prepare the lecture as suggested for "Explore the Story of Simeon and Anna."

LEADING THE CLASS

(1) Gather to Learn

❖ Welcome the class members and introduce any guests.

❖ Pray that in this season of Christmas the students will find new hope in Christ and share that hope with others.

❖ Encourage the students to reflect on the meaning of Christmas by talking with a small group. Divide the class into several groups and assign each one a set of questions. You may want to write these on newsprint prior to the session.

Group 1: What hope does the Christ child bring into the world? Who is seeking the hope that he brings? Why do they need this hope?

Group 2: Where do many people in today's world seek hope? Do you feel these are good choices? If not, why not? What can you do to help people look elsewhere?

❖ Call the class together and note that Simeon and Anna, two elders in whom God's Spirit dwelled mightily, believed that Israel's hope of salvation had been fulfilled in the birth of Jesus, who they recognized as the Messiah.

❖ Read aloud today's focus statement: **People need a sense of hope. Where do they find it? According to Simeon and Anna, hope lies in the Christ child.**

(2) Explore the Story of Simeon and Anna

❖ Select a volunteer to read Luke 2:22-24.

❖ Invite the class to comment on what they know about Jesus' parents from these three verses.

❖ Share information from verses 22, 23, and 24 in the Understanding the Scripture portion. Use this information either to round out the discussion or as a lecture. Drive home the point that although Mary and Joseph were clearly not wealthy, they were observant Jews who acted as the law required.

❖ Read aloud Luke 2:25-35, which tells about Simeon.

❖ Distribute paper and pencils. Ask the students to close their Bibles and list as much as they know about: (a) the character of Simeon, (b) what the Holy Spirit had revealed to Simeon, and (c) what he believed and said about Jesus. Discuss these ideas, or present them yourself in a lecture, using information from Understanding the Scripture.

❖ Choose one of the following options, or allow the adults to select the option they prefer. Provide time for the students to share with other class members what they have drawn or written.

Option 1: Distribute paper and pencils or drawing implements and ask them to sketch the scene in the Temple.

Option 2: Distribute paper and pencils and encourage the students to write a diary entry as if they were Mary after hearing Simeon's words about her newborn son.

❖ Choose a volunteer to read about Anna in Luke 2:36-38 and then discuss these questions.

(1) What do you know about Anna?

(2) What might you surmise about her from the little that you know?

(3) How did Anna respond to the hope that she had in the Messiah?

❖ Conclude this portion of the session by asking two people to role-play a discussion between Simeon and Anna of what they had experienced as a result of their encounter with Jesus in the Temple.

(3) Celebrate the Hope That Christ's Birth Brings

❖ Distribute slips of paper and pencils. Encourage the students to write down one hope that they have because Jesus came into the world. Collect the papers, shuffle them, and read several at random.

❖ Sing several Christmas carols that reveal the hope that Christ Jesus' birth brings to the world. You may want to select these carols yourself, or invite the students to suggest ones that speak to them of hope.

(4) Identify Ways to Be Bearers of Hope to Others

❖ Note that Anna and Simeon proclaimed to others the hope that they had in the Messiah. We, too, are called to be bearers of hope to others.

❖ Create a project that offers hope to those in need by following these steps.

Step 1: Brainstorm groups of people within your community who need hope. The list may include the hungry, homeless, lonely, grieving, AIDS patients, or battered spouses and their children who have sought shelter.

Step 2: Zoom in on one group that the class members feel they could assist.

Step 3: Create a plan of action that indicates what you will do, for whom, when, how much it will cost, the steps involved, who will be responsible for ensuring that each step is complete, and a means of evaluation to determine how well the project has met its goal.

Step 4: Deploy class members to take action. Ask them to report back at whatever time the group has set. Likely, they will need several weeks to work.

(5) Continue the Journey

❖ Read together Simeon's words known as the "Nunc Dimittis," found in Luke 2:29-32. Hymnals often include these words as a reading as, for example, *The United Methodist Hymnal*, no. 225.

❖ Read aloud this preparation for next week's lesson. You may also want to post it on newsprint for the students to copy. **Prepare for next week's session by reading Mark 1:14-28, which is both the background and lesson scripture for "Spreading the Good News." Keep this** focus in mind as you prepare: **People are looking for good news. Where can we hear good news? In Mark, we see that Jesus proclaimed God's good news.**

❖ Read aloud the following three ideas. Challenge the students to commit themselves to use these activities as a springboard to spiritual growth.

(1) **Share the good news of hope with at least one person this week. If appropriate, invite this individual to worship with you on Sunday.**

(2) **Write in a journal about a spiritual rite of passage that had great meaning for you. Perhaps it was your own confirmation or the baptism of a child. Why was this event so meaningful? What hope did it give you?**

(3) **Create a dance or simple movements that express your joy in the coming of Jesus. Pray as you dance, thanking God for the hope that you have in God's Messiah.**

❖ Sing or read aloud "My Master, See, the Time Has Come," which is based on Luke 2:29-32.

❖ Ask the students to echo this benediction as you read it phrase by phrase: **Grant, O Lord, that what has been said with our lips we may believe in our hearts, and that what we believe in our hearts we may practice in our lives; through Jesus Christ our Lord. Amen.**

UNIT 2: THE CALL OF JESUS AND HIS FOLLOWERS (MARK)
SPREADING THE GOOD NEWS

PREVIEWING THE LESSON

Lesson Scripture: Mark 1:14-28
Background Scripture: Mark 1:14-28
Key Verse: Mark 1:17

Focus of the Lesson:
People are looking for good news. Where can we hear good news? In Mark, we see that Jesus proclaimed God's good news.

Goals for the Learners:
(1) to summarize the good news that Jesus was proclaiming.
(2) to explore why this is good news for our time.
(3) to consider ways the church helps to spread this good news.

Pronunciation Guides:
Capernaum   (kuh puhr' nay uhm)   Zebedee   (zeb' uh dee)

Supplies:
Bibles, newsprint and marker, paper and pencils, Bible commentaries and/or Bible dictionaries, hymnals

---

READING THE SCRIPTURE

NRSV
Mark 1:14-28

14 Now after John was arrested, Jesus came to Galilee, proclaiming the good news of God, 15 and saying, "The time is fulfilled, and the kingdom of God has come near; repent, and believe in the good news."

16 As Jesus passed along the Sea of Galilee, he saw Simon and his brother Andrew casting a net into the sea, for they were fishermen. **17 And Jesus said to them, "Follow me and I will make you fish for people."** 18 And immediately they left their

NIV
Mark 1:14-28

14After John was put in prison, Jesus went into Galilee, proclaiming the good news of God. 15"The time has come," he said. "The kingdom of God is near. Repent and believe the good news!"

16As Jesus walked beside the Sea of Galilee, he saw Simon and his brother Andrew casting a net into the lake, for they were fishermen. 17"Come, follow me," Jesus said, "and I will make you fishers of men."

nets and followed him. 19 As he went a little farther, he saw James son of Zebedee and his brother John, who were in their boat mending the nets. 20 Immediately he called them; and they left their father Zebedee in the boat with the hired men, and followed him.

21 They went to Capernaum; and when the Sabbath came, he entered the synagogue and taught. 22 They were astounded at his teaching, for he taught them as one having authority, and not as the scribes. 23 Just then there was in their synagogue a man with an unclean spirit, 24 and he cried out, "What have you to do with us, Jesus of Nazareth? Have you come to destroy us? I know who you are, the Holy One of God." 25 But Jesus rebuked him, saying, "Be silent, and come out of him!" 26 And the unclean spirit, convulsing him and crying with a loud voice, came out of him. 27 They were all amazed, and they kept on asking one another, "What is this? A new teaching—with authority! He commands even the unclean spirits, and they obey him." 28 At once his fame began to spread throughout the surrounding region of Galilee.

[18]At once they left their nets and followed him.

[19]When he had gone a little farther, he saw James son of Zebedee and his brother John in a boat, preparing their nets. [20]Without delay he called them, and they left their father Zebedee in the boat with the hired men and followed him.

[21]They went to Capernaum, and when the Sabbath came, Jesus went into the synagogue and began to teach. [22]The people were amazed at his teaching, because he taught them as one who had authority, not as the teachers of the law. [23]Just then a man in their synagogue who was possessed by an evil spirit cried out, [24]"What do you want with us, Jesus of Nazareth? Have you come to destroy us? I know who you are—the Holy One of God!"

[25]"Be quiet!" said Jesus sternly. "Come out of him!" [26]The evil spirit shook the man violently and came out of him with a shriek.

[27]The people were all so amazed that they asked each other, "What is this? A new teaching—and with authority! He even gives orders to evil spirits and they obey him." [28]News about him spread quickly over the whole region of Galilee.

UNDERSTANDING THE SCRIPTURE

Mark 1:14. Mark makes it clear that Jesus did not begin his ministry of preaching, teaching, and healing until after John the Baptist was arrested. Jesus comes into Galilee, which was the scene of most of his ministry, proclaiming the gospel or "the good news of God." The "gospel" is not a compendium of teachings by Jesus, but the proclamation that God has acted in Christ to save humanity. It is a message about Jesus rather than a message by him.

Mark 1:15. Jesus proclaims that the age of salvation foretold by the preaching of John the Baptist has begun. The time for which humanity has been waiting has arrived! The

kingdom of God is now replacing the age of strife and evil and opposition to God. The new age for which the people of Jesus' day had longed is now "at hand."

Jesus' call to repentance continues the theme that something new is happening in the world. The word "repent" comes from the Greek *metanoia*, which literally means "a change of mind." The coming of Jesus changes the whole way we look at life, for Jesus' ministry inaugurates the coming of the kingdom of God.

We are called to believe in the good news that God has acted in Jesus Christ to overpower our enemies, to redeem us from our lost and helpless state and from our slavery to sin.

Mark 1:16. The first disciples that Jesus calls are Simon, whom he will later give the name of Peter (see Mark 3:16), and his brother Andrew. Peter will become the leader of the disciples, while Andrew will be known as one who continually brought others to Jesus. There is every indication that they were common, ordinary folks.

Mark 1:17. Jesus calls the fishermen to begin a new chapter in their lives using an analogy from their present profession. He wants them to "fish for people."

Mark 1:18. There is a sense of urgency in Mark's Gospel. The fact that these men drop occupation and family obligations to follow the one who summons them demonstrates that the call comes from God. In a traditional society, such a break with family and occupation is extraordinary. Yet Mark indicates that Peter and Andrew left *immediately* to follow Jesus. For Mark, the action of these two fishermen toward Jesus presents us with the ideal response of every person. When Jesus calls, we should drop everything and follow him.

Mark 1:19-20. The call is repeated with another pair of brothers: James and John. Their response is the same: they leave everything behind and follow Jesus. In the Old Testament, reference to hooks and nets generally carried a negative overtone. God set traps for those who deserved judgment. Jesus calls the disciples to share in his mission, which involves healing, preaching, and exorcism. Those who are "caught" by this new fishing activity are saved, not destroyed. Just as the preaching of Jesus shifts away from the tone of judgment associated with John the Baptist to one of fulfillment, so also the metaphor of fishing for people is used in a way to suggest the positive function of preaching: bringing the good news to others.

Mark 1:21. The city of Capernaum, located on the northwest shore of the Sea of Galilee, was apparently the headquarters of Jesus'

mission (see Mark 2:1). The Gospels all witness to Jesus' loyalty to the synagogue. He apparently made no effort to establish a new type of worship, but worked only to purify the old.

Mark 1:22. The very first event of Jesus' ministry is one that expresses his authority. The scribes were the experts in the laws of the first five books of the Bible. As such, people often consulted them when the authority of Moses was desired or questioned. In the introduction to the healing story, Jesus appears "as one having authority," in contrast to the scribes. The Greek word of "authority" means "out from himself." No scribe ever gave a decision on his own. If he made a statement he would buttress it with citation after citation from the great legal masters of the past. The last thing he ever gave was an independent judgment. How different was Jesus! When Jesus spoke, he did not quote the authorities, but acted like an authority himself. He spoke with the finality of the voice of God. The positive certainty of Jesus was the very antithesis of the careful quotations of the scribes. By this opening event in the ministry of Jesus, Mark conveys to the reader that Jesus is no ordinary human being. He is the Son of God, who has come to rescue humanity from the demonic forces that enslave us.

Mark 1:23. The term "unclean spirit" is common in the New Testament for a demon. Demon possession was widely held responsible for many of humanity's ills in Jesus' time. Humans were at the mercy of these demons, unless under the protection of some stronger, spiritual power.

Mark 1:24. The designation "Jesus of Nazareth" would imply to the ancient reader that Jesus was born in Nazareth, although "Nazareth" (literally, "the Nazarene") could refer to a party (such as Simon the Zealot) rather than a place (see Acts 24:5). "Have you come to destroy us?" is the basic question. Mark's answer clearly is "Yes, he has!" "The Holy One of God" is an excellent and appropriate title for Jesus. It is ironic that the demons recognize Jesus and obey instantly, while human beings are far less perceptive and responsive. All the way through Mark's Gospel, only the demons recognize Jesus as he really is!

Mark 1:25. Jesus' rebuke is intended to silence the demon, not to deny that Jesus is "The Holy One of God."

Mark 1:26. The fact that the demon obeys the command of Jesus and comes out demonstrates the power of Jesus over the forces of evil. The end of demonic power is a sign that the present evil age is coming to a close.

Mark 1:27. Sadly, the fact that all the people are amazed does not mean that they have come to believe in Jesus. Jesus has piqued their curiosity, but they have not grasped the theological significance of this demonstration of the good news they have just witnessed.

Mark 1:28. Good news is almost impossible to keep quiet! Word about what happened begins to spread. The ministry of Jesus has begun!

INTERPRETING THE SCRIPTURE

Jesus Proclaims the Good News

In a world of crime, disease, terrorism, deceit, and broken promises, people are longing to hear good news. It was true in Jesus' day. It is true in the twenty-first century as well. In first-century Galilee, the religious authorities had developed such a tedious and cumbersome interpretation of the Law of Moses that it was no longer seen by many as a blessing from God, but rather as a burden. In addition, the preaching of John the Baptist seemed to emphasize God's judgment more than it demonstrated God's grace. In like manner, modern media has been used to spread the message that we are "sinners in the hands of an angry God." A narrow interpretation of the Scriptures and judgmental preaching have put a negative spin on Christian theology for many.

We need to proclaim with every atom of our beings that the gospel is good news, literally and figuratively! The word "gospel" means "good news." The message that God has acted in Jesus Christ to give us new and abundant life is the best news we can ever hear. It makes the promises of a better life that we hear through television commercials pale by comparison.

Craig Miller, of The United Methodist Board of Discipleship, has developed a video entitled "Now Is the Time!" His message is that we need to prepare for the influx of children who are now preschool age and are candidates for our Sunday school and youth ministries. We don't have a lot of time to reach these children, for they are growing up before our very eyes.

Mark's message carries a similar note of urgency. God's plan of salvation for humanity has culminated in the person and work of Jesus Christ. The new age is dawning. Now is the time to respond to the gospel message.

When we are confronted with the good news that there is a better way to live, our natural response is to repent, to express regret for our past mistakes, and to receive the gift of new life that Jesus offers. There is no need to wait! We are invited to believe this message and begin a new life today.

Believing always involves a leap of faith. A man in my congregation told me that he researched various religions before he was willing to commit himself to the Christian faith. He realized that it was not possible to have proof for what our faith teaches. But he chose to believe that the message of the gospel is true. Each of us is called to make a similar decision.

Jesus Calls the First Disciples

From the outset, Jesus called people to follow him and to share in his ministry of preaching, teaching, and healing. The first persons who Jesus called were the fishermen: Simon and Andrew, James and John. The text implies that these fishermen were wealthy enough to own homes and employ other workers. They were established, relatively prosperous businessmen. However, there is no indication that there was anything special about them. While they were not impoverished nor persons on the margins of society, neither were they part of the wealthy and privileged aristocracy. Certainly they were people with character flaws, as later stories will attest.

Thus the call of God comes to ordinary people as we go about our daily tasks. There is no hint in Mark's Gospel that these fishermen did anything to attract the attention of Jesus. They were doing business as usual the day they were called. Jesus saw in them qualities that God could use in spreading the message of salvation to all people. It is a basic Christian teaching that God can use each of us in the service of God's kingdom. Jesus' call to the disciples is his call to you and to me today: "Follow me, and I will use your abilities and your expertise to minister to the needs of my people."

The Disciples Respond to Jesus' Call

The invitation to "fish for people" involved a major career change for the disciples. Leaving their nets meant leaving their gainful employment. For James and John, to leave their father Zebedee "in the boat with the hired men" signaled possible difficulties for the family business. Yet Mark clearly tells us that the disciples left their fishing business immediately.

According to British Bible scholar William Barclay, "following Christ is like falling in love." It is more than a calculated, intellectual response to a well-reasoned set of postulates. It is a total commitment that defies every attempt at complete explanation.

The story of Jesus calling the fishermen reminds us that when we meet Jesus we are confronted with a decision. We cannot remain neutral about the gospel. Either we follow, or we stay in the boat. The gospel demands a response.

We are also reminded that discipleship always has a cost. If we are willing to follow Jesus, we must be ready to give up something in order to bring the good news to others. The Bible does not tell us what happened to the family fishing business the disciples left behind. Nor does Mark share how arrangements were made to shift the burdens of family and business details to others. The disciples likely would have had Jesus' blessing and encouragement to care for family matters. Jesus modeled tenderness in his concern for his own mother (John 19:26-27), and the entire gospel message proclaims respect and compassion for all persons.

Yet there can be no doubt that Mark wants his readers to understand that Simon, Andrew, James, and John made a total commitment to Jesus that day—a commitment that changed their lives from top to bottom. Clearly, the good news is so compelling that it demands our total allegiance from the moment we hear God's gracious invitation. The first disciples responded in faith. Will we?

Jesus Heals a Man with an Unclean Spirit

Mental and emotional problems plagued the people of Jesus' day as they do our own. "One in every five Americans experiences a mental disorder in any given year, and half of all Americans have such disorders at some time in their lives," according to Susan Gregg-Schroeder, writing in the January/February 2003 issues of *Circuit Rider* magazine. In our day, typically someone who offers help for those with mental and emotional problems is warmly received. Such a person was even more eagerly welcomed in the first century when knowledge and understanding of illness and disease was much more primitive than it is today. Those in the Capernaum synagogue soon learned that Jesus had power over the demons of mental and emotional distress.

Jesus' preaching was compelling; his teaching made sense; and his healing power made him attractive to those who had been without hope. Not surprisingly, "his fame began to spread throughout the surrounding region of Galilee" (1:28). It's not surprising that news of Jesus and his ministry spread like wildfire! People instinctively want to share a message so wonderful. Good news is hard to contain.

What is the best way to share the gospel today? First-century witnesses are instructive. When lives are changed, people will want to share that message with others. I believe that Jesus' words are just as compelling and as life-changing today as they were in A.D. 30. Jesus promises help and hope for all who "repent and believe in the good news" (1:15). He has authority over the powers that would keep us from being the people God created us to be. Jesus' message is too good *not* to be true! When we grasp its significance, we want to share the good news with all that we meet.

✓

SHARING THE SCRIPTURE

PREPARING TO TEACH

Preparing Our Hearts

This week's devotional reading is found in Matthew 4:18-25. Here we read Matthew's account of Jesus' calling of the first disciples and the beginning of his ministry. Imagine yourself among the first followers of Jesus? What attracted you to him? Had you been James or John, why would you have left your dad and the hired help in the boat to go follow Jesus? Why was Jesus good news for you?

Pray that you and your students will not only hear the good news but also be willing to spread the news.

Preparing Our Minds

Study the background and lesson scripture, both of which are in Mark 1:14-28. Spend some time comparing Mark's account with Matthew's account, found in the devotional reading.

Write on newsprint: the preparation for next week's session.

Collect commentaries and Bible dictionaries if you plan to do option 1 under "Summarize the Good News Jesus Proclaimed."

Plan any minilectures that you will do.

LEADING THE CLASS

(1) Gather to Learn

❖ Welcome the class members and introduce any guests.

❖ Pray that the students will be open to the good news that Jesus proclaimed and allow this good news to permeate their very being.

❖ Encourage the students to share any good news they heard or read this week. This news may be personal, or it may have an impact on the community, nation, or world.

❖ Discuss how good news can change one's outlook on life.

❖ Move toward today's session by noting that Jesus proclaimed good news about

God's kingdom. Moreover, Jesus himself was the good news.

❖ Read aloud today's focus statement: **People are looking for good news. Where can we hear good news? In Mark, we see that Jesus proclaimed God's good news.**

(2) Summarize the Good News Jesus Proclaimed

❖ Invite several students who use different translations to read aloud Mark 1:14-15. Discuss the following questions, or work them into a lecture based on material found in Mark 1:14 and 15 in the Understanding the Scripture portion.

(1) **When did Jesus begin to proclaim good news?**

(2) **What difference do you think this timing makes?**

(3) **What response does Jesus invite people to make to the good news?**

❖ Read aloud Mark 1:16-20. Suggest that the students close their eyes and imagine what they can see, hear, taste, touch, or feel. The purpose here is to help the adults envision themselves as new recruits with Jesus. After the reading, talk with them about what they could sense. Ideas include: briny water, dead fish, slapping of water against boats, heavy fishing nets, birds hovering overhead, Zebedee's face, sun beating down on sweaty skin, and Jesus' voice.

❖ Discuss the following questions, or use the information under "Jesus Calls the First Disciples" in the Interpreting the Scripture section, and Mark 1:16-17, 18, and 19-20 in Understanding the Scripture to create a brief lecture to help the students understand what was entailed in answering Jesus' call.

(1) **What did James and John leave behind when they got out of their father's boat?**

(2) **Why do you think Jesus called fishermen, rather than people who had greater status?**

(3) **In the Bible, what images or ideas do we usually associate with nets and hooks?**

❖ Read Mark 1:21-28 as a drama by selecting one person to read the narrator's part, one the voice of the unclean spirit, and one to read Jesus' words. The entire class should read the words of the crowd in verse 27.

Option 1: Divide the class into small groups, and make sure that each one has paper, pencils, a Bible dictionary and/or commentary. Assign at least one of these words to each group: *authority, scribes,* and *unclean spirit/demon.* Allow time for the students to work and then report back to the entire class.

Option 2: Do Option 1 yourself and create a lecture from your findings.

Option 3: Provide paper and pencils. Invite the students to write about or draw a representation of a "demon" within them that is creating problems for them. Assure them that they will not be asked to share this information with anyone, only to identify it for themselves. Offer a prayer for healing at the conclusion of this activity.

(3) Explore Why This Is Good News Today

❖ Encourage the students to review Mark 1:14-28. Brainstorm with them the good news that they hear preached or enacted within these verses. List their ideas on newsprint.

❖ Suggest that the students think about the kind of world that we could have if people heard and heeded and Jesus' good news. Challenge them to name songs, movies, or paintings that might describe such a world.

(4) Consider Ways the Church Helps to Spread Good News

❖ Discuss these five questions.

(1) **Why are Jesus' teachings and actions good news today?**

(2) **Who needs to hear this good news?**

(3) **How is your church currently spreading the good news?**
(4) **What else can your congregation do to show and tell the good news?**
(5) **What are you personally willing to do to spread the good news?**

❖ Commission the students to go out as evangelists. First, remind them that Greek word, *evangel*, means good news. Then prayerfully read these words: **We ask you, O God, to bless these your servants whom we commission this day. Fill their hearts with the power of the Holy Spirit that they may go forth as messengers of the good news of Jesus Christ, in whose name we pray. Amen.**

(5) Continue the Journey

❖ Read aloud this preparation for next week's lesson. You may also want to post it on newsprint for the students to copy. **Prepare for next week's session by reading Mark 2:13-17 for our session entitled "Sharing God's Hospitality." Keep in mind this focus as you read: People often feel unaccepted. Where can we find true acceptance? Jesus called a despised tax collector as a disciple, showing God's acceptance of all. He demonstrated that acceptance by extending and receiving hospitality despite the disapproval of others.**

❖ Read aloud the following three ideas. Challenge the students to commit themselves to use these activities as a springboard to spiritual growth.

(1) **Seek opportunities to spread the good news in word or in deed this week. In doing so, remember the commission you received in class to go forth as a messenger of Christ.**
(2) **Be alert for good news in the media. How might this good news show that God's kingdom is present, even though it is not fully here yet?**
(3) **Pray for someone (even yourself) who needs healing. Trust that God is working in that person's life even if his or her physical condition remains unchanged. Remember that healing can come even when a cure does not.**

❖ Sing or read aloud "Silence, Frenzied, Unclean Spirit."

❖ Ask the students to echo this benediction as you read it phrase by phrase: **Grant, O Lord, that what has been said with our lips we may believe in our hearts, and that what we believe in our hearts we may practice in our lives; through Jesus Christ our Lord. Amen.**

SHARING GOD'S HOSPITALITY

PREVIEWING THE LESSON

Lesson Scripture: Mark 2:13-17
Background Scripture: Mark 2:13-17
Key Verse: Mark 2:17

Focus of the Lesson:
People often feel unaccepted. Where can we find true acceptance? Jesus called a despised tax collector as a disciple, showing God's acceptance of all. He demonstrated that acceptance by extending and receiving hospitality despite the disapproval of others.

Goals for the Learners:
(1) to study the story and explain why tax collectors were hated in Jesus' day.
(2) to explore the acceptance they have in Jesus and the way that challenges them to accept others.
(3) to identify some ways they can reach out to people who are deemed unacceptable.

Pronunciation Guide:
Alphaeus   (al fee' uhs)

Supplies:
Bibles, newsprint and marker, paper and pencils, commentaries and/or Bible dictionaries, hymnals

---

READING THE SCRIPTURE

NRSV
Mark 2:13-17

13 Jesus went out again beside the sea; the whole crowd gathered around him, and he taught them. 14 As he was walking along, he saw Levi son of Alphaeus sitting at the tax booth, and he said to him, "Follow me." And he got up and followed him.

15 And as he sat at dinner in Levi's house, many tax collectors and sinners were also

NIV
Mark 2:13-17

[13]Once again Jesus went out beside the lake. A large crowd came to him, and he began to teach them. [14]As he walked along, he saw Levi son of Alphaeus sitting at the tax collector's booth. "Follow me," Jesus told him, and Levi got up and followed him.

[15]While Jesus was having dinner at Levi's

sitting with Jesus and his disciples—for there were many who followed him. 16 When the scribes of the Pharisees saw that he was eating with sinners and tax collectors, they said to his disciples, "Why does he eat with tax collectors and sinners?" 17 When Jesus heard this, he said to them, "Those who are well have no need of a physician, but those who are sick; **I have come to call not the righteous but sinners."**

house, many tax collectors and "sinners" were eating with him and his disciples, for there were many who followed him. [16]When the teachers of the law who were Pharisees saw him eating with the "sinners" and tax collectors, they asked his disciples: "Why does he eat with tax collectors and 'sinners'?"

[17]On hearing this, Jesus said to them, "It is not the healthy who need a doctor, but the sick. **I have not come to call the righteous, but sinners."**

UNDERSTANDING THE SCRIPTURE

Mark 2:13. Jesus began his ministry in the synagogue, but increasingly taught in open-air settings, notably by the Sea of Galilee. Undoubtedly his message was too controversial to be accepted within the walls of the institutions of Jewish orthodoxy. But also, the size of the crowds that were drawn to Jesus probably forced him to abandon teaching in buildings and use outdoor settings.

Actually, walking by the lakeside and teaching was not uncommon for Jewish teachers in Jesus' day. As the rabbis walked the roads from one place to another, or as they strolled in the open air, their disciples grouped themselves around them and walked with them and listened as they talked. Jesus was doing what any rabbi might have done.

Mark 2:14. Galilee was one of the great road centers of the ancient world. Palestine is the land bridge between Europe and Asia, and all traffic went through this area. At the time of Jesus, Judea was a Roman province under a Roman procurator; Galilee was ruled by Herod Antipas, a son of Herod the Great; and the eastern territory was ruled by Philip, another of Herod's sons. On the way from Philip's territory to Herod's domain, Capernaum was the first town to which the traveler came. Because of that it was a cus-

toms' center. Levi's occupation as a tax collector was to collect customs due on goods crossing the border. He, like other tax collectors, would need to collect the amount required in his contract to pay the Roman authorities. However, the toll collector could demand more and retain the extra money for himself. Although chief tax collectors could become rich, most toll collectors were not wealthy. Nevertheless, many people—especially those who had numerous taxable goods—viewed toll collectors as a dishonest lot.

It is difficult to identify this disciple. He does not appear in any of the official lists of the Twelve (see Mark 3:13-19). He is identified in Mark 2:14 as the "son of Alphaeus." He may be related to, or the same person as "James son of Alphaeus," listed in Mark 3:18. Luke retains the name "Levi," but not "son of Alphaeus" (Luke 5:27). Matthew replaces "Levi" with "Matthew" (Matthew 9:9), and does not mention Alphaeus at all. Most commentators assume that "Levi" and "Matthew" refer to the same person. That there is considerable confusion in the manuscripts where these names occur shows that clarification of this disciple's identity has been problematic from the earliest days.

In any case, the story of Levi's call and his response is the Gospel writer's prime concern (and ours as well). The account of Levi's call to discipleship has a number of parallels with the earlier story about the call of the fishermen (Mark 1:16-20). Like the fishermen, Levi is by the sea, engaged in his usual occupation. Like the fishermen, at Jesus' call Levi drops everything to follow Jesus.

Mark 2:15. Just as Jesus dined at Simon's house, so now he goes to the home of Levi and eats with "tax collectors and sinners." The expression "sinner" reflects the social contempt in which these toll collectors were held. The orthodox religious people such as the Pharisees would have referred not only to tax collectors as sinners, but also the people of the land, who did not observe all the rules and regulations of conventional Pharisaic piety. These "sinners" are not criminals or moral degenerates, but rather those who were not scrupulous in observance of the details of ritual law. It was customary for the Pharisees to avoid contact with these people. By going to Levi's house and sitting at his table and associating with his friends, Jesus was defying the orthodox customs of his day.

Mark 2:16. "The scribes of the Pharisees" can be more accurately understood as "the scribes of the Pharisees' party." Although there were no explicit prohibitions against persons such as Jesus and his disciples eating with those fellow Jews who were engaged in a despised trade such as toll collecting, the Pharisees, who sought to maintain a higher standard of holiness than ordinary people, would probably not have done so. Meals played an important part in the religious and social life of ancient peoples, and further, Jewish meals had to comply with Kosher laws.

Typically, a number of houses in a town were grouped together around a central courtyard, making it easy for outsiders to look in and learn what the inhabitants were doing. When the scribes of the Pharisaic sect discovered Jesus dining with "sinners," they voiced their objections to Jesus' disciples.

Mark 2:17. Jesus' response is in two parts. First, Jesus responds to their objection by citing a common proverb: "Those who are well have no need of a physician." Jesus' intention is to provide a cure for those who are sick in soul. Doesn't that include everybody? Yes, it does. But Jesus is able to help only those who recognize their need and are open to the "cure" that he provides. Jesus can do little for people who think that they are so good that nothing needs to be done for them. Only those who are sinners and know it, and who long for a cure are open to the healing touch of Jesus.

The second half of Jesus' response applies the proverb to Jesus' own ministry: He did not come to call the righteous. "The righteous" to which Jesus is probably referring are those who are sincerely attempting to follow the way of life set forth in the Law. "Sinners" are those who deliberately reject the Law. The wicked do not have any concern for religious matters. They are not part of the crowd that came to Jesus. Instead, Jesus seeks them out!

Jesus' message is for all people. God is ready to heal and forgive. In this story Jesus seeks out those whom society considers *evil*. He accepts their hospitality and offers forgiveness to those who are rejected by the "righteous" people of his day. Thus, when Jesus eats at the home of Levi he is symbolically breaking down the barriers that have been erected around the gracious love of God.

INTERPRETING THE SCRIPTURE

Jesus Calls Levi, a Tax Collector

There are probably persons within every congregation who attend worship regularly, and give generously of their time, talent, and financial resources, yet who are not members of the church. Some do not want to commit themselves; others have a difference of opinion with some part of the church's doctrine, and therefore feel they cannot in good conscience take the membership vows. Still others have a deep sense of unworthiness that keeps them from formal membership in the Body of Christ. Early in my ministry I remember inviting a woman to join the church. She looked toward the floor and replied, "No, pastor, I cannot join. I am not worthy."

What is the barrier that keeps some people from accepting God's grace in Jesus Christ? Is it early learning? Is it failure to hear the word of forgiveness for past mistakes and offenses against God and other human beings? Is prejudice so ingrained in some people's thinking that they believe they are unworthy to participate in the community of faith?

The story of Levi helps us to understand that God accepts even those that society ostracizes. No occupation need keep one from the outstretched arms of Jesus. No past history need prevent a person from discipleship. What did Jesus see in Levi that caused him to ask this toll collector to leave his post and become part of his ministry? What gifts does God see in us?

Suffice it to say that God is not put off by the prejudices and opinions of society. We do not know whether Levi had earned the reputation of being a cheater of his fellow Jews and therefore deserved to be ostracized from polite society. Jesus accepted this tax collector, forgave his past, and opened to him a new life of love and service in God's kingdom. Jesus makes the same invitation to you and to me.

Guess Who's Coming to Dinner?

Levi was so excited about his new calling from God that he invited Jesus to dinner, and Jesus accepted! What would it be like to have Jesus as a dinner guest? There is an old poem that reminds us that in reality Jesus is a guest at every meal we eat. The question is not, "Will Jesus come to our house?" He is already there! The issue we need to face is whether or not we are acknowledging his presence in our thoughts, our speech, and our actions every day.

Meals play an important role in defining the new community that is beginning to form around the preaching, teaching, and healing of Jesus. After Simon and Andrew became disciples, Jesus healed Simon's mother-in-law, and then she served them a meal. Now that Levi has been included in the circle of disciples, he invites his friends to a banquet, attended by Jesus. These meal scenes contribute to our understanding of the two meals that will define the Christian community: the Lord's Supper and the heavenly banquet that will be celebrated when God's kingdom is fully realized (Mark 14:25).

Are all people welcome at the Lord's table? Denominations vary in their answer to that question. In The United Methodist Church, for example, the words of invitation state that all who intend to lead a new life in Christ are invited to participate. We pride ourselves on being an inclusive church. Yet, do non-United Methodists see us that way? What barriers have we erected? Is the manner in which we serve the Sacrament inclusive of people with physical limitations? Are our services offered at times when those who are employed as "toll collectors" are able to attend? Are our worship services joyous celebrations of the gracious activity of God in our midst or are they stiff and solemn occasions that make people uncomfortable and thwart the Spirit's work?

Whenever Jesus attends a banquet or dinner party, there should be excitement in the house! How is Jesus' presence celebrated in your home and in your place of worship?

Jesus Is Criticized

By his actions in attending Levi's dinner party, Jesus offended the most conscientious followers of the Law. When we go against normal social conventions, there is always criticism and misunderstanding. Many see in this story a parallel in our day between those segments of the church that seek to uphold a particular interpretation of certain doctrines, as opposed to those who feel that Jesus' teaching on inclusiveness should break down all barriers.

In his own ministry, Jesus never violated the Torah, the Laws of Moses found in the first five books of the Bible. However, Jesus refused to be bound by the social customs that had developed through the years that placed barriers between some people and the manifestations of God's grace that he saw all around.

How much do we spend on buildings that are designed to help us focus our thoughts on God, and how much do we spend on feeding the hungry people that God created and for whom Christ died? How much do we spend on outreach, and how much on the pastoral care of those who are already members? What is our budget for hospitality? No matter what we do, there is always someone who will criticize our actions.

Jesus took a bold step when he went to Levi's house for dinner. He sent a message of inclusiveness and acceptance when he had table fellowship with Levi's relatives and friends. "How far does God's love reach?" we ask. Jesus drew the circle wide and demonstrated God's acceptance of all persons at Levi's table and on the cross.

Jesus Seeks to Interpret His Actions

How often Jesus was misunderstood in the Gospel accounts. How easily the actions of the church can be misinterpreted in our own day. How do we extend the love and compassion of Christ to all persons without giving the impression that we have no moral standards or solid criteria upon which to base our actions? The challenge is ever before us.

One of the major themes running through the Gospels is that of hospitality. God invites all persons to a new life. Though we erect barriers and obstacles in many ways, God always stands ready to receive us, to forgive us our past mistakes, and to set us on a path of love and service in anticipation of God's coming kingdom. How do we show concern for our neighbors, strangers, and newcomers? How do we communicate God's love to others?

Those who respond to God's invitation are called into a fellowship that is supposed to be different from the typical clubs and fraternal organizations of secular society. In God's fellowship, status doesn't matter. Social position, wealth, education—these things should not be used to include some and exclude others. Yet human nature being what it is, we sometimes allow the value system of the world to invade the church, and the struggles for power and position that occur outside the church occur on the inside as well. Jesus calls us to an inclusive community where all are made to feel welcome. No one is beyond the love and care of God. Whether we see ourselves as "righteous Pharisees" or as "tax collectors and sinners," the invitation is the same: "Follow me." We who hear the summons and heed the message are called to demonstrate God's hospitality in every area of our lives.

SHARING THE SCRIPTURE

PREPARING TO TEACH

Preparing Our Hearts

This week's devotional reading is found in Ephesians 4:25-32. The writer—possibly Paul or one of his associates—comments on how we are to live together in community. We are admonished to "put away" negative behavior. Instead, we are to forgive others and live together harmoniously. What negative behavior do you need to "put away"? How can you show love and hospitality to others? What actions will you take today?

Pray that you and your students will live peaceably and hospitably so that all will feel welcomed into God's household.

Preparing Our Minds

Study the background and lesson scripture, both of which are in Mark 2:13-17. Although this passage about the call of Levi is short, it raises numerous points concerning Jesus' acceptance of all people, the response of the religious leaders to this "unacceptable" tax collector, and Jesus' response to them.

Write on newsprint:

the preparation for next week's session.

Plan a brief lecture for the section "Study the Story and Explain Why Tax Collectors Were Hated" to explore possible identities for Levi, using the second paragraph under Mark 2:14 in Understanding the Scripture.

Provide commentaries and/or Bible dictionaries that include information on tax collectors. Or, create a lecture to discuss their roles, duties, and reception among the Jewish populace.

LEADING THE CLASS

(1) Gather to Learn

❖ Welcome the class members and introduce any guests.

❖ Pray that all who have come today will feel welcomed and included, for Jesus wants each of us to show hospitality one to another.

❖ Encourage group members to recall a time when they were in a setting that was new to them. Perhaps they began to attend a new church, or moved to a new community, or accepted a new job, or joined a new organization. Ask them to talk with a partner about how they were received. Did they feel welcomed and included, invisible, or excluded? How did they respond to the treatment they received?

❖ Bring the class together and brainstorm ideas as to the kinds of actions and attitudes that make people feel welcomed. List these ideas on newsprint.

❖ Move into today's session by noting that Jesus called all sorts of people to follow him, including ones who the religious leaders of the day refused to accept.

❖ Read aloud today's focus statement: **People often feel unaccepted. Where can we find true acceptance? Jesus called a despised tax collector as a disciple, showing God's acceptance of all. He demonstrated that acceptance by extending and receiving hospitality despite the disapproval of others.**

(2) Study the Story and Explain Why Tax Collectors Were Hated

❖ Choose volunteers to read Mark 2:13-17 as a drama. You will need to appoint people to read the parts of the narrator, Jesus, and the scribes.

❖ Present the brief lecture you have created on the identity of Levi, son of Alphaeus.

❖ Explore the duties of tax (toll) collectors, noting why they were very much disliked, especially by people who were among the "haves" and why the religious people considered them "sinners."

Option 1: Divide into groups. Distribute paper and pencils, commentaries, and/or Bible dictionaries. Ask the groups to locate pertinent information and report back to the class.

Option 2: Create a lecture on this topic, using the first paragraph for Mark 2:14 in the Understanding the Scripture portion and any other information you can locate.

❖ Wrap up this section of the lesson by noting that Levi was a very unlikely choice as a disciple, but Jesus called him nonetheless, and Levi responded by inviting Jesus to dinner.

(3) Explore the Impact of Jesus' Acceptance

❖ Point out that Jesus offers the invitation to "follow me" to all sorts of people. Not everyone chooses to accept, but all are invited.

❖ Ask the students to focus on your congregation and your class as they address these questions.

(1) What efforts do we make to welcome, accept, and include anyone who comes to our church?

(2) As we look at the racial, ethnic, and age makeup of our community, can we honestly say that our church is reaching out to everyone who is in our community? If not, what steps do we need to take?

(3) What barriers exist in our church to keep people from wanting to unite with us? (These barriers may be literal, such as a lack of facilities for those with handicapping conditions, or structural, such as the time and day(s) of the services, or atmospheric,

such as unwritten policies that create barriers to full participation by all members.)

(4) What bridges have we built within the community to indicate our commitment to accepting everyone, just as Jesus did?

(4) Identify Ways to Reach Out to People Deemed "Unacceptable"

❖ Note that Jesus reached out to Levi, a person whom, as we have already seen, was not accepted by the staunchly religious people of the day. Jesus called Levi and was willing to have a meal with this tax collector.

❖ Encourage the students to plan a project by following these three steps.

Step 1: Identify a group in your community that most people would label as "unacceptable," such as homeless people, prisoners, hungry people, the unemployed, unwed teenage mothers, or people who depend upon public support or housing.

Step 2: Brainstorm ways that the class could do something to show that they accept these others, just as Jesus would.

Step 3: Decide on a way to help some members of the group identified and implement the plan.

❖ Encourage the adults to commit themselves to action that will enable all of God's children to feel loved and accepted. They may do this by letting a legislator know of their support for a bill that will help "unacceptable" people. Or they may choose to volunteer time to help those who society has shunned or left behind. Or they may contribute to church and nonprofit groups who help those at the margins of society.

❖ Distribute paper and pencils and ask the students to write down what they will try to do within the next month. Do not ask them to show their written commitment to anyone, but do ask that they put this paper in their Bibles where they will see it each day.

(5) Continue the Journey

❖ Pray that the class members will be open to all persons and help them feel welcomed and included.

❖ Read aloud this preparation for next week's lesson. You may also want to post it on newsprint for the students to copy. **Prepare for next week's session, "Preparing for the Job," by reading Mark 6:6***b***-13 and 3:13-19. Keep this focus in mind as you read: People need to be equipped to deal with the tasks to which they are called. How can Christians be adequately equipped for their tasks, especially proclaiming the good news? As with the Twelve, Jesus calls us to a relationship with God that prepares us for ministry in many forms.**

❖ Read aloud the following three ideas. Challenge the students to commit themselves to use these activities as a springboard to spiritual growth.

(1) Identify at least one person or group with whom you have a personal, theological, or social disagreement. Pray for this person, and for yourself, asking God to help you find ways to reach out to this individual.

(2) Invite someone to worship and/or Sunday school who for whatever reason does not feel accepted in the church. Introduce your guest to others and help him or her to feel welcomed.

(3) Participate in whatever way(s) you are able in the class project designed to show others that they are persons of worth, accepted by Jesus and also by you.

❖ Ask the students to turn first to the person on their left, and then to the person on their right and say, "Jesus loves and accepts you, and so do I."

❖ Sing or read aloud "Help Us Accept Each Other."

❖ Ask the students to echo this benediction as you read it phrase by phrase: **Grant, O Lord, that what has been said with our lips we may believe in our hearts, and that what we believe in our hearts we may practice in our lives; through Jesus Christ our Lord. Amen.**

PREPARING FOR THE JOB

PREVIEWING THE LESSON

Lesson Scripture: Mark 6:6b-13; 3:13-19
Background Scripture: Mark 6:6b-13; 3:13-19
Key Verse: Mark 3:14

Focus of the Lesson:
People need to be equipped to deal with the tasks to which they are called. How can Christians be adequately equipped for their tasks, especially proclaiming the good news? As with the Twelve, Jesus calls us to a relationship with God that prepares us for ministry in many forms.

Goals for the Learners:
(1) to review the tasks that Jesus set for the disciples and the way those tasks help to equip them for ministry.
(2) to explore the skills needed for ministry and affirm how Jesus continues to equip his followers.
(3) to celebrate their skills for ministry and to commit to strengthening them.

Pronunciation Guide:
Boanerges   (boh' uh nuhr' jeez)

Supplies:
Bibles, newsprint and marker, paper and pencils, hymnals

READING THE SCRIPTURE

NRSV
Mark 6:6b-13

6b Then he went about among the villages teaching. 7 He called the twelve and began to send them out two by two, and gave them authority over the unclean spirits. 8 He ordered them to take nothing for their journey except a staff; no bread, no bag, no money in their belts; 9 but to wear sandals and not to put on two tunics. 10 He said to

NIV
Mark 6:6b-13

6bThen Jesus went around teaching from village to village. 7Calling the Twelve to him, he sent them out two by two and gave them authority over evil spirits.

8These were his instructions: "Take nothing for the journey except a staff—no bread, no bag, no money in your belts. 9Wear sandals but not an extra tunic. 10Whenever you them, "Wherever you enter a house, stay there until you leave the place. 11 If any place will not welcome you and they refuse to hear you, as you leave, shake off the dust that is on your feet as a testimony against them." 12 So they went out and proclaimed that all should repent. 13 They cast out many demons, and anointed with oil many who were sick and cured them.

Mark 3:13-19

13 He went up the mountain and called to him those whom he wanted, and they came to him. **14 And he appointed twelve, whom he also named apostles, to be with him, and to be sent out to proclaim the message,** 15 and to have authority to cast out demons. 16 So he appointed the twelve: Simon (to whom he gave the name Peter); 17 James son of Zebedee and John the brother of James (to whom he gave the name Boanerges, that is, Sons of Thunder); 18 and Andrew, and Philip, and Bartholomew, and Matthew, and Thomas, and James son of Alphaeus, and Thaddaeus, and Simon the Cananaean, 19 and Judas Iscariot, who betrayed him.

enter a house, stay there until you leave that town. [11]And if any place will not welcome you or listen to you, shake the dust off your feet when you leave, as a testimony against them."

[12]They went out and preached that people should repent. [13]They drove out many demons and anointed many sick people with oil and healed them.

Mark 3:13-19

[13]Jesus went up on a mountainside and called to him those he wanted, and they came to him. **[14]He appointed twelve—designating them apostles—that they might be with him and that he might send them out to preach** [15]and to have authority to drive out demons. [16]These are the twelve he appointed: Simon (to whom he gave the name Peter); [17]James son of Zebedee and his brother John (to them he gave the name Boanerges, which means Sons of Thunder); [18]Andrew, Philip, Bartholomew, Matthew, Thomas, James son of Alphaeus, Thaddaeus, Simon the Zealot [19]and Judas Iscariot, who betrayed him.

UNDERSTANDING THE SCRIPTURE

Mark 6:6b. The call of the disciples is placed in the context of Jesus' teaching ministry. Desirous that all hear the gospel, Jesus went "from village to village" (NIV). As he traveled, he chose others to help him.

Mark 6:7. From the earliest tradition it is reported that Jesus chose twelve disciples. The number twelve makes this group representative of the twelve tribes of Israel, indicating that Jesus has come to restore Israel. Missionary pairs appear to have been a characteristic of early Christianity. The danger associated with first-century travel made such arrangements necessary. Some commentators suggest that the use of pairs was associated with the legal requirements for two witnesses to testify in a case

(Deuteronomy 19:15). The disciples are to be an extension of the ministry of Jesus, and as such they are full participants in Jesus' mission. Their purpose is twofold: to cast out demons (6:7) and to preach repentance (6:12). As his emissaries, Jesus gives the disciples the power to accomplish the tasks. Like Jesus, they speak and act with authority.

Mark 6:8. The fact that the lists of provisions for the journey vary from Gospel to Gospel (see Matthew 10:9-10; Mark 6:8; Luke 9:3; 10:4) suggests that the earliest Christians recognized the need to adapt to the circumstances in which they found themselves. The purpose of the staff is unclear, and the parallel accounts (Matthew 10:10 and Luke 9:3) forbid taking a staff.

Mark 6:9. The disciples are not permitted to carry money or extra provisions from one place to another. They are not engaged in preaching and healing in order to make money, which would have subjected them to the charge of being religious charlatans or magicians. The admonition to wear sandals seems to imply a long journey. A second tunic would have provided protection from the cold night air, and is not permitted. Rather the disciples are to trust God to provide lodging each night.

Mark 6:10. The disciples are to depend on local hospitality. The admonition to remain in the first house that welcomed them may mean that they were to be satisfied where they were and not seek better or more luxurious accommodations elsewhere.

Mark 6:11. Hospitality was a sacred duty in the East. When a stranger entered a village, it was not his or her duty to search for hospitality; it was the duty of the village to offer it. If hospitality was refused, Jesus told his disciples to shake the dust of that place from their feet when they left, which would have been understood in Jesus' day as a gesture of cursing a place. It was a testimony before God that the town had refused to hear God's word.

Mark 6:12. The disciples went out and proclaimed God's truth. The word that is used is literally the word for a herald's proclamation. The message was "Repent!" To repent means to change one's mind, and then fit one's actions to this new reality. Repentance is no sentimental feeling sorry. Repentance is a revolutionary thing. It frequently means changing the entire way we live our lives. Note that the disciples' proclamation is not limited to one class or group. The text says clearly, *"all* should repent."

Mark 6:13. While the admonition of Jesus to repent may seem difficult and painful to enact, the disciples also brought Jesus' message of help and healing. His words brought liberation to poor, demon-possessed men and women. Anointing with oil was a com-

mon practice in ancient times, and was used by the early church as a vehicle to impart the power of Christ to the sick (see James 5:14).

Mark 3:13. In the Bible, mountains have particular significance as places of prayer and divine revelation. The implication of the text is that there was a larger group with Jesus, and that out of these he chose twelve.

Mark 3:14-15. Jesus appoints this group to accompany him and to share his mission. He not only commissions the Twelve to preach, but also confers on them authority over demons. The disciples have two purposes: "to be with him, and to be sent out." Before being sent on their mission, they will receive special instruction from Jesus. As his disciples, it is expected that they will remain true to Jesus as his steady and consistent companions. They will also be his representatives, telling others about him. Jesus gives them his message to share and the power to do his work in the world.

Mark 3:16. There are variations in the lists of disciples in the New Testament, and scholars are not agreed as to the reasons. It is strange that Simon Peter is separated from his brother Andrew. Mark may have chosen this arrangement to give precedence to the three who seem to have been the most prominent leaders: Peter, James, and John. Giving Simon the surname "Rock" ("Peter" in Greek, "Cephas" in Aramaic) is not reported as a special event in Mark as in Matthew 16:17-18. However, following this verse, Mark refers to Simon as "Peter" throughout the remaining chapters of his Gospel, except in 14:37.

Mark 3:17. The surname "Boanerges" or "Sons of Thunder" probably refers to a personality trait in the two brothers.

Mark 3:18. In the list of disciples, Matthew has replaced Levi, who was called earlier (2:14) but is not included in the list. The Gospel of Matthew (10:3) identifies Matthew as "the tax collector." Luke uses the name Levi in the story of the tax collector's call (Luke 5:27-28). In Mark 3:18, James the son of Alphaeus is identified this way to distinguish him from James the son of Zebedee. Since Levi was earlier identified as "the son of Alphaeus" some have guessed that James and Levi refer to the same person. Simon the Cananaen was a political zealot, one who wanted to overthrow the Roman government by force.

Mark 3:19. The final name on the list carries an onerous ring. Judas Iscariot will betray Jesus. The surname "Iscariot" is obscure in meaning and might mean "man of Kerioth," a village either in Hebron or Moab.

INTERPRETING THE SCRIPTURE

Jesus Gives Instructions to the Twelve

When we read about Jesus calling the twelve disciples and his instructions to them, we realize that we are living in a day and time far removed from ancient Galilee. Ours is an age of specialization and sophistication. We receive training and certification before we proceed with our work. Information is growing so rapidly that continuing education is a way of life. It is now common for persons to change careers several times during their adult lives, and the person who works at one company from high school graduation until retirement is a rarity.

In such a culture, to read about Jesus walking along the lakeside and calling untrained and unlettered fishermen, tax collectors, revolutionaries, and the like to follow him, and then sending them out two by two seems a far cry from the way we operate today. In The United Methodist Church, for example, it may take from seven to ten years from the time a person first responds to God's call to ministry until he or she is ordained as a deacon or an elder. In addition to the college and seminary requirements, there are psychological tests, doctrinal examinations, and a host of interviews with committees on ministry all along the way.

Can Jesus' instructions inform our modern practice? I once had a pastor tell me that she couldn't work with the youth in her church because she had not had a course on youth ministry in seminary. What skills and educational experiences are required for service in the church? I would not want to appear unsophisticated or anti-intellectual, but it seems to me that the basic requirement needed for ministry with the people God loves is first of all to experience the call that comes from God, and then to have the willingness to go where God leads.

Educational experiences are important. But more important is a love for people and a commitment to share God's word. The first disciples trusted God to tell them what to say and how to respond. We are called to do likewise.

The Twelve literally heard Jesus speak to them. I believe that if we seek God's will for our lives, we too will feel God calling us to be Christian witnesses in the world. Certainly training and education are essential in today's world. But now, as then, the willingness to go where God sends us is paramount.

"Travel light" is the word of Jesus. On a backpacking trip, the less equipment one takes, the easier the hiking will be, and the less fatigued one will be at the end of the day. By taking nothing for the journey, we will not be bogged down with all the concerns that worldly possessions cause us to have. Traveling light will also force us to trust in God for our provisions. That is a risky way to travel, but it is theologically sound.

The Disciples Are Sent Out

When we take Jesus seriously, more often than not, we find that people are receptive to the message. The disciples had results from their ministry. The Bible tells us, "they cast out many demons, and anointed with oil many who were sick and cured them" (Mark 6:13). When we take Jesus seriously, and follow his instructions, we will find many receptive hearts. Too often the naysayer and those who are not open to the gospel message put us off. Why is it that we let negative comments affect us so? More often than not, the first comment I will share at the dinner table is the critical remark someone made, the negative letter, the irate phone call. I will fail to tell about the many positive comments that folks have shared with me that day. Why?

Again, the words of Jesus are instructive, and as helpful in the twenty-first century as they were to Jesus' original audience. If folks refuse to listen to and heed the gospel message, shake the dust off your feet and move on! Jesus does not want us to waste our resources on those who are unreceptive. Others are waiting to hear the gospel. Spend your time and energy with them.

The Job Description of a Disciple

Jesus asks three things of those who would be his disciples: "to be with him, and to be sent out to proclaim the message, and to have authority to cast out demons" (Mark 3:15). At first glance, these commands seem contradictory. It is virtually impossible, we surmise, to stay with Jesus and at the same time to go out. Yet through the years, Christians in every age have found that both dimensions are vitally important if we are to be faithful followers of Jesus.

We can't read our Bibles for very long without feeling compelled to witness to what we have seen and heard. The gospel demands proclamation, and the world is hungry for the message of Christ. Yet at the same time, we can't be in ministry for very long until we are driven back to Bible study, meditation, and prayer in order to sustain our evangelistic and missionary efforts. Both action and contemplation are necessary components in the life of faith. In our day as in every other, we must strive for balance in our walk with God.

The Twelve That Jesus Chose

The Christian faith began with a group. Jesus called individuals to be part of a movement, rather than to be isolated followers. Christianity is to be lived out in fellowship with others. The essence of the way of the Pharisees was that it separated persons from others. (The very name "Pharisee" means "the separated one.") The whole essence of Christianity is that it binds folks together and calls them to live with one another and for one another.

Not only is Christianity designed to be lived out in community, but it also has been from the outset a diverse group. In following Christ, extremes are brought together. Levi (or Matthew) was a tax collector, and therefore an outcast. He was a renegade and a traitor to his fellow countrymen. Simon the Cananaen, or Simon the Zealot, as Luke calls him (Luke 6:15), was one of the band of fiery and violent nationalists who were pledged even to murder and assassination in order to cleanse their country of its foreign yoke. The man who had practically become a traitor to his people and the fanatical patriot were both called by Jesus, and both lived and worked together as part of the company of those who spent time with our Lord. Christianity began by insisting that the most diverse people should live together. They were enabled to do so because they were all living with Jesus.

We are continually challenged in our day to relate the gospel to all persons and to learn to live together amidst diverse expressions of the Christian faith. When we share the gospel message with others, we must be careful not to allow God's message of love and forgiveness to become limited by our cultural trappings. The principle that the gospel comes to bring healing, peace, and good news to people means that we must adapt to the culture of those we are seeking to serve. At the same time we must not permit the culture to rob Christianity of its life-giving message of freedom and hope. Christians must never become agents of the culture. We must always maintain our first and ultimate allegiance to God as revealed in Jesus Christ. In our day, as in every age, that is a serious challenge. Even as the Twelve were chosen, the Gospel writer notes that Judas would betray his Lord. Will we?

SHARING THE SCRIPTURE

PREPARING TO TEACH

Preparing Our Hearts

This week's devotional reading is found in Luke 9:1-6. This passage is a parallel to the account we will read from Mark for today's session. What does Jesus call the disciples to do? What traveling orders does he give them? How are they to conduct themselves when they reach a town? Why do you suppose that Jesus tells them to "shake the dust off [their] feet" if the towns-people are unreceptive to their message? What implications do Jesus' directions have for your own ministry as a disciple?

Pray that you and your students will heed Jesus' call, be open to the gifts that he gives to equip you, and step out in faith to minister.

Preparing Our Minds

Study the background and lesson scripture, both of which are in Mark 6:6b-13 and 3:13-19. As you read, think about how Jesus calls and equips us for ministry today.

Write on newsprint:
the preparation for next week's session.
litany response for gifts, found under "Celebrate One's Ministry Skills."

Plan the lecture suggested under "Review Tasks for Ministry Jesus Set for the Disciples," if you choose not to use the discussion questions.

LEADING THE CLASS

(1) Gather to Learn

❖ Welcome the class members and introduce any guests.

❖ Pray that the students will seek new ways to prepare for whatever work God calls them to do.

❖ Invite the class to talk about the ways that people prepare for a job. Some members may tell stories of how they were equipped for their vocation. Include as many ideas as possible, such as apprenticeship, internship, other on the job training programs, post–high school training, college degree, military service, or learning from a family member.

❖ Mention that Jesus called his disciples and helped them to prepare for the job by being with him, learning from his word and deed, and receiving power from him to do their work.

❖ Read aloud today's focus statement: **People need to be equipped to deal with the tasks to which they are called. How can Christians be adequately equipped for their tasks, especially proclaiming the good news? As with the Twelve, Jesus calls us to a relationship with God that prepares us for ministry in many forms.**

(2) Review Tasks for Ministry Jesus Set for the Disciples

❖ Read aloud Mark 6:6b-13. Then discuss the following questions with the class, or create a lecture that will answer all of these questions. Use information from Understanding the Scripture to augment the discussion, or as the basis for your lecture. You may want to draw a chart on newsprint and fill it in as the class responds or as you speak.

(1) **What did Jesus call the Twelve to do?**

(2) **How were they equipped and sent out?**

(3) **Who were they to visit?**

(4) **What were they to do when they arrived in a town?**

(5) **What were they to do when they left a town where people refused to hear them?**

(6) **How would you evaluate the success of their mission?**

❖ Point out that from what we know about these disciples, they were ordinary people called for extraordinary ministry.

❖ Read Mark 3:13-19. Encourage the students to talk about what this passage tells them about the disciples and their mission. Use the information in Understanding the Scripture to broaden the discussion. Be sure to note that Jesus called Simon "Peter," and that he called Zebedee's sons, James and John, "Boanerges." Explore what traits these names suggest.

(3) Explore Ministry Skills Jesus Gives His Followers

❖ Challenge the students to brainstorm types of ministry to which persons (laity and clergy) are called. List these ideas on newsprint, but be sure to leave additional room to write next to each type.

❖ Review the list and add to it the kinds of gifts that people need to undertake each ministry. For example, someone who chairs a committee must have good organizational

skills, be able to relate to people, understand how to solve a problem and resolve a conflict, and have a passion for what the committee does. As another example, someone called to a ministry of intercessory prayer needs to have genuine concern for persons in need and be willing to lift up those persons on a regular basis.

❖ Conclude this section of the lesson by talking about ways that the church (including but not limited to your congregation) equips its people for ministry. Lift up any upcoming training events, and encourage students who could benefit from them to attend. In addition to courses and training events, talk about other ways that you believe God is equipping contemporary disciples.

(4) Celebrate One's Own Ministry Skills

❖ Distribute paper and pencils. Invite the students to list the gifts and skills that they have for ministry. Remind them that while ministry is certainly conducted in the church it is also spread beyond the four walls. One may, for example, have a ministry of caring for sick family members or neighbors. Collect these papers. Shuffle them and give them out to other members of the class.

❖ Create a litany of thanksgiving for the gifts and skills that each member brings. Post newsprint on which you have written this response: **We give you thanks and praise, O God, for these gifts for you ministry.** Have individual students call out the gifts that are listed on the paper that they were given. The class will then affirm these gifts by reading the response in unison. Continue the litany until everyone's gifts have been read aloud and affirmed. If the class is large, do this activity with groups of five to seven people.

(5) Continue the Journey

❖ Pray that each of the class members will hear God's call upon their lives and be willing to respond with a resounding "yes," trusting that God will equip them with the resources they need to do the task.

❖ Read aloud this preparation for next week's lesson. You may also want to post it on newsprint for the students to copy. **Prepare for next week's session by reading Mark 8:27-38, which is both our background and scripture passage for the session entitled "Giving Your All." As you read, keep this focus in mind: We all are willing to commit to people and causes we care about. What is the highest commitment we can make? Jesus described the total commitment due to God's Messiah.**

❖ Read aloud the following three ideas. Challenge the students to commit themselves to use these activities as a springboard to spiritual growth.

(1) **Take a gifts inventory, if you have not already done so, to determine the areas in which you would serve most effectively. Check Cokesbury or another Christian bookstore to select one of the many inventories available.**

(2) **Ponder how much "baggage" you carry with you in your spiritual life. Are you traveling light as Jesus commands his disciples to do, or are you heavily laden with burdens that prevent you from being an active, faithful witness? What changes do you need to make?**

(3) **Seek opportunities to get training in the area of ministry to which you have been called. Perhaps your church, district, conference, or diocese offers such training for laity.**

❖ Sing or read aloud "Here I Am, Lord."

❖ Ask the students to echo this benediction as you read it phrase by phrase: **Grant, O Lord, that what has been said with our lips we may believe in our hearts, and that what we believe in our hearts we may practice in our lives; through Jesus Christ our Lord. Amen.**

GIVING YOUR ALL

PREVIEWING THE LESSON

Lesson Scripture: Mark 8:27-38
Background Scripture: Mark 8:27-38
Key Verse: Mark 8:34

Focus of the Lesson:
We all are willing to commit to people and causes we care about. What is the highest commitment we can make? Jesus described the total commitment due to God's Messiah.

Goals for the Learners:
(1) to investigate what Jesus says about the commitment his followers must have.
(2) to identify some of the other commitments that compete for time and attention today.
(3) to evaluate their other commitments in light of the call of Jesus Christ.

Pronunciation Guide:
Caesarea Philippi   (ses' uh ree' uh fil ip' i)

Supplies:
Bibles, newsprint and marker, paper and pencils, hymnals

READING THE SCRIPTURE

NRSV
Mark 8:27-38

27 Jesus went on with his disciples to the villages of Caesarea Philippi; and on the way he asked his disciples, "Who do people say that I am?" 28 And they answered him, "John the Baptist; and others, Elijah; and still others, one of the prophets." 29 He asked them, "But who do you say that I am?" Peter answered him, "You are the Messiah." 30 And he sternly ordered them not to tell anyone about him.

NIV
Mark 8:27-38

27Jesus and his disciples went on to the villages around Caesarea Philippi. On the way he asked them, "Who do people say I am?"

28They replied, "Some say John the Baptist; others say Elijah; and still others, one of the prophets."

29"But what about you?" he asked. "Who do you say I am?"

Peter answered, "You are the Christ."

31 Then he began to teach them that the Son of Man must undergo great suffering, and be rejected by the elders, the chief priests, and the scribes, and be killed, and after three days rise again. 32 He said all this quite openly. And Peter took him aside and began to rebuke him. 33 But turning and looking at his disciples, he rebuked Peter and said, "Get behind me, Satan! For you are setting your mind not on divine things but on human things."

34 He called the crowd with his disciples, and said to them, "If any want to become my followers, let them deny themselves and take up their cross and follow me. 35 For those who want to save their life will lose it, and those who lose their life for my sake, and for the sake of the gospel, will save it. 36 For what will it profit them to gain the whole world and forfeit their life? 37 Indeed, what can they give in return for their life? 38 Those who are ashamed of me and of my words in this adulterous and sinful generation, of them the Son of Man will also be ashamed when he comes in the glory of his Father with the holy angels."

30Jesus warned them not to tell anyone about him.

31He then began to teach them that the Son of Man must suffer many things and be rejected by the elders, chief priests and teachers of the law, and that he must be killed and after three days rise again. 32He spoke plainly about this, and Peter took him aside and began to rebuke him.

33But when Jesus turned and looked at his disciples, he rebuked Peter. "Get behind me, Satan!" he said. "You do not have in mind the things of God, but the things of men."

34Then he called the crowd to him along with his disciples and said: "If anyone would come after me, he must deny himself and take up his cross and follow me. 35For whoever wants to save his life will lose it, but whoever loses his life for me and for the gospel will save it. 36What good is it for a man to gain the whole world, yet forfeit his soul? 37Or what can a man give in exchange for his soul? 38If anyone is ashamed of me and my words in this adulterous and sinful generation, the Son of Man will be ashamed of him when he comes in his Father's glory with the holy angels."

UNDERSTANDING THE SCRIPTURE

Mark 8:27. The setting for the story is the Gentile region of Caesarea Philippi, twenty-five miles north of the Sea of Galilee. Perhaps Jesus took the disciples to this region to get away from the crowds that attended to his every move earlier in his ministry. There Jesus asked the Twelve what effect his ministry was having on the people. What had the disciples been hearing?

Mark 8:28. They answer by reporting the popular rumors. Some believe Jesus is John the Baptist come back to life. Others think that he is Elijah. It was a popularly held belief at that time that before God's Messiah would appear there would be a time when the world was torn in pieces. The physical

and moral order would collapse, and into this chaos would come Elijah, as the forerunner and herald of the Messiah. He was to heal the breaches and bring order into the chaos to prepare the way for the Messiah to come.

Mark 8:29. Jesus is most interested in his disciples' understanding of who he is. Peter, as the spokesperson for the group, responds, "You are the Christ (or the Messiah.)" "Messiah" is the Hebrew and "Christ" is the Greek for "the Anointed One." Three groups of persons were anointed in Jewish society: prophets, priests, and kings. Anointing represented God's affirmation that the person was the divinely chosen leader of the people. It is important for us to remember that "Christ" is not a name; it is a title. Peter's confession of faith is the first correct human statement about Jesus' identity in the Gospel of Mark. The demons had earlier recognized who Jesus was. Now Peter and the other disciples appear to have reached the correct insight that Jesus is the Messiah. However, their understanding falls far short of Jesus' understanding that the Messiah is destined to suffer and die.

Mark 8:30. Just as Jesus has silenced the demons earlier in the Gospel story, so now he forbids the disciples to reveal his messiahship. Several commentators suggest that Jesus instructs the Twelve to tell no one who he is so that he can teach them what his messiahship really means.

Mark 8:31. This is the first of three predictions that Jesus makes to his disciples to prepare them for his death and resurrection (see also 9:31 and 10:33-34). All three are in vain, for Mark portrays the disciples as consistently failing to understand. The point of this threefold prediction is to establish firmly in the mind of the reader that the disciples, while making a confession of faith, have a totally inadequate understanding of Jesus' significance.

The passion prediction uses the title "Son of Man" for Jesus rather than "Messiah" or "Son of God." The Old Testament image of a heavenly "son of man" (Daniel 7:13-14) ascending to the divine throne provided a framework for understanding the resurrection of Jesus and the expectation that Jesus would return as judge. In Daniel, the "Son of Man" is identified with the righteous of Israel who suffer. In Mark's passion prediction the Son of Man does not identify with the righteous from the distance of heaven, but actually experiences their plight.

Mark 8:32. To leave no excuse for the disciples' failure to grasp the significance of Jesus, Mark stresses that Jesus no longer speaks in parables and in figures of speech, but "spoke plainly about this" (NIV). The reaction of Peter illustrates his lack of understanding and makes it necessary to view his confession of faith in Jesus as Messiah as less than a full comprehension.

Mark 8:33. Jesus, in turn, gives Peter his most serious personal rebuke, calling him Satan and accusing him of not being on the side of God. The phrase "get behind me" is a Jewish way of saying "begone."

Mark 8:34. What follows is a paragraph of several short sayings of Jesus, arranged by Mark to give some standards for true discipleship. They are appropriate here because they speak to Peter's failure to grasp the significance of Jesus' coming crucifixion. The "crowd" should be understood as including the reader of the Gospel. One is struck by the startling honesty of Jesus. Jesus did not try to bribe anyone by offering an easy way. Instead he sought to challenge those who would be his disciples. The picture of a condemned criminal carrying the cross bar to the place of his execution paints a shocking description of that which is required for discipleship. However, Jesus did not ask anyone to do or to face anything that he was not prepared to do and face himself. Just as Jesus invited the disciples to "deny themselves and take up their cross," so Jesus demonstrated a life of sacrifice for others and a willingness to bear the cross for the sins of the world.

Mark 8:35. Paradoxical as it may sound, there are certain things in life that are lost by being kept and saved by being used. A talent that a person possesses is a good example. If one uses the talent, it will develop more and more. If one refuses to use the talent, in time he or she will lose it. God gave us life to spend and not to keep. Those who live carefully, protecting themselves, always thinking first of their own profit, ease, comfort, and security are losing life all the time. But those who spend their lives for others, forgetting health, wealth, and comfort in their desire to do something for Jesus and the people for whom Jesus gave his life, will gain immeasurably.

Mark 8:36-37. Nothing is gained by

rejecting Jesus and saving one's life, since those who turn away from discipleship will be condemned.

Mark 8:38. This verse reflects the situation Christians faced under Roman persecution. To deny Christ is to be saved in this world but to be lost in the next. Those who remain faithful can be confident that they will be among the elect at the judgment, for the Jesus whom they follow is the exalted one who will testify about his followers before God. Those who are ashamed of Jesus will discover that their Savior treats them in the same way. Thus Christians are encouraged to remain faithful through suffering, confident that they will eventually participate in God's coming kingdom where all wrongs will be addressed and where peace and goodness will prevail forever.

INTERPRETING THE SCRIPTURE

Peter's Confession of Faith

I remember the story of a costume party. Everyone was watching for the guest of honor to arrive. Because the partygoers were all in costume and wearing masks, no one's identity was known. In fact, those at the party later learned that the guest of honor had arrived and was milling about, socializing with the others incognito! No one was aware that the guest of honor was already in their midst.

What an appropriate illustration of the coming of Jesus into the country villages of first-century Palestine! The people were looking for God's Messiah to appear. Through the years they had dreamed of a king like David who would arise and make their nation great again. The prophets foretold the coming of a great leader for God. The people looked for this leader to rid them of the domination of foreign powers, which had oppressed them for centuries. Most expected that this leader would totally destroy the foreign powers and set up a kingdom with Jerusalem as the capital. Palestine would be the center of the world, and all the nations would be subject to it. After her enemies were broken, Israel would enjoy a new age of peace and prosperity that would last forever. All the signs pointed toward the present hour as the time of God's dramatic intervention. Yet when Jesus appeared, claiming to be God's Messiah, most did not recognize him.

"Who do people say that I am?" asked Jesus. Clearly the crowds did not comprehend that he was the Messiah. After all, he did not conduct himself in the manner in which they were expecting God's Messiah to act.

But, queried Jesus, did the disciples understand? Yes, apparently they did, for Peter, speaking for the group responded by saying, "You are the Christ; you are the Messiah." We will subsequently learn that Peter and the others had an inadequate understanding of Jesus' messianic role. However, Peter's confession makes it clear that he and the disciples understood that Jesus was God's Anointed One who would bring God's salvation to the world.

From a Christian perspective, the question "Who do you say that I am?" is the single most important question facing every human being. How we answer that question not only determines our future, it also shapes the way we live our lives each day. Each of us must decide, based on the evidence we have, whether we believe Jesus is the Messiah. As with the first disciples, our understanding is always inadequate and incomplete. Based on what he knew and what he had experienced, Peter declared his faith. We are called to do likewise.

Jesus Foretells His Suffering and Death

One of the themes running through the Gospels is the idea that Jesus was not the kind of messiah that people were looking for. The people expected a conquering hero; Jesus came as a humble servant. The people expected the Messiah to throw his weight around and show Rome who was boss; Jesus turned the other cheek. This concept of a suffering messiah, while part of the Old Testament prophecies (see Isaiah 49, 50, 52:13–53:12), did not seem to be part of the popular thinking in the first century, even among the disciples. That Jesus' kingdom would begin in the hearts of the believers rather than in the government chambers was a difficult concept for the early followers of Jesus to understand. Still today Christians tend to measure power and influence using the methods of the world. It is hard for us to understand that God is at work when evil forces seem to have the upper hand and to perceive the power of the suffering servant.

The Tempter Speaks Through a Friend

Commentators tell us that when Peter took Jesus aside and rebuked him, people would have been horrified, for disciples never treated their teachers in that manner. Such behavior would have been an unthinkable response to the teaching of a first-century rabbi. Yet Peter's intent was not to show disrespect. Peter said what he did because he loved Jesus. He could not bear the thought of Jesus suffering and dying. Furthermore, he did not want his leader treated with contempt. How humiliating that would be! The movement could never succeed if the Messiah was destroyed. Didn't Jesus see that?

How hard it must have been for Jesus to stay true to his calling. He had weathered the storm in the wilderness. The tempter had approached him from every angle.

Satan had tried his best to get Jesus to compromise his ideals. Jesus held firm.

Now Satan was back. This time the Tempter was working through one of Jesus' closest friends. Peter thought he was looking out for Jesus' best interests. He felt Jesus was misguided and that he was making a mistake. Peter was only seeking Jesus' own good. Jesus had to resist the temptation to listen to Peter's words, spoken in love, and listen instead to the voice of God.

How do we discern the voice of God in a world filled with the sounds of so many voices? God often works through other people to share God's message. But so does the Evil One! Jesus was able to stay true to God's calling. Discerning God's call and following God's direction is a challenge for believers in every age.

Taking Up the Cross

During the first part of Mark's Gospel, Jesus calls the disciples and shares with them his ministry of preaching, teaching, and healing. Just as he brings help and hope to those who are in need of encouragement, understanding, and wholeness, so Jesus empowers his disciples to continue his ministry in the world.

Not everyone received Jesus with open arms. For some, his message caused anger and hostility rather than peace and goodwill. Good news for the poor implied bad news for the rich. Those who were enlightened no longer were content to maintain the status quo. Those who were healed began to live their lives in new ways.

Opposition to Jesus mounted. When Jesus began to predict his eventual suffering and death his disciples reacted negatively, which is no surprise. No one wants to see their heroes harassed and humiliated. Yet not only did Jesus predict his own demise, he also taught that his disciples would encounter a similar fate. Those who participate in Jesus' ministry of preaching, teaching, and healing must also be willing to participate in his ministry of suffering.

The world did not understand Jesus. The world still does not understand the way of sacrificial love. When a family member gives up activities that are personally fulfilling to care for a child or an aging parent, when a faithful Christian gives up a lucrative career to follow a path of service, when an overworked executive volunteers to help the less fortunate, then we come to understand, in part, the meaning of Jesus' call to "take up the cross."

These are hard sayings. I suspect that "denying self" was no more popular in Jesus' day than it is in our own. Yet we are called to live in such a way that we will not be ashamed of ourselves in the life to come. Let us make that goal a reality in our lives so that, with God's help, we will live today and everyday satisfied that we are serving our Lord as best we can.

SHARING THE SCRIPTURE

PREPARING TO TEACH

Preparing Our Hearts

This week's devotional reading is found in Matthew 16:24-28. Here, Jesus tells his followers what true discipleship means. They must take up their cross, deny themselves, and be ready to give their life for Jesus' sake. These words are difficult to read, and even more challenging to live by. Which of us really wants to set aside our own comforts and agendas to follow Christ into situations we would prefer to avoid? Yet, crossbearing and its attendant suffering is at the heart of true discipleship. What does your life show about your willingness to make the kind of sacrificial commitment that Christ requires?

Pray that you and your students will take Jesus' commands seriously and be willing to live the sacrificial discipleship to which Christ calls us.

Preparing Our Minds

Study the background and lesson scripture, both of which are found in Mark 8:27-38. To make comparisons with the other Synoptic Gospels, you may also want to read the story of Peter's confession in Matthew 16:13-23 and Luke 9:18-22, as well as Jesus' teaching on discipleship in Matthew 16:24-28 (our devotional reading) and Luke 9:23-27.

Write on newsprint:

steps 1-6 under "Identify Competing Commitments."

the preparation for next week's session.

Plan the Bible study under "Investigate Commitment to Jesus."

LEADING THE CLASS

(1) Gather to Learn

❖ Welcome the class members and introduce any guests.

❖ Pray that the students will live as faithful disciples who are willing to give their all for the sake of the gospel.

❖ Brainstorm a list of commitments that class members have. List these ideas on newsprint, and leave the list posted during class. The students may include generic commitments, such as to family, work, or church. Or, they may be very specific in naming organizations they support, such as Rotary International.

❖ Discuss these questions with the class, or try to answer them yourself in a brief lecture concerning a group that is important to you.

(1) What attracts you to this group?

(2) What motivates you to support this group?

(3) How much of your time, money, and talent are you willing to donate to this cause?

❖ Note that in today's passage we will explore what it means to make a commitment to Jesus and the priority that such a commitment requires.

❖ Read aloud today's focus statement: **We all are willing to commit to people and causes we care about. What is the highest commitment we can make? Jesus described the total commitment due God's Messiah.**

(2) Investigate Commitment to Jesus

❖ Choose a volunteer to read Mark 8:27-38.

❖ Use the information in Understanding the Scripture for Mark 8:28 to comment on why people thought Jesus was John the Baptist or Elijah.

❖ Discuss the following questions.

(1) What does the word "messiah" really mean? (See Understanding the Scripture, Mark 8:29.)

(2) Do you think Peter really understood what it meant for Jesus to be the Messiah? Support your answer.

❖ Do a brief Bible study to enlarge the class's understanding of the role and mission of the "Messiah."

Point 1: In Mark 8:31, Jesus predicts his passion. Look at the two other instances where he states what will happen in Mark 9:31 and 10:33-34. What additional information do you learn?

Point 2: In Mark 8:31, Jesus refers to himself as "the Son of Man." Read Daniel 7:13-14 to find out additional information about this image.

Point 3: Jesus' words teach us that the Messiah must be prepared to suffer and die for the sake of God's kingdom. Since Peter and other Jews of his day were looking for a messiah who would liberate them from Roman rule, Peter has trouble accepting Jesus' prediction.

Point 4: Jesus' rebuke of Peter indicates that Jesus perceives Peter's words as a continuation of Satan's temptation in the wilderness. See Matthew 4:1-11, Mark 1:12-13, and Luke 4:1-13 for other Gospel accounts of this event in the wilderness. What similarities do you see between the wilderness temptation and Peter's challenge?

❖ Provide a few moments of silent time for the students to consider how they define "messiahship" and whether or not they are truly ready to follow Jesus all the way to the cross.

(3) Identify Competing Commitments

❖ Distribute paper and pencils. Ask the students to look again at the list of commitments they brainstormed earlier and follow these steps. For this activity, do not include your commitment to God. We'll do that later.

Step 1: Write your personal list of commitments. You may use the brainstormed list for ideas, but you are not limited to it.

Step 2: Rank these commitments by numbering the most important ones from 1 to 10 (more or less).

Step 3: Mentally review your calendar for the last three or four weeks. Next to each item, write an approximate amount of time you devoted to the commitment over the last month or so.

Step 4: Compare your ranking for each item with the actual time you spent.

Step 5: Evaluate whether your time is being spent appropriately in light of your perceived commitments.

Step 6: Consider any changes you need to make to bring your stated priorities in line with the actual amount of time you spend.

(4) Evaluate Other Commitments in Light of Jesus' Call

❖ Distribute another sheet of paper to each student. Encourage them to write down whatever they do that specifically relates to their commitment to God through Jesus Christ. The list may include spiritual disciplines, such as prayer and Bible study, as well as missions/outreach projects and time spent doing church work. Note that much work for Christ goes on outside the walls of the church. Also ask them to note the approximate time per month they spend on each item.

❖ Suggest that they hold this sheet of paper side by side to the one from the previous activity. Encourage the students to talk with a partner or small group about what these two activities reveal about their true priorities.

(5) Continue the Journey

❖ Draw the class together and pray that the students will seek God's guidance in determining whether or not their priorities are in order, and trust God to help them make whatever rearrangements are necessary.

❖ Read aloud this preparation for next week's lesson. You may also want to post it on newsprint for the students to copy. **Prepare for next week's session, "Moving Toward Greatness," by reading the back-**ground passage from Mark 10:13-45. Look especially at the lesson scripture in Mark 10:32-45. As you read pay particular attention to the focus of the session: Everybody wants to be great. What is the way of greatness? Jesus says that true greatness comes through serving others.**

❖ Read aloud the following three ideas. Challenge the students to commit themselves to use these activities as a springboard to spiritual growth.

(1) **Identify those causes for which you are willing to die for, suffer for, be inconvenienced for, or contribute to. How do each of these causes fit in with your commitment to Christ?**

(2) **Play a word association game by listing whatever comes to mind when you hear the words "commitment," "loyalty," and "suffering."**

(3) **Recall or read about someone who has lived a sacrificial life, one whose life has been poured out for the sake of the gospel. How can this person be a role model for you?**

❖ Sing or read aloud "Take Up Thy Cross."

❖ Ask the students to echo this benediction as you read it phrase by phrase: **Grant, O Lord, that what has been said with our lips we may believe in our hearts, and that what we believe in our hearts we may practice in our lives; through Jesus Christ our Lord. Amen.**

MOVING TOWARD GREATNESS

PREVIEWING THE LESSON

Lesson Scripture: Mark 10:32-45
Background Scripture: Mark 10:13-45
Key Verses: Mark 10:43*b*-44

Focus of the Lesson:
Everybody wants to be great. What is the way of greatness? Jesus says that true greatness comes through serving others.

Goals for the Learners:
(1) to hear Jesus' teachings about service and true greatness.
(2) to compare greatness as defined by culture and media with greatness as defined by Jesus.
(3) to identify opportunities for service in one's church and community and to name ways participants can be involved.

Supplies:
Bibles, newsprint and marker, paper and pencils, hymnals; optional magazines/pictures, scissors, glue, poster board; butcher paper (for a mural), markers, tape

---

READING THE SCRIPTURE

NRSV
Mark 10:32-45

32 They were on the road, going up to Jerusalem, and Jesus was walking ahead of them; they were amazed, and those who followed were afraid. He took the twelve aside again and began to tell them what was to happen to him, 33 saying, "See, we are going up to Jerusalem, and the Son of Man will be handed over to the chief priests and the scribes, and they will condemn him to death; then they will hand him over to the Gentiles; 34 they will mock him, and spit upon him, and flog

NIV
Mark 10:32-45

³²They were on their way up to Jerusalem, with Jesus leading the way, and the disciples were astonished, while those who followed were afraid. Again he took the Twelve aside and told them what was to happen to him. ³³"We are going up to Jerusalem," he said, "and the Son of Man will be betrayed to the chief priests and teachers of the law. They will condemn him to death and hand him over to the Gentiles, ³⁴who will mock him and spit on him, flog him and kill him. Three days later he will rise."

him, and kill him; and after three days he will rise again."

35 James and John, the sons of Zebedee, came forward to him and said to him, "Teacher, we want you to do for us whatever we ask of you." 36 And he said to them, "What is it you want me to do for you?" 37 And they said to him, "Grant us to sit, one at your right hand and one at your left, in your glory." 38 But Jesus said to them, "You do not know what you are asking. Are you able to drink the cup that I drink, or be baptized with the baptism that I am baptized with?" 39 They replied, "We are able." Then Jesus said to them, "The cup that I drink you will drink; and with the baptism with which I am baptized, you will be baptized; 40 but to sit at my right hand or at my left is not mine to grant, but it is for those for whom it has been prepared."

41 When the ten heard this, they began to be angry with James and John. 42 So Jesus called them and said to them, "You know that among the Gentiles those whom they recognize as their rulers lord it over them, and their great ones are tyrants over them. 43 But it is not so among you; **but whoever wishes to become great among you must be your servant, 44 and whoever wishes to be first among you must be slave of all.** 45 For the Son of Man came not to be served but to serve, and to give his life a ransom for many."

[35]Then James and John, the sons of Zebedee, came to him. "Teacher," they said, "we want you to do for us whatever we ask."

[36]"What do you want me to do for you?" he asked.

[37]They replied, "Let one of us sit at your right and the other at your left in your glory."

[38]"You don't know what you are asking," Jesus said. "Can you drink the cup I drink or be baptized with the baptism that I am baptized with?"

[39]"We can," they answered.

Jesus said to them, "You will drink the cup and be baptized with the baptism I am baptized with, [40]but to sit at my right or left is not for me to grant. These places belong to those for whom they have been prepared."

[41]When the ten heard about this, they became indignant with James and John. [42]Jesus called them together and said, "You know that those who are regarded as rulers of the Gentiles lord it over them, and their high officials exercise authority over them. [43]Not so with you. **Instead whoever wants to become great among you must be your servant, [44]and whoever wants to be first must be slave of all.** [45]For even the Son of Man did not come to be served, but to serve, and to give his life a ransom for many."

UNDERSTANDING THE SCRIPTURE

Mark 10:13. In Mark 9:33-37 Jesus made an example of a little child to overturn the disciples' arguments about which of them was the greatest. In the first century world children were not considered persons in their own right. They had no status or power. This episode begins with the disciples' attempt to enforce the standard social mores: Children should not be allowed to disturb a teacher and his students.

Mark 10:14. Once again their behavior demonstrates that the disciples did not understand Jesus' ministry, which is inclusive, not exclusive.

Mark 10:15. Jesus warns the disciples that they must give up the normal human calculations of greatness if they are to participate in the rule of God. Just as a young child is totally dependent upon the parents for any status or inheritance, so the disciples are radically dependent upon God's grace. The disciples do not set the conditions for entering God's kingdom.

Mark 10:16. Commentators suggest that women who had responsibility for the care of young children brought them to Jesus so that he could touch them, for they believed that his touch might protect the children from evil.

Mark 10:17-18. When the rich man runs to Jesus and addresses him as a "good teacher," Jesus immediately switches the focus from himself to God. It is as if Jesus is saying, "No flattery, please! Don't call me good. Save that word for God!" Salvation does not lie in obedience, for even if that could be accomplished, human beings still lack the essential requirement of salvation: complete renunciation of all worldly dependence and acceptance of salvation in trust and faith as God's gift.

Mark 10:19-20. That the man claims to have kept all the commandments since his youth seems to display a rather interesting naïveté as well as a lack of humility.

Mark 10:21. Jesus extends to the man the call to join the circle of disciples. To do so, he must first divest himself of his property. A disciple possesses only the basic items of clothing (see Mark 6:9). Furthermore, a disciple cannot be a rich person with all the accompanying complex socioeconomic ties and relationships. This invitation also illustrates the earlier saying about becoming like a child, insofar as it requires setting aside all the elements that confer status and power over others.

Mark 10:22. Despite the rich man's devotion to the word of God, he cannot bring himself to accept the call. The sadness with which he departs distinguishes him from the enemies of Jesus, who are hostile when they leave.

Mark 10:23. The story shifts from the public encounter to Jesus' instruction to the disciples. These sayings highlight the conflict between wealth and discipleship.

Mark 10:24. People naturally assumed that the wealthy were the recipients of God's blessings and were therefore closer to God than other people. Jesus' lament that it is very difficult for persons of means to "enter the kingdom" truly shocks his hearers.

Mark 10:25. Jesus' proverbial comment about the difficulty of a camel passing through the eye of a needle should be taken literally, according to commentators. The explanation that there was a needle's eye gate into Jerusalem that a camel could enter only on its knees is not factual. Further, it misses the point that it is impossible for the rich to enter the kingdom of God, a teaching that is confirmed in verses 26-27.

Mark 10:27. This axiom was well known in antiquity, in which stock examples of impossible things were used to contrast the world of nature and human experience with the divine. God's power is not limited by any constraints. Jesus' miracles demonstrate that he possesses the power of God to do things that are otherwise impossible.

Mark 10:28-30. Peter claims, on behalf of all the disciples, that they have done what the rich man refused to do—left everything and followed Jesus. Jesus replies that renunciation of things in this world will eventually bring everything in return, both in this life and in the next. Christians can look forward to inclusion in the new family gathered around Jesus.

Mark 10:31. This saying reminds us that human values are not necessarily God's values, and in particular, that the Twelve may not be entitled to any special priority.

Mark 10:32. They are "on the road" and Jesus is depicted as moving at the head of a single file of disciples, which in first-century Palestine would have customarily been arranged according to seniority.

Mark 10:33-34. This third prediction of the Passion, which Jesus makes privately and personally to the Twelve, follows the pattern of the first two (8:31-33; 9:30-32). There is no hint that the disciples understand what Jesus is sharing with them.

Mark 10:35-37. James and John are represented as selfishly seeking the chief seats in the house.

Mark 10:38. The phrase "drink the cup" is idiomatic for martyrdom. The cup of wine symbolizes the blood of Jesus, which will be shed to establish the new covenant. Jesus' prayer to be spared the cup if it is God's will makes the cup stand for all the suffering of the Passion. "Baptism" is also a metaphor for suffering.

Mark 10:39. The confident assertion that they can share Jesus' suffering strikes us as naive. However, Jesus predicts that they will share his suffering. Acts 12:2 informs us that James was martyred in Jerusalem. The circumstances surrounding John's death are less certain. However, commentators note that this prediction is itself the best evidence, for had it not been fulfilled, it probably would not have been preserved.

Mark 10:40. Jesus does not determine the positions people have in the Kingdom. God is the one who will decide who will share Jesus' glory.

Mark 10:41. The indignation of the ten disciples at James and John emphasizes the inappropriateness of their behavior.

Mark 10:42-45. The meaning of discipleship is not privilege but service. This final saying points to the Son of Man as one who has come to serve, rather than to receive the glory the disciples had in mind. It also states the reason for Jesus' death: "a ransom for many."

INTERPRETING THE SCRIPTURE

Again Jesus Predicts His Death and Resurrection

A seminary professor often told our class, "Never fear repetition." Television advertisers have learned that lesson well. How many times have we seen the "golden arches" or been lured to own a "piece of the rock"? By consistent repetition, certain images become ingrained in our minds. Thus, repetition is an effective teaching tool.

Today's lesson begins with the third "passion prediction" of Jesus. For the third time Jesus shares with his disciples confidentially and frankly "what was to happen to him" (10:32). In order to follow the mission that Jesus believes God has set before him, Jesus must leave the pleasant hillsides and lakeshore of Galilee, where hundreds and even thousands of people have enthusiastically received his preaching, teaching, and healing ministries. Now, he repeats, he must go to Jerusalem where his message will receive a different response. In Jerusalem he will be harassed and condemned to death. He will be killed, but after three days he will rise again.

In the Gospels the disciples are depicted as a rather unperceptive lot. There is no indication that the Twelve grasped what Jesus was saying. In fact, the request of James and John makes it clear that the sons of Zebedee had completely failed to understand Jesus.

We marvel at the response of the disciples, yet do we understand the implications of the gospel any better than did the first hearers? Two thousand years after Jesus' message brought the promise of peace, joy, and love to the world, we are still at war. We are still unhappy, and we are still struggling with human relationships in our homes, schools, offices, and churches. We have not integrated the message of Jesus into the fabric of our daily lives.

Even though the disciples repeatedly failed to understand, Jesus did not waver. He did not compromise his message, nor did he alter his course. We are called to study, to pray, and to listen for God's voice.

We, too, must follow where God leads. Even when people do not understand, we must not quit trying to share the gospel message. We must not allow the message of the gospel to be watered down, nor can we let the world cause us to waver in our response to God's call.

The Request of James and John

Hardly had Jesus finished speaking about his suffering and death when James and John made their infamous request, "to sit, one at your right hand and one at your left, in your glory" (10:37). Glory? Jesus had just explained that his mission would involve humiliation, mocking, folks spitting on him, flogging him, and killing him. How discouraging it must have been for Jesus to hear these "concerns" after he had just explained for the third time where his ministry was leading.

The brothers were not envisioning heavenly glory. They were still thinking in terms of Jesus taking control of the government of Judea and setting himself up to rule the world from Jerusalem. Earlier in this chapter the rich man turned away from following Jesus because he could not let go of his socioeconomic prestige to be a disciple. Ironically, the argument about greatness among the disciples and the request of James and John suggest that they might have preferred a form of discipleship that would have permitted them some sort of prestige or influence as well.

Sadly, ambition always has the potential of influencing human relationships, even in the church. James and John are no different from others who desire power and status in human organizations. Each of us must examine our motives when we make requests of Jesus. This story is somewhat embarrassing to the Christian church, because it casts a poor light on the disciples. Ambition always makes persons of faith look shabby in the eyes of the world. Christians need to beware of the selfish desire that can cloud our vision and tarnish our witness.

Jesus Responds to Human Ambition

A wise and thoughtful woman in my first parish once gave me this advice. "Don't pray for patience." "Why not?" I naively asked. "Well," she said, "You know how you get it!" Be careful what you pray for! That is what Jesus is telling James and John. Essentially, Jesus says, "Sitting at my right hand and left hand is not mine to grant, but in order to be eligible, you are going to have to endure the same suffering that is about to befall me."

Discipleship is not a matter of power and prestige, but a matter of service. Oftentimes these days we talk of empowering groups within the church and in society. That some persons and groups have been ill-treated through the years is beyond question. Certainly we want to work to help redress the wrongs of the past. Certainly God intends that the rights of every person be respected. Certainly we are called to advocate for the rights of the marginalized and the oppressed. But fundamentally, God's kingdom is not about power; it is about serving others. It involves voluntary self-sacrifice in order that the entire community can be enhanced. Jesus makes it clear that power comes from God alone. Jesus is attempting to be faithful to God's call, and he expects the same devotion from his disciples. The disciples must surrender their ingrained ideas of honor and dishonor, power and weakness. Jesus' twenty-first century disciples need to surrender our ingrained ideas as well. As long as we measure our successes and failures by the standards of the world, we will fail to grasp the essence of Jesus' teaching.

Jesus Defines True Greatness

How hard it is to make the shift from power to servanthood as the measure of true greatness. Everything we have been taught pulls us the other way. All of our empirical evidence is on the side of the world. Yet upon reflection we see the logic in Jesus' teaching.

Recall Saint Francis of Assisi, who stripped himself of every stitch of clothing his cloth merchant father had given him, and devoted his life to the poor. Recall Mother Teresa, who spent her life on the streets of Calcutta ministering to those society had left abandoned to die. Each of us can name persons who are far less famous, yet whose faithful and devoted service has been an inspiration to us. These folks will have a far greater impact upon the world than the contemporary leaders of business and government who are enjoying a brief season in the spotlight of worldly power.

In the end, Jesus gave his life as "a ransom for many" (10:45). Jesus made the ultimate sacrifice. He served God's purposes even in death. His example of selfless love is a pattern in which his followers are called to participate. For some in our day, as in the first century, following Jesus may lead to martyrdom. For all of us, following Jesus means allowing God to change our value system, reorder our priorities, and use our lives in faithful service. Ultimately, living for Jesus may be just as costly as dying for him. The way of self-sacrifice is never easy. Jesus shows us the way. May each of us have the courage to follow.

SHARING THE SCRIPTURE

PREPARING TO TEACH

Preparing Our Hearts

This week's devotional reading is found in Matthew 20:20-28. The story of James and John's mother asking Jesus to honor her sons creates quite a stir among the other ten disciples. As you read this passage, envision yourself at the scene. How are you like each of the characters? Which character are you most like? How do you see yourself as a servant— or do you shun this role? How are Jesus' teachings about service as the path to greatness in conflict with the messages your culture sends?

Pray that you and your students will seek greatness by following Jesus' example and humbly serving others.

Preparing Our Minds

Study the background scripture, Mark 10:13-45, especially verses 32-45, which comprise today's lesson passage. Compare Mark's version with the account in Matthew 20:20-28. What similarities and differences do you note?

Write on newsprint:

the preparation for next week's session.

Plan a lecture, if you choose that option, for "Hear Jesus' Teachings About Service and True Greatness."

Gather the supplies you will need if you plan to do the collage(s) for Gather to Learn.

LEADING THE CLASS

(1) Gather to Learn

❖ Welcome the class members and introduce any guests.

❖ Pray that the students will strive to become great people, as Jesus describes greatness.

❖ Brainstorm with the class answers to this question: **What are the marks of true greatness according to our society?** You may do this activity in one of two ways.

Option 1: List ideas on newsprint. Leave the newsprint posted and refer to it as the session continues.

Option 2: Provide magazine pictures, scissors, glue, and poster board. Invite the students to make one (or more, depending on the size of the class) collage showing examples of people our society would label as great. These do not have to be famous people, but they should look like people who have money, status, and power. Artistic ability is not important to make this collage; pictures are arranged at random and glued to the poster board. Display the collages where everyone can see them throughout the session.

❖ Raise the idea that Jesus had a different idea of greatness. Today we'll focus on his teachings about the relationship between service and greatness.

❖ Read aloud today's focus statement: **Everybody wants to be great. What is the way of greatness? Jesus says that true greatness comes through serving others.**

(2) Hear Jesus' Teachings About Service and True Greatness

❖ Choose volunteers to read Mark 10:32-45 as a drama. You will need a narrator and people to read the parts of Jesus, James, and John.

❖ Invite the class members to envision themselves within the scene as they answer these questions. Use information from Understanding the Scripture either to augment the discussion, or as the foundation for a lecture that you will give based on these questions.

(1) **Do you think the disciples, especially James and John, really understood what Jesus had told them in verses 32-34? What are the reasons for your answer?**

(2) **Why do you suppose James and John made the request? What did they expect to gain?**

(3) **What would you have said privately to James and John had you been one of the other ten disciples?**

(4) **How might you have responded to Jesus' teachings that service is the key to greatness?**

(3) Compare Definitions of Greatness

❖ Call attention to the list of words or collage(s) made earlier in the session to illustrate society's understanding of greatness.

❖ Talk frankly about the challenges Christians face in living in a society where greatness is often measured in terms of one's status, power, and material possessions.

❖ Post a sheet of newsprint. Encourage the students to suggest ways that society's definition of "greatness" needs to be changed in order to conform to Jesus' understanding of greatness. Record their ideas.

❖ Pose this question for discussion in pairs or small teams: **What changes can we make as individuals and as a group to live more faithfully according to Jesus' teachings on greatness?**

❖ Bring the class together and discuss their ideas. Encourage the class members to commit themselves to trying at least one of these ideas.

(4) Identify Opportunities for Service

❖ Create a graffiti board on a wall by posting butcher paper or several sheets of newsprint. Set out markers.

❖ Ask the students to go to the graffiti board and write the name and/or a brief description of at least one service project within the church or community. If the group is large, ask three people to go to the board and take turns writing ideas as students make suggestions.

❖ Give the students a few moments to look at everything that has been written. Ask them to write their names near any project that they personally support. If the group is large, you may have to omit this step.

❖ Discuss these questions.

(1) **What do these projects suggest about what our church or community thinks is important?**

(2) **What does the amount of support (financial and volunteer) that we are giving to these projects suggest about our commitment to them?**

(3) **What are some other ways that we might become involved in these projects?**

(4) **Would Jesus say that our commitments of time, talent, and money to these projects are moving us toward greatness? Support your answer.**

❖ Distribute paper and pencils. Encourage the students to consider prayerfully whatever additional individual commitments they can make to these projects. Ask them to write down their intention.

(5) Continue the Journey

❖ Call the group back together and pray that as Christians we may take Jesus' teachings regarding greatness seriously and so commit ourselves to giving as much of our time and resources as possible to serving others.

❖ Suggest that the students put their written commitments in their Bibles, wallets, handbags, or some other place where they will see and remember them.

❖ Read aloud this preparation for next week's lesson. You may also want to post it on newsprint for the students to copy. **Prepare for next week's session, "Overcoming Grief," by reading Ruth 1, especially 1:3-8 and 14-18. Keep this focus in mind as you read: People are sometimes** overwhelmed by a devastating loss. **How do we deal with significant losses? In committing herself to Naomi, Ruth embraced the God of Israel, who helped them overcome their hardships. Within her grief, Ruth reached out to Naomi in support and true friendship.**

❖ Read aloud the following three ideas. Challenge the students to commit themselves to use these activities as a springboard to spiritual growth.

(1) **Commit yourself to some form of service, perhaps one that is new to you. Periodically check the written commitment that you made on Sunday to see how faithfully you are fulfilling your promise.**

(2) **Make a list in words or pictures of the kinds of service that you currently perform.**

(3) **Page through your calendar for the previous month (or the upcoming month). Estimate the amount of time you spend serving others. Reflect on whether your commitment to service is in keeping with God's call on your life. If not, what changes will you make?**

❖ Sing or read aloud "Lord, Whose Love Through Humble Service."

❖ Ask the students to echo this benediction as you read it phrase by phrase: **Grant, O Lord, that what has been said with our lips we may believe in our hearts, and that what we believe in our hearts we may practice in our lives; through Jesus Christ our Lord. Amen.**

UNIT 3: WHOSOEVER WILL—COME!
OVERCOMING GRIEF

PREVIEWING THE LESSON

Lesson Scripture: Ruth 1:3-8, 14-18
Background Scripture: Ruth 1
Key Verse: Ruth 1:16

Focus of the Lesson:
People are sometimes overwhelmed by a devastating loss. How do we deal with significant losses? In committing herself to Naomi, Ruth embraced the God of Israel, who helped them overcome their hardships. Within her grief, Ruth reached out to Naomi in support and true friendship.

Goals for the Learners:
(1) to encounter the story of Ruth and Naomi.
(2) to identify some of the significant losses people face today.
(3) to identify and express gratitude for sources of support that can help them when facing significant loss.

Pronunciation Guide:

Chilion	(kil'ee uhn)	Mahlon	(mah'lon)
Elimelech	(i lim' u lek)	Moab	(moh'ab)
Ephrathite	(ef' ruh thit)	Orpah	(or'puh)
levirate	(lev' uh rit)	Tamar	(tay' mahr)

Supplies:
Bibles, newsprint and marker, paper and pencils, hymnals

READING THE SCRIPTURE

NRSV
Ruth 1:1-3, 14-18

In the days when the judges ruled, there was a famine in the land, and a certain man of Bethlehem in Judah went to live in the country of Moab, he and his wife and two sons. 2 The name of the man was Elimelech and the name of his wife Naomi, and the names of his two sons were Mahlon and

NIV
Ruth 1:1-3, 14-18

In the days when the judges ruled, there was a famine in the land, and a man from Bethlehem in Judah, together with his wife and two sons, went to live for a while in the country of Moab. ²The man's name was Elimelech, his wife's name Naomi, and the names of his two sons were Mahlon and

Chilion; they were Ephrathites from Bethlehem in Judah. They went into the country of Moab and remained there. 3 But Elimelech, the husband of Naomi, died, and she was left with her two sons.

14 Then they wept aloud again. Orpah kissed her mother-in-law, but Ruth clung to her.

15 So she said, "See, your sister-in-law has gone back to her people and to her gods; return after your sister-in-law." **16 But Ruth said,**

**"Do not press me to leave you
    or to turn back from following you!
Where you go, I will go;
    where you lodge, I will lodge;
your people shall be my people,
    and your God my God.**

17 Where you die, I will die—
    there will I be buried.
May the LORD do thus and so to me,
    and more as well,
if even death parts me from you!"

18 When Naomi saw that she was determined to go with her, she said no more to her.

Kilion. They were Ephrathites from Bethlehem, Judah. And they went to Moab and lived there.

³Now Elimelech, Naomi's husband, died, and she was left with her two sons.

¹⁴At this they wept again. Then Orpah kissed her mother-in-law good-by, but Ruth clung to her.

¹⁵"Look," said Naomi, "your sister-in-law is going back to her people and her gods. Go back with her."

¹⁶**But Ruth replied, "Don't urge me to leave you or to turn back from you. Where you go I will go, and where you stay I will stay. Your people will be my people and your God my God.** ¹⁷Where you die I will die, and there I will be buried. May the LORD deal with me, be it ever so severely, if anything but death separates you and me." ¹⁸When Naomi realized that Ruth was determined to go with her, she stopped urging her.

UNDERSTANDING THE SCRIPTURE

Ruth 1:1. The book of Ruth is a short story that begins with a "once upon a time" flavor. The fact that this story takes place "in the days when judges ruled" may indicate that the narrator wants to connect the beginning of Ruth with the end of the Judges. From Bethlehem will come King David, a descendant of Ruth, who will rule Israel in a much more competent way than that of the Judges. That the account of Ruth is based on a solid historical tradition is generally accepted. The story of David's Moabite ancestry is hardly something that would have been invented in the postexilic period.

As Abraham and Jacob went to Egypt in time of famine, so Elimelech and his wife

Naomi and their two sons take refuge in Moab.

Ruth 1:2. Elimelech's family are said to be "Ephrathites," which in this context seems to be the name of a clan. Other places in the Old Testament are mentioned too. Ephrathath is simply another name for Bethlehem. To the ears of an Israelite audience, almost any reference to Moab would have carried negative connotations, as Moab was a country that was continually cast in a negative light in biblical narratives written earlier.

Ruth 1:3-5. The names given Naomi's sons are symbolic of the short-lived role they will play in the story. According to commentators, "Mahlon" sounds like the disease that hit the Egyptians before the Exodus, and "Chilion" seems to come from the root meaning "to perish." Both Mahlon and Chilion took foreign wives, a practice condemned in Nehemiah 13:25.

Ruth 1:6-7. Although she and her family had looked for a more abundant life in Moab, Naomi experienced the devastating blow of death there instead. So the three widows set out to return to Bethlehem.

Ruth 1:8-10. Naomi wants her sons' brides to remarry. Her statement in verse 9 makes it clear that urging each of them to go back to their "mother's house" is equivalent to encouraging them to look for new husbands. Going back to the mother's house is a first step in the process that will allow them to find "rest" or "security" in another husband's home. Naomi's wish implies that both of her son's wives have been kind and loyal to their husbands and to her beyond the call of duty. Naomi hopes the Lord will follow *their* example. The affection of Ruth and Orpah for their Judean mother-in-law is shown by their desire to go with her and by their tears.

Ruth 1:11-13. When the younger women say they would rather return with Naomi to her home than return to their own homes, Naomi tries to argue persuasively that they would be better off going back to their own mothers' houses. Naomi's reasoning is apparently based on what was known as the "levirate marriage" practice. According to Deuteronomy 25:5-10, if an Israelite man died before he produced any offspring, his brother was expected to marry his widow and to allow the firstborn son of that union to be considered the son of his deceased brother. Naomi knows that she is not able to provide Orpah and Ruth with the husbands she thinks they need. The questions Naomi asks in verse 13 remind the reader of the story of Tamar and Judah (Genesis 38), which illustrates how levirate marriage customs were supposed to work. Naomi's final argument has to do with her own apparently hopeless situation. The future may seem uncertain for Orpah and Ruth, but Naomi thinks her own situation is worse than theirs. They might remarry and have children, but Naomi seems to have no hope. Naomi is bitter, and she blames the Lord for bringing about the situation in which she finds herself. She does not think the Lord has dealt kindly with her at all.

Ruth 1:14. Both daughters-in-law weep. Orpah, having been persuaded by Naomi's argument, kisses Naomi good-bye. But unlike Orpah, Ruth is not persuaded. She "clings" to her mother-in-law.

Ruth 1:15. The persistence of Naomi in trying to dissuade Ruth from accompanying her emphasizes Naomi's concern for Ruth's welfare. Naomi does not chide Orpah for returning to her own gods. Her interest is in the welfare of her daughters-in-law, not in making proselytes.

Ruth 1:16-17. Unlike Orpah, who is not given a speaking part in the story, Ruth makes a lengthy, forceful, and impassioned speech that dismisses all Naomi's arguments as irrelevant. Ruth is indignant because Naomi urges her to abandon her present loyalties and to turn her back on her previous commitments. The word translated "leave" connotes "changing primary allegiance." Ruth uses verbs that state her intentions for the future: "I will go"; "I will lodge"; "I will die," and "I will be buried." She has already committed herself to the family into which she married. In effect, Ruth is saying, "Your God *is* my God, and your people *are* my people, therefore where you go I will go, and where you lodge I will lodge."

Ruth 1:18. The Hebrew can be understood in two ways. Either Naomi stopped urging Ruth to go back, or Naomi stopped speaking to Ruth altogether.

Ruth 1:19. Was the whole town stirred because Naomi was accompanied by an outsider?

Ruth 1:20-21. Naomi tells her story. Her change of name indicates a change in status. She has formerly been known as "the pleasant one." Now she will be known as "bitter."

Ruth 1:22. In the homecoming scene (1:19-21), Naomi is so focused on her own bitterness that she ignores the presence of Ruth. Now the narrator reminds us that

Ruth is very much in the picture. Naomi has returned empty, but it is "the beginning of the barley harvest" in Bethlehem. The promise of better days for Ruth and Naomi is on the horizon.

INTERPRETING THE SCRIPTURE

A Family Is Faced with Devastating Loss

Part of the reason the Bible continues to be a best-seller is that its stories are true to life. We read Naomi's story with interest, for all of us have experienced the pain of loss in our lives. Early in my ministry a two-year old boy was shot as the result of a robbery and police chase. He was the innocent victim of the evil of others. His tragic wounding shocked the entire community. More recently, several large companies in our greater metropolitan area have announced plans for reorganization that will result in significant job losses in our area. Nearly every week I hear of someone in our community who has lost a job. Unfortunately, in contemporary society, because so much of our self-worth is tied to our work, job loss often brings loss of self-esteem as well.

No wonder Naomi was bitter. She and her family had gone to Moab in order to escape the famine in Israel. They had pulled up stakes and moved, seeking a better life. Instead of prospering, Naomi's husband died, followed by both of her sons. In my congregation last fall a woman died of medical complications. Six weeks later her husband died. The grief experienced by the extended family soon became almost overwhelming. A year before, they had celebrated Christmas together in the family homestead. Last Christmas there were no parents and grandparents with them to celebrate.

Several years ago some psychologists developed a chart of stressors and assigned a number to each, approximating the level of trauma a person would experience in each crisis. Change of job, for example, would be lower on the list than divorce or loss of a spouse. The idea was to help people look at their lives and assess their level of stress. When we face devastating loss, where and to whom do we turn?

The Widows Seek to Comfort One Another

On September 11, 2001, the world changed. On that day any naïveté that Americans had about our invulnerability was shattered as terrorists attacked the World Trade Center, a symbol of our economy, and the Pentagon, a symbol of our government and military prowess. It is fair to say that the entire world was shaken by these events. For those in the caring professions the events of September 11 proved to be especially challenging. Not only did our workload suddenly increase dramatically, but we were also dealing with our own feelings of devastation and loss.

Naomi and her daughter-in-law had to deal with the loss of their own spouses. They also sought to console each other. They were not afraid to share their grief, for the text tells us that "they wept aloud" (1:14). I worry when people experience the death of a loved one, but shed no tears. Tears can bring relief and help begin the healing process. In spite of the fact that stoicism is often held up as the ideal in our society, I believe that it takes a stronger person to allow the tears to flow, and to admit one's vulnerability. That Ruth, Orpah, and

Naomi expressed their grief openly was therapeutic for them and instructive for us.

The widows used different methods in coping with their losses. Naomi blamed God for her plight. Note that she was not condemned or criticized for her statements. Biblical people expressed their anger with God. That can be therapeutic! God can handle our anger. If we shake our fist at God, we are in good company. The psalmist, the prophets, and many other biblical characters expressed their frustration with God as well.

Orpah decided to return to her family. Again, the biblical narrator does not condemn Orpah for her actions, nor should we. Sometimes we need to take a step back when trouble comes into our lives. What in our past do we need to reclaim? How can we draw upon our past for the resources we need to help us through times of current crisis?

Ruth, on the other hand, "clung" to Naomi. That Ruth desired to stay with Naomi shows not only her love for her mother-in-law, but also hints at the strength she obviously drew from the faith that she had learned through their relationship.

I know three different families within a single congregation who have recently lost a young family member to cancer. They are receiving the ministry of the church, but they are also ministering to one another. They know the pain of loss that the others are bearing. As theologian and writer Henri Nouwen observed, they are "wounded healers." Naomi, Ruth, and Orpah ministered to one another's needs, while drying the tears from their own eyes.

Ruth Pledges Her Loyalty to Naomi

"Where you go, I will go; where you lodge, I will lodge; your people shall be my people, and your God my God" (1:16, today's key verse). These beautiful and moving words are often spoken or sung at weddings at the couple's request.

Prospective brides and grooms are sometimes surprised to learn that originally these words were spoken not by lovers in a candlelight ceremony, but by a young widow addressing her mother-in-law. After the death of her husband, Ruth was neither legally required nor expected to remain with her mother-in-law. Thus her speech must be understood as an act showing love and loyalty over and above what was considered customary.

From time to time I hear reports of relatives, friends, and even neighbors who demonstrate caring beyond the normal expectation. In our contemporary society, where family members may be separated by hundreds of miles, persons in the community often rise to the occasion and care for one another in times of need. Such stories rarely make the six o'clock news. But love and loyalty are still the keys to the healing process when people experience grief and loss. Ruth could not be dissuaded from staying with Naomi in her hour of need. Her devotion is instructive, not only for newlyweds, but also for us all.

Naomi Accepts Ruth's Ministry of Love

My mother had a friend who was always doing nice things for her and for our family. The problem was, the friend would never let my mother do anything in return. Once my mom baked a pie and took it to the friend's home to say "thank you" for her many kindnesses. The next day, the friend showed up at our door with a seven-layer cake! When my mom took this friend to lunch, her friend insisted on picking up the check. Some people have a hard time accepting the ministry of others. Can you think of anyone who fits that description?

Naomi did her best to convince Ruth to go back home. Maybe Naomi did not want to have to explain a Moabite daughter-in-law, for Naomi's people had despised the Moabites for generations. Perhaps Naomi felt she had enough to deal with, without the burden of confronting the prejudices of her hometown. Certainly the story demonstrates that Naomi was looking out for Ruth's welfare, too. She did not want to see Ruth suffer the poverty of widowhood, which was almost inevitable in that society. If Ruth went back to her own people, Naomi reasoned, Ruth would have a better chance of getting remarried.

However, Ruth refused to take "no" for an answer. Perhaps Ruth sensed that Naomi needed the care and attention of someone she knew and trusted. Ruth had also adopted the religion of her husband's family, a faith that brought her great comfort. She could practice her faith more openly if she returned to Bethlehem with Naomi.

Finally Naomi gave in. She allowed Ruth to accompany her and accepted Ruth's ministry of love. If we are going to experience healing after we have suffered loss in this life, we need to accept the ministry of others. It is a basic tenet of our Judeo-Christian faith that God works through other people. Will we resist the ministry of others, or will we open ourselves to what God may be trying to do through them?

SHARING THE SCRIPTURE

PREPARING TO TEACH

Preparing Our Hearts

This week's devotional reading is found in Psalm 31:9-15. In this lament, the psalmist cries out in his grief, trusting God to deliver him. What grief have you had to bear, especially in the last year? Did you turn toward or turn away from God in the midst of your sorrow? What have you learned from experiences of grief? Can you truly say with the psalmist, "My times are in your hand?"

Pray that you and your students will be willing to trust God to be present with you in grief and to help you overcome your sadness.

Preparing Our Minds

Study the background from Ruth 1 and the lesson scripture from Ruth 1:3-8, 14-18.

The book of Ruth is short, so if you have time this week, try to skim all four chapters. Consider why this book, which only tells us about a single family, is important enough to be included in the Bible.

Write on newsprint:

    the preparation for next week's session.

Plan lectures and also a Bible study, as suggested under "Encounter the Story of Ruth and Naomi."

LEADING THE CLASS

(1) Gather to Learn

❖ Welcome the class members and introduce any guests.

❖ Encourage the students to talk about losses that their country or community has experienced in recent years. They may think about losing a sense of security after the events of September 11, 2001, or about losing armed forces personnel in a war with Afghanistan or Iraq. Be sensitive to personal losses that class members have experienced recently. Some may want to speak about their individual grief.

❖ Note that loss and death and grief are part of the human condition. We all have grieved and/or will grieve losses. Therefore, the story we will study today speaks not only of the losses one family sustained centuries ago but also addresses the same kinds of losses that we continue to experience.

❖ Read aloud today's focus statement:

People are sometimes overwhelmed by a devastating loss. How do we deal with significant losses? In committing herself to Naomi, Ruth embraced the God of Israel, who helped them overcome their hardships. Within her grief, Ruth reached out to Naomi in support and true friendship.

(2) Encounter the Story of Ruth and Naomi

❖ Ask a volunteer to read Ruth 1:3-8.

❖ Create a lecture using information from Understanding the Scripture to explain:

Point 1: why Elimelech's Judean family was in Moab.

Point 2: what is known about Mahlon and Chilion.

Point 3: Naomi's reason for returning to Judah.

Point 4: what Naomi was really saying to Orpah and Ruth when she told them to return to their mother's houses. (If time permits, include an explanation of levirate marriage, from verses 11-13 in Understanding the Scripture, and why this type of marriage would not be possible for Orpah and Ruth.)

Point 5: the kind of relationship the reader can surmise that Naomi had with her daughters-in-law, based on what she tells them.

❖ Do a Bible study of the following verses to show the provisions that were to be made in the face of the powerlessness and economic hardship that widows faced: Exodus 22:22-24; Deuteronomy 24:19-22; Isaiah 1:17; Jeremiah 7:5-7, 22:3; Zechariah 7:8-10. Either present this information in a lecture, or divide the class into groups, assign each group one passage, and have the groups report to the entire class.

❖ Choose a narrator and two other volunteers, one to read the words of Naomi and one to read Ruth's part. Ask them to read Ruth 1:14-18 as a drama.

❖ Invite the class to discuss these points. Use information from "The Widows Seek to Comfort One Another" in the Interpreting the Scripture to add to the discussion. Or, create a lecture from this information.

(1) The way the three women coped with their grief.

(2) Ruth's extraordinary pledge of loyalty.

(3) Naomi's reluctance to accept Ruth's offer.

(4) Naomi's acceptance of Ruth's ministry of love.

(3) Identify Significant Losses People Face Today

❖ Invite the students to brainstorm a list of losses that people face today. List these ideas on newsprint. Some losses will be universal, such as the death of a loved one or loss of one's own health. Others may be more related to the society in which we live, such as the loss of a spouse due to divorce, financial losses on the stock market, loss of a job due to downsizing, loss of one's home due to bankruptcy.

❖ Encourage the students to talk about how people cope with various losses. You may want to divide into small groups so that everyone has an opportunity to participate.

(4) Express Gratitude for Support in Times of Loss

❖ Distribute paper and pencils. Ask the students to recall a significant loss. Encourage them to express gratitude for support they received by doing one of these activities.

Option 1: Write a thank-you note to someone who offered support to you. You may even choose to write to someone who is now deceased. The point here is to express your gratitude.

Option 2: Play joyous music and invite the students to move and/or dance to it as they recall with gratitude help they have received.

Option 3: Talk with a partner about how God helped you deal with a significant loss. Close the discussion by expressing gratitude to God in prayer.

❖ Bring the class back together and invite the students to comment on any insights related to how comfort and support during time of loss can strengthen one's faith.

(5) Continue the Journey

❖ Pray that the students will walk closely with God in times of loss and grief, and that they will support others as they work to overcome their grief.

❖ Read aloud this preparation for next week's lesson. You may also want to post it on newsprint for the students to copy. **Prepare for next week's session, "Overcoming Pride," by reading background scripture from 2 Kings 5, especially the lesson scripture from 5:1-5, 9-15a. As you read, pay particular attention to this focus statement: Pride is often hard to overcome. How do we overcome pride to receive the help we need? When Naaman overcame his reluctance to listen to advice, he received healing and accepted the God of Israel.**

❖ Read aloud the following three ideas. Challenge the students to commit themselves to use these activities as a springboard to spiritual growth.

(1) Offer comfort and support to someone who is grieving a significant loss.

(2) Volunteer your time and talent or send financial support to a reputable agency that assists persons who are displaced because of difficult circumstances in their own country.

(3) Consider joining a caregivers support group, a widows group, or other support group where you can share your experiences and also learn from others how to cope with similar situations.

❖ Sing or read aloud "Come, Ye Disconsolate" or "You Are Mine."

❖ Ask the students to echo this benediction as you read it phrase by phrase: **Grant, O Lord, that what has been said with our lips we may believe in our hearts, and that what we believe in our hearts we may practice in our lives; through Jesus Christ our Lord. Amen.**

OVERCOMING PRIDE

PREVIEWING THE LESSON

Lesson Scripture: 2 Kings 5:1-5, 9-15*b*
Background Scripture: 2 Kings 5
Key Verses: 2 Kings 5:13-14

Focus of the Lesson:
Pride is often hard to overcome. How do we overcome pride to receive the help we need? When Naaman overcame his reluctance to listen to advice, he received healing and accepted the God of Israel.

Goals for the Learners:
(1) to encounter the story of Naaman.
(2) to explore ways that pride and prejudice keep us from hearing God's voice in others today.
(3) to examine ways that pride can be destructive to relationships and list ways to overcome it.

Pronunciation Guide:

Abana	(ab' uh nuh)	Elisha	(i li' shuh)
Aram	(air' uhm)	Naaman	(nay' uh muhn)
Aramean	(air uh mee' uhn)	Pharpar	(fahr' pahr)

Supplies:
Bibles, newsprint and marker, paper and pencils, optional drawing supplies, hymnals

---

READING THE SCRIPTURE

NRSV
2 Kings 5:1-5, 9-15*b*

Naaman, commander of the army of the king of Aram, was a great man and in high favor with his master, because by him the LORD had given victory to Aram. The man, though a mighty warrior, suffered from leprosy. 2 Now the Arameans on one of their

NIV
2 Kings 5:1-5, 9-15*b*

Now Naaman was commander of the army of the king of Aram. He was a great man in the sight of his master and highly regarded, because through him the LORD had given victory to Aram. He was a valiant soldier, but he had leprosy.

raids had taken a young girl captive from the land of Israel, and she served Naaman's wife. 3 She said to her mistress, "If only my lord were with the prophet who is in Samaria! He would cure him of his leprosy." 4 So Naaman went in and told his lord just what the girl from the land of Israel had said. 5 And the king of Aram said, "Go then, and I will send along a letter to the king of Israel."

9 So Naaman came with his horses and chariots, and halted at the entrance of Elisha's house. 10 Elisha sent a messenger to him, saying, "Go, wash in the Jordan seven times, and your flesh shall be restored and you shall be clean." 11 But Naaman became angry and went away, saying, "I thought that for me he would surely come out, and stand and call on the name of the LORD his God, and would wave his hand over the spot, and cure the leprosy! 12 Are not Abana and Pharpar, the rivers of Damascus, better than all the waters of Israel? Could I not wash in them, and be clean?" He turned and went away in a rage. **13 But his servants approached and said to him, "Father, if the prophet had commanded you to do something difficult, would you not have done it? How much more, when all he said to you was, "Wash, and be clean?" 14 So he went down and immersed himself seven times in the Jordan**, according to the word of the man of God; his flesh was restored like the flesh of a young boy, and he was clean.

15 Then he returned to the man of God, he and all his company; he came and stood before him and said, "Now I know that there is no God in all the earth except in Israel."

[2]Now bands from Aram had gone out and had taken captive a young girl from Israel, and she served Naaman's wife. [3]She said to her mistress, "If only my master would see the prophet who is in Samaria! He would cure him of his leprosy."

[4]Naaman went to his master and told him what the girl from Israel had said. [5]"By all means, go," the king of Aram replied. "I will send a letter to the king of Israel." So Naaman left, taking with him ten talents of silver, six thousand shekels of gold and ten sets of clothing.

[9]So Naaman went with his horses and chariots and stopped at the door of Elisha's house. [10]Elisha sent a messenger to say to him, "Go, wash yourself seven times in the Jordan, and your flesh will be restored and you will be cleansed."

[11]But Naaman went away angry and said, "I thought that he would surely come out to me and stand and call on the name of the LORD his God, wave his hand over the spot and cure me of my leprosy. [12]Are not Abana and Pharpar, the rivers of Damascus, better than any of the waters of Israel? Couldn't I wash in them and be cleansed?" So he turned and went off in a rage.

[13]**Naaman's servants went to him and said, "My father, if the prophet had told you to do some great thing, would you not have done it? How much more, then, when he tells you, 'Wash and be cleansed!' [14]So he went down and dipped himself in the Jordan seven times,** as the man of God had told him, and his flesh was restored and became clean like that of a young boy.

[15]Then Naaman and all his attendants went back to the man of God. He stood before him and said, "Now I know that there is no God in all the world except in Israel."

UNDERSTANDING THE SCRIPTURE

2 Kings 5:1. The story of the healing of Naaman is one of the most fascinating in the book of Kings. It is an entertaining drama with a rich cast of characters, a well-developed plot, many ironic twists and turns, keen insights into human flaws, and a satisfying conclusion. The story begins with Naaman, a military commander of Damascus, who is favored by the king of Aram (ancient Syria). Naaman's army has been victorious over Israel. Israel's defeat is explained by saying that Naaman's victory has been granted by the Lord, for in Israelite theology no foreign army can be victorious over Israel unless it is by the will of God. Naaman is a "great man" but he is also a leper. Most scholars now agree that the Hebrew word for "leprosy" does not refer to what we know as Hansen's disease, but to skin afflictions of various sorts that carried a social stigma and the threat of death.

2 Kings 5:2. Ironically, help for this "great man" will come by way of a "young girl" from Israel, captured by the Arameans on one of their raids.

2 Kings 5:3. Elisha has already gained a reputation for performing miracles.

2 Kings 5:4-6. The young girl's proposal makes it all the way to the king of Aram, who sends a letter to the king of Israel, presumably Jehoram (3:1). Diplomatic arrangements were necessary in order for the Aramean general who squelched Israel to be allowed to visit Samaria in a time of peace. Naaman goes to Samaria with an extravagant load of gifts and a letter to the king.

2 Kings 5:7. The king of Israel is greatly disturbed by the letter, for the king assumes that he is expected to perform the miracle himself. The king knows that curing Naaman is not something any human being can accomplish. Only God has the power of life and death. Is this a new challenge from the Arameans? The king sees the letter as a political threat. He does not seem to know that there is a prophet in Israel who can perform the miracle.

2 Kings 5:8. Hearing of the king's despair, Elisha sends a messenger to convey his willingness to help, in order that Naaman "may learn that there is a prophet in Israel."

2 Kings 5:9-10. Naaman arrives at Elisha's house with an impressive entourage, but Elisha does not even come out to meet this "great man." Elisha merely sends instructions through a messenger that Naaman should wash seven times in the Jordan River, promising that his flesh will be restored as the result, and that Naaman will then be free of the dread disease. "Seven times" is consistent with the instructions for ritual cleansing in Leviticus 14.

2 Kings 5:11-12. Naaman is indignant with what he perceives as rude treatment by Elisha. In his mind's eye, the general had pictured the healing: Elisha would come out, call on the name of the Lord, wave his hand over the spot and cure Naaman's leprosy. According to commentators, the order of the words in Hebrew suggests a wounded ego: "I thought that *for me* he would surely come out." Naaman's honor and his national pride are offended. If he merely must wash in a river, he could have done that in his own country. Why make the trip to Israel? Surely the local rivers of Damascus—the Abana and the Pharpar—are better than the muddy Jordan. So he turns away in rage.

2 Kings 5:13. Naaman's servants point out that he would no doubt have gone to great lengths to do what Elisha instructed had it been something difficult. Why not give the simple directions a chance to succeed?

2 Kings 5:14. To his credit, for all Naaman's greatness and pride, he is able to listen to the advice of his servants. Thus, Naaman follows Elisha's instructions and is healed, just as the prophet had promised. His flesh is restored like that of a "young boy" and Naaman is free of leprosy. His body is whole!

2 Kings 5:15-16. Naaman now recognizes that "there is no God in all the earth except in Israel." In gratitude for his healing, Naaman wishes to give Elisha a gift, but Elisha persistently refuses.

2 Kings 5:17-19a. Naaman assumes that Israel's God can be worshiped only on

Israelite soil. Hence his proposal to take some of that soil home, since he does not want to offer burnt offerings and sacrifices to other gods. At the same time, he asks pardon in advance for one exception to his vow. On state occasions Naaman, as the Syrian king's right-hand man, will have to accompany the king to worship Rimmon, the stormgod or "thunderer," the patron god of the Arameans. Elisha replies with neither condemnation nor permission, but tells Naaman to "go in peace."

2 Kings 5:19b-20. Elisha has been firm that he will not accept any gifts from Naaman. Elisha's servant Gehazi thinks that the prophet has been too easy on Naaman, and decides to seize this opportunity for personal gain.

2 Kings 5:21-24. Gehazi lies to Naaman by saying that Elisha has changed his mind about the gift because two prophets have suddenly arrived, and Elisha needs the gifts in order to provide adequate hospitality. Gehazi's lie is credible because his request is relatively modest. He asks for only a small fraction of what Naaman had brought. Gehazi's deviousness stands in contrast to the graciousness of Naaman, who urges him to take twice the amount of cash requested, packages the money and clothing nicely, and has his servants carry the packages for Gehazi. As soon as Gehazi returns to the capital he sends the helpers away and hides the gifts.

2 Kings 5:25-27. When questioned, Gehazi proceeds to lie to Elisha, saying that he has not gone anywhere. However, Elisha knows differently. As punishment, Gehazi will be afflicted with Naaman's leprosy, as will his descendants.

INTERPRETING THE SCRIPTURE

Is There Hope for Naaman?

The older we get, the more important health and wellness issues become. The Bible tells us that Naaman, the commander of the Aramean king's army, was a capable and highly respected leader. In short, he was a "great man." However, Naaman suffered from the dread disease of leprosy. Although they were unsure of its origin and ignorant of how it spread, biblical people feared this skin disease, and forced those who exhibited its symptoms to live apart from the rest of the community. In Leviticus, the people were given specific instructions for dealing with leprosy: "The person who has the leprous disease shall wear torn clothes and let the hair of his head be disheveled; and he shall cover his upper lip and cry out, 'Unclean, unclean' " (Leviticus 13:45).

Obviously, it was a disease that everyone feared. As a diagnosed leper, it was only a matter of time until Naaman would have been forced to leave his position of prominence in the king's army and move to a leper colony.

It is hard to imagine an equivalent to the ancient treatment of lepers in our society today. The fear of AIDS has caused many to ostracize those whose medical condition they do not understand. Hopefully, education and compassion will carry the day in cases where our brothers and sisters are afflicted with such deadly diseases.

The tone of 2 Kings 5 is one that emphasizes the inclusive love of God. It never occurred to the young girl who is a captive of the Arameans that her God would refuse to cure Naaman because he was a "foreigner." The God she knew was a God of love who showed compassion for all persons. In like manner, Elisha erects no barriers of race, class, or creed. He offers God's healing to Naaman without expecting the Aramean army general to make a confession of faith.

Is there hope for Naaman? According to the young Israelite girl and the prophet Elisha, there is. As persons of faith we are called to affirm that God's saving grace is available to all people. God can bring help and healing to those who suffer from physical and spiritual ills. There is hope for every person whom God created. There is hope for you and for me.

Naaman's Pride Interferes

Have you ever been lost? Perhaps you have observed that when most *women* are lost, they will readily ask for directions, while most *men* are reluctant to do so. Someone once asked Daniel Boone if he had ever been lost. "I have never been lost," he replied, "But I will have to admit to being confused for several weeks."

What is it about human nature that makes us reluctant to seek and to accept the advice of others? Naaman was insulted by the response of Elisha. His pride kept him from going to the muddy Jordan and washing as Elisha suggested. Pride is deadly. Pride keeps folks from moving ahead in life and overcoming barriers that would bring healing to their bodies, minds, and spirits. Pride keeps us from learning more about one another so that we can break down prejudices and work together toward common goals. Pride keeps us from hearing and seeing what God is trying to do in our midst. Pride keeps nations at war and reconciliation from being achieved. How much devastation has our world suffered because of pride?

Naaman's Servants Reason with Him

It is a basic tenet of our Judeo-Christian faith that we must be respectful and attentive to every person, for we do not know through whom God will choose to speak. In the story of Naaman, first God used a young Israelite girl to speak to the commander of the king's army. Then, when Naaman refused to wash in the muddy waters of the Jordan, God used Naaman's servants to reason with him.

Naaman is portrayed as a "great man." One of the characteristics of true greatness is a caring and a sensitivity toward persons in all walks of life. Naaman must have been such a person, for his servants obviously cared deeply for him, and demonstrated their concern for his welfare. They were not afraid to reason with Naaman.

To his great credit, Naaman listened to the word of the young captive girl, and he listened to the word of his servants. He was not too proud to recognize the voice of reason when it was offered. Are we willing to listen to what God may be saying to us, even when it comes through those who are our subordinates, or through those who are younger than we are? Or does our pride get in the way?

Naaman Is Healed in Body and Spirit

When Naaman was able to swallow his pride, he received the healing that Elisha had instructed and that God intended. That day Naaman discovered that God often works not through dramatic performances, but through acts of simple obedience. How does God work in our lives? Many times we expect God to be revealed to us in ways that are larger than life. We hear testimonies of how the heavens opened and God spoke to someone in an audible way, or how someone's life was changed through miraculous happenings, and we lift up that type of experience as normative. Then we wonder why God does not perform that way in our lives. Naaman's story reminds us that many times God uses ordinary people and ordinary events to accomplish God's purposes. Rather than looking for out-of-the-ordinary and spectacular events, we should become more attuned to the spectacular things that God is doing in the world every day. It was Elizabeth Barrett Browning who observed, "every common bush afire with God." Are our eyes open to that reality? Pride kept Naaman from seeing. What keeps our eyes from perceiving the presence and power of God in our world and in our lives today?

When Naaman was able to let go of his agenda and accept what God was willing to do in his life, he found physical healing and spiritual clarity. Not content to be healed and then go on his way, Naaman committed his life to the God who had cured him of leprosy. Physical healing led to fresh spiritual insight. Thus Naaman was not only cured of his leprosy, he also was cured of the pride that kept him from being the person God intended that he become.

More significant than Naaman's clean skin was his fresh perspective and his new lease on life. Naaman had not only been cured of a physical disease; he was a changed man. When we allow God to work within our lives, we will find that God is able to transform us completely. "Be careful what you pray for," someone has said. Naaman asked God to heal his body, but God gave him new spiritual insight as well. When we allow God to work within our lives, we will find that God gives us spiritual clarity too. When we allow God's spirit to overcome the pride that is in our hearts, like God did with Naaman, God will enable us to move forward as whole persons in fullness of life.

SHARING THE SCRIPTURE

PREPARING TO TEACH

Preparing Our Hearts

This week's devotional reading is found in Mark 7:17-23. Here Mark records Jesus' teaching about what constitutes true defilement. Jesus declares that what comes from within us defiles us. One of the evils listed—pride—is the focus of today's session. In your spiritual journal, write about an incident that distanced you from God as a result of your pride. What did you learn about overcoming pride?

Pray that you and your students will be aware of how harmful pride is to you and to your relationship with God and others. Ask God's help in overcoming your pride.

Preparing Our Minds

Study the background scripture from 2 Kings 5, noting especially verses 1-5, 9-15*a*.

Write on newsprint:

the list of quotes concerning pride for the Gather to Learn portion.

the preparation for next week's session.

Plan which activities you will use. You may need to write some brief lectures.

LEADING THE CLASS

(1) Gather to Learn

❖ Welcome the class members and introduce any guests.

❖ Pray that the students will be aware of how pride affects their lives and find ways to minimize the damage.

❖ Post the following quotations on pride so that everyone can see them.

(1) **"He is so full of himself that he is quite empty" (Anonymous).**

(2) **"He who sings his own praise is usually off key" (Anonymous).**

(3) **"Temper gets people into trouble. Pride keeps them there" (Anonymous).**

(4) **"A proud man is always looking down on things and people; and, of course, as long as you're looking down, you can't see something that's above you" (C. S. Lewis, 1898–1963).**

(5) "Pride is a form of selfishness" (D. H. Lawrence, 1885–1930).

(6) "The proud hate pride—in others (Benjamin Franklin, 1706–1790).

(7) "Things average out: if you think too much of yourself, other people won't" (Anonymous).

(8) "Pride is the ground in which all the other sins grow, and the parent from which all the other sins come" (William Barclay, 1907–1978).

(9) "Pride goes before destruction, and a haughty spirit before a fall" (Proverbs 16:18).

❖ Invite the class members to comment on these quotations, or you may talk about them in a lecture. **Which ones "ring true"? Which ones seem to best describe or define "pride"? If you were to write one sentence about pride, what would you say?**

❖ Note that in today's session from 2 Kings 5 concerning Naaman, we will see a good example of pride and how it was overcome.

❖ Read aloud today's focus statement: **Pride is often hard to overcome. How do we overcome pride to receive the help we need? When Naaman overcame his reluctance to listen to advice, he received healing and accepted the God of Israel.**

(2) Encounter the Story of Naaman

❖ Read 2 Kings 5:1-5 yourself.
❖ Discuss these questions with the class, or suggest answers in a lecture. The Understanding the Scripture portion will provide information.

(1) **What does this passage tell you about Naaman?**

(2) **What does this passage tell you about the young Israelite girl?**

(3) **What does this passage suggest about Elisha?**

(4) **What does this passage suggest about Israel's understanding of the way God acts in human history?**

❖ Choose volunteers to read 2 Kings 5:9-15*b* as a drama. You will need a narrator, Elisha's messenger, Naaman, two or more servants of Naaman.

❖ Encourage several volunteers to role-play a conversation among Naaman's servants after Naaman walked away in a rage, according to verse 12. Tell the "servants" to assume that Naaman is not within earshot. The "servants" may discuss what they think about Naaman's behavior and how they plan to encourage him to follow Elisha's instructions. If the class is large, you may want to have several groups for role-play.

❖ Point out that verse 15 reports that Naaman acknowledges Israel's God.

❖ Ask each student to choose one of these four options to consider further Naaman's story.

Option 1: Distribute paper and pencils. Ask the students to imagine themselves as Naaman and to write a letter to a friend explaining what had happened. Include comments about pride and how Naaman had to overcome that in order to be healed by Israel's God.

Option 2: Work with a partner or team to plan a video production of Naaman's story. Who might be the main actors? What kind of music would you have in different parts of the story? What special effects would you use?

Option 3: Distribute paper and pencils. Write a song, based on a familiar tune, which retells Naaman's story. Consider a chorus that speaks about the dangers of pride.

Option 4: Distribute unlined paper and crayons, markers, or colored pencils. Mentally divide Naaman's story into scenes. Choose one or more of the scenes to illustrate.

❖ Bring everyone together and call for several volunteers to read their letter, tell about their plans for a video, sing their song, or show their picture.

*(3) Explore How Pride Keeps Us
from Hearing God*

❖ Read aloud the second paragraph under "Naaman's Pride Interferes."

❖ Write the words "Cause" and "Effect" as the headings for two columns on a sheet of newsprint. Invite the students to list as many causes of pride as they can name. Do the same for effects.

❖ Remind the class that Naaman's reluctance to wash in the Jordan was based on his unwillingness to listen impartially to Elisha's messenger. Then ask students to discuss answers to these questions with a partner or small group:

(1) **When has your pride made it difficult for you to hear God's voice?**

(2) **How have racial, gender, religious, linguistic, or other prejudices interfered with your ability to hear God speaking to you through someone else?**

(3) **How have you been able to overcome pride in order to hear God's message for you?**

(4) Examine the Destructiveness of Pride

❖ Read aloud this fictitious case study: **A prominent pianist was scheduled to give a concert in a major city, but had to renege on the contract just three weeks before the event due to an injury. The organizers contacted another accomplished soloist who really wanted to do the concert but felt insulted because he was not chosen originally.**

❖ Divide the class into groups and tell them that they are to envision themselves as the concert organizers. Ask them to brainstorm ways that they can help the pianist overcome pride and be willing to accept this—and future—contracts from these organizers.

❖ Bring the groups together and hear their ideas.

❖ Conclude this portion of the session by talking about how pride can be destructive to current and future relationships. Create a list on newsprint of how pride can

be overcome. Encourage students to add ways that have worked for them.

(5) Continue the Journey

❖ Pray that class members will be able to identify pride and find ways to overcome it with God's help.

❖ Read aloud this preparation for next week's lesson (you may also want to post it on newsprint for the students to copy): **Prepare for next week's session, "Overcoming Uncertainty," by reading background scripture from John 3:1-21. Pay particular attention to verses 1-16. Keep this focus in mind as you read: People often ask questions about their relationship to God. How do we find these answers? Jesus told Nicodemus that the answers are found in a relationship with God through Jesus Christ.**

❖ Read aloud the following three ideas. Challenge the students to commit themselves to use these activities as a springboard to spiritual growth.

(1) **Be alert for media stories of persons who allowed pride to rule them. What prompted this pride? What consequences did this pride have for the individual and for others? How was it overcome?**

(2) **Interview someone who you believe embodies Christian humility. Find out how this person is able to overcome pride.**

(3) **Write an opinion essay on pride, giving examples of how pride can destroy relationships.**

❖ Sing or read aloud "I Want a Principle Within."

❖ Ask the students to echo this benediction as you read it phrase by phrase: **Grant, O Lord, that what has been said with our lips we may believe in our hearts, and that what we believe in our hearts we may practice in our lives; through Jesus Christ our Lord. Amen.**

OVERCOMING UNCERTAINTY

PREVIEWING THE LESSON

Lesson Scripture: John 3:1-16
Background Scripture: John 3:1-21
Key Verses: John 3:5-6

Focus of the Lesson:
People often ask questions about their relationship to God. How do we find these answers? Jesus told Nicodemus that the answers are found in a relationship with God through Jesus Christ.

Goals for the Learners:
(1) to explore the story of Jesus and Nicodemus.
(2) to contrast the understandings that Jesus and Nicodemus had concerning new birth, and state their own understandings.
(3) to celebrate the new life God offers through Christ.

Pronunciation Guide:
Nicodemus   (nik uh dee' mus)

Supplies:
Bibles, newsprint and marker, paper and pencils, hymnals

READING THE SCRIPTURE

NRSV
John 3:1-16

Now there was a Pharisee named Nicodemus, a leader of the Jews. 2 He came to Jesus by night and said to him, "Rabbi, we know that you are a teacher who has come from God; for no one can do these signs that you do apart from the presence of God." 3 Jesus answered him, "Very truly, I tell you, no one can see the kingdom of God without being born from above." 4 Nicodemus said to him, "How can anyone be born after

NIV
John 3:1-16

Now there was a man of the Pharisees named Nicodemus, a member of the Jewish ruling council. [2]He came to Jesus at night and said, "Rabbi, we know you are a teacher who has come from God. For no one could perform the miraculous signs you are doing if God were not with him."
[3]In reply Jesus declared, "I tell you the truth, no one can see the kingdom of God unless he is born again."

having grown old? Can one enter a second time into the mother's womb and be born?" **5 Jesus answered, "Very truly, I tell you, no one can enter the kingdom of God without being born of water and Spirit. 6 What is born of the flesh is flesh, and what is born of the Spirit is spirit.** 7 Do not be astonished that I said to you, 'You must be born from above.' 8 The wind blows where it chooses, and you hear the sound of it, but you do not know where it comes from or where it goes. So it is with everyone who is born of the Spirit." 9 Nicodemus said to him, "How can these things be?" 10 Jesus answered him, "Are you a teacher of Israel, and yet you do not understand these things?

11 "Very truly, I tell you, we speak of what we know and testify to what we have seen; yet you do not receive our testimony. 12 If I have told you about earthly things and you do not believe, how can you believe if I tell you about heavenly things? 13 No one has ascended into heaven except the one who descended from heaven, the Son of Man. 14 And just as Moses lifted up the serpent in the wilderness, so must the Son of Man be lifted up, 15 that whoever believes in him may have eternal life.

16 "For God so loved the world that he gave his only Son, so that everyone who believes in him may not perish but may have eternal life."

⁴"How can a man be born when he is old?" Nicodemus asked. "Surely he cannot enter a second time into his mother's womb to be born!"

⁵**Jesus answered, "I tell you the truth, no one can enter the kingdom of God unless he is born of water and the Spirit. ⁶Flesh gives birth to flesh, but the Spirit gives birth to spirit.** ⁷You should not be surprised at my saying, 'You must be born again.' ⁸The wind blows wherever it pleases. You hear its sound, but you cannot tell where it comes from or where it is going. So it is with everyone born of the Spirit."

⁹"How can this be?" Nicodemus asked.

¹⁰"You are Israel's teacher," said Jesus, "and do you not understand these things? ¹¹I tell you the truth, we speak of what we know, and we testify to what we have seen, but still you people do not accept our testimony. ¹²I have spoken to you of earthly things and you do not believe; how then will you believe if I speak of heavenly things? ¹³No one has ever gone into heaven except the one who came from heaven—the Son of Man. ¹⁴Just as Moses lifted up the snake in the desert, so the Son of Man must be lifted up, ¹⁵that everyone who believes in him may have eternal life.

¹⁶"For God so loved the world that he gave his one and only Son, that whoever believes in him shall not perish but have eternal life."

UNDERSTANDING THE SCRIPTURE

John 3:1. Nicodemus was a member of the Pharisees, those who set themselves apart from ordinary life in order to keep every detail of the Jewish law. He was also a "leader of the Jews," a member of the Sanhedrin, the seventy-member supreme court concerning religious matters. We can also assume that Nicodemus was wealthy, for when Jesus died Nicodemus brought for his body "a mixture of myrrh and aloes, weighing about a hundred pounds" (John 19:39). Only a person of means could have done that.

John 3:2. The fact that Nicodemus came to Jesus by night is significant, for "night" is used in John's Gospel to represent separation from the presence of God. Jesus had piqued Nicodemus's interest. Yet if people saw him talking with Jesus, they might lose respect for Nicodemus, because many of his colleagues had dismissed Jesus as a charlatan. But Nicodemus had concluded otherwise, and wanted Jesus' help and advice. Nicodemus probably assumed that if he approached Jesus secretly, he could learn the answers to his questions without the embarrassment of having others know that he had been with Jesus.

Nicodemus may also have come to Jesus at night because he wanted a private time with Jesus. During the day there would be interruptions. The rabbis taught that the best time to study the law was at night when a person was undisturbed. In the darkness of the night, Nicodemus could seek illumination for the deepest yearnings of his heart.

The dialogue between Jesus and Nicodemus is one of mutual respect. Nicodemus addresses Jesus as "rabbi," acknowledging Jesus as "a teacher who has come from God" (3:2). Nicodemus also speaks to Jesus in the first person plural ("we know"), implying that he is speaking as a leader of a community that shares respect for Jesus.

John 3:3. Jesus goes right to the heart of the matter with his pronouncement that no one can see the kingdom of God without being "born from above" (NRSV) or "born again" (NIV). The Greek word has both meanings, speaking of the time of birth (again) and the place (from above). Jesus' expression challenges Nicodemus (and us) to move beyond the surface to a deeper meaning. Coming to faith is to undergo such a radical change in life that it is analogous to the birth experience itself. It is to have something happen to the soul that can only be described as starting all over again. The new birth is more than a human achievement. It involves the grace and power of God.

In John's Gospel, the kingdom of God is not only a future possibility, but also a present reality. Being part of the kingdom of God is to be perfectly in tune with God's will as well as looking forward to the day when the whole world will acknowledge the presence and power of God.

John 3:4. Nicodemus takes Jesus literally, protesting that what Jesus suggests is physiologically impossible. Nicodemus does not grasp the layers of meaning implied by Jesus' response.

John 3:5-7. Because Nicodemus does not understand, Jesus shares a fresh set of images. The idea of being born of water and the Spirit reinforces the two layers of meaning that Jesus has developed earlier. All of us are born in the water of a womb. Water is a symbol of life and a symbol of cleansing. When Jesus takes possession of our lives, the sins of the past are forgiven and forgotten. The Spirit is a symbol of power. When Jesus takes possession of our lives, we receive a new power that enables us to be and do what by ourselves would be impossible.

John 3:8. Jesus' image of the wind helps explain the birth of which he speaks. The Greek word has two inherent meanings: wind and spirit. The wind/spirit blows where it wills; human beings can detect its presence but cannot chart its precise movement. Thus Jesus' offer of new birth is a mystery beyond total human knowledge and control.

John 3:9. Nicodemus still does not understand. Once again his preconceived ideas prevent him from understanding the new idea that Jesus is proposing.

John 3:10. Jesus' response points out the fact that neither Nicodemus's credentials as a Pharisee and member of the Sanhedrin nor his self-professed knowledge have brought him any closer to understanding the message of Jesus for his life.

John 3:11-13. Jesus knows about heavenly things because he has descended from heaven. Verse 13 refers to Jesus' ascension in the past tense. The Gospels were written after the Resurrection, and this allusion reminds us of what is to come.

John 3:14. On their journey through the wilderness, the people of Israel complained and regretted that they had left Egypt. To punish them God sent a plague of deadly, fiery serpents. When the people cried for mercy, God instructed Moses to make an image of a serpent and hold it up in the midst of the camp. Those who looked at the serpent were healed and their lives were saved.

Jesus shares that he will be "lifted up." He is alluding, of course, to his crucifixion. This humiliating act will actually become a saving act, for when Jesus is lifted up on the cross, eternal life will become possible for those who believe.

John 3:15. Clearly "whoever" believes will have eternal life. There are no restrictions or exclusions in the gospel message.

John 3:16-18. God gives Jesus as an act of love to all people, but only believers accept that gift. If we believe, we are reborn into a new relationship with God; if we do not believe, we perish. God sends the Son into the world in love in order to save it, not condemn it. Yet the very presence of Jesus confronts the world with a decision: to believe or not to believe. Making that decision is the moment of judgment. God does not make this judgment, but rather ratifies the decision that people make for themselves.

John 3:19-21. Light and darkness are presented as a metaphor. Those who believe "come to the light" while those who do not remain in darkness. God sent Jesus to save the world, but each person must decide whether to accept that offer of salvation. The' world thereby judges itself in its response to Jesus.

INTERPRETING THE SCRIPTURE

Nicodemus Seeks Jesus' Counsel

The story of Jesus and Nicodemus provides us with an understanding of the Gospel message and demonstrates how we can have a relationship with God through Jesus Christ. In spite of his education, his prestigious position in the community, his prudent investments, and his devout religious practice, Nicodemus was painfully aware that there was something lacking in his life. All of his responsible actions had not brought him the happiness and contentment that he was seeking.

Nicodemus decided to meet with Jesus personally and ask what he needed to do to enter the kingdom of God that Jesus was proclaiming. As a Jew, he was used to certain rules and concrete rituals one could follow and then be assured of moving in the right direction. Probably for political reasons Nicodemus came to Jesus at night. Nicodemus no doubt assumed that if he approached Jesus secretly, he could learn the answers to his questions without the embarrassment of having others know that he had been with Jesus.

Is it possible to follow Jesus secretly? Perhaps, for a while. British Bible scholar and theologian William Barclay's comment is that ultimately, there can be no secret disciples of Jesus. "Either the witness will kill the silence or the silence will kill the witness."

How many of us can relate to Nicodemus? Some people live in families where being a believer is simply not acceptable. For others, expressing one's faith openly would be frowned upon at work, or become problematic from a legal perspective. For all of us, I believe there is an uncertainty and a nervousness that makes Jesus seem distant and far away. The Jesus we may have learned about in Sunday school doesn't seem adequate for a world where terror seems to reign, a world where we stand in line for hours in airports with armed guards in every corner, a world where we fear for our children's safety every time they leave our side. If we seek Jesus today, we too will be approaching him in the midst of a dark and uncertain time, when the forces of evil seem to have gotten the upper hand, a time when many of us know well what is often described as the "dark night of the soul."

Jesus Explains the New Birth

"What do I need to do in order to have peace of mind in these troubled times?" a modern Nicodemus asks Jesus. Jesus' reply is simply this, "You must be born again." Some of us have heard that language since we were children. For some, it means a narrow, restrictive lifestyle consisting of more "don't's" than "do's." Others have no idea what Jesus is talking about. Jesus says that coming to faith is a lot like the process of being born.

Birth is a traumatic experience. For nine months we are in the warmth of a womb, where our every need is met. All of a sudden, we are ushered into the cold, cruel world. No wonder babies cry! If they only knew what was ahead. Life in the Spirit is not an easy road either. The way of self-giving love meant the cross for Jesus. His followers cannot expect a life free from challenge and sacrifice.

For some, being born is easy—a couple hours of labor, and a healthy baby arrives. For others, labor goes on and on, and the baby has to be born by Caesarean section, then rushed to the neonatal intensive care unit. Some people come to faith easily and naturally. Some people cannot pinpoint a time and a place when they became Christians. For others, the experience of faith comes at the end of a long and painful struggle.

Babies cannot make it in this world on their own. If they are not fed and cared for properly, they will die. When people come to faith, they will not survive very long without help and nurture and support.

Statistics show that within six months of joining a church, half the new members will become inactive if they do not become involved in the life of the congregation. If parents neglect their children, charges can be brought against them. Could God bring charges against us for failing to reach out to those who are new to the faith and to the church?

Nicodemus Does Not Understand

As is true with many persons in our world today, Nicodemus does not understand Jesus' concept of new birth. Nicodemus takes Jesus literally, and finding it impossible to "enter a second time into the mother's womb" continues to scratch his head.

Many people enjoy intellectual discussions concerning religion. Yet they hesitate when it comes to making a commitment to Christ and the Christian way of life. I am wary of those who talk about God as though they had just had lunch with the Deity. Faith remains a mystery, and God is always beyond our total comprehension. Yet there comes a time when we must make a decision, based on what we know. Someone once asked Mark Twain if it bothered him that there were so many passages of Scripture that he did not understand. "The passages that bother me are those I do understand," replied Twain.

John's Gospel is not clear as to whether Nicodemus eventually became a disciple. He accompanied Joseph of Arimathea, a secret disciple of Jesus, when Joseph approached Pilate for the body of Jesus. That may be an indication that Nicodemus, too, revealed his discipleship following the Crucifixion (John 19:39-42). We do not hear of Nicodemus again following this story.

At any rate, there is no indication that Nicodemus's initial encounter with Jesus caused him to come to faith. The scholarly debate apparently did not produce a disciple. It rarely does. Jesus was describing an experience when he used the birth analogy. He was speaking of a new way of life for which there are no precedents. Nicodemus didn't get it. Will we?

Jesus Explains the Believer's Relationship with God

"Let me try another analogy," Jesus seems to be saying. Then Jesus compares the wind to the Spirit of God, pointing out that we can see the effects of the wind, but we cannot restrict it. Both the wind and the Spirit come from God, whose creative genius is beyond our ability to fathom.

Drawing on a story that Nicodemus would recall, Jesus reminds him of the serpent that Moses lifted up in the wilderness. By looking at this image, the people's faith and hope was restored, and they were healed of their infirmities. In like manner, when Christ is lifted up on the cross, everyone who believes will receive new life.

Much of the problem in the church today is that there are a lot of people in our congregations who have never made a clear and decisive commitment to follow Jesus Christ. Even those of us who have given our lives to Christ need to renew our commitment from time to time, for God is always calling us to deeper and fuller levels of discipleship. The new birth is not a one-time experience, but a continual process of committing the best that we have to the highest that we know. Only those who refuse the gift stand outside the new life that God offers.

SHARING THE SCRIPTURE

PREPARING TO TEACH

Preparing Our Hearts

This week's devotional reading is found in John 3:17-21, which is part of the background scripture. This passage clearly states that God's purpose in sending Jesus is to save the world. How, then, do we fall under condemnation? John declares that those who refuse to walk in the light of Jesus condemn themselves. In other words, all are invited to come to God through Jesus, but anyone can choose to refuse the invitation. Ponder this scripture passage. Where do you see yourself in it? Where do you want to see yourself?

Pray that you and your students will make good choices in responding to the invitation to come to God.

Preparing Our Minds

Study the background lesson from John 3:1-21, especially verses 1-16. Martin Luther referred to John 3:16 as "the Gospel in miniature." Would you agree with him? Why or why not?

Nicodemus is mentioned in only two other places in the Bible: John 7:50 and 19:39. Read these verses so as to gain more insight into how Nicodemus must have responded to his conversation with Jesus in chapter 3.

Write on newsprint:

the litany of celebration.

the preparation for next week's session.

Plan a brief lecture about Nicodemus, as suggested under "Explore the Story of Jesus and Nicodemus."

LEADING THE CLASS

(1) Gather to Learn

❖ Welcome the class members and introduce any guests.

❖ Pray that students will freely raise

questions so as to be able to overcome any uncertainty about their relationship with Jesus.

❖ Distribute paper and pencils. Encourage the students to imagine that they could have a private conversation with Jesus. They are to write one or two pressing questions that they would want to have answered. Collect the papers and read aloud as many questions as time allows.

❖ Ask the students to classify the types of questions they have heard and make a list of these types. For example, some questions may have to do with the kingdom of God, others with why God has allowed certain things to happen, others with learning about who Jesus is, others with the meaning of sin and evil, and so on. There are no hard and fast categories here. Your purpose is to discover some broad areas of interest.

❖ Point out that today our session will focus on Nicodemus, a man who so desired to know more about Jesus that he went to him during the night to ask questions in the hope of clearing up his uncertainties.

❖ Read aloud today's focus statement: **People often ask questions about their relationship to God. How do we find these answers? Jesus told Nicodemus that the answers are found in a relationship with God through Jesus Christ.**

(2) Explore the Story of Jesus and Nicodemus

❖ Select three volunteers to read John 3:1-16 as a drama. One reader is the narrator, one reads the part of Jesus, and one the part of Nicodemus.

❖ Present a brief lecture using information for verses 1 and 2 from Understanding the Scripture to help the students understand who Nicodemus was, why he chose to come at night, what he hoped to learn, and how the two men treated one another. Note that Nicodemus is only mentioned in the Gospel of John.

❖ Pose these questions for discussion. If your class prefers a lecture, ponder the

answers yourself and write a lecture based on your ideas.

(1) What does this encounter between Nicodemus and Jesus tell you about Jesus?

(2) What does it tell you about God?

(3) Assuming that Nicodemus can stand for anyone who is searching for God, what does this passage say about humanity's quest for God?

(3) Contrast Understandings Concerning New Birth

❖ Read the information from John 3:3 in the Understanding the Scripture portion. Your main purpose is to clarify the two meanings of the Greek word *(anothen)* that is translated "born from above" (NRSV) or "born again" (NIV).

❖ Invite the students to describe Nicodemus's understanding of "new birth." Write these ideas on the left side of a sheet of newsprint.

❖ Encourage the class to list Jesus' understandings of "new birth" in the right column.

❖ Talk with the group about the major similarities and differences that they perceive between these two points of view. One important difference is that Nicodemus takes Jesus' words literally, whereas Jesus is speaking more metaphorically.

❖ Persuade the group members to give their own interpretation of "new birth" and how it affects their understanding of salvation. Try to get them to include ideas related to time of birth and place of birth. Remember that while some people can name an exact moment when they were "born again," others have grown gradually in faith throughout their lifetimes.

(4) Celebrate the New Life God Offers Through Christ

❖ Invite the students to read aloud this litany of celebration from 1 Peter 1:3-5, 8-9.

Be sure to copy the litany onto newsprint prior to class.

Group 1: Blessed be the God and Father of our Lord Jesus Christ!

Group 2: By his great mercy he has given us a new birth into a living hope through the resurrection of Jesus Christ from the dead,

Group 1: and into an inheritance that is imperishable, undefiled, and unfading, kept in heaven for you,

Group 2: who are being protected by the power of God through faith for a salvation ready to be revealed in the last time.

Group 1: Although you have not seen him, you love him;

Group 2: and even though you do not see him now, you believe in him and rejoice with an indescribable and glorious joy,

All: for you are receiving the outcome of your faith, the salvation of your souls.

(5) Continue the Journey

❖ Pray that the students will continue to seek answers to their questions of faith so that they may find greater certainty in their relationship with Christ.

❖ Read aloud this preparation for next week's lesson. You may also want to post it on newsprint for the students to copy. **Prepare for next week's session, "Overcoming Prejudice," by reading the story of the Samaritan woman found in John 4:1-42. Our lesson will concentrate on verses 7-10, 19-26. The key verse is Galatians 3:28. Consider this focus as you read: It is often difficult to overcome barri**ers raised by prejudice. Whom are we prejudiced against, and how is God calling us to change this? Neither Jesus nor the Samaritan woman lets prejudice interfere with their conversation. As a result, Jesus identified himself to her and she spread the good news.**

❖ Read aloud the following three ideas. Challenge the students to commit themselves to use these activities as a springboard to spiritual growth.

(1) Reconsider the questions you raised in this week's "Gather to Learn" activity. Search the Scriptures and ponder what you think Jesus would say in answer to those questions.

(2) Listen to Johann Sebastian Bach's Cantata 68, "Also hat Gott die Welt geliebt" ("Thus has God loved the world"), which includes a musical interpretation of John 3:16-21. How does Bach's music help you to "feel" your way into the passage?

(3) Recall that Jesus challenged Nicodemus's way of thinking. In what ways does Jesus need to challenge your thinking?

❖ Sing or read aloud "Wash, O God, Our Sons and Daughters."

❖ Ask the students to echo this benediction as you read it phrase by phrase: **Grant, O Lord, that what has been said with our lips we may believe in our hearts, and that what we believe in our hearts we may practice in our lives; through Jesus Christ our Lord. Amen.**

OVERCOMING PREJUDICE

PREVIEWING THE LESSON

Lesson Scripture: John 4:7-10, 19-26
Background Scripture: John 4:1-42
Key Verse: Galatians 3:28

Focus of the Lesson:
It is often difficult to overcome barriers raised by prejudice. Whom are we prejudiced against, and how is God calling us to change this? Neither Jesus nor the Samaritan woman lets prejudice interfere with their conversation. As a result, Jesus identified himself to her and she spread the good news.

Goals for the Learners:
(1) to examine the story of Jesus and the Samaritan woman.
(2) to discern reasons for prejudice.
(3) to identify some barriers that prejudice creates in our world today and to consider ways to break down those barriers.

Supplies:
Bibles, newsprint and marker, paper and pencils, hymnals

READING THE SCRIPTURE

NRSV
John 4:7-10, 19-26

7 A Samaritan woman came to draw water, and Jesus said to her, "Give me a drink." 8 (His disciples had gone to the city to buy food.) 9 The Samaritan woman said to him, "How is it that you, a Jew, ask a drink of me, a woman of Samaria?" (Jews do not share things in common with Samaritans.) 10 Jesus answered her, "If you knew the gift of God, and who it is that is saying to you, 'Give me a drink,' you would have asked him, and he would have given you living water."

NIV
John 4:7-10, 19-26

7When a Samaritan woman came to draw water, Jesus said to her, "Will you give me a drink?" 8(His disciples had gone into the town to buy food.)

9The Samaritan woman said to him, "You are a Jew and I am a Samaritan woman. How can you ask me for a drink?" (For Jews do not associate with Samaritans.)

10Jesus answered her, "If you knew the gift of God and who it is that asks you for a drink, you would have asked

19 The woman said to him, "Sir, I see that you are a prophet. 20 Our ancestors worshiped on this mountain, but you say that the place where people must worship is in Jerusalem." 21 Jesus said to her, "Woman, believe me, the hour is coming when you will worship the Father neither on this mountain nor in Jerusalem. 22 You worship what you do not know; we worship what we know, for salvation is from the Jews. 23 But the hour is coming, and is now here, when the true worshipers will worship the Father in spirit and truth, for the Father seeks such as these to worship him. 24 God is spirit, and those who worship him must worship in spirit and truth." 25 The woman said to him, "I know that Messiah is coming" (who is called Christ). "When he comes, he will proclaim all things to us." 26 Jesus said to her, "I am he, the one who is speaking to you."

Galatians 3:28

28 There is no longer Jew or Greek, there is no longer slave or free, there is no longer male and female; for all of you are one in Christ Jesus.

him and he would have given you living water."

19"Sir," the woman said, "I can see that you are a prophet. 20Our fathers worshiped on this mountain, but you Jews claim that the place where we must worship is in Jerusalem."

21Jesus declared, "Believe me, woman, a time is coming when you will worship the Father neither on this mountain nor in Jerusalem. 22You Samaritans worship what you do not know; we worship what we do know, for salvation is from the Jews. 23Yet a time is coming and has now come when the true worshipers will worship the Father in spirit and truth, for they are the kind of worshipers the Father seeks. 24God is spirit, and his worshipers must worship in spirit and in truth."

25The woman said, "I know that Messiah" (called Christ) "is coming. When he comes, he will explain everything to us."

26Then Jesus declared, "I who speak to you am he."

Galatians 3:28

28There is neither Jew nor Greek, slave nor free, male nor female, for you are all one in Christ Jesus.

UNDERSTANDING THE SCRIPTURE

John 4:1-3. To the Pharisees, Jesus' ministry appeared to be more "successful" than that of John the Baptist, so to avoid misunderstanding Jesus decides to travel back to Galilee.

John 4:4-6. The most direct route from Judea to Galilee is through Samaria. The schism between the Jews and the Samaritans was quite bitter. It can be traced to the Assyrian occupation of northern Palestine in 721 B.C. (see 2 Kings 17). By about 200 B.C., the subject of contention was the correct location of the center of worship life. The Samaritans had built a temple on Mount Gerizim near Sychar, the site of

Jacob's well, a piece of property with historical ties to Jacob and Joseph. The Jews, of course, held that Jerusalem was the proper place of worship. In 128 B.C., the Jewish Maccabean ruler John Hyrcanus destroyed the Samaritan temple and attempted to suppress the separate Samaritan cult. When the Romans took control of Palestine in 64–63 B.C., the Samaritans were free to restore their independent religious customs.

John 4:7-8. To the ears of first-century readers, the following narrative would have been shocking, even scandalous as: (1) Jews did not invite contact with Samaritans; (2) a Jewish man did not initiate conversation with an unknown woman; and (3) a Jewish teacher did not engage in public conversation with a woman.

John 4:9. Jesus' discourse with the woman, like that with Nicodemus (John 3:1-15), develops on two levels. The woman thinks of water in earthly terms. In Palestine, where the water supply is not always sufficient, having adequate water is a natural concern. Jesus, however, speaks of living or flowing water as a sign of eternal life, whose source is God, and whose abundance is assured in the promise of the coming kingdom of God.

John 4:10. Instead of answering the woman's question directly, Jesus invites her to answer herself. If the woman could recognize the identity of the person with whom she speaks, she would be the one to request water.

John 4:11-12. The woman challenges Jesus' ability to match the gift of Jacob, one of the patriarchs of the faith.

John 4:13-14. Jesus focuses on the effect of the two waters. Jacob's gift, while its abundance was legendary, could not quench people's thirst permanently. Jesus' gift of living water will accomplish that purpose. Those who drink from Jesus' water "will never be thirsty" because his water "will become in them a spring of water gushing up to eternal life."

John 4:15. The Samaritan woman responds enthusiastically to Jesus' words, but her enthusiasm misses the point. She continues to think in terms of physical thirst and does not grasp the meaning of "living water."

John 4:16. Jesus introduces a new topic, focusing on the woman's own life.

John 4:17-19. We should read these verses carefully. The text does not portray this woman as a sinner, nor does Jesus judge her. There are many possible reasons for her marital history other than moral laxity. (Remember the custom of levirate marriage from the lesson on Ruth.) At any rate, the reasons for her marital history do not concern Jesus. The conversation is an example of Jesus' ability to see and know all things. It is also a moment of revelation for the woman. Jesus' insight into her words and life leads her to declare him to be a prophet.

John 4:20. In light of her recognition of Jesus as a prophet, the Samaritan woman puts before him the most pressing theological problem that stands between the Jews and her people—the proper place for divine worship. This topic should not be seen as a psychological ploy to evade the issues of her own life. Rather the woman anticipates that the prophet Jesus will be able to speak an authoritative word on the subject.

John 4:21. Jesus directs her attention away from the present and focuses on the future.

John 4:22. Jesus reminds the woman of Israel's place as God's chosen people in order to caution her that by rejecting the Jews, she risks rejecting God's offer of salvation.

John 4:23-24. "God is Spirit," not bound to any place or people. Jesus' presence in the world initiates this transformation of worship, because Jesus' presence changes the moment of anticipation ("the hour is coming") to the moment of the in-breaking of the kingdom of God ("is now here").

John 4:25. The woman's response indicates that she has heard the note of promise in Jesus' words, but not the message about fulfillment.

John 4:26. The discussion closes with Jesus' dramatic revelation, which is simple and bold. The Greek translation is "I am," identifying Jesus as the one in whom God is known.

John 4:27. The disciples' reaction to Jesus is similar to the woman's initial response: shock that Jesus is violating social conventions.

John 4:28. That the woman leaves her water jar indicates that her concern about water has been superseded by the revelation of Jesus' identity.

John 4:29. The first evangelist in John's Gospel story is a Samaritan woman! In response to her conversation with Jesus, she goes into town and bears witness to what she has seen and heard. She invites her fellow townspeople to "come and see."

John 4:30. She is a credible witness, for upon hearing her story, the townspeople come to Jacob's well to meet Jesus.

John 4:31-34. Jesus' conversation with his disciples follows a similar pattern to his conversation with the woman. The disciples take Jesus at face value, while Jesus is speaking of an inner and spiritual meaning. A great task can lift a person beyond bodily needs. Jesus was nourished by the fact that he was doing the will of God.

John 4:35-38. Jesus uses the traditional biblical image of the harvest to illustrate his point that the time of waiting is over. The Kingdom is at hand. The "crop" of Samaritan believers is proof that the harvest is ready. In John's Gospel, the mission to "outsiders" does not wait until after Jesus' death and resurrection.

John 4:39. As the story concludes, John focuses on the success of the Samaritan mission. The people who have heard the woman's testimony come to faith in Jesus.

John 4:40. Having Jesus stay is to enter into relationship with him.

John 4:41-42. Many more persons come to faith because of Jesus' stay, and the woman's witness diminishes in importance when the Samaritans have their own experience of Jesus. The acclamation of Jesus as "the Savior of the world" is the most profound confession of faith found thus far in John's Gospel. Religious differences that have kept people apart are overcome through the salvation that is available in Jesus.

Galatians 3:28. In his letter to the church at Galatia in which Paul focuses on the theme of Christian liberty, he asserts that all are one in Christ Jesus. All persons are to be viewed without prejudice, for all are equal before God.

INTERPRETING THE SCRIPTURE

Jesus Shocks a Samaritan Woman

When I was a United Methodist district superintendent, each fall I would visit all the churches under my supervision and conduct the annual charge conference, the basic yearly business meeting of the congregation. During my first year, I innocently drove to one of the churches, greeted the parishioners, and began the meeting. We had barely begun when one man began an angry barrage of accusations. I had never met him before, but he attacked me bitterly. Others joined in the discussion. Finally, when it was obvious that we had reached an impasse, I offered to have lunch with the man who had instigated the attack so that we could discuss his issues in a less emo-tionally charged setting. He agreed. At that lunch, and in subsequent meetings with other leaders of that congregation, it became clear to me that those folks were having trouble dealing with me because I represented the hierarchy of the denomination. They had already decided they didn't like me before I ever came to town. It was the office of district superintendent that they detested. Anyone who came in that capacity was vulnerable to attack.

I have experienced age prejudice, education prejudice, and racial prejudice, but I don't believe I have ever been quite as aware of prejudice as I was in my dealings with that particular church. That congregation refused to see me as a person. Their focus was on what I represented.

Today's lesson cuts to the core of barriers raised by prejudice. Jesus shocked the Samaritan woman by approaching her at Jacob's well. First, Jews had no dealings with Samaritans. Because of age-old issues that had grown through the years, a breach had developed between the two groups that resulted in a prohibition of all social intercourse. Moreover, in respectable society, a Jewish man did not initiate conversation with an unknown woman, and a Jewish teacher did not engage in public conversation with a woman. A rabbi might not even speak to his own wife or daughter or sister in public. For a rabbi to be seen speaking to a woman in public was the end of his reputation. Yet Jesus spoke to this woman. In that very act Jesus took a great step toward breaking down barriers and overcoming the prejudices of his day.

When Jesus spoke to the woman, and she responded, they were able to overcome some of the barriers that had previously kept their respective nationality groups apart. The Samaritan woman was shocked, but she responded to the initiative of Jesus. Walls began coming down, and the inclusiveness of the gospel was demonstrated, not in theory, but in action.

The Samaritan Woman Is Intrigued by Jesus

To her great credit, the Samaritan woman was not put off by Jesus. That he was willing to engage her in conversation surprised her, but she was willing to respond. Her initial response was wariness, which was probably appropriate, considering the situation. After all, Jesus was a total stranger. Yet the woman was slow to grasp the idea that Jesus' words had a deeper meaning.

Many times I encounter people whose grasp of religious ideas is extremely superficial. Someone finds out that I am a minister, and immediately I can see the person making several assumptions based on their previous learning. Sometimes someone that I have just met for the first time will ask a question that reveals very little understanding of the things of faith. There is a difference between interest in religion and making a confession of faith. When the Samaritan woman asked Jesus about the "living water," her question revealed the fact that she did not grasp the deeper meaning of Jesus' responses. As the story progresses, and as the dialogue continues, she gains a greater knowledge of the things of faith. Eventually she comes to understand who Jesus is and the difference he can make in her life. Thus the Samaritan woman is for us a model of growing in faith.

Jesus Explains "True Worship"

I believe that the woman's question about where one should worship is sincere. She had been taught to regard Mount Gerizim as the most sacred spot in the world and to despise Jerusalem. She knew that the Jews taught that the temple on Mount Zion was the place where folks should worship. Her question was simply this: Who was right?

According to Jesus, true worship does not happen in one place or another. It involves more of the spirit of the worshiper than it does the physical space. Fundamentally, the Samaritan woman was asking, "Where can I find God?" Jesus responded by saying in essence that she did not need to offer sacrifices in some special place. True worship finds God in every place.

If God is Spirit, God is not confined to things. Therefore idol worship is not only irrelevant, it is an affront to the very nature of God. If God is Spirit, God is not confined to places, and so to limit the worship of God to Jerusalem or to any other place is to set limits on God who is greater than all limitations. If God is Spirit, then our gifts to God must be gifts of the Spirit. The only gifts that are appropriate to the nature of God are the gifts of love, loyalty, devotion, and obedience. True and genuine worship occurs when we, through our spirits, attain friendship and intimacy with God.

Jesus Reveals His Identity

At the conclusion of their conversation, Jesus reveals his identity more completely. In so doing, he demonstrates that he is able to fulfill the Samaritan woman's expectations concerning who the Messiah will be, while at the same time challenging her assumptions and prejudices. The same is true for us.

When we meet Jesus, our cultural prejudices should fall. However, the history of the church witnesses to the fact that too often the church has been held hostage by the prevailing culture. Our key verse for this lesson is Galatians 3:28: "There is neither Jew nor Greek, slave nor free, male nor female, for you are all one in Christ Jesus." Yet that ideal was not always visible in the early church, nor is it operative today. Sunday morning at 11 o'clock is still the most segregated hour of the week in many communities. Even in the church, wages for women are often less than for men doing the same work. Ethnic prejudices abound, and while slavery has been outlawed worldwide, many people are forced to work for less than a living wage. The church has often been silent when its voice for justice and compassion was needed.

In order to overcome the massive problems that prejudice causes in our day, we need to keep our worship and spiritual lives focused on Jesus, as did the woman at the well. Jesus helped her examine her life. By her own report, Jesus told her everything she had ever done. That helped her with examining her own prejudices and overcoming some of the barriers that she had erected along life's way. We will not overcome prejudice unless and until we take a good look at our past, examine our presuppositions, and ask for forgiveness where we have acted inappropriately. Then we must ask God to help us move forward in faith.

SHARING THE SCRIPTURE

PREPARING TO TEACH

Preparing Our Hearts

This week's devotional reading is found in John 4:35-42, which is part of the background scripture. In a world where enmity between Jews and Samaritans had existed for centuries, we may be amazed to find a woman who is so able to overcome her prejudice against the Jews that she witnesses to her people about finding the Messiah, the Jewish Jesus. She leads her neighbors to him, and they accept Jesus as "the Savior of the world." When have prejudices deafened your ear to a messenger? How have you overcome those biases, perhaps even helping others to dispel their prejudices as well?

Pray that you and your students will be open to hear the voice of God, no matter who the messenger may be. Ask that Christians work together so that we might truly be of one mind, living in unity with Christ.

Preparing Our Minds

Study the background scripture from John 4:1-42, which tells the story of the encounter between Jesus and the Samaritan woman. Look especially at verses 7-10, 19-26, which we will highlight in our session.

If time permits, do some additional reading from a Bible dictionary or handbook on the Samaritans.

Write on newsprint:

the preparation for next week's session.

LEADING THE CLASS

(1) Gather to Learn

❖ Welcome the class members and introduce any guests.

❖ Pray that the students will be open to all persons and willing to overcome prejudice so as to hear God's voice in whomever God sends.

❖ Read today's key verse from Galatians 3:28. Invite the students to talk about how they see these verses being lived out in the contemporary church. Are all Christians truly one? If not, what divides us?

❖ Note that in today's scripture lesson of the encounter between Jesus and the woman of Samaria we find divisions over where people are to worship. Such divisions created prejudice and animosity that had existed for centuries before Jesus and the woman met.

❖ Read aloud today's focus statement: **It is often difficult to overcome barriers raised by prejudice. Whom are we prejudiced against, and how is God calling us to change this? Neither Jesus nor the Samaritan woman lets prejudice interfere with their conversation. As a result, Jesus identified himself to her and she spread the good news.**

(2) Examine the Story of Jesus and the Samaritan Woman

❖ Choose a volunteer to read John 4:7-10.

❖ Discuss these questions, or answer them in a lecture. You will find helpful information in the Understanding the Scripture portion for these verses, as shown in parentheses.

(1) **Why would John's readers have found this encounter between Jesus and the Samaritan woman shocking?** (4:7-8)

(2) **How is this conversation similar to the one that Jesus had with Nicodemus?** (4:9)

(3) **What was the relationship between the Jews and Samaritans?** (4:4-6)

❖ Select persons to read the parts of Jesus and the woman in verses 19-26, and then answer these questions.

(1) **What does this dialogue reveal to you about worship?**

(2) **What does it reveal to you about Jesus?**

(3) **Are we as the church living up to Jesus' unconditional acceptance of all who come seeking salvation? Give reasons to support your answer.**

(3) Discern Reasons for Prejudice

❖ Read aloud the first paragraph under "Jesus Shocks a Samaritan Woman." Discuss the apparent reasons for this congregation's prejudice against a district superintendent whom they did not yet personally know.

❖ Brainstorm types of prejudice that people may hold (such as racial, cultural, religious, age, or gender biases). List these ideas on newsprint.

❖ Consider reasons for the identified prejudices by using the following information as the basis for a lecture.

Point 1: *Prejudice* is a negative attitude.

Point 2: Prejudice occurs when people try to divide others into categories or groups, such as the following.

■ Those who are part of the *in-group* favor their own group members and reject all others, who comprise the *out-group*.

■ People assume that members of one *out-group* are all alike.

■ People assume that members of the *in-group* are somehow special and unique.

■ People make judgments based on a few members of an *out-group* and then attribute those characteristics to everyone in the group, resulting in stereotyping.

Point 3: Prejudice is learned and, therefore, can be changed.

❖ Distribute paper and pencils. Provide a few moments of quiet time for students to identify and write their personal prejudices. Assure them that this information is only between themselves and God.

(4) Identify Barriers That Prejudice Creates and Ways to Break Those Barriers

❖ Divide the class into teams and distribute paper or newsprint. Ask each team to identify a prejudice (for example, bias against a particular ethnic group) and list ways that this prejudice creates barriers. Also ask the teams to brainstorm ideas for ways that these barriers may be broken.

❖ Call the groups back together and invite each one to report on the highlights of their ideas.

(5) Continue the Journey

❖ Pray that the students will strive to see all persons as "one in Christ," so as not to be swayed by personal prejudices.

❖ Read aloud this preparation for next week's lesson. You may also want to post it on newsprint for the students to copy. **Prepare for next week's session, "None Is Righteous," by reading the background and lesson scripture from Romans 1:16-20; 3:9-20. This session begins our spring quarter, "God's Project: Effective Christians," with a unit entitled "Saved by God." Keep this focus in mind as you read: People often find themselves doing something hurtful to themselves or others, despite their best intentions to "be a good** person." **Why do we keep doing things we know we shouldn't, especially when we want to do good? Paul explains that we are sinful by nature.**

❖ Read aloud the following three ideas. Challenge the students to commit themselves to use these activities as a springboard to spiritual growth.

(1) **Be alert for news articles outlining how prejudice has been harmful to someone's opportunities for employment, for education, or for social and economic advancement. What do you think Jesus would say about each of the situations you discovered?**

(2) **Learn more about the Samaritans and their relationship with the Jews. You can find information in Bible dictionaries and handbooks, as well as on the Internet.**

(3) **Find ways to challenge prejudices that exist in your family, workplace, community, or church. Help people to understand that prejudice is incompatible with the teachings and behaviors of Jesus.**

❖ Sing or read aloud "Christ, from Whom All Blessings Flow." The fifth and sixth verses, as they appear in *The United Methodist Hymnal* (no. 550), are based on today's key verse, Galatians 3:28.

❖ Ask the students to echo this benediction as you read it phrase by phrase: **Grant, O Lord, that what has been said with our lips we may believe in our hearts, and that what we believe in our hearts we may practice in our lives; through Jesus Christ our Lord. Amen.**

THIRD QUARTER
God's Project: Effective Christians

MARCH 6, 2005–MAY 29, 2005

During the Spring Quarter we will investigate Paul's Letters to the churches in Rome and Galatia. Paul considers how one becomes a Christian and what it means to live faithfully as a disciple.

Unit 1, "Saved by God," includes four sessions that look at sin, judgment, justification, and redemption. Together, these sessions explore the basic conditions that form the framework of becoming effective Christians. We begin on March 6 with "None Is Righteous," which is an exploration of Paul's understanding of sin as found in Romans 1:16-20 and 3:9-20. The lesson for March 13, "God Judges All People," examines Paul's teachings in Romans 2:1-16 concerning God's judgment. In "Justified by Faith," the session for Palm Sunday on March 20, we will encounter Paul's teachings on justification by faith as set forth in Romans 5:1-11, 18-21. The final lesson for this unit is "Victory over Death." Since this is our Easter session, we will delve into John 20:1-10, which is a portion of John's account of the first Easter. We will also study Romans 6:1-14 where Paul interprets the meaning of the Resurrection.

In Unit 2, "The Christian Life," we will spend four weeks unpacking Paul's understandings of what it means to live as Christians. In "Power for Living," the session for April 3 that focuses on Romans 8:1-17, Paul contrasts what it means to live in the Spirit with what it means to live in the flesh. The lesson for April 10, "Affirming Christ as Lord," discerns Paul's teachings about salvation as recorded in Romans 10:5-21. The familiar passage from Romans 12:1-21 is the basis of the session for April 17, "Living the Christian Life." In this lesson, our goal will be to examine Paul's description of a life consecrated to God. "Living in Harmony" looks at Romans 14:1-13 and 15:5-6 on April 24. Here, as we conclude Unit 2, we will explore Paul's instructions about living nonjudgmentally and harmoniously in Christ.

In Unit 3, "Set Free," we turn to Paul's Letter to the Galatians to study his theology of freedom in Christ. This unit begins on May 1 with "Hanging on to God's Good News," based on Galatians 1. In this session we will study Paul's defense of both his authority and the gospel that he preaches. "Living on Faith," the session for May 8, examines Galatians 2:15–3:5 where Paul sets forth his understanding of what it means to be justified by faith. The session for May 15, "From Slave to Heir," is rooted in Galatians 3:19–4:7. During this lesson we will explore Paul's teachings about the purpose of the law. "Free to Serve," an examination of Paul's ideas about Christian liberty, looks at Galatians 5:1-15 on May 22. The spring quarter ends on May 29 with a study of Paul's teachings about how Christians are to live together. This session, "Life Together," is based on Galatians 5:22–6:10.

MEET OUR WRITER

DR. NANCY CLAIRE PITTMAN

Nancy Claire Pittman grew up in the wide, flat spaces of the Texas Panhandle before moving with her family to Oklahoma City during her high school years. After graduating from Putnam City High School, she returned to Texas to attend Texas Christian University in Fort Worth. There she earned a bachelor of arts degree in religion and psychology, and a master of divinity degree. While pursuing her education, she served as a summer youth minister in various churches in the region and as the youth minister of the Fort Worth area congregations of the Christian Church (Disciples of Christ).

Pittman was ordained to the ministry by the Christian Church (Disciples of Christ) in the Southwest on April 1, 1984. After serving as associate minister of Oak Cliff Christian Church in Dallas, she pursued doctoral studies at Southern Methodist University, where she completed her doctorate in New Testament studies in 1997, with a dissertation on Christology in the book of Revelation.

Engaged often as a preacher and lecturer in congregations and at regional and national events, in 1994 (when writing her doctoral dissertation), she and her husband, Don, were commissioned as overseas missionaries by the Common Board of Global Mission of the Christian Church (Disciples of Christ) and the United Church of Christ to serve on the faculty of Tainan Theological College and Seminary, a highly respected school in East Asia related to the Presbyterian Church of Taiwan. There, Pittman learned to speak Taiwanese and taught biblical Greek, introduction to the Synoptic Gospels, Johannine literature, and various exegetical courses. She also chaired the Worship Committee of the school, which provided oversight for nine worship services each week.

Having returned to the United States after almost seven years in Taiwan, Pittman is currently pastor of First Christian Church in Tahlequah, Oklahoma, the capital of the Cherokee nation and the ending point of the "Trail of Tears." She also serves as an adjunct professor of New Testament at Phillips Theological Seminary in Tulsa, an ecumenical seminary affiliated with the Christian Church (Disciples of Christ), where her husband is dean and William Tabbernee Professor of the History of Religions. They have a fifteen-year-old daughter, Merillat, who loves school, music, and her church youth group.

GOD'S PROJECT: EFFECTIVE CHRISTIANS

I have often observed that students of the New Testament, lay or clergy, professional or amateur, either love to study Paul's Letters or stay away from them with steadfast determination. In the last ten years before accepting this assignment, I could have been placed in the second group. Throughout my doctoral studies and in my teaching, I had focused my energy on other parts of the New Testament, particularly the Gospels and Revelation. And yet in the back of my mind I continued to contemplate Paul's sometimes difficult understandings of Christ and the church. I continued to mull over my disagreements with some of his views, or more precisely, the views of centuries of his interpreters.

So I accepted the assignment to work on this curriculum because it was time for me to look afresh at this challenging apostle, preacher, and letter-writer. It may be time for you as well to look again at these fascinating, puzzling, thought-provoking letters. They offer us a glimpse of the soul of a man on fire for God and of his passionate relationship with some of the earliest churches. Furthermore, through reading carefully what Paul has to say to those Roman and Galatian Christians we might also gain insight into our own congregational struggles and joys. We might also learn that some problems were as thorny for the first generation of Christians as they remain for us today. But the central solution is also the same.

Christ Is the Answer

A respected New Testament scholar has claimed that Paul discovered this solution long before he was aware of the plight of humankind or the troubles of congregations that he addresses so vividly in his letters. The solution is Jesus Christ. Out there on the road to Damascus, Saul the zealous Jew encountered the risen Lord. Up to that moment this man had never questioned the rightness of his crusade against Christians, nor had he ever wondered about his own sinfulness. He was convinced that he was pursuing a righteous cause, God's cause. All that changed when the grace of God through the crucifixion and resurrection of Jesus was revealed to him on that road. In that moment, everything that he had previously believed about God, humanity, and the people of God was transformed into an unwavering faith in Christ. This is the starting point and the ending point of the theological claims and ethics found in Paul's Letters.

It follows, according to one commentator, that the plight must correspond to this solution. Paul's profound experience of Christ convinced him that God had provided a savior, not just to Jews but to all humanity. In fact, such a savior must have been necessary. But why? Why does the whole world need Jesus the Messiah who died on a cross and then was resurrected? Through the eyes of faith Paul began to discern just how far humanity had fallen away from God. An immeasurable, unbridgeable gulf divided God from creation. From generation to generation, people chose to worship created things rather than the Creator

(Romans 1:20-25). People chose to break the primal covenant God had established with humanity and to follow their own desires, their own passions, the urgings of their own flesh. Again and again, every human being, with one exception, followed his or her own nature and not the ways of God.

The Jewish law could not bridge this gap. Although at one time in his life he practiced the law with great enthusiasm and care, Paul now saw that his efforts were futile. Neither he nor anyone else could carry out the commandments of the law so completely that they could actually build a bridge across the chasm to God. More important, Paul came to see that such efforts were not only ineffective but also needless. The grace of God, as it was manifested in the gift of Jesus to an unloving but greatly loved world, was more than sufficient. Through this gift God was offering a new covenant in which God not only kept God's side of the bargain but also gave the means through which humans could keep their side.

That meant, according to Paul, the faith of Jesus Christ. In the formula "faith of Christ," the word "of" is significant because it has two meanings. On the one hand, it refers to the faith that Jesus himself possessed in God, a faith that would empower him to move all the way to the cross. On the other hand, "of" refers to the faith that believers gain when they turn away from the sinful claims of a world gone so badly awry and turn toward that cross. When they make the decision to trust this event as the revelation of God's grace to them and to the whole world, when they believe with their whole hearts that through Christ, God has provided access to God's very self, then they possess this "faith of Christ."

This faith is all that is required for individuals to enter into the new covenant with God. By holding fast to this faith we are made righteous in the eyes of God. Paul expressed this same idea in another common claim: through faith we are justified. In Greek, the words translated "righteous" and "justified" are from the same root word, which simply stated means, "being made right" (see lesson 3, "Justified by Faith"). In this context, Paul was saying that our covenant with God is restored because God has wiped the slate clean and made us right.

In Paul's view, this is surely a matter between individuals—no matter their gender, race, or legal status—and God. But it is more than that. It is also a communal matter between the community of the faithful and God. And that still does not reach the limits of the issue. For it is ultimately a cosmic matter. Through Christ all creation will be renewed, made whole and beautiful and good in the fullness of time. This work, in all three of the ways listed here, is not yet complete. Our hope for our churches, our world, and ourselves has not yet been fulfilled. So we look forward, not back, to the day in which the gulf between God and creation will completely disappear and all things will be made new in and through Jesus Christ (see Romans 8:18-25).

The Formation of a New People

In the meantime, Paul recognized that God's project has not yet been completed. We are imperfect, infallible, limited creatures who have faith and yet fall away, who love God and yet are easily wooed by other attractions. That project is to build effective Christians, people of faith who can proclaim the gospel of Jesus Christ with untiring steadiness of purpose and commitment. Further, this effectiveness must be cultivated within a community of dedicated Christians, which we have come to call the church. For Paul did not envision isolated individuals crying alone in the wilderness; he saw a new people of God banded together by nothing other than a common faith in the salvation offered in Christ.

In order to understand just how radical Paul's conception of a new people was for his time, we must remember that in his world people were primarily identified and described by their membership within a family, nationality, and race. People were not seen as unique individuals with their own hopes and schemes for life. They were viewed as parts of a larger whole—as the multigenerational family, the nation-state or the ethnic group into which they were born. These groupings determined the place of a person within society and how others would judge her or him. That is why Paul reminded his readers on several occasions of his own ethnic identity and religion: "I myself am an Israelite, a descendant of Abraham, a member of the tribe of Benjamin" (Romans 11:1; see also Philippians 3:5). His affirmation of his affiliation to this group supported the particular point he is trying to make.

Yet now that he had truly seen the work of God in Christ he no longer counted his membership in the Jewish nation as his primary identity. He was now a part of the new community of God as are all who believe in Christ. And he was trying, with varying degrees of success, to shape and grow this community in accordance with the gospel that has been revealed in God's Son. This was not easy. Its members were drawn from many nationalities and races, from the Jews of Israel and the diaspora to Greeks scattered across the Greco-Roman world to the Romans who ruled the Western hemisphere to people from various smaller nations and ethnic enclaves. They did not come from the same social class—rich, poor, and middle-class persons were all drawn to the power of the gospel.

Further, both inside local congregations and among congregations across Asia Minor (Paul's primary sphere of activity), Christians often had little in common. They ate different foods; they followed different customs; they had varying opinions about conduct and morality. They were always tempted to make judgments about one another based first on gender, then ethnic origin, then physical characteristics and last, if at all, the content of character or belief. Moreover, at this stage in the development of the Christian churches, they claimed very little of the same memories, traditions, or teachings. When disagreements threatened their unity, they could not appeal to a constitution or book of worship because they had none. They could not even take refuge in reminiscence and the long history of their church because their community was so new, so recently called into being.

In this context, Paul is trying to form a new community and to shape a new identity for its members, an identity as children of God whose membership is based solely on faith in Christ. This identity would form and inform the beliefs, practices, and behavior of the new community. As God has first loved the believers, so they are to love one another. Everything they do and say to one another and to the world is to be rooted in this love. The Jewish law as a norm for human behavior, which had no power to save or transform even its staunchest adherents, would be relegated to a place behind this ethic of love.

But Paul knew that such a community could not be achieved without the participation of God in the project. The Spirit is Paul's way of talking about that participation. The Spirit, as the representative of God's will for communion with one another and with God, opposes the flesh, a code word for the desires of humanity to pursue their own interests and ways. The Spirit also makes possible love and all the other gifts essential for the formation of such a community. Without it, the church is merely another group among guilds, ethnic enclaves, and other gatherings of people with common origins and family ties. With it, the church becomes the Body of Christ.

Christians in Rome

The first letter by Paul in the New Testament is also the longest, the Epistle to the Romans. Scholars generally agree that it is among the last, if not the last, letters Paul wrote at a time late in his career when he was planning to go to Jerusalem to deliver the offering he was collecting for the church there (Romans 15:25). It can be dated some time in the middle to late 50s. From Judea he intended to travel to Spain and on the way stopped in Rome to greet the Christians who lived in the capital city of the Roman Empire (Romans 15:23-24).

We know little about the group of believers to whom Paul wrote. That he had many friends and acquaintances there is evident from the long list of greetings in Romans 16. Perhaps through them he may have learned that this community had been troubled by uneasy relationships between Christian Jews and Christian Gentiles. About seven to ten years earlier the emperor Claudius had expelled from Rome the Jews, including those who had embraced the Christian faith, because he believed they had caused a riot. In 54 C.E., Nero, Claudius's successor, had allowed them to come back. The Christian Gentiles may have grown accustomed to the absence of their Jewish brothers and sisters. Now they all had to learn again to live and work with one another. In these circumstances Paul found it necessary to explore the place of both Jew and Gentile within God's household and their respective roles within God's intention for human salvation.

The letter also served as an introduction of his own understanding of the gospel to Christians who were not acquainted with him, the larger portion of the Roman community. In it he affirms repeatedly the availability of the gospel and its power to all, regardless of ethnic origin. In Romans 1:16-17 he states the theme of the letter and, indeed, of much of his ministry: "For I am not ashamed of the gospel; it is the power of God for salvation to everyone who has faith, to the Jew first and also to the Greek. For in it the righteousness of God is revealed through faith for faith."

In the first eight lessons of this unit, we will have the opportunity to look at individual units within this majestic letter. A broad outline in which these passages can be situated looks like this:

Romans 1:1–4:25   The Enduring Faithfulness of God
Romans 5:1–8:39   The Saving Faith of Christ and the New People of God
Romans 9:1–11:36   God's Faithfulness to the First Covenant People of God
Romans 12:1–16:27 The Practice of Faith

Trouble in Galatia

Paul only knew a few individual Christians in Rome; in contrast, he knew well the churches in Galatia because he had worked with them since the beginning of their movement. With these people he had an intimate and long-standing relationship based first on their care for him when he ended up in Galatia on account of a "physical infirmity" (Galatians 4:13). So when he heard of trouble in these communities, he writes a sometimes angry, sometimes exhorting, always passionate letter to them.

Apparently, a group of people who disagreed with Paul about some critical matters had come to prominence in Galatia. Scholars of an earlier era called them the "Judaizers" and described them as people who wanted the Galatians to practice all aspects of the Jewish law, including circumcision. Although more recent scholars still accept this simple description of their message, they have rejected the term "Judaizers." This is largely because it obscures the fact that the argument being discussed in the pages of this letter was between two groups of Jewish Christians, not between Jews and non-Jews. Paul represented one Jewish group that believed that God's action in Christ makes the specific commandments of Torah irrelevant and unnecessary. The other Jewish group continued to treasure these commandments and believed that somehow they brought those who kept them even closer to God. In lessons 9-13 I will follow Richard B. Hays's lead and call them the "Missionaries." Both groups were trying to persuade Gentile Christians, who comprised the majority of the Galatian churches, to adopt their viewpoints. Eventually, as we know from history, Paul was to win this argument, but not without much emotion and pain. Christians were indeed set free from the Jewish law.

As a way to place the passages of lessons 9-13 within the context of the letter as a whole, here is an outline of the larger sections of Paul's Letter to the Galatians:

Galatians 1:1–2:21 Paul's Divine Call to the Gospel and the Mission to the Gentiles
Galatians 3:1–5:1   Doing Law Versus Claiming Faith
Galatians 5:2–6:10 Life in the Freedom of the Spirit
Galatians 6:11-18   Final Words

UNIT 1: SAVED BY GOD
NONE IS RIGHTEOUS

PREVIEWING THE LESSON

Lesson Scripture: Romans 1:16-20; 3:9-20
Background Scripture: Romans 1:16-20; 3:9-20
Key Verse: Romans 3:10

Focus of the Lesson:
People often find themselves doing something hurtful to themselves or others, despite their best intentions to "be a good person." Why do we keep doing things we know we shouldn't, especially when we want to do good? Paul explains that we are sinful by nature.

Goals for the Learners:
(1) to explore Paul's understanding of sin.
(2) to consider their responses and the responses of others to the gospel.
(3) to rejoice in the freedom and forgiveness they have in Christ.

Supplies:
Bibles, newsprint and marker, paper and pencils, hymnals

READING THE SCRIPTURE

NRSV
Romans 1:16-20

16 For I am not ashamed of the gospel; it is the power of God for salvation to everyone who has faith, to the Jew first and also to the Greek. 17 For in it the righteousness of God is revealed through faith for faith; as it is written, "The one who is righteous will live by faith."

18 For the wrath of God is revealed from heaven against all ungodliness and wickedness of those who by their wickedness suppress the truth. 19 For what can be known about God is plain to them, because God has

NIV
Romans 1:16-20

[16]I am not ashamed of the gospel, because it is the power of God for the salvation of everyone who believes: first for the Jew, then for the Gentile. [17]For in the gospel a righteousness from God is revealed, a righteousness that is by faith from first to last, just as it is written: "The righteous will live by faith."

[18]The wrath of God is being revealed from heaven against all the godlessness and wickedness of men who suppress the truth by their wickedness, [19]since what may be

shown it to them. 20 Ever since the creation of the world his eternal power and divine nature, invisible though they are, have been understood and seen through the things he has made. So they are without excuse.

Romans 3:9-20

9 What then? Are we any better off? No, not at all; for we have already charged that all, both Jews and Greeks, are under the power of sin, 10 as it is written:

"There is no one who is righteous, not even one;
11 there is no one who has understanding,
there is no one who seeks God.
12 All have turned aside, together they have become worthless;
there is no one who shows kindness,
there is not even one."
13 "Their throats are opened graves;
they use their tongues to deceive."
"The venom of vipers is under their lips."
14 "Their mouths are full of cursing and bitterness."
15 "Their feet are swift to shed blood;
16 ruin and misery are in their paths,
17 and the way of peace they have not known."
18 "There is no fear of God before their eyes."

19 Now we know that whatever the law says, it speaks to those who are under the law, so that every mouth may be silenced, and the whole world may be held accountable to God. 20 For "no human being will be justified in his sight" by deeds prescribed by the law, for through the law comes the knowledge of sin.

known about God is plain to them, because God has made it plain to them. [20]For since the creation of the world God's invisible qualities—his eternal power and divine nature—have been clearly seen, being understood from what has been made, so that men are without excuse.

Romans 3:9-20

[9]What shall we conclude then? Are we any better? Not at all! We have already made the charge that Jews and Gentiles alike are all under sin. [10]As it is written:

"There is no one righteous, not even one;
[11] there is no one who understands,
no one who seeks God.
[12] All have turned away,
they have together become worthless;
there is no one who does good,
not even one."
[13] "Their throats are open graves;
their tongues practice deceit."
"The poison of vipers is on their lips."
[14] "Their mouths are full of cursing and bitterness."
[15] "Their feet are swift to shed blood;
[16] ruin and misery mark their ways,
[17] and the way of peace they do not know."
[18] "There is no fear of God before their eyes."

[19]Now we know that whatever the law says, it says to those who are under the law, so that every mouth may be silenced and the whole world held accountable to God. [20]Therefore no one will be declared righteous in his sight by observing the law; rather, through the law we become conscious of sin.

UNDERSTANDING THE SCRIPTURE

Romans 1:16-17. After greeting the Roman church with a typical salutation (1:1-7) and words of thanksgiving and encouragement (1:8-14), Paul writes in verse 15 that he is eager to come to Rome to proclaim the gospel. Verses 16 and 17 clarify the rea-

sons for his eagerness and so serve as the theme of the entire letter.

Paul is so eager to work with the Roman Christians whom he has never met because, as he states in verse 16, he is not ashamed of the gospel. According to the Greek text, this is the fourth time he has used the word *gospel* since he began the letter. (The NRSV adds an additional *gospel* in verse 3 to make the meaning clearer.) In verse 1 Paul says this good news is of God; in verses 3 and 8 he presents Jesus Christ, God's son, as the content of this news. The gospel is the announcement of the fulfillment of God's promises as the future arrives in the person of Christ. Paul is not embarrassed to report this great event.

Paul proclaims the gospel because it is the power of God for salvation. Notice that the gospel does not merely point to God's power; the gospel *is* the power itself unleashed, revealed, made real and concrete. It is the power for deliverance (the basic meaning of the Greek word for salvation), deliverance from evil, captivity, danger, oppression, and even poor health.

Everyone who has faith, everyone who believes and receives the truth of the gospel, can receive this salvation. For Jews of Paul's era, "everyone" could be divided into two groups: ethnic Jews who receive first the opportunity to respond to God's act in Christ, and Greeks (here a synonym for Gentiles) who also get a chance. This order of reception of the gospel is an important motif in Romans.

Everyone who believes can receive this salvation because through the gospel the righteousness of God is revealed. Righteousness, for Paul, connotes not simply God's justice but also God's faithfulness in offering renewed relationship with all humanity. It is God's determination to hold fast to the covenant God made with all of creation, no matter how often humans fail to faithfully keep it.

Finally, this righteousness is revealed, as Paul writes in an idiomatic phrase, "through faith for faith," which has been translated in many ways. In *The New Interpreter's Bible*, N. T. Wright suggests that "from God's faithfulness to human faithfulness" is a good, clear way to understand this idiom.

Paul closes this theme statement by quoting Habakkuk 2:4 as confirmation of what he has just said. He is also underscoring his earlier point in verse 16 that both Jew and Greek are saved—are made righteous—through faith, and not birth or actions.

Romans 1:18-20. Having stated the central message of the letter, at verse 18 Paul begins to explicate his understanding of the human situation before God. Not only is the righteousness of God revealed (1:17), but the wrath of God is also exposed. Wrath here is not uncontrollable, vengeful rage. It is, rather, a verdict on the guilt of humankind. As such it is the opposite of salvation. And it demonstrates God's zealous concern for creation and the justice—or lack thereof—that is displayed within it. Further, it is revealed in the present time, just as salvation is.

This wrath is directed against all humans who suppress the truth in wickedness and ungodliness. At this point, however, Paul is talking specifically to Gentiles who do not have the advantage of knowing the law. Nonetheless, they have been shown God's truth through the created order. They know what God desires, but they have ignored it. They have chosen instead to pursue the things that take them away from God. Paul states explicitly that there is no excuse for such a decision and in the following verses lists the consequences of it.

Romans 3:9-20. These verses follow a lengthy treatment of the righteous judgment of God (see "God Judges All People," lesson 2) and the advantage—or lack thereof—that the law offers to Jews in facing such judgment. In short, Jews like Gentiles must face God's wrath. So Paul begins this section with another rhetorical question: "What then? Are we (meaning himself and his Jewish brothers and sisters) any better off?" His answer is a resounding no. Every single person is under the power of sin.

This is the first time "sin," as a noun, is employed in this letter; it appears as a verb in 2:12. The fundamental meaning for the root of both the verb and the noun is "missing the mark." So when Jews sin against the law, they miss the goal of keeping it carefully and precisely. The word throughout Greek literature also denotes transgression against moral customs, social mores, and laws.

Paul gives the word "sin" an explicitly theological twist and uses it in two ways. The first sense is similar to the meanings just described—sin as an action against God and God's creation. But Paul also uses the word in a second sense, as a power or a master over which we have no control. Sometimes, in an extension of this second meaning, he even uses the word to connote a place, a realm, in which everyone who does not have faith lives without recourse (see 6:1 and following).

To prove his point that all people, Jew and Greek alike, are held in bondage to sin, he offers a series of scriptural references. These verses are taken from Ecclesiastes (7:20); the Psalms (14:1-2; 53:1-2; 5:9; 140:3; 10:7; 36:1); and the prophet Isaiah (59:7-8), with the point being that even the sacred writings of the Jews bear witness to Paul's claims. Not a single person can be reckoned as righteous in all creation. All have missed the mark; all have fallen captive to sin's unbreakable hold.

In verses 19-20 Paul concludes this appeal to scripture for support by returning to the subject of the law. Those who are "under the law," that is, Jews, are directly addressed by it. But that fact does not excuse Gentiles, for everyone in the whole world must answer to God for their sinful actions. In verse 20, Paul makes one last appeal to the Jewish scriptures by quoting Psalm 143:2. Law reveals sin and no one can escape.

INTERPRETING THE SCRIPTURE

The Main Points

As we work through Paul's Letter to the Romans we will encounter words that are sublimely clear and inspirational, as well as ideas that are difficult to understand or to accept. Keeping Paul's theme statement of 1:16-17 in front of us can serve as a polar star as we navigate through the complexities. In these two verses he succinctly asserts the primary topics that will guide the entire letter.

First, God plays the leading role in the great drama of creation, history, and salvation. And God always keeps God's promises, especially the promise of renewed relationship between God's self and humanity. It is this promise-keeping dependability that constitutes the righteousness of God, a quality that is of utmost importance to Paul's understanding of the divine.

Second, God keeps this pledge through the death and resurrection of Jesus Christ, events that changed forever the course of history by defeating sin and death and ushering in the age to come of God's peace. This action is the content of the gospel and it alone has the power to deliver us from all bondage, especially that of sin and death, and to bring us into the relationship that God so desires. Just uttering the gospel sets free its force for salvation. Thus, it is not the human effort of proclamation that makes the accomplishment of God's purposes possible; it is solely God's work in and through the gospel.

Third, our role in this story of salvation is to believe, to receive, and to trust—meanings encompassed by Paul's use of the word "faith." Through faith we have the eyes to see just how righteous and just God really is and just how far God will go to be in right relationship with us. Through faith in what God has done we are also made whole and righteous, as we will see in subsequent lessons.

*"Not Having Your Cake and
Not Eating It Too!"*

One of the difficulties in this letter has to do with Paul's definition of "sin." As described in the Understanding the Scripture portion, Paul uses the word in two senses: as a deliberate action or attitude that misses the standard God has set up and also as an almost personalized power that holds humanity in thrall. Before we can explore a difficulty that arises in this double meaning, we should consider more fully what each sense means.

In the first sense, sin is an active choice to suppress the truth (1:18), the truth that only God is the creator, the redeemer, and giver of life and all its gifts. Any action that betrays that truth is a sin. To pretend that we ourselves are the independent providers of abundant living is a sin. To claim that other gods or creatures might actually control creation, or a part thereof, is a sin. To view ourselves as masters of the world, and not stewards of what God has made, is a sin. To reject the truth God has revealed in Christ is a sin. The vices that Paul lists in 1:24-32 are results of sin, not the basic sin itself.

In the second sense, sin is a power that controls us and over which we can hardly gain mastery. It is inevitable and inescapable by human efforts, taking on a malevolent life of its own as it exercises authority over humanity, creates a kind of solidarity among sinners, and leads people away from God. Notice that in these verses Paul does not use the figure of Satan as an explanation or personification for sin in these texts. Sin is powerful, but it is rooted in the human condition (see "Justified by Faith," lesson 3).

The difficulty in Paul's twofold understanding of sin lies in the fact that, on the one hand, while we are under sin's control,

on the other hand, we have no excuse for our sinful behavior. We certainly cannot claim ignorance: Paul repeatedly claims that all humanity is sinful and knows it (see 1:19). Nor can we appeal to the thralldom in which sin holds us. He never allows us to say "the devil made me do it." So as I ponder this problem, I begin to think that not only can we not have our cake, we cannot eat it either.

Thus it seems rather unjust to blame us for missing the mark in some way if we are fully under sin's power. Yet to quibble over such an injustice is to miss Paul's primary point: all of us, regardless of our ethnic background, our education, our accomplishments, are sinners. We are trapped in the same inexplicable web of sin as both cause and effect in our lives. And we need God's help in overcoming the barriers that sin places between us and God. The means God chose to destroy that barrier is the cross of Christ Jesus. Our part is to believe in that means.

Good News: We're All Sinners!

When I was growing up, many youth ministers were influenced by a theory of human relationships known as "transactional analysis." It was popularized in a book entitled *I'm OK, You're OK* by Thomas A. Harris. Those of us who participated in workshops on transactional analysis and tried to apply it in our lives were quite tempted to interpret it as a kind of radical relativism. We sometimes viewed it as a license to do whatever we wanted as long as we were not hurting anyone else. After all, we were all fundamentally OK, we reasoned, and so actions that were not overtly hurtful must also be OK.

I still remember a sermon preached one Sunday morning by our senior minister who had heard enough of our relativism. The gist of it was this: in many respects we are not OK, and what we are doing to ourselves and to others is not OK either. In fact, he said quite frankly, we are sinners and we are sinning in certain ways, even if we cannot immediately see the harmful consequences of our actions. By reminding us of this fact, he was echoing Paul who challenges us in the same way in these passages.

At the time, my friends and I were quite taken aback by his attack of our theory *du jour* and believed that he was being harsh and critical. What I grew to understand in college and seminary was that our minister was trying to speak a good word to us, a freeing word. I learned, and am still learning, that no matter how good I tried to act, no matter how well-intentioned I was in my relationships with others, no matter how much I tried to control my jealous, lazy, wasteful impulses, I was unable to attain

fully the goals I had set for righteous, moral, loving behavior. What was wrong with me? Why could I not fix myself? Paul's answer is simple. I could not solve my dilemma myself because I was under the power of sin.

Paradoxically, I find this to be good news. Not because it releases me from the obligation to pursue good, but because it reminds me that I am not God. I am not perfect and God already knows that. I find it good news also because it enables me to give others a break as well, to stop demanding that they be sinless in all things. And finally I find it good news because God, through faith, forgives my past and empowers me to deal with sin's always threatening enslavement.

SHARING THE SCRIPTURE

PREPARING TO TEACH

Preparing Our Hearts

This week's devotional reading is found in Psalm 59:1-5. Evil and enemies abound. Hence, the psalmist cries out to God, lamenting his situation and fervently praying that God will deliver him. We may share in the writer's feelings, for we too are surrounded by evil. We can proclaim, as Paul does in today's lesson, that not one person is righteous—including ourselves. Identify difficult relationships that you are now facing. Why are these relationships so challenging for you?

Pray that God will show you and your students how to deal lovingly with people who oppose them.

Preparing Our Minds

Study the background and lesson scripture, both found in Romans 1:16-20 and 3:9-

20. Try to discern Paul's theme for this letter. What is Paul saying about sin? Do you agree with his definitions and concerns?

Write on newsprint:
    information for next week's lesson, found under "Continue the Journey."

Plan a lecture concerning Paul's definitions of "sin," if you choose to do this optional activity under "Explore Paul's Understanding of Sin."

LEADING THE CLASS

(1) Gather to Learn

❖ Welcome the class members and introduce any guests.
❖ Pray that the participants will recognize that no one is righteousness, but that through faith they can experience God's gracious love.
❖ Invite the students to identify actions or attitudes that help to define what it means to be a human being. List their ideas on newsprint. If time permits, discuss those

attributes that set humans apart from the rest of the animal kingdom.

❖ Note that in today's lesson we will see how Paul talks about sin as being part of our human nature. Humans can actually plan to sin; we can also try hard not to sin and still find ourselves sinning anyway.

❖ Read aloud today's focus statement: **People often find themselves doing something hurtful to themselves or others, despite their best intentions to "be a good person." Why do we keep doing things we know we shouldn't, especially when we want to do good? Paul explains that we are sinful by nature.**

(2) Explore Paul's Understandings of Sin

❖ Choose two volunteers, one to read Romans 1:16-20 and another to read Romans 3:9-20.

❖ Use one of the following activities to explore Paul's teachings concerning sin.

- **Activity 1:** Use the information under Romans 3:9-20 and also under "Not Having Your Cake and Not Eating It Too!" to create a lecture that focuses on the two main ways that Paul defines sins.

- **Activity 2:** Divide the class into two groups and ask each group to focus on one of the readings. In what ways does Paul use the word "sin" in the assigned passage? Bring the two groups together to report their findings. Help them to recognize Paul's two uses of the word "sin" and how these two understandings are in conflict with one another.

- **Activity 3:** Divide the class into several groups. Give each group pencils and papers. The groups are to define the word "sin," based on what Paul says in the two assigned readings from Romans. Provide time for the students to read their definitions to one another and receive feedback on their ideas.

❖ Encourage the students to give exam-

ples of (1) sins that we choose to commit and (2) sin as a force of evil in the world. List their ideas under these headings on a sheet of newsprint.

❖ Conclude this portion of the session by pointing out that Paul is clear about our status before God: we are all sinners; no one is righteous.

(3) Consider Learners' Responses to the Gospel

❖ Read or retell the information under "The Main Points" and ask these questions. Information for verses 16-17 and 18-20 in Understanding the Scripture may be helpful as you lead the discussion.

- **(1) Do you agree with Paul's understanding as expressed here? Why or why not?**
- **(2) Paul says that he is not ashamed of the gospel. He responds to the gospel by boldly proclaiming Jesus Christ. How does your church respond to the gospel? How do you respond as an individual believer?**
- **(3) What does this passage suggest concerning human accountability before God?**

(4) Rejoice in Freedom and Forgiveness in Christ

❖ Retell the information under "Good News: We're All Sinners!"

❖ Invite the students to comment on their own efforts to make sin relative or to lessen its importance. Discuss the success, or failure, of these efforts.

❖ Distribute paper and pencils. Ask the students to record examples of struggles that they have in trying to do what is right. Be clear that this information is confidential.

❖ Lead the students in a guided imagery exercise. Ask them to respond silently when you pause.

- **Imagine yourself standing before God as you are about to give an account of your life. Think of some** words to describe how you are feeling right now. (Pause)

- You hear God ask you these two questions and try to find words to answer them: What struggles have you had in trying to do good? What barriers have prevented you from doing what you know is right? (Pause)
- Finally, you hear God saying that divine grace is sufficient for you. Tell God how you have experienced such amazing grace in your own life. (Pause)

❖ Invite the students to speak aloud a word of praise to God for the freedom and forgiveness they have experienced in Christ.

(5) Continue the Journey

❖ Pray that the students will recognize that although they are sinners, by God's grace they can have a relationship with God through Jesus Christ.

❖ Read aloud this preparation for next week's lesson. You may also want to post it on newsprint for the students to copy. **Prepare for next week's session, "God Judges All People," by reading Romans 2:1-16, which is both the background and scripture lesson. Keep this focus in mind as you prepare: People are sometimes tempted to pass judgment on others and to** consider themselves superior. Do we have a valid basis to judge others in this way? Paul says that we do not because we all stand under God's judgment and are found wanting. The good news is that God can help us to do what is pleasing to God.

❖ Read aloud the following three ideas. Challenge the students to commit themselves to use these activities as a springboard to spiritual growth.

(1) **Be aware this week of times when you miss the mark of God's standard and fall into sin. As you reflect on your shortcomings, consider what you can do to avoid the same problems in the future?**

(2) **Write in your spiritual journal about the ways that you see God's grace at work in your life this week. Offer a prayer of thanks for God's grace.**

(3) **Offer forgiveness to someone who has sinned against you and/or seek forgiveness from someone you have wronged.**

❖ Sing or read aloud "Only Trust Him."

❖ Say one phrase of this prayer at a time and ask the class to repeat it so that they will quickly learn it: **Grant, O Lord, that we may go forth to serve you as faithful disciples who not only hear the word but also do it in the name of Jesus. Amen.**

GOD JUDGES ALL PEOPLE

PREVIEWING THE LESSON

Lesson Scripture: Romans 2:1-16
Background Scripture: Romans 2:1-16
Key Verse: Romans 2:16

Focus of the Lesson:
People are sometimes tempted to pass judgment on others and to consider themselves superior. Do we have a valid basis to judge others in this way? Paul says that we do not because we all stand under God's judgment and are found wanting. The good news is that God can help us to do what is pleasing to God.

Goals for the Learners:
(1) to examine Paul's teachings concerning God's judgment.
(2) to analyze their tendencies to judge others.
(3) to make a commitment to prepare for God's judgment.

Supplies:
Bibles, newsprint and marker, paper and pencils, hymnals

READING THE SCRIPTURE

NRSV
Romans 2:1-16

Therefore you have no excuse, whoever you are, when you judge others; for in passing judgment on another you condemn yourself, because you, the judge, are doing the very same things. 2 You say, "We know that God's judgment on those who do such things is in accordance with truth." 3 Do you imagine, whoever you are, that when you judge those who do such things and yet do them yourself, you will escape the judgment of God? 4 Or do you despise the riches of his kindness and forbearance and patience? Do you not realize that God's kindness is meant

NIV
Romans 2:1-16

You, therefore, have no excuse, you who pass judgment on someone else, for at whatever point you judge the other, you are condemning yourself, because you who pass judgment do the same things. ²Now we know that God's judgment against those who do such things is based on truth. ³So when you, a mere man, pass judgment on them and yet do the same things, do you think you will escape God's judgment? ⁴Or do you show contempt for the riches of his kindness, tolerance and patience, not realizing that God's kindness leads you toward repentance?

to lead you to repentance? 5 But by your hard and impenitent heart you are storing up wrath for yourself on the day of wrath, when God's righteous judgment will be revealed. 6 For he will repay according to each one's deeds: 7 to those who by patiently doing good seek for glory and honor and immortality, he will give eternal life; 8 while for those who are self-seeking and who obey not the truth but wickedness, there will be wrath and fury. 9 There will be anguish and distress for everyone who does evil, the Jew first and also the Greek, 10 but glory and honor and peace for everyone who does good, the Jew first and also the Greek. 11 For God shows no partiality.

12 All who have sinned apart from the law will also perish apart from the law, and all who have sinned under the law will be judged by the law. 13 For it is not the hearers of the law who are righteous in God's sight, but the doers of the law who will be justified. 14 When Gentiles, who do not possess the law, do instinctively what the law requires, these, though not having the law, are a law to themselves. 15 They show that what the law requires is written on their hearts, to which their own conscience also bears witness; and their conflicting thoughts will accuse or perhaps excuse them **16 on the day when, according to my gospel, God, through Jesus Christ, will judge the secret thoughts of all.**

[5]But because of your stubbornness and your unrepentant heart, you are storing up wrath against yourself for the day of God's wrath, when his righteous judgment will be revealed. [6]God "will give to each person according to what he has done." [7]To those who by persistence in doing good seek glory, honor and immortality, he will give eternal life. [8]But for those who are self-seeking and who reject the truth and follow evil, there will be wrath and anger. [9]There will be trouble and distress for every human being who does evil: first for the Jew, then for the Gentile; [10]but glory, honor and peace for everyone who does good: first for the Jew, then for the Gentile. [11]For God does not show favoritism.

[12]All who sin apart from the law will also perish apart from the law, and all who sin under the law will be judged by the law. [13]For it is not those who hear the law who are righteous in God's sight, but it is those who obey the law who will be declared righteous. [14](Indeed, when Gentiles, who do not have the law, do by nature things required by the law, they are a law for themselves, even though they do not have the law, [15]since they show that the requirements of the law are written on their hearts, their consciences also bearing witness, and their thoughts now accusing, now even defending them.) [16]**This will take place on the day when God will judge men's secrets through Jesus Christ, as my gospel declares.**

UNDERSTANDING THE SCRIPTURE

Romans 2:1-5. Paul slightly changes the subject at 2:1, immediately after he concludes the catalogue of consequences for ignoring God (1:24-32). Now he begins to discuss the act of judging others. And the first thing he reminds us is that judgment is a prerogative that belongs exclusively to God. It is not something in which humans can indulge.

Paul makes this point through "diatribe"—an ancient form of argumentation used in speeches and debates in which the speaker set up an imaginary opponent in order to instruct his audience. We can assume his use of this device because suddenly, after using the third person plural "they" throughout 1:18-32, he switches to the second person singular "you" in 2:1-5.

Also, in 2:1 and 3 he uses a Greek phrase translated by the NRSV as "whoever you are," indicating that he has no specific person in mind. The imaginary opponent is probably Gentile. We can say that because this section immediately follows a direct address to Gentiles without signaling any change of addressees.

Teachers should nonetheless be aware that since the time of Augustine commentators have frequently assumed that Paul is addressing a fictitious Jew in these verses. Occasionally this has contributed to anti-Semitic attitudes and actions. Therefore, it seems best to look at the evidence in the text and think about this person who Paul is describing as a Gentile who is quite judgmental toward others.

In Romans 2:1-2 Paul states the problem. This person may believe herself (or himself) to be superior to others because she possesses a superior law. She believes herself to know the truth about such things and about God's judgment upon them. And so she passes judgment, eagerly moralizing and accusing others for the things they do.

As Paul points out in 2:3, she may herself be participating in these evil activities. Yet somehow she thinks that her knowledge of right and wrong, whether it is based on Torah or Gentile law codes, lifts her above all condemnation. Paul will have nothing to do with such hypocrisy. Regardless of knowledge or station in life or ethnicity, all will see and experience the judgment of God.

This propensity to pass judgment on others while ignoring one's own unrighteousness tests God's tolerance, implies Paul in 2:4. He asks his imaginary opponent, who is indulging in the same wickedness as those she so eagerly scorns, if she looks down on the riches of God's kindness, forbearance, and patience? Are you above the blessings of God, Paul asks?

He continues with the pointed rhetorical questions that are a part of diatribe. Paul probes to find out if the opponent realizes

that God's kindness is meant to lead to repentance? God is patient in order that the imaginary opponent will have a chance to turn away from her unrighteous life, not so that she might have further opportunity to participate in wickedness and ungodliness.

If she persists in judging others while behaving badly, Paul announces in 2:5, then she also will face the consequences of God's wrath. For the day will come in which God will do the judging and the unrighteousness of all, Jew and Gentile, will be revealed.

In mentioning this "day of wrath," Paul is drawing upon an ancient Jewish tradition about a day when God will come to judge the evil of the earth and destroy it. For example, the prophet Isaiah says, "See, the day of the LORD comes, cruel, with wrath and fierce anger, to make the earth a desolation, and to destroy its sinners from it" (Isaiah 13:9). Jeremiah (Lamentations 1:12); Ezekiel 7:19; and Zephaniah 1:14-15, among others, also refer to this terrible day. The early Christians remembered this tradition and often connected it to the Second Coming of Christ. Paul uses it primarily to talk about a future event as he does here (see also Romans 2:16 and 5:9; 1 Corinthians 4:5; 2 Corinthians 5:10; 1 Thessalonians 1:9-10). Occasionally, however, he suggests that the judgment of God is a reality already present in our midst (see Romans 1:18).

Romans 2:6-11. In this section Paul offers a more detailed description of God's judgment on the day of wrath. What is especially striking about this text is his emphasis on judgment according to the works of each person. "For [God] will repay according to each one's deeds," he writes in 2:6. However, before we accuse Paul of being inconsistent with his dictum that we are saved through faith (Romans 3:28), we should note where this sentence comes from. He is quoting here Psalm 62:12 and Proverbs 24:12. Both of these passages counsel dependence upon God and not upon one's own actions or knowledge. Actions and words betray our deepest allegiances;

they demonstrate how much we are trusting God.

So, says Paul in 2:7-8, those who do good while seeking glory, honor, and immortality (all positive motives in the ancient Western world) will be rewarded with eternal life. Those who seek only their own pleasure, those who do wickedness, will be the recipients of God's anger. And, Paul reiterates in 2:9-11, it matters not if one is Jewish or Greek, for God shows no partiality. God does not play favorites.

Romans 2:12-16. Paul continues the same theme of judgment upon both Jew and Gentile in this section. For the first time in this letter, he talks about "law." Joseph Fitzmeyer explains that throughout Romans Paul employs the word "law" in four different ways: generically, as in a command or rule; figuratively, as in a principle of some kind; as a reference to the entire Hebrew Bible; and as a reference to the Jewish Law, the Torah. In this passage Paul is using "law" to refer to the Torah.

For those who are "apart from the law,"

namely the Gentiles, God will judge them by standards that are also "apart from the law." God will use a different criterion for those "under the law," namely Jews, because they know the law but they do not live it.

Furthermore, in 2:14-15 we learn that it is possible for Gentiles who do not know the law to be justified, that is, to be placed in right relationship with God. They can receive such reward because even without the Jewish law, it is possible for them to depend upon the one true God and do what is right. They also can show the true requirement of Torah: that it becomes so much a part of a person's life that it is engraved upon his or her heart.

Romans 2:16 refers again to that day of judgment in which God will judge "the secret thoughts of all." Notice that this time Paul adds explicitly Christian motifs. This statement is a part of the gospel that he preaches, and God will carry out this judgment through Jesus Christ.

INTERPRETING THE SCRIPTURE

Judgment and the Day of Wrath

In Romans 2:5 Paul begins to draw upon a theme already prominent in Jewish tradition and Hebrew Scripture: the wrath of God expressed on one terrible and future day. First, we should recognize that for Paul and his Jewish antecedents, wrath is not primarily the uncontrolled emotion of fury that we moderns often associate with the word, especially if we are familiar with Jonathan Edwards's famous sermon, "Sinners in the Hands of an Angry God." It is rather an action, God's action of judgment against sinful humanity. As such it is the opposite of God's deliverance from sin.

Second, Paul conceives of God's wrath and judgment, like salvation, as having a

past dimension as well as a future one. Scholars often refer to this as the "already-not-yet" quality of much of Paul's thought. On the one hand, as noted in last week's lesson, Paul said in Romans 1:24-32 that the punishment for sin is God's nondeliverance from its power. God, out of wrath, gave sinners up to their sin. Judgment begins the minute we choose evil over good.

On the other hand, Paul points to a day when God's wrath will be fully revealed and judgment will be fully realized. Echoes of Jewish prophetic and apocalyptic ideas are heard in his description of what will happen to those who do evil and those who do good. In fact, these ideas pervade early Christian understandings of a future that would climax at any time with the Second

Coming of Christ. Passages such as Daniel 7:13-14 and Psalm 2 enabled ancient Christians to depict Christ as the one who would on God's day of wrath inaugurate judgment as well as salvation.

Facing Sin Seriously

I have always been deeply uncomfortable with the image of God as a judge pouring out wrath upon sinners. I prefer to think of God as love, in the words of the author of 1 John (1 John 4:8, 16). And I want God's love to be as unconditional as that of the extravagantly loving father in the parable of the prodigal son (Luke 15:11-32). Further, I myself respond much better and am much more likely to change my problematic behavior if I am rewarded for what I do right than punished for what I do wrong. I know I am not the only one who wishes that words about God's judgment were not in the Bible.

But we only have license to ignore God's judgment if we are also willing to ignore sin and its evil consequences in ourselves and in our world. Paul will not allow us to do this. He takes sin seriously. And he is not talking merely about the sins of individuals against God. He is also talking about sin throughout human society, the kind of sin that leads to oppression and death for many.

When we remember the Holocaust, the Rwandan genocide, the 9/11 attacks on New York and Washington D.C., among many other atrocities of our generation, we must long for judgment on those people who perpetrated such acts against humankind. In the face of such enormous evil we can only hope that God will indeed summon those who have done such injustice to account for their actions. We ourselves have few, if any, tools to do this and can only look to God for rectification of such terrible things.

Yet it is not only these obvious enormous evils that face us. Sin pervades and influences our individual lives as well. Our children face bullies at school; we face capricious bosses and faceless institutions that sometimes do not wish us well. We deal daily with the consequences of the sinful acts of ourselves and of others. Again, is it not appropriate, even at some level satisfying, to turn to God with our hopes that the petty injustice and unrighteousness all around us will be challenged and brought to nothing? If we ourselves cannot be judges, as Paul urges us to remember, isn't it natural to want God to play that role? Paul reminds us of how seriously God takes sin and evil and asks us only to do the same.

Yet Another Apparent Contradiction

In the previous lesson we looked at a logical difficulty in Paul's understanding of sin. In this passage we are presented with another apparent contradiction, this time in Paul's understanding of how we are justified, that is, brought into right relationship with God. Throughout this letter Paul emphasizes his belief that salvation comes through faith, not works (see for example 1:16-17; 3:28; 4:1-25). Yet here in the second chapter Paul says quite directly, "[God] will repay according to each one's deeds" (2:6); and "For it is not the hearers of the law who are righteous in God's sight, but the doers of the law who will be justified" (2:13).

Several resolutions to this logical inconsistency have been suggested. Some scholars have claimed that Paul is addressing only Christians after having been justified by faith in these texts. But the fact that Paul never indicates such a shift away from talking about the universal human condition to the situation of faithful Christians counts strongly against this explanation. Others suggest that Paul believes there are people, Jew or Gentile, who do not have faith in Christ and yet are so righteous that God grants them "glory and honor and immortality" (2:7) anyway.

Again our drive for consistency obscures two fundamental truths that Paul is trying to convey. First, all of us, Jew or Greek, stand on equal footing before a God who does not play favorites. Whether we know the law of the Jews or the law of other peoples, all of us must face God and account for what we have done with our knowledge of right and wrong.

This leads to the second truth: human actions do indeed matter. Paul knows this as surely as Matthew knows it in the recounting of the last judgment (Matthew 25:31-46), as surely as James knows it when he says that faith without works is dead (James 2:17). Can our actions ultimately save us? Paul despairs of such an impossibility. Nonetheless, he calls all humanity to act as righteously and justly as possible in order to indicate what lies in our hearts. God will take care of the rest.

Letting God Be the Judge

The human tendency to judge others when we ourselves are engaged in our own kinds of sin is so strong that we need constant reminders to refrain from this favorite pastime. Paul's parody of the judgmental person in 2:1-5 is similar to Jesus' humorous stab at those who with logs in their own eyes still want to judge the faults of others (Matthew 7:1-5). Do these passages ask us to refrain from speaking the truth about sinful and damaging actions when we encounter them? I do not think so. They do, however, call us to examine our own consciences, motives, and behavior first before humbly criticizing those things that are harmful to individuals and deleterious to the community. And they remind us that in all things God alone is the final judge of all people—including ourselves.

SHARING THE SCRIPTURE

PREPARING TO TEACH

Preparing Our Hearts

This week's devotional reading is found in Psalm 50:1-15. Here the psalmist writes about God's coming judgment. God does not need the numerous sacrifices that the people have brought but instead desires to receive their thanks and hear their prayers. As you read this psalm, begin to think about what you believe concerning God's judgment, which is the theme for our lesson from Romans. Do you expect God to judge you personally? If so, what do you think God's verdict will be?

Pray that you and your students will recognize that God will call each of us to account and we therefore need to be ready.

Preparing Our Minds

Study the background and lesson scripture, both of which are from Romans 2:1-16.
Write on newsprint:
   information for next week's lesson, found under "Continue the Journey."
Plan a lecture if you choose that option in the "Examine Paul's Teaching Concerning God's Judgment" section.

LEADING THE CLASS

(1) Gather to Learn

❖ Welcome the class members and introduce any guests.
❖ Pray that the students will discern from this lesson that God's judgments are just.
❖ Note that many television shows deal with real-life and fictional courtroom dra-

mas. Invite students to comment on any of these types of shows that they watch. Why are these shows intriguing? What motivates people to watch such shows? Do people accept responsibility for their actions and hold themselves accountable? Is justice well served in most of these cases?

❖ Point out that just as Judge Judy, or another popular television judge, must render a verdict, so too God renders a verdict about each of our lives.

❖ Read aloud today's focus statement: **People are sometimes tempted to pass judgment on others and to consider themselves superior. Do we have a valid basis to judge others in this way? Paul says that we do not because we all stand under God's judgment and are found wanting. The good news is that God can help us to do what is pleasing to God.**

(2) Examine Paul's Teaching Concerning God's Judgment

❖ Choose a volunteer to read Romans 2:1-11.

❖ Either discuss the following questions, or answer them yourself in a lecture. You can find information in "Understanding the Scripture" in verses 1-5 and 6-11.

(1) Paul uses an ancient form of argument called "diatribe" to make his point. In a diatribe, the speaker or writer usually sets up an imaginary opponent. Describe the kind of person who is Paul's opponent here. Give reasons to support the kind of person you choose.

(2) On what basis does this imaginary opponent make judgments?

(3) What does Paul say will happen to those persons who are unrepentant before God?

(4) What clues do other Bible passages give us concerning "the day of wrath"? (You may want to invite the students to turn to passages mentioned in Understanding the Scripture.)

❖ Ask several students who have different translations to read Romans 2:12-16.

(1) Distribute paper and pencils. Provide a time limit for students to meditate on these five verses. Encourage them to write something that stands out for them in this passage. They may think of an interpretation, a new insight, or a question.

(2) Ask the students to work with a partner or small team to discuss whatever thoughts have occurred to them.

(3) Bring the class together and invite volunteers to share what they have learned.

(4) If you prefer to lecture, omit steps 1-3 and summarize your own interpretations, insights, and questions.

(3) Analyze Personal Tendencies to Judge Others

❖ Read aloud these words and phrases, pausing after each one.
- Unwed parent
- Convicted felon
- Drug addict or alcoholic
- Married man or woman having an affair
- Person who gossips

(1) Ask students to call out whatever comes to their minds when they hear these words. List their ideas on newsprint.

(2) Look back over the newsprint to discern which words sound empathetic and which ones sound judgmental.

(3) Read the list aloud again, this time asking the students to respond with words that Jesus might use. List these ideas on another sheet of newsprint.

(4) Post the newsprint sheets side by side. Discuss how Jesus' words and the students' words differ.

❖ Read aloud Romans 2:1: **"Therefore you have no excuse, whoever you are, when you judge others; for in passing judgment on another you condemn your-**

self, because you, the judge, are doing the very same things."

❖ Provide time for the students to ponder ways in which they are judgmental and to offer their silent prayers to ask for God's forgiveness and to seek God's guidance in avoiding such judgments. Close this quiet time with the word "amen."

(4) Make a Commitment to Prepare for God's Judgment

❖ Point out that we have tried to recognize and root out our own tendencies to judge others.

❖ Invite the students to complete this sentence, either aloud or silently: **To prepare for God's judgment, I will commit myself to. . . .**

(5) Continue the Journey

❖ Pray that the students will remember that because we all stand under God's judgment we are not to judge others. Instead, we are to prepare ourselves for God's judgment, which is just.

❖ Read aloud this preparation for next week's lesson. You may also want to post it on newsprint for the students to copy. **Prepare for next week's Palm Sunday session, "Justified by Faith," by reading Romans 5:1-11, 18-21. Center your thoughts on this focus as you read: Many people have experienced the joy of reconciliation after a once-loving relationship is shattered and then restored. How can we expe-**rience this reconciliation with God after we have sinned? Paul reminds us that Jesus has already achieved this for us by dying for us.

❖ Read aloud the following three ideas. Challenge the students to commit themselves to use these activities as a springboard to spiritual growth.

(1) **Be alert for times this week when you judge others. What kinds of attitudes or behaviors do you see in another that causes you to judge that person? Whenever you feel tempted to judge someone else, pray that God will give you kind and loving words to say instead of judgmental ones.**

(2) **Keep a list of your actions and attitudes for three days. Try to view the list through God's eyes. Are you patiently doing good, or are you self-serving? What changes do you need to make?**

(3) **Meditate on the salvation that God offers through Jesus Christ. Consider how your life would be different if you did not know Christ. Give thanks for God's saving and sanctifying work in your life.**

❖ Sing or read aloud "O Day of God, Draw Nigh."

❖ Say one phrase of this prayer at a time and ask the class to repeat it so that they will quickly learn it: **Grant, O Lord, that we may go forth to serve you as faithful disciples who not only hear the word but also do it in the name of Jesus. Amen.**

JUSTIFIED BY FAITH

PREVIEWING THE LESSON

Lesson Scripture: Romans 5:1-11, 18-21
Background Scripture: Romans 5:1-11, 18-21
Key Verse: Romans 5:1

Focus of the Lesson:
Many people have experienced the joy of reconciliation after a once-loving relationship is shattered and then restored. How can we experience this reconciliation with God after we have sinned? Paul reminds us that Jesus has already achieved this for us by dying for us.

Goals for the Learners:
(1) to encounter Paul's teachings on justification by faith.
(2) to identify the effects of justification on their lives.
(3) to demonstrate their reliance on God's grace.

Pronunciation Guide:
justification   (jus te fa ka' shun)   reconciliation   (re ken si le a' shun)

Supplies:
Bibles, newsprint and marker, paper and pencils, hymnals

READING THE SCRIPTURE

NRSV
Romans 5:1-11, 18-21

Therefore, since we are justified by faith, we have peace with God through our Lord Jesus Christ, 2 through whom we have obtained access to this grace in which we stand; and we boast in our hope of sharing the glory of God. 3 And not only that, but we also boast in our sufferings, knowing that suffering produces endurance, 4 and endurance produces character, and character produces hope, 5 and hope does not

NIV
Romans 5:1-11, 18-21

Therefore, since we have been justified through faith, we have peace with God through our Lord Jesus Christ, ²through whom we have gained access by faith into this grace in which we now stand. And we rejoice in the hope of the glory of God. ³Not only so, but we also rejoice in our sufferings, because we know that suffering produces perseverance; ⁴perseverance, character; and character, hope. ⁵And hope does not disappoint us, because God's love has been poured into our hearts through the Holy Spirit that has been given to us.

6 For while we were still weak, at the right time Christ died for the ungodly. 7 Indeed, rarely will anyone die for a righteous person—though perhaps for a good person someone might actually dare to die. 8 But God proves his love for us in that while we still were sinners Christ died for us. 9 Much more surely then, now that we have been justified by his blood, will we be saved through him from the wrath of God. 10 For if while we were enemies, we were reconciled to God through the death of his Son, much more surely, having been reconciled, will we be saved by his life. 11 But more than that, we even boast in God through our Lord Jesus Christ, through whom we have now received reconciliation.

18 Therefore just as one man's trespass led to condemnation for all, so one man's act of righteousness leads to justification and life for all. 19 For just as by the one man's disobedience the many were made sinners, so by the one man's obedience the many will be made righteous. 20 But law came in, with the result that the trespass multiplied; but where sin increased, grace abounded all the more, 21 so that, just as sin exercised dominion in death, so grace might also exercise dominion through justification leading to eternal life through Jesus Christ our Lord.

disappoint us, because God has poured out his love into our hearts by the Holy Spirit, whom he has given us.

[6]You see, at just the right time, when we were still powerless, Christ died for the ungodly. [7]Very rarely will anyone die for a righteous man, though for a good man someone might possibly dare to die. [8]But God demonstrates his own love for us in this: While we were still sinners, Christ died for us.

[9]Since we have now been justified by his blood, how much more shall we be saved from God's wrath through him! [10]For if, when we were God's enemies, we were reconciled to him through the death of his Son, how much more, having been reconciled, shall we be saved through his life! [11]Not only is this so, but we also rejoice in God through our Lord Jesus Christ, through whom we have now received reconciliation.

[18]Consequently, just as the result of one trespass was condemnation for all men, so also the result of one act of righteousness was justification that brings life for all men. [19]For just as through the disobedience of the one man the many were made sinners, so also through the obedience of the one man the many will be made righteous.

[20]The law was added so that the trespass might increase. But where sin increased, grace increased all the more, [21]so that, just as sin reigned in death, so also grace might reign through righteousness to bring eternal life through Jesus Christ our Lord.

UNDERSTANDING THE SCRIPTURE

Introduction. In the first four chapters of Romans Paul described the situation of enmity that exists between God and God's creatures. All human beings have sinned in their insistent, stubborn clinging to idols and in their unjust, unrighteous adherence to their own selfish standards of right and wrong. Both Jew and Greek are guilty; and

there appears to be nothing, not even the Jewish law, that will protect or save them from the wrath of God that will come as the result of their own actions.

Paul claimed that only one thing can save us from our bondage to the power of sin and place us in a righteous, just relationship with God: the grace of God that is offered through faith in Christ Jesus. To prove this point he appealed to God's impartiality and to the example of Abraham who trusted God's promise-keeping character long before he was circumcised—a work of the law. Abraham is thus the ancestor of many nations through his faith, not through his adherence to the Jewish law.

At 5:1 Paul begins a second major section of the letter, a section in which he deals with individual and corporate life in Christ. This section continues through 8:39. Today's verses deal with the theme of justification and its results for Christian living.

Romans 5:1-11. The first eleven verses of chapter 5 belong together as a unit. We can see this through Paul's use of an inclusio, a rhetorical bracket in which the theme of 5:1 and 2, boasting in our newfound peace with God, is restated in 5:11. In the unit Paul discusses the results of our justification through faith by God.

The first clause of the first verse provides a strong summary of what Paul has said previously. "Therefore, since we are justified by faith," he states confidently. In Greek the words "justify" and "justification" are forms of the same word for "righteous" and "righteousness." A literal translation of the first clause of verse 1 would thus be something like "therefore, having been made righteous [or treated as righteous] through faith."

The Greek word for this constellation of words has two linguistic contexts. On the one hand, it comes from the language of the law courts: a judge is considered righteous or just; and the judge can decide to declare a person accused of a crime "righteous" or, in modern English, not guilty, in the eyes of the law. On the other hand, this same Greek word is found in covenantal contexts. God is deemed righteous because God always keeps God's promises to humanity, especially those in which all creation will one day be put right with God. By treating human beings as righteous even though they have repeatedly broken their promises,

God restores God's always-intended covenantal relationship. In justifying us God makes our relationship with God right, just, and good, even though we do not deserve it.

Because God has made us righteous and restored our relationship with God through our faith, we have peace with God. We are no longer in the situation of antagonism depicted in chapters 1–4. It is Jesus Christ who has made this cessation of hostilities possible. So in 5:2 we learn that through him we also live within the realm of God's abiding grace. We can also now boast, as we could not in 3:27, because the object of our bragging is what God has done and will do for us, not what we have done for ourselves.

Romans 5:3-5 contains one long sentence concerning the present state of our life in Christ. Not only can we boast in our hope, but we can also boast in our sufferings. Grace may well be a hallmark of the Christian life, but in Paul's view, so is suffering. However, the suffering is not meaningless for three reasons. First, it places us within the context of Jesus' suffering. Through suffering we are brought nearer to Jesus' life and death. Second, early Christians often believed that suffering is a sign of the beginning of the end. The future, in the death and resurrection of Christ, has broken in on the world. The sufferings of believers are a sign of that future.

Finally and most obviously in this passage, suffering serves as a means to spiritual growth in the Christian life. For in suffering we learn endurance; endurance generates character; character leads to hope. This hope is not ungrounded optimism or false buoyancy about prospects for the future. It is a clear-eyed realization that suffering indeed does not last forever but God's faithfulness does. This kind of hope does not disappoint us (5:5), because God instills it in us through the agency of the Holy Spirit.

All of this is made possible by the death of Christ. Jesus' experience on the cross is, for Paul, the critical moment in history because it demonstrates fully God's love for the unrighteous, which, as we have already seen, is a category that includes everyone. Paul marvels in 5:6-11 at this proof of God's vast love. And since we have been made right with God, justified, through the shedding of Jesus' blood, we will be saved from that day of wrath described in Romans 2. This brings us back to Paul's starting point: now through the Lord Jesus Christ we have reconciliation with God.

Romans 5:18-21. Romans 5:18-19 summarizes what Paul introduces in 5:12-20—a contrast between Adam, the first human, and Christ, the perfect one. In the commentary series *Interpretation,* Paul Achtemeier states the opposition like this: "Here the choices [for human beings] are two: Belong to the humanity whose destination is determined by Adam or belong to the humanity whose destination is determined by Christ." Adam through his disobedience brought sin and condemnation into the world; Christ through his faithful obedience brought justification and life.

At 5:20 Paul reintroduces the subject of the Jewish law. Although Jews might have hoped to escape the results of Adam's trespass through obedience to the law, Paul claims that the inevitable inability to live the law invites a counsel of despair (see Romans 7:5-25). The law creates opportunity for sin in its breaking and intensifies awareness of the impossibility of keeping it. Nonetheless, sin results not simply in death; it also brings further occasion for God's grace until at last grace exercises "dominion through justification leading to eternal life through Jesus Christ our Lord" (5:21).

INTERPRETING THE SCRIPTURE

From Justification to Reconciliation

Paul's classic dictum that we are justified by faith has been a foundation for Christian faith, especially in its Protestant forms, through the centuries. Nonetheless, the English word "justification" can be baffling. In common usage, we talk about justifying our actions by which we mean explaining ourselves (in a positive sense) or making excuses (in a negative sense) for our bad behavior.

Knowing that the root of the Greek word that we translate "justification" is the same as that of "righteousness" helps us get beyond that sense of rationalizing or defending ourselves that the English word conveys. Further, Paul uses the Greek word for "justification" in a passive voice, a reminder that "justifying" is not something we do ourselves in an active way. It is something that is done for us—in this case, by God. God justifies us. But God is not making excuses for us or defending us; God is actually making us righteous. When we also consider the law court and covenant contexts mentioned previously, we come to an even clearer understanding of God's action. God, as judge, is declaring us, by virtue of our faith, to be righteous. God, in acknowledging us as one party in a covenantal relationship, is also holding up both sides of the bargain. Thus, I find it helpful to substitute the words "being made right with God" for "justification" when I encounter the word in Paul's Letters.

Because through God's gracious action in Jesus we are now made right with God, we have peace with God. This peace is not a ceasefire, a pause for two warring parties to catch their breath and check their wounds. It is permanent, in Paul's view, and brings about a new state of affairs as surely as V.J. Day changed everything for post–World War II America and Japan. Paul calls us to greet such a change with the same kind of joy that Americans (if not the Japanese) displayed when the bells rang to announce the signing of the peace treaty.

We also are no longer at odds with tools like the law that God brought into the world to help us understand our sinfulness. Moreover, in this new state of reconciliation we can learn to work with God, not against God. No longer do we have to labor against God as if God were our enemy. Now we can act with and on behalf of God, seeking the good for God and God's creation as God has sought and continues to seek our own good.

Peace, Yes; Absence of Pain, No

Hostilities with God may have ceased, but pain and suffering continue even in our newly reconciled state. This paradox is often difficult to understand and accept because we humans are psychologically wired to avoid pain and to pursue pleasure. We seem to believe that the things that hurt us are, practically speaking, evil. And we Christians can compound the problem as we too casually equate good fortune and periods of relative calm and prosperity in our life with signs of God's blessings.

Paul makes no pretense that the faith that is the foundation of our salvation protects or preserves us from affliction. Indeed, for him suffering is an unavoidable part of the Christian life. It is a fact. Christians cannot escape the traumas of childhood, the aches and pains of old age, the disease and natural disaster that mark all of human life. Nor are we protected from the anguish that too often we inflict on one another.

So we have a choice: we can be frustrated and disappointed by it; or, we can learn and grow from it. We can grow bitter and desperate; or, we can gain the endurance, the character, and the hope that Paul says grow out of suffering. We can come to embrace the counterintuition that God is with us even as we face the finitude of our bodies, the vicissitudes of nature, and the outra-

geous evil perpetrated among members of the human race.

The Rev. C. M. Kao, a Taiwanese pastor and friend, models this lesson for us. In the 1970s Taiwan was making a tumultuous and painful shift to democracy from military rule and dictatorship under Chiang Kai-shek and his son. Rev. Kao played a key part in bringing the international Christian community's attention to the plight of the majority of the Taiwanese. When he helped to hide a prodemocracy leader from government agents, he was arrested and sent to prison for a number of years. Because he stood up for the principles of freedom and self-determination in the name of Christ, he suffered the kind of persecution that Paul often encountered.

While in prison, he wrote the poem: "Cactus and Caterpillars," reprinted here with permission from *Testimonies of Faith: Letters and Poems from Prison in Taiwan*, Studies from the World Alliance of Reformed Churches, No. 5 (Geneva: WARC, 1984).

> I asked the Lord
> to give me a bunch of flowers.
>
> But
>
> the Lord gave me
> a cactus, ugly and full of thorns.
>
> I asked the Lord
> to give me lovely butterflies.
>
> But
>
> the Lord gave me
> Hairy caterpillars, horrible and obscene.
>
> I was shocked
>   disappointed
>   grieved!
>
> After many days
> suddenly I saw cactus burst into bloom.
> Those hairy caterpillars also turned
> into lovely butterflies
> flying and dancing in the spring wind.
>
> How unfathomable God's purpose is!

Uneven Odds

In Romans 5 Paul introduces a comparison between Adam and Christ and offers his readers a choice between the two. According to his reading of Genesis 2:4*b*-3:24, Adam brings sin into the world through his disobedience. (Notice how Paul keeps Eve out of it!) That sin, says Paul, brought condemnation and death for all of Adam's descendants. Thus Adam is a type, or a foreshadowing figure, of "the one who was to come" (5:14). Paul's use of such a type follows a common form of rabbinic midrash and illuminates his understanding of the significance of Christ. As such Christ, Adam's antitype, brings grace and life into the world. Just as Adam's act of disobedience made all of us sinners, so Christ's act of obedience made us righteous.

The issue here for Paul is not really a question of the origin of sin, of how sin came into the world through the defiance of an actual historical figure named Adam and cursed us all. The issue, for Paul, is rather the contrast between a humanity that refuses to trust God's grace, for which Adam serves as a convenient representative, and Christ who trusts it even to death. Further, we now have a choice concerning the type to which we will belong.

Yet, lest we consider that the odds between the two are even, that one choice is as good as another, Paul reminds us that grace is a much greater power than sin. Grace abounds, even as the law itself, transgressed and disobeyed as it is, multiplies sin and its occasions. Those who follow Adam will always be dealt a losing hand, no matter how hard they play or how lucky they seem in life. For Adam has, after all, died as do all those who play his game. Christ lives now and forever—and opens the door to eternity for all who choose to accept him.

SHARING THE SCRIPTURE

PREPARING TO TEACH

Preparing Our Hearts

This week's devotional reading is found in 2 Corinthians 3:4-11. What difference does it make in your life to know that God has made you "competent to be ministers of a new covenant"? How do you envision "the ministry of justification abound(ing) in glory"? Write your thoughts in your spiritual journal.

Pray that you and your students will give thanks for God's amazing action of justification through Jesus Christ.

Preparing Our Minds

Study the background and lesson scripture, both found in Romans 5:1-11, 18-21.

Write on newsprint:

sentence stems for "Identify Effects of Justification on Learners' Lives."

information for next week's lesson, found under "Continue the Journey."

Plan lectures on:

the meaning of "justification," based on the second and third paragraphs under Romans 5:1-11 in the Understanding the Scripture portion.

possible answers to the questions under the heading "Encounter Paul's Teachings on Justification by Faith."

LEADING THE CLASS

(1) Gather to Learn

❖ Welcome the class members and introduce any guests as you gather for this Palm Sunday session.

❖ Pray that on this Palm Sunday adults

will experience the joy of reconciliation with God, made possible for us by Jesus Christ.

❖ Invite several volunteers to use the word "justified" or "justification" in a sentence. Write the sentences on newsprint. Consider how the word is used in each instance. Then, in a brief lecture based on the second and third paragraphs of Romans 5:1-11 in the Understanding the Scripture portion, explain how Paul would have understood this word. Also point out the relationship between "justification" and "righteousness" in Greek.

❖ Read aloud today's focus statement: **Many people have experienced the joy of reconciliation after a once-loving relationship is shattered and then restored. How can we experience this reconciliation with God after we have sinned? Paul reminds us that Jesus has already achieved this for us by dying for us.**

❖ Note that as we begin Holy Week, we are reminded that the events of this week lead to the celebration of God's supreme act of justification and reconciliation through the death and resurrection of Jesus Christ.

Encounter Paul's Teachings on Justification by Faith

❖ Select a volunteer to read Romans 5:1-11.

❖ Consider the following questions by (a) discussing them with the entire class, (b) discussing them within small groups, or (c) giving a brief lecture.

(1) **What benefits are bestowed on believers as a result of justification by faith?** (Be sure to consider peace with God or reconciliation, hope of glory, opportunities to build character and hope born of suffering, God's love poured out upon us by the power of the Holy Spirit, and salvation.)

(2) **What does this passage say to you about humanity?**

(3) **What does this passage say about**

God and God's will for humanity?

❖ Provide a few moments for the class as a whole to share insights or raise questions.

❖ Choose a volunteer to read Romans 5:18-21.

❖ Make a chart on newsprint with two labels at the top: *Adam* and *Christ*. Ask the class members to first list how Adam and Christ are alike. Then list how they are different. Ask: **What difference does it make that Christ was very much like Adam and yet also quite different?**

(3) Identify the Effects of Justification on Learners' Lives

❖ Brainstorm with the students the characteristics of a person who has been reconciled with God. List ideas on newsprint.

❖ Distribute paper and pencils. Invite the students to complete these three sentence stems, which you may want to post on another sheet of newsprint:

■ Before I truly accepted Christ as Savior and Lord, I tried to reconcile myself with God by. . . .

■ In regard to justification, I now believe. . . .

■ My justified relationship with God shows forth in my life in the following ways. . . .

❖ Encourage the students to talk with a partner or small group about their answers.

(4) Demonstrate Reliance on God's Grace

❖ Read aloud each of the following scenarios. Ask the students to comment on how the persons involved might demonstrate their faith by relying on God's grace.

■ Alyson Chambers had lost her mother and sister to breast cancer. She has just received confirmation that a lump in her breast is most likely cancerous. How might her response to this news demonstrate her reliance on God's grace?

■ Roger Ross recently lost a good job,

and his prospects for finding a similar one seem bleak. How might his response to this situation demonstrate that through his faith he has peace with God?

- Timothy Thompson, the seven-year-old son of Kevin and Kendra Thompson, is having major behavioral problems at home and at school. Neither loving discipline nor medication seems to help this child who is a constant source of anxiety and embarrassment for his parents. How might Kevin and Kendra let their faith demonstrate their reliance on God's grace?

❖ Provide time for the students to meditate silently on these questions that you will need to read aloud slowly, pausing after each one.

- **Like Alyson, Roger, Kevin, and Kendra, we all have situations in our lives that challenge our faith, perhaps to the point where we have trouble believing that we truly are justified by faith. What circumstances in your own life challenge you in this way?**

- **What steps will you take to demonstrate that you truly live in a reconciled relationship with God through Jesus Christ?**

(5) Continue the Journey

❖ End the meditation time by praying that the students will experience God's peace, which is available to them once they are justified by faith in Christ.

❖ Read aloud this preparation for next week's lesson. You may also want to post it on newsprint for the students to copy. **Prepare for next week's Easter session,**

"Victory over Death," by reading John 20:1-10 and Romans 6:1-14. Our session will focus on John 20:1-10 and Romans 6:1-11, 13. Consider this focus statement as you study: People often need help to achieve things beyond their personal power or ability. Where can we find the power to help us fight our own sinful natures? Paul says that we have been given the power through Jesus' resurrection, and John describes that joyous first Easter.

❖ Read aloud the following three ideas. Challenge the students to commit themselves to use these activities as a springboard to spiritual growth.

(1) **Write a story or poem about how reconciliation among church members positively affects the ministry of the church.**

(2) **Recall the chart created during the session that listed characteristics of a person who was reconciled with God. Contemplate these characteristics in light of your own life. Which of these characteristics will you pray that God will give or strengthen in your own life?**

(3) **Tell an unchurched person about your beliefs concerning justification and reconciliation with God through Jesus Christ. Invite that person to attend worship and Sunday school with you so as to seek God's gift for himself or herself.**

❖ Sing or read aloud "Grace Greater than Our Sin."

❖ Say one phrase of this prayer at a time and ask the class to repeat it so that they will quickly learn it: **Grant, O Lord, that we may go forth to serve you as faithful disciples who not only hear the word but also do it in the name of Jesus. Amen.**

VICTORY OVER DEATH

PREVIEWING THE LESSON

Lesson Scripture: John 20:1-10; Romans 6:1-11, 13
Background Scripture: John 20:1-10: Romans 6:1-14
Key Verse: Romans 6:9

Focus of the Lesson:
People often need help to achieve things beyond their personal power or ability. Where can we find the power to help us fight our own sinful natures? Paul says that we have been given the power through Jesus' resurrection, and John describes that joyous first Easter.

Goals for the Learners:
(1) to delve into John's account of the Easter story and Paul's interpretation in Romans.
(2) to consider how Christ's dying and rising relates to them.
(3) to celebrate their victory in Christ.

Pronunciation Guide:
Ostern   (German—o' sten)

Supplies:
Bibles, newsprint and marker, paper and pencils, hymnals

READING THE SCRIPTURE

NRSV
John 20:1-10

Early on the first day of the week, while it was still dark, Mary Magdalene came to the tomb and saw that the stone had been removed from the tomb. 2 So she ran and went to Simon Peter and the other disciple, the one whom Jesus loved, and said to them, "They have taken the Lord out of the tomb, and we do not know where they have laid him." 3 Then Peter and the other disciple set out and went toward the tomb. 4 The two were running together, but the other disciple

NIV
John 20:1-10

Early on the first day of the week, while it was still dark, Mary Magdalene went to the tomb and saw that the stone had been removed from the entrance. ²So she came running to Simon Peter and the other disciple, the one Jesus loved, and said, "They have taken the Lord out of the tomb, and we don't know where they have put him!"

³So Peter and the other disciple started for the tomb. ⁴Both were running, but the other disciple outran Peter and reached the tomb

outran Peter and reached the tomb first. 5 He bent down to look in and saw the linen wrappings lying there, but he did not go in. 6 Then Simon Peter came, following him, and went into the tomb. He saw the linen wrappings lying there, 7 and the cloth that had been on Jesus' head, not lying with the linen wrappings but rolled up in a place by itself. 8 Then the other disciple, who reached the tomb first, also went in, and he saw and believed; 9 for as yet they did not understand the scripture, that he must rise from the dead. 10 Then the disciples returned to their homes.

Romans 6:1-11, 13

What then are we to say? Should we continue in sin in order that grace may abound? 2 By no means! How can we who died to sin go on living in it? 3 Do you not know that all of us who have been baptized into Christ Jesus were baptized into his death? 4 Therefore we have been buried with him by baptism into death, so that, just as Christ was raised from the dead by the glory of the Father, so we too might walk in newness of life.

5 For if we have been united with him in a death like his, we will certainly be united with him in a resurrection like his. 6 We know that our old self was crucified with him so that the body of sin might be destroyed, and we might no longer be enslaved to sin. 7 For whoever has died is freed from sin. 8 But if we have died with Christ, we believe that we will also live with him. **9 We know that Christ, being raised from the dead, will never die again; death no longer has dominion over him**. 10 The death he died, he died to sin, once for all; but the life he lives, he lives to God. 11 So you also must consider yourselves dead to sin and alive to God in Christ Jesus.

13 No longer present your members to sin as instruments of wickedness, but present yourselves to God as those who have been brought from death to life, and present your members to God as instruments of righteousness.

first. 5 He bent over and looked in at the strips of linen lying there but did not go in. 6 Then Simon Peter, who was behind him, arrived and went into the tomb. He saw the strips of linen lying there, 7 as well as the burial cloth that had been around Jesus' head. The cloth was folded up by itself, separate from the linen. 8 Finally the other disciple, who had reached the tomb first, also went inside. He saw and believed. 9 (They still did not understand from Scripture that Jesus had to rise from the dead.)

10 Then the disciples went back to their homes.

Romans 6:1-11, 13

What shall we say, then? Shall we go on sinning so that grace may increase? 2 By no means! We died to sin; how can we live in it any longer? 3 Or don't you know that all of us who were baptized into Christ Jesus were baptized into his death? 4 We were therefore buried with him through baptism into death in order that, just as Christ was raised from the dead through the glory of the Father, we too may live a new life.

5 If we have been united with him like this in his death, we will certainly also be united with him in his resurrection. 6 For we know that our old self was crucified with him so that the body of sin might be done away with, that we should no longer be slaves to sin—7 because anyone who has died has been freed from sin.

8 Now if we died with Christ, we believe that we will also live with him. **9 For we know that since Christ was raised from the dead, he cannot die again; death no longer has mastery over him**. 10 The death he died, he died to sin once for all; but the life he lives, he lives to God.

11 In the same way, count yourselves dead to sin but alive to God in Christ Jesus. . . . 13 Do not offer the parts of your body to sin, as instruments of wickedness, but rather offer yourselves to God, as those who have been brought from death to life; and offer the parts of your body to him as instruments of righteousness.

UNDERSTANDING THE SCRIPTURE

John 20:1-10. John tells the familiar story of the empty tomb through the eyes of three characters: Mary Magdalene, Peter, and the unnamed disciple frequently called "the one whom Jesus loved." Early Sunday morning Mary Magdalene went to the place where only a few days before Jesus had been buried. In every Gospel she was the first or among the first to go to the tomb. According to John's Gospel, when she arrived she saw that the stone that sealed the tomb had been removed and ran back to tell the disciples what she has seen. Although she then disappears for the remainder of today's reading, she returns in 20:11-18 to play a significant role in the unfolding drama.

In the meantime, John narrates what happens between Peter and the beloved disciple, a mysterious figure who is never named. In fact, he does not even make an appearance until late in the Gospel at John's version of the Last Supper. He is the one disciple who remained at the cross when the others run away. It is to him that Jesus entrusts his mother and him to her as he hung on the cross (19:26-27).

Why is he never named in the Gospel that is now so closely associated with him (see John 21:24)? We do not know the answer—perhaps the community for which the Gospel was written already knew who he was and had no need to have his name spelled out. Maybe he is the apostle John for whom the Gospel was named, although not until a century after its writing. Or, maybe he is anonymous to help us identify with him. No name can be anyone's name, including our own.

When Mary found Peter and the beloved disciple, the two instantly jumped up and ran to the tomb to see for themselves. They ran together, writes John, until the beloved sprinted ahead and reached the tomb first.

He peered in, saw the linen wrappings that had covered the body of Jesus neatly folded, yet remained outside. When Peter caught up, he went all the way in and saw not only what the beloved saw but also the head cloth rolled up in a corner. Only after Peter had already gone in did the beloved step inside the door. And when he looked around he believed. The fact that his belief is mentioned gives the impression that at that moment Peter did not believe. At the same time, John says that neither understood the scripture concerning the Resurrection as they returned home.

Romans 6:1-14. In Romans 5:20 Paul makes the startling claim that the more sin increased the more grace multiplied and grew. It is, after all, the stronger power. In 6:1 a problematic implication of such a statement has occurred to him and he hastens to clear it up in the following verses.

After hearing his words in 5:20 his readers might be tempted to conclude that it would be good to trespass against the law, to sin as it were, so that grace might proliferate all the more. Paul voices such a conclusion as he asks rhetorically, "Should we continue in sin in order that grace may abound?" Then he answers his question with an emphatic, "By no means! How can we who died to sin go on living in it?" (6:2).

This remark opens the door for Paul to discuss believers' participation in the death and resurrection of Christ through baptism. Commentators generally agree that as Paul writes this passage he has in mind the practice of baptism by total immersion. At that time people who confessed Christ were led into water, dipped completely under, and then lifted back up out of the water. So in verses 3 and 4 Paul envisions the act of placing a candidate for baptism under the water as a representation of Christ's death and the lifting up as resurrection into new life.

This involvement in the two crucial moments of Christ's life changes everything for believers as they are brought into a newness of life that begins in the here and now and not in the somewhere else and later. According to 6:5, baptism unites them in the death of Christ and consequently assures them of union in his resurrection as well.

Further, in Romans 6:6-7, the old self has been crucified with Christ. This is the self that followed the destiny of Adam discussed in the last lesson. With the death of the old self the "body of sin," as the Greek phrase is translated in both the NRSV and the NIV, is destroyed. As N. T. Wright explains in *The New Interpreter's Bible*, this "body" is best understood as a person's "solidarity with sin." Now believers are no longer slaves to sin. In 6:8-11, Paul returns to the theme of new life that he started to explore in verse 5. Through baptism his audience, with Christ, comes into the new life that is begun in the present time and is free from the power of sin and death.

Paul began this section in 6:1 with the warning that the Roman Christians cannot continue to sin. He returns to this point in 6:12-14, admonishing his readers not to allow sin to rule over their bodies. The Greek word that Paul uses here for "bodies" encompasses the entire person or personality and not simply flesh and blood. Through Christ believers no longer have to be enslaved to the power of sin or to the desires of their bodies. Now they can present their whole selves to God as tools (or weapons) for righteousness, and not for wickedness. In other words, since they have been freed from the power of sin, they should take control over the things that might lead them into evil. It is now their responsibility to say no to sin. It is now their opportunity to offer themselves to God as instruments in God's quest for righteousness in the human community.

INTERPRETING THE SCRIPTURE

And the Winner Is . . .

Every time I read John 20:1-10, I puzzle over why these two men, the unnamed beloved and Peter, race to the tomb. I find it easier to guess at the beloved's motives—he had been with Jesus all through the last events of his life and was now merely continuing to demonstrate his faithfulness. But why was Peter racing? Only a few days before he could not get away from Jesus fast enough; he was too busy running in the opposite direction. So why was he running toward Jesus' location now, when it was way too late to make amends for his desertion?

Maybe Peter was running due to sheer jealousy. The beloved had already proved his loyalty to Jesus and been identified as the one that Jesus loved. Thus Peter wanted to get to the tomb faster than the beloved to show that he was still the leader, still the number one disciple.

Or maybe Peter was running because of guilt. After all, he was the one who denied Jesus shortly after boasting of his loyalty and devotion to him. Just in case Jesus was lurking about, he hoped to confess his sins to Jesus before anyone else had a chance to tell him and then say how sorry he was.

These possibilities lead me to consider another motive. Maybe he ran out of hopeful curiosity. Peter was surely present when Jesus revived Lazarus from the dead. Maybe, he thought as he was running, Jesus could do the same thing for himself. And he wanted to be the first on the scene to see it all.

Whatever their motives, the two arrived at the tomb, one ahead of another, and surveyed the situation, taking in the same facts, the same data. Then they returned home, walking this time I imagine, and in much different moods. The beloved strode in joy and hope, for he has seen and believed, if not understood. Peter plodded along in despair, for he had just seen and not believed and certainly not understood. He had needed to see Jesus so badly one more time to be reassured that he was also loved, to be forgiven, to be relieved of the burden of sadness. And all he saw was a bunch of old cloths lying around a tomb. He was the loser in this sad race to what turned out to be nothing.

Not Cheating But Defeating Death

Most of us know what it is like to lose people we really love, be they grandparents, parents, siblings, spouses, children, favorite relatives, or friends. We have tasted the same sorrow and bitterness that was in the mouth of Peter. We have been oppressed by the ache of despair and loneliness, the throb of emotions too complicated to sort out and too real to ignore in the face of death. Perhaps we have felt guilty for not being present, for not saying the right things; or we have felt hurt by things that our loved ones said or did before they died. Because we also have known the terrible finality of death, we can understand what Peter and all of Jesus' friends were feeling. They had lost everything, even his body, and there was nothing they could do about it.

But God could and would do something. What God would do was not simply revive Jesus, breathe back life into a broken body so that he could continue to live as he had been before the Crucifixion. No, God had something else in mind. God resurrected Jesus. There is a difference between revival and resurrection. Reviving Jesus would be just cheating death for a little while; resurrecting Jesus would be defeating death, once and for all time.

In resurrecting Jesus, God obliterated for-

ever the distinction between life and death, a distinction that God never made so sharply in the first place and was now teaching the followers of Jesus not to make either. When the resurrected Jesus finally does appear to Peter, the beloved, Mary Magdalene, and all the rest, he is alive in a new way. And he is holding the door open for all of us to walk through into the same new life—a life that not even death can extinguish.

We know from the end of the Fourth Gospel and from Acts that Peter was transformed by the resurrection of his Lord. He changed from one who did not understand or believe into the first preacher of the gospel. To everyone who would listen he spoke of how Jesus was alive and how all the guilt and despair of death now had no meaning in the face of his awesome power to forgive and to love. And in the end Peter finally understood that he himself was also a winner, the recipient of greater awards and accolades than he ever knew at the beginning. Christ had made him victorious through the power of God's love.

From Death to Life to Righteous Action

In this passage Paul is also talking about the significance of the Easter event for believers. Just as Peter was transformed by his faith in the overwhelming power of the Resurrection, so Paul tells us that we also are transformed by the same power. It is through baptism that we fully realize our transformation because it provides the avenue through which we symbolically participate in the death and resurrection of Christ. In Frederick Buechner's words in *Wishful Thinking*: "Going under symbolizes the end of everything about your life that is less than human. Coming up again symbolizes the beginning in you of something strange and new and hopeful. You can breathe again." Thus we, like Peter and the earliest apostles, are freed from the dominion of sin and free to become people who can be used by God for righteousness.

Although early Christian communities practiced the immersion of adults who confessed Jesus as Lord, many Christian churches from ancient times have practiced sprinkling or pouring rather than immersion. They have also baptized infants unable to make such a confession. The symbolism, regardless of method, remains the same. Whether or not we can fully understand what is happening to us at baptism, whether or not we were pushed under water or had water poured over us, through baptism we become a very real part of God's story of salvation for humankind.

But if it is the case that in baptism God does something for us, then after baptism we must begin to do something for God. Released from slavery to sin, we are now free to live lives worthy of such grace. That is why Paul urges us to stop allowing sin to have its way with us—our bodies, our minds, our souls. That is why we cannot continue to sin as if God would multiply the kind of "cheap grace" that Dietrich Bonhoeffer warned us about in *The Cost of Discipleship*. This is "the grace which amounts to the justification of sin without the justification of the repentant sinner who departs from sin and from whom sin departs." The grace that Christ offers through his death and resurrection is costly— not only for him but for us as well. It is costly because it beckons us to follow him through the denial of selfish desires, through trial and test, through renunciation of sin.

SHARING THE SCRIPTURE

PREPARING TO TEACH

Preparing Our Hearts

This week's devotional reading is found in Romans 6:15-23. In this passage, which follows today's background scripture, Paul writes that we have "been set free from sin." Instead of reaping the wages of sin, we have received eternal life—the free gift of God. Paul uses the term "sanctification" in verse 22 to describe the process of transforming growth in the holiness of God through the power of the Spirit. How might this transforming process prepare you for victory over death? Where in your life do you see evidence of sanctification? In what other areas of your life do you need to be transformed?

Pray that you and your students will seek the Spirit's transforming power so that as a sanctified believer you will be prepared to accept God's free gift of eternal life.

Preparing Our Minds

Study the background, John 20:1-10 and Romans 6:1-14, and lesson scripture, John 20:1-10 and Romans 6:1-11, 13.

Write on newsprint:

questions in the section "Consider How Christ's Dying and Rising Relates to the Learners."

information for next week's lesson, found under "Continue the Journey."

Plan any lectures that you want to use.

Be prepared for unusual circumstances that might have an impact on your Easter session, such as choir members being absent or leaving early.

LEADING THE CLASS

(1) Gather to Learn

❖ Welcome the class members and introduce any guests.

❖ Pray that all who have joined with you today will celebrate their personal victory in Jesus as together we celebrate his victory over death this Easter Sunday.

❖ Note that the English word "Easter," like the German word "Ostern," comes from a source that refers to the east, the direction of the sunrise. Some Christian traditions use the word "Pascha," related to the Hebrew word "Pesach," which is the name for Passover. Even Christian groups who do not use "Pascha" for the day of Resurrection, refer to Jesus as the Paschal Lamb. In the eighth century, a Christian writer named Venerable Bede mistakenly related the word "Easter" to an ancient goddess of spring because with the spring sun came new life. Later scholars question that such a goddess existed, but even if she did Christians have transferred the meaning of the life-giving new sun to the day of the resurrection of Jesus, who brings us new life.

❖ Invite the students to work with a partner or small group to say what Easter signifies for them.

❖ Bring the groups back together and read aloud today's focus statement: **People often need help to achieve things beyond their personal power or ability. Where can we find the power to help us fight our own sinful natures? Paul says that we have been given the power through Jesus' resurrection, and John describes that joyous first Easter.**

(2) Delve into John's Account of the Easter Story and Paul's Interpretation in Romans

❖ Choose volunteers to read the parts of a narrator and Mary Magdalene. Ask them to read John 20:1-10 as a drama.

❖ Discuss these questions with the class, or answer them yourself in a lecture.

(1) **What did Simon Peter see? What conclusions did he draw?**

(2) **What did the disciple whom Jesus loved see? What conclusions did he draw?**

(3) **What did Mary Magdalene see? What conclusions did she draw?**

(4) **As you read John's account what conclusions do you draw about what happened that first Easter morning? How do those events affect your life?**

❖ Choose someone to read Romans 6:1-11, 13. Ask the class to listen, just as the members of the church at Rome would have listened to this letter being read.

❖ Invite the students to discuss their understandings of what Paul was writing. Add the following points to their discussion, or work them into a lecture.

Point 1: Paul taught that salvation was God's free gift. Here, Paul rejects his opponents' conclusion (possibly based on the ideas in 5:20) that he was encouraging others to sin.

Point 2: Through baptism, believers participate in the dying (going under the water) and rising (coming up from the water) of Christ.

Point 3: In baptism, believers die to sin.

Point 4: As a result of baptism, believers are united with Christ and experience the newness of life in God that Christ's resurrection makes possible.

Point 5: Believers are to live righteously before God as a result of their dying and rising with Christ.

(3) Consider How Christ's Dying and Rising Relates to the Learners

❖ Encourage the students to recall their baptisms or their confirmation in which they publicly professed and claimed the vows made on their behalf at the time of their baptism. You may wish to read those vows as your own church states them. They are found in the hymnals of many denominations.

❖ Distribute paper and pencils. Encourage the students to work individually to write answers to these questions, which you may want to post on newsprint.

(1) What does the fact that I have died and been raised up in baptism (either literally as in immersion, or figuratively as in sprinkling or pouring) mean to me?
(2) How does this act affect my life?
(3) How might my life be different had I not been baptized?

(4) Celebrate Victory in Jesus

❖ Post a sheet of newsprint. Work with the students to write a litany in which they celebrate the victory over sin and death that is theirs through Christ Jesus. Suggest that they use ideas from the papers they wrote in the previous activity to add to the litany. They will need to create a refrain to be used after each item, such as "we give thanks for your victory, O Christ." If the class is large, you will need to divide into groups to write several litanies.

❖ When the litany is completed and agreed upon by consensus, ask the group members to stand, if able, and hold hands with one another as they read their litany.

(5) Continue the Journey

❖ Pray that the students will continue to claim for their own lives the victory of death that Christ has won.

❖ Read aloud this preparation for next week's lesson. You may also want to post it on newsprint for the students to copy. **Prepare for next week's session, "Power for Living," by reading Romans 8:1-17, especially verses 1-16. Consider this focus as you read: Sometimes life overwhelms** us and we find ourselves without strength or wisdom to know what to do or where to turn. Where can we find help in such times? Paul writes that the power of God's Spirit is available to those who are in Christ.

❖ Read aloud the following three ideas. Challenge the students to commit themselves to use these activities as a springboard to spiritual growth.

(1) **Identify an area of your life that needs to be freed from sin. Through contemplation, prayer, and Bible study seek God's guidance to win victory over this problem.**
(2) **Recall an activity that you tried and failed and then tried and succeeded in doing. What did you do to overcome failure? What lessons can you use from that experience to overcome defeat in the future?**
(30 **Read the Easter accounts from all four Gospels. Note the differences in details. Recognize that all point to Jesus' victory over death. Be aware that although most Christians have a favorite account, all of the Gospels record a momentous event that has life-changing consequences for all who believe.**

❖ Sing or read aloud "We Know That Christ Is Raised."

❖ Say one phrase of this prayer at a time and ask the class to repeat it so that they will quickly learn it: **Grant, O Lord, that we may go forth to serve you as faithful disciples who not only hear the word but also do it in the name of Jesus. Amen.**

UNIT 2: THE CHRISTIAN LIFE

POWER FOR LIVING

PREVIEWING THE LESSON

Lesson Scripture: Romans 8:1-16
Background Scripture: Romans 8:1-17
Key Verse: Romans 8:14

Focus of the Lesson:
Sometimes life overwhelms us and we find ourselves without strength or wisdom to know what to do or where to turn. Where can we find help in such times? Paul writes that the power of God's Spirit is available to those who are in Christ.

Goals for the Learners:
(1) to contrast Paul's teachings on life in the flesh and life in the Spirit.
(2) to cite examples of the Spirit's activity in their lives and church.
(3) to seek empowerment to live in the Holy Spirit.

Supplies:
Bibles, newsprint and marker, paper and pencils, hymnals

READING THE SCRIPTURE

NRSV
Romans 8:1-16

There is therefore now no condemnation for those who are in Christ Jesus. 2 For the law of the Spirit of life in Christ Jesus has set you free from the law of sin and of death. 3 For God has done what the law, weakened by the flesh, could not do: by sending his own Son in the likeness of sinful flesh, and to deal with sin, he condemned sin in the flesh, 4 so that the just requirement of the law might be fulfilled in us, who walk not according to the flesh but according to the

NIV
Romans 8:1-16

Therefore, there is now no condemnation for those who are in Christ Jesus, 2because through Christ Jesus the law of the Spirit of life set me free from the law of sin and death. 3For what the law was powerless to do in that it was weakened by the sinful nature, God did by sending his own Son in the likeness of sinful man to be a sin offering. And so he condemned sin in sinful man, 4in order that the righteous requirements of the law

Spirit. 5 For those who live according to the flesh set their minds on the things of the flesh, but those who live according to the Spirit set their minds on the things of the Spirit. 6 To set the mind on the flesh is death, but to set the mind on the Spirit is life and peace. 7 For this reason the mind that is set on the flesh is hostile to God; it does not submit to God's law—indeed it cannot, 8 and those who are in the flesh cannot please God.

9 But you are not in the flesh; you are in the Spirit, since the Spirit of God dwells in you. Anyone who does not have the Spirit of Christ does not belong to him. 10 But if Christ is in you, though the body is dead because of sin, the Spirit is life because of righteousness. 11 If the Spirit of him who raised Jesus from the dead dwells in you, he who raised Christ from the dead will give life to your mortal bodies also through his Spirit that dwells in you.

12 So then, brothers and sisters we are debtors, not to the flesh, to live according to the flesh—13 for if you live according to the flesh, you will die; but if by the Spirit you put to death the deeds of the body, you will live. **14 For all who are led by the Spirit of God are children of God**. 15 For you did not receive a spirit of slavery to fall back into fear, but you have received a spirit of adoption. When we cry, "Abba! Father!" 16 it is that very Spirit bearing witness with our spirit that we are children of God.

might be fully met in us, who do not live according to the sinful nature but according to the Spirit.

[5]Those who live according to the sinful nature have their minds set on what that nature desires; but those who live in accordance with the Spirit have their minds set on what the Spirit desires. [6]The mind of sinful man is death, but the mind controlled by the Spirit is life and peace; [7]the sinful mind is hostile to God. It does not submit to God's law, nor can it do so. [8]Those controlled by the sinful nature cannot please God.

[9]You, however, are controlled not by the sinful nature but by the Spirit, if the Spirit of God lives in you. And if anyone does not have the Spirit of Christ, he does not belong to Christ. [10]But if Christ is in you, your body is dead because of sin, yet your spirit is alive because of righteousness. [11]And if the Spirit of him who raised Jesus from the dead is living in you, he who raised Christ from the dead will also give life to your mortal bodies through his Spirit, who lives in you.

[12]Therefore, brothers, we have an obligation—but it is not to the sinful nature, to live according to it. [13]For if you live according to the sinful nature, you will die; but if by the Spirit you put to death the misdeeds of the body, you will live, **[14]because those who are led by the Spirit of God are sons of God.** [15]For you did not receive a spirit that makes you a slave again to fear, but you received the Spirit of sonship. And by him we cry, "*Abba*, Father." [16]The Spirit himself testifies with our spirit that we are God's children.

UNDERSTANDING THE SCRIPTURE

Introduction. Today's reading is a part of the conclusion of the second major section of Romans that began at 5:1 and will end at 8:31-39 in a hymn of praise to the unconquerable love of God in Jesus Christ. In this section Paul is discussing the new life

Christians have found now that they have peace with God (see "Justified by Faith," lesson 3). In 5:18-21, he sets up a contrast between Christ and Adam in order to demonstrate both the effects of Christ's crucifixion and resurrection on the destiny of all humankind and the choice that Christians have concerning that destiny. Will they belong to the children of Adam? Or will they join the family of God through their brother Jesus?

In Romans 8:1-17 Paul continues to open up the contrast between these two possibilities for human life. However, in place of the Adam/Christ contrast that we saw in 5:18-21, in this text he uses a flesh/Spirit distinction. In fact, throughout this section Paul discusses his dichotomy of human destinies through the use of a wide range of metaphors and images. Sometimes it seems as though he is contrasting places: the dominion of sin versus the dominion of grace. Other times he is working with a distinction in eras or ages in the world: the old age of Adam and death versus the new of Christ and life. Thus it is important to remember that in Christ believers live under the authority of God's grace in a new age—one which, as we will see, is guided not by law or by the flesh, but by the Spirit.

Romans 8:1-11. In this first part of today's lesson, Paul is reminding the Roman Christians of their new status in Christ Jesus. In the first verse he reiterates the fact that now they no longer face condemnation because they have received God's promises through faith in Christ. The "now" is a signal of his understanding that the new eschatological age has begun.

Christians are now free from this final judgment of God against all unrighteousness and injustice because they are now under "the law of the Spirit of life" and not "the law of sin and death." Notice the opposition of the kinds of law that Paul is making here. He is probably not referring in either case to the Torah, but rather referring to a principle or figure of speech (see "God Judges All People," lesson 2). It is hardly conceivable that Paul would understand that the Spirit brings a new law to supplant Torah or any other human form of law. Rather, he is making a point that believers are no longer enslaved to the powers of sin and death because the Spirit now reigns.

This is the first extended passage in Romans where the Spirit serves as a major theme. Although Paul has mentioned it earlier, he now begins to work with it as a major force in believers' lives. We should keep in mind that he probably did not have the same concept of the Trinity that we do today; this was a doctrine to be developed later by Christians in subsequent centuries. Nonetheless, he certainly operated with a sense of the Spirit as the very presence of God in the lives of the faithful.

In 8:3 Paul returns to the subject of the Torah and what it was not able to accomplish, that is, to destroy the power of sin. Its inability to do this was not due to any inherent weakness in the law. This is important to understand because it reminds us that Paul does not think of the law in and of itself as evil. Instead, the ineffectiveness of the law is due to the flesh. Again we must remember that "flesh" for Paul does not denote human physicality with its attendant drives and needs, but the self's determination to rebel against God. It is the force that opposes the Spirit. Although the Torah could not accomplish the purposes of God, Christ Jesus, the Son of God could. "In the likeness of sinful flesh" the Son was sent by God to deal with sin, to break its power and redeem all who believe from its death-grip.

Because God has done this, believers can now walk according to the Spirit and not according to their own self-determination (8:4-8). In them is fulfilled the "just requirement of the law," which might be better translated as "righteous verdict" as opposed to the condemnation of 8:1. Now believers can pay attention to the ways of the Spirit and ignore those of the flesh. They can put away all the old stuff that led them along the path of death and take on the life-giving habits and virtues of the Spirit. In this way they can please God. Paul continues to reinforce the opposition between Spirit and flesh throughout 8:9-11 in his description of Christian life now that sin is dead.

Romans 8:12-17. These verses begin to answer the "so what" question implied in the preceding section. This is signaled by the "therefore" (NIV) or "so then" (NRSV) at the beginning of Romans 8:12. If the faithful are no longer living according to the flesh, then how are they to act, what are they to do? First, says Paul, they are to recognize that they no longer have any obligations to the demands or the longings of the flesh. Again, he underscores the fact that to live according to those things ensures death, but to live in the Spirit is life.

At 8:14 he introduces another result of life in the Spirit: to be led by the Spirit is to become children of God. No longer are believers slaves to some power or another, including God. They are now full members of God's family with all the rights and responsibilities that go with such a status. They do not have to be afraid as slaves who have no control over their own lives. They have been adopted, a legal procedure that brings them under the full protection and care of the one who has adopted them—God. And as children they can call God, "Abba! Father!" This ability to call on God by the same means that Jesus used confirms their new life in the Spirit. In the first half of 8:17 Paul concludes this thought by claiming that if they are children, they are also heirs with Christ himself.

INTERPRETING THE SCRIPTURE

The War of the Worlds Within

The old Orson Wells radio drama, *War of the Worlds*, tells the story of a man in Great Britain who watches alien forces from Mars attack his beloved homeland. The horrible monsters from outer space seem completely unconquerable as they land, build huge weapons of mass destruction, and proceed to suck the life out of every human they can reach with their machines. In the end they are vanquished, not by force, but by bacteria foreign to their systems that they ingest while digesting humanity. The bacteria kill the aliens and Earth is spared further devastation.

Paul also conceives of a humanity that plays a role in the cosmic battle between God's righteousness and forces of evil. In Paul's vision, we are not quite as helpless as those in Wells's story because we can choose our destiny in a way that the hapless Britons could not. Further, we are not powerless because Christ through his death and resurrection vanquishes the powers of death and sin and thus provides us the choice of destiny. Through him we are not doomed to destruction.

Nevertheless, a war continues to wage within us—a war between our own desires that will lead us ultimately to pain and ruin and an enthusiasm for the will of God that will lead to life and grace. Although the die has been cast in our initial decision to believe, the struggle within remains. Every day, in every particular of our lives, we must choose to walk according to the Spirit or according to the flesh. God has provided the power to choose, but has left us with the daily decisions to follow Christ.

A Native American story illustrates this constant struggle. A wise Cherokee grandfather was once teaching his grandson about life. He said, "A terrible fight is going on inside me like a fight between two wolves. One wolf is jealousy, anger, bitterness, regret, pride, self-pity, and cruelty. The other is joy, peace, hope, love, truth, humility, compassion, justice and generosity."

"But I am not the only person in this world in which this battle is going on. I imagine wolves are also fighting in you, just as they are in people all around us."

After listening to his grandfather and thinking about it for a while, the grandson asked, "Which wolf will win?" And the old man answered, "The one you feed."

A Passion for Destruction

In her discussion of the "passions" as described by the early church fathers and mothers, Roberta Bondi, in her book *To Love as God Loves*, provides another way to think of Paul's concept of "flesh." A "passion" for these ancient Christians was anything we do or feel that keeps us away from the grace of God. It "has as its chief characteristics the perversion of vision and the destruction of love." It can take the form of gluttony, anger, greed, impurity of thought, pride, laziness, a habit of sadness and gloom. Passions are often the things we turn to when we cannot cope with what life is handing out to us. They comprise the way of the flesh and when we seek to live by them or gratify them, even when we are overwhelmed by difficulties, we are choosing self-destruction and death.

When Life Is Overwhelming

When life seems too busy, when problems seem too intractable, when failures are too frequent and successes too sporadic, where do we turn if not to the things of the flesh? How do we stop the multiplication of trouble that follows gratification of momentary desires, passions?

Believers live in the Spirit, says Paul, not the flesh. Even when the pressures around us are unstinting, we live in the Spirit. Even when we have failed miserably at something that mattered deeply to us, we live in the Spirit. Even when we can hardly recognize its presence in our lives, we live in the Spirit. And it is the Spirit that will take us away from the things destroying us and lead us on paths of life-giving grace.

A friend has been struggling with life as a member of the in-between generation—in between aging parents whose health is failing and growing children whose demands on time and energy are only increasing in their teenage years. For relief from these pressures she often turned late at night to Internet chat rooms. There she could pretend to be someone without all the minor and very unglamorous problems of her daily life. A few minutes before bed checking her e-mail began to turn into an hour and then a few hours. Before she knew what was happening, she was spending every evening she was home until 2:00 or 3:00 in the morning in front of her computer.

Finally, her daughter could no longer take her mother's absorption in her on-line life. One night she asked her mother if she could move in with her grandparents just so she would have someone to talk to in the evenings. That got her mother's attention. She shut off the computer, realizing that she had given into her passions—though she would not have put it in those words. With help from the whole family and some friends, she resumed a life lived according to the demands of the Spirit.

The Gift of Prayer

We are accustomed to thinking of prayer as another item on a long list of things to be accomplished each day. Many days, if we find a minute or two, we sit down to pray so that we can say "Well, I got that done. Next?" At the same time, when we do get a chance to pray we give God a list of things God needs to do—take care of this problem at work, heal my friend, find a few extra dollars for the family, give me some rest, and guard and guide my children all day since I can't!

Behind Paul's words in this passage is a different view of prayer. To him it is not an obligatory task, but a gift, a privilege offered by God because we are now brothers and sisters of Jesus and children of the One he called "Father." To understand the full import of this fact, we must realize that to some degree Paul's concept of the household of God was based on the common household organizations of his day. A wealthy home would be led by the patriarch of the family and include his wife, his children, perhaps a few close friends and other extended family members, and an assortment of freed servants and slaves. A hierarchy of manners governed who might approach whom with petitions and requests for favors. The lowest members of the household could rarely approach the leading members. Slaves could rarely if ever approach the master without being summoned first by someone higher up in the rankings. Children, especially the (male) heirs, could approach him with greater ease.

So when Paul asserts that with Jesus we have become children of God he is showing us that now we have the right of approach to God. And we can approach him with familial intimacy. We can call him "Our Father"; we can place before him the same concerns that his Son addressed to him. Further, this ability to speak as precious child to God confirms the presence of the Spirit with us.

The next time we make a commitment to pray, it might be helpful to remember Paul's understandings. And it might be easier to pray (and find time for it) if we think of it not as something we *have* to do, but something we *get* to do. Through the power of the Holy Spirit we can live and pray as God's children.

SHARING THE SCRIPTURE

PREPARING TO TEACH

Preparing Our Hearts

This week's devotional reading is found in Romans 7:1-6. Here Paul draws a comparison between a woman, who is no longer bound in marriage to her dead husband, and the law, which likewise does not bind people to it after their deaths. Paul goes on to say that we live not as slaves "but in the new life of the Spirit." What does his message mean to you? What insights does this reading give you into living the Christian life in the Spirit?

Pray that you and your students will desire to be freed from the flesh and live in the Spirit.

Preparing Our Minds

Study the background scripture, found in Romans 8:1-17. Our session will focus on verses 1-16.

Write on newsprint:

information for next week's lesson, found under "Continue the Journey."

LEADING THE CLASS

(1) Gather to Learn

❖ Welcome the class members and introduce any guests.

❖ Pray that all of today's participants will choose to live in the Spirit.

❖ Invite volunteers to tell the class anecdotes about times they needed—and found—strength to face a challenge. This strength could be physical, emotional, intellectual, or spiritual. Where did they find the necessary strength? How did they feel when they were able to overcome the problem?

❖ Note that in today's lesson, Paul teaches that if we live in the Spirit, rather than in the flesh, we have all the power we need for living.

❖ Read aloud today's focus statement: **Sometimes life overwhelms us and we find ourselves without strength or wisdom to know what to do or where to turn. Where can we find help in such times? Paul writes that the power of God's Spirit is available to those who are in Christ.**

(2) Contrast Paul's Teachings on Life in the Flesh and Life in the Spirit

❖ Choose three volunteers to read Romans 8:1-8, 9-11, and 12-16 (or 17), respectively.

❖ Post a sheet of newsprint that has been divided into two columns. On the left side write "Life in the Spirit," and on the right, "Life in the Flesh." Encourage the students to list as many specific examples as they can think of under each heading.

❖ Review the plot of Orson Wells's *War of the Worlds*, and read the story of the Cherokee grandfather, both found under "The War of the Worlds Within" in the Interpreting the Scripture portion. Invite the students to comment on how the Wells's story and the Native American story illustrate Paul's contrast between life in the Spirit and life in the flesh.

❖ Conclude this portion of the session by asking the students to think of other stories, paintings, or songs that show a similar contrast.

(3) Cite Examples of the Spirit's Activity in Learners' Lives and Church

❖ Distribute paper and pencils. Provide quiet time. Ask each student to identify two or three items under each heading on the newsprint that relate to their own lives. They are to make a note of how each item they have selected on the left empowers them to live faithfully. Next to the items selected on the right, they are to write how each item acts as a barrier between themselves and God.

❖ When time is up for this activity, ask the students to fold their papers and put them in their Bibles so they can refer to them during the week.

❖ Encourage the students to cite examples of the Spirit's activity within their congregation, denomination, or the church at large. You may want to list these ideas on newsprint.

❖ Discuss these questions with the class.
(1) **If we were to live as a Spirit-empowered church, what other evidence of the Spirit's activity might we see?**
(2) **What actions or attitudes might be hindering the work of the Spirit?** (Be careful to talk in generalities here. Citing specific names or incidents will likely be harmful, not helpful.)
(3) **What steps can we take to change these actions and attitudes?**

(4) Seek Empowerment to Live in the Holy Spirit

❖ Do this guided imagery activity with the students. Begin by asking them to get comfortable in their chairs and invite them to close their eyes to concentrate better.

(1) **Envision yourself in a house church in Rome. You have just heard one of your church leaders reading Paul's letter to you. Imagine how you are feeling and responding to the news that you are no longer under condemnation because as a believer you live in the Spirit.** (pause)
(2) **You cry out "Abba! Father!" because you recognize that you are not a slave to sin, but an heir of God. Visualize the kind of life you can lead as God's son or daughter who is empowered by the Holy Spirit.** (pause)
(3) **Suddenly you realize that you do not live as you imagine you could. You know that you struggle at times and don't know where to turn for help. Offer a silent prayer of confession.** (pause)
(4) **In your mind's eye, see the Holy Spirit resting upon you as a dove or tongue of fire. Keep this picture as you think about a difficult situation you currently face. Give thanks to God for the gift of the Holy Spirit. Claim the Spirit's power in your life.** (pause)
(5) **Open your eyes when you are ready.**

❖ Invite volunteers to share any insights they gleaned from this activity.

(5) Continue the Journey

❖ Pray that the participants will experience the power of the Spirit's presence at all times.

❖ Read aloud this preparation for next week's lesson. You may also want to post it on newsprint for the students to copy. Prepare for next week's session, "Affirming Christ As Lord," by reading background scripture from Romans 10:5-21, giving particular attention to verses 5-17. Read carefully with this focus in mind: People often look for good news to balance all the bad news they read and hear about in the media. What's the best possible news we could read or hear about? Paul announces the good news that anyone who confesses Jesus as Lord will be saved.

❖ Read aloud the following three ideas. Challenge the students to commit themselves to use these activities as a springboard to spiritual growth.

(1) Recall that Paul teaches that when believers live in the Spirit they experience freedom and new life as God's children. Write answers to these questions in your spiritual journal: In what way(s) do I perceive myself as a child of God? What difference does this perception make in my relationship with God?

(2) Make a list of compulsive behaviors that bar you from enjoying life in the Spirit. In addition to praying about these behaviors, what other steps can you take to control them?

(3) Perform some beneficial deed this week that clearly demonstrates that you are living in the Spirit.

❖ Sing or read aloud "Holy Spirit, Truth Divine."

❖ Say one phrase of this prayer at a time and ask the class to repeat it so that they will quickly learn it: **Grant, O Lord, that we may go forth to serve you as faithful disciples who not only hear the word but also do it in the name of Jesus. Amen.**

AFFIRMING CHRIST AS LORD

PREVIEWING THE LESSON

Lesson Scripture: Romans 10:5-17
Background Scripture: Romans 10:5-21
Key Verse: Romans 10:9

Focus of the Lesson:
People often look for good news to balance all the bad news they read and hear about in the media. What's the best possible news we could read or hear about? Paul announces the good news that anyone who confesses Jesus as Lord will be saved.

Goals for the Learners:
(1) to discern Paul's teachings about salvation.
(2) to plumb the depth of their confession that Jesus is Lord.
(3) to tell God's good news.

Supplies:
Bibles, newsprint and marker, paper and pencils, hymnals

READING THE SCRIPTURE

NRSV
Romans 10:5-17

5 Moses writes concerning the righteousness that comes from the law, that "the person who does these things will live by them." 6 But the righteousness that comes from faith says, "Do not say in your heart, 'Who will ascend into heaven?'" (that is, to bring Christ down) 7 "or 'Who will descend into the abyss?'" (that is, to bring Christ up from the dead). 8 But what does it say?

"The word is near you,
    on your lips and in your heart"

(that is, the word of faith that we proclaim); **9 because if you confess with your lips that Jesus is Lord and believe in your**

NIV
Romans 10:5-17

5Moses describes in this way the righteousness that is by the law: "The man who does these things will live by them." 6But the righteousness that is by faith says: "Do not say in your heart, 'Who will ascend into heaven?'" (that is, to bring Christ down) 7"or 'Who will descend into the deep?'" (that is, to bring Christ up from the dead). 8But what does it say? "The word is near you; it is in your mouth and in your heart," that is, the word of faith we are proclaiming: **9That if you confess with your mouth, "Jesus is Lord," and believe in your heart that God raised him from the dead, you will be saved.**

heart that God raised him from the dead, you will be saved. 10 For one believes with the heart and so is justified, and one confesses with the mouth and so is saved. 11 The scripture says, "No one who believes in him will be put to shame." 12 For there is no distinction between Jew and Greek; the same Lord is Lord of all and is generous to all who call on him. 13 For, "Everyone who calls on the name of the Lord shall be saved."

14 But how are they to call on one in whom they have not believed? And how are they to believe in one of whom they have never heard? And how are they to hear without someone to proclaim him? 15 And how are they to proclaim him unless they are sent? As it is written, "How beautiful are the feet of those who bring good news!" 16 But not all have obeyed the good news; for Isaiah says, "Lord, who has believed our message?" 17 So faith comes from what is heard, and what is heard comes through the word of Christ.

¹⁰For it is with your heart that you believe and are justified, and it is with your mouth that you confess and are saved. ¹¹As the Scripture says, "Anyone who trusts in him will never be put to shame." ¹²For there is no difference between Jew and Gentile—the same Lord is Lord of all and richly blesses all who call on him, ¹³for, "Everyone who calls on the name of the Lord will be saved."

¹⁴How, then, can they call on the one they have not believed in? And how can they believe in the one of whom they have not heard? And how can they hear without someone preaching to them? ¹⁵And how can they preach unless they are sent? As it is written, "How beautiful are the feet of those who bring good news!"

¹⁶But not all the Israelites accepted the good news. For Isaiah says, "Lord, who has believed our message?" ¹⁷Consequently, faith comes from hearing the message, and the message is heard through the word of Christ.

UNDERSTANDING THE SCRIPTURE

Introduction. The third major section of Paul's Letter to the Romans begins at 9:1 and concludes at 11:36. Today's passage, 10:5-21, is embedded in this lengthy discussion concerning the salvation of the Jews. Paul opens the section with a cry of anguish over the knowledge that many Jews have not accepted Jesus as the Messiah through faith (9:2-3). How can the chosen people of God, the physical descendants of Abraham, be cut off from the covenant?

As he ponders this issue he becomes increasingly aware that neither he nor any other human is able to comprehend fully the will and the ways of God (9:20-21). God is beyond human understanding (11:33-36). Paul also affirms that even as most of his kindred reject the offer of salvation through faith in Christ, their rejection allows that same offer to be made available to Gentiles—more evidence of God's incomprehensible grace. Through it all he remains convinced that Christ Jesus is the fulfillment of the promises of God that are recorded in the Hebrew Scriptures. These writings, in Paul's view, point to the pivotal decision by most Israelites not to accept Jesus as Lord and the inclusion of the Gentiles within God's family through their faith in him. At 10:4 Paul reaffirms that "Christ is the end of the law so that there may be righteousness for everyone who believes." This is where today's lesson begins.

Romans 10:5-13. In Romans 10:5-13 Paul employs a form of midrash to expound his point that it is possible for everyone to be saved through faith in Christ. "Midrash" is based on a Hebrew word meaning "inquiry" and simply denotes exegesis. In this instance, Paul is using the kind of midrash that was performed in the Qumran community. To this group of first-century sectarian Jews, "scripture [was] seen as a prophetic mystery that could only be rightly understood in relationship to their eschatological crisis," write James L. Bailey and Lyle D. Vander Broek in *Literary Forms in the New Testament*. Although Paul was not associated with this group, he similarly understands that his own community is facing an "eschatological crisis" brought about by the death and resurrection of Christ. In these events God has inaugurated a new age. Thus Paul interprets the Hebrew Scriptures through the lens of this eschatological crisis and concludes that they point toward Christ as the fulfillment of God's promises and the Jewish rejection of that accomplishment.

Paul begins his interpretive explanation in verse 5 with an allusion to Leviticus 18:5. He points to this verse to emphasize that whatever righteousness is found in the law comes from doing it. Then in 10:6-8 he quotes another passage from the Hebrew Bible, Deuteronomy 30:12-14. In this part of Deuteronomy Moses is speaking about what will happen to the Israelites after they have been unfaithful and forced into exile. They will be restored to their land, saved from their enemies, and given a new opportunity to live out the law that God has given them. In the verses Paul quotes here, Moses is reminding the people that the law is not some impossibly difficult prescription for behavior. Rather, the law serves as a renewal of the covenant for the people. It is so close to them that it is already in their hearts and mouths.

Paul's purpose in using these two scripture passages is not to show that Leviticus and Deuteronomy stand in opposition to one another or that Moses was unable to make a consistent argument. He is instead interpreting these verses through his faith in Christ. The commandment of which Moses spoke in Deuteronomy has become for Paul Christ himself in 10:6-8. This means that the righteousness that comes from the law mentioned in Leviticus 18:5 is no longer necessary. It is "the word of faith" that is now so near to us.

Thus the Roman Christians are not called to pursue righteousness and salvation through practice of the law, but through faith. In verses 9 and 10 he makes this simple and yet comprehensive point: salvation comes through a faith that is so unified and complete that it can be confessed from the mouth and believed in the heart in one movement.

At this point Paul makes a distinction between being justified (being made right with God) and being saved. In *The New Interpreter's Bible* N. T. Wright explains the difference like this: "'Righteousness' denotes the status people have on the basis of faith: a present legal status that anticipates the future verdict of the divine law court, a present covenantal status that anticipates final affirmation of membership in God's people. 'Salvation' denotes the actual rescue from sin and death effected in the future by the promised resurrection, and likewise anticipated in the present." Paul returns to the Hebrew Bible in verse 11, quoting Isaiah 28:16 as confirmation of what he has just said.

In 10:12-13 Paul repeats the claim made earlier in his discussion of sin (3:22-23): God, the Lord of all people, does not distinguish between Jew and Greek. This is as true for salvation as it was for sin. Again he uses a scriptural quotation for confirmation of this point. The context for Joel 2:32, which he quotes here, is a description of the coming day of the Lord. Paul's use of it to conclude this section of the passage underlines both the possibility of God's universal salvation and the eschatological crisis presented to each person in Jesus Christ.

Romans 10:14-21. A new section of this passage begins with a burst of rhetorical questions in 10:14-15*a*. In essence, Paul wonders how "they," which refers to the "everyone" in verse 13, will ever be saved if they do not believe, or have never heard the news, or have no one to proclaim it, or have never received a messenger who was sent to them. The questions culminate in a quotation of Isaiah 52:7: "How beautiful are the feet of those who bring good news!" The questions and quotation serve as rationale for Paul's own mission to the Gentiles. He, his companions, and all Christian missionaries are the ones who have been sent to proclaim the good news so that it can be heard and obeyed (10:16*a*). Another quotation from Isaiah (53:1) reminds him that not all have received what missionaries have offered. Faith remains the necessary ingredient. And it grows out of the proclamation of the word of Christ. Finally, in verse 18, he asks himself if everyone has had the opportunity to hear this proclamation. He answers affirmatively with the quotation of Psalm 19:4.

In 10:19-21 Paul returns to the issue of his fellow Jews. He wonders how Israel could not have understood its own Scriptures. After all, Moses himself, in Deuteronomy 32:21, says that God will use people who are not a nation, that is, Gentiles, to make the Israelites jealous and angry. Further, Isaiah, in 65:1, points out that God has been found by those who were not even looking, again referring to Gentiles. Finally, Paul uses Isaiah's words yet again to call the Jews a "disobedient and contrary people." How did they miss such allusions to what was to come and thus fail to believe in Christ? Ultimately, Paul has no fully satisfactory answer.

INTERPRETING THE SCRIPTURE

Keeping the Goodness in the Good News

The key verse of this passage, Romans 10:9, encapsulates Paul's understanding of what is good about his message to the Roman Christians. First, it is possible for us to be saved from our powerlessness over sin, from death and darkness, from hopeless alienation from God. Second, the possibility comes not through our following of the Jewish law or any other law, but through faith. All we have to do is confess with our mouths and believe in our hearts that what God has done through Jesus makes a profound difference to us and to the world. We are released from all bondage and servitude to human passions and desires and to imperfect human constructs and understandings of what the divine wants.

Our faith serves as an entrance into our lives through which God can make us right (justification) and begin the work of bringing us wholeness and peace. All we have to do is hold the door open as God moves in, and then keep it open through the challenges, the times of tediousness and boredom, and the changing circumstances of our lives.

The difficulty for most mature Christians lies in the fact that eventually the newness and the goodness of Paul's message wears off. Most of us cannot always live in a state of excitement about the relationship with God made possible through faith, no matter how seriously we want to take it. We find ourselves yawning through its announcement every Easter and Christmas; our minds wander in Sunday school and Bible studies. And no matter how impassioned the announcer is about this best of all news, we wonder about winning the lottery, learning that our children achieved great scholastic success, or our own promotions and raises.

As a professional announcer of this good news I try always to keep in front of me one of Fred Craddock's dictums for preachers:

"Do not expect everything [you preach] to be confirmed by your pulse. How you feel about a matter may not be a true register of its importance, or its merit. Some things are true even when we are asleep."

Perhaps the measure of the worth of this good news that Paul offers is found not so much in fevered enthusiasm but in the fact we can take it for granted. Regardless of whether we win a million dollars, whether our children attend Harvard, or whether we climb the ladder of success, we can rely on the salvation that God is holding out for us if we confess and believe that Jesus is Lord.

The Cost of Faith

Of course confessing and believing in Jesus has its own demands. For some people in this world these costs can be quite high. While my husband and I were serving as missionaries in Taiwan, we helped in the leadership of an English-speaking worship service on Sunday afternoons. This service attracted many Taiwanese people for a variety of reasons. Some came to practice their English skills; others came because they had become Christian while studying abroad and needed a place to worship in their adopted language.

One Taiwanese woman came because she was attracted to the good news of faith in Jesus. For a couple of months, she came every Sunday afternoon to sing the hymns, pray the prayers, and listen intently to the message. We struck up a friendship over the weeks and talked regularly about what she was hearing in church. The time came, I thought, when she was ready to confess her faith and be baptized and so I invited her to consider it.

Immediately she rejected my offer. "It was impossible," she said and turned to go. When I went after her I asked her what was so difficult about such a simple step, one she seemed so ready to take. Cornered, she explained that if she accepted Christ, her mother would reject her. She would be excluded from the family gatherings at Lunar New Year and Mid-Autumn Festival because she could no longer participate in the rituals before the ancestors and the gods. She would also be cut out of the family will. So strongly did her mother believe that Christianity was a Western invention at best and a false religion at worst that she had made it very clear to her daughter that following the way of Christ would have dire consequences.

The woman never came back to church after that and I never saw her again. Perhaps privately she has believed in her heart. Publicly, to my knowledge, she has never been able to confess with her mouth.

"Beautiful Feet"

The challenging rhetorical questions in Romans 10:14-17 have inspired countless missionaries through the centuries to leave their homes and travel to places unknown to proclaim the word of Christ. When I was a child, our congregation often welcomed missionaries on furlough to come and speak to us about their work overseas. I was entranced. It seemed so soul stirring to be sent to exotic cultures to proclaim the good news that Jesus saves. And it seemed so exalting to get to be a part of God's missionary enterprise. "How beautiful are the feet of those who bring good new!" I wanted my feet also to be acclaimed beautiful.

Now that I have had the opportunity to serve God in such a way, I have learned that such work is not always exciting and romantic. In fact, the steady task of proclaiming the gospel and caring for people in Taiwan was sometimes as prosaic and demanding as it is at home in the U.S. I also learned that God calls all of us, not just people who are sent to other countries by their mission boards, to do this announcing of the good news. It is our shared task wherever we are. And honestly, if we cannot speak of Christ or show his face to the neighbor across the fence, then we probably will be unable to do it in China, Sudan, or Argentina.

But the most important thing I learned in Taiwan was this: Neither I nor any other missionary was bringing God to some God-forsaken place. God had already arrived, long before we entered the picture. And God stays even after we leave and go home. The missionary task is not ever to say, "We have something that you do not." Instead our job consists of pointing out the places where God is already dwelling, announcing the truth that God's love is revealed in Jesus Christ, and acting out that love in our everyday lives. If we do these things, everywhere we go, we can be counted among those with beautiful feet, and a beautiful faith.

SHARING THE SCRIPTURE

PREPARING TO TEACH

Preparing Our Hearts

This week's devotional reading is found in Hebrews 5:5-10. In verse 8 the writer affirms that Jesus is God's Son and in verse 9 that he is "the source of eternal salvation for all who obey him." By what words and deeds do you affirm that salvation is available through Christ, who is Lord? What difference does your affirmation make in the way you live?

Pray that you and your students will be able to confess that Jesus is Lord and the source of salvation.

Preparing Our Minds

Study the background scripture as found in Romans 10:5-21 and the lesson scripture, Romans 10:5-17.

Look up the Old Testament quotations, noted in the Understanding the Scripture portion, that Paul uses in these verses. The context of these verses in the Old Testament may help you better understand Paul's use of them in his letter.

Write on newsprint:

information for next week's lesson, found under "Continue the Journey."

Plan any lectures that you plan to use, based on the suggestions provided.

LEADING THE CLASS

(1) Gather to Learn

❖ Welcome the class members and introduce any guests.

❖ Pray that the adults will be able to affirm that Jesus is Lord and claim that he is Lord of their own lives.

❖ Note that a popular slogan reminds us to "talk the talk and walk the walk." Invite the students to discuss what this might mean in terms of their lives as Christians.

❖ State that although Paul did not know this slogan, he certainly would understand its intent and agree with its message: We need to proclaim what we live and live what we proclaim.

❖ Read aloud today's focus statement: **People often look for good news to balance all the bad news they read and hear about in the media. What's the best possible news we could read or hear about? Paul announces the good news that anyone who confesses Jesus as Lord will be saved.**

(2) Discern Paul's Teachings About Salvation

❖ Choose a volunteer to read Romans 10:5-13 and another to read 14-17.

❖ Discuss the following questions, or prepare a lecture based on their answers.

(1) For Paul, what are the essential

requirements for salvation? How does Paul's belief square with your own? (See key verse, Romans 10:9.)

(2) **In verse 10 Paul seems to make a distinction between "justification" and "salvation." What contrast do you think he is trying to draw here?** (See paragraph 5 under Romans 10:5-13 in Understanding the Scripture.)

(3) **What is the connection between hearing and believing?** (Note verses 14-17.)

(4) **Paul emphasizes the importance of the role of preaching and proclamation. Do you believe the Christian faith could survive if people could not hear others speak about faith? Give reasons for your answer.**

(5) **What are you willing to do, individually or as a member of the class, in response to verses 14-17?**

❖ Read Psalm 96. If your hymnal includes a Psalter (the Psalms), distribute hymnals so that the class can read responsively. Then discuss whatever relationship you can discern between Psalm 96 and Paul's teachings in Romans 10.

(3) Plumb the Depths of One's Confession That Jesus Is Lord

❖ Distribute hymnals and point out several creeds (such as the Apostles' Creed or Nicene Creed) that are familiar. Either do a lecture or lead the class in a discussion to discern the important points in each creed. Invite comment as to which points students find troubling or questionable, as well as points they can strongly affirm.

❖ Distribute paper and pencils. Invite the students to write a brief confession of their own faith. Ask them to read these confessions in small groups. Bring the class together and note important themes or ideas that were lifted up in many of the confessions.

❖ Note that according to our key verse, Romans 10:9, we only have to confess with our lips and believe in our hearts. Yet, many people believe that a confession must be made in both word and deed. Invite the students to discuss whether the Christian faith is best expressed in words, in action, or a combination of both. Encourage them to give examples to support their answers.

(4) Tell the Good News

❖ Read Romans 10:15, noting that the quotation is from Isaiah 52:7.

❖ Read or retell the information under "Beautiful Feet" in the Interpreting the Scripture portion.

❖ Distribute paper and pencils. Provide time for quiet meditation. Ask the students to identify at least one person who needs to hear the truth that God's love is revealed in Jesus Christ. **Suggest that they ponder this question: How can you tell the good news in words and live it out in actions so as to draw the person you have identified to Christ?** Encourage the students to write the first name of the person they have identified on their paper and how they plan to approach this person with God's good news.

❖ Close the meditation time by again reading Romans 10:15.

❖ Go around the room and ask the students to give just the first name, even an initial, of the person each has identified. Write these names on newsprint. Invite the students to keep these individuals and each other in prayer this week as they go forth to share the good news.

(5) Continue the Journey

❖ Pray that the students and those whom they have identified will believe in their hearts that God raised Jesus from the dead and also take every appropriate opportunity to confess that Jesus is Lord so that others may hear the good news. If time permits, include each name on the list in your prayer.

❖ Read aloud this preparation for next week's lesson. You may also want to post it on newsprint for the students to copy. **Prepare for next week's session entitled "Living the Christian Life" by reading Romans 12:1-21, giving particular attention to verse 1-2 and 9-21. Keep this focus in mind as you read: People sometimes find it hard to express the love they feel for another. How do Christians show the love we are commanded to have for one another? Paul gives concrete suggestions for attitudes and behavior befitting a Christian lifestyle.**

❖ Read aloud the following three ideas. Challenge the students to commit themselves to use these activities as a springboard to spiritual growth.

(1) **Ponder the roles of teaching, preaching, writing, and other forms of verbal expression that led you to the Christian faith and helped you to grow deeper into the faith. What verbal expressions can you share with others to assist them in their faith journeys?**

(1) **Struggle with the following question and write your answers in a spiritual journal: What do you believe are the requirements for salvation? Then think about what Paul might say in response to your answers.**

(3) **Sing or repeat the affirmation, "Jesus is risen from the dead and is Lord," several times each day. As you hear these words, ponder what they truly mean to you.**

❖ Sing or read aloud "He Is Lord."

❖ Say one phrase of this prayer at a time and ask the class to repeat it so that they will quickly learn it: **Grant, O Lord, that we may go forth to serve you as faithful disciples who not only hear the word but also do it in the name of Jesus. Amen.**

LIVING THE CHRISTIAN LIFE

PREVIEWING THE LESSON

Lesson Scripture: Romans 12:1-2, 9-21
Background Scripture: Romans 12:1-21
Key Verses: Romans 12:9-10

Focus of the Lesson:
People sometimes find it hard to express the love they feel for another. How do Christians show the love we are commanded to have for one another? Paul gives concrete suggestions for attitudes and behavior befitting a Christian lifestyle.

Goals for the Learner:
(1) to examine Paul's description of a life consecrated to God.
(2) to consider how faith makes a difference in how they live.
(3) to evaluate personal attitudes and actions in light of what Paul urges.

Supplies:
Bibles, newsprint and marker, paper and pencils, hymnals

READING THE SCRIPTURE

NRSV
Romans 12:1-2, 9-21

I appeal to you therefore, brothers and sisters, by the mercies of God, to present your bodies as a living sacrifice, holy and acceptable to God, which is your spiritual worship. 2 Do not be conformed to this world, but be transformed by the renewing of your minds, so that you may discern what is the will of God—what is good and acceptable and perfect

9 Let love be genuine; hate what is evil, hold fast to what is good; 10 love one another with mutual affection; outdo one another in showing honor. 11 Do not lag in zeal, be ardent in spirit, serve the Lord.

NIV
Romans 12:1-2, 9-21

Therefore, I urge you, brothers, in view of God's mercy, to offer your bodies as living sacrifices, holy and pleasing to God—this is your spiritual act of worship. [2]Do not conform any longer to the pattern of this world, but be transformed by the renewing of your mind. Then you will be able to test and approve what God's will is—his good, pleasing and perfect will.

[9]**Love must be sincere. Hate what is evil; cling to what is good. [10]Be devoted to one another in brotherly love. Honor one another above yourselves.** [11]Never be lacking in zeal, but keep your spiritual fervor,

12 Rejoice in hope, be patient in suffering, persevere in prayer. 13 Contribute to the needs of the saints; extend hospitality to strangers.

14 Bless those who persecute you; bless and do not curse them. 15 Rejoice with those who rejoice, weep with those who weep. 16 Live in harmony with one another; do not be haughty, but associate with the lowly; do not claim to be wiser than you are. 17 Do not repay anyone evil for evil, but take thought for what is noble in the sight of all. 18 If it is possible, so far as it depends on you, live peaceably with all. 19 Beloved, never avenge yourselves, but leave room for the wrath of God; for it is written, "Vengeance is mine, I will repay, says the Lord." 20 No, "if your enemies are hungry, feed them; if they are thirsty, give them something to drink; for by doing this you will heap burning coals on their heads." 21 Do not be overcome by evil, but overcome evil with good.

serving the Lord. [12]Be joyful in hope, patient in affliction, faithful in prayer. [13]Share with God's people who are in need. Practice hospitality.

[14]Bless those who persecute you; bless and do not curse. [15]Rejoice with those who rejoice; mourn with those who mourn. [16]Live in harmony with one another. Do not be proud, but be willing to associate with people of low position. Do not be conceited.

[17]Do not repay anyone evil for evil. Be careful to do what is right in the eyes of everybody. [18]If it is possible, as far as it depends on you, live at peace with everyone. [19]Do not take revenge, my friends, but leave room for God's wrath, for it is written: "It is mine to avenge; I will repay," says the Lord. [20]On the contrary:

"If your enemy is hungry, feed him;
  if he is thirsty, give him something to
  drink.
In doing this, you will heap burning coals
  on his head."

[21]Do not be overcome by evil, but overcome evil with good.

UNDERSTANDING THE SCRIPTURE

Romans 12:1-2. "Therefore" is the word Paul uses to transition to this fourth and last major section of his Letter to the Romans. This "therefore" follows the moving doxology of Romans 11:33-36 with which Paul concludes his long discussion of the salvation of the Jews in Romans 9–11. Because God's wisdom and power are unknowable and infinite, because "from him and through him and to him are all things" (11:36), believers should respond with an openness to the ways of God and love toward one another.

"Therefore" also, in some measure, follows all that Paul has been discussing throughout the letter: a right relationship with God, the gift of life in the Spirit, the ability to defeat the power of sin—all things

that have been made possible through Christ. To paraphrase: "now that we have received this grace upon grace from our amazing and inscrutable God, we ought to live the lives God has intended for us all along."

The imperatives for responsive action are summed up in verses 1 and 2: "Present your bodies as a living sacrifice"; and "do not be conformed to this world, but be transformed." The background to the first command is found in the sacrificial rites of the Jerusalem Temple. Paul was surely aware of the rules for sacrifice that many faithful Jews practiced. As we might expect, he would have nothing to do with such a system in the new order established in Christ. In place of sheep, bulls, doves, and first fruits, Paul calls believers to present their bodies, their very selves, to God. (This is not a radically new concept to Jewish tradition. Echoes of Micah 6:6-8 resonate in these words.)

In presenting themselves to God, believers participate in "spiritual worship." The original Greek meaning for the word translated by both the NIV and the NRSV as "spiritual" actually means "logical" or "rational." As Paul Achtemeier writes in the volume on Romans of the *Interpretation* series commentary, the presentation of their very selves in worship "is the logical response . . . to the history of God's grace he has been reciting."

The second imperative, "do not be conformed to this world," draws upon the dualism we have already seen in this letter. "This world" ("this age" in some manuscripts) is the world of the flesh where sin reigns. Paul exhorts the faithful not to continue to pattern themselves on the values and goals of the cultures around them. Rather, he encourages them to let their whole being be made over by the Spirit through the mind's assent to faith.

Romans 12:3-8. This kind of transformation takes place in the faithful community and in the individual. Not only do believers find themselves in a new relationship with God, they are also now in a new relationship with one another. This bond is, or should be, based on respect, mutual regard, and an awareness of the gifts that each one offers to this newly constituted family of God. Here Paul gives guidance for ordering this family and for living together in harmony. Above all, its members must remember that they are brought together by Christ and comprise his body (see also 1 Corinthians 12 and Philippians 2).

Paul's first word of advice comes in verse 3: "I say to everyone among you not to think of yourself more highly than you ought to think." Paul is calling for a bit of humility in Christian relations. In *Wishful Thinking* Frederick Buechner captures the sense of

Paul's meaning in his definition of humility: "True humility doesn't consist of thinking ill of yourself but of not thinking of yourself much differently from the way you'd be apt to think of anybody else." Notice also that in his use of the word "think" Paul is again accentuating the role of intelligence and logic in the Christian life as he did in verses 1 and 2. Further, the standard for measuring each person is faith and nothing else, including the standards that the world holds up to assess the worth of people.

In 12:4-8 Paul employs the metaphor of the body in discussing why each person should not exalt himself or herself over others. He reminds his readers that all Christians are a part of something much greater, the Body of Christ, and not a totality in and of themselves. God has given each person different gifts that must be used in service to the whole. Without each gift, the community is bereft of something it needs. Conversely, without the gifts of others in the community, the individual is also incomplete.

Paul then lists various gifts: prophecy, ministry (service), the abilities to teach and encourage, generosity, leadership, and compassion. The list is not exhaustive; elsewhere, notably 1 Corinthians 12, he lists other gifts. Rather it is suggestive—offering examples of some of the gifts that are necessary for a church to function as Christ's body in the world.

Romans 12:9-21. We can organize Paul's words of advice in this section into two smaller groupings: verses 9-13 deal primarily with relations within the Christian community and verses 14-21 generally concern the ways Christians should approach the outside world. Although here is overlap between these two groupings, this distinction helps us understand and remember Paul's overarching imperatives.

In 12:9-13, Paul commands the Roman Christians to love and honor one another, placing the needs and hopes of others above one's own. He calls for perseverance and zeal in prayer and service. He demands generosity and hospitality to all who require it, saints (believers) with whom they are acquainted and strangers who are visiting the community.

In the second grouping, verses 14-21, Paul turns his attention to the problems Christians might face in their dealings with non-believers. He is realistic about the difficulties believers might encounter, but nonetheless expects the same standard of conduct outside as within the warmth of the believing fellowship. And in laying out these expectations, he quotes from the teachings of Jesus, one of the few places in all his letters where he demonstrates knowledge of these traditions.

When the faithful meet persecution, they should bless the persecutors (compare Luke 6:28). Whether their neighbors are joyful or sorrowful, they should stand empathetically with them. They should continue to display the same humility outside the church as they do inside. They should strive to live at peace with everyone, never attempting to extract revenge or repayment for evil (compare Matthew 5:44; 25:35; Luke 6:27).

The meanings in Paul's commands throughout Romans 12:9-21 are fairly straightforward and require little explanation. The difficulty is in the doing of these ethical and moral instructions, not in the comprehending! And in Paul's view, only by living out these words do Christians demonstrate actively the faith that brought them into a new relationship with God and with one another in the first place.

INTERPRETING THE SCRIPTURE

Walking the Walk

In Romans 12 Paul shows how the theology that he has been explaining up to this point becomes the foundation for ethical and moral behavior. If Christ has indeed brought us before God in a transformed relationship, then faith can no longer be a nice Sunday morning abstraction. It is, for Paul, an every-day, every-hour, every-place concern. We are called by him "to walk the walk" in the same way that we have "talked the talk" that is held in our hearts and confessed with our mouths.

So Paul offers this list of concrete advice about how we are to treat one another within and outside of the community. In a sense the items on the list are extensions of Jesus' commands that we love our neighbors as ourselves (Matthew 22:39) and that we treat others as we would have them treat us (Matthew 7:12). These ideas are also not unique to the teachings of Paul, or Jesus for that matter. Similar words of wisdom about human relations are found in the Old Testament and throughout the writings of the ancient Greeks and Romans. However, the fact that they can be discovered in other religious traditions does not make them any less important for Christians—or any less demanding to follow. As mentioned above, the true difficulty of Romans 12 is not in understanding its meanings but in making a commitment to live out these imperatives in every particularity of our lives.

Occasionally in my life I have had to make it a priority to lose weight. When the scales remind me that I must do something, I make a commitment and start to follow through. I attend Weight Watcher meetings; I watch and record every bite taken; I give up (for a time) fat-filled desserts, chocolate, and French fries. In short, I attack this problem with enormous energy and dedication.

In the last round of weight loss, I began to think about what might happen if I attacked other problems in my life with the same zeal. For example, what if I treated my fellow church members exactly as Paul recommends? And what if I worked on these relationships with the same enthusiasm as I watch my weight? What if I kept a record of how I was doing in the humility and kindness departments? What if I considered with fellow Christians the implications of my actions as carefully as I consider the effects of what I eat at a weight loss meeting?

Although a side effect of such intense scrutiny of my own behavior might be an over-attention upon myself, it might also result in a powerful dedication to the task of improving my witness through action. The marks of a true Christian that Paul sets out in Romans 12 are quite high, but if I can lose a few pounds now and then surely I can also work diligently on the quality of my friendships within and outside the church.

Unity, Not Uniformity

An old Taiwanese folktale makes the point that Paul is trying to make in this passage about living as one body in Christ. It goes like this: Everyone knows that the mouth governs eating, the stomach digestion, the hands what we do, and the feet where we go. And when they work together, everything in a body runs smoothly. But what would happen if the parts refused to work together? One day one particular body found out when everything began to fall apart.

It started with the mouth when it wondered out loud, "If I don't eat the food there is no way the body can exist, can it?" The stomach, overhearing these musings, mockingly responded, "And if I refuse to digest the food, you cannot eat anything and would quickly become useless!"

When the hand heard their conversation, it quickly cried out, "Everything that the mouth eats and the stomach digests comes from my labor. If I decide not to work, what will you eat? What will you digest?"

The foot would not be left out of this discussion. When it heard what the others were saying, it became angry and boastful. And it said to all of them, "If I choose not to go any place where there is food in front of all of you, the hand could not get it, the mouth could not eat, and the stomach could not digest. What would you do then?"

And so it was that each of these parts of the body dramatized its own importance and refused to yield to one another. Each was unwilling to say that the others were as important as it was. The mouth announced that it was not going to take another bite. And the stomach said it would no longer digest even a morsel. The hand claimed that its refusal was just as well because it would not pick up the food. The foot said that was okay with it because it wasn't moving anyway.

While these parts of the body went on strike and took a hard line on the issue, hunger began to run its course through the body and it grew weaker and weaker. Nonetheless, no one would give in or admit that it needed another part to survive.

At last, the eye opened and decided to get involved in the matter. It said, "Taken together, all parts of the body make up a family that cannot be divided for anyone's benefit. We must therefore get along, each performing the function it was created to perform so that the entire body can work properly. Each of you is necessary and the rest of us are dependent upon what you do for us. So stop this fighting, and get back to work! If you don't the entire body will die."

When the quarreling parts heard these words, they at last made up and once again took up their work. Now they understood that if they did not work together, they would indeed fall apart.

"The Greatest of These Is Love"

Paul describes the church as a body in need of many kinds of gifts elsewhere, in his first Letter to the Corinthian church. Immediately following this more elaborate explanation of the Body of Christ, he speaks of the one gift, love, without which no community of faith can survive. With enduring eloquence he writes of its manifestations and implications for the Christian life (1 Corinthians 13).

Romans 12 speaks of the same gift but in a much more prosaic style. Here he spells out in simple language exactly what it means to live a life of love among believers. It is not easy. In fact, the modern Western individualism that pervades our culture makes the job even more difficult than it was for the first-century Romans. In our world of "if it feels good do it" and "I did it my way" we have a built-in aversion to mutual humility and deference.

Nevertheless, we are not let off the hook. To be a true follower of Christ is to belong to a community that embodies his mission. And to belong to a community requires daily, selfless acts of sacrifice of one's own way to the wishes of others, of one's own desires for the needs of others, of one's own self-interest for the good of a community. That is what it means to demonstrate our faith in the love of Jesus and our love for one another.

SHARING THE SCRIPTURE

PREPARING TO TEACH

Preparing Our Hearts

This week's devotional reading is found in Romans 12:3-8, which is part of our background reading. Think about the church as the Body of Christ, with each member using his or her gifts to function for the benefit of the entire body. What changes might you expect to see if the church were to take more seriously this organic image of the body, with all parts working together? What marks of a true Christian do you find in these verses from Romans?

Pray that you and your students will identify and use the spiritual gifts that have been entrusted to you for the building up of the Body of Christ.

Preparing Our Minds

Study the background scripture from Romans 12:1-21 and lesson scripture, Romans 12:1-2, 9-21.

Review, if time permits, Paul's teachings on the gifts of the Spirit in 1 Corinthians 12 through 14. Note similarities between what Paul writes in these chapters and what he writes to the Christians in Rome.

Write on newsprint:

information for next week's lesson, found under "Continue the Journey."

Plan a lecture on the gifts of the Spirit that Paul discusses in 1 Corinthians 12 through 14, if you choose to use this option under "Examine Paul's Description of a Life Consecrated to God."

LEADING THE CLASS

(1) Gather to Learn

❖ Welcome the class members and introduce any guests.

❖ Pray that the students will identify the marks of a true Christian and commit themselves to live consecrated unto God.

❖ Encourage the students to think about the attributes of persons who in their opinion are truly living Christ-centered lives. Write these ideas on newsprint.

❖ Note that in today's lesson we will discover what Paul has to say to the church at Rome concerning the marks of the true Christian.

❖ Read aloud today's focus statement: **People sometimes find it hard to express** the love they feel for another. **How do Christians show the love we are commanded to have for one another? Paul gives concrete suggestions for attitudes and behavior befitting a Christian lifestyle.**

(2) Examine Paul's Description of a Life Consecrated to God

❖ Select a volunteer to read Romans 12:1-2.

■ Brainstorm answers to this question and write the students' responses on newsprint: **How would you describe a person who has been transformed and is no longer conformed to the world's ways?**

■ Look at the list and invite the students to evaluate the "average Christian" in terms of their list.

■ Discuss reasons why many Christians continue to be conformed to the ways of the world rather than transformed by the power of God.

❖ Choose someone to read Romans 12:9-13.

■ Read or retell the folktale under "Unity, Not Uniformity" in the Interpreting the Scripture portion.

■ If you choose to lecture, briefly add information about the spiritual groups and their role in building up the Body of Christ as found in 1 Corinthians 12 through 14.

■ Invite the students to assess whether they think that most Christians identify and use their gifts for the purposes God intended. If not, why do people fail to use their gifts? How could the church be different if everyone responded to the call to use his or her gifts?

❖ Enlist a volunteer to read Romans 12:14-21.

■ Note that Paul writes to people well acquainted with persecution and opposition. These verses explain how

they are to respond to such negative behavior and evil.

■ Discuss these questions.

(1) **What echoes of Jesus' teachings do you hear in these verses?** (See Matthew 5:44; 25:35; Luke 6:27-28.)

(2) **What changes would you notice in interpersonal relationships if all Christians took Paul's words seriously?**

(3) **What do these verses suggest to Christians who are willing to try to sway political decisions regarding hostilities with other countries?**

❖ Look back at the list of traits the group brainstormed at the beginning of the session. Invite the students to add or delete any characteristics so as to be in keeping with Paul's teaching concerning the marks of a true Christian.

❖ Sum up Paul's emphasis on love as a mark of the true Christian by reading responsively "Canticle of Love" (*The United Methodist Hymnal*, no. 646) or by reading in unison 1 Corinthians 13.

(3) Consider How Faith Makes a Difference in Learners' Lives

❖ Point out that according to Paul's teachings faithful Christians are to be genuinely (that is, without hypocrisy) committed to doing good through acts that are rooted in selfless love. They are to use their gifts to build up the Body of Christ.

❖ Distribute paper and pencils. Ask the students to list challenges to their faith that they often encounter and how their faithfulness enables them to overcome these obstacles. Challenges could include society's emphasis on individualism, success, power, influence, and money. The learners are not to discuss their ideas but rather keep their lists where they can periodically review them and note changes in their own thinking and behavior.

(4) Evaluate Personal Attitudes and Actions in Light of What Paul Urges

❖ Encourage the students to look again at Romans 12:9-13. Look especially at the action words (verbs). Provide quiet time for the participants to examine their own lives to see how they are living up to Paul's teaching and where they need to seek God's guidance to live more faithfully. End this quiet time with these words: **"Now, O God, transform my words and deeds to reflections of your love so that others may see Jesus in me. Amen."**

❖ Invite the adults to look again at Romans 12:14-21. Note that Paul, as Jesus, teaches that we are to bless our enemies, refrain from repaying evil with evil, and live peaceably insofar as that is in our power. These teachings would have been very real to early Christians facing persecution. Encourage the students to discuss with the class or in small groups whether Paul is speaking here only of interpersonal behavior, or is suggesting that Christians are not to condone war. Ask them to consider what actions they should take in light of their understanding of Paul's teaching.

(5) Continue the Journey

❖ Pray that the students will live as transformed persons whose lives bear the marks of those who claim Jesus as Savior and Lord.

❖ Read aloud this preparation for next week's lesson. You may also want to post it on newsprint for the students to copy. **Prepare for next week's session entitled "Living in Harmony" by reading Romans 14:1-13 and 15:5-6, which serve as both our** background and lesson scriptures. **As you read, keep this focus statement in your thoughts: People often become impatient with those of a different opinion or perspective, particularly if it is perceived as juvenile or ill conceived. How can Christians bear with one another when we have different opinions of what constitutes a faithful lifestyle? Paul encourages us to have patience with one another.**

❖ Read aloud the following three ideas. Challenge the students to commit themselves to use these activities as a springboard to spiritual growth.

(1) **Contemplate Paul's teaching that we are to be living sacrifices. What does this mean to you? What specific examples can you point to of sacrificial living in your own life? Write your ideas in a spiritual journal.**

(2) **Be alert for accounts of persons who have overcome evil with good. Occasionally such stories appear in the media. You may know someone who has responded with goodness to evil. How can such persons be role models for you?**

(3) **Evaluate your own class or congregation in terms of Paul's teachings in Romans 12. Where does the group measure up and where does it fall short? What can you do to help the group live more lovingly?**

❖ Sing or read aloud "Take My Life, and Let It Be."

❖ Say one phrase of this prayer at a time and ask the class to repeat it so that they will quickly learn it: **Grant, O Lord, that we may go forth to serve you as faithful disciples who not only hear the word but also do it in the name of Jesus. Amen.**

LIVING IN HARMONY

PREVIEWING THE LESSON

Lesson Scripture: Romans 14:1-13; 15:5-6
Background Scripture: Romans 14:1-13; 15:5-6
Key Verses: Romans 15:5-6

Focus of the Lesson:
People often become impatient with those of a different opinion or perspective, particularly if it is perceived as juvenile or ill conceived. How can Christians bear with one another when we have different opinions of what constitutes a faithful lifestyle? Paul encourages us to have patience with one another.

Goals for the Learners:
(1) to explore Paul's instructions about living nonjudgmentally and harmoniously in Christ.
(2) to identify situations where they need to apply Paul's instructions.
(3) to make a commitment to live harmoniously in Christ.

Supplies:
Bibles, newsprint and marker, paper and pencils, hymnals

READING THE SCRIPTURE

NRSV
Romans 14:1-13

Welcome those who are weak in faith, but not for the purpose of quarreling over opinions. 2 Some believe in eating anything, while the weak eat only vegetables. 3 Those who eat must not despise those who abstain, and those who abstain must not pass judgment on those who eat; for God has welcomed them. 4 Who are you to pass judgment on servants of another? It is before their own lord that they stand or fall. And

NIV
Romans 14:1-13

Accept him whose faith is weak, without passing judgment on disputable matters. 2One man's faith allows him to eat everything, but another man, whose faith is weak, eats only vegetables. 3The man who eats everything must not look down on him who does not, and the man who does not eat everything must not condemn the man who does, for God has accepted him. 4Who are you to judge someone else's servant? To his own master he stands or falls. And he will they will be upheld, for the Lord is able to make them stand.

5 Some judge one day to be better than another, while others judge all days to be alike. Let all be fully convinced in their own minds. 6 Those who observe the day, observe it in honor of the Lord. Also those who eat, eat in honor of the Lord, since they give thanks to God; while those who abstain, abstain in honor of the Lord and give thanks to God.

7 We do not live to ourselves, and we do not die to ourselves. 8 If we live, we live to the Lord, and if we die, we die to the Lord; so then, whether we live or whether we die, we are the Lord's. 9 For to this end Christ died and lived again, so that he might be Lord of both the dead and the living.

10 Why do you pass judgment on your brother or sister? Or you, why do you despise your brother or sister? For we will all stand before the judgment seat of God. 11 For it is written,

"As I live, says the Lord, every knee
    shall bow to me,
  and every tongue shall give praise
    to God."

12 So then, each of us will be accountable to God.

13 Let us therefore no longer pass judgment on one another, but resolve instead never to put a stumbling block or hindrance in the way of another.

Romans 15:5-6
5 May the God of steadfastness and encouragement grant you to live in harmony with one another, in accordance with Christ Jesus, 6 so that together you may with one voice glorify the God and Father of our Lord Jesus Christ.

stand, for the Lord is able to make him stand.

[5]One man considers one day more sacred than another; another man considers every day alike. Each one should be fully convinced in his own mind. [6]He who regards one day as special, does so to the Lord. He who eats meat, eats to the Lord, for he gives thanks to God; and he who abstains, does so to the Lord and gives thanks to God. [7]For none of us lives to himself alone and none of us dies to himself alone. [8]If we live, we live to the Lord; and if we die, we die to the Lord. So, whether we live or die, we belong to the Lord.

[9]For this very reason, Christ died and returned to life so that he might be the Lord of both the dead and the living. [10]You, then, why do you judge your brother? Or why do you look down on your brother? For we will all stand before God's judgment seat. [11]It is written:

"'As surely as I live,' says the Lord,
  'every knee will bow before me;
    every tongue will confess to God.'"

[12]So then, each of us will give an account of himself to God.

[13]Therefore let us stop passing judgment on one another. Instead, make up your mind not to put any stumbling block or obstacle in your brother's way.

Romans 15:5-6
[5]May the God who gives endurance and encouragement give you a spirit of unity among yourselves as you follow Christ Jesus, [6]so that with one heart and mouth you may glorify the God and Father of our Lord Jesus Christ.

UNDERSTANDING THE SCRIPTURE

Romans 14:1-6. Throughout Romans 13 Paul continues to write about the issues he discussed in Romans 12, namely, how Christians are to get along with others inside and outside the community. In Romans 14 he reframes his argument around the themes of welcome and judgment. Again, as in the previous lesson, the underlying demand is that Christians love one another as God has loved them. Here he employs yet another imperative to underscore this point.

"Welcome those who are weak in faith," he writes, "but not for the purpose of quarreling over opinions." In other words, do not invite people to dinner in order to bait them, argue with them, and prove them wrong! Granted that the readers are not going to be so rude, the implicit question in this verse becomes this: Precisely who are the "weak in faith" and who are the strong?

Paul does not seem to make this division along Jewish and Gentile lines. There is no prohibition in the Jewish Scriptures against eating meat, so the weak probably cannot be identified as Jews who eat only vegetables. Nor was there widespread vegetarianism in the Gentile world, making it unlikely that Gentiles were the weak ones Paul had in mind. Moreover, he does not make this division based on those who are new to the community against those who have been Christian for a long time. No mention is made of how recently the weak or the strong have made a commitment to faith.

In fact, Paul's definition of those who are weak in faith is quite surprising. For him they are Christians who are abstaining from eating certain foods based on ill-conceived religious convictions. In contrast, the strong are those who have come to believe that food itself has no intrinsic cleanness or uncleanness and provides neither access nor barrier to the presence of God. Because they believe that only faith in Christ brings people closer to God, what they eat is irrelevant to their relationship with God. Thus he considers their faith to be stronger.

Nonetheless, Paul exhorts his listeners to treat one another with respect regardless of dietary practice or, for that matter, regardless of whether or not one observes any holy days (14:5). The rationale for such a non-judgmental attitude in this passage is two-fold. First, as Paul implies in verse 4, Christians cannot reprove those who belong not to them but to another master, namely Christ. It is only the master's responsibility to correct his servants. Second, those who eat meat and those who do not, those who observe the Sabbath or any other day as holy and those who believe all days are alike, do so "in honor of the Lord." Their intentions are to glorify and express gratitude to God. Such a noble motivation justifies these kinds of choices.

Romans 14:7-9. Paul amplifies his rationale for mutual acceptance in this central section of the chapter. He reminds the Roman Christians that they do not live to themselves as the ultimate goal of life or for themselves as the ultimate inspiration for life. Their reason for doing what they do is grounded in the fact that they now belong to Christ—together they are his servants. Whether they are alive or dead, in whatever circumstance they find themselves, Christ is now their ruler. This is why he was crucified and resurrected, "so that he might be Lord of both the dead and the living."

Romans 14:10-13. Paul begins this concluding section with two rhetorical questions: Why do you judge your sister or brother? And why do you despise her or him? He is not expecting a spirited response to these queries. Rather, he is setting his readers up for the final argument against judging others. All believers will one day stand before the judgment seat of God; no one will be exempt. And to underscore the point, as he does so frequently, Paul quotes scripture, this time from Isaiah 45:23, where Isaiah proclaims the word of the Lord. Paul continues by reminding his readers that God alone is the judge of all people and to God alone are they accountable. If they judge one another, they are taking over a prerogative that belongs only to God; they are setting themselves up as God. This usurping of God's authority is utterly unacceptable. (See also Philippians 2:10-11.)

Verse 13 both summarizes the previous

twelve verses and offers yet another recommendation for community life. "Therefore," Paul concludes, "no longer pass judgment on one another." Instead, he adds, decide now not to place any kind of stumbling block in the path of others. To put it another way, Paul urges believers not only to refrain from judgment, a relatively passive action, but also to seek actively to help keep those who are "weak in faith" from breaking their own convictions. Paul encourages Christians to make the way smooth for other believers, rather than insisting on one's own desires and beliefs.

Romans 15:5-6. The final verses of this lesson, and of our study of Romans, comprise a prayer for harmony among all believers. This is only the second time Paul has turned to prayer language in his communication with the Roman church. (The first was in Romans 1:9-12, part of the greeting section of the letter.) He asks that God give the community the unity its members need to live in peace, knowing that without God's aid such peace cannot be attained. However, he is not seeking harmony for its own sake but for the purpose of glorifying God and Christ Jesus. The Christian community does not exist to perpetuate itself and to satisfy its own goals. It exists for service to the world as the Body of Christ and for the worship of the God who calls it into existence.

INTERPRETING THE SCRIPTURE

Welcome First, Judge Later

In this passage Paul opposes two actions that I had never considered before as opposites: welcome and judgment. I am not sure why I was so startled. After all, to welcome someone into your home is in some sense to accept him as he is and to reserve judgment about his actions and beliefs. To shun a person is to do the exact opposite: make a judgment about him prior to opening your door to him. Paul urges us to train ourselves to be instinctively open and hospitable to those with whom we disagree or who have done something we view as problematic. We should strive to overcome the knee-jerk, visceral impulses toward rejection that are so much a part of our nature. The act of judgment should be exercised only long after we have first embraced the one with whom we differ.

A young woman in my congregation decided for various reasons that she must divorce the man she had married five years earlier. She dreaded going home to tell her parents about her decision. She was certain that they would not understand, that they would insist that she try to get back with a man with whom she could no longer live. Only one other member of her extended family had sought a divorce, and he was no longer warmly received at family gatherings.

The plane ride to her parents' home was interminable. When she arrived, she went to the luggage carousel where she found her mother looking for her. "Your father is waiting in the car," she said. Then for the first time she looked into her daughter's eyes and saw something seriously wrong. "What on earth is the matter?" she asked. Her daughter blurted the news as tears started down her face. The mother was too shocked to say anything and in silence they went out to the car.

As soon as they got in, my friend's father knew that something was not right but he gave only the usual greetings. As he steered the car through the airport traffic, and the silence became unbearable, she finally said from the backseat, "Dad, Mark and I are getting a divorce." Her father slowly steered the car to the side of the road, stopped it, and turned around. "There are two things you need to know," he said. "One—your mother and I will always love you. And two—you can always come home."

This kind of instinctive welcome, one that places discussion of differences and options on the back burner, is what Paul is asking us to practice in the faithful community.

When and How to Judge

This passage in which Paul so eloquently exhorts us not to judge one another is a favorite for all who would much rather live and let live than deal seriously with the behavior of other believers. I find myself quoting it, at least in my head, when parishioners question the morals, attitudes, or actions of others in my presence. Most of the time, they question things that to me are unworthy of serious reflection and then wonder aloud whether the people in question can participate in our congregation. Of course they can, I generally respond, whether they eat meat, have a glass of wine with dinner, or do not like to wear a tie to worship.

There are issues in our churches, however, that deserve, even demand, serious reflection and, perhaps at some point in time, judgment. The issue of the ordination of homosexuals comes to mind because it has received so much attention in recent years, but there are many others. Can a faithful Christian drive an SUV? Can she work at a plant that manufactures weapons or other defense-industry-related products? Can he be involved in the selling of cigarettes, alcohol, and lottery tickets?

What we learn from Paul in this passage is not that these issues, as well as those he is discussing, are unimportant or irrelevant to faith. Rather, we learn that they should never serve as tests of fellowship, as bases for offering hospitality to another believer. That is to say, we are brought together by faith in Christ. That is the first and most important claim on our lives. The second claim, repeated by Paul in various ways in these chapters, is this: whether or not we agree, whether or not we keep certain commandments, whether we live out the same standards of conduct, we must love one another. This means that we must first welcome one another. Then together, with prayer and sensitivity and a willingness to listen and to speak the truth in love, we decide together how our community will live out its faith. And sometimes we decide that for whatever reason at this point in time we cannot decide.

Unity in the Midst of Conformity

When Paul was writing to the Roman church he was addressing his advice to a tiny minority in the general population. Most Romans had not even heard of Jesus much less of the small sect that was gathering in his name every week. In modern-day Taiwan we lived in a similar situation. Most people there practice some form of Buddhism or reverence to a particular deity in Taiwanese folk religion. Christians made up only 2 percent of the population. Unity in the midst of this kind of pluralistic environment is easier to maintain than it is here. Christians throughout Asia understand well that what unites them to one another is radically different from the surrounding truth claims. So they cling to one another even as they argue a bit about the kind of issues that Paul is addressing in this letter.

The strength of this bond is much harder to feel in a nation in which most people declare themselves to be, in one way or another, Christian. Because most of our society espouses to some degree Judeo-Christian faith and norms, we are much more aware of our differences within that conformity. And these differences are always threatening to undo us—within our local congregations, within our denominations, and among churches of various confessions and creeds.

Our challenge is to listen even more carefully to Paul's words about hospitality and put them into practice. The mainline churches, in spite of widespread agreement that their numbers have declined in the last twenty years, continue to be one of the few places in our society where people of various political persuasions, socio-economic classes, ideological backgrounds, races, and theological points of view, come together around a common commitment to Christ.

We are likely to find within our Sunday school classes diverse opinions on the issues that confront us. We are likely to see in our sanctuaries people of many different occupations sitting in the pews. My prayer is that we will cling to one another, as tightly as those Asian Christians who struggle with being a minority in their cultures, and live out Paul's challenge to reserve judgment, to welcome each person to the table, and to live together in harmony.

SHARING THE SCRIPTURE

PREPARING TO TEACH

Preparing Our Hearts

This week's devotional reading is found in James 4:7-12. Here James warns Christians about judging others. This theme also appears in today's session from Romans. What argument does James make against making judgments? When have you judged others? How have you felt when others have judged you, perhaps incorrectly? How do judgments and nasty words disrupt the harmony of life in the community of faith?

Pray that you and your students will be aware of words of judgment that hurt individuals or groups and create discord within the Body of Christ.

Preparing Our Minds

Study the background and lesson scripture, both of which are found in Romans 14:1-13 and 15:5-6.

Write on newsprint:

questions under "Explore Paul's Instructions About Living In Christ."

information for next week's lesson, found under "Continue the Journey."

Plan any lectures you will use. Decide which activities are most appropriate for your students.

LEADING THE CLASS

(1) Gather to Learn

❖ Welcome the class members and introduce any guests.

❖ Pray that today's participants will recognize how detrimental judgment is to the community of faith and vow to do all in their power to live in harmony.

❖ Invite the students to talk with the class, a small group, or a partner about a situation in which they became (or witnessed someone else become) impatient and judge others whose ideas differed from theirs. Note that such situations often arise in our family, workplace, and church settings. If these situations are not handled well, the result can be a serious rupture in the cohesiveness of the group. Encourage the students to state what the situation was, how the student or person involved handled it, and what the final outcome was.

❖ Read aloud today's focus statement: **People often become impatient with those of a different opinion or perspective, particularly if it is perceived as juvenile or ill conceived. How can Christians bear with one another when we have different opinions of what constitutes a faithful lifestyle? Paul encourages us to have patience with one another.**

(2) Explore Paul's Instructions About Living in Christ

❖ Divide the class into groups and make the following assignments. Write the questions and group assignments on newsprint and post it. Each group is to answer all three questions and report back to the class. If you prefer to lecture, do each assignment yourself. You will find ideas in the Understanding the Scripture portion.

(1) **What is Paul saying to his readers in Rome? Summarize his ideas in your own words.**

(2) **How would you apply Paul's comments to your community in the twenty-first century?**

(3) **What implications do these verses have for living harmoniously in Christ?**

Here are the group assignments:

- **Group 1:** Romans 14:1-4.
- **Group 2:** Romans 14:5-6.
- **Group 3:** Romans 14:7-9.
- **Group 4:** Romans 14:10-13.

❖ Invite the students to look together at our key verses from Romans 15:5-6.

(1) **What does this passage tell you about God?**

(2) **What does it tell you about God's expectations for the church?**

(30 **How does the image of the choir reinforce Paul's meaning?**

(3) **What favorite hymn(s) could be sung together in harmony to glorify God?**

(3) Identify Situations Where Learners Need to Apply Paul's Instructions

❖ Choose one of the following two activities.

- **Activity 1:** Read aloud the following case studies and invite the students to discuss the dilemma, perhaps relating it to a similar situation in their lives, and answer the questions.

  Case Study 1: Emily and Ron are a thirty-something couple with three young children. Although they would like to attend church regularly, their two older children are avid soccer players who are only eligible for a league that practices and plays on Sunday mornings. How can Ron and Emily be true to their faith while considering the needs of their children?

  Case Study 2: The members of Community Church are divided over the use of music in worship. One group wants to dispense with the organ and use a praise team exclusively, while the other group is absolutely opposed to instruments such as guitars, drums, and a keyboard. What can this church do to honor the diverse preferences of its members while still remaining a unified body of believers who do not belittle different ideas?

- **Activity 2:** Read or retell "Welcome First, Judge Later" in the Interpreting the Scripture portion. Encourage the students to talk about the example of the young woman from her point of view, from the point of view of her mother, and the point of view of her father. How does this story illustrate Paul's admonition to welcome others rather than judge them?

❖ Distribute paper and pencils. Ask the students to reflect on these questions and write answers that will not be shared. You will need to read these questions aloud and/or post them on newsprint. Conclude the activity by encouraging the students to talk about any insights they gained from their contemplation.

(1) **How have I adjusted my behavior to be more considerate of family members, coworkers, and/or church members?**

(2) **How did my adjustment help to bring harmony? If it didn't bring harmony, what might be the reason?**

(3) **How did I feel about making this adjustment?**

(4) What would Jesus say about the adjustment I made?

(4) Make a Commitment to Live Harmoniously in Christ

❖ Brainstorm answers to this question: **What changes do we as a class or congregation have to make in order to live more harmoniously in Christ?** Insist that the answers be kept general so that no one person or group is cast in a negative light.

❖ Encourage the adults to identify the individual changes they are willing to make. In some classes, the trust level may be high enough to share these comments, but in others, this activity may be done in silence.

❖ End this activity by reading Romans 14:13 and challenging the students to make personal commitments in silence to live harmoniously in Christ.

(5) Continue the Journey

❖ Pray the words in today's key verses, Romans 15:5-6. Either read them yourself or invite the adults to join you in this prayer.

❖ Read aloud this preparation for next week's lesson. You may also want to post it on newsprint for the students to copy. **Prepare for next week's session entitled "Hanging On to God's Good News" by reading Galatians 1, focusing on verses 1-12. Note that we are moving into Unit 3, which is a study of Galatians entitled "Set Free." Keep this focus in mind as you read: When faced with several different claims about what is true, people often become confused and uncertain over what to believe. As Christians, what are we to believe is true? Paul says that there is only** one gospel, and that is the one received from Christ.

❖ Read aloud the following three ideas. Challenge the students to commit themselves to use these activities as a springboard to spiritual growth.

(1) Look carefully at the way other Christians live out their faith commitments. If you see actions or hear words with which you do not agree, decide why you disagree. How did you react? If you are willing to accept Paul's teaching that an issue for one Christian may not be an issue for another, would you feel inclined to change your opinion if you had reacted negatively? Why or why not?

(2) Compare and contrast Matthew 18:15-20, which speaks about pointing out faults to church members, with Paul's writings about being nonjudgmental. These two teachings seem to be in tension with each other. Reflect on how you can reconcile them. Write your ideas in your spiritual journal.

(3) Seek ways to honor the diversity within your congregation while still maintaining the unity of the Body of Christ. Find at least one specific action you can take this week to bring believers together.

❖ Sing or read aloud "Help Us Accept Each Other."

❖ Say one phrase of this prayer at a time and ask the class to repeat it so that they will quickly learn it: **Grant, O Lord, that we may go forth to serve you as faithful disciples who not only hear the word but also do it in the name of Jesus. Amen.**

UNIT 3: SET FREE (GALATIANS)
HANGING ON
TO GOD'S GOOD NEWS

PREVIEWING THE LESSON

Lesson Scripture: Galatians 1:1-12
Background Scripture: Galatians 1
Key Verse: Galatians 1:11

Focus of the Lesson:
When faced with several different claims about what is true, people often become confused and uncertain over what to believe. As Christians, what are we to believe is true? Paul says that there is only one gospel, and that is the one received from Christ.

Goals for the Learners:
(1) to study Paul's defense of both his authority and the gospel.
(2) to evaluate their willingness to believe in one gospel in a world that accepts many "gospels."
(3) to affirm their commitment to the Christian gospel.

Pronunciation Guide:
Galatia   (guh lay'shuh)

Supplies:
Bibles, newsprint and marker, paper and pencils, hymnals

READING THE SCRIPTURE

NRSV
Galatians 1:1-12

Paul an apostle—sent neither by human commission nor from human authorities, but through Jesus Christ and God the Father, who raised him from the dead—2 and all the members of God's family who are with me,

To the churches of Galatia:

3 Grace to you and peace from God our

NIV
Galatians 1:1-12

Paul, an apostle—sent not from men nor by man, but by Jesus Christ and God the Father, who raised him from the dead—²and all the brothers with me,

To the churches in Galatia:

³Grace and peace to you from God our Father and the Lord Jesus Christ, ⁴who gave

Father and the Lord Jesus Christ, 4 who gave himself for our sins to set us free from the present evil age, according to the will of our God and Father, 5 to whom be the glory forever and ever. Amen.

6 I am astonished that you are so quickly deserting the one who called you in the grace of Christ and are turning to a different gospel—7 not that there is another gospel, but there are some who are confusing you and want to pervert the gospel of Christ. 8 But even if we or an angel from heaven should proclaim to you a gospel contrary to what we proclaimed to you, let that one be accursed! 9 As we have said before, so now I repeat, if anyone proclaims to you a gospel contrary to what you received, let that one be accursed!

10 Am I now seeking human approval, or God's approval? Or am I trying to please people? If I were still pleasing people, I would not be a servant of Christ.

11 For I want you to know, brothers and sisters, that the gospel that was proclaimed by me is not of human origin; 12 for I did not receive it from a human source, nor was I taught it, but I received it through a revelation of Jesus Christ.

himself for our sins to rescue us from the present evil age, according to the will of our God and Father, 5 to whom be glory for ever and ever. Amen.

6 I am astonished that you are so quickly deserting the one who called you by the grace of Christ and are turning to a different gospel—7 which is really no gospel at all. Evidently some people are throwing you into confusion and are trying to pervert the gospel of Christ. 8 But even if we or an angel from heaven should preach a gospel other than the one we preached to you, let him be eternally condemned! 9 As we have already said, so now I say again: If anybody is preaching to you a gospel other than what you accepted, let him be eternally condemned!

10 Am I now trying to win the approval of men, or of God? Or am I trying to please men? If I were still trying to please men, I would not be a servant of Christ.

11 I want you to know, brothers, that the gospel I preached is not something that man made up. 12 I did not receive it from any man, nor was I taught it; rather, I received it by revelation from Jesus Christ.

UNDERSTANDING THE SCRIPTURE

Galatians 1:1-5. Paul opens this letter, as he does his others, with three elements: two direct statements concerning who he is and to whom he is writing and a brief greeting. In doing this he is following the letter-writing conventions of his day, making the important information known to his readers from the very beginning.

First, Paul declares his identity, "Paul an apostle"—his primary distinction. He will defend this claim about himself throughout the letter. The basic definition of "apostle" is "one who is sent." So next he makes clear who has sent him: "neither by human commission nor from human authorities, but

through Jesus Christ and God the Father, who raised him from the dead" (1:1). Paul is preparing his readers to receive his message and take it to heart by first establishing his own credentials. In this case, his authority comes straight from the God who raised Christ.

After establishing his identity and authority, he names the addressees of his letter: "to the churches of Galatia." These churches might have been located in the southern half of Galatia, close to the Mediterranean Sea or further north in what is now central Turkey. Based on the way Paul talks to them in 4:8-9, 5:2-3, and 6:12-13 we can ascertain that most of the Galatian Christians were Gentiles who knew something about Jewish beliefs and practices. We can also get a glimpse of the situation of these churches when Paul wrote to them (see next section).

Finally, Paul writes words of blessing that contain a description of his understanding of Jesus Christ: "Grace to you and peace from God our Father and the Lord Jesus Christ, who gave himself for our sins to set us free from the present evil age" (1:3-4*a*). The theme for this study unit is taken from these verses. Through Christ believers are made free. Free to do what will come clearer in subsequent lessons.

Galatians 1:6-9. Here Paul launches into the subject of the letter and the reason for writing. He also deviates from his usual introductions in that he offers no thanksgiving for the Galatians as he does for the addressees in other letters. He is angry with these Christians in Galatia and he is not wasting his time with insincerities. They are deserting "the one who called [them]," God, and turning to some other "gospel" that Paul completely rejects.

Recall that "gospel" for Paul is the good news of what God has done and will do through Jesus Christ (see "None Is Righteous," lesson 1). The gospel has power that transforms those who speak and those who hear it. The emphasis lies on the gracious, life-giving activity of God on behalf of a humanity that does not deserve it. But in Galatia someone, or a group of people, is distorting this understanding. They are putting the emphasis on human action, on things that humans should do to ensure the promises of God.

In 1:7 Paul refers for the first time to these people in Galatia "who are confusing you and want to pervert the gospel of Christ." As I explained in the background article at the beginning of this study, these people are Jews who believe that the keeping of the Jewish law somehow brings even Christians closer to God and maintains that relation-

ship. Throughout this and subsequent lessons, I will refer to Paul's opponents as "Missionaries."

In 1:8-9 Paul continues his angry denunciation of the message that the Missionaries have brought to the Galatian communities. Even if an angel had told them what the Missionaries have said, Paul would deny the truth of it. He delcares that he has given them what they need to know; what others add or change is wrong and they should be cursed. This strong language conveys Paul's fury at a situation that he cannot be present to rectify.

Galatians 1:10-12. Paul is finished for now with the name-calling, even changing tone a bit by referring to his audience as "brothers and sisters" (1:11). He returns to the subject of the source of his gospel. It does not come from himself or from any other human, but "through a revelation of Jesus Christ" (1:12). The Greek word for "revelation" signifies the divine nature of his gospel. God does this kind of revealing, not humans. And Jesus is the content of the revelation (see 1:16).

Paul also reminds his audience that he is not seeking their approval by preaching a gospel that seems easier to follow than the message of the Missionaries. Perhaps this group had suggested that Paul watered down the true gospel so that the Galatians would like him. Maybe they called him a "people-pleaser" because he did not urge them to follow the precepts of Torah, which were sometimes difficult. In response, Paul claims that he is striving to please only God and to serve only Christ as faithfully as possible.

Galatians 1:13-24. To support this claim, Paul offers a rare glimpse into his past life and actions. He tells of his zeal for persecuting Christians that grew out of his commitment to the traditions of his Jewish forebears (1:13-14). Then in 1:15-16 he mentions the revelation of the risen Christ that he received from God. Notice that Paul gives none of the details that Luke relates in Acts

9, 22, and 26. In this context the incidents of the revelation are of no importance to him. What matters is the fact that God is the source of the encounter with Christ and the gospel he is proclaiming to the Gentiles. Further, he notes parenthetically that God had set him apart for this mission before he was born. Paul is underscoring here the divine source and nature of his ministry.

Next, in 1:16b-17, Paul tells of what he did immediately after the revelatory experience of Christ. He most emphatically did not "confer with any human being" (1:16) nor did he seek counsel from the apostles in Jerusalem (1:17). Instead, he went into Arabia, presumably alone, perhaps to preach the gospel. Paul tells nothing of his

purpose for that trip or for his return to Damascus. The point of his telling his readers these things is to remind them that he did not need the permission or the authority of any other human being to carry out the work God had given him. Only after three years does Paul finally go to Jerusalem and consult with "Cephas," better known to us as Peter (1:18).

Finally, Paul says that he continued his missionary work by traveling to Syria and Cilicia. There he heard rumors from Christians in Judea about his spreading fame: The former persecutor has become preacher of the gospel he tried to stamp out (1:23). And, he concludes, they were glorifying God because of him (1:24).

INTERPRETING THE SCRIPTURE

Paul and the Galatian Christians

Paul can speak so candidly with the Galatian Christians because he has had a long relationship with them. Apparently, he had come to them some years before by accident when a physical ailment forced him to make an unplanned stop in Galatia (4:13). Some people, probably Gentiles who were attracted to the synagogue (usually called "God-fearers"), welcomed and cared for him while he regained his strength. Paul took advantage of the opportunity to preach the gospel to them and draw them into the growing Christian movement. Because he was the first Christian evangelist to work among them, he perceives himself as their spiritual father and feels accountable for them. It is his job, indeed his fundamental responsibility, to make sure they understand the true nature of the gospel. That is why he believes that he can address them so openly and with such emotion.

Paul is deeply disturbed to learn that they are being pulled away from the path he laid for them. He is angry with them for

being so easily led astray; he is even angrier with the Missionaries who are leading them down the wrong road. For Paul what is at stake is not the temporary pain of circumcision or the inconvenience of following the dietary regulations of the Hebrew Bible. What matters is that the Galatians believe that the gospel frees them from such things; it does not enslave them further to another set of human restrictions. And it is equally important that the Galatians see that God does the work on their behalf. They do not have to meet specific requirements to receive God's grace; indeed, there is nothing they can do to merit this gift.

Relationship Is the Key

In our dealings with one another within the church we would do well to learn from Paul's approach in this letter. All of us encounter situations in which some members of our congregation are not behaving or believing in ways that reflect our fundamental commitment to Christ. We wring our hands and ask one another what we ought to do. Often one of two things then occurs: either we ignore the problem and pray that it will go away, or someone confronts the wrongdoers—usually with disastrous results.

Paul can dare to challenge the Galatian Christians because in the past he has made the effort to cultivate a relationship with them. When he was with them he gratefully received their hospitality and their ministrations on his behalf. They became friends— he reminds them of that fact in 4:12 and 6:1. Now, as the Galatians seem to stray from the gospel he preached among them, he can call on that past connectedness and remind them what they have meant to one another.

Too often we wade into difficult situations without first building this kind of friendship with one another. We should learn to understand, to care for, and to trust one another when times are good so that we can draw on that reservoir of goodwill when things turn sour. In fact, such cultivation of friendships within the church, among persons of differing opinions and practices, may help us avoid the kind of conflict that tears churches apart when disagreements become more heated.

"Not What You Know, But Who You Know"

The content of Paul's gospel is not doctrine or law. It is the man Jesus who embodies for Paul the life-giving, sacrificial desire of God to have a relationship with us. In the name of that man, there are many "Missionaries" today who are distorting Paul's message, his "gospel." There are some who claim that we need to believe that God will bless us with prosperity in order to receive wealth and possessions. This kind of preaching has no place in Paul's gospel. There are some who claim that we must draw very clear lines among believers based on our view of whether or not the Bible is inerrant. This kind of distinction cannot be found in Paul's gospel. There are others who single out specific verses in the Bible

and make them binding law. This kind of thinking is contradicted by Paul's gospel.

The key test for Paul is simply this: Do you know Jesus? And do you know him in such a way that you are allowing his power to transform your life in accordance with his life and death? And do you know him in such a way that you are actively seeking the power of this gospel for the good of your community of faith, of your world?

"... And Who Knows You"

In the song "I Am a Town," Mary Chapin Carpenter describes musically a small town in one of the Carolinas. She sings of the religion of a small town in the South, mostly Baptist, and affirms that Jesus knows its name. This last phrase, whenever I hear the song, makes me ask myself afresh the question: does Jesus know *my* name?

For Paul it is never enough to simply know Jesus and the God he reveals so fully. We must also be known by God. Paul makes this point explicit in Galatians 4:9 when he writes, "Now, however, that you have come to know God, or rather to be known by God" (see also 1 Corinthians 8:3; 13:12). God is always the lead partner in the dance of faith—the one who knows first who and what we are and who then imparts that knowledge to us.

What does God know about me, I ask? Are we on a first-name basis? Along with the troublesome parts of myself that I would just as soon God not know, are there some things worth knowing? What are they? Does God find in me a fundamental trust in the fact that Jesus has brought us together and that only my refusal to join the dance will separate us?

In the end this is the gospel that Paul preaches: not only does Jesus make God known to us, but he also makes us known to God. No other rules or beliefs can do this. As we will see in the remainder of these lessons on the Letter to the Galatians, faith in this simple affirmation will set us free from all other efforts to get God's attention and will lead us down the road to an intimate knowledge of one another that cannot be surpassed.

SHARING THE SCRIPTURE

PREPARING TO TEACH

Preparing Our Hearts

This week's devotional reading is found in Acts 13:26-33. Here Paul preaches the good news of Jesus to those assembled in the synagogue of Antioch in Pisidia. He wants his Jewish listeners to know that this Jesus, whom God raised from the dead, fulfills God's promise to their ancestors. Moreover, Paul quotes Psalm 2:7 to affirm that Jesus is the very Son of God. This good news has the power to set people free. How is the news of God's promised Messiah, whom God has resurrected, good news for you? Are you willing to hang on to this gospel, or do you set it aside in favor of other so-called words of good news that our society preaches? Talk with God about your relationship and seek to strengthen it by the power of the Holy Spirit.

Pray that you and your students will experience freedom in Christ as you allow God's good news to direct your life.

Preparing Our Minds

Study the background, which includes all of Galatians 1, and lesson scripture, which focuses on verses 1-12.

Write on newsprint:

list of sentences under "Affirm Commitment to the Christian Gospel."

information for next week's lesson, found under "Continue the Journey."

Plan how you will do the suggested activities. Prepare any lectures you choose to do.

LEADING THE CLASS

(1) Gather to Learn

❖ Welcome the class members and introduce any guests.

❖ Pray that all who attend today will be able to clearly identify God's gospel and turn away from the many "gospels" that our society preaches.

❖ Point out that we are living in what many people term the postmodern era. One important aspect of postmodernism is that people do not accept the idea of absolute truth. Nor do they accept the notion that they must choose one religious faith. They prefer to pick and choose ideas from many different faiths. And yet, as Bible-believing Christians, we are called to accept the truth of God's word. Furthermore, we proclaim only one gospel and do not accept a patchwork quilt of religious ideas, though we do recognize that many legitimate beliefs can fall under the umbrella of Christianity.

❖ Invite the students to talk about the other "gospels," such as the gospel of success or wealth, which confront them daily. How do the class members hang on to God's good news when so many other "gospels" compete for our attention?

❖ Read aloud today's focus statement: **When faced with several different claims about what is true, people often become confused and uncertain over what to believe. As Christians, what are we to believe is true? Paul says that there is only one gospel, and that is the one received from Christ.**

(2) Study Paul's Defense of Both His Authority and the Gospel

❖ Choose a volunteer to read Galatians 1:1-5. Raise these discussion questions, or answer them in a lecture that you will prepare prior to class.

(1) **What does this passage tell you about Jesus?**

(2) **What does this passage tell you about Paul?**

(3) **If you had been present when this letter was first read to the church, would you listen to Paul as a credible authority? Why or why not?**

❖ Read Galatians 1:6-12 as if you were Paul actually speaking to the church. Choose whichever of these activities will best engage your class.

Activity 1: Discuss why Paul is angry at this church. Outline on newsprint whatever teachings of Paul's opponents that can be discerned from verses 6-12.

Activity 2: Invite several volunteers to role-play a response from the Galatian church to Paul's charges.

Activity 3: Paul speaks about receiving revelation from Christ. Some people believe that Paul is arrogant because he claims to have divinely given knowledge. Invite the adults to talk with a partner or small group concerning what they believe about the source of Paul's knowledge.

(3) Evaluate Learners' Willingness to Believe In One Gospel

❖ Imagine that Paul were alive and writing to your church today. What kinds of "other gospels" would he be railing against in the twenty-first century because of their corrupting influence? Write these ideas on newsprint.

❖ Set up a debate on the following statement: **We live in a pluralistic, global village where many faiths must coexist peaceably. Paul's insistence that people** **must believe only in the gospel he preaches creates discord in our world.** You need not stage a formal debate, but invite persons willing to speak to both sides of this issue to do so. The proposition is framed so that most class members will disagree, but you will likely have a lively discussion.

❖ Lead the learners through this guided imagery.

■ **Imagine yourself in your sanctuary at worship with your congregation when suddenly the apostle Paul appears and begins to berate your beliefs. Listen to what he is saying to you. How do you feel about his accusations?** (Pause)

■ **Paul insists that Christ has revealed to him the gospel that he shares with you. He says to you, "Will you believe?" How do you answer him?** (Pause)

■ **The next day, after Paul has gone, you begin to think about the answer you gave. How does your life show what you truly believe, or that you have questions about what you believe?** (Pause)

■ **Open your eyes when you are ready.**

❖ Invite the students to share insights they gained from any of these activities.

(4) Affirm Commitment to the Christian Gospel

❖ Note that one's commitment, no matter who or what that commitment is to, can be seen in the way one lives.

❖ Distribute paper and pencils. Ask the students to look at newsprint that you will now post on which you have already written the following information. The class members are to copy these sentence stems and complete them as they choose.

(1) **I have questions about the gospel Paul preaches because _____.**

(2) **I believe strongly that Paul's gospel tells the good news from God about Jesus Christ because _____.**

(3) I am willing to tell others that I believe _____.

(5) Continue the Journey

❖ Pray that the students will hang on to God's good news, which sets them free.

❖ Read aloud this preparation for next week's lesson. You may also want to post it on newsprint for the students to copy. **Prepare for next week's session entitled "Living on Faith" by reading Galatians 2:15–3:5. These verses are both our background and scripture lesson. As you read, keep this focus in mind: People tend to treasure acts of grace that are extended to them by others. Where do we encounter such acts of grace in the church? Paul says that God has already given us the greatest grace possible through the gift of Christ.**

❖ Read aloud the following three ideas. Challenge the students to commit themselves to use these activities as a springboard to spiritual growth.

(1) **Look back on your own life. When have you sensed God's call? What were the circumstances? How did you respond to the call—or did you** choose not to? What happened as a result of this call and your positive or negative response to it?

(2) Be alert for new ideas, especially those that may affect your spiritual life. How can you discern which ones fit within the framework of Christianity and which ones are "other gospels"? Identify pressures placed on you to accept ideas that are out of bounds for you as a Christian. Consider how you can respond politely but firmly to demands that you accept non-Christian "gospels."

(3) Commit yourself to spending more time than usual reading the Bible this week so that you can delve more deeply into the gospel that sets you free.

❖ Sing or read aloud "How Firm a Foundation."

❖ Say one phrase of this prayer at a time and ask the class to repeat it so that they will quickly learn it: **Grant, O Lord, that we may go forth to serve you as faithful disciples who not only hear the word but also do it in the name of Jesus. Amen.**

LIVING ON FAITH

PREVIEWING THE LESSON

Lesson Scripture: Galatians 2:15–3:5
Background Scripture: Galatians 2:15–3:5
Key Verse: Galatians 2:20

Focus of the Lesson:
People tend to treasure acts of grace that are extended to them by others. Where do we encounter such acts of grace in the church? Paul says that God has already given us the greatest grace possible through the gift of Christ.

Goals for the Learners:
(1) to delve into Paul's understanding of justification by faith.
(2) to consider what "justification by faith" means in their own lives.
(3) to affirm their faith in Christ.

Supplies:
Bibles, newsprint and marker, paper and pencils, hymnals

READING THE SCRIPTURE

NRSV
Galatians 2:15-21

15 We ourselves are Jews by birth and not Gentile sinners; 16 yet we know that a person is justified not by the works of the law but through faith in Jesus Christ. And we have come to believe in Christ Jesus, so that we might be justified by faith in Christ, and not by doing the works of the law, because no one will be justified by the works of the law. 17 But if, in our effort to be justified in Christ, we ourselves have been found to be sinners, is Christ then a servant of sin? Certainly not! 18 But if I build up again the very things that I once tore down, then I demonstrate that I am a transgressor. 19 For

NIV
Galatians 2:15-21

15"We who are Jews by birth and not 'Gentile sinners' 16know that a man is not justified by observing the law, but by faith in Jesus Christ. So we, too, have put our faith in Christ Jesus that we may be justified by faith in Christ and not by observing the law, because by observing the law no one will be justified.

17"If, while we seek to be justified in Christ, it becomes evident that we ourselves are sinners, does that mean that Christ promotes sin? Absolutely not! 18If I rebuild what I destroyed, I prove that I am a lawbreaker. 19For through the law I died to the law so through the law I died to the law, so that I might live to God. I have been crucified with Christ; 20 and it is no longer I who live, but it is Christ who lives in me. **And the life I now live in the flesh I live by faith in the Son of God who loved me and gave himself for me**. 21 I do not nullify the grace of God; for if justification comes through the law, then Christ died for nothing.

Galatians 3:1-5

You foolish Galatians! Who has bewitched you? It was before your eyes that Jesus Christ was publicly exhibited as crucified! 2 The only thing I want to learn from you is this: Did you receive the Spirit by doing the works of the law or by believing what you heard? 3 Are you so foolish? Having started with the Spirit, are you now ending with the flesh? 4 Did you experience so much for nothing?—if it really was for nothing. 5 Well then, does God supply you with the Spirit and work miracles among you by your doing the works of the law, or by your believing what you hear?

that I might live for God. [20]I have been crucified with Christ and I no longer live, but Christ lives in me. **The life I live in the body, I live by faith in the Son of God, who loved me and gave himself for me.** [21]I do not set aside the grace of God, for if righteousness could be gained through the law, Christ died for nothing!"

Galatians 3:1-5

You foolish Galatians! Who has bewitched you? Before your very eyes Jesus Christ was clearly portrayed as crucified. [2]I would like to learn just one thing from you: Did you receive the Spirit by observing the law, or by believing what you heard? [3]Are you so foolish? After beginning with the Spirit, are you now trying to attain your goal by human effort? [4]Have you suffered so much for nothing—if it really was for nothing? [5]Does God give you his Spirit and work miracles among you because you observe the law, or because you believe what you heard?

UNDERSTANDING THE SCRIPTURE

Introduction. In last week's lesson we saw how strongly Paul asserted that the gospel he handed on to the Galatian Christians was received from God and not humans. We also saw how strongly he believed that he in no way owed the Christian leaders in Jerusalem obedience or allegiance as their disciples. In 2:1-10, he tells of a meeting with the other apostles in Jerusalem. Together they agreed that just as Peter was to be the apostle to the circumcised, Paul was to be the apostle to the uncircumcised. The only thing they asked of Paul was that he would collect an offering for "the poor"—perhaps a designation for Jewish-Christians in Jerusalem—from among the Gentile churches in which he worked.

Apparently some time after this meeting in Jerusalem, Paul and Peter had an uncomfortable encounter in Antioch. There, Paul accused Peter of being hypocritical, of eating with Gentiles at first and then drawing back from them when some Jewish people from James arrived. Before everyone gathered there, Paul asked him, "If you, though a Jew, live like a Gentile and not like a Jew, how could you compel the Gentiles to live like Jews?" (2:14). This question introduces the verses in our lesson today.

Galatians 2:15-21. This difficult passage contains the interpretive crux of the entire letter: everyone, Jew and Gentile, is justified through faith and not works of the law. Though simply stated, almost every significant word in this summary is ambiguous and weighted in Paul's usage. So we turn to a detailed examination of these seven verses.

Paul begins with his theological interpretation of what happened between Peter and him in Antioch. He, like Peter, is a Jew and not a Gentile "sinner"—a common designation for all who live outside the covenant between God and those who keep Torah. Paul appears to be using "sinner" ironically in this context. Although Gentiles may be a part of the covenant people, they know in the deepest sense that their status before God does not depend upon "works of the law." For they have been "justified" by other means. Recall from the lesson on Romans 5:1-11 ("Justified by Faith," lesson 3) that the Greek word translated "justified" here basically means, "being made righteous." God is the one who makes humanity righteous, who does not hold their sins against them and establishes in Christ an eternal covenant with humanity.

What does Paul mean by "works of the law" in this passage? Scholars of an earlier era, influenced by Martin Luther's interpretation, explained that it referred to any human attempt to make oneself righteous. They saw Pharisaic Jews as the paradigms of such attempts. Recently, however, scholars have argued that these ideas do not capture Paul's actual meaning. On the one hand, no first-century Jew claimed that the practice of the law made him righteous before God. The practice of the law was always a response to what God had first done in establishing the covenant and giving the law.

On the other hand, the context of the phrase "works of the law" within the letter argues against such a broad interpretation. Remember that immediately before Galatians 2:15-16 Paul discusses Peter's withdrawal in Antioch from table-fellowship—a withdrawal that signified his intention to maintain the boundaries that separate Jew from Gentile even after the Christ-event. These kinds of acts that emphasize Jewish distinctiveness seem to be the content for Paul's use of the phrase "works of the law." Perhaps the Missionaries in Galatia were advocating a similar adherence to the rules of ethnic separation and identity. The boundaries could only be breached, they claimed, through circumcision.

In 2:16 Paul insistently opposes such an assertion. In no way can believers be put into right relationship with God by practicing laws that separate them from Gentiles. Rather, they are justified by "faith in Jesus Christ." He is not talking about simple intellectual assent, but about a trust and commitment in Jesus' redemption of both Jew and Gentile that shapes and challenges every other activity or idea of a believer.

In Galatians 2:17 Paul considers a possible implication of his own rejection of the laws of separation. To understand the thrust of his question, we have to remember that in this passage "sinner" seems to be synonymous with "Gentile" (see 2:15). We also have to consider that in the background of this rhetorical question are issues of table-fellowship, raised both by Paul's encounter with Peter in Antioch and by the Missionaries' teachings in Galatia. Paul thus asks: If we are trying to live out our belief that in Christ God has made all of us righteous and whole, and yet are found to be like Gentile sinners, does this make Christ a servant of sin? (The NRSV translates literally the Greek phrase "found to be sinners"; the NIV does not.) Observant Jews who see Jewish Christians eating with Gentile sinners might claim that these Christians, the representatives of Christ, are thereby bringing Christ into contact with unclean people and things. In Richard B. Hays's words in *The New Interpreter's Bible*, they would be "making [Christ] an accomplice in sinful actions—and therefore, in effect, the table-waiter of sin!"

Paul rejects this logic (2:17). And he takes matters a step further. If he does not eat with Gentiles, he builds up again the walls of separation that Christ himself destroyed. And he becomes the hypocrite whose actions nullify the gospel of salvation for all that he preached in the first place. The law no longer has any claim on him. For he, like all believers, has participated in the crucifixion of Christ. His own desires based on the will of the flesh have been killed; Christ now lives within him. That is possible only through faith in Christ, "the Son of God, who loved me and gave himself for me" (2:20). Otherwise, if being made right with God were possible through performing acts of the law, the death of Christ would have been absolutely pointless.

Galatians 3:1-5. Paul concludes this tightly woven, complex text with a series of angry rhetorical questions. "Who has bewitched you in spite of the fact that you have seen Christ crucified in your very midst?" (3:1; he is probably referring to the vividness of the gospel he proclaimed when he was with them). "How did you receive the Spirit, through following the law or through faith in the gospel you heard?" he demands to know. Of course the answer he expects is "faith." "Then," to paraphrase Paul, "why are you returning to the ways of the flesh when you started your journey of faith with the Spirit?" (See "Power for Living," lesson 5, for Paul's use of the categories "flesh" and "Spirit".) In 3:4 he wonders if they experienced the presence of the Spirit for nothing in the same way that Christ died for nothing (2:21). And then he restates the essential point of this paragraph: Do you know the Spirit and its power by keeping the law or by faith in the gospel you have heard?

INTERPRETING THE SCRIPTURE

Unconditional Love

A Jew by birth and a Pharisee by training, Paul was well aware of "the rules" he and his people followed to express their devotion to God. He had come to believe that God loved and approved of him solely because he followed the rules.

Then he met Jesus Christ on the road to Damascus.

His theology and practices were suddenly up for grabs. Following "the rules" was no longer necessary for wresting salvation from God. He had found unconditional love in Jesus, and he placed his full faith and confidence in his Lord. Now he wanted everyone—Jew and Gentile alike—to know that faith in Jesus was the pathway to salvation. No longer were the legalisms of his Pharisaical background necessary. All anyone has to do to be in a right relationship with God is to live by faith.

Paul's message is indeed good news for us as well. Before we criticize the Pharisees for their reliance upon "the rules," we must remember that many Christian groups are just as quick to depend upon legalities and codes. They have numerous rules that must be obeyed, many of which equal or excel the requirements of Pharisaical living. Paul writes that we do not have to live by these legalisms because we can never be reconciled to God by obeying laws. That relationship can only come about when we have faith in Christ.

Do Paul's teachings mean "anything goes"? Are there no longer any standards for moral and ethical behavior? Can't we just live as we want to, knowing that our faith in Christ, not our works, is what puts us in a right relationship with God? Paul's response to such arguments is an emphatic "no!" Christ is not "a servant of sin" (2:17). If we don't need to live by the law, and if we only need faith in Christ, what then governs our behavior?

"Christ Crucified"

Paul answers that question in Galatians 2:20 where he passionately exclaims, "It is no longer I who live, but it is Christ who lives in me." The resurrection faith that Paul preached consists of two elements: an affirmation that the Crucified One has indeed been raised from the dead and a conviction that he dwells within the daily lives of those who receive this good news.

To say that we are crucified with Christ requires us to first acknowledge that Christ himself was crucified and then resurrected by the gracious power of God. Christ loved us so much that he gave himself up to be crucified so that we might be put right with God.

Paul argues that if we believe that we can be put right by obeying the law, then Christ's death was absolutely pointless. The Galatians are obviously having trouble holding on to this idea. They apparently accepted it once, when Paul preached to them. Now, however, they are swayed by Missionaries who clearly are pushing them to revert to their legalistic practices. Paul will have none of this! He insists that the graciousness of God extended toward them—and us—must be believed in faith.

The apostle wants us to recognize that our lives have been transformed by the grace of God through the crucifixion of Jesus Christ. As you and I are crucified with Christ in the waters of baptism, Christ lives in us. Paul is not saying that the Christian's personality is snuffed out so that Christ alone lives within us. Rather, as Christ lives in us, he is able to shape and transform who we are so that we grow closer to the image of God in which we were created. As we are conformed to God's image, we do not need to have the law to guide us, for we will act in accordance with divine ways.

Do we stand with the foolish Galatians who insist that all manner of legalisms must be followed in order to please God? Or do we stand with Paul, believing that we are saved and live by faith in the one who was willing to die for us and whom God resurrected? A "yes" to legalism means that we must strive constantly to know every iota of the law and to follow it rigorously, knowing all the while that we cannot possibly do this. Is this fleshly life the one we really want to live? Or, are we willing to say yes to "faith," believing that our crucified and risen Lord now lives within us and is himself working to mold us into the person that God intends us to be as we live within the community of faith?

"He Lives!"

Once an earnest young Jewish student attending a Christian evangelistic meeting asked hymnist Alfred H. Ackley (1887–1960), "Why should I worship a dead Jew?" Ackley responded, "He lives! I tell you, He is not dead, but lives here and now! Jesus Christ is more alive today than ever before. I can prove it by my own experience, as well as the testimony of countless thousands."

This conversation later inspired Ackley to write the gospel Easter hymn "He Lives!" The famous chorus allows its singers to affirm that Jesus lives within us and that he remains with us through all of life's wonders and difficulties.

As one of a thousand songs that Ackley wrote, the hymn captures the sense of Paul's assertion in this passage from the Letter to the Galatians. But before we get too wrapped up in our individual involvements with Jesus, we should remember that Paul always includes a communal dimension to the indwelling of Christ and his Spirit. This is evident in Galatians 3:1-5 where Paul is upbraiding his audience for ignoring the source of the Spirit. All those pointed "yous" are plural, though the English cannot properly convey this. Christ not only lives in me as I claim the gospel message; Christ also lives in us as we together hold fast to our faith.

SHARING THE SCRIPTURE

PREPARING TO TEACH

Preparing Our Hearts

This week's devotional reading is found in Galatians 3:6-14. These verses immediately follow today's scripture lesson. Paul uses Abraham, who lived long before the law was given, as an example of "those who believe" (3:9). Abraham's faith, Paul argues, not his works, is what made him righteous before God. So, too, those who have faith in God are both descendants of Abraham and justified by their faith. What does it mean to you to say that you are made right with God (justified) on the basis of your faith? How does the way you live demonstrate what you believe?

Pray that you and your students will affirm your faith in God and live righteously as Abraham did.

Preparing Our Minds

Study the background and lesson scripture, Galatians 2:15–3:5. Paul insists that both Jews and Gentiles are saved by faith in Jesus Christ, not by the law. Read Galatians 2:1-14 to see ways this teaching has implications for how people live together. In verses 11-14 Paul upbraids Peter for his hypocritical attitudes toward table-fellowship with Gentiles.

Write on newsprint:

　　quotations on "justification," found under "Consider What 'Justification by Faith' Means in Learners' Lives."

　　information for next week's lesson, found under "Continue the Journey."

Plan any lectures that you choose to use.

LEADING THE CLASS

(1) Gather to Learn

❖ Welcome the class members and introduce any guests.

❖ Pray that those who gather today will recognize that Christians live by faith in Jesus Christ, the Crucified One.

❖ Read the following words that pastors in The United Methodist Church speak to their congregations as an introduction to the Sacrament of Baptism. (Or, read similar words from your own faith tradition.) **Brothers and sisters in Christ: Through the Sacrament of Baptism we are initiated into Christ's holy church. We are incorporated into God's mighty acts of salvation and given new birth through water and the Spirit. All this is God's gift, offered to us without price.**

❖ Discuss these questions:
(1) **What does this introduction say to you about God?**
(2) **What does this introduction suggest to you about how one is saved or justified?**

❖ Read aloud today's focus statement: **People tend to treasure acts of grace that are extended to them by others. Where do we encounter such acts of grace in the church? Paul says that God has already given us the greatest grace possible through the gift of Christ.**

(2) Delve into Paul's Understanding of Justification by Faith

❖ Choose a volunteer to read Galatians 2:15-21.

❖ Ask the adults to work in small groups to discern what Paul is trying to say here.

■ Distribute paper and pencil to each group. Encourage a recorder to write one or two sentences that summarize in the group's own words Paul's message to the Galatians in these verses.

■ Invite a spokesperson for each group to read aloud the group's understanding of Paul's teachings.

- Wrap up this activity by reading in unison today's key verse, Galatians 2:20.
- ❖ Select someone to read Galatians 3:1-5.
- Give a brief lecture on the meaning of Galatians 3:1-5. Use information in Understanding the Scripture for these verses.
- Invite the students to brainstorm what Paul's message to today's church might be. In what ways have we been "bewitched"? Write their ideas on newsprint.
- Consider how the contemporary church could reverse its "bewitched" state. What would have to happen? List ideas on newsprint.

(3) Consider What "Justification by Faith" Means in Learners' Lives

❖ Read aloud or post on newsprint the following quotations on justification. Invite the students to comment on which one(s) best capture their belief about justification. If time permits, encourage them to talk about how Paul would respond to each of these ideas.

- "The courage to be is the courage to accept oneself as accepted in spite of being unacceptable . . . this is the genuine meaning of the Paulinian-Lutheran doctrine of justification by faith" (Paul Tillich, 1886–1965, *The Courage to Be*).
- "The whole doctrine of justification by faith hinges, for me, on my painfully reluctant realisation that my Father is not going to be more pleased with me when I am good than when I am bad. He accepts me and delights in me as I am. It is ridiculous of him, but that is how it is between us" (Anglican Bishop John V. Taylor, *The Go-Between God*).
- "God does not justify us because we are worthy, but by justifying us makes us worthy" (Thomas Watson, circa 1557–1592).

- "Justification means 'just-as-if-I-never-sinned' " (Anonymous).
- "The doctrine of justification is the foundation that supports all of the other benefits we receive from Christ" (Erwin W. Lutzer, 1941–).

❖ Distribute paper and pencils. Encourage each adult to write what "justification by faith" means in his or her own life. This is to be a personal definition, not something meant for a textbook. Some volunteers may be willing to share their thoughts with the class.

(4) Affirm Faith in Christ

❖ Invite the students to affirm their faith in Christ in at least one of these ways.
- **Activity 1:** Look at the "Apostles' Creed" and/or "The Nicene Creed." (You will find these historic creeds in many hymnals.) Talk about what the creed(s) mean to the students, especially in regard to faith in Christ. Recite one of these creeds together with heartfelt expression.
- **Activity 2:** Encourage the students to call out ideas that can be used to develop their own creed or litany of faith. Suggest that they incorporate some of the ideas they wrote on "justification by faith" in an earlier activity. Write their ideas on newsprint. When the litany or creed is complete, read it together.
- **Activity 3:** Provide quiet time for the students to meditate on this idea, which you will need to read aloud: **I affirm that my life is centered in Christ who was crucified, and who now lives in me. What examples can I give to show that my faith in my Lord and Savior Christ is evident in my life?**

(5) Continue the Journey

❖ Pray that the students will live by faith in Christ Jesus the Lord, who willingly gave himself so that those who believe in him might be put right with God.

❖ Read aloud this preparation for next week's lesson. You may also want to post it on newsprint for the students to copy. **Prepare for next week's session entitled "From Slave to Heir" by reading Galatians 3:19–4:7. Study especially Galatians 3:19-29 and 4:4-7. Keep this focus in mind as you read: In general, societies have laws to ensure that everyone is treated well. The Bible affirms that God's law was given to help people know how to live according to God's will. What hope do we have when we are unable to follow God's law as we should? Paul says God has released us from life under the law by sending Christ to make us true children of God.**

❖ Read aloud the following three ideas. Challenge the students to commit themselves to use these activities as a springboard to spiritual growth.

(1) **Think about the rules of a favorite game of yours. What happens if you ignore any of these rules? Do you understand the Christian life to be like this game, complete with rules that must be obeyed? Ponder how your understanding of the Christian life is different from and similar to Paul's understanding.**

(2) **Draw a picture or create a list of phrases that shows how Christ lives in you. How does your faithfulness shine through so that others may see Christ in you?**

(3) **Contemplate what it means to love unconditionally. Does Jesus' unconditional love for us mean that we no longer need to have self-discipline or standards of conduct? What would Paul say in response to your thoughts?**

❖ Sing or read aloud "My Faith Looks Up to Thee."

❖ Say one phrase of this prayer at a time and ask the class to repeat it so that they will quickly learn it: **Grant, O Lord, that we may go forth to serve you as faithful disciples who not only hear the word but also do it in the name of Jesus. Amen.**

FROM SLAVE TO HEIR

PREVIEWING THE LESSON

Lesson Scripture: Galatians 3:19-29; 4:4-7
Background Scripture: Galatians 3:19–4:7
Key Verses: Galatians 4:4-6

Focus of the Lesson:
In general, societies have laws to ensure that everyone is treated well. The Bible affirms that God's law was given to help people know how to live according to God's will. What hope do we have when we are unable to follow God's law as we should? Paul says God has released us from life under the law by sending Christ to make us true children of God.

Goals for the Learners:
(1) to explore Paul's teachings about the purpose of the law.
(2) to express feelings about being a child of God.
(3) to celebrate their freedom as members of God's inclusive family.

Pronunciation Guide:
Abba   (ah' buh *or* ab' uh)

Supplies:
Bibles, newsprint and marker, paper and pencils, hymnals

READING THE SCRIPTURE

NRSV
Galatians 3:19-29

19 Why then the law? It was added because of transgressions, until the offspring would come to whom the promise had been made; and it was ordained through angels by a mediator. 20 Now a mediator involves more than one party; but God is one.

21 Is the law then opposed to the promises of God? Certainly not! For if a law had been

NIV
Galatians 3:19-29

[19]What, then, was the purpose of the law? It was added because of transgressions until the Seed to whom the promise referred had come. The law was put into effect through angels by a mediator. [20]A mediator, however, does not represent just one party; but God is one.

[21]Is the law, therefore, opposed to the

given that could make alive, then righteousness would indeed come through the law. 22 But the scripture has imprisoned all things under the power of sin, so that what was promised through faith in Jesus Christ might be given to those who believe.

23 Now before faith came, we were imprisoned and guarded under the law until faith would be revealed. 24 Therefore the law was our disciplinarian until Christ came, so that we might be justified by faith. 25 But now that faith has come, we are no longer subject to a disciplinarian, 26 for in Christ Jesus you are all children of God through faith. 27 As many of you as were baptized into Christ have clothed yourselves with Christ. 28 There is no longer Jew or Greek, there is no longer slave or free, there is no longer male and female; for all of you are one in Christ Jesus. 29 And if you belong to Christ, then you are Abraham's offspring, heirs according to the promise.

Galatians 4:4-7

4 But when the fullness of time had come, God sent his Son, born of a woman, born under the law, 5 in order to redeem those who were under the law, so that we might receive adoption as children. 6 And because you are children, God has sent the Spirit of his Son into our hearts, crying, "Abba! Father!" 7 So you are no longer a slave but a child, and if a child then also an heir, through God.

promises of God? Absolutely not! For if a law had been given that could impart life, then righteousness would certainly have come by the law. [22]But the Scripture declares that the whole world is a prisoner of sin, so that what was promised, being given through faith in Jesus Christ, might be given to those who believe.

[23]Before this faith came, we were held prisoners by the law, locked up until faith should be revealed. [24]So the law was put in charge to lead us to Christ that we might be justified by faith. [25]Now that faith has come, we are no longer under the supervision of the law.

[26]You are all sons of God through faith in Christ Jesus, [27]for all of you who were baptized into Christ have clothed yourselves with Christ. [28]There is neither Jew nor Greek, slave nor free, male nor female, for you are all one in Christ Jesus. [29]If you belong to Christ, then you are Abraham's seed, and heirs according to the promise.

Galatians 4:4-7

[4]But when the time had fully come, God sent his Son, born of a woman, born under law, [5]to redeem those under law, that we might receive the full rights of sons. [6]Because you are sons, God sent the Spirit of his Son into our hearts, the Spirit who calls out, "Abba, Father." [7]So you are no longer a slave, but a son; and since you are a son, God has made you also an heir.

UNDERSTANDING THE SCRIPTURE

Galatians 3:19-25. In this passage Paul is wrestling with an issue that is troubling both him and the Galatian community: the place of the law in God's plan of salvation for humankind. As an observant Jew before Christ was revealed to him, Paul had treasured the law as God's most holy and complete revelation. Now he faced the Missionaries who were preaching almost the same belief he had before he met Christ.

(We can assume they were not preaching exactly the same thing because they were also Christian.) At the same time, he cannot believe that the law was some sort of mistake on God's part. But if Christ is the fullest revelation of the love of God and the means through which we are made right with God, what is the place of the law in God's view and in human life?

In 3:19 Paul asks: "Why then the law?"

Three possibilities suggest themselves to him. First, Paul says, "it was added because of transgressions." This obscure phrase probably means the law both identifies sin and restrains human sinfulness, checking its power. The law functioned in these ways until the "offspring" (NRSV) or "Seed" (NIV), both translations referring to Jesus, comes to fulfill God's promises.

In Galatians 3:19b-20, Paul claims that the law was given through angels. He may be remembering Deuteronomy 33:2, which claimed that angels were present at the giving of the law at Sinai. The mediator mentioned at the end of 3:19 is, of course, Moses. Paul seems to be arguing that the law is a product of a committee that mediated between God and humanity and therefore represents a less direct revelation. This somehow diminishes its importance, especially when compared to God's revelation in Christ. Yet, lest his readers get the wrong impression, Paul quickly affirms in 3:21 that the law is very much a part of God's promises.

The second function of the law that Paul offers is found in 3:22-23. Here Paul introduces a different metaphor for the law, the law as prison warden: "But the scripture has imprisoned all things under the power of sin" (3:22; notice that he uses "scripture" as a synonym for law). The law is in charge as a divine agent, even of sin, and it makes clear that humans are in bondage to sin. It remains in a position of authority, allowing the power of sin to hold all things captive, until "faith would be revealed" (3:23) in Jesus Christ. Only then would the promises of God be fulfilled and the authority of the law cease.

At 3:24 Paul brings in yet another metaphor to illustrate a third function of the law in God's plan. The law is a "disciplinarian" (NRSV; the NIV does not directly translate this rich Greek image). This word actually refers to a slave in a Greco-Roman family who guided, educated, and protected the children until they reached maturity.

The implication is that people were children while they were under the authority of the law. Faith brings them into maturity; then they no longer need the law. The arrival of Jesus Christ brings the law's guardianship to a close (3:25).

Galatians 3:26-29. In Greek the word translated "for" in the NRSV signals the underlying explanation for the end of the law's primary authority. In Christ believers are now children of God. They are no longer slaves to sin or its overlord, the law, but have been made children of God, brothers and sisters of Christ. This same idea is present in Romans 8:14-17 (see "Power for Living," lesson 5).

What is different in this Galatians text is the surprising reference to baptism at this point. As if he is thinking about how faith brings believers into the family of God, Paul suddenly introduces the entryway into that family, namely baptism. Moreover, he introduces a new explanatory image: baptism into Christ is like wearing Christ. In the *Galatians* volume of the Abingdon New Testament Commentaries series, Sam K. Williams says that this figure of speech, drawn from the Old Testament, carries a sense of being characterized "by the named quality or attribute"(see, for example, Psalm 93:1). Thus, if all believers have put on Christ, they are now wearing the same thing. Distinctions like ethnicity, legal status, and gender no longer matter in the baptized community. For all are wearing Christ, belong to Christ, and are true heirs to the promises of God.

Galatians 4:1-7. Paul returns in 4:1 to the point he has been trying to make throughout this passage. Because they have been minor children, the heirs of the promises of God, namely the Jews, were the same as slaves in Paul's view of God's plan for redemption. They had to remain under the guardianship of something else, in this case, the law, until God's appointed day arrived. The same is true for the Gentiles to whom Paul refers to as "us" in 4:3. Although the law did not enslave them, they remained in bondage to the "elemental spirits." What Paul means by this phrase is difficult for us to determine. Perhaps it is a reference to traditions and principles of moral behavior found in Hellenistic culture (see Colossians 2:8, 20 in which the same phrase appears). But when God was ready, God sent the Son, human ("born of a woman") and Jewish ("born under the law") so that those already guarded by the law might now come into their full inheritance (4:4-5). Through the redemption of the "natural" children of God, namely the Jews, Gentiles are adopted as children into God's family.

Since all believers, whether they were originally Jew or Gentile, are now God's children, God sends them the gift of the Spirit, a gift that enables them to cry out to God as the Father. Paul seems to echo Jesus' own prayer to God in his use of the Aramaic word for father, "Abba." The Spirit is also confirmation that those who have faith in Christ are no longer slaves, possessed by evil or guarded by the law, but children and thus heirs of God's gift of salvation.

INTERPRETING THE SCRIPTURE

Following the Law/Following Christ

Since the days of Paul, Christians have struggled with the place of the Jewish law in the Christian life. On the one hand, we have done our best to teach and to adhere to certain sections of that law. The Ten Commandments are a natural favorite for following and teaching to our children. So are portions that Jesus himself held dear, especially the commandments to love God and love neighbor. On the other hand, we have rejected or put aside other parts of the law, with the help of early Jewish Christians like Paul. We do not practice the dietary regulations (Leviticus 11); we do not put to death persons caught in the act of adultery (Leviticus 20:10); we do not sacrifice animals on an altar before the Lord (Leviticus 4–7). (We should note that modern Jews do not practice the last two examples; many do not practice the first.)

It is easy to see why we would reject these parts of the law, but there are parts we do not follow and probably should. The practice of the Year of Jubilee comes to my mind (Leviticus 25). And a very well-known commandment that most of us simply ignore to our detriment is that of honoring the Sabbath by resting and worshiping God.

How do we decide which laws to obey and which to ignore? Jesus gives us one clue, which I mentioned above: the two central commandments upon which all else hangs are to love God and to love neighbor. Paul in this letter to the Galatians offers other clues. Commandments that separate us into higher and lower classes, which keep us apart, are to be avoided.

Most important, Paul argues that whenever we claim that following a particular law somehow leads to our righteousness in the eyes of God we have completely misunderstood faith in Christ and the function of the law. When we claim that someone must do thus and so to achieve salvation, we have missed the whole point of Jesus' death and faith in that death. So we follow aspects of the law not to gain righteousness but in response to the love of God that we meet in Jesus. The law is a wonderful resource for understanding and keeping the ethics and morals of God's reign. Paul has no problem with these practices. What we cannot do is establish them as an entrance to that reign. Faith alone provides that doorway.

The Lines of Baptism

Through the centuries baptismal practices have served as a primary means for making distinctions between Christians and determining who is closer to heaven. It strikes me as quite ironic that this very thing that Paul says makes us the same in the eyes of God has become the way we measure our differences. Some groups practice infant baptism; others baptize adult believers. Some pour water on the one being baptized; others sprinkle from a baptismal font; still others immerse in a tub-like baptistery or a natural body of water such as a river or lake. Some insist that the water must be flowing; others claim that it must be sanctified and blessed by one set apart for such duties. All of these differences have been used to make the claim that "our church" is more scriptural, or more faithful to Christian tradition, or more relevant to the lives of its congregants.

In my own tradition, the Christian Church (Disciples of Christ) we practice immersion of "believers," a practice I believed to be the most valid until my husband and I served the larger Body of Christ in Taiwan. There, my husband and I were part of the leadership team of a small English-speaking congregation. All kinds of Christians from around the world gathered every Sunday afternoon. In that context we were once asked by some friends from Canada to baptize their newborn son in accordance with their tradition, the United Church of Canada. If we accepted their request, it would be the first time either of us had baptized an infant. We were reluctant to go against the practice of our own church. One evening in a phone call home, I told my father about our dilemma. He reminded me that in such a circumstance we did not represent just our denomination; we represented the whole Body of Christ. As such it was not only permissible but also obligatory to perform the baptism in a way that many Christians throughout the world have practiced for centuries.

The following Sunday our friends brought the child to the front of the little church. There they made the baptismal vows for him until he was old enough to confirm them. And there Don and I baptized him by sprinkling water across his forehead in the name of the Father, and the Son, and the Holy Ghost. The distinctions that Paul feared disappeared. We were one again as we put on the clothes of Christ at baptism.

The Current Equivalents

We may be tempted to view Paul's concern about the way the Missionaries were preaching the practice of the law as irrelevant to modern Christian living. After all, we know very few, if any, Christians who would argue that circumcision is necessary to be justified before God! Yet in our church board meetings, Sunday school classes, and everyday unreflective conversations we may also be preaching the need to observe some law or another in order to be saved. I do not think that we necessarily draw them from the body of Jewish law that we find in the Torah. We have other equivalents in our practice of the faith. The above example concerning baptism is but one.

I once had a conversation with a parishioner concerning tithing. A friend had told him that Christians must tithe (give 10 percent) to the church—that is the law. My parishioner, however, had other thoughts. He gave a portion of his income to several causes, including the church and the support of his disabled younger sister. He believed that because the total percentage of his gifts equaled about 10 percent of his gross income that he was meeting the requirement for tithing. What did I think, he asked.

As a minister of a congregation always in need of money I was inclined to agree with the friend! Nonetheless, after stalling to get my thoughts together, I said that I did not believe God *required* us either to tithe or to give 10 percent of our income to persons less fortunate. God's grace was free—we don't pay for it in any way. At the same time, the use of our money should reflect the faith of our lives. If it doesn't, something is wrong—not so much with our salvation, which is in God's hands, but with our acceptance of that salvation. Maybe in our heart of hearts we do not really believe that what Christ has done for us is more wonderful than the new car out on the driveway. And if we can't believe that, then we can't respond appropriately with our money, our time, and our energy.

Paul urges us to receive God's love as the grace-filled gift that it is. There are no strings attached, except to accept it with faith. Once we have begun the process of believing, then we can respond. Yet even the ability to respond is a gift—a gift of the Spirit that leads us ever deeper into trust and dependence upon God and releases from the tyranny of selfishness and greed.

SHARING THE SCRIPTURE

PREPARING TO TEACH

Preparing Our Hearts

This week's devotional reading is found in Romans 3:27-31. Here Paul emphatically tells us that only by faith in Jesus Christ can we be put right with God. Paul sums up the gospel message in verse 28: "For we hold that a person is justified by faith apart from works prescribed by the law." Yet, the apostle does not teach that we are to dispense with the law; rather, we are to uphold it. What, then, is he saying about the purpose of the law? What is its relationship to faith? Ponder what Paul is saying. Compare what he writes to whatever you believe about the law and faith.

Pray that you and your students will recognize that the law is not the basis for our salvation. Instead, we are to trust God's gift of grace.

Preparing Our Minds

Study the background from Galatians 3:19–4:7 and lesson scripture, Galatians 3:19-29 and 4:4-7. Here Paul writes at length about the purpose of the law.

Write on newsprint:

words suggested at the end of "Celebrate Freedom as Members of God's Family."

information for next week's lesson, found under "Continue the Journey."

Plan a lecture, as suggested under "Explore Paul's Teachings About the Purpose of the Law," to help class members understand the purpose of the law. You may also want to prepare a lecture to impart information related to Galatians 4:4-7.

LEADING THE CLASS

(1) Gather to Learn

❖ Welcome the class members and introduce any guests.

❖ Pray that today's learners will recognize that they are no longer slaves but God's own heirs, thanks to God's gracious gift of salvation through Jesus Christ.

❖ Encourage the students to cite civil laws that focus on creating a more just society where everyone is treated equally. List these ideas on newsprint. As the class reviews what they have suggested, invite them to note groups who may not be protected by the laws they have named. Are there additional laws that protect them, or are some people excluded from protection?

❖ Read aloud today's focus statement: **In general, societies have laws to ensure that everyone is treated well. The Bible affirms that God's law was given to help** people know how to live according to God's will. What hope do we have when we are unable to follow God's law as we should? Paul says God has released us from life under the law by sending Christ to make us true children of God.

(2) Explore Paul's Teachings About the Purpose of the Law

❖ Choose someone to read Galatians 3:19-29 as if reading to the church at Galatia.

- Use information from Understanding the Scripture to prepare a lecture that will help students identify and understand the three purposes of the law Paul suggests here: "it was added because of transgressions"; it serves as a prison warden since humans are in bondage to sin; it operates as a disciplinarian ("babysitter") until a child reaches maturity and no longer needs to be watched.

❖ Discuss these questions in regard to verses 27-31.

(1) Why might Paul introduce the idea of baptism here?

(2) Why is being clothed in Christ a suitable image in light of verse 28?

(3) Do you honestly believe that all people see themselves as equals in Christ, or do some feel "more equal than others"? Explain your answer.

❖ Ask the class to read in unison Galatians 4:4-7. Note that 4:4-6 are today's key verses.

- Discuss these questions, or prepare a lecture to answer them yourself.

(1) What kind of treatment would you expect if you were God's slave?

(2) What kind of treatment would you expect if you were God's son or daughter?

(3) What is the good news that you hear in these Bible verses?

(3) Express Feelings About Being a Child of God

❖ Invite the students to think silently about these ideas. Jesus called God "Abba," a term of endearment often translated as "Daddy." What associations come to your mind when you think of God as "Daddy"? If you cannot make this connection, what barriers prevent you from doing so? Is there any way you can overcome these barriers?

❖ Break the silence by distributing paper and pencils.

- Ask the students to sketch themselves in relation to God. State at the outset that artistic ability is unimportant and that this picture will not be shared.

- Suggest that the students look at their picture and explore the image that they have drawn. Do they just see the eye of God upon them? Are they holding God's hand? Are they groveling at God's feet? What size do they see themselves in relationship to God? Ask them to answer these questions silently: What clues do your drawings give as to how you relate to God? Are you seeing yourself as a child of God or as a slave or in some other relationship? What changes, if any, do you need to make in how you envision yourself with God?

(4) Celebrate Freedom as Members of God's Family

❖ Invite the participants to gather in a circle and hold hands if possible. Take the lead by turning to the person on your left and saying "_____(name), you are a beloved child of God." Continue clockwise around the circle until all persons have been told that they are members of God's family. If the class is large, make several circles. If persons do not know each other, omit the name.

❖ End this time by asking the class to say these words, which you may want to post on newsprint prior to class: **We give thanks that we are no longer slaves but heirs of God through Jesus Christ and affirm our love for one another as brothers and sisters.**

(5) Continue the Journey

❖ Pray that the participants will accept and give thanks for their place in God's family as adopted sons and daughters.

❖ Read aloud this preparation for next week's lesson. You may also want to post it on newsprint for the students to copy. **Prepare for next week's session entitled "Free to Serve" by reading Galatians 5:1-15, which is both our background and scripture lesson. Keep in mind this focus as you prepare for next week's session: People have mixed ideas about what real freedom is and how it relates to love. What is the nature of Christian freedom and how does it relate to love? Paul says that our freedom lies not in self-indulgence but in expressing love to others, especially other Christians.**

❖ Read aloud the following three ideas. Challenge the students to commit themselves to use these activities as a springboard to spiritual growth.

(1) **Explore how you believe law, sin, and grace relate not only to our codes of morality and ethics but also to our relationship with God. What does your experience suggest?**

(2) **Talk with members of your Sunday school class and congregation about the implications that calling yourselves "children of God" has for your life together as a community of faith. What changes could occur if people really believed that they were all God's children?**

(3) **Identify ways that you can be an advocate for groups of people who do not have full civil rights. Select one or two groups that you feel you could help by sending letters to elected officials, convincing the congregation to work for justice on behalf of these persons, or taking other appropriate action.**

❖ Sing or read aloud "I Want to Walk as a Child of the Light."

❖ Say one phrase of this prayer at a time and ask the class to repeat it so that they will quickly learn it: **Grant, O Lord, that we may go forth to serve you as faithful disciples who not only hear the word but also do it in the name of Jesus. Amen.**

FREE TO SERVE

PREVIEWING THE LESSON

Lesson Scripture: Galatians 5:1-15
Background Scripture: Galatians 5:1-15
Key Verse: Galatians 5:13

Focus of the Lesson:
People have mixed ideas about what real freedom is and how it relates to love. What is the nature of Christian freedom and how does it relate to love? Paul says that our freedom lies not in self-indulgence but in expressing love to others, especially other Christians.

Goals for the Learners:
(1) to examine Paul's ideas about Christian liberty.
(2) to identify ways Christian love guides their personal ethics.
(3) to act on their Christian freedom by lovingly serving others.

Pronunciation Guide:
eschatology   (es kuh tol' uh jee)   eschatological   (es kat uh loj' i kuhl)

Supplies:
Bibles, newsprint and markers, paper and pencils, hymnals

READING THE SCRIPTURE

NRSV
Galatians 5:1-15

For freedom Christ has set us free. Stand firm, therefore, and do not submit again to a yoke of slavery.

2 Listen! I, Paul, am telling you that if you let yourselves be circumcised, Christ will be of no benefit to you. 3 Once again I testify to every man who lets himself be circumcised that he is obliged to obey the entire law. 4 You who want to be justified by the law have cut yourselves off from Christ; you

NIV
Galatians 5:1-15

It is for freedom that Christ has set us free. Stand firm, then, and do not let yourselves be burdened again by a yoke of slavery.

²Mark my words! I, Paul, tell you that if you let yourselves be circumcised, Christ will be of no value to you at all. ³Again I declare to every man who lets himself be circumcised that he is obligated to obey the whole law. ⁴You who are trying to be justi-

have fallen away from grace. 5 For through the Spirit, by faith, we eagerly wait for the hope of righteousness. 6 For in Christ Jesus neither circumcision nor uncircumcision counts for anything; the only thing that counts is faith working through love.

7 You were running well; who prevented you from obeying the truth? 8 Such persuasion does not come from the one who calls you. 9 A little yeast leavens the whole batch of dough. 10 I am confident about you in the Lord that you will not think otherwise. But whoever it is that is confusing you will pay the penalty. 11 But my friends, why am I still being persecuted if I am still preaching circumcision? In that case the offense of the cross has been removed. 12 I wish those who unsettle you would castrate themselves!

13 For you were called to freedom, brothers and sisters; only do not use your freedom as an opportunity for self-indulgence, but through love become slaves to one another. 14 For the whole law is summed up in a single commandment, "You shall love your neighbor as yourself." 15 If, however, you bite and devour one another, take care that you are not consumed by one another.

fied by law have been alienated from Christ; you have fallen away from grace. [5]But by faith we eagerly await through the Spirit the righteousness for which we hope. [6]For in Christ Jesus neither circumcision nor uncircumcision has any value. The only thing that counts is faith expressing itself through love.

[7]You were running a good race. Who cut in on you and kept you from obeying the truth? [8]That kind of persuasion does not come from the one who calls you. [9]"A little yeast works through the whole batch of dough." [10]I am confident in the Lord that you will take no other view. The one who is throwing you into confusion will pay the penalty, whoever he may be. [11]Brothers, if I am still preaching circumcision, why am I still being persecuted? In that case the offense of the cross has been abolished. [12]As for those agitators, I wish they would go the whole way and emasculate themselves!

[13]**You, my brothers, were called to be free. But do not use your freedom to indulge the sinful nature; rather, serve one another in love.** [14]The entire law is summed up in a single command: "Love your neighbor as yourself." [15]If you keep on biting and devouring each other, watch out or you will be destroyed by each other.

UNDERSTANDING THE SCRIPTURE

Galatians 5:1-6. Paul, as we saw in the last lesson concerning Galatians 3:19–4:7, has claimed that believers are no longer slaves to the law but heirs of the promises of God. In the remainder of Galatians 4 he illustrates his point by drawing upon the story of Hagar and Sarah and interpreting it rather subversively. You, he says to the Gentile believers, are the metaphorical children of Hagar who are in danger of being oppressed by the metaphorical children of Sarah, those like the Missionaries who preach the practice of the entire law. Galatians 5:1 serves as the dramatic con-

clusion to this illustration as well as the theme statement of our passage today. In fact, the resounding statements, "For freedom Christ has set us free. Stand firm, therefore, and do not submit again to a yoke of slavery," contain the central message of the entire letter. Note that the emphasis lies upon Christ's action, Paul's customary starting point. He then urges these Christians not to accept the teachings of the Missionaries that would yoke them into slavery to the law and ultimately to sin.

"Listen," demands Paul in 5:2. "It is I myself," Paul seems to be saying, "who is telling you not to allow yourselves to be circumcised." He is placing himself right there in their midst by referring to himself so strongly here. His pressing tone continues throughout 5:3-6. If the Galatians are circumcised, then they place themselves under the whole law. In his view there is no picking or choosing about which individual commandments one would prefer to obey. If they accept the premise that circumcision is necessary, than the logical corollary is that the entire law is necessary and should be explicitly obeyed. In this way they step out of the realm of grace ("fallen away from grace," 5:4) and into the realm of law. Thus, whatever Christ has done would be of little consequence to them. They would have made their choice to be in bondage to slavery; the freedom that Christ offers through his death would be irrelevant to their quest for righteousness through the law.

In complete contrast to this attitude, Paul says in 5:5, that "we," that is he and his adherents, are still waiting in the Spirit and in hope for the righteousness of God to come to them. The process of making believers right with God that Christ has begun on the cross will be fulfilled in the future, God's future. In the meantime, he concludes, "in Christ Jesus neither circumcision nor uncircumcision counts for anything. The only thing that counts is faith working through love," Paul proclaims in 5:6.

This is the first time the word "love" in a noun form appears in the letter. Paul used it as a verb in 2:20 where he wrote, "And the life I now live in the flesh I live by faith in the Son of God, who loved me and gave himself for me." "Faith" and "love" appear in the same thought there as they do here in 5:6; clearly to Paul they are intertwined. The perfect portrait of love is found in the self-sacrifice of Jesus on the cross. The perfect model of faith is found in his willingness to die for the world. Jesus' example of faith in love is the standard for all Christians; nothing else, including the law, must interfere with the effort faithfully to live up to it.

Galatians 5:7-12. Again, as he has done so frequently in this letter, Paul addresses the Galatian community directly with the plural "You" that begins 5:7. "You *were* running well," he backhandedly commends them as he implies that they are not doing so any longer. His use of an athletic metaphor here is similar to his usage in other letters (see 1 Corinthians 9:24-27; Philippians 3:12-14; 2 Timothy 4:7). Then, rhetorically, he asks, "Who cut in on you?" (5:7 NIV)—a continuation of the image of a race in which one racer has cut off another. "Who prevented you from obeying the truth?" (5:7 NRSV). Paul clarifies the point of his metaphor with this question. Galatians 5:8 is a reminder that the Missionaries, who are preventing the Galatians from obeying the truth, are not from God. Their teachings do not come from "the one who calls you," namely God (see 1:6).

As he does so frequently, in 5:9 Paul suddenly changes metaphors, leaving the athletic image and moving to a proverb that draws upon baking imagery (see 1 Corinthians 5:6 in which Paul quotes the same proverb). The Missionaries are like a bit of yeast that changes the whole batch of bread. The job of the Galatians is to cast out this yeast. In a rhetorical flourish, Paul says in 5:10 that he is confident that they will agree with him and do just this. Further, the punishment will be placed upon the chief offenders, the Missionaries who are confusing these Christians with their unsound teaching.

The next two verses, 5:11-12, are difficult to understand. Were Paul's opponents claiming that Paul himself had recommended circumcision in other settings? If they were spreading such rumors, Paul wonders, then why were they persecuting him since he evidently agreed with them? If this were true then the offense has disappeared. We can detect his sarcasm in these remarks concerning "offense." The offense to the Missionaries, implies Paul, is the cross itself.

He concludes his remarks about this group with a harsh and crude wish, a play on the act of circumcision.

Galatians 5:13-15. In these verses Paul returns to the theme of freedom that permeates this letter: "For you were called to freedom, brothers and sisters." You were called to freedom from a law that would constrain you beneath its yoke and keep you from experiencing fully the benefits of Christ's love. However, this precious freedom carries responsibility: "Only do not use your freedom as an opportunity for self-indulgence, but through love become slaves to one another" (5:13).

Paul does not want to do away with ethical imperatives in the Christian life. Although he preaches freedom from the strictures of the Jewish law, he by no means preaches freedom from any sort of responsibility, especially toward one another. To underscore the point, he repeats in 5:14 Jesus' own teaching: "For the whole law is summed up in a single commandment, 'You shall love your neighbor as yourself.'" Love, not rules and laws that separate believers, forms the ties that bind that Christian community into one. Then Paul adds his own warning about quarreling in the community and how it leads to destruction.

INTERPRETING THE SCRIPTURE

Not Freedom From . . ., But Freedom For . . .

Today we often speak of freedom as the personal liberty to do whatever the individual wants to do if the activity does not harm anyone. The classic American point of reference is Thomas Jefferson's words in the Declaration of Independence: "We hold these truths to be self-evident, that all men are created equal, that they are endowed by their Creator with certain unalienable Rights, that among these are Life, Liberty and the pursuit of Happiness."

The modern interpretations of these words that place the emphasis upon the individual and his or her right to pursue pleasure and autonomy were unknown to Paul. He did not define freedom in quite that way. On the one hand, he would not have placed the individual in the center of the quest from freedom. For him, and indeed his whole culture, the individual was primarily a part of collectives that included the family, the community, and the society as a whole. On the other hand, freedom was not a warrant for lawlessness or licentiousness to his mind. Thus for cen-

turies biblical scholars have talked about Paul as advocating not so much a freedom from constraints of any kind but a freedom for loving God and loving neighbor.

Through faith in Christ we are of course set free from the necessity of following the law in order to become children of God. We are set free from the impossibly heavy burden of fulfilling requirements in order to obtain God's salvation. But the freedom we gain is not a license to live shamefully, rudely, or carelessly. For in fact we are now granted a license to live in peace with one another and to focus on caring for sisters and brothers.

"Love Is the Answer"

For Paul, love is the "more excellent way" or expression of the presence of the Spirit (1 Corinthians 12:31; Galatians 5:22). It is also the more difficult way of relating to one another and to God. So it is ironic that his opponents in Galatia were accusing him of making entrance into the community of faith too easy. They claimed that he was trying to please the people and so had taught them that it was unnecessary to be circumcised or observe the more difficult commandments in the law. But Paul knew that loving one another was the hardest thing of all and still the basic answer to all the problems within the community.

Love, in Paul's usage, does not simply denote an emotional state, although surely at times we can and do feel love. It has little to do with romance or any sort of sexual conduct, though our culture would have us believe that those things fully encompass the meaning of love. Love is not uncritical acceptance of all kinds of behaviors and expressions of individuality, though our teenagers would want us to believe that it is. For Paul, love is a realistic and sometimes grim determination to hold on to, even cherish in concrete acts, one another in our communities of faith, in our families, in the world. It is sometimes a monumental effort to care for people not always because of who they are, but many times in spite of who they are.

I find expressing this love extremely difficult and exhausting a good deal of the time. If you are honest perhaps you will admit the same is true for you. We all know of church meetings and gatherings at which the one thing we did not want to do is love, in sacrificial form, the person who is spouting ignorance or venom or an alternative plan to our own well-thought-out arrangements. We know people who have left our church or someone else's church precisely because they were not loved and were unable to see anyone else being loved in that community. They have told us that the church was the most unloving place on earth. Sometimes they have been correct.

Yet, Paul preaches, if we are to be faithful to Christ the very embodiment of love then we must love one another. We do that by relinquishing our need to control things in the church, by challenging one another to live more faithful lives, by forgiving and then forgiving again those who have sinned against us. In this way, love serves as the only antidote to our problems within the community. And it propels us to reach outward, to express the same care for those beyond our walls and boundaries.

A Future Yet to Come

In Galatians 5:5 Paul says that believers "eagerly wait for the hope of righteousness." He is reminding us that the process begun by faith and through which God makes us righteous has not yet been completed. That fulfillment will come in God's future. This verse illustrates the strong "eschatological" thrust of Paul's teaching. ("Eschatology" and its adjective form refer to beliefs about the end of time and history.)

For several reasons many of us would prefer not to study this dimension of Paul's thought. Some Christians have given eschatology a bad name—they have focused on the judgment of God that is coming very soon and all the terrible things that will happen to those who do not believe as they do. In doing this they have selected certain passages primarily out of Revelation, 1 Thessalonians, Daniel, and Ezekiel, put them together according to their own interpretive principles, and sold their interpretations as God's plan for our lifetime.

Others have thought about the dilemma of Christians at the end of the first century, some forty years after Paul died, namely this: Why hasn't Christ returned as he promised and do away with the evil of this world? We may have wondered that ourselves, and then put the question away as unanswerable. Still others have constricted the future coming of Christ into a personal meeting with him after we die.

Paul's concern that we not forget our future arises, I think, out of a deep awareness of the present state of affairs. The truth is that neither the Galatian Christians nor we live in a consummated reign of God. Evil remains all around us and occasionally crops up within us. Although we may have professed faith in Jesus, we still struggle to live good, faithful, loving lives. Since this is the case, our present situation cannot be God's final answer to our need for the Son to come and make things fully right.

God's project of building a covenantal community built on the faith of Christ and bound together by faith in Christ is not yet complete. So we wait—eagerly sometimes, other times complacently—for God to finish what God started. And while we wait, we hope, we believe, we serve, and we love.

SHARING THE SCRIPTURE

PREPARING TO TEACH

Preparing Our Hearts

This week's devotional reading is found in 1 Peter 2:11-17. Here Peter writes about how we are to live as God's servants. Peter, like Paul, affirms our freedom in Christ. Yet, that freedom does not give us license to do wrong. Instead, we are to honor and serve others. Whom have you served today? How did you do that? What role did your belief that you are God's servant play in your willingness to serve? Ponder these questions. Write in your spiritual journal three ways that you could serve others this week.

Pray that you and your students will be open to opportunities to serve others in love.

Preparing Our Minds

Study the background and lesson scripture, both of which are found in Galatians 5:1-15.

Write on newsprint:

sentence stems in the section "Identify Ways Christian Love Guides the Learners' Personal Ethics."

information for next week's lesson, found under "Continue the Journey."

Plan a lecture from Understanding the Scripture for the section entitled "Examine Paul's Ideas About Christian Liberty."

LEADING THE CLASS

(1) Gather to Learn

❖ Welcome the class members and introduce any guests.

❖ Pray that those who have come together this morning to study and fellowship will be aware that they are free in Christ to lovingly serve others.

❖ Post a sheet of newsprint on which you have written the words "Freedom is. . . ." Have several markers available. As the learners enter the room, invite them to complete the sentence. If the class is so large that this is not feasible, do this activity as a brainstorming session when everyone has gathered.

❖ Review what has been written. Discuss whether these ideas are all similar, or whether some contradict others. Leave the paper posted for future reference.

❖ Read aloud today's focus statement: **People have mixed ideas about what real freedom is and how it relates to love. What is the nature of Christian freedom and how does it relate to love? Paul says that our freedom lies not in self-indulgence but in expressing love to others, especially other Christians.**

(2) Examine Paul's Ideas About Christian Liberty

❖ Ask four volunteers to read Galatians 5:1, 2-6, 7-12, and 13-15.

❖ Use information from Understanding

the Scripture to create a lecture that will help the students understand what Paul believes about the nature of Christian freedom.

❖ Note that today the issue of circumcision that was so important to Paul plays no role in Christian churches. Instead, we have different issues that can divide us. Name some of these issues and list them on newsprint. Then look at each issue individually and answer these questions, either working with the entire class or in small groups.

(1) How does this issue divide us?

(2) Is there any middle ground that we can stand on and still be true to our beliefs?

(3) How can we "love [our] neighbor as [ourselves]" even if we cannot find common ground on this issue?

❖ Look again at the newsprint where you have definitions of freedom written. Invite the class to make additions, modifications, or deletions, based on what they have learned from Paul.

(3) Identify Ways Christian Love Guides the Learners' Personal Ethics

❖ Point out that for Paul "faith working through love" (5:6) is essential because it is through this love that we sacrificially serve others through the power of the Holy Spirit. We follow Christ who sacrificially gave himself up for us on the cross.

❖ Distribute paper and pencils. Invite the students to write a response to each of the following ideas. You may read these aloud and wait for the students to respond or post them on newsprint so they can work at their own pace.

■ When I sense that a person needs someone to listen to his or her problems, I tend to. . . .

■ When I know that someone needs money, I often. . . .

■ When I hear that a group of persons is being treated unjustly, I respond by. . . .

■ When I go to a church meeting and people are acting rudely toward one another, I. . . .

■ When I meet another Christian whose beliefs and practices are different from mine, I. . . .

■ When I attend a Bible study and hear interpretations of scripture that don't square with mine, I. . . .

■ When I hear jokes, stories, or gossip that paints others in an unkind way, I. . . .

❖ Talk with the group about possible answers. Some students may be willing to volunteer their ideas. No one answer is correct for each item, but help the students recognize that Christ has set them free in order that they may be able to respond to others in love. Often that love requires sacrifice.

❖ Provide a few moments for silent reflection. Invite the students to consider any ways they need to change their responses in light of the class discussion.

(4) Act on Christian Freedom by Lovingly Serving Others

❖ Identify, or ask the students to identify, some outreach projects that your congregation supports. List these projects on newsprint.

❖ Encourage the class to zero in on one project that they could work together on to lovingly serve others. Brainstorm ways that this could happen, and write these ideas on newsprint. Push the class to go beyond simply collecting money for a missions project. Suggest that they consider how they could become personally involved. For example, would they be willing to help build a Habitat for Humanity house, or go to a mission site to work in Central America, or feed people at a soup kitchen in their community?

❖ Select one or two ideas and ask the students to pray about them over the next several weeks. Appoint volunteers to get further information about the selected projects. Choose a time to get together outside of class to plan what the group will do, to set a date, and to create a task force to handle the details. Perhaps persons who are unable to travel or do manual work could participate by gathering information and serving on the task force.

(5) Continue the Journey

❖ Pray that the students will take the freedom they have in Christ seriously as a means of lovingly serving others.

❖ Read aloud this preparation for next week's lesson. You may also want to post it on newsprint for the students to copy. **Prepare for next week's session entitled "Life Together" by reading Galatians 5:22–6:10. This passage serves as our background and lesson scripture. Think about this focus as you read: Most people long for respect and kindness, but not everyone is willing to extend such treatment to others. Is there some way we can develop the art of respect for others? Paul says that God's Spirit can fill us with the attitudes we should have.**

❖ Read aloud the following three ideas. Challenge the students to commit themselves to use these activities as a springboard to spiritual growth.

(1) **Commit yourself to serve voluntarily at least one person or group who could benefit from the skills and talents you have to offer.**

(2) **Recall a church meeting you have recently attended. Would you say that people acted with love toward one another and eagerly tried to serve one another? If not, what negative behaviors did you participate in and/or observe? Pray that God will change the atmosphere in future meetings so attendees will act in love as brothers and sisters.**

(3) **Identify a person, idea, or event that has caused confusion for you in regard to your belief as a Christian. Determine whether this person or idea is truly shaking your faith, or simply causing you to re-think some stance you thought you had already settled. Try to formulate some questions. If possible, arrange a time to meet with someone who is knowledgeable about whatever concerns you.**

❖ Sing or read aloud "Go Forth for God."

❖ Say one phrase of this prayer at a time and ask the class to repeat it so that they will quickly learn it: **Grant, O Lord, that we may go forth to serve you as faithful disciples who not only hear the word but also do it in the name of Jesus. Amen.**

LIFE TOGETHER

PREVIEWING THE LESSON

Lesson Scripture: Galatians 5:22–6:10
Background Scripture: Galatians 5:22–6:10
Key Verse: Galatians 6:2

Focus of the Lesson:
Most people long for respect and kindness, but not everyone is willing to extend such treatment to others. Is there some way we can develop the art of respect for others? Paul says that God's Spirit can fill us with the attitudes we should have.

Goals for the Learners:
(1) to study Paul's teachings about how Christians are to live together.
(2) to evaluate evidence of the Spirit in their lives.
(3) to commit themselves to live a Spirit-filled life.

Supplies:
Bibles, newsprint and marker, paper and pencils, hymnals, construction paper

---

READING THE SCRIPTURE

NRSV
Galatians 5:22-26

22 By contrast, the fruit of the Spirit is love, joy, peace, patience, kindness, generosity, faithfulness, 23 gentleness, and self-control. There is no law against such things. 24 And those who belong to Christ Jesus have crucified the flesh with its passions and desires. 25 If we live by the Spirit, let us also be guided by the Spirit. 26 Let us not become conceited, competing against one another, envying one another.

Galatians 6:1-10

My friends, if anyone is detected in a

NIV
Galatians 5:22-26

22But the fruit of the Spirit is love, joy, peace, patience, kindness, goodness, faithfulness, 23gentleness and self-control. Against such things there is no law. 24Those who belong to Christ Jesus have crucified the sinful nature with its passions and desires. 25Since we live by the Spirit, let us keep in step with the Spirit. 26Let us not become conceited, provoking and envying each other.

Galatians 6:1-10

Brothers, if someone is caught in a sin,

MAY 29

transgression, you who have received the Spirit should restore such a one in a spirit of gentleness. Take care that you yourselves are not tempted. **2 Bear one another's burdens, and in this way you will fulfill the law of Christ.** 3 For if those who are nothing think they are something, they deceive themselves. 4 All must test their own work; then that work, rather than their neighbor's work, will become a cause for pride. 5 For all must carry their own loads.

6 Those who are taught the word must share in all good things with their teacher.

7 Do not be deceived; God is not mocked, for you reap whatever you sow. 8 If you sow to your own flesh, you will reap corruption from the flesh; but if you sow to the Spirit, you will reap eternal life from the Spirit. 9 So let us not grow weary in doing what is right, for we will reap at harvest time, if we do not give up. 10 So then, whenever we have an opportunity, let us work for the good of all, and especially for those of the family of faith.

you who are spiritual should restore him gently. But watch yourself, or you also may be tempted. [2]**Carry each other's burdens, and in this way you will fulfill the law of Christ.** [3]If anyone thinks he is something when he is nothing, he deceives himself. [4]Each one should test his own actions. Then he can take pride in himself, without comparing himself to somebody else, [5]for each one should carry his own load.

[6]Anyone who receives instruction in the word must share all good things with his instructor.

[7]Do not be deceived: God cannot be mocked. A man reaps what he sows. [8]The one who sows to please his sinful nature, from that nature will reap destruction; the one who sows to please the Spirit, from the Spirit will reap eternal life. [9]Let us not become weary in doing good, for at the proper time we will reap a harvest if we do not give up. [10]Therefore, as we have opportunity, let us do good to all people, especially to those who belong to the family of believers.

UNDERSTANDING THE SCRIPTURE

Galatians 5:22-26. In order for members of the faithful community to avoid biting and devouring one another (5:15), they must learn to walk by the Spirit, the opponent of the flesh. As we saw in his Letter to the Romans, Paul understands the Spirit and the flesh to be competing spheres of influence. The believer must choose which sphere she will live in. If she gives into the flesh, she will perform the works that Paul lists in 5:19-21. These actions tear apart not only the individual but the community as well.

In contrast to the ruin to which living by the flesh leads is the fruit of the Spirit. If the works of the flesh include envy, anger, fornication, strife, and impurity, life in the

Spirit produces the opposites of these destructive forces: "[T]he fruit of the Spirit is love, joy, peace, patience, kindness, generosity, faithfulness, gentleness, and self-control" (5:22-23).

Although space does not permit discussing each of these in depth, we should take note of two features of the list. First, the "fruit" Paul lists are not character traits that can be produced consistently and over a long period of time through human will and exertion. They are products of the Spirit's work in a believer's life. In fact, many are attributes of God noted in other places in scripture. Even self-control, a virtue highly prized by people of that age and viewed as something an individual could cultivate for himself or herself, is seen here as a gift. Second, these qualities actually enhance the life of the community, in contrast to the works of the flesh that destroy it. They bring life and energy to a community; they enable it to focus on reaching out to others in mission.

The remainder of 5:23 is a puzzle. Paul is probably assuring the Galatian Christians that the law certainly does not forbid such fruit to those who choose to live in the Spirit. In 5:24 he continues to draw the contrast between flesh and Spirit by reminding his readers that the flesh has been crucified with Jesus. But the Spirit will supplant it as a guide for those who seek it; competition, envy, and boasting thus have no place in their dealings with one another (5:24-25).

Galatians 6:1-10. Paul ends the previous section with prohibitions, concrete reminders to the Galatians not to conduct themselves according to the flesh. In the first six verses of this new section he gives positive commandments for living according to the Spirit. He is listing things the members of the community should do to and for one another. Supporting these commands is the understanding that his readers are more than fellow believers; they are family. The correct translation for Paul's term of address is "brothers," which in other instances the NRSV translates as "brothers and sisters." Here the "friends" of the NRSV obscures the fundamental relationship of family that characterizes the faithful community.

Brothers and sisters in Christ will commit transgressions. It is unavoidable even for those in the Spirit. When they do, the family members should reprove the transgressors, gently and with humility, and then bring them back into the community. This restores not only the individuals who have done wrong but also the entire Body of Christ. Commentators differ about whether the phrase "you who have received the Spirit" in 6:1 refers to all believers or to a select group who are somehow more spiri-

tual than the others. Because Paul generally talks about the Spirit as something to which all believers have access, I think he is referring to the entire community. He concludes the first verse of this instruction with a warning to all not to be tempted.

The teaching in 6:2 follows the same sense as 6:1: to bear one another's burdens means to take on the weaknesses and transgressions of others in the community. When the sisters and brothers do this they fulfill the law of Christ. We might wonder what law Paul is talking about here. After all, aren't the law and Christ opposites in his view? Here he seems to be referring to the fulfillment of the law in 5:14. In that verse the Greek word translated "summed up" is the same word that is used here in 6:2 as "fulfill." To bear one another's burdens is to fulfill Jesus' command, repeated from Leviticus 19:18, to love your neighbor as yourself.

Paul continues in 6:3-5 with an admonition to these Christians to think of themselves realistically and humbly. No one should consider herself more important than she actually is. Each person should examine his own motivations and contributions to the community and not focus on those of his fellow believer. Only then will he have justified reason for pride in his own work. Although 6:5, the counsel that each person bears her own load, seems to contradict 6:2, the command to bear one another's burdens, in fact the two statements may balance each other. On the one hand, Christians must form communities in which all things are shared, even weakness and fault. On the other hand, each member of the community must use the gifts God has given for its edification.

Galatians 6:6 stands alone thematically in this passage. Paul is asking that teachers within the community should be financially remunerated for their work. It is important to remember that for Paul teaching is a gift among others given by the Spirit (see Romans 12:7; 1 Corinthians 12:4-11; 28).

Because the exercise of this gift takes long hours away from opportunities to earn money, he is urging them to support their teachers.

In the last paragraph of this section, comprised by 6:7-10, Paul concludes his words of advice to this community. He employs a familiar image of sowing and reaping. Not only does this image point to the present work of each believer; it is also a reminder of a future judgment made according to how each one performs the work given to him or her. The effect, in the words of Richard B. Hays in *The New Interpreter's Bible*, is to send this kind of message: "Remember, this is *God* you are dealing with here, not some image of your own construction. Don't think you can get away with anything, for God judges everything in the end." Paul's final sentence before closing the letter repeats themes that have run throughout Galatians 5:22–6:10: care for one another, respect one another, and work for the good of all.

INTERPRETING THE SCRIPTURE

The Art of Tending an Orchard

When Paul lists the fruit of the Spirit in Galatians 5:22-23, he is not talking about qualities that can be produced by our own efforts. This fruit is produced only when we live in and by the Spirit. That statement does not mean that there is nothing we can do to bear this fruit in our lives. It just means that we do not have to do everything.

So what can we do to bring love, joy, peace, and so on into our lives? The first clue is found in the last part of today's scripture in the words concerning sowing and reaping, drawn also from the imagery of tending crops. We can tend the orchard of our souls with care and persistence. We start by sowing seeds, doing the small things that will lead to something bigger. We can speak words of patience and kindness even when we are not feeling particularly compassionate or tolerant. We can utter short prayers for self-control in trying circumstances. We can turn away, even slightly, from the lures of the flesh (always remembering that we are talking here about envy, strife, anger, and so on).

We can be vigilant in guarding against the ugly worms and weeds that want to take over the orchard. Anger at those with whom we disagree grows quickly into resentment and grudge bearing. These will choke the life out of new shoots of generosity and faithfulness if we do not root them out when they first appear. Gluttony and drunkenness, such common vices in our culture that we shudder to label them as such, will eat at the buds of self-control that are trying to break out of the soil.

And then we wait. That's the point of acknowledging that this fruit comes from the Spirit. We simply wait in soulful quiet for the Spirit to do the larger part of this work. It may take a long time; it may come quickly. But it will only be done if we make room for God's breath by waiting and watching and planting the seeds.

"R-E-S-P-E-C-T"

I have been listening to Aretha Franklin sing her most famous song most of my life so that now I can hardly think the word "respect" without singing the letters in my head. But it is much harder to live out "r-e-s-p-e-c-t" than to spell it. It grows out of Jesus' simple dictum to do unto others as we would have them do unto us. It takes shape as we learn that we are just like the "others" that Jesus warns about. And it develops into a way of life as we follow the rules that Paul lays out in this passage.

Sometimes respect is difficult to recognize. I once served as the pastor of a small church in a large city, a congregation whose members had a long history of relationship patterns with one another. It took me a while to get used to the informal ways these people talked about and to one another. At first I thought many of them were terribly judgmental behind one another's backs and just plain rude to their faces.

The relationship of two prominent members seemed especially to reflect the adage that familiarity breeds contempt. If Doris was not in my office complaining about the recent antics of Clint, then he was there hashing old history. If Clint was telling me of Doris's high control needs one day, she was saying how Clint thought he owned the church the next.

Then one day Doris fell and broke her arm. The first person she asked to help her finish some things she was doing for the church was Clint. That's because he was the first person to get to the emergency room after hearing from the grapevine what had happened. By the time I arrived, Clint was helping her to his car so he could take her home and telling me to ask some of the women of the church to get food prepared for her for the next few days. As I watched the two of them grumble and fuss, I realized how much they cared for one another. Their previous words were just a casual blowing off of steam, an acknowledgment of their own faults in one another. Their words were not a true reflection of the profound regard they felt for each other. For their actions truly spoke louder than their words.

Being the God-people

One Saturday morning, after a week of battling a cold, I woke up without a voice. The cold had settled into my chest and I was unable to get out anything more than a squeak. When my husband, also a minister, saw that I would not be able to lead worship the next day, he graciously volunteered to preach a sermon from his barrel. The next day, at church, the kindergarten Sunday school teacher told her students that Pastor Nancy would not be preaching that day. One of the little boys in the class worried aloud: "If Pastor Nancy is sick, who is going to be the God-person?"

The answer, of course, is that all of us are called to be the God-people—the people who represent God and God's sacrificial love to one another and to the world. Although Paul does not use that phrase to characterize Christians, his point is the same. As Christians we are set apart through our faith in Christ, not so that we can follow a set of laws or principles, not so that we can hold ourselves above others, but so that we can take up the ministry of Christ to the world. We cannot do his work if we are governed by the flesh and not the Spirit. Nor can we do it if we are wasting time envying, or being angry at, or fighting with one another.

God's Project: Effective Christians

The theme of this quarter's study has been "God's Project: Effective Christians." In these Letters to the Romans and the Galatians, Paul has shown us how to join this project, how to continue to be a part of it, and how to make it our own. We join it through faith in the one who was faith personified, Jesus Christ, not through audition or lengthy application. Nor do we have to demonstrate competence or effectiveness or efficiency or ability before God takes us on.

We remain a part of God's project through the power of the Spirit. By turning away from selfishness and self-centeredness, what Paul calls the flesh, we can become vessels of that Spirit. We make God's project our project through love, a love that places the needs of the others before our own, a love that is perfected by constant practice and prayer.

So Paul cajoles and comforts us with

these words as he did those early Christians so many centuries ago. He dares to ask more of us than we think we can give, to promise more than we believe God will do. And always he holds before us his gospel— the good news—that through the death and resurrection of Jesus our relationship with God and one another is made whole and beautiful. And all we have to do is believe it.

SHARING THE SCRIPTURE

PREPARING TO TEACH

Preparing Our Hearts

This week's devotional reading is found in 1 John 3:14-23. Here John writes that we are to love one another because Jesus, who loved us enough to lay down his life for us, commands us to do so. John is not just speaking about a "warm fuzzy" kind of feeling; but rather, the kind of love that acts on behalf of another. Where does John's writing touch your life? What changes in attitude or behavior does this passage nudge you to make?

Pray that you and your students will love one another with the kind of active love that seeks the best for others and willingly makes sacrifices on their behalf.

Preparing Our Minds

Study the background and lesson scripture, Galatians 5:22–6:10.

Write on newsprint:

information for next week's lesson, found under "Continue the Journey."

Plan a lecture about the contrast between bearing burdens and carrying one's own burdens for the section "Study Paul's Teachings About How Christians Are to Live Together."

Cut out enough construction paper doves so that each student has one. Try to enlist help during the week to do this task.

LEADING THE CLASS

(1) Gather to Learn

❖ Welcome the class members and introduce any guests.

❖ Pray that the students will recognize and engage in the kind of life that Christ calls them to live together as a covenant people.

❖ Distribute paper and pencils. Challenge the students to sketch or write about the ideal Christian. Those who choose to sketch could draw an arrow to the mouth, for example, and write the words "speaks kindly of others." An arrow to the hands, for example, could have the words "willing to bear the burdens of others."

❖ Invite the participants to share their ideas and/or drawings with a small group and talk about why they think the attributes they have chosen to highlight are important in the life of a Christian. (We will talk more about these ideas in the next activity.)

❖ Read aloud today's focus statement: **Most people long for respect and kindness, but not everyone is willing to extend such treatment to others. Is there some way we can develop the art of respect for others? Paul says that God's Spirit can fill us with the attitudes we should have.**

(2) Study Paul's Teachings About How Christians Are to Live Together

❖ Read aloud Galatians 5:22-26 yourself.
■ Write the fruit of the Spirit (love, joy, peace, patience, kindness, generosity, faithfulness, gentleness, and self-control) on a sheet of newsprint. If you are artistic, draw them as if they are hanging on a tree.
■ Encourage the students to look again at the descriptions they drew or wrote

about earlier. Which of the fruit have they included, even if they described it differently? Which have the omitted?

- What else, if anything, would they add to Paul's list to describe the ideal Christian?

❖ Choose a volunteer to read Galatians 6:1-10.

- Talk about how the church (in general or your particular congregation) would be different if everyone abided by Paul's teachings.
- Encourage the class members to talk about how the class as a whole and as individuals "work for the good of all, and especially for those of the family of faith" (6:10).
- Discuss, or create a lecture from the Understanding the Scripture portion, the apparent contrast between 6:2 ("Bear one another's burdens") and 6:5 ("For all must carry their own loads").

❖ Sum up this portion of the session by asking individuals to identify what Paul is saying to them about living within the community of faith.

(3) Help Learners Evaluate Evidence of the Spirit in Their Lives

❖ Note that Paul writes in 6:8 that we will reap what we sow. Ask students to call out something that they might sow, such as "love" or "patience." Then ask others to call out what they might reap from that seed.

❖ Provide quiet time for individuals to reflect on what they have just heard. Ask them to consider what they are sowing and reaping. Then invite them to evaluate whether or not what they are sowing gives evidence of the Spirit's presence in their lives.

❖ Break the silence by offering a brief prayer that the adults will give thanks for the good that they have sown and be open to change when what they are reaping gives evidence that they have not sown in the Spirit.

(4) Commit to Living a Spirit-filled Life

❖ Remind the learners that in this session they have defined the ideal Christian, they have studied what Paul has to say about the good fruit that grows in the soil of a Spirit-filled life, and they have considered what they sow and reap in relation to a Spirit-filled life.

❖ Distribute to the learners pencils and construction paper cut in the shape of a dove. Ask them to write on this representation of the Holy Spirit something that they will commit themselves to do this week that will help them to live a more Spirit-filled life. What they write may relate to the fruit of the Spirit, such as "I commit myself to greater generosity of my time, talent, and treasure." Or, it might relate to a person or group with whom they have a covenant relationship, such as "I will not grow weary in helping my grandson who lives with me."

❖ Conclude this activity by asking the students to read together in a whisper the words they have written and then place the doves in their Bibles as a reminder of their commitment.

(5) Continue the Journey

❖ Pray that the participants will commit themselves to live a Spirit-filled life in which the fruit of the Spirit is evident daily.

❖ Read aloud this preparation for next week's lesson. You may also want to post it on newsprint for the students to copy. **Prepare for next week's session entitled "Preparing for Leadership" by reading Mark 1:4-13, which is our background and scripture lesson. Next week we begin our summer quarter, "Jesus' Life, Teachings, and Ministry," which is a study of Matthew, Mark, and Luke. Keep this focus statement in mind as you study next Sunday's lesson: People respond best to leaders who have appropriate credentials and qualifications to lead *and* who** demonstrate a genuine understanding of their followers. What credentials and qualifications *and* understanding does Jesus demonstrate for those who would minister in his name? Jesus' authority was declared—by human and divine voices—at the time of his baptism. In facing and responding to temptations, Jesus established his understanding of the human condition.

❖ Read aloud the following three ideas. Challenge the students to commit themselves to use these activities as a springboard to spiritual growth.

(1) **Ponder the covenants you are attempting to live out in your own life. These might include covenants with a spouse, children, parents, employers, and the church. As you live out these covenants, what evidence do you see that the fruit of the Spirit are ripening in your life?**

(2) **Make a list of persons or groups whose burdens you bear. Next to each one, write a phrase or two to describe how you feel about carrying this burden. As you review your list, how do you think Jesus would react to your descriptions?**

(3) **Commit some random act of kindness for a stranger this week, but do not tell others what you have done.**

❖ Sing or read aloud "O Church of God United."

❖ Say one phrase of this prayer at a time and ask the class to repeat it so that they will quickly learn it: **Grant, O Lord, that we may go forth to serve you as faithful disciples who not only hear the word but also do it in the name of Jesus. Amen.**

FOURTH QUARTER
Jesus' Life, Teachings, and Ministry

JUNE 5, 2005–AUGUST 28, 2005

During the thirteen weeks of the summer quarter we will explore Mark, Matthew, and Luke to discover "Jesus' Life, Teachings, and Ministry." We will look at Jesus' life as recorded in the book of Mark, his teachings as documented in Matthew, and his ministry of compassion as recounted in Luke. Each of these Gospels is written by a different author for a different audience. Collectively, these three books are known as the "Synoptic Gospels." "Synoptic" means "seeing together." Since these three books tell the same story in basically the same order and often in the same words, they are referred to as "Synoptic Gospels."

Unit 1, "Jesus' Life" (Gospel of Mark), begins on June 5 with a session concerning Jesus' baptism and temptations entitled "Preparing for Leadership," which is based on Mark 1:4-13. The lesson for June 12, "Healed to Wholeness," looks at the healing of a paralyzed man, as retold in Mark 2:1-12, that demonstrates the depth of Jesus' caring for others and his power to bring healing to situations that otherwise seem hopeless. We continue on June 19 with a lesson from Mark 14:53-65 and 15:1-5, "The Prevailing Good," which encourages us to be faithful to God despite the cost. "Hope in the Midst of Despair," the session for June 26, based on Mark 16, demonstrates God's power as we encounter Jesus' empty tomb.

Unit 2, "Jesus' Ministry of Teaching" (Gospel of Matthew), begins on July 3 with a session on the Beatitudes, "Experiencing True Happiness," from Matthew 5:1-16. On July 10 we explore Matthew 6:1-18, which helps us in "Practicing Genuine Piety." In "Learning to Listen," the session for July 17 from Matthew 13:1-23, we overhear Jesus telling his disciples why he spoke in parables. The parable of the unforgiving servant, the focus of "Free to Forgive" from Matthew 18:21-35 on July 24, teaches that we are to have a spirit of unconditional forgiveness toward others. Unit 2 ends on July 31 with a session entitled "Meeting Human Needs." This session, which explores Matthew 25:31-46, discerns that we are accountable to Jesus for aiding those persons in need.

The final unit, "Jesus' Ministry of Compassion" (Gospel of Luke), begins on August 7 with "What Is My Calling?" That session delves into Luke 4:14-30 to explore Jesus' calling to bring good news to those who are oppressed and marginalized. "Hope for Healing," the session for August 14, explores two stories of healing from Luke 8:40-56: Jairus's daughter and the woman with the issue of blood. On August 21 we will study the beloved parable of the good Samaritan, found in Luke 10:25-37, in the session entitled "Stretching Our Love." Luke 14:7-24 is the basis for "Building Community," a session that focuses on two parables concerning table fellowship that teach us about humility and hospitality. This session for August 28 concludes the summer quarter and this year's *New International Lesson Annual.*

MEET OUR WRITER

DR. ROSS WEST

Ross West lives in Rome, Georgia, where he offers publishing consulting services, writes, and leads seminars as president of Positive Difference Communications. West is the author of *Go to Work and Take Your Faith Too!*, *How to Be Happier in the Job You Sometimes Can't Stand*, and numerous adult Bible study materials. He has written for two previous editions of *The New International Lesson Annual*.

West is an adjunct instructor at Shorter College in Rome, Georgia, and teaches several courses related to Christian ministry. He conducts seminars and workshops across the nation in his specialties of adult Christian education and how to live one's faith on the job.

He previously served as director of Creative Services for the national organization of the Boy Scouts of America; as pastor and associate pastor of churches in Georgia, Louisiana, Virginia, Arkansas, and Kentucky; and as an editor and manager at a religious publishing house.

West earned the doctor of ministry degree from New Orleans Baptist Theological Seminary and the master of divinity degree from The Southern Baptist Theological Seminary in Louisville, Kentucky. His undergraduate degree is from Louisiana Tech University in Ruston, Louisiana.

West is a member of the Coalition for Ministry in Daily Life, an international ecumenical partnership that encourages ministry in daily life, especially in the workplace. He is also associated with the Cooperative Baptist Fellowship.

West's wife, Dr. Martha West, is associate professor of early childhood education at Shorter College. Their son, daughter-in-law, and two grandchildren live in Ann Arbor, Michigan.

MARK, MATTHEW, AND LUKE— UNIQUE WITNESSES TO JESUS

How Many Gospels Do We Need?

Wouldn't one Gospel have been enough? Why do we need four in our Bibles? Sometimes people may ask such questions as they read the Gospels and try to "harmonize" the differences among them. When we study the Gospels seriously, as we have an opportunity to do this quarter, we see that the incidents and teachings may not appear in quite the same way in each Gospel, if they even appear in more than one Gospel.

So why do we need four Gospels—Matthew, Mark, Luke, and John? Wouldn't it be better if we had only one Gospel so we could be sure what happened and when and what exactly was said? If the answer to this question were yes, though, which one would you like to keep and which three would you like to discard?

Attempts have been made through the years to produce harmonies of the four Gospels, trying to put the events in each in a single chronological scheme. As well meant and as helpful as these may be, the fact is that these harmonies are human documents that represent only the best guesses of human interpreters of the Bible. Furthermore, attempting to coordinate all the varying details and outline a definite chronology of Jesus' life reflects only our needs. Such attempts to coordinate the details may well be the least important and least relevant way of studying the Gospels. The greater reality to consider is what we have in the New Testament are four distinct Gospels. The early Christians seem not to have been disturbed by this reality. Rather than wishing for one account, either by discarding three of the four Gospels or trying somehow to meld them together, we would benefit more if we sought to understand the unique way in which each Gospel witnesses to Jesus.

The life of the church and of individual Christians would be so much poorer if we did not have all four of the Gospels. Each bears witness to Jesus in a unique way.

Information We Would Miss

If we did not have the Gospel of Matthew, for example, we would not have the story of the Wise Men (Matthew 2:1-12). Neither would we have Jesus' statement, "Come to me, all you that are weary and are carrying heavy burdens, and I will give you rest" (11:28). Neither would we have a number of parables (see Matthew 13:24-30, 44-50, for example) or many of the details of Jesus' teachings (see Matthew 5–7).

If we did not have the Gospel of Luke, we would not have the angel's announcement to the shepherds of Jesus' birth (Luke 2:1-20). We would not have the story of the prodigal son (Luke 15:11-32) or of Lazarus the beggar (Luke 16:19-31).

If we did not have the Gospel of Mark, what would we miss? For one thing, we would miss much of Matthew and Luke since the Gospels of Matthew and Luke evidently used the

Gospel of Mark as a source, as suggested in the following paragraphs. All but a few verses in Mark appear also in either Matthew or Luke.

If we did not have the Gospel of John, we would not know that Jesus' ministry lasted more than one year, for only John refers to three celebrations of Passover (John 2:13; 6:4; 11:55). We would not know of the raising of Lazarus (John 11:1-44), or of Jesus' conversation with Nicodemus (John 3) or with the Samaritan woman (John 4).

Unique Perspectives for Unique Needs

The unique contributions of each of the Gospels go beyond providing us with information that we would not have if we did not have these Gospels. Each Gospel makes a unique contribution to our understanding of and perspective on Jesus in the way that it presents and interprets the information about Jesus.

Each Gospel presents its understanding of Jesus in a different way. All four of the Gospels, in fact, are literary works that "interpret the *theological* meaning of a concrete *historical* event to people in a particular historical situation," according to M. Eugene Boring in *The New Interpreter's Bible*. Look at the elements of that quote a moment. The Gospels are not biographies of Jesus. Their purpose is not to record the details of Jesus' life as a biographer would. Rather each of the Gospels seeks to convey "the *theological* meaning" of who Jesus was and what he did. That is why it seems to have been of little concern for the Gospel writers to try to match their Gospels so that the same event appears at the same place in each or so that each detail about an event is the same when it appears in more than one Gospel. The concern was not with the details but with the theological meaning.

Next, the Gospels focus on "a concrete *historical* event." Although the Gospel writers were more concerned with the meaning than with making the details consistent, there was no doubt that their focus was on something that really happened in the person of Jesus of Nazareth. The third major element in the quote has to do with the audience to which the Gospels were written. Each was written "to people in a particular historical situation." Matthew, Mark, Luke, and John each wrote to a particular set of people in a particular historical situation. As proclaimers of the good news about Jesus, each Gospel writer sought to focus that message in such a way that it would be most helpful to the first readers. That is another reason each Gospel provides different details and gives different slants to similar stories and sayings. Each Gospel was meant to help meet the specific needs of the readers in a particular faith community.

Sometimes when we are participating in a worship service, we may hear a familiar hymn text set to a new tune. Often when this happens, we give attention to the words in a new and fresh way. We might think of the four Gospels as setting the same hymn text to different tunes. The basic message that each conveys is the same even though the tunes are different and we may thus experience different feelings and thoughts as we give attention to them. In the case of the Gospels, the words themselves may be different—quite different in the case of the Gospel of John.

People may become disturbed when they take the time to compare similar scripture passages in the Gospels and find that an incident may be treated differently in one Gospel from the way it is treated in another. The unique perspective that each Gospel provides on Jesus need not be disturbing to us, however. Each Gospel treatment was meant to convey the specific message about Christ that would have spoken most pointedly to Christians in a specific situation in the first-century world. As we study these passages more deeply and recognize this fact, we may be led to see how each Gospel speaks pointedly to a situation that is special to our own situation. Furthermore, when the Gospels differ either in the chronological order of various incidents or in the details, the question is not, *which one is true*. The answer is that all of them are true, for all of them convey the true theological message about Jesus. The difference in chronology, in details, or in the words used has no bearing on whether one account is "more true" than another. They are all true as they help us understand and interpret who Jesus is.

Sources for Each Gospel

Another reason for the uniqueness of each Gospel has to do with the sources behind each of them. Although no Gospel writer left a footnoted manuscript telling the source of each verse, we can make fairly good guesses about these sources.

The view that seems to fit the evidence in the Gospels best is that the Gospel of Mark was the first one written. Then the Gospel of Mark was used in the writing of Matthew and Luke. As indicated previously, one reason for this view is that almost all of Mark appears in either Matthew or Luke. Another reason is that Mark seems to provide the chronological order for Matthew and Luke, where chronological order is apparent. Still another reason for Mark being considered the first Gospel written is Matthew and Luke never agree together when alterations from Mark are made, thus suggesting that Mark was a respected source for each of them.

The traditional view of the writing of the Gospel of Mark is that Mark took the preaching of Peter about Jesus, compiled it, and used it to speak directly to persecuted Christians in Rome during the late 60s of the first century A.D. Why the late 60s? In A.D. 64, the great fire in Rome occurred. When Nero needed someone to blame it on, he blamed Christians and began to persecute them. Thus the Gospel of Mark may have been written about A.D. 65–67 especially to provide encouragement to persecuted Christians. If the Gospel of Mark were written about this time, then it would have been available for use in Matthew and Luke, which likely were written in the 70s and 80s. According to these ideas about the writing of the Gospel of Mark, the basics of primitive Christian preaching as we see it recorded in Acts 10:36-40 became the outline for Mark's Gospel.

What about the Gospel of Matthew? When we look at this Gospel, we can see that it makes much use of Mark and that it is also much longer than Mark (28 chapters in Matthew, whereas only 16 chapters in Mark). We also see that some things in Matthew are not in any of the other Gospels and that Matthew and Luke have some things that Mark does not have. Why is this? How does it fit together? The best thought on the matter at this point suggests that the writer of Matthew had available the Gospel of Mark plus a source sometimes referred to as *Q* that Luke also had plus a source to which only Matthew had access, referred to as *M*. (*Q* simply is an abbreviation of the German word *Quelle*, which means *source*.) So the equation for the writing of the Gospel of Matthew goes like this: Matthew = Mark + *Q* + *M*. The Gospel of Matthew has a special interest in connecting Jesus with the Old Testament. It contains many Old Testament quotes and is the most Jewish of the Gospels. Matthew likely was written in the late 70s to 80s A.D. to speak particularly to Jewish-oriented readers or to provide information for witnessing to the Jewish community.

What about the Gospel of Luke? As did Matthew, Luke also had Mark plus the source we call *Q* containing materials that appear in both Matthew and Luke. Luke also had a special source available only to him. Scholars generally refer to that source in a sort of shorthand by calling it *L*. *L* simply refers to information that appears only in Luke. The equation for the writing of the Gospel of Luke would thus go like this: Luke = Mark + *Q* + *L*. The Gospel of

Luke connects with the Gentile world, showing familiarity with Gentile concerns, thus seeking to reach out to Gentiles. It also, though, still is quite in touch with the world of Judaism. The Gospel of Luke likely was written sometime in the A.D. 80s to the mid-90s.

These three Gospels—Mark, Matthew, and Luke—are called the *Synoptic* Gospels. *Synoptic*—what does that mean? The word "optic" is familiar to us, referring to the eyes. The prefix "syn" means with or together with. Thus, the word "synoptic" literally means see together. This name was given to the Gospels of Matthew, Mark, and Luke because they seemed to be similar in their presentation of the story of Jesus.

The Gospel of John, on the other hand, is different from the other three in many ways. The Gospel of John is the latest of the Gospels, likely appearing sometime in the 90s. The Gospel of John has a special concern to relate both to people familiar with Judaism and to people familiar with Greek philosophical thought.

Unique Emphases

As we study and teach the verse selections from the Gospels of Mark, Matthew, and Luke, you will find it helpful to keep in mind the unique emphases of each Gospel.

Unit 1, "Jesus' Life," is from the Gospel of Mark. Although the scripture selections for this unit could have been taken from the other Gospels, using selections from the Gospel of Mark is highly appropriate since Mark is especially concerned to give a fast-paced survey of Jesus' actions. Indeed, Mark uses one word twenty-seven times to keep the story of Jesus' life moving quickly: "immediately" (see Mark 1:12, 18, 20, 42, for example). Mark's way of presenting and interpreting the story of Jesus suggests that this Gospel was meant to provide a kind of survival kit for Christians under great pressure. The emphasis was on providing quickly and briefly what Christians under pressure, perhaps facing persecution, would need to understand about Jesus. They might need encouragement quickly, and they might need to make a quick decision as to whether commitment to Jesus was truly worth it.

Unit 2, "Jesus' Ministry of Teaching," is from the Gospel of Matthew. Choosing scriptures from Matthew for this unit reflects Matthew's strong emphasis on Jesus' teachings. Indeed, the Gospel of Matthew is organized around five extensive blocks of teachings (Matthew 5–7; 10; 13; 18; 24–25). This outline may be a further connection of Matthew's Gospel with Judaism, since these five sections would remind readers of Jewish background of the fact that the Pentateuch also had five books.

Unit 3, "Jesus' Ministry of Compassion," is from the Gospel of Luke. Luke is especially concerned with ministry to people who were left out, and the scripture passages chosen for this study reflect that emphasis. Luke's major emphases include reaching out to Gentiles (see Luke 14:15-24); providing justice for the poor and oppressed (see Luke 1:46-55; 4:16-30; 7:11-17; 16:19-31); showing compassion for outcasts (see Luke 2:8-12; 5:27-32; 7:36-38; 10:25-37; 14:7-24; 18:9-14); and lifting the status of women (see Luke 8:2-3, 40-56; 10:38-42; 21:1-4).

These lessons from Mark, Matthew, and Luke provide an opportunity to get in touch with the unique message of each of these Gospels. The message is about the same Jesus, of course, and it is the same message of good news. The studies focus, though, on three different aspects of the story of Jesus—his life, his teachings, his compassion—and the story is told from three unique perspectives.

Each Gospel is important, and each Gospel is unique. Furthermore, each Gospel is true, in spite of the differing details, for we learn the truth about Jesus from each. Too, we hear Jesus' instructions and his call to us uniquely through each Gospel.

UNIT 1: JESUS' LIFE (GOSPEL OF MARK)
PREPARING FOR LEADERSHIP

PREVIEWING THE LESSON

Lesson Scripture: Mark 1:4-13
Background Scripture: Mark 1:4-13
Key Verse: Mark 1:11

Focus of the Lesson:
People respond best to leaders who have appropriate credentials and qualifications to lead *and* who demonstrate a genuine understanding of their followers. What credentials and qualifications *and* understanding does Jesus demonstrate for those who would minister in his name? Jesus' authority was declared—by human and divine voices—at the time of his baptism. In facing and responding to temptations, Jesus established his understanding of the human condition.

Goals for the Learners:
(1) to study the stories of Jesus' baptism and temptations.
(2) to examine their responses to Jesus' credentials as the Messiah.
(3) to claim their identity as Christians qualified to minister to others.

Supplies:
Bibles, newsprint and marker, paper and pencils, hymnals

READING THE SCRIPTURE

NRSV
Mark 1:4-13

4 John the baptizer appeared in the wilderness, proclaiming a baptism of repentance for the forgiveness of sins. 5 And people from the whole Judean countryside and all the people of Jerusalem were going out to him, and were baptized by him in the river Jordan, confessing their sins. 6 Now John was clothed with camel's hair, with a leather belt around his waist, and he ate locusts and

NIV
Mark 1:4-13

⁴And so John came, baptizing in the desert region and preaching a baptism of repentance for the forgiveness of sins. ⁵The whole Judean countryside and all the people of Jerusalem went out to him. Confessing their sins, they were baptized by him in the Jordan River. ⁶John wore clothing made of camel's hair, with a leather belt around his waist, and he ate locusts and wild honey.

wild honey. 7 He proclaimed, "The one who is more powerful than I is coming after me; I am not worthy to stoop down and untie the thong of his sandals. 8 I have baptized you with water; but he will baptize you with the Holy Spirit."

9 In those days Jesus came from Nazareth of Galilee and was baptized by John in the Jordan. 10 And just as he was coming up out of the water, he saw the heavens torn apart and the Spirit descending like a dove on him. **11 And a voice came from heaven, "You are my Son, the Beloved; with you I am well pleased."**

12 And the Spirit immediately drove him out into the wilderness. 13 He was in the wilderness forty days, tempted by Satan; and he was with the wild beasts; and the angels waited on him.

[7]And this was his message: "After me will come one more powerful than I, the thongs of whose sandals I am not worthy to stoop down and untie. [8]I baptize you with water, but he will baptize you with the Holy Spirit."

[9]At that time Jesus came from Nazareth in Galilee and was baptized by John in the Jordan. [10]As Jesus was coming up out of the water, he saw heaven being torn open and the Spirit descending on him like a dove. **[11]And a voice came from heaven: "You are my Son, whom I love; with you I am well pleased."**

[12]At once the Spirit sent him out into the desert, [13]and he was in the desert forty days, being tempted by Satan. He was with the wild animals, and angels attended him.

UNDERSTANDING THE SCRIPTURE

Mark 1:4. The first verse of Mark's Gospel describes Jesus as "Christ" and "Son of God." Mark then moves immediately in verses 2-3 to connect Jesus' coming with Isaiah's prophecy of "a messenger" who would "prepare the way of the Lord" (see Isaiah 40:3). "Lord" refers to the coming Messiah.

Who was the "messenger"? In 1:4, we see that he was this strange and strangely compelling character called "John the baptizer." We find him first "in the wilderness," just as Isaiah 40:3 had said. As a geographical location, "the wilderness" in which John proclaimed his message was the rugged area in the southern portion of the valley of the Jordan River. "The wilderness," however, has theological as well as geographical meaning in this verse, as the reference to "the wilderness" in Isaiah 40:3 suggests.

John was "proclaiming a baptism of repentance for the forgiveness of sins" (1:4). John called people to engage in the ritual act of baptism in water to signify their repen-

tance of their sins. The Jews baptized proselytes to Judaism, and the Essenes at Qumran used baptism as an initiation rite. Still, John's baptism was unique, though, especially in its meaning—repentance.

John's preaching of repentance placed him solidly in the line of God's prophets. The prophets were calling for repentance when they called the people to "turn" or "return" to God (see, for example, Jeremiah 3:12; 4:1; 18:11; 25:5; 35:15). So John the Baptist was challenging the people to "turn" or "return" to God. The Greek word translated "repentance" amplifies this idea. This word has to do with "changing one's mind." Repentance thus calls for a radical change of life. Repentance means doing an about-face in how one lives and returning to God and God's ways.

The result of such repentance is "the forgiveness of sins." John's message was for the people to turn back to God and for them to symbolize that act by being baptized. On the basis of the people's repentance, God would forgive their sins. Thus the way would be prepared for the coming of the Messiah.

Mark 1:5. Judea was the southern region of the land of Israel. The city of Jerusalem was within Judea. The people of Judea and Jerusalem were responding to John's message by "confessing their sins" and being "baptized by him in the river Jordan." The literal meaning of the Greek word translated "confessing" is saying the same. Thus, in confessing one's sins, one says the same thing about one's wrong actions and attitudes as God does. One admits that these acts and attitudes are wrong, just as God says they are.

Mark 1:6. John's unusual appearance would have reminded the people of Elijah (see 2 Kings 1:8), whose return had been promised (Malachi 4:5-6). John's diet would not have been unusual for a person who lived a nomadic desert life. Even John's diet would thus have demonstrated his participation in the life of the wilderness, where the way of the Lord was being prepared.

Mark 1:7. Lest anyone be confused about John's role in God's plan, John made clear his relation to the Messiah. He affirmed that he was not the Messiah. Rather, he was not worthy even "to stoop down and untie the thong of his sandals." In Jewish life, even servants were not required to remove the sandals of their masters. John was saying that he was not even up to the level of being worthy to be a servant to the Messiah.

Mark 1:8. John further pointed out the distance between himself and the Messiah by contrasting his baptism with the Messiah's baptism. John baptized merely in water; the Messiah would "baptize you with the Holy Spirit." John's baptism in water was merely preparatory to the coming of the Lord, but the Messiah's baptism would relate the person to God's Spirit.

Mark 1:9. During the time when John the Baptist was preaching, Jesus came to John to be baptized. Jesus had been living in "Nazareth of Galilee." Nazareth is in the northern portion of the land of Israel. It was the town in which Joseph and Mary had lived prior to Jesus' birth (Luke 1:26-28). They had returned there after their sojourn in Egypt (Matthew 2:23). There, Jesus had grown up (Luke 2:39-40; 4:16).

Mark gives no hint that Jesus' baptism by John was a matter of concern even though John's baptism was based on repentance (compare Matthew 3:13-15). Still, we wonder about the meaning of Jesus' baptism at the hands of John. Perhaps it signified Jesus' identification with a world that needed to get ready for the Lord's coming, which was taking place at that very moment.

Mark 1:10-11. John the Baptist, in line with the prophets of the Old Testament, was placing his stamp of approval on Jesus through baptizing him. At the same time, God placed God's stamp of approval on Jesus. The sights—"the heavens torn apart and the Spirit descending like a dove on him"—and the sound—"a voice came from heaven"—at Jesus' baptism signified that Jesus was indeed the One who was fully qualified as "Christ, the Son of God" (1:1). The words attributed to the "voice," referring to God, echo Psalm 2:7 and Isaiah 42:1. These texts are used often in the New Testament to provide understanding of Jesus' identity (see Matthew 12:18; 17:5; Mark 9:7; Luke 9:35; 2 Peter 1:17).

Mark 1:12-13. The temptation experience of Jesus provides yet another affirmation of Jesus' identity as "Christ, the Son of God" (1:1). Jesus' time in "the wilderness" was a time of testing. Unlike the ancient Israelites, who had been tested in the wilderness during their journey to the promised land, Jesus proved faithful, as verses 12-13 imply (see also Matthew 4:1-11; Luke 4:1-13).

The statement that Jesus "was with the wild beasts; and the angels waited on him" indicates Jesus' faithfulness to God when faced with Satan's tempting. Perhaps the implication of this statement is also that through Jesus' faithfulness to God and resistance to Satan, the wilderness was turned into paradise. The image suggests life as it was before sin brought disharmony into the world (Genesis 3). It also suggests life in the messianic age, when "the wolf shall live with the lamb" (Isaiah 11:6).

INTERPRETING THE SCRIPTURE

Affirmed by John

One of the greatest motivations to do something important or be someone significant is to have someone believe that we are capable. No one climbs the ladder of accomplishment alone. If we get very far or overcome many obstacles, one reason is that there is at least one person whom we can look back to or up to and know that that person believes in us.

Dare we say that John the Baptist was a key person filling such a function for Jesus? We like to think of Jesus as being self-sufficient and needing no one. At the most critical moment of his life, everyone deserted Jesus, and he faced it alone. It is also true, however, that as Jesus struggled with the most difficult decision of his life, he sought the encouragement of human companionship. Jesus was human as well as divine.

John the Baptist filled the role of preparing "the way of the Lord" (Mark 1:3), preparing the people for the coming of the Messiah. John's message, his manner of dress, and even his diet served to stake out the radical claim that something new and different was happening. The people should get ready for it. What should they do? Repent—turn to God—and show that repentance by being baptized. Such actions would prepare people for the Messiah who was soon to burst upon the scene.

When Jesus came to John the Baptist to be baptized, Jesus in a sense was paying tribute to John for John's role in the ministry of the Messiah and for John's affirmation of his ministry. Jesus did not engage in his mission in a Lone Ranger fashion but connected what he was about to do with what John the Baptist already was doing. John the Baptist's affirmation of Jesus' ministry as well as Jesus' receiving that affirmation remind us of the importance of having someone believe in us as well as the importance of having the humility to know that we, too, need others as we seek to minister and to lead. When people who have accomplished much look back on the reasons for their accomplishments, at their best they realize that they have stood on others' shoulders. At critical times, others provided the support, encouragement, and validation that they needed.

The recent movie, *A Beautiful Mind*, told the story of the brilliant mathematician John Nash. As a young person, he sought to achieve much, often brashly thinking he could do it alone because of his great intellectual capacities. Bouts with paranoid schizophrenia, though, almost destroyed him. In the movie's rendering of Nash's receiving the Nobel Prize, Nash paid tribute to his wife for her encouragement and love through the horrendous difficulties of his life. He recognized not only that he had not succeeded alone but also that he owed his very survival to her.

Affirmation from others who believe in us can encourage and motivate us to overcome difficulties in our lives and to move forward with our God-given tasks. Indeed, it is a necessity.

Approved by God

At Jesus' baptism, God placed his stamp of approval on Jesus. Parents know the pride they feel when a child does well or makes the right choice. In colloquial terms we can almost hear God saying, *That's my child!*

Mark pictures "the Spirit descending like a dove on him" (1:10) and tells of the "voice from heaven" saying, "You are my Son, the Beloved; with you I am well pleased" (1:12).

Mark does not tell what these occurrences meant to Jesus. Perhaps we would not go too far astray, however, by suggesting that they must have meant much to the human Jesus who was seeking to do God's will. Surely every person seeking to do God's will desires some sort of affirmation from God that he or she is on the right track. Such a desire applies to individual decisions and actions we may be contemplating. It also applies as we look back on our lives as we grow older. Have we made the right choices? Have we taken the best course? Is God pleased with what we have decided, said, and done?

We are grateful when we sense some sort of affirmation from God that we are on the right track. Surely as Jesus experienced the sights and the sound from God at his baptism, he felt affirmed in the knowledge that, indeed, he was on the right track.

Think further about this matter of God's affirmation by considering this question. What would a video camera have captured if it had been trained on the scene? That is, if we were to see a videotape of that event, would we see "a dove"? The biblical text is careful to say "like a dove," not "in a dove." The text is clear, too, that "he saw." The only certain meaning is that Jesus saw. What about the sound? What would we hear on the videotape? Would we hear God speaking in an audible voice? The text does not indicate that anyone else heard the voice. In another instance in which "a voice came from heaven" (John 12:28), the crowd "heard it and said that it was thunder" (John 12:29). Only at the Transfiguration do the Gospels indicate that someone else— Peter, James, and John—heard the voice (Matthew 17:5-6; see Luke 9:35-36).

As we seek approval by God for our mission, decisions, words, and actions, we should recognize that this sense of approval generally is a private, inner experience. So how can we be sure that God will say of what we have done or are planning to do, "With you I am well pleased" (Mark 1:11)? People have done strange, crazy, and evil things and claimed they were doing God's will. How can we test such inner experiences? Perhaps the most basic way of evaluating these experiences is to ask ourselves whether the actions we have taken or are contemplating are in line with God's purposes as we see them in the Scriptures. We can also evaluate these actions by what we think the best Christians we know about have done or would do. We should also consider the effect these actions would have on others. Would these actions demonstrate genuine love? We should be willing to test our inner experiences by how they square with love for God as we have come to know God in Jesus Christ and love for people in the ways Jesus loved people.

Confirmed by Experience

Just because we have been affirmed by others and have sensed God's approval and direction doesn't mean that only smooth sailing lies ahead. That was certainly not the case with Jesus. "The Spirit immediately drove him out into the wilderness" (1:12). There, Jesus faced tempting by Satan. Only after Jesus had resisted the tempting did Jesus' time in the wilderness become a time of spiritual victory. Surely, though, the experience of being victorious over Satan's tempting served as additional confirmation for Jesus' ministry.

Positive spiritual experiences can also provide confirmation for our ministry. Among the benefits of growing older, in addition to a consideration of the alternative, is being able to look back on the difficult experiences one has survived and to recognize that surviving such experiences has made one stronger. When one is a teenager, every bump, including on one's face, can seem like the end of the world. When we have survived a few bumps on our faces and elsewhere, we begin to realize that we may be able to deal with the next bump, too, however big it may be. Experiences of spiritual success can help to confirm our choices and direction.

SHARING THE SCRIPTURE

PREPARING TO TEACH

Preparing Our Hearts

This week's devotional reading is found in Matthew 12:17-21. Here we find a quotation from Isaiah 42:1-4, a passage that is commonly called the First Servant Song. Many scholars believe that this song originally referred to Israel's calling during its exile in Babylonia to bring light to the Gentiles. Later, Christian interpreters have seen this description of God's chosen servant being fulfilled in Jesus. What do you think this passage means? How can you relate it to Jesus? What difference does Jesus' work as God's servant make in your life?

Pray that you and your students will recognize that Jesus is not only God's chosen servant but also God's beloved Son.

Preparing Our Minds

Study the background and lesson scripture found in Mark 1:4-13.

Write on newsprint:

information for next week's lesson, found under "Continue the Journey."

Plan a lecture related to John the Baptist as suggested under "Study the Stories of Jesus' Baptism and Temptations."

LEADING THE CLASS

(1) Gather to Learn

❖ Welcome the class members and introduce any guests.

❖ Pray that the students will recognize that Jesus needed to prepare for leadership, just as we do.

❖ Brainstorm with the class answers to this question: **What personal attributes and skills does a good leader need?** Write ideas on newsprint.

❖ Discuss ways people prepare to be leaders.

❖ Read aloud today's focus statement: **People respond best to leaders who have appropriate credentials and qualifications to lead *and* who demonstrate a genuine understanding of their followers. What credentials and qualifications *and* understanding does Jesus demonstrate for those who would minister in his name? Jesus' authority was declared—by human and divine voices—at the time of his baptism. In facing and responding to temptations, Jesus established his understanding of the human condition.**

(2) Study the Stories of Jesus' Baptism and Temptations

❖ Choose a volunteer to read Mark 1:4-8.

■ Invite the students to raise questions that this passage brings to mind for them. Record their questions on newsprint.

■ Use the information from Understanding the Scripture, verses 4-8, to create a lecture that will help to explain the reading by introducing John, his message, and his relationship with Jesus.

■ Review the newsprint with the students and see if there are unanswered questions. Encourage the students to suggest answers. Those who have study Bibles may find pertinent information in the footnotes. If questions remain unanswered, challenge the students to locate pertinent information during the week.

❖ Select someone to read the story of Jesus' baptism from Mark 1:9-11 and then discuss the following questions.

(1) **What does this passage tell you about Jesus?**

(2) **Where else in the Scripture do you see words similar to verse 11?** (See Psalm 2:7; Matthew 3:17; Luke 9:35, Jesus' transfiguration; John 1:32-34; 2 Peter 1:17. You may want to have these verses read aloud.)

(3) **John came offering "a baptism of repentance for forgiveness of sins," yet Jesus would not have needed baptism for this reason. Why do you think he chose to be baptized?**

❖ Ask a volunteer to read the story of Jesus' temptation, as recorded in Mark 1:12-13.

■ Do a comparative Bible study by dividing into groups and asking half of the groups to read Matthew 4:1-11 and the other half to look at Luke 4:1-13. Tell the groups to consider how their passage is similar to and different from Mark's report.

■ Bring the students together and ask the groups working on each Gospel to give a report.

■ Close by asking: **Why might Mark's Gospel give such a brief report with so few details?**

(3) Examine Learners' Responses to Jesus' Credentials As the Messiah

❖ Ask the students to identify the marks of a modern leader. What kinds of skills, talents, experience, and education do such people usually have to offer?

❖ Invite the students to identify the credentials that they believe Jesus has for ministry, according to Mark's Gospel. You may want to list these ideas on newsprint.

❖ Compare these credentials with those they previously discussed concerning contemporary leaders. Invite the students to speculate on the chance Jesus would have for becoming a major leader in our day.

❖ Encourage the learners to talk with a partner or small groups about their own responses to Jesus' credentials as the Messiah that Mark offers. Suggest that they discuss whether or not they would have accepted Jesus as the Messiah had they only known the information contained in today's scripture reading.

❖ Provide an opportunity for volunteers to comment on insights discerned by their groups.

(4) Claim Identity As Christians Qualified to Minister to Others

❖ Distribute paper and pencils. Invite the students to jot down words or phrases they would use to identify themselves as Christians. This list might include: *disciple, steward, follower of Christ, child of God,* or *believer.*

❖ Ask the students to turn to Romans 12:6-8 and 1 Corinthians 12:8-10, 28; and read the lists of gifts.

❖ Suggest that the class members discern which gifts they have been given individually and collectively to build up the community of faith. They may want to list these gifts on their papers.

❖ Conclude this portion of the lesson by asking the adults to identify ways that they are—or could be—using their gifts in ministry to others. You may want the students to reflect on their gifts, or to discuss them with a small group.

(5) Continue the Journey

❖ Pray that the participants will perceive their own baptism as part of their preparation for leadership and offer whatever leadership they can to the faith community.

❖ Read aloud this preparation for next week's lesson. You may also want to post it on newsprint for the students to copy. **Prepare for next week's session entitled "Healed to Wholeness" by reading Mark 2:1-12, 3:1-6, and 8:1-10, focusing especially on Mark 2:1-12. Keep this focus in mind as you read: Many people suffer in some area of their life, and often they—and those who would like to help—feel overwhelmed and powerless. Are we doomed to live with this sense of helplessness? The miracles affirm the depth of Jesus' caring for others and his power to bring healing to situations others would write off as hopeless.**

❖ Read aloud the following three ideas. Challenge the students to commit themselves to use these activities as a springboard to spiritual growth.

(1) **Ponder these questions and write your reflections in your spiritual journal: What does baptism mean to you? What role does baptism play in your spiritual life? How might you be different if you had not been baptized?**

(2) **Name several temptations that you face on a relatively consistent basis. How have you been able to overcome these temptations? What help do you need to resist them?**

(3) **Find at least one way this week to use one or more of your spiritual gifts in service to the world.**

❖ Sing or read aloud "When Jesus Came to Jordan."

❖ Say these words from 1 Peter one phrase at a time and ask the class to repeat them: **Prepare your minds for action; discipline yourselves; set all your hope on the grace that Jesus Christ will bring you when he is revealed.**

HEALED TO WHOLENESS

PREVIEWING THE LESSON

Lesson Scripture: Mark 2:1-12
Background Scripture: Mark 2:1-12; 3:1-6; 8:1-10
Key Verse: Mark 2:11

Focus of the Lesson:
Many people suffer in some area of their life, and often they—and those who would like to help—feel overwhelmed and powerless. Are we doomed to live with this sense of helplessness? The miracles affirm the depth of Jesus' caring for others and his power to bring healing to situations others would write off as hopeless.

Goals for the Learners:
(1) to delve into the story of Jesus' healing the paralyzed man.
(2) to explore ways that Jesus heals their lives.
(3) to identify ways they can be instruments of God's healing in the world and to commit themselves to action.

Supplies:
Bibles, newsprint and marker, paper and pencils, hymnals

READING THE SCRIPTURE

NRSV
Mark 2:1-12

When he returned to Capernaum after some days, it was reported that he was at home. 2 So many gathered around that there was no longer room for them, not even in front of the door; and he was speaking the word to them. 3 Then some people came, bringing to him a paralyzed man, carried by four of them. 4 And when they could not bring him to Jesus because of the crowd, they removed the roof above him; and after having dug through it, they let down the mat on which the paralytic lay. 5 When Jesus

NIV
Mark 2:1-12

A few days later, when Jesus again entered Capernaum, the people heard that he had come home. ²So many gathered that there was no room left, not even outside the door, and he preached the word to them. ³Some men came, bringing to him a paralytic, carried by four of them. ⁴Since they could not get him to Jesus because of the crowd, they made an opening in the roof above Jesus and, after digging through it, lowered the mat the paralyzed man was lying on. ⁵When Jesus saw their faith, he said to the saw their faith, he said to the paralytic, "Son, your sins are forgiven." 6 Now some of the scribes were sitting there, questioning in their hearts, 7 "Why does this fellow speak in this way? It is blasphemy! Who can forgive sins but God alone?" 8 At once Jesus perceived in his spirit that they were discussing these questions among themselves; and he said to them, "Why do you raise such questions in your hearts? 9 Which is easier, to say to the paralytic, 'Your sins are forgiven,' or to say, 'Stand up and take your mat and walk'? 10 But so that you may know that the Son of Man has authority on earth to forgive sins"—he said to the paralytic—**11 "I say to you, stand up, take your mat and go to your home."** 12 And he stood up, and immediately took the mat and went out before all of them; so that they were all amazed and glorified God, saying, "We have never seen anything like this!"

paralytic, "Son, your sins are forgiven."

6 Now some teachers of the law were sitting there, thinking to themselves, 7 "Why does this fellow talk like that? He's blaspheming! Who can forgive sins but God alone?"

8 Immediately Jesus knew in his spirit that this was what they were thinking in their hearts, and he said to them, "Why are you thinking these things? 9 Which is easier: to say to the paralytic, 'Your sins are forgiven,' or to say, 'Get up, take your mat and walk'? 10 But that you may know that the Son of Man has authority on earth to forgive sins. . . ." He said to the paralytic, —11 **"I tell you, get up, take your mat and go home."** 12 He got up, took his mat and walked out in full view of them all. This amazed everyone and they praised God, saying, "We have never seen anything like this!"

UNDERSTANDING THE SCRIPTURE

Mark 2:1. After Jesus' temptation in the wilderness and then John's arrest, Jesus had returned to Galilee, the northernmost region of the land of Israel (1:16). He had gone specifically to the city of Capernaum (1:21). He had then traveled "throughout Galilee, proclaiming the message in their synagogues and casting out demons" (1:39). Now Jesus was back "at home" in Capernaum (2:1), and his presence became known in the area. Whose "home" it was remains uncertain. Actually, the literal translation of the Greek expression is simply "in a house" rather than "at home" (NJB and KJV, "in the house").

Mark 2:2. Exactly what the house in which Jesus was staying was like is uncertain. Archaeological work in Capernaum has unearthed simple one- and two-room houses around a courtyard. A crowd had gathered that was so large that it had filled the small house and spilled out the front door. News of Jesus' fame had already

spread beyond Capernaum to all of Galilee (1:28, 32, 45). Within the house, Jesus "was speaking the word to them" (2:2). This "word" was "the good news of God" (see 1:14-15).

Mark 2:3. As Jesus taught inside the house, something was happening outside the house. "Some people"—at least four—came carrying a "paralyzed" man who was unable to walk. For people to bring people in need of healing to Jesus had happened before in Capernaum (1:21-34). What made this incident so memorable was what happened when the four friends were unable to get their paralyzed friend to Jesus because of the crowd.

Mark 2:4. Houses in Palestine often had an outside stairway leading to the roof. The roof was flat and composed of packed-down earth and sticks. A literal translation of the Greek terms describing the actions of the paralytic's friends is that they "unroofed the roof" by digging a hole through it. They then lowered the paralytic, still lying on the mat, into the room where Jesus was.

Mark 2:5. Jesus recognized "their faith," evidently referring to the faith of the friends and of the paralytic himself. Then Jesus spoke to the paralytic, telling him, "Son, your sins are forgiven." The statement seems to come from out of the blue. What surely the paralytic and his friends had hoped and prayed to hear was, *Son, you are healed.* The paralytic, his friends, and the rest of the gathered crowd must have been waiting for an explanation. Of course, the Old Testament tells of healing and forgiveness being related (see 2 Chronicles 7:14; Psalm 103:3). Too, the book of Job is a long argument about whether there is a connection between sin and suffering, including physical difficulties. The book teaches that Job's suffering had not come because of his sin. Even so, the view continued into New Testament times that suffering, including physical difficulties, came because of sin (see John 9:1). We must beware of tending toward this erroneous view ourselves. We are on surer ground when we see that the incident shows the man's physical condition and his need for forgiveness represented concerns of God, for each in its own way kept the man from wholeness of life. The basic message that everyone gathered around would soon see was that Jesus' healing the man, which could be observed, validated Jesus' forgiveness of the man's sins, which could not be observed.

Mark 2:6-7. The "scribes," most of whom were Pharisees, were experts in the Jewish law. Their opposition to Jesus' statement that the man's sins were forgiven was based on their all-consuming emphasis on keeping all the details of the law as defined by the Jewish traditions. These traditions had been developed after the return from the Exile in order to keep any similar punishment from ever happening to the nation again. Their motives may have been good, but their method led only to a self-absorbed legalism rather than to God. The logic of

their argument was since only God could forgive sin, then Jesus as a human being could not forgive sin. Therefore, Jesus was blaspheming God by claiming to forgive sin. They failed to recognize a second set of ideas was also logical: Since only God can forgive sins and Jesus forgives sins, then Jesus is "the Christ, the Son of God" (1:1).

Mark 2:8-9. Jesus challenged the scribes to consider the second logical approach. He did this by inviting them to evaluate whether forgiving or healing was more difficult.

Mark 2:10-11. Jesus told the scribes that he was going to heal the man as a demonstration of his authority to forgive. Jesus' healing of the paralytic, while surely done in response to the man's physical need, confirmed his identity as "the Christ, the Son of God" (1:1).

Mark 2:12. In response to Jesus' command, the paralyzed man "stood up, and immediately took the mat and went out before all of them." He was healed! No one could miss what Jesus had done. Furthermore, the scribes and others would need to ponder the meaning of what he had done. The logical conclusion was Jesus' healing the man, which was visible to all, meant Jesus' pronouncement of forgiveness of sins was also valid.

Who were "they" who "were all amazed"? The amazed ones might not have included the scribes, for Mark shortly would picture them as questioning Jesus again. Whatever the case, the result of the encounter in the crowded home was the people "glorified God" and said, "We have never seen anything like this!"

Mark 3:1-6. The healing of the man with the withered hand is the fifth incident of conflict in Mark 2:1–3:6. As with the other four incidents (2:1-12; 2:13-17; 2:18-22; 2:23-28), a question was raised about the way in which Jesus was conducting his ministry. In this case, the conflict occurred because Jesus healed the man on the Sabbath. Jesus made helping the man a higher priority than keeping religious customs. Jesus' breaking the Sabbath law was so offensive to the Pharisees that they sought "to destroy him" (3:6).

Mark 8:1-10. Jesus' second feeding miracle in the Gospel of Mark (see also 6:30-44) indicated again his concern for human need. This incident likely occurred in Gentile territory and indicates Jesus' concern for all people in need.

INTERPRETING THE SCRIPTURE

A Human Problem

People with problems are all around us. Perhaps we have only to look in the mirror to see such a person. The problem may be a physical difficulty we were born with or that occurred as a result of accident or disease.

Perhaps this difficulty is something we've somehow managed to make the best of if not overcome. Lou Gehrig, one of the greatest baseball players ever, found he had ALS (amyotrophic lateral sclerosis), which has become known as Lou Gehrig's disease. He began his farewell speech in Yankee Stadium by saying, "Fans, for the past two weeks you've been reading about a bad break I got. Yet today I consider myself the luckiest man on the face of the earth." He went on to talk of the blessings he had experienced in his life and concluded by saying, "I have an awful lot to live for."

Did such a positive attitude characterize the paralytic whose friends brought him to Jesus one day? We don't know. Likely, though, he was not happy with his situation in life, and he wanted Jesus to change it. That's why his friends brought him to Jesus. We, too, may have the best attitude possible about whatever difficulty with which we are struggling, but still we may want the difficulty to be alleviated. Paul felt this way when he talked about his "thorn." "Three times I appealed to the Lord about this, that it would leave me, but he said to me, 'My grace is sufficient for you, for power is made perfect in weakness' " (2 Corinthians 12:8-9). Paul's experience should caution us about connecting physical difficulty to sin. It should also keep us from thinking that lack of faith is the reason that we, or others, have not been healed. We would certainly consider Paul to be a person of faith, and yet his "thorn"— whatever it was—was not removed.

Faith is important in the restoration of the paralytic in this passage, but we must not turn the thought around and suggest that a person's lack of faith is what is preventing that person's restoration to wholeness. We simply do not know why Jesus brought physical restoration to some people but not all, and why all people are not restored physically today.

Likely it was out of the universal desire to be restored and to learn from One who was able to bring restoration that the people flocked to Jesus when they heard he was back in Capernaum. After all, they knew what he had done previously there (see Mark 1:21-34). Further, Jesus had gone throughout Galilee, doing similar deeds (1:39), even healing a leper (1:40-45). Jesus' works verified and confirmed his words.

Human Helpers

To this crowded setting in Capernaum, the paralytic's friends brought him to Jesus to be healed. People have focused vision and a fixed purpose when something of great importance to them is at stake, especially their health or that of a friend or family member. They may take off work, rearrange their schedules, drive or fly hundreds of miles, spend whatever money they have, and generally do whatever it takes when matters of health are involved.

Everything else, even things they had considered important, pales into insignificance. Just so, for the paralyzed man and his friends the center of their universe became one little room in their small village.

The crippled man was blessed to have friends to care for him as they did. Not only did they bring him to where Jesus was, but also they were willing to go to any lengths actually to get him to Jesus. *There's a crowd at the door and we can't get in? That's a problem, but we'll find a way.* Perhaps as they looked around for what to do, one of them suggested, *I know. How about the roof?* No one evidently said, *Well, climbing the stairs will be problem. Besides, how do you think the homeowner will feel if we tear up his roof?* No one made such comments or asked such questions. They didn't stand around thinking of all the reasons they could never do what needed to be done as we sometimes do. Too, as far as we know, when the paralyzed man saw the crowd blocking the way, he didn't say, *Well, fellows, thanks for trying. You can just take me back home.* They just did it. First thing you know they had climbed the stairs, dug a hole in the roof, and lowered their friend into the room where Jesus was. Then they looked down on the scene as the paralyzed man looked up at Jesus, who was probably smiling.

What the friends did has been referred to as a "stretcher ministry." They brought their friend to Jesus so their friend could receive the help he needed. Churches today are going to need to develop "stretcher ministries" as they attempt to minister to our world. Academics and others are calling the world Christians are dealing with today a "postmodern" world. One of the things ministering in a postmodern world means is that the church can no longer count on people coming to church just because it's "the thing to do." Too, the church can't count on the culture giving special treatment to it any longer. What the church must do is what the four friends did. The church, groups within it, and individual Christians must search

out human need and find ways to bring such need under the care of Jesus. Many churches will need to find ways to stop just being the church on Sunday at their church property and to start being the kind of church that ministers to human need seven days a week, and not just on church property. The church must also focus its efforts and ministries more on people's real needs than on simply encouraging participation because people "ought to."

Divine Restoration

What happens when people with needs are brought to Jesus? One result is that Jesus does something about their needs. In this case, Jesus restored the man spiritually. Later he restored him physically. Jesus always grants restoration, though not always physically, when people come to him in faith.

A second thing often happens when people with needs are brought to Jesus and he grants restoration to them. Some people don't like it. They may even complain about it. In this case, the people who didn't like it were the scribes. Is anyone in your church ever reluctant to see God's hand at work in unusual ways? Sometimes people have good reasons for opposing changes in how their church engages in ministry. Other times people have only bad reasons. Still other times church folk oppose change just because they have difficulty dealing with change. We would be wise to question ourselves vigorously when we find ourselves opposing changes in how our church engages in ministry to people. At the very least, we ought to encourage the intent and look for ways to improve the effort rather than simply being negative as the scribes were.

At least one more result occurs when people with needs are brought to Jesus and Jesus restores them. People glorify God. Obviously that's the response the text affirms in verse 12.

SHARING THE SCRIPTURE

PREPARING TO TEACH

Preparing Our Hearts

This week's devotional reading is found in Mark 7:31-37. This story of healing is similar to today's lesson concerning the healing of the paralyzed man. Presumably a group of friends, known only as "they," bring a deaf man to Jesus, who heals him. When the man spoke, the crowd was "astounded beyond measure" (7:37), praising Jesus for his marvelous works. As you read, ponder what it means to be healed to wholeness. Where does Jesus need to touch you so that you too will be healed and made whole? Talk with God about your needs.

Pray that you and your students will seek God's healing touch, both for your friends and for yourselves.

Preparing Our Minds

Study the background lesson, found in Mark 2:1-12 (healing of the paralyzed man), 3:1-6 (healing of the man with the withered hand), and 8:1-10 (Jesus feeding the four thousand). Our session will focus on Mark 2:1-12.

Write on newsprint:

chart for the activity under "Delve into the Story of Jesus' Healing the Paralyzed Man."

information for next week's lesson, found under "Continue the Journey."

LEADING THE CLASS

(1) Gather to Learn

❖ Welcome the class members and introduce any guests.

❖ Pray that those who have gathered will recognize that Jesus wants to heal them unto wholeness and has the power to do so.

❖ Distribute paper and pencils. Invite the students to list their own infirmities/sufferings and/or those of a friend. Assure them that this information will not be shared with the class.

❖ Do this guided imagery. Suggest that the students close their eyes as they envision these scenes.

■ **See yourself before Christ, assuming whatever posture seems most comfortable for you. Silently share the list of infirmities/sufferings you have written.** (Pause)

■ **Look at Christ. What does his facial expression tell you? What can you hear him saying to you?** (Pause)

■ **Imagine yourself responding to Christ. How would you describe your emotions at this moment?** (Pause)

■ **Open your eyes when you are ready.**

❖ Read aloud today's focus statement: **Many people suffer in some area of their life, and often they—and those who would like to help—feel overwhelmed and powerless. Are we doomed to live with this sense of helplessness? The miracles affirm the depth of Jesus' caring for others and his power to bring healing to situations others would write off as hopeless.**

(2) Delve into the Story of Jesus' Healing the Paralyzed Man

❖ Choose volunteers to read the parts of the narrator and Jesus in Mark 2:1-12. The rest of the class will read the part of the scribes (2:7) and that of all the people (2:12).

❖ Provide background information by creating a brief lecture from the verses for Mark 2:1-12 in the Understanding the Scripture portion.

❖ Ask the class to complete this chart, which you will want to write on newsprint prior to class. Distribute paper and pencils so that the students can copy the information and fill in their own charts as they work individually or with a team. They are to refer to Mark 2:1-12 in their Bibles to complete this activity.

Scene	Characters	Action	Reaction

❖ Discuss these questions with the class.

(1) What does this story suggest concerning Jesus' relationship with the people?

(2) What motivates people to go out of their way for others, as the friends of the paralyzed man did for him?

(3) Why do the scribes, the lawyers and overseers of the law, treat Jesus so shabbily? Had you been in their sandals, what would you have said or done?

(4) Had you been present at this healing, what would your response to Jesus have been?

(5) What is the relationship between healing and forgiveness? What pitfalls do we have to avoid today when talking about healing and forgiveness?

(3) Explore Ways That Jesus Heals Learners' Lives

❖ Ask the students to name or briefly describe biblical healing stories that they find comforting.

❖ Invite volunteers to share stories of God's healing in their own lives or in the lives of people they know of or know personally.

❖ Pay special attention to students with handicapping conditions and/or chronic illnesses, who may feel left out or unloved by God because they have not been totally

healed of their infirmity. Differentiate between "cure," which may or may not occur, and "healing," which is God's power at work to bring wholeness into one's life even if an infirmity remains.

❖ Close this portion by using information from "A Human Problem" in Interpreting the Scripture to illustrate that one's attitude toward one's infirmity makes a huge difference in one's quality of life and relationship with God.

(4) Be Instruments of Healing in God's World

❖ Brainstorm with the class ways that they can be instruments of healing in God's world. Point out that "healing" need not be limited to physical ailments. Some people are mentally ill and need supportive friends just as surely as the paralyzed man did. Some people long for emotional healing, perhaps from painful memories of trauma or abuse. Encourage the adults to think of a wide variety of ways that they could help those in need of healing. List the ideas on newsprint.

❖ Ask the students to review the list silently and select one suggestion that they could implement in the coming week.

❖ Distribute paper and pencils and request that the adults write this sentence: *"With God's help, I will commit myself to. . . ."* The sentence should be completed with whatever activity they intend to do this week.

❖ Suggest that the students put this piece of paper in their Bible so that they will be reminded of their commitment during the week.

(5) Continue the Journey

❖ Create on newsprint a prayer list of persons who need healing. First names are sufficient, and the reason for the prayer need not be made known so as to protect the patient's privacy.

❖ Pray that the students will seek and

help to make God's healing power available to others. Ask that God empower them to keep faith with the commitment they made to assist someone who needs healing. Include the name of each person on the list in your prayer.

❖ Read aloud this preparation for next week's lesson. You may also want to post it on newsprint for the students to copy. **Prepare for next week's session entitled "The Prevailing Good" by reading the background scripture from Mark 14:53-65 and 15:1-5. The session will zoom in on Mark 14:53-65 and 15:1b-3. Keep yourself focused on this idea as you read: Those who do what is right are often viewed as a threat to society—and even as threats to the status quo of the religious community. Why should we not give up in despair and avoid the demands and sacrifices of doing "what is right"? By submitting to his arrest, Jesus showed us that living in faithfulness to God's plan can indeed lead to rejection and persecution. Ultimately, however, that rejection and persecution fulfill God's plan.**

❖ Read aloud the following three ideas.

Challenge the students to commit themselves to use these activities as a springboard to spiritual growth.

(1) **Pray for healing for yourself and others this week. This healing may be physical, but can also include mental and emotional healing.**

(2) **Read a book by an author, such as Larry Dosey, that deals with the connection between spirituality and healing. How does this connection work in your life? What evidence do you have?**

(3) **Offer to help someone who is having medical problems. Perhaps you could provide transportation to a doctor, or share a home-cooked meal with someone who is recuperating.**

❖ Sing or read aloud "Heal Me, Hands of Jesus."

❖ Say these words from 1 Peter one phrase at a time and ask the class to repeat them: **Prepare your minds for action; discipline yourselves; set all your hope on the grace that Jesus Christ will bring you when he is revealed.**

THE PREVAILING GOOD

PREVIEWING THE LESSON

Lesson Scripture: Mark 14:53-65; 15:1*b*-3
Background Scripture: Mark 14:53-65; 15:1-5
Key Verse: Mark 14:55

Focus of the Lesson:
Those who do what is right are often viewed as a threat to society—and even as threats to the status quo of the religious community. Why should we not give up in despair and avoid the demands and sacrifices of doing "what is right"? By submitting to his arrest, Jesus showed us that living in faithfulness to God's plan can indeed lead to rejection and persecution. Ultimately, however, that rejection and persecution fulfill God's plan.

Goals for the Learners:
(1) to examine Mark's account of Jesus' arrest and questioning by Pilate.
(2) to consider their experience of rejection in light of Jesus' persecution.
(3) to identify and use sources of faith and strength to do the right thing even in adversity.

Pronunciation Guide:
Sanhedrin   (san hee' druhn)

Supplies:
Bibles, newsprint and marker, paper and pencils, hymnals

READING THE SCRIPTURE

NRSV
Mark 14:53-65

53 They took Jesus to the high priest; and all the chief priests, the elders, and the scribes were assembled. 54 Peter had followed him at a distance, right into the courtyard of the high priest; and he was sitting with the guards, warming himself at the fire. **55 Now the chief priests and the whole council were looking for testimony against**

NIV
Mark 14:53-65

53They took Jesus to the high priest, and all the chief priests, elders and teachers of the law came together. 54Peter followed him at a distance, right into the courtyard of the high priest. There he sat with the guards and warmed himself at the fire.

55The chief priests and the whole Sanhedrin were looking for evidence

Jesus to put him to death; but they found none. 56 For many gave false testimony against him, and their testimony did not agree. 57 Some stood up and gave false testimony against him, saying, 58 "We heard him say, 'I will destroy this temple that is made with hands, and in three days I will build another, not made with hands.'" 59 But even on this point their testimony did not agree. 60 Then the high priest stood up before them and asked Jesus, "Have you no answer? What is it that they testify against you?" 61 But he was silent and did not answer. Again the high priest asked him, "Are you the Messiah, the Son of the Blessed One?" 62 Jesus said, "I am; and

'you will see the Son of Man
seated at the right hand of the Power,'
and 'coming with the clouds of heaven.'"

63 Then the high priest tore his clothes and said, "Why do we still need witnesses? 64 You have heard his blasphemy! What is your decision?" All of them condemned him as deserving death. 65 Some began to spit on him, to blindfold him, and to strike him, saying to him, "Prophesy!" The guards also took him over and beat him.

Mark 15:1b-3

They bound Jesus, led him away, and handed him over to Pilate. 2 Pilate asked him, "Are you the King of the Jews?" He answered him, "You say so." 3 Then the chief priests accused him of many things.

against Jesus so that they could put him to death, but they did not find any. [56]Many testified falsely against him, but their statements did not agree.

[57]Then some stood up and gave this false testimony against him: [58]"We heard him say, 'I will destroy this man-made temple and in three days will build another, not made by man.'" [59]Yet even then their testimony did not agree.

[60]Then the high priest stood up before them and asked Jesus, "Are you not going to answer? What is this testimony that these men are bringing against you?" [61]But Jesus remained silent and gave no answer.

Again the high priest asked him, "Are you the Christ, the Son of the Blessed One?"

[62]"I am," said Jesus. "And you will see the Son of Man sitting at the right hand of the Mighty One and coming on the clouds of heaven."

[63]The high priest tore his clothes. "Why do we need any more witnesses?" he asked. [64]"You have heard the blasphemy. What do you think?"

They all condemned him as worthy of death. [65]Then some began to spit at him; they blindfolded him, struck him with their fists, and said, "Prophesy!" And the guards took him and beat him.

Mark 15:1b-3

They bound Jesus, led him away and handed him over to Pilate.

[2]"Are you the king of the Jews?" asked Pilate.

"Yes, it is as you say," Jesus replied.

[3]The chief priests accused him of many things.

UNDERSTANDING THE SCRIPTURE

Mark 14:53. Just prior to the event described in this verse, Jesus had been arrested in the Garden of Gethsemane (Mark 14:32-50). His disciples had fled, and

now Jesus was alone at this gathering of first-century Israel's version of "the establishment." Everyone was there—"the high priest; and all the chief priests, the elders, and the scribes" (14:53). This group constituted the Sanhedrin, the ruling council of Judaism (see 14:55). The "high priest" was the leader. "The chief priests" included men who formerly had been high priest plus current Temple officials. "The elders" represented the leading families in Jerusalem. "The scribes" were experts in the law. Most scribes were Pharisees while the other members of the Sanhedrin tended toward the views of the Sadducees. The Pharisees were concerned with strict adherence to religious obligations. The Sadducees were the upper-class aristocrats and were concerned with maintaining the status quo to hold on to their lofty position of wealth and power.

Mark 14:54. To Peter's credit, at least he followed Jesus "at a distance." In fact, he came "right into the courtyard of the high priest." Peter courageously had gotten as close to the Sanhedrin meeting as permitted.

Mark 14:55. The goal of the Sanhedrin was to put Jesus to death. Their plan for arriving at their goal was muddled, though. They could not find sufficient testimony against Jesus to warrant putting him to death. A nighttime meeting of this council would have been highly unusual.

Mark 14:56-59. Those who testified falsely against Jesus could not get their stories together (14:56). The law required more than one witness to put a person to death (Numbers 35:30; Deuteronomy 17:6) or in fact to convict of any crime (Deuteronomy 19:15).

The accusation in Mark 14:57-59 evidently represented a twisting, or at least a misunderstanding, of a statement of Jesus. For example, Jesus' statement in 13:2 could have been distorted into the idea that Jesus himself would destroy the temple. An exchange similar to that in John 2:18-21 could have been the basis for the false testimony against Jesus (see also Mark 15:29).

Mark 14:60. In spite of the lack of validity in the testimony against Jesus, the high priest persisted. His questions were off base since the testimony had not met the legal requirements of being from a minimum of two witnesses whose testimony agreed.

Mark 14:61. Why did Jesus not answer the high priest's question? Perhaps Jesus saw that any response to such a question was futile since the Sanhedrin was not adhering to the law in its eagerness to do away with him. We are reminded of Isaiah 53:7 in which the Servant maintains his silence, "like a lamb that is led to the slaughter."

The high priest then pointedly demanded Jesus to tell him whether he was "the Messiah, the Son of the Blessed One" (15:61). What was the source of this charge? Perhaps Judas had reported to the chief priests that Jesus claimed to be the Messiah (see 14:10-11) based on Jesus' conversation with the disciples at Caesarea Philippi (see 8:29-30). Perhaps the word had simply gotten out. Perhaps the Jewish leaders themselves had observed Jesus' words and deeds and had deduced for themselves that these words and deeds indicated such a claim.

Mark 14:62. To the question of whether he was the Messiah, Jesus responded, "I am." He continued by combining the ideas of Daniel 7:13 and Psalm 110:1. "Son of Man" indicates exaltation and was messianic in nature. Jesus uniquely, however, poured new meaning into this term by connecting the exalted figure of the Son of Man with suffering and service (see Mark 10:45). "Seated at the right hand of the Power" refers to enthronement at the right hand of God. "The right hand" indicates the place of power, since a person's right hand generally is stronger than the left. "Coming with the clouds of heaven" in the context of Daniel 7:13 refers to the Son of Man's being presented in exaltation to "the Ancient One," God. The message of verse 62 thus is that although Jesus was on trial and about to be crucified, the Sanhedrin (plural "you") would soon become aware of God's exaltation of Jesus.

Mark 14:63-64. The high priest and the

rest of the Sanhedrin considered Jesus' claim to be the Messiah to make him liable to death. Their logic went like this: *Jesus has claimed to be the Messiah. Since, however, Jesus does not conform to our idea of what the Messiah is to be like, then Jesus must not be the Messiah. Therefore, since Jesus has claimed falsely to be the Messiah, he is worthy of death.* "All of them" pronounced that he deserved death (but see Luke 23:50-51).

Mark 14:65. The members of the Sanhedrin joined in spitting on and hitting Jesus, having blindfolded him. Then "the guards" physically beat him (see 14:54).

Mark 15:1. This "consultation" seems to be more official in nature than the gathering described in 14:53-65. The Sanhedrin next sent Jesus to Pilate, the Roman governor of Judea, to secure his official approval for Jesus to be put to death.

Mark 15:2. Pilate focused on the question that was important in his role as the Roman governor. Was Jesus "the King of the Jews"? A literal translation of the Greek words of Jesus' answer is, *You yourself say.* The NRSV translation, "You say so," preserves better the mysterious nature of the reply than the NIV translation, which interprets it as "Yes, it is as you say." Jesus' reply appears to indicate resistance to the idea of being "King of the Jews," certainly as Pilate would have understood it. Pilate would have seen the kingship as political and militaristic in nature. Thus, if Jesus had vigorously said *yes* to Pilate's question, Pilate likely would have found ample reason to convict him immediately rather than continuing the trial and in fact seeking to release Jesus. In addition, seeing the statement as being more enigmatic is in line with the theme of silence in 14:61 and 15:4-5.

Mark 15:3-5. Just as Jesus had been silent in the face of the accusations before the Sanhedrin, Jesus the Suffering Servant also was silent as the leaders of the Sanhedrin made further accusations against him before Pilate. The result was that Pilate, the Roman governor, "was amazed" at Jesus.

INTERPRETING THE SCRIPTURE

On Trial

The events of life constantly put people on trial. The greatest challenge, though, is not in itself that the events of life put us on trial for who we really are, what we truly believe, and what we actually are willing to do to see that right is done and good prevails. The greatest challenge is for us to recognize that we indeed are on trial and respond accordingly.

Jesus knew he was on trial. Evidently the gathering described in 14:53-65 was an informal, back-room assembly rather than an official trial. Even so, all the evidence pointed to Jesus' being on trial. He had been arrested, and testimony against him was given.

Jesus had told his disciples earlier that he "must undergo great suffering, and be rejected by the elders, the chief priests, and the scribes, and be killed" (Mark 8:31). Before Jesus was put on trial by the Sanhedrin and by Pilate, he already in a sense had been on trial on many occasions. He had been on trial, for example, in the temptation experience in the wilderness (1:13); in the five conflict situations with the scribes and Pharisees recorded in 2:1–3:6; in his hometown by the people who "took offense at him" (6:3); in his discussions with the Pharisees and scribes over keeping "the tradition of the elders" (7:5) and with the Pharisees over a question about marriage and divorce (10:2-12); in the Temple as he challenged the moneychangers (11:15-18); and then in the last week of his life in his encounters with everybody in the Jewish establishment, meaning the chief priests, and scribes, the elders, the Herodians, and the Sadducees (11:27–12:44). So for Jesus to be literally on trial after his betrayal by Judas was but a continuation of all that he had faced before.

When we consider how Jesus faced these trials, we generally want to run quickly to his divinity and say that his divinity was what enabled him to be victorious. While not denying Jesus' divinity, we would be closer to the mark if we recognized that it was not his divinity but his determined and committed humanity that Jesus called upon for courage. For us to appeal to Jesus' divinity is to make it too easy to absolve ourselves of any need to be faithful under trial ourselves.

We ourselves might be led to greater faithfulness when the times of testing come if we would decide in advance not to be surprised by such trials and also to decide that, come what may, we will seek to be faithful (see 1 Peter 4:12). We should also recognize that although the time of trial may come with a big demand being placed on us, it may also come in the seemingly small, day-to-day challenges of life. It may come in questions such as these: How will we treat the person who is different from us? Will we speak up or will we keep silent when we see injustice occurring? Will we be honest in all the relationships of our lives, including at work? Will we repeat—or start—a bit of hurtful talk even though we're not quite sure whether it is true? (It's called gossip and may even qualify as slander or libel, even when Christians do it, even when it's about celebrities or political leaders.) Will we speak of our commitment to Christ when opportunity presents itself, or will we fade into the woodwork? Will we be a "24/7" committed Christians or merely "Sunday Christians"?

We often seem to think that being committed to Christ is like being asked to plunk down a large sum of money—say $100,000—once, and once and for all. We may indeed be asked to make such a commitment, perhaps of money, perhaps of something even more valuable, our very lives. That kind of Christian commitment may be called for, in which on a given day Christ may call us to take a stand for him in a way that will cost us much. It's also likely, too, that we will be asked to pay out our commitment a bit at a time—$5 here, $10 there—in the smaller, daily commitments and choices that Christ calls us to make. However we find ourselves "on trial" as Christians, theologian Georgia Harkness said succinctly and well what our task is. She wrote, "To be a Christian is to seek to do the will of God at all costs."

Accused

Jesus' accusers went to great lengths to get a conviction. They first sought false witnesses against Jesus. Alas, "their testimony did not agree" (14:59). The tactics shifted when Jesus refused to respond to his accusers. Then the high priest asked Jesus (14:61), "Are you the Messiah, the Son of the Blessed One?" Jesus confessed, "I am" (14:62).

When Jesus was accused of being the Messiah, there was indeed plenty of evidence that he was. Early on, Jesus' contemporaries had recognized that "he taught them as one having authority, and not as the scribes" (1:22). Then, after he had pronounced to the paralytic that his sins were forgiven, he had healed him, saying, "So that you may know that the Son of Man has authority on earth to forgive sins" (2:10). Many other incidents had occurred to back up Jesus' statement of who he was.

Couched in modern language, the following question puts the matter pointedly as we seek to apply this statement and Jesus' response to our lives: *If you were arrested for being a Christian, would there be enough evidence to convict you?* Jesus' statement of his identity, plus Jesus' words and deeds that backed up the statement, call us to consider the extent to which our lives give evidence of our profession of commitment to Christ.

Condemned but Faithful

Jesus' statement that he was indeed the Messiah brought immediate condemnation by the high priest. He "tore his clothes" (14:63). This action demonstrated his belief that Jesus' claim was blasphemous. He put this belief into words in 14:64, "You have heard his blasphemy."

The Sanhedrin seized on the charge that Jesus was guilty of blasphemy as the opportunity to send Jesus to Pilate to obtain conviction by the Roman government. Before Pilate, the chief priests accused Jesus "of many things" (15:3). Pilate would take some time to try to manipulate his way out of the situation, but Jesus would stand condemned in the end.

Several decades ago, missionary nurse Mavis Pate was shot and killed when guerrillas ambushed, evidently by mistake, the car in which she was riding in the nation in which she was serving. A pastor on the personnel committee of the mission-sending agency recalled what she had said when she had sought appointment as a missionary. When asked why she wanted to be a missionary, he recalled her saying, "I'm really trying to find something big enough to die for. I think being a missionary is the answer."

In the final analysis, all of us are deciding for ourselves what is "big enough to die for." We would be wise to make sure our answer is worth our lives.

When Martin Luther was on trial before the Diet of Worms for his acts on behalf of the Christian faith, he said, "On this I take my stand; I can do no other. God help me." Let us pray that in the daily as well as the ultimate challenges to our faith, we too will be completely faithful.

SHARING THE SCRIPTURE

PREPARING TO TEACH

Preparing Our Hearts

This week's devotional reading is found in Mark 14:17-21. Here we see a scene of intimate hospitality. The disciples are reclining at the table as was customary, eating the Passover meal with Jesus for the last time. Jesus' announcement of betrayal must have hit all but one of the Twelve as a thunderbolt. They immediately responded by asking one another, "Surely, not I?" (14:19). Jesus faced the ultimate opposition to his ministry by one of his closest friends. How do you handle trials and opposition, especially situations of betrayal? What is the worst trial you have undergone? How did you get through it?

Pray that you and your students will seek God's grace to handle opposition even as you seek to enable good to prevail.

Preparing Our Minds

Study the background from Mark 14:53–65 and 15:1-5. The lesson scripture focuses on Mark 14:53-65 and 15:1b-3.

Write on newsprint:

the thought questions for the "Identify and Use Sources of Faith and Strength to Do the Right Thing Even in Adversity" portion.

information for next week's lesson, found under "Continue the Journey."

Plan the lectures as suggested in the portion entitled "Examine Mark's Account of Jesus' Arrest and Questioning by Pilate."

LEADING THE CLASS

(1) Gather to Learn

❖ Welcome the class members and introduce any guests.

❖ Pray that the students will recognize the need to stand firm in the face of opposition so they can continue to do whatever is right and good.

❖ Consider current examples of persecution, particularly against members of specific religious groups, which exist around the world.

- Brainstorm with the students some examples of such persecution.
- Identify students' questions concerning persecution. Write these questions on newsprint and post it where everyone can see.

❖ Read aloud today's focus statement: **Those who do what is right are often viewed as a threat to society—and even as threats to the status quo of the religious community. Why should we not give up in despair and avoid the demands and sacrifices of doing "what is right"? By submitting to his arrest, Jesus showed us that living in faithfulness to God's plan can indeed lead to rejection and persecution. Ultimately, however, that rejection and persecution fulfill God's plan.**

(2) Examine Mark's Account of Jesus' Arrest and Questioning by Pilate

❖ Study Mark 14:53-65.

- Select volunteers to portray a narrator, someone giving false testimony (verse 58), the high priest, and Jesus. These actors are to read Mark 14:53-65 as a drama. Ask the class members to imagine that they are part of the Sanhedrin as these proceedings are occurring.
- Discuss these questions with the class.
  (1) According to the text, why was it so important to the religious officials to get rid of Jesus?
  (2) What other motives might have the religious leaders had for their actions?

- Create a lecture to help the learners understand who the members of the council were, the problem with the false testimony, the questions about whether or not Jesus was the Messiah, and the charges the Sanhedrin could use to claim Jesus was deserving of death. You will find information in the Understanding the Scripture section to help you write this lecture.

❖ Study Jesus' questioning before Pilate.
- Choose three persons to read the parts of Pilate, Jesus, and a narrator. They are to read Mark 15:1b (start with "They bound") through verse 3.
- Create a lecture on Mark 15:1-5, based on ideas in the Understanding the Scripture portion, to help the students understand why Pilate and Jesus acted as they did.

(3) Consider Learners' Experiences of Rejection in Light of Jesus' Persecution

❖ Invite the students to talk with the class or a small group about experiences that they have had of being rejected or ridiculed for taking a stand on a particular issue related to their religious beliefs. Encourage the speakers to state:
- the nature of the incident.
- the ways in which they were ridiculed for their stance.
- how they were able to stand firm.
- how this situation was finally resolved.

❖ Discuss this question with the entire class: **When you are being ridiculed for your beliefs or your stance on an issue that is informed by your beliefs, how does your knowledge of Jesus' response to persecution empower you to stand firm?**

(4) Identify and Use Sources of Faith and Strength to Do the Right Thing Even in Adversity

❖ Distribute paper and pencils. Post newsprint on which you have previously written the following thought questions.

Provide quiet time for the students to reflect on these questions. You may want to conclude this activity by asking the students to comment on their responses.

(1) **When you face adversity or ridicule, where do you find the strength to withstand the taunts hurled against you?**

(2) **How does your faith become a source of strength for you?**

❖ Look again at the list of names or groups that was brainstormed at the beginning of the class. Invite the students to express information and/or opinions about the sources of faith and strength that have sustained these people.

❖ Ask the students to write on their sheet of paper these words, which you will need to read aloud, and complete the sentence: **When people ridicule me for my religious beliefs, I commit myself to rely on the following sources of faith and strength: . . . .**

(5) Continue the Journey

❖ Pray that the participants will do what is right, regardless of the sacrifices they must make to do so.

❖ Read aloud this preparation for next week's lesson. You may also want to post it on newsprint for the students to copy. **Prepare for next week's session entitled "Hope in the Midst of Despair" by reading Mark 16 as the background scripture and studying verses 1-8 and 12-15 most carefully. Focus your attention on this idea: When** things continue to go from bad to worse to worst, people tend to accept the situation as inevitable and hopeless. Is our human situation bound to be one of hopelessness and helplessness? Jesus' empty grave bears witness to God's ultimate power to exceed all human expectations.

❖ Read aloud the following three ideas. Challenge the students to commit themselves to use these activities as a springboard to spiritual growth.

(1) **Encourage someone who is facing ridicule or persecution for his or her religious beliefs to stand firm.**

(2) **Pray for persons around the world who are being persecuted for their religious beliefs. If you can contact any of these persons, let them know that your prayers for faith and courage are with them.**

(3) **Examine your own life. Are you living an alternative or countercultural lifestyle compared to others who do not profess faith in Christ? What lengths are you willing to go to remain faithful, even in the face of adversity?**

❖ Sing or read aloud "Stand By Me."

❖ Say these words from 1 Peter one phrase at a time and ask the class to repeat them: **Prepare your minds for action; discipline yourselves; set all your hope on the grace that Jesus Christ will bring you when he is revealed.**

HOPE IN THE MIDST OF DESPAIR

PREVIEWING THE LESSON

Lesson Scripture: Mark 16:1-8, 12-15
Background Scripture: Mark 16
Key Verse: Mark 16:6

Focus of the Lesson:
When things continue to go from bad to worse to worst, people tend to accept the situation as inevitable and hopeless. Is our human situation bound to be one of hopelessness and helplessness? Jesus' empty grave bears witness to God's ultimate power to exceed all human expectations.

Goals for the Learners:
(1) to examine Mark's account of Jesus' resurrection.
(2) to relate to feelings and reactions of Jesus' followers at the empty tomb.
(3) to identify how the Resurrection provides hope amid difficult situations and prompts them to act.

Supplies:
Bibles, newsprint and marker, paper and pencils, hymnals, newpapers and/or news magazines

READING THE SCRIPTURE

NRSV
Mark 16:1-8, 12-15

When the sabbath was over, Mary Magdalene, and Mary the mother of James, and Salome bought spices, so that they might go and anoint him. 2 And very early on the first day of the week, when the sun had risen, they went to the tomb. 3 They had been saying to one another, "Who will roll away the stone for us from the entrance to the tomb?" 4 When they looked up, they saw that the stone, which was very large, had already been rolled back. 5 As they entered the tomb, they saw a young man,

NIV
Mark 16:1-8, 12-15

When the Sabbath was over, Mary Magdalene, Mary the mother of James, and Salome bought spices so that they might go to anoint Jesus' body. ²Very early on the first day of the week, just after sunrise, they were on their way to the tomb ³and they asked each other, "Who will roll the stone away from the entrance of the tomb?"

⁴But when they looked up, they saw that the stone, which was very large, had been rolled away. ⁵As they entered the tomb, they saw a young man dressed in a white robe

dressed in a white robe, sitting on the right side; and they were alarmed. **6 But he said to them, "Do not be alarmed; you are looking for Jesus of Nazareth, who was crucified. He has been raised; he is not here. Look, there is the place they laid him.** 7 But go, tell his disciples and Peter that he is going ahead of you to Galilee; there you will see him, just as he told you." 8 So they went out and fled from the tomb, for terror and amazement had seized them; and they said nothing to anyone, for they were afraid.

12 After this he appeared in another form to two of them, as they were walking into the country. 13 And they went back and told the rest, but they did not believe them.

14 Later he appeared to the eleven themselves as they were sitting at the table; and he upbraided them for their lack of faith and stubbornness, because they had not believed those who saw him after he had risen. 15 And he said to them, "Go into all the world and proclaim the good news to the whole creation."

sitting on the right side, and they were alarmed.

6"Don't be alarmed," he said. "You are looking for Jesus the Nazarene, who was crucified. He has risen! He is not here. See the place where they laid him. 7But go, tell his disciples and Peter, 'He is going ahead of you into Galilee. There you will see him, just as he told you.' "

8Trembling and bewildered, the women went out and fled from the tomb. They said nothing to anyone, because they were afraid.

12Afterward Jesus appeared in a different form to two of them while they were walking in the country. 13These returned and reported it to the rest; but they did not believe them either.

14Later Jesus appeared to the Eleven as they were eating; he rebuked them for their lack of faith and their stubborn refusal to believe those who had seen him after he had risen.

15He said to them, "Go into all the world and preach the good news to all creation."

UNDERSTANDING THE SCRIPTURE

Mark 16:1-2. The Sabbath began at sunset on Friday and ended at sunset on Saturday. After sunset on the Sabbath, the women "bought spices, so that they might go and anoint him" (16:1). Then the women came to the tomb on Sunday "very early . . . when the sun had risen" (16:2).

Mary Magdalene witnessed Jesus' crucifixion (15:40) and burial (15:47). She had been "cured of evil spirits" (Luke 8:2; see Mark 16:9). Mary was the mother of James, although which James is uncertain. Perhaps it was "James son of Alphaeus," one of the Twelve (Mark 3:18). This Mary's other son was Joses (see Matthew 27:56 where his name is written as "Joseph"), and thus she was the "Mary the mother of Joses" who had joined Mary Magdalene in observing where Jesus was buried (Mark 15:47). Who

was Salome? The suggestion has been made that Salome was the mother of James and John, the sons of Zebedee (see Matthew 27:56). Such a connection is uncertain, however.

Why did the women go to anoint Jesus' body on Sunday when he had been buried on Friday? To anoint a body after it had been in the tomb so long would have been unusual. Perhaps the women felt Jesus' body had not been cared for appropriately when Joseph of Arimathea had buried it on Friday as the Sabbath approached (Mark 15:46). Or perhaps in Friday's confusion the women were unaware that Joseph and Nicodemus had indeed cared for the body (see John 19:38-40). Perhaps the women simply wanted to demonstrate their care.

As we try to understand the circumstances of Jesus' resurrection, we often seek to coordinate the differing details of the four Gospels' accounts. Doing so is difficult if not impossible. Our understanding of Jesus' resurrection would be helped if we kept in mind that although we may not be able to coordinate the details, the message of the reality and meaning of Jesus' resurrection is what is most important.

Mark 16:3-4. On their way to the tomb, the women were talking about how they would gain access. Particularly for the more well-to-do, as Joseph of Arimethea was described in Matthew 27:57, the custom was to bury the body in a cave-like site that had been hollowed out or constructed. Archaeological discoveries have revealed that a large, wheel-like stone that was rolled down a grooved track would have blocked the entrance to such a tomb. Moving the stone would have required strength beyond that of the women. When the women arrived, the large stone "had already been rolled back."

Mark 16:5. The women "entered the tomb." Then they saw "a young man, dressed in a white robe." The women were alarmed by the fact that he was there and Jesus' body was not. The figure was an angel, as is implied by the white robe (see also Matthew 28:2-7; Luke 24:4-7, 22-23; John 20:12-13).

Mark 16:6. The "young man" comforted the women. He then connected what the women knew—that Jesus had been crucified—with the information that Jesus had "been raised; he is not here." As if to verify and affirm this message, he pointed out "the place they laid him."

Mark 16:7. The young man commissioned the women to bear the news of Jesus' resurrection to "his disciples and Peter." Singling out Peter likely was intended to indicate that Peter's denials would not prevent him from continued service (14:66-72).

The mention that the resurrected Jesus was "going ahead of you to Galilee" confirmed Jesus' promise in 14:28. Still, this statement has puzzled interpreters through

the centuries, since many of Jesus' resurrection appearances occurred in and near Jerusalem (Luke 24:13-52; John 20:19-29; Acts 1:1-12). Matthew records no resurrection appearances to the disciples in Jerusalem but makes much of Galilee (Matthew 28:7-10, 16-20; see also John 21, which takes place in Galilee).

Mark 16:8. How did the women respond to these alarming circumstances? Basically, they were afraid, recognizing the evidence of God's activity. The Greek word for fear in this verse is used elsewhere in Mark to refer to fearful awe in response to God's activity in Jesus (see 4:41; 5:15, 33, 36; 6:50; 9:6, 32).

The best manuscript evidence indicates that the Gospel of Mark ends with this verse. That is why most modern translations—including NRSV and NIV—print material after this verse in a separate section, indicating it is not original to Mark. Some Bible students suggest that the last lines of Mark could have been lost since they would have been at the end of the scroll and that these "lost" verses would have told of the Resurrection appearances. Other commentators wonder whether Mark meant to write more but was interrupted. Such speculation is intended mainly to explain what appears to be an abrupt ending to Mark's Gospel. Perhaps, though, Mark meant to end the Gospel on this note of fear and amazement in order to confront readers with questions such as: *What about you? Will you believe?* The challenge would then be to move to faith in the risen Christ without having seen him, as the women thus were challenged.

Mark 16:9-11. These verses and those that follow are part of what is known as the longer ending of Mark. This material was added to Mark later, with the first references to it dating only to the second-century A.D. John 20:1-2, 11-19 contains something of a parallel to the experience of Mary Magdalene in these verses.

Mark 16:12-15. A parallel to verses 12-13 can be seen in Luke 24:13-35. A gathering similar to that in 16:14 is described in Luke 24:36-49 and John 29:19-29. Verse 15 reminds us of Matthew 28:19.

Mark 16:16-20. Similar meanings to that in verse 16 can be found by combining such verses as John 3:18; Acts 2:38; 10:47; Romans 10:9. References can be found in other New Testament literature to exorcisms (see Acts 8:6-7) and to speaking in tongues (see Acts 2:4-11; 1 Corinthians 12:27-30; 14:1-40).

Healing the sick was also part of the church's ministry (see Acts 28:8; 1 Corinthians 12:9; James 5:14-15). No parallels exist in the New Testament to the statement about handling snakes and drinking poison. The only possible reference to handling snakes is in what the natives of Malta observed about Paul (Acts 28:1-6). Parallels to some of the ideas in verses 19-20 can be found in Luke 24:50-52 and Acts 1:1-11.

INTERPRETING THE SCRIPTURE

Doing the Next Thing

Sometimes when things look hopeless, the best we can do to deal with our hopelessness is to turn to the next practical thing to be done and do it. On September 11, 2001, that is what many people found themselves doing. They did what they needed to do to survive, they helped one another with their wounds, they looked for survivors, and they did the thousand other things that would bring aid and recovery to people who had lost much.

Perhaps that is what the three women were doing. They had followed and loved Jesus, but he had been crucified and buried. They must have felt the loss as much as anyone ever grieved the loss of someone dear. Darkness and sorrow surely had engulfed them as they watched his body be laid in the tomb (see Mark 15:47; Matthew 27:56). Anyone who has gone through the funeral of someone dear can identify with their sorrow.

Yet as the Sabbath ended and a new day began, they felt they had to do something. For one reason or another, they believed they needed to do something to care for Jesus' body. So they made plans to go to the tomb (Mark 16:1).

The women were doing what people need to do when things seem hopeless—just do something. Simply taking action to do the next thing that needs to be done can do much to help us deal with our hopelessness when a great blow has struck us.

The prophet Elijah found himself in a situation of great hopelessness (see 1 Kings 19). King Ahab and Queen Jezebel were seeking his life. Elijah felt so bereft of hope that he wanted to die. Instead of dying, though, Elijah soon found himself doing some very practical things. He slept a while. Then, at the encouragement of an angel of the Lord, he ate and drank. Not long after, the Lord commanded him to get back to work fulfilling the commission he had given him.

Sometimes when life seems at its darkest, simply taking action of some sort can help us move on. Of course, there is a place and a time for letting ourselves and others grieve deeply. God has so made us that feeling and expressing grief is a necessary part of dealing with the loss of someone dear. Great harm can occur in our lives if we do not allow ourselves to do so. Still, there is also a place and a time for taking practical action to help us move on with our lives.

Looking for an Answer

On their way to the tomb, the women knew that the stone across the entrance was too heavy for them to roll away. Then they received the first of a number of surprises. The stone already had been rolled away.

Looking into the tomb, they received a second surprise. They saw "a young man, dressed in a white robe" (16:5). The other Gospels state what Mark hints at: The "young man" was an angel, a messenger from God (Matthew 28:2-7; Luke 24:4-7, 22-23; John 20:12-13). He gave them the surprising news that Jesus "has been raised" (16:6). Still another surprise was the message that they would see Jesus again, just as Jesus had promised.

How did the women respond? Verse 8 uses multiple descriptive words—"fled," "terror," "amazement," "afraid." No human being had ever experienced anything comparable to what these women experienced. Anyone who has ever heard the shocking news of a loved one's death knows what a blow such news is. Those who have experienced great tragedy speak of how it seemed the world itself was coming apart. The news the women received was even more shocking. The news of a loved one's death is a great blow, but it is a blow that others have felt. The news of Jesus' resurrection, though, was of a different order entirely, beyond the bounds of human experience. No wonder the women were afraid. They were facing the issue of how to make sense of life and death.

When a loved one dies, in the midst of our grief we may ask ourselves about the nature of life and death. We may even think about our own death. We may find ourselves pondering the meaning of our lives and considering death as it relates quite personally to us. We may come to recognize that dying is not just something that happens to someone else. The only answer that comes close to satisfying our quest for understanding what both life and death are all about is found in Jesus' resurrection. If our hope is not in Jesus and in what God did in raising him from the dead, what hope do we have?

Receiving Confirmation

These verses speak of incidents that remind us of incidents in the other Gospels.

The verses tell of Jesus' resurrection appearances. The mention of the two disciples who "were walking into the country" reminds us of Jesus' appearance to the two disciples on the road to Emmaus (Luke 24:13-35). The reference to the Eleven at a meal reminds us of more than one occasion recorded in the other Gospels (see Luke 24:36-49; John 20:19-29). These experiences of the disciples with the risen Jesus confirmed for them and for us the reality of Jesus' resurrection.

Do we need such confirmation? Yes, for death is an unknown, a great unknown, and we want whatever confirmation we can find that death is not the end. Jesus' resurrection is the great confirmation that good triumphs over evil, hope overcomes despair, and life goes on beyond death. The blows of life come, but we can live through them, and we can live forever, even beyond death, because of Christ.

Obeying the Commission

How shall we respond to Jesus' resurrection? We are to tell others. The women first received the command to "tell" (16:7). Then Jesus commanded the Eleven, "Go into all the world and proclaim the good news to the whole creation" (16:15).

The revolutionary news of Jesus' resurrection needs to be told, for Jesus' resurrection provides an entirely new perspective on life. When we recognize what a difference the news makes, we will obey Jesus' command to tell it.

Joseph Cardinal Bernardin of Chicago died of pancreatic cancer in November 1996, only thirteen days after completing his remarkable book, *The Gift of Peace*. During the time between diagnosis of the disease in June 1995 and his death in November 1996, he continued to minister to people, developing a special ministry to cancer patients. In a news conference after the cardinal received news that his condition had worsened, a reporter asked whether he had anything special he wanted to accomplish during his remaining time. The cardinal initially responded that he would continue to work as much as he could and that he also wanted to visit relatives. Then he replied that demonstrating in his life the way he prepared for death would be the most important thing he could accomplish for the benefit of people.

Preparing for death has to do with what we believe about death and what we believe about life. Jesus' life, death, and resurrection help us know both how to live and how to die. In fact, Jesus' resurrection shows us that when we know how to die we also know how to live. Such a message of hope is worth telling—and living.

SHARING THE SCRIPTURE

PREPARING TO TEACH

Preparing Our Hearts

This week's devotional reading is found in Matthew 28:16-20. In a postresurrection appearance, Jesus commissions his disciples to go into the world and make disciples. Matthew notes that some of the disciples "doubted." And can we blame them? They knew with certainty that Jesus had died on the cross. They must have been filled with grief and pain. In the midst of their despair, Jesus appears and commands them to undertake a worldwide ministry. What evidence can you give to show that you as an individual and your church as a body are intentional about fulfilling the Great Commission? What else could you do?

Pray that you and your students will recognize that through faith we can have hope and see a bright future, even in the midst of despair.

Preparing Our Minds

Study the background scripture, which is Mark 16. Look carefully at the lesson scripture in Mark 16:1-8, 12-15.

Review the Easter morning story as told in Matthew 28:1-15, Luke 24:1-12, and John 20:1-18. Look for similarities and differences among the four accounts.

Write on newsprint:

    sentence stem for the Gather to Learn portion.

information for next week's lesson, found under "Continue the Journey."

Collect newspapers and magazines for the activity under "Identify How the Resurrection Provides Hope and Prompts Action Amid Difficult Situations." Call several students and ask them to bring these publications as well.

Plan a lecture to conclude "Examine Mark's Account of Jesus' Resurrection."

LEADING THE CLASS

(1) Gather to Learn

❖ Welcome the class members and introduce any guests.

❖ Pray that the students will find hope in the midst of despair as they consider how Jesus' resurrection brings new life and faith.

❖ Begin to consider beliefs about resurrection. Remember that not all Christians share the same views, so if someone voices a minority opinion ensure that his or her idea is not simply dismissed.

■ Post this sentence stem on newsprint: **My belief about resurrection from the dead is that. . . .**

■ Invite students to call out endings to the sentence. Write ideas on the newsprint. If the class is large, work in small groups to do this.

■ Try, if possible, to categorize or group statements so as to summarize the main points.

❖ Read aloud today's focus statement: **When things continue to go from bad to worse to worst, people tend to accept the situation as inevitable and hopeless. Is our human situation bound to be one of hope-lessness and helplessness? Jesus' empty grave bears witness to God's ultimate power to exceed all human expectations.**

(2) Examine Mark's Account of Jesus' Resurrection

❖ Select a volunteer to read Mark 16:1-8.

■ Encourage the students to act as news reporters and let them brainstorm questions that they would ask the women. List their ideas on newsprint. Invite the group to answer as many questions as possible.

■ Make note of the comments in the Understanding the Scripture portion for Mark 16:8 and 16:9-11 concerning what scholars believe may be the orig-inal ending of Mark in verse 8 and the additional verses that were likely added later to change the negative ending to a positive one.

■ Invite the students to comment on their impression of the Easter story if it were to end at verse 8.

❖ Choose someone to read Mark 16:12-15.

■ Use the information in Understanding the Scripture to compare Mark 16:12-15 to the other three Gospels. If time per-mits, include comparisons for other verses of Mark. You may want to do this as a lecture, or involve the students in a discussion.

(3) Relate to Feelings and Reactions of Jesus' Followers at the Empty Tomb

❖ Distribute paper and pencils. Ask the students to write a letter to God expressing their reactions to and feelings about death— their own that will come some day, or that of a loved one who is already deceased. If some adults seem reluctant to do this because they have negative feelings about death, remind them that the psalmists often expressed negative emotions, for they trusted God to be receptive to all their needs and feelings. (If someone has recently lost a loved one and chooses not to participate in this activity, honor that decision.)

❖ Invite volunteers to share words or phrases from their letters that express their reactions and/or feelings. Write these ideas on newsprint.

❖ Ask the adults to identify words or phrases that Jesus' followers might also have written on the Saturday between Good Friday and Easter Sunday. (The class may choose to add other ideas to the newsprint.) Discuss how the class members' reactions to and feelings about the loss of a loved one relate to those of Jesus' followers.

❖ Wrap up by surveying the students to see how (or if) they can relate their loved one's death to the hope of Easter that Jesus' original followers experienced in the midst of their despair.

(4) Identify How the Resurrection Provides Hope and Prompts Action Amid Difficult Situations

❖ **Option 1:** Help the adults to identify how resurrection faith provides hope amid difficult world or local situations.

■ Provide newspapers and news magazines. Ask the class members individually or in groups to scan these publications to find information about challenging local, national, and global situations.

■ Ask individuals or groups to report their findings.

■ Discuss these questions:
   (1) **What hope can you discern in this situation?**
   (2) **What role does Jesus' resurrection play in giving you hope that this situation can be resolved?**
   (3) **If you can affirm hope based on**

Jesus' resurrection, what action can you take to help resolve the difficult situation(s) you have identified?

❖ **Option 2:** Help the adults to identify how resurrection faith gives them hope in the midst of personal crises.

- Distribute paper and pencils. Invite the adults to write about a crises or difficult situation they are facing.
- Suggest that they look at this situation in light of their faith in Jesus' resurrection to discern where they can see glimmers of hope.
- Encourage the adults to make a silent commitment to God concerning any action they will take.

(5) Continue the Journey

❖ Pray that the participants will be able to find hope in the midst of difficult situations by recalling Jesus' resurrection from the dead.

❖ Read aloud this preparation for next week's lesson. You may also want to post it on newsprint for the students to copy. **Prepare for next week's session entitled "Experiencing True Happiness" by reading the Beatitudes from Matthew 5:1-16. Keep this focus in mind as you read: Culture and the media reinforce each other in equating "the good life" with material wealth, unbeatable power, and sensual**

pleasures. Still, people feel there is never enough; there must be more! Where and how can people find that which brings true happiness and real living? Jesus taught that true happiness is found not in what one possesses and controls, but in the spirit in which one gives and lives, and how one's life glorifies God.

❖ Read aloud the following three ideas. Challenge the students to commit themselves to use these activities as a springboard to spiritual growth.

(1) **Comfort someone who is mourning. Remind the bereaved one that Jesus' resurrection brings hope to us amid our grief and despair.**

(2) **Write in your spiritual journal about your own beliefs concerning death and resurrection. Search your Bible to find passages that support or challenge your beliefs.**

(3) **Survey friends, coworkers, and others to find out what they believe about the possibility of resurrection and life after death. You may want to share your own beliefs, but do so in a winsome way.**

❖ Sing or read aloud "He Lives."

❖ Say these words from 1 Peter one phrase at a time and ask the class to repeat them: **Prepare your minds for action; discipline yourselves; set all your hope on the grace that Jesus Christ will bring you when he is revealed.**

UNIT 2: JESUS' MINISTRY OF TEACHING (GOSPEL OF MATTHEW)
EXPERIENCING TRUE HAPPINESS

PREVIEWING THE LESSON

Lesson Scripture: Matthew 5:1-16
Background Scripture: Matthew 5:1-16
Key Verse: Matthew 5:6

Focus of the Lesson:
Culture and the media reinforce one another in equating "the good life" with material wealth, unbeatable power, and sensual pleasures. Still, people feel there is never enough; there must be more! Where and how can people find that which brings true happiness and real living? Jesus taught that true happiness is found not in what one possesses and controls, but in the spirit in which one gives and lives, and how one's life glorifies God.

Goals for the Learners:
(1) to analyze the Beatitudes and explain each in its context.
(2) to compare their ideas of happiness with those of the media and of the Beatitudes.
(3) to apply at least one Beatitude to a current situation.

Pronunciation Guide:
Beatitude   (bee at' uh tyood)

Supplies:
Bibles, newsprint and marker, paper and pencils, hymnals, optional commentaries

---

READING THE SCRIPTURE

NRSV
Matthew 5:1-16

When Jesus saw the crowds, he went up the mountain; and after he sat down, his disciples came to him. 2 Then he began to speak, and taught them, saying:

3 "Blessed are the poor in spirit, for theirs is the kingdom of heaven.

4 "Blessed are those who mourn, for they will be comforted.

NIV
Matthew 5:1-16

Now when he saw the crowds, he went up on a mountainside and sat down. His disciples came to him, 2and he began to teach them, saying:

3 "Blessed are the poor in spirit,
for theirs is the kingdom of heaven.

4 Blessed are those who mourn,
for they will be comforted.

5 "Blessed are the meek, for they will inherit the earth.

6 "Blessed are those who hunger and thirst for righteousness, for they will be filled.

7 "Blessed are the merciful, for they will receive mercy.

8 "Blessed are the pure in heart, for they will see God.

9 "Blessed are the peacemakers, for they will be called children of God.

10 "Blessed are those who are persecuted for righteousness' sake, for theirs is the kingdom of heaven.

11 "Blessed are you when people revile you and persecute you and utter all kinds of evil against you falsely on my account. 12 Rejoice and be glad, for your reward is great in heaven, for in the same way they persecuted the prophets who were before you.

13 "You are the salt of the earth; but if salt has lost its taste, how can its saltiness be restored? It is no longer good for anything, but is thrown out and trampled under foot.

14 "You are the light of the world. A city built on a hill cannot be hid. 15 No one after lighting a lamp puts it under the bushel basket, but on the lampstand, and it gives light to all in the house. 16 In the same way, let your light shine before others, so that they may see your good works and give glory to your Father in heaven."

5 Blessed are the meek,
   for they will inherit the earth.

**6 Blessed are those who hunger and thirst
   for righteousness,
   for they will be filled.**

7 Blessed are the merciful,
   for they will be shown mercy.

8 Blessed are the pure in heart,
   for they will see God.

9 Blessed are the peacemakers,
   for they will be called sons of God.

10 Blessed are those who are persecuted
      because of righteousness,
   for theirs is the kingdom of heaven.

11 "Blessed are you when people insult you, persecute you and falsely say all kinds of evil against you because of me. 12 Rejoice and be glad, because great is your reward in heaven, for in the same way they persecuted the prophets who were before you.

13 "You are the salt of the earth. But if the salt loses its saltiness, how can it be made salty again? It is no longer good for anything, except to be thrown out and trampled by men.

14 "You are the light of the world. A city on a hill cannot be hidden. 15 Neither do people light a lamp and put it under a bowl. Instead they put it on its stand, and it gives light to everyone in the house. 16 In the same way, let your light shine before men, that they may see your good deeds and praise your Father in heaven."

UNDERSTANDING THE SCRIPTURE

Matthew 5:1. From Matthew 4:23-25 we learn that "the mountain" is in Galilee. Galilee is the northern portion of the land of Israel. "The crowds" refers to the people who "followed him from Galilee, the Decapolis, Jerusalem, Judea, and from beyond the Jordan" (4:25). Having ascended the mountain, Jesus "sat down," the familiar practice of a teacher.

Matthew 5:2. Verse 1 states that "his dis-

ciples came to him." At the end of the Sermon on the Mount, however, we see also that "the crowds were astounded at his teaching" (7:28). Jesus "taught" them, providing instruction in living "the good news of the kingdom" that he proclaimed (see 4:23).

Matthew 5:3. This verse begins the Beatitudes, which are recorded in verses 3-11. The word "beatitudes" refers to statements about happiness or blessedness. Each verse in 5:3-11 begins with a word that refers to this quality. These statements describe the truly happy or blessed people. These people have responded to the good news of the Kingdom as taught by and exemplified in Jesus Christ. Jesus contrasted these Kingdom people to those who follow the world's ways. The Beatitudes describe characteristics of Kingdom people rather than categories of people who are happy or blessed.

Who are "the poor in spirit"? They are the people who feel keenly their need of God's help and acknowledge this need. Such people receive the blessings of God's kingdom. Matthew's Gospel speaks of "the kingdom of heaven" in referring to the kingdom of God, likely because Matthew's Gospel is concerned to relate Jesus' teachings and ministry to Judaism. Matthew thus uses "heaven" as a way of speaking of God reverently, without mentioning God's name.

Matthew 5:4. "Those who mourn" are those who grieve over the gap between what God wishes and the conditions they see about them and in themselves. This beatitude assures that they "will be comforted." That is, they will be consoled and encouraged as the blessings of the Kingdom come to pass. These blessings will come as God's will is done, "on earth as it is in heaven" (6:10).

Matthew 5:5. The word that often comes to mind in conjunction with the word "meek" is "mouse." We would be helped in our understanding if we thought of *Moses*, though, for "meek" is how Moses is described (see KJV, Numbers 12:3). The beatitude refers to people who are "gentle" or "humble." Psalm 37:10-11 provides a commentary on this beatitude, suggesting the great contrast between those who are faithful to God and those who grasp for themselves.

Matthew 5:6. This beatitude promises satisfaction and fulfillment to those who desire "righteousness" as much as a hungry person desires food or a thirsty person desires water. "Righteousness" refers basically to seeking God and God's will (see 6:33; Isaiah 51:1). The concept also includes the ideas of justice and goodness.

Matthew 5:7. "The merciful" refers to those who minister to people in need as well as to those who offer forgiveness to people who have wronged them. Those who act mercifully toward others shall themselves be shown mercy. As with the blessing portions of the previous Beatitudes, the passive expression—"be mercied" or be shown mercy—should be understood to indicate that God is the source of this blessing. For other references to this concept, see Micah 6:8; Matthew 9:13; 12:7; 18:35; 25:31-46. Since being merciful is how God acts, people who seek to do God's will act like this also (see Luke 6:36).

Matthew 5:8. "The pure in heart" live in faithfulness to God by loving God with their whole heart, soul, and mind (see 22:37). Also included are the kinds of actions that characterize such faithful love for God (see Psalm 24:3-4). The blessing of seeing God refers to spiritual fellowship now, with the ultimate fulfillment occurring when God's kingdom fully comes.

Matthew 5:9. People who have truly responded to the good news of the Kingdom are "peacemakers." By their actions, they bring the peace of God's reign into the life of the world. Such peace does not refer merely to the absence of conflict but to the achievement of reconciliation. The blessing is that such people are called "children of God." Again, the passive indicates that God is the one who describes them as "children of God." Calling them "children of God" means that God acknowledges that they are like God and belong to God as descendants.

Matthew 5:10. This beatitude and the next show how radically different are those who truly have responded to the good news of the Kingdom. They are "persecuted." The blessing of such a life is "the kingdom of heaven." Although persecuted, the citizen of the Kingdom is part of God's eternal, victorious reign.

Matthew 5:11-12. The meaning of this concluding beatitude is similar to that of the previous one. It expands the mistreatment of persecution to include insults ("revile") and slander ("utter all kinds of evil against you falsely"). Because of the lack of manuscript certainty about the word "falsely," the NRSV includes "falsely" with a note while the NIV does not include it at all. The blessing of this beatitude is expressed as an imperative ("Rejoice"), a different format than that of the other Beatitudes. Rejoicing is appropriate for two reasons: (1) "your reward is great," understood to be provided by God; and (2) receiving such mistreatment puts one in line with God's prophets in the past.

Matthew 5:13. In using the metaphor "the salt of the earth" to describe people of the Kingdom, Jesus focused on the uselessness of salt when it loses its taste. Salt can loses its taste when it is mixed with other elements, as those who heard Jesus speak would have known. The call thus is for people of the Kingdom to live in accord with the Kingdom's values.

Matthew 5:14-16. The emphatic "you" in the image of light in verse 14 and that of salt in verse 13 emphasizes the contrast between people of the Kingdom and those who had not responded to the good news of the Kingdom. The image of light carries a challenge similar to that of the image of salt. People of the Kingdom are so to live that others are attracted to the God of the Kingdom.

INTERPRETING THE SCRIPTURE

Gathering a Crowd

Why did the crowds seek Jesus, follow after him, and come to the mountain where Jesus taught them? Although we should not think of Jesus as being grouchy and grim, he was not in the entertainment business. The crowds did not come because Jesus offered them entertainment. Jesus' Sermon on the Mount was not preceded by a band of excited musicians, an appearance by a celebrity, a routine by the first-century equivalent of a stand-up comic, or some combination of these.

So how in the world did Jesus "get a crowd"? The Scriptures imply that the crowds came to Jesus because they were desperate and hopeful that he could help them. They needed healing, and they hungered to hear what Jesus was proclaiming, "the good news of the kingdom" (4:23). The crowds were not disappointed that they came. At the end of the Sermon on the

Mount, "the crowds were astounded at his teaching, for he taught them as one having authority, and not as their scribes" (7:28-29).

Churches often wonder how to get a crowd these days. One layperson was heard talking in a derogatory manner about the church's pastor. The layperson said that what they really needed was a drawing card. Of course, no preacher or teacher wants to be dull, not with such an astounding message to preach or teach. Dull worship services or Bible study classes do no credit to the gospel. Still, to attempt to make entertainment, whether in the worship service or the teaching session, the drawing card is to miss both the point and the boat. Jesus didn't feel the need to be a drawing card and in fact rejected such a role (see 16:21-23).

So what should we do to get a crowd? Rather than either emphasizing entertainment or expecting people to come just because it's the custom, maybe we should do what Jesus did. He focused on people and on their real needs—physical as well as spiritual—and on the good news of God's grace and God's way to live.

Reversing the World's Standards

The disciples along with the gathered crowd had only to hear the first sentence of Jesus' teaching to know that the message of the day was going to be unusual. What Jesus taught about the qualities and blessings of Kingdom people would not fit into the familiar categories of how to get ahead in this world. Indeed, the message describing qualities of Kingdom people began with poverty and concluded with persecution. Along the way were various ideas that ran counter to the ideas of the world. These ideas meant downward mobility, not upward mobility. Jesus was reversing the world's standards as he described how people acted when they truly responded to the good news of the Kingdom.

The values Jesus attributed to such people include:

- being poor in spirit rather than self-sufficient (5:3).
- sorrowing for one's spiritual shortcomings and those of the world rather than boasting of one's goodness or ignoring wrongs (5:4).
- being humble and refusing to make claims for themselves, rather than engaging in self-promotion and exalting themselves about others (5:5).
- desiring fervently to do God's will, rather than focusing on the world's values (5:6).
- extending mercy toward those in need and forgiveness toward those who had done them wrong, rather than either passing such people by or holding a grudge (5:7).
- loving God with complete faithfulness rather than living with divided loyalties (5:8).
- working for reconciliation of conflict,

rather than either ignoring problems or seeking revenge (5:9).
- being so at odds with the world's values as to risk persecution, rather than going along to get along (5:10-12).

Our temptation is to treat the Beatitudes the way we try to treat almost everything else—as useful tools for our goals. Do we recognize how selfish and how out of touch with the spirit and intent of the Beatitudes such an approach is? The Beatitudes are not self-help methods to make us happy or at least happier immediately. If they were, surely Jesus would have left out the part about persecution.

What are the results of such actions and qualities? In each case, such actions and qualities of Kingdom people are rewarded, though not necessarily immediately. The rewards are prophetic and eschatological in nature. The Beatitudes are not a set of how-to instructions, calling people to come and do these things and they will be rewarded. Rather, Jesus in the Beatitudes simply stated that when people respond to the good news, then these qualities are evident and these results occur. The qualities are not entrance requirements for the Kingdom. Rather they describe how people who have responded to the gospel of the Kingdom see themselves and act.

In the Beatitudes, Jesus reversed the world's values and turned them upside down. Living in such a manner means that one goes against the grain of the world's standards, and thus a price must be paid. Never mind, though. God honors and blesses the values in the Beatitudes and the people who practice them. This outcome will be revealed in the coming fullness of God's kingdom. The question the Beatitudes call us to ask of ourselves is whether we believe what Jesus teaches to the extent that our lives reflect the qualities of the Beatitudes.

Challenging, Not Suggesting

When we read with honesty the Beatitudes as well as the rest of the Sermon on the Mount, we find ourselves asking whether anyone can live up to these majestic thoughts. Perhaps we might even come to the conclusion that these Beatitudes must be only for a select few if for anyone. The qualities seem so out of reach that perhaps they are for super disciples.

The text does not give us this easy out, though. Note in 5:13 that Jesus said, "You are the salt of the earth," and that in 5:14 he said, "You are the light of the world." In the Greek of 5:13 and 5:14 this word "you" is emphatic. The Greek expression means, *You yourselves* "are the salt of the earth," and *You yourselves* "are the light of the world." How easy it is for us to pass the buck of responsibility. The challenge is to us, even though we might consider ourselves quite ordinary Christians.

Note what Jesus did *not* say. He did not say, *You ought to be* the salt of the earth, and neither did he say, *You ought to be* the light of the world. Further, to paraphrase Dietrich Bonhoeffer, Jesus did not say, *You have the salt and the light*. Rather we simply *are* the salt and the light, like it or not, if we are Kingdom people. The only question is whether we will be unsalty salt or hidden light, both of which are contradictions in terms. Both unsalty salt and hidden light are useless. People who have heard and responded to the call of the good news of the Kingdom do not have the option of deciding whether they will be salt or light but only whether they will be salty salt or useless salt, or useful light or hidden light. Salt and light are metaphors for influence and witness that continually gives glory to God. Jesus calls us to such a life.

SHARING THE SCRIPTURE

PREPARING TO TEACH

Preparing Our Hearts

This week's devotional reading is found in Luke 6:17-23. Often referred to as Jesus' Sermon on the Plain, these verses echo Matthew's record of Jesus' Sermon on the Mount. Read this passage in light of the Beatitudes found in Matthew 5:1-16. Note the similarities and differences. Note also that Matthew records more Beatitudes than Luke does. How do Luke's different words change Matthew's meaning? If you read Luke 6:24-26 you will also notice woes, curses upon people, indicating a reversal of fortune.

Pray that you and your students will be open to receiving the blessings that God is ready to pour out upon those who live as Kingdom people.

Preparing Our Minds

Study the background and lesson scripture, both of which are found in Matthew 5:1-16.

Write on newsprint:
   information for next week's lesson, found under "Continue the Journey."

LEADING THE CLASS

(1) Gather to Learn

❖ Welcome the class members and introduce any guests.

❖ Pray that participants will experience the blessedness that living in God's reign has to offer them.

❖ Read aloud today's focus statement: **Culture and the media reinforce one another in equating "the good life" with material wealth, unbeatable power, and sensual pleasures. Still, people feel there** is never enough; there must be more! Where and how can people find that which brings true happiness and real living? Jesus taught that true happiness is found not in what one possesses and controls, but in the spirit in which one gives and lives, and how one's life glorifies God.

(2) Analyze the Beatitudes and Explain Each in Its Context

❖ Choose ten volunteers to read Matthew 5:1-12. One will read verses 1-2, one will read verses 11-12, and the rest will each read one verse of verses 3-10.

- Divide the class into three groups and distribute paper and pencils. Assign verses 3-6 to one group, 7-9 to a second group, and 10-12 to the third group. Provide commentaries if you have them available. Also, suggest that students who have study Bibles (that is, Bibles that have many footnotes) check them to learn more about the meaning of their assigned verses.
- Encourage the students to discern the meaning of their assigned beatitudes. Then, they are to rewrite them in contemporary English. This activity may take some time as group members each offer their own interpretations.
- End this part of the session by calling on each of the groups to report their findings. Invite listeners to challenge or question interpretations.

❖ Solicit two volunteers, one to read Matthew 5:13 and another to read verses 14-16.

- Discuss the characteristics of salt and what Jesus might be saying here when he compares his followers to salt, particularly tasteless salt.
- Discuss the characteristics of light and what Jesus might be saying here when he compares his followers to light.
- Provide quiet time for the adults to reflect on these two questions: **How well do the metaphors "salt" and "light" describe me? What steps do I**

need to take to add more of Christ's zest to others' lives and to allow him to shine brightly through me?

(3) Compare Learners' Ideas of Happiness with Those of the Media and of the Beatitudes

❖ Ask the students to complete this statement: **"I believe happiness is. . . ."** List their ideas on newsprint. Try to classify the ideas, using such categories as wealth, power, or pleasure.

❖ Encourage the students to complete this statement: **"The media teach us that happiness is. . . ."** List their ideas on a second sheet of newsprint.

❖ Invite the students to complete this statement: **"The Beatitudes teach that happiness is. . . ."** List their ideas on a third sheet of newsprint.

❖ Post all the sheets of newsprint so that they class can see them side-by-side. Distribute paper and pencils. Suggest that the learners select the top three definitions of "happiness."

❖ Conclude this portion of the session by asking the learners to consider prayerfully if they are experiencing true happiness or only a short-lived imitation. Invite them to pray about any disparity between how they are experiencing happiness, how they would prefer to experience it, and how God wills for them to experience it.

(4) Apply at Least One of the Beatitudes to a Current Situation

❖ Distribute paper and pencils if you have not already done so. Ask the students to each choose one of the Beatitudes and to write briefly how they perceive that this one can be applied to a current situation. How might the world be different, for example, if Christians took the role of peacemaker and worked hard for reconciliation in the Middle East? Or, how might we be different if we were "pure in heart," single-mindedly focused on God? Set a time limit on this independent work.

❖ Invite the students to share their ideas with a partner or small group.

❖ Ask the class to suggest ways that members could commit themselves to living as Kingdom people, and invite them to make that commitment. If an action has been discerned that the whole class could undertake, you may want to consider how the group could live out a particular beatitude together.

(5) Continue the Journey

❖ Pray that the participants will discern what it means to live as Kingdom people and act in those ways so that they will be blessed with true happiness.

❖ Read aloud this preparation for next week's lesson. You may also want to post it on newsprint for the students to copy. **Prepare for next week's session entitled "Practicing Genuine Piety" by reading background scripture from Matthew 6:1-18. The class session will focus on verses 1-14. As you read this passage from the Sermon on the Mount, keep this focus in mind: Our society tends to recognize and reward people who make visible their religious activities and practices. How can people engage in the important and vital spiritual disciplines without falling into the temptation of doing so to be seen by others? Jesus emphasized the importance of engaging in spiritual disciplines that sustain and strengthen a close personal** relationship with God rather than in public displays designed for recognition.

❖ Read aloud the following three ideas. Challenge the students to commit themselves to use these activities as a springboard to spiritual growth.

(1) **Notice television and magazine ads this week. What do they tell you that you need to do or buy in order to be a happy person? How are the values in these ads in conflict with Jesus' teachings in Matthew 5? Are there any ways in which the values of these ads reflect Jesus' teachings?**

(2) **Speak with others about their ideas of what brings happiness. Share your ideas and the reasons why you prefer Jesus' teachings on Kingdom living over society's "me first" values.**

(3) **Identify ways in which you are salt and light. Write in your spiritual journal about how your "saltiness" and "light" provide zest and illumination for the lives of others. Write specific examples to illustrate your points.**

❖ Sing or read aloud "This Little Light of Mine."

❖ Say these words from 1 Peter one phrase at a time and ask the class to repeat them: **Prepare your minds for action; discipline yourselves; set all your hope on the grace that Jesus Christ will bring you when he is revealed.**

PRACTICING GENUINE PIETY

PREVIEWING THE LESSON

Lesson Scripture: Matthew 6:1-14
Background Scripture: Matthew 6:1-18
Key Verse: Matthew 6:1

Focus of the Lesson:
Our society tends to recognize and reward people who make visible their religious activities and practices. How can people engage in the important and vital spiritual disciplines without falling into the temptation of doing so to be seen by others? Jesus emphasized the importance of engaging in spiritual disciplines that sustain and strengthen a close personal relationship with God rather than in public displays designed for recognition.

Goals for the Learners:
(1) to reflect on Jesus' teachings about giving and prayer.
(2) to express feelings about private and corporate actions.
(3) to commit themselves to the daily practice of spiritual disciplines.

Pronunciation Guide:
piety   (pi e tee')

Supplies:
Bibles, newsprint and marker, paper and pencils, hymnals, optional books on spiritual disciplines

---

READING THE SCRIPTURE

NRSV
Matthew 6:1-14

"Beware of practicing your piety before others in order to be seen by them; for then you have no reward from your Father in heaven.
2 "So whenever you give alms, do not sound a trumpet before you, as the hypocrites do in the synagogues and in the

NIV
Matthew 6:1-14

"Be careful not to do your 'acts of righteousness' before men, to be seen by them. If you do, you will have no reward from your Father in heaven.
2"So when you give to the needy, do not announce it with trumpets, as the hypocrites

streets, so that they may be praised by others. Truly I tell you, they have received their reward. 3 But when you give alms, do not let your left hand know what your right hand is doing, 4 so that your alms may be done in secret; and your Father who sees in secret will reward you.

5 "And whenever you pray, do not be like the hypocrites; for they love to stand and pray in the synagogues and at the street corners, so that they may be seen by others. Truly I tell you, they have received their reward. 6 But whenever you pray, go into your room and shut the door and pray to your Father who is in secret; and your Father who sees in secret will reward you.

7 "When you are praying, do not heap up empty phrases as the Gentiles do; for they think that they will be heard because of their many words. 8 Do not be like them, for your Father knows what you need before you ask him.

9 "Pray then in this way:
Our Father in heaven,
   hallowed be your name.
10   Your kingdom come.
   Your will be done,
      on earth as it is in heaven.
11   Give us this day our daily bread.
12   And forgive us our debts,
      as we also have forgiven our debtors.
13   And do not bring us to the time of trial,
      but rescue us from the evil one.
14 For if you forgive others their trespasses, your heavenly Father will also forgive you."

do in the synagogues and on the streets, to be honored by men. I tell you the truth, they have received their reward in full. [3]But when you give to the needy, do not let your left hand know what your right hand is doing, [4]so that your giving may be in secret. Then your Father, who sees what is done in secret, will reward you.

[5]"And when you pray, do not be like the hypocrites, for they love to pray standing in the synagogues and on the street corners to be seen by men. I tell you the truth, they have received their reward in full. [6]But when you pray, go into your room, close the door and pray to your Father, who is unseen. Then your Father, who sees what is done in secret, will reward you. [7]And when you pray, do not keep on babbling like pagans, for they think they will be heard because of their many words. [8]Do not be like them, for your Father knows what you need before you ask him.

[9]"This, then, is how you should pray:
" 'Our Father in heaven,
   hallowed be your name,
[10] your kingdom come,
   your will be done
      on earth as it is in heaven.
[11] Give us today our daily bread.
[12] Forgive us our debts,
      as we also have forgiven our debtors.
[13] And lead us not into temptation,
      but deliver us from the evil one.'
[14]For if you forgive men when they sin against you, your heavenly Father will also forgive you."

UNDERSTANDING THE SCRIPTURE

Matthew 6:1. This verse serves as a heading for Jesus' instructions on three religious practices of that day—almsgiving (6:2-4), prayer (6:5-15), and fasting (6:16-18). The key element in the misuse of these practices was not their public nature—doing them "before others"—but rather their motivation—"to be seen by them." Jesus praised the widow who publicly "came and put in two small copper coins" (Mark 12:42-44). He also spoke positively of the tax collector's public prayer for God's mercy (Luke 18:13-14). Too, Jesus did not condemn the practice of fasting itself but only when it was done in an attention-getting manner (see Matthew 9:14-15). In 5:16, Jesus had called for Kingdom people to let their "light shine before others, so that they may see your good works." The purpose, though, was for those who saw to "give glory to your Father in heaven" (5:16).

In the case of each hypocritical religious act, the idea that one has no reward from the Father in heaven appears (6:1; see 6:2, 5, 16). The word translated "reward" implies the idea of payment or wages.

Matthew 6:2. Jesus' statement about blowing a trumpet to call attention to one's giving probably was intended to show how ludicrous a display of false piety was. "Hypocrite" refers to one who plays a role different from what he or she really is, just as an actor would. Jesus' statement that "they have received their reward" indicates that since they had wanted recognition from people and had received it, then that was all the reward they could expect. No praise from God would be forthcoming.

Matthew 6:3. The injunction about "not let(ting) your left hand know what your right hand is doing" is a teaching device. Physically doing this would be impossible. The meaning is that the one who gives (with the right hand, for example) should be unconcerned with receiving praise from others (the left hand, for example).

Matthew 6:4. One should give as if giving in secret, anonymously. God knows how much people give and will reward them accordingly for their generosity. The emphasis is not necessarily on material rewards but rather the rewards of God's kingdom, especially in an eschatological sense. The best texts do not include "openly," and thus no contrast is intended between one's giving secretly and God's responding openly.

Matthew 6:5-6. Jesus condemned people's praying "so that they may be seen by others." These instructions do not prohibit public prayer. The Bible contains many positive examples of public prayer, and Jesus himself prayed in public (see 19:13). Jesus' teaching that disciples should "go into your room and shut the door and pray to your Father who is in secret" emphasizes prayer as communication with God, not done to receive praise from others.

Matthew 6:7-8. As 6:5-6 condemned the kind of hypocritical praying generally associated with some Jewish people's practice, so verse 7 condemned the kind of praying generally associated with Gentile practice. The former sort of hypocritical praying attempted to impress other people, while the latter sort of hypocritical praying attempted to impress and thus manipulate the gods. As attempting to impress others with one's praying was wrong, so also attempting to impress God with one's praying was misguided. Such prayers have the misguided purpose of informing God of what needs to be done and even manipulating God, but "your Father knows what you need before you ask him."

Matthew 6:9. The instructions in 6:9-13 about genuine prayer provide positive guidance related to Jesus' warnings in 6:5-8. Verses 9-10 focus on God, and verses 11-13 are requests about human needs.

To call God "Father" was a familiar way of speaking of God in that culture. "Father" implies care and provision rather than gender. To call God "our" Father stands in contrast to the self-centered, hypocritical prayer condemned in verses 5-8. "In heaven" and "hallowed be your name" indicate that God is set apart from human beings and is to be recognized as such. "Name" refers to God's nature, identity, and personhood, rather than to a specific word by which one calls God.

Matthew 6:10. The phrases "your kingdom come" and "your will be done on earth as it in heaven" have parallel meaning. When God's kingdom truly comes, then God's will shall be done on earth as it is in heaven. Similarly, whenever God's will is done on earth as it is in heaven, then to that extent God's kingdom has come on earth.

Matthew 6:11. In each of the petitions in 6:11-13, the focus is not on "me" but on "us" and "we." Such an emphasis provides an additional contrast to the self-centered praying condemned in 6:5-7. Verse 11 focuses on the meeting of physical need, which is capsuled in the request for "daily bread." The word translated "daily" appears only twice in the New Testament (Matthew 6:11; Luke 11:3) and only rarely in the rest of ancient literature. Thus commentators are uncertain about the meaning and debate whether the reference is to bread for today or bread for the coming day. Basically the reference is to *the bread we need* or *what is needed to sustain life.*

Matthew 6:12. Our forgiveness of others is integrally related to our receiving forgiveness (see 18:23-35). Verses 14-15 of chapter 6 underscore this concept. People who refuse to forgive others show that they have not truly turned to God in repentance and thus are incapable of receiving the forgiveness God offers. "Debts" refers to sins—ours against God and others' against us.

Matthew 6:13. The request, "do not bring us to the time of trial," calls us to recognize our weakness in facing trial and the snares of "the evil one." It is an expression thus of humility and trust. Jesus' followers must call on God and seek God's deliverance rather than relying on their strength. Note again how greatly this concept contrasts with the kind of hypocritical, self-centered prayer Jesus condemned in 6:5-7.

Matthew 6:14-15. See the comments on verse 12.

Matthew 6:16-18. As with giving alms and praying, the emphasis in the concern about fasting is on motivation. Those who fast in order to call others' attention to their piety "have received their reward" (6:16). People who were fasting might wear sackcloth and place ashes on their heads as signs of mourning and repentance for their spiritual condition before God. Jesus instructed that people who fast should continue to be joyful in their demeanor and appearance rather than to use the practice of fasting to impress others with their piety.

INTERPRETING THE SCRIPTURE

Seeking Praise for Piety

"Beware," Jesus said, of seeking to be known for your piety. That seems to be rather different from the ordinary encouragements we often get and give about religious activities. Don't we want people to engage in religious acts, including giving and praying? Don't we want people to be Christian openly rather than secretly and to witness openly of their faith to others? Only a few sentences earlier Jesus had encouraged people to "let your light shine before others, so that they may see your good works" (5:16).

So what is the difference between letting "your light shine before others, so that they may see your good works" (5:16) and "practicing your piety before others in order to be seen by them" (6:1)? The difference is in the motivation. Jesus encouraged being openly, actively, and even courageously Christian so that God is glorified and not ourselves. The religious practices Jesus warned against were those that people engaged in so that others would glorify *them* for being so religious.

This passage calls us to ask a hard question of ourselves. Do we engage in religious acts so others will see and think how good we are at performing them, how worthy of praise we are for doing them, or at least how respectable we are?

One wonders sometimes whether our Christianity is any more real than little children playing the game of church. As children play church, they may appear to sing, preach, pray, take up the offering, and otherwise engage in all the visible displays of worship. Perhaps such a game is amusing in young children, but in the rest of us such game-playing is deadening to authentic religion. Real religion cannot penetrate our lives when we are engaging in acts that appear religious while actually we are just going through the motions.

In this verse and in the verses about giving and praying that follow, Jesus is teaching us that at the heart of real religion must be reality rather than sham. These verses call us to be more honest with God, with ourselves, and with our fellow human beings. Such honesty is the threshold for genuine religious experience that is more than a public display aimed at seeking praise from others.

Giving Without Seeking Credit

Jesus' instructions in this passage about giving contain several basic thoughts. First, Jesus evidently assumes we will give, expecting us to do so. Giving alms refers to giving money to the needy. Only a few verses prior, Jesus had taught, "Give to everyone who begs from you" (5:42). Jesus later challenged a young man seeking eternal life to "go, sell your possessions, and give the money to the poor" (19:21). Scripture clearly calls for us to give (see also James 2:15-16).

A second basic thought of Matthew 6:2-4 is that we are to give without seeking the praise of others. This teaching cuts across the grain of many modern church practices with regard to financial giving. People sometimes give to get public recognition for the gift, and churches sometimes encourage such giving. For example, people some-

times seek to get their names or their family's name on a plaque for giving a certain item—perhaps a musical instrument, perhaps a building. How does that square with Jesus' instruction in this passage? At the very least this passage teaches that if people give to be recognized by other people, then that is the only recognition they should expect. Should we give more attention to this teaching in this day when many fund-raising campaigns openly seek large donors by enticing such gifts with the promise of providing public recognition? Have the fund-raising ways of the world infiltrated the church? Do we dare to pay attention to what Jesus said when most churches need money badly? How important is "getting the money" when placed beside being faithful to Jesus' teachings?

A third thought in this passage is that God rewards those who give gifts without concern for others knowing about their generosity. Furthermore, God's reward counts for eternity, lasting longer than any plaque.

A remarkable act of giving occurred in a southern state several years ago. In fact, the act was so profoundly touching that it came to be known simply as "the gift." The gift was to the local university, and it was for a substantial amount—$150,000. More impressive than the amount, though, was the person who gave it and the spirit in which she gave it. Oseola McCarty was in her late eighties, and she had spent her life washing other people's clothes. This elderly black woman had scrimped and saved her whole life, living simply.

One day the person at the bank who handled her affairs broached the subject of what she wanted done with her money after her death, since she had no living relatives. She decided she wanted to give it to the local university for student scholarships. Further, she wanted to give it now, before she died, keeping only a little for living expenses. She asked for nothing in return—no plaques, no recognition of any kind.

The honors that came to her after word

got out came as a great surprise to this simple, unassuming woman. A university official said of her, "She's just different. When you're around her, you just feel better." Doesn't that sound a lot like letting your light shine without "practicing your piety before others in order to be seen by them" (6:1)?

Praying Authentically

As with Jesus' instructions about giving, these instructions about authentic prayer emphasize its unselfish nature. People engaging in genuine prayer are not interested in calling attention to themselves, either in where they pray or in what is in their prayers.

In a day when most people who are called on to pray in public do so with fear and trembling, how do Jesus' teachings about prayer speak to us? Perhaps these instructions should remind us that even public prayer is intended first of all simply to be communication with God rather than a performance to impress others. Jesus' teachings on authentic prayer should also challenge us to make sure that our prayers, whether public or private, are in line with the content of the prayer about which Jesus said, "Pray then in this way" (6:9).

Consider these major teachings in the prayer Jesus taught us to pray in 6:9-13. First, our prayers should focus on God and seek the doing of God's will in our lives and in all the world. Second, our prayers should remind us that we depend on God for our most basic needs and express trusting hope that God will meet those needs. Third, our prayers should confess our need for forgiveness from God and our willingness to forgive others. Too, our prayers should emphasize our humble dependence on God in dealing with the evils of our world and with "the evil one" (6:13). Praying in such a manner would keep us from merely listing our self-centered desires and trying to glorify such selfishness by hypocritically calling it prayer.

Are we truly praying with humility of spirit of a desire to communicate with God? Are we allowing Jesus' teachings to instruct us in praying as Kingdom people, or do we choose to follow the world's need to receive public recognition for anything we do, including our offering of prayers?

SHARING THE SCRIPTURE

PREPARING TO TEACH

Preparing Our Hearts

This week's devotional reading is found in Luke 11:5-13. Here we find a parable that Jesus uses to teach perseverance in prayer. What is Jesus' point in this parable? What do you learn about God—and yourself—from this parable?

Pray that you and your students will experience prayer as a relationship with our loving God, not a required exercise that must be done at a certain time each day.

Preparing Our Minds

Study the background from Matthew 6:1-18 and lesson scripture from Matthew 6:1-14. The lesson scripture looks at two spiritual practices, almsgiving and prayer. The background scripture also includes the discipline of fasting.

Write on newsprint:

information for next week's lesson, found under "Continue the Journey."

Plan to do the suggested lectures in "Reflect on Jesus' Teachings About Giving and Prayer."

Collect as many books on spiritual disciplines as possible. Your Christian bookstore and/or your pastor or church librarian can help you locate books on this topic that are available. Bring these books to the session.

LEADING THE CLASS

(1) Gather to Learn

❖ Welcome the class members and introduce any guests.

❖ Pray that God's Spirit will empower you to learn more about the disciplines of giving and prayer so that the participants may go forth to engage in these important practices.

❖ Suggest these definitions of "piety," which you may choose to write on newsprint: (1) reverence and love of God; (2) loving obedience to God's will; (3) devotion to God's service; (4) observance of religious principles; (5) respect for one's parents and willingness to fulfill obligations to them.

❖ Discuss the kinds of religious principles that a pious person may choose to observe. List these ideas on newsprint. (NOTE: This list may look remarkably like spiritual disciplines, such as prayer, Bible study, meditation, giving, participating in church sacraments, and so on.)

❖ Point out that today's session focuses on acts of piety and how they should—or should not—be done.

❖ Read aloud today's focus statement: **Our society tends to recognize and reward people who make visible their religious activities and practices. How can people engage in the important and vital spiritual disciplines without falling into the temptation of doing so to be seen by others? Jesus emphasized the importance of engaging in spiritual disciplines that sustain and strengthen a close personal relationship with God rather than in public displays designed for recognition.**

(2) Reflect on Jesus' Teachings About Giving and Prayer

❖ Choose a volunteer to read Matthew 6:1-4.

- Help the class discern what Jesus is saying here by preparing a short lecture based on information in the Understanding the Scripture portion. Be sure to point out that the term "hypocrites" did not carry the negative meaning we assign to it. Rather, the Greek word referred to actors who were playing a role instead of showing their true selves.

- Note that Jesus definitely does not condemn almsgiving, but is concerned that it be motivated by a desire to serve God by serving others, not a need to have others notice how wonderful the giver is.

- Invite the class to comment on some contemporary ways that people blow their own horns about what they have given. ("Giving Without Seeking Credit" in Interpreting the Scripture includes ideas.) Consider how these recognitions help or hinder true giving. Use the example of Oseola McCarty that is cited in "Giving Without Seeking Credit."

❖ Select a volunteer to read Matthew 6:5-8.

- Discuss how Jesus' teaching on prayer is similar to his teaching on giving alms (that is, charitable giving).

❖ Choose one person to read Matthew 6:9-14 and another to read Luke 11:2-4.

- Discuss these questions.
  (1) How are these versions similar and different?
  (2) How are they similar to and different from the way that you pray the Lord's Prayer?

- Use information for verses 9-13 in Understanding the Scripture to help the class unpack the meaning of Jesus' prayer. You may wish to present this information in a lecture.

■ Consider the relationship between us forgiving others and God forgiving us.

(3) Express Feelings About Private and Corporate Actions

❖ Ask the students to work with a partner or small team. Read each of the following phrases aloud, pausing to give the team time to discuss their reactions to the idea.

■ Listening to someone pray in public.
■ Volunteering to pray aloud on behalf of a group.
■ Giving to the church.
■ Knowing what other people give to the church, just as they know what you give.
■ Expecting recognition for what you do.
■ Receiving public recognition even though you did not expect or want it.

❖ Invite the groups to come together and say which item they had greatest agreement about, and which one the group disagreed with the most. What reasons can they give for their agreement or disagreement?

(4) Commit to the Daily Practice of Spiritual Disciplines

❖ Look again with the class at the newsprint on which they had brainstormed ideas about spiritual practices. List whatever other ideas you can to this list. Books on spirituality, such as Richard Foster's *Celebration of Discipline,* list a variety of spiritual disciplines, such as prayer, fasting, Bible study, meditation, and living simply. Add additional ideas to your list.

❖ Set out any books you have been able to collect on spiritual disciplines. You may want to say a word about the books and the disciplines they outline. Invite the students to pass these books around. Perhaps some will want to borrow a book, if possible, to study a discipline in more depth.

❖ Distribute paper and pencils. Ask the students to write and complete this sentence on their paper: **"I will study the spiritual dis-**

cipline of . . . and seek to practice it daily for the next month."** When they have finished, ask the students to put these papers in their Bibles so that they will be regularly reminded of the commitment they have made.

(5) Continue the Journey

❖ Pray that the students will commit themselves faithfully to practices such as giving and praying.

❖ Read aloud this preparation for next week's lesson. You may also want to post it on newsprint for the students to copy. **Prepare for next week's session entitled "Learning to Listen" by reading the background scripture from Matthew 13:1-23 and the session scripture from 13:9-17. Learn why Jesus chose to speak in parables by concentrating on this focus statement: Most people's discussions about the meaning of life can seem complex, abstract, and impractical. How can we find a way to communicate and explore that which concerns us most deeply? Jesus taught in parables that drew from the everyday life of everyday people and yet made plain the deeper truth he sought to communicate.**

❖ Read aloud the following three ideas. Challenge the students to commit themselves to use these activities as a springboard to spiritual growth.

(1) **Give an anonymous gift to help someone else.**
(2) **Read aloud the Lord's Prayer slowly, pausing to think about what each phrase means.**
(3) **Use a concordance to search what the Scriptures have to say about "prayer." Also look up "pray(s)," "praying," and "prayed."**

❖ Sing or say aloud "The Lord's Prayer."

❖ Say these words from 1 Peter one phrase at a time and ask the class to repeat them: **Prepare your minds for action; discipline yourselves; set all your hope on the grace that Jesus Christ will bring you when he is revealed.**

LEARNING TO LISTEN

PREVIEWING THE LESSON

Lesson Scripture: Matthew 13:9-17
Background Scripture: Matthew 13:1-23
Key Verse: Matthew 13:9

Focus of the Lesson:
Most people's discussions about the meaning of life can seem complex, abstract, and impractical. How can we find a way to communicate and explore that which concerns us most deeply? Jesus taught in parables that drew from the daily life of ordinary people and so made plain the deeper truth to those willing to follow him.

Goals for the Learners:
(1) to understand why Jesus taught in parables.
(2) to explore how routine experiences can point toward spiritual truths.
(3) to talk with others about Jesus in understandable terms.

Supplies:
Bibles, newsprint and marker, paper and pencils, Bible commentaries, hymnals

---

READING THE SCRIPTURE

NRSV
Matthew 13:9-17

[Jesus said,] **9 "Let anyone with ears listen!"**

10 Then the disciples came and asked him, "Why do you speak to them in parables?" 11 He answered, "To you it has been given to know the secrets of the kingdom of heaven, but to them it has not been given. 12 For to those who have, more will be given, and they will have an abundance; but from those who have nothing, even what they have will be taken away. 13 The reason I speak to them in parables is that 'seeing

NIV
Matthew 13:9-17

[Jesus said,] **9 "He who has ears, let him hear."**

[10]The disciples came to him and asked, "Why do you speak to the people in parables?"

[11]He replied, "The knowledge of the secrets of the kingdom of heaven has been given to you, but not to them. [12]Whoever has will be given more, and he will have an abundance. Whoever does not have, even what he has will be taken from him. [13]This is why I speak to them in parables:

they do not perceive, and hearing they do not listen, nor do they understand.' 14 With them indeed is fulfilled the prophecy of Isaiah that says:

'You will indeed listen, but never understand,
and you will indeed look, but never perceive.
15 For this people's heart has grown dull,
and their ears are hard of hearing,
and they have shut their eyes;
so that they might not look with their eyes,
and listen with their ears,
and understand with their heart and turn—
and I would heal them.'
16 But blessed are your eyes, for they see, and your ears, for they hear. 17 Truly I tell you, many prophets and righteous people longed to see what you see, but did not see it, and to hear what you hear, but did not hear it."

"Though seeing, they do not see;
though hearing, they do not hear or understand.
14 In them is fulfilled the prophecy of Isaiah:
"'You will be ever hearing but never understanding;
you will be ever seeing but never perceiving.
15 For this people's heart has become calloused;
they hardly hear with their ears,
and they have closed their eyes.
Otherwise they might see with their eyes,
hear with their ears,
understand with their hearts
and turn, and I would heal them.'
16 But blessed are your eyes because they see, and your ears because they hear. 17 For I tell you the truth, many prophets and righteous men longed to see what you see but did not see it, and to hear what you hear but did not hear it."

UNDERSTANDING THE SCRIPTURE

Matthew 13:1. This verse establishes the setting for the teachings in Matthew 13. The exact reference of "that same day" is uncertain. Likely Matthew did not intend actually to refer to the activities of a certain day, thus enabling us to trace into the previous chapter the events of that exact day. If it was so intended, though, how far back that day went is unclear, but perhaps at least to 12:38. In sitting down, Jesus was assuming the position of a respected teacher (see 5:1). "The sea" refers to the Sea of Galilee (see 4:13, 15, 18).

Matthew 13:2. As had occurred on other occasions, "great crowds gathered around him" (see 4:25; 5:1; 7:28; 8:1, 18; 9:33; 12:23). This gathering was so large that Jesus found it necessary to sit in a boat and teach the crowd from there.

Matthew 13:3. "Parables" are mentioned here in Matthew for the first time. Rather than being simple stories to be enjoyed and appreciated, parables were intended to stimulate serious thought and to call for decision. Moreover, a parable was not meant to contain an obvious moral but to cause the hearer to consider its meaning. Parables compare one thing and another and invite thought about that comparison. Since the nature of that comparison might not be readily apparent, a parable is in a sense mysterious (see 13:11). In Jewish use, a parable could have the qualities of a riddle.

How should parables be interpreted? In the earlier history of the interpretation of parables, interpreters often sought the meaning of every single detail of a parable. Such an approach turns the parables into allegories, which is not the way parables were considered in Jewish culture. Too, with such an approach, evaluating whether a given allegorical point is correct is not possible, especially when the parable is extracted from its biblical setting. While some parables have allegorical elements and even approach being allegories, assigning meaning to each detail is not appropriate. A better approach is to recognize that a parable generally has only one main meaning and to minimize allegorical interpretation.

Matthew states that Jesus "told them many things in parables" (13:3). The first parable Matthew singles out is of a sower who "went out to sow" (13:3).

Matthew 13:4. In that time, the sower would broadcast the seed and then cultivate the soil. Some seeds fell on the path that ran through the field. These seeds were unable to take root in the packed soil and were eaten by the birds.

Matthew 13:5-6. The "rocky soil" was soil that had a thin layer of earth over a rocky base. Thus the seeds sprouted quickly. When the sun's scorching heat struck them, they "withered away" since they did not have sufficient roots.

Matthew 13:7. Other seeds fell among the thornbushes. The thornbushes choked out the seeds.

Matthew 13:8. In contrast, some seeds fell on good soil. The seeds that fell on good soil produced abundantly, some superabundantly.

Matthew 13:9. This verse called Jesus' hearers and Matthew's readers to their responsibility to consider the parable personally.

Matthew 13:10. The disciples were puzzled about Jesus' use of parables, especially why Jesus told them to the crowds. The implication is that the disciples understood the parables while the crowds did not.

Matthew 13:11. In the setting of chapter 13 in the Gospel of Matthew, a division was occurring in Israel about Jesus. This division can be seen in chapter 11 in the discussion about John the Baptist. It can also be seen in

Matthew 12 in Jesus' discussion with the Pharisees (12:1-45) and in Jesus' remarks about his true family (12:46-50). The ability to understand the parables thus was based on one's response to Jesus. Even so, understanding the parables was not the result of human achievement but was God's gift. Here as elsewhere in Matthew, the emphasis is on God's gift of revelation (see 11:27).

Matthew 13:12-13. Understanding or not understanding Jesus' parables further marks the division between those who are responsive to Jesus and those who are not. Those who do not perceive who Jesus is fail to understand the meaning of the parables. These verses and verses 10-17 as a whole remind us that relating to Jesus is based both on God's grace, over which we human beings have no control, and our responsiveness. God's grace always comes first, however, both in order and in importance (see Matthew 16:17; 1 John 4:19).

Matthew 13:14-15. This quotation from Isaiah 6:9-10 states what happens when people close their ears and eyes to what God is doing. On one level, they may hear the words and see what is happening, but they "never understand" and "never perceive."

The quotation emphasizes God's sovereignty in providing revelation but at the same time people's responsibility for perceiving it.

Matthew 13:16-17. In contrast, Jesus' disciples had responded to the revelation of God. In a beatitude, Jesus described them as "blessed" (13:16). They were seeing what "many prophets and righteous people" (13:17) through the centuries had longed to see as they saw Jesus proclaiming and demonstrating "the good news of the kingdom" (4:23).

Matthew 13:18-23. The interpretation of the parable given in these verses has allegorical elements. The attention shifts from the seed to the kind of soil. The packed soil of the path is interpreted as referring to those who resist God's revelation (13:4, 18).

The "rocky ground" (13:20; see 13:5) refers to those who accept God's message quickly but not deeply. The soil of the thorns refers to those who allow "the cares of the world and the lure of wealth" to "choke out the word" (13:22; see 13:7). Some soil, however, is "good soil," and the seeds sown on this soil bear a great harvest (13:23; see 13:8). As in 13:10-17, the interpretation of the parable includes both God's sovereignty and people's responsibility.

The combination of the parable and its interpretation suggests two main meanings. First, as the Kingdom is proclaimed, disciples of every age should not become discouraged. God's harvest is certain, and it will be phenomenal (13:8, 23). Furthermore, as the Kingdom is proclaimed, how people respond is crucial. Will they participate in the harvest by letting the seeds of the Kingdom take root in them?

INTERPRETING THE SCRIPTURE

The Responsibility for Listening

The picture in the parable of the sower is of the sower broadcasting seed in every direction (13:3-8). The picture implies that no one is left out or passed by but that the opportunity to hear is open to all. This implication thus suggests that the responsibility to listen is placed on all. That responsibility is seen in verse 9 also.

On the television show *Inside the Actor's Theatre*, which appears on the Bravo channel, the interviewer uses a list of ten questions with each guest near the conclusion of the interview. One of the questions is, "When you enter heaven, if there is a heaven, what do you hope to hear God say?" When the interviewer asked this question of renowned movie director Steven Spielberg, Spielberg replied, "Thanks for listening." Spielberg then explained by calling attention to Deuteronomy 6:4, which begins, "Hear, O Israel."

What is our first responsibility to God? We might state an answer to this question in several ways, but listening to God certainly should come high on the list. Only when we listen to God can we live in trusting obedience and faithfulness.

Many of our attempts to figure out life falter and fail because we do not have the right perspective to begin with. We have failed to listen, first of all to God.

Our problem is that we move in our own world and forget we are in God's world. So we focus our thoughts and our efforts on our world, which is largely the material world, and fail to get a perspective on the larger world. Our vision, focused largely on ourselves, is too limited.

What is our first responsibility to other people if we would communicate to them our concern for them, including our concern that they know the spiritual realities that are important to us? At the top of the list should be to listen to them.

Many of our attempts to communicate to others falter and fail because our focus is on our message and ourselves. We do not listen to others and respond to them in terms of their needs and level of understanding. We waste much time as Christians and as churches in answering questions important to no one but us and doing so in language that makes little sense to anyone but us.

If we truly want to communicate spiritual truths to others, we must recognize that the responsibility for communicating begins with us. So how can we do that?

Our first step toward actually communicating spiritual truths, rather than just intellectualizing about them in the abstract, must be to clear away the debris of our lives that keeps us from listening to God ourselves. Thus we must begin by examining with honesty our interior lives. As we do so, we come to recognize again the depth of our need of God's grace and the greatness of God's love in wanting to share that grace. We learn, too, that our relationship with God is intended to be more important than anything else—possessions, status, and participation in a given culture, even church culture. As we experience the nurture such a relationship with God provides, then we are ready to seek to communicate the spiritual realities we have found.

Our second step must be to listen to other people for the ways in which they are struggling with questions that at bottom are spiritual in nature. When we have listened, then maybe we will be ready to respond in ways appropriate to what we have heard.

A recently retired insurance company executive said that when he began his career the emphasis in recruiting salespeople was placed on finding people who could talk well. Now, he said, the emphasis is on finding people who can listen well. If listening is important in business, surely it's important in the spiritual realm.

The Reality of Unresponsiveness

People are responsible for listening, but the reality is that people respond to the message in different ways. The disciples' question in verse 10 and Jesus' reply in verses 11-15 remind us that some listen responsively and some do not. Those who listen responsively understand more and more, while those who do not do so find their understanding blocked by their own misperceptions.

Jesus made this point in the parable of the sower and its interpretation (13:3-8, 18-23). Some seed fell on the hardpacked soil of the path and could not penetrate it. "The birds came and ate them up" (13:4), an action that Jesus compared to the work of "the evil one" who "comes and snatches

away what is sown in the heart" (13:19). Have we not seen—and perhaps experienced—the reality of this teaching? The more often people say no to God, the more resistant to the gospel their lives often become.

Some seed fell on "rocky ground," ground that featured only a few inches of soil on top of a rocky layer of subsoil (13:5, 20). This kind of soil can be compared to halfhearted would-be disciples who are excited initially about the Christian faith. They show their lack of genuine faith when difficulty comes. Their commitment is so shallow as to be nonexistent. They are like the friends of the little red hen in the children's story. They're there for the party, but not for the hard work.

Some seed fell "among thorns" (13:7, 22). Jesus pointedly compared this kind of soil to those who let "the cares of the world and the lure of wealth choke the word" (13:22). Such folk really want more to be comfortable, or at least not to be so uncomfortable, than truly to be Christian.

Why do we sometimes find discussing spiritual matters to be difficult? Sometimes it is because we are fearful that our message and we ourselves will be rejected. The parable of the sower reminds us that not all communication of the gospel is accepted. That, however, is not the complete story.

The Joy of Truly Hearing

We can almost hear the elation in Jesus' voice as he pronounced a blessing on his disciples. They had seen and heard what "many prophets and righteous people" of old had longed to see and hear (13:17). Furthermore, they had responded positively to what they had seen and heard.

Parallel in meaning to the blessing in these verses is Jesus' description in verse 8 of the abundant harvest and his interpretation of that harvest in verse 23. Jesus' point is that some will hear and respond even though others do not.

We sometimes are discouraged at the lack of responsiveness to and even the seeming failure of the church's efforts. Certainly we should be concerned when the church experiences a decline in converts, influence, and resources and when the darkness of worldliness deepens. Recall Jesus' good news in this parable, though. There *will* be a harvest. An abundant response to the work of the gospel is certain, in fact, however unlikely it may appear in light of what we presently see.

We sometimes wonder what to say in discussing spiritual matters. We may be reluctant to begin to do so, in fact. We will find the right approach as we listen to God and to others, buoyed by the knowledge that the harvest is certain. As we grow in our willingness to discuss our faith and our ability to do so, our lives will be enriched, and others will have an opportunity to hear and respond and thus be part of the harvest themselves.

SHARING THE SCRIPTURE

PREPARING TO TEACH

Preparing Our Hearts

This week's devotional reading is found in Mark 4:10-20. Here, as in today's lesson from Matthew, Jesus talks about the purpose of the parables within the context of the parable of the sower. Jesus' words in verses 11-12 may strike us as harsh. Isn't the kingdom of God supposed to be open to everyone? Yet, Jesus is talking in terms of "insiders" and "outsiders." Scholars debate the interpretation of this difficult passage. What does it say to you?

Pray that you and your students will listen with understanding to Jesus as you read and study his parables.

Preparing Our Minds

Study the background from Matthew 13:1-23 and lesson scripture, Matthew 13:9-17. Note that although the parable of the sower is included in the background scripture, the focus of the lesson is on Jesus' purpose in using parables.

Write on newsprint:

information for next week's lesson, found under "Continue the Journey."

Gather several Bible commentaries for use in class. Perhaps you have some you would be willing to share. Check with your pastor and in the church library/media center. Many public libraries also have such references that can be checked out.

Make notes for a lecture if you decide to use Option 2 in the "Understand Why Jesus Taught in Parables" section.

LEADING THE CLASS

(1) Gather to Learn

❖ Welcome the class members and introduce any guests.

❖ Pray that the participants will be attuned to the voice of God, listening for the word of the Lord as it comes through the Scriptures and through interaction with one another.

❖ Invite the volunteers to recall favorite stories from their childhood. If you have a wide range of ages in the group, the stories may need to be briefly retold so they become familiar to everyone.

❖ Encourage the students to answer these questions.

(1) What makes stories that you read or heard decades ago so memorable?

(2) Why do you think that many people

find stories an effective means by which to teach and learn?

❖ Read aloud today's focus statement: **Most people's discussions about the meaning of life can seem complex, abstract, and impractical. How can we find a way to communicate and explore that which concerns us most deeply? Jesus taught in parables that drew from the daily life of ordinary people and so made plain the deeper truth to those willing to follow him.**

(2) Understand Why Jesus Taught in Parables

❖ Set the scene for today's lesson by noting that Jesus was sitting beside the Sea of Galilee when he told the parable of the sower. Briefly help the class recall the types of soil the seed fell on. Do not spend much time on the parable itself, though, because this is not the thrust of the session.

❖ Choose a volunteer to read Matthew 13:9-17.

❖ Unpack the meaning of this passage by using one of these two plans.

Option 1

- Divide the class into teams. Distribute paper and pencils to each student. Give each team at least one commentary.
- Challenge each team to read Matthew 13:9-17 again in whatever Bible translations they have and check one or more commentaries to see how it might be interpreted.
- Suggest that the students individually take notes as they hear the Bible and commentaries read. Encourage each student to write words, phrases, questions, or insights that he or she finds helpful in interpreting the passage.
- Ask each group to talk together to develop one or more interpretations of this passage. Each student will have ideas to contribute.
- Provide time for each group to share its interpretation and for the rest of the class to respond to it.

Option 2

- Prepare a lecture in which you share interpretations of this passage according to several commentators.
- Invite the students to comment on these interpretations, raise questions, and/or give their own insights.

(3) Explore How Routine Experiences Can Point Toward Spiritual Truths

❖ Invite the students to brainstorm some routine experiences (for example, eating breakfast, walking the dog, going to work, shopping for groceries, singing in the shower). List their ideas on newsprint.

❖ Challenge the class members to find spiritual truths in the experiences they have listed. Here are three examples you can use as discussion starters.

- While eating breakfast we are reminded that God provides our daily bread.
- While walking the dog early in the morning we are reminded that God's creative work continues each day and that we are called to be stewards of that creation.
- While singing in the shower, we are reminded that the psalmist calls us to sing a new song to the Lord.

❖ Wrap up this portion of the lesson by noting that Jesus used ordinary experiences, such as the ones we have, to teach us about the kingdom of God.

(4) Talk with Others About Jesus in Understandable Terms

❖ Invite volunteers to role-play a conversation among several people, at least one of whom takes the role of a Christian and one of whom makes no claim to Christ. In the conversation use common experiences to talk with about Christ and what he means in the life of a believer.

❖ Ask the class to listen carefully to the conversation for the use of words that persons who make no claim to Christ likely do not know. These words include theological terms such as *salvation, grace, repentance,* and *eternal life.*

❖ Repeat the role-play with different volunteers, as time permits.

❖ After each role-play, invite the class members who watched to comment on how understandable they believe the conversation would have been to someone who is not Christian.

❖ Sum up this activity by encouraging class members to state insights they have gleaned from this activity that will help them as they speak to others about Christ.

(5) Continue the Journey

❖ Pray that all who have participated in today's lesson will follow Jesus so closely that they might hear and understand whatever message(s) he has for them, and then share God's good news with others.

❖ Read aloud this preparation for next week's lesson. You may also want to post it on newsprint for the students to copy. **Prepare for next week's session entitled "Free to Forgive" by reading Matthew 18:21-35, which is both our background and lesson scripture. Keep this focus in mind as you study your lesson: Most of us desire forgiveness when we have wronged another, but we often find it difficult to forgive others when they have wronged us. Can we afford the consequences of living with such inconsistencies? The parable of the unforgiving slave goes beyond a limited view of forgiveness; it calls for a spirit of unconditional forgiveness toward others.**

❖ Read aloud the following three ideas. Challenge the students to commit themselves to use these activities as a springboard to spiritual growth.

(1) **Monitor your response to those who need you to listen to them. Do you really listen, focusing your full attention on the speaker and his or her concern? Are you interruptible? Do you need to offer unsolicited advice? What would Jesus say about your ability to listen? What changes do you need to make?**

(2) **Be alert for differences in interpretation of a conversation, meeting, newscast, or other situation in which you and others heard the same words spoken but disagreed about what they meant. What could you learn from other people's interpretations? Did their ideas change your interpretation?**

(3) **Notice when and how adults use stories to communicate. Do you find that stories help you to learn something? How often do you tell stories yourself? Jesus often used stories to communicate spiritual truths. How could you use a story to convey your own experiences of God?**

❖ Sing or read aloud "The Voice of God Is Calling."

❖ Say these words from 1 Peter one phrase at a time and ask the class to repeat them: **Prepare your minds for action; discipline yourselves; set all your hope on the grace that Jesus Christ will bring you when he is revealed.**

FREE TO FORGIVE

PREVIEWING THE LESSON

Lesson Scripture: Matthew 18:21-35
Background Scripture: Matthew 18:21-35
Key Verse: Matthew 18:27

Focus of the Lesson:
Most of us desire forgiveness when we have wronged another, but we often find it difficult to forgive others when they have wronged us. Can we afford the consequences of living with such inconsistencies? The parable of the unforgiving slave goes beyond a limited view of forgiveness; it calls for a spirit of unconditional forgiveness toward others.

Goals for the Learners:
(1) to unpack the meaning of the parable of the unforgiving slave.
(2) to consider why they sometimes find it difficult to forgive others.
(3) to recall and celebrate times when they sought and received forgiveness.

Supplies:
Bibles, newsprint and marker, paper and pencils, hymnals

READING THE SCRIPTURE

NRSV
Matthew 18:21-35

21 Then Peter came and said to him, "Lord, if another member of the church sins against me, how often should I forgive? As many as seven times?" 22 Jesus said to him, "Not seven times, but, I tell you, seventy-seven times.

23 "For this reason the kingdom of heaven may be compared to a king who wished to settle accounts with his slaves. 24 When he began the reckoning, one who owed him ten thousand talents was brought to him;

NIV
Matthew 18:21-35

[21]Then Peter came to Jesus and asked, "Lord, how many times shall I forgive my brother when he sins against me? Up to seven times?"

[22]Jesus answered, "I tell you, not seven times, but seventy-seven times.

[23]"Therefore, the kingdom of heaven is like a king who wanted to settle accounts with his servants. [24]As he began the settlement, a man who owed him ten thousand talents was brought to him. [25]Since he was

25 and, as he could not pay, his lord ordered him to be sold, together with his wife and children and all his possessions, and payment to be made. 26 So the slave fell on his knees before him, saying, 'Have patience with me, and I will pay you everything.' **27 And out of pity for him, the lord of that slave released him and forgave him the debt.** 28 But that same slave, as he went out, came upon one of his fellow slaves who owed him a hundred denarii; and seizing him by the throat, he said, 'Pay what you owe.' 29 Then his fellow slave fell down and pleaded with him, 'Have patience with me, and I will pay you.' 30 But he refused; then he went and threw him into prison until he would pay the debt. 31 When his fellow slaves saw what had happened, they were greatly distressed, and they went and reported to their lord all that had taken place. 32 Then his lord summoned him and said to him, 'You wicked slave! I forgave you all that debt because you pleaded with me. 33 Should you not have had mercy on your fellow slave, as I had mercy on you?' 34 And in anger his lord handed him over to be tortured until he would pay his entire debt. 35 So my heavenly Father will also do to every one of you, if you do not forgive your brother or sister from your heart."

not able to pay, the master ordered that he and his wife and his children and all that he had be sold to repay the debt.

^{26}"The servant fell on his knees before him. 'Be patient with me,' he begged, 'and I will pay back everything.' **^{27}The servant's master took pity on him, canceled the debt and let him go.**

^{28}"But when that servant went out, he found one of his fellow servants who owed him a hundred denarii. He grabbed him and began to choke him. 'Pay back what you owe me!' he demanded.

^{29}"His fellow servant fell to his knees and begged him, 'Be patient with me, and I will pay you back.'

^{30}"But he refused. Instead, he went off and had the man thrown into prison until he could pay the debt. ^{31}When the other servants saw what had happened, they were greatly distressed and went and told their master everything that had happened.

^{32}"Then the master called the servant in. 'You wicked servant,' he said, 'I canceled all that debt of yours because you begged me to. ^{33}Shouldn't you have had mercy on your fellow servant just as I had on you?' ^{34}In anger his master turned him over to the jailers to be tortured, until he should pay back all he owed.

^{35}"This is how my heavenly Father will treat each of you unless you forgive your brother from your heart."

UNDERSTANDING THE SCRIPTURE

Matthew 18:21. This verse continues the teachings of Jesus in this chapter, which contains the fourth of five major discourses of Jesus in Matthew (chapters 5–7; 10; 13; 18; 23–25). Jesus' teachings in Matthew 18 focus on relationships, especially relationships in the community of faith. In verses 15-20, Jesus had described how to deal with church members whose sins threatened to disrupt the fellowship of the church. Lest the teaching in verses 15-20 be used too readily or in too punitive a manner, verses 21-35 remind Matthew's readers of the importance of restoring relationships through forgiveness rather than simply following the regulations. The implication of Peter's question is that he thought he was being generous in saying "as many as seven times."

Matthew 18:22. Jesus' reply to Peter's

question indicates generosity far beyond what Peter had proposed. The expression "seventy-seven times" may be related to Genesis 4:24, where the expression is "seventy-seven" in the ancient Greek translation. The question is not whether Jesus called for forgiveness seventy-seven times (NRSV, NIV) or four-hundred-and-ninety times (KJV). Jesus' point was not about specific numbers but about paying no attention to specific numbers. Jesus called for generous, lavish, seemingly excessive forgiveness rather than being quick to blame, hold a grudge, and seek revenge.

Matthew 18:23. Review the discussion of parables in the lesson for July 17 on Matthew 13:3 in Understanding the Scripture. Note especially that a parable compares one thing and another and is intended to stimulate thought. Note, too, that the interpretation of a parable generally has one main meaning. To interpret a parable allegorically was not the method the people of Jesus' day would have used to think about and understand the parable. Thus neither should we attempt to find a parallel to every detail of the parable.

The "kingdom of heaven" is Matthew's expression for the kingdom of God. The parable is about "a king who wished to settle accounts with his slaves." The word translated "slaves" in the NRSV can also be translated "servants," as in the NIV. Although either translation of the word is appropriate, the image seems more likely to be of a king settling accounts with those who served him as administrators rather than necessarily referring to people the king owned as slaves.

Matthew 18:24. The settlement of accounts revealed that one administrator "owed him ten thousand talents." The note in the NRSV that a talent was equivalent to fifteen years' wages of a laborer suggests the greatness of the debt—thus 150,000 years of work. A talent was the largest unit of money and was worth six thousand drachmas. A drachma was equivalent to a denarius, which was the daily pay of a laborer. Thus, figured in terms of the denarius, the size of the debt would be equivalent to sixty million days' pay. The amount could have been even larger, since another measurement of the value of the talent is that it was equivalent to ten thousand denarii, which would mean the size of the debt was equivalent to one hundred million days' pay. The point is that the size of the debt was simply inconceivable.

Matthew 18:25. Selling a person and his family for payment of debt was practiced in the Gentile, but not the Jewish world. In the Jewish world, a thief could be sold for repayment for what he had stolen, but the thief's wife could not (Exodus 22:1). Even by selling the whole family and all this debtor's possessions, though, the amount recovered would not approach the greatness of the debt in the parable in Matthew. The price of a slave in that day would have been only as high as about 2,000 denarii. Thus, the debtor had absolutely no hope of repaying the debt.

Matthew 18:26. In desperation, the debtor "fell on his knees" and asked for patience. He must have known how impossible it was to fulfill the promise, "I will pay you everything." In light of the rest of the parable, are we to think of this behavior as manipulation, desperation, or both?

Matthew 18:27. "Out of pity" is the key thought in this verse. The word refers to being moved with compassion. Indeed, no motive other than compassion can be found.

Matthew 18:28. How would the forgiven debtor live now that the king had forgiven him? His behavior toward a fellow servant who was in his debt was as shocking as the amount of debt he had once owed. He attacked his fellow servant physically and violently. The sum the fellow servant owed would have been considered substantial. A "hundred denarii" was equivalent to a hundred days' pay for a laborer. The sum, however, was inconsequential in comparison to what the forgiven debtor had once owed.

Matthew 18:29-30. The fellow servant sought mercy, using the words the forgiven debtor had used. The forgiven debtor rejected the request for mercy and put his fellow servant in prison until the debt was paid.

Matthew 18:31-33. On hearing the report from the other servants about what the forgiven debtor had done, the king angrily took action. The meaning of the parable hinges on the king's question in verse 33, "Should you not have had mercy on your fellow slave, as I had mercy on you?"

Matthew 18:34. The king took back his earlier forgiveness of the debt and cast the debtor into prison until the debt was repaid. Obviously the debtor had no hope of ever repaying the debt.

Matthew 18:35. The word "so" brings the comparison in the parable to a focus. Exactly what is the point of comparison? Is every detail, including the king's taking back the forgiveness earlier extended, a part of the point of comparison? Especially important here is the previous warning about treating a parable as an allegory. Consider the meaning of the parable in the context of Peter's question in verse 21 and Jesus' response in verse 22. Doesn't the parable teach that we are to be generous in extending forgiveness to our fellow human beings? To fail to extend such forgiveness to people who have wronged us is completely out of touch with Jesus' teachings.

INTERPRETING THE SCRIPTURE

Calculating Forgiveness

Peter's question to Jesus revealed what he really thought about forgiveness. Even though he was willing to go beyond what his culture had taught him, he felt that surely there had to be a limit to forgiveness.

In our minds and hearts, don't we feel the same way? We certainly like to think of ourselves as people who do not act nearly as negatively as others when a wrong is done to us. Don't we have real questions, though, about forgiving heinous or continual wrongs against others and ourselves?

Jesus' teaching about forgiveness is just not that easy to practice, is it? That's why we find many Christians readily joining others in calling for retaliation when a building is bombed and for revenge when a crime is committed. If we indeed are to behave as Christians, we must ask ourselves where calling for revenge or holding grudges is in line with Jesus' teachings about forgiveness.

Calculating forgiveness—limiting forgiveness to certain kinds of wrongs or to certain numbers of wrongs—is foreign to the teaching of Jesus in this verse. Like it or not, Jesus' teaching about forgiveness in this verse calls us to forgive the person who keeps being obnoxious, even hateful, toward us. Can any act against us be too great for us to refuse to forgive the wrongdoer who committed it? We should recall that scripture records Jesus saying, "Father, forgive them," even while he was being crucified (see Luke 23:34).

Seeking and Receiving Forgiveness

Exactly what is forgiveness anyway? In the relationship of the king and his servants, particularly the one servant who owed an astronomical sum, we can see at least a glimmer of what it is. To combine the ancient parable and our modern practice, being forgiven is like the bank saying to us that although we once owed them a billion dollars and were on our way to bankruptcy or jail, it has forgiven that debt. The bank no longer has a record of it. In fact, our credit record is now unblemished.

You may be wondering what the name of that bank is. It's the bank of heaven, for that's what God has done for us. Paul wrote of such forgiveness when he said, "God proves his love for us in that while we still were sinners Christ died for us" (Romans 5:8).

The main reason we do not recognize our responsibility to forgive others is that we do not appreciate how far God had to come to forgive us. We think our wrongs against God were small so that forgiving us was pretty easy, a light thing, really. When we think and feel this way, we ignore four words in the verse Paul wrote. Those four words are, "Christ died for us" (Romans 5:8).

We must avoid interpreting this parable in an allegorical manner and letting the king represent God and the heavily indebted servant represent people. After all, do we really want to think of God as selling a person's wife and children because of that person's sins? Even as we try to avoid the danger of allegorical interpretation, however, it is difficult not to let the king's forgiveness of the servant's enormous debt remind us of what God in Christ has done for us.

Against such a background, the parable takes on added meaning as we let it lead us to consider how we are to treat people who have wronged us. Simply put, we are to extend forgiveness to them in the same manner in which the king forgave the enormous debt and in which God offers forgiveness to us.

Is such an approach soft? You can take that up with Jesus, if you wish. The fact is, however, that no other approach breaks the chain of wrong that binds our world. As long as nations, peoples, and individuals continue to return evil for evil, the chain of evil will continue. Only forgiveness can break the chain.

Have you ever been caught up in a situation in which wrongs were done and then wrongs were done in return so that the conflict continued? Almost any church conflict, or any conflict situation at all, is based on such behavior. As long as the blaming and the wrongs continue, the problem continues. The conflict can be resolved only when someone says, "I'm sorry," and someone else says, "I forgive you. Let's start again."

Denying Forgiveness

The parable reminds us that truly receiving forgiveness means practicing forgiveness ourselves. The forgiven debtor showed that his request to the king for forgiveness was just manipulation and his receiving the king's forgiveness was just another successful slick deal.

In church relationships and in other human relationships attempts at reconciliation sometimes don't work or don't last. Why is that? One reason is that one or the other party didn't consider the reconciliation very real to begin with. It was only a truce until one side or the other gained strategic advantage, rather than being a genuine forgiveness of wrongs.

What should have happened in this parable? The forgiven debtor should have been so affected by the king's forgiveness of his enormous debt that he took the first opportunity he had to be kind and merciful to someone who owed him a substantial amount, too. When the opportunity came, though, the forgiven debtor revealed that he had failed to get the message.

In the same manner, when we fail to extend forgiveness to those who have wronged us, we indicate that we have not gotten the message about forgiveness.

Extending Genuine Forgiveness

The comment in verse 35 comes after the king has taken back his forgiveness of the debtor because of the debtor's treatment of his fellow servant. The comment reminds us of the importance of being generous in our relationships with people who have wronged us. If there is agreement with this idea, we now have at least three possibilities for applying Jesus' teaching about unlimited forgiveness.

One possibility is to give lip service to Jesus' teaching on forgiveness but continue to live just as we prefer. That happens day in and day out in personal relationships, in the work setting, in community affairs, in national and international situations, and, yes, even in church relationships. We simply accept the approach of our culture, which holds that getting back at those who have wronged us is appropriate.

A second possibility is to seek to put forgiveness into practice as a law and observe it strictly and legalistically, with no regard for specific circumstances. We treat wrong actions lightly, condoning them and allowing the wrongdoer to continue to run roughshod over others and us, and call that

forgiveness. Such an approach leaves us with some difficult issues, though. For example, is the child molester—in the church as well as elsewhere—to be "forgiven" over and over and be turned loose to continue to prey on innocent children? Surely not.

A third possibility is to seek ways to be faithful to Jesus' teaching in each circumstance we face. Keep in mind that the context for the teaching in 18:21-22 is the preceding discussion about discipline and correction in the church (18:15-17). Forgiving others continually does not mean condoning their actions continually. Forgiving certainly means avoiding revenge, as Jesus clearly taught (see 5:38-48), but it may well include correction of wrongdoers' actions and protection of people wrongdoers might harm.

SHARING THE SCRIPTURE

PREPARING TO TEACH

Preparing Our Hearts

This week's devotional reading is found in 2 Corinthians 2:5-11. Consider what Paul has to say about forgiving someone who has apparently caused him pain. What does Paul tell the congregation to do? How does Paul interpret a lack of forgiveness? Are there similar situations in your congregation? If so, how can you work toward resolution of the problem and forgiveness of the one(s) who have caused others pain?

Pray that you and your students will be open to forgiving others and yourselves.

Preparing Our Minds

Study the background and lesson scripture, Matthew 18:21-35.

Write on newsprint:

questions under "Consider Why the

Learners Sometimes Find It Difficult to Forgive Others."

information for next week's lesson, found under "Continue the Journey."

Plan how you will present the information from the Understanding the Scripture portion as suggested in the section entitled "Unpack the Meaning of the Parable of the Unforgiving Slave."

LEADING THE CLASS

(1) Gather to Learn

❖ Welcome the class members and introduce any guests.

❖ Pray that the students will hear God speaking to them about forgiveness as we study today's lesson.

❖ Invite the class to talk about how they feel when they experience or read about cases of:

■ road rage that results in an accident or

argument that leads to serious injury or death.

- rage in a school, possibly leading to the death and serious injury of students and/or staff.
- rage in the workplace when a current or former employee responds to a grievance by killing or injuring others.

❖ Lead a brief discussion on these questions.

(1) How might forgiveness on the part of the enraged person have tempered any of these situations?

(2) What role might forgiveness play in the lives of the loved ones or victims of the enraged person?

❖ Read aloud today's focus statement: **Most of us desire forgiveness when we have wronged another, but we often find it difficult to forgive others when they have wronged us. Can we afford the consequences of living with such inconsistencies? The parable of the unforgiving slave goes beyond a limited view of forgiveness; it calls for a spirit of unconditional forgiveness toward others.**

(2) Unpack the Meaning of the Parable of the Unforgiving Slave

❖ Read Matthew 18:21-22.

- Use the information for these two verses from Understanding the Scripture to create a brief lecture about Jesus' teaching on forgiveness in response to Peter's question.

❖ Move to the parable in verses 23-35 that Jesus uses to illustrate his point by asking for volunteers to read the parts of the first debtor, second debtor, king, and narrator.

- Retell information from Matthew 18:24 and 18:25 in Understanding the Scripture to help the students understand the enormous debt that the first debtor owed.
- Discuss these questions.

(1) What might Jesus' listeners have

thought when they heard the sum of money owed to the king by the first debtor?

(2) What might they have thought when they heard the debt owed by the second servant?

(3) What motivated the king to act on behalf of the first servant by forgiving his debt?

(4) What motivated the king to change his mind?

(5) Do you think the king's responses were fair? Why or why not?

(6) What do you think Jesus' "take home" message is for you today?

- Retell or read the information found under "Extending Genuine Forgiveness." You may want to list on newsprint the three ways of applying Jesus' teachings: lip service; legalistic application; faithfulness to Jesus' teachings.
- Invite the students to respond to these ideas.

(3) Consider Why the Learners Sometimes Find It Difficult to Forgive Others

❖ Brainstorm with the class answers to this question: **Why is it sometimes difficult to forgive those who have wronged us?** Write their ideas on newsprint.

❖ Distribute paper and pencils. Ask the students to work independently to write about a person/situation that they find difficult to forgive. Suggest that they write answers to these questions, which you will want to post on newsprint. Note that their answers will not be shared.

(1) What happened to cause a rupture in your relationship?

(2) What impact did this situation have on you?

(3) What impact did this situation appear to have on the one who may have caused the problem?

(4) What barriers make it difficult for you to forgive this individual?

(5) How might offering forgiveness to this person change you?

❖ Encourage the students to write a closing sentence in which they offer forgiveness, as if writing to this individual.

❖ Challenge the students to act on what they have written.

❖ Try to extend the idea of personal forgiveness to encompass larger groups who have difficulty forgiving. Note that in the section entitled "Calculating Forgiveness" we have said that practicing forgiveness is not easy. Often Christians join the call "for retaliation when a building is bombed and for revenge when a crime is committed." Encourage the students to comment on how the world could be different if Christians began to take Jesus' teachings on forgiveness seriously.

(4) Recall and Celebrate Times of Forgiveness

❖ Encourage the class members to recall silently a time when they needed to receive forgiveness from someone else and that person responded by forgiving.

❖ Invite the students to talk about how they feel when someone forgives them. (Be sure to keep the discussion focused on feelings, not on the incidents that prompted the need for forgiveness.)

❖ Give the students an opportunity to express thanks for times when they have been forgiven, and to recall how forgiveness brought them a sense of wholeness.

(5) Continue the Journey

❖ Pray that the students will give, seek, and receive forgiveness this week.

❖ Read aloud this preparation for next week's lesson. You may also want to post it on newsprint for the students to copy.

Prepare for next week's session entitled "Meeting Human Needs" by reading Matthew 25:31-46, which is both the background and lesson scripture. Focus your study on these ideas: Many people claim there is a tension between religious devotion and involvement in such social concerns as poverty, hunger, and compassion for those who are rejected. How can we best express our devotion and commitment? Christ, to whom we are finally accountable, meets us in our world today through those who are in need.

❖ Read aloud the following three ideas. Challenge the students to commit themselves to use these activities as a springboard to spiritual growth.

(1) Recall any debts that are owed to you. If you are financially able to do so, would you be willing to forgive any of this debt? If so, find an appropriate way to let the debtor know. (Be careful, though, about forgiving debts if doing so will prompt the debtor to act irresponsibly, thus doing more harm than good.)

(2) Spend time with God in prayer examining your own faults and sins. Experience God's gracious forgiveness. Afterward, forgive someone who has wronged you.

(3) Make a deliberate effort to ask forgiveness for a wrong you have committed against someone else.

❖ Sing or read aloud "Forgive Our Sins as We Forgive."

❖ Say these words from 1 Peter one phrase at a time and ask the class to repeat them: **Prepare your minds for action; discipline yourselves; set all your hope on the grace that Jesus Christ will bring you when he is revealed.**

MEETING HUMAN NEEDS

PREVIEWING THE LESSON

Lesson Scripture: Matthew 25:31-46
Background Scripture: Matthew 25:31-46
Key Verse: Matthew 25:40

Focus of the Lesson:
Many people claim there is a tension between religious devotion and involvement in such social concerns as poverty, hunger, and compassion for those who are rejected. How can we best express our devotion and commitment? Christ, to whom we are finally accountable, meets us in our world today through those who are in need.

Goals for the Learners:
(1) to study Jesus' teaching regarding the Great Judgment.
(2) to explore how their acts of service to others have spiritual implications.
(3) to identify and implement plans to serve God through helping others

You will need these supplies:
Bibles, newsprint and marker, paper and pencils, hymnals

READING THE SCRIPTURE

NRSV
Matthew 25:31-46

31 "When the Son of Man comes in his glory, and all the angels with him, then he will sit on the throne of his glory. 32 All the nations will be gathered before him, and he will separate people one from another as a shepherd separates the sheep from the goats, 33 and he will put the sheep at his right hand and the goats at the left. 34 Then the king will say to those at his right hand, 'Come, you that are blessed by my Father, inherit the kingdom prepared for you from the foundation of the world; 35 for I was hungry and you gave me food, I was thirsty

NIV
Matthew 25:31-46

31"When the Son of Man comes in his glory, and all the angels with him, he will sit on his throne in heavenly glory. 32All the nations will be gathered before him, and he will separate the people one from another as a shepherd separates the sheep from the goats. 33He will put the sheep on his right and the goats on his left.

34"Then the King will say to those on his right, 'Come, you who are blessed by my Father; take your inheritance, the kingdom prepared for you since the creation of the world. 35For I was hungry and you gave me and you gave me something to drink, I was a stranger and you welcomed me, 36 I was naked and you gave me clothing, I was sick and you took care of me, I was in prison and you visited me.' 37 Then the righteous will answer him, 'Lord, when was it that we saw you hungry and gave you food, or thirsty and gave you something to drink? 38 And when was it that we saw you a stranger and welcomed you, or naked and gave you clothing? 39 And when was it that we saw you sick or in prison and visited you?' **40 And the king will answer them, 'Truly I tell you, just as you did it to one of the least of these who are members of my family, you did it to me.'** 41 Then he will say to those at his left hand, 'You that are accursed, depart from me into the eternal fire prepared for the devil and his angels; 42 for I was hungry and you gave me no food, I was thirsty and you gave me nothing to drink, 43 I was a stranger and you did not welcome me, naked and you did not give me clothing, sick and in prison and you did not visit me.' 44 Then they also will answer, 'Lord, when was it that we saw you hungry or thirsty or a stranger or naked or sick or in prison, and did not take care of you?' 45 Then he will answer them, 'Truly I tell you, just as you did not do it to one of the least of these, you did not do it to me.' 46 And these will go away into eternal punishment, but the righteous into eternal life."

something to eat, I was thirsty and you gave me something to drink, I was a stranger and you invited me in, 36I needed clothes and you clothed me, I was sick and you looked after me, I was in prison and you came to visit me.'

37"Then the righteous will answer him, 'Lord, when did we see you hungry and feed you, or thirsty and give you something to drink? 38When did we see you a stranger and invite you in, or needing clothes and clothe you? 39When did we see you sick or in prison and go to visit you?'

40"**The King will reply, 'I tell you the truth, whatever you did for one of the least of these brothers of mine, you did for me.'**

41"Then he will say to those on his left, 'Depart from me, you who are cursed, into the eternal fire prepared for the devil and his angels. 42For I was hungry and you gave me nothing to eat, I was thirsty and you gave me nothing to drink, 43I was a stranger and you did not invite me in, I needed clothes and you did not clothe me, I was sick and in prison and you did not look after me.'

44"They also will answer, 'Lord, when did we see you hungry or thirsty or a stranger or needing clothes or sick or in prison, and did not help you?'

45"He will reply, 'I tell you the truth, whatever you did not do for one of the least of these, you did not do for me.'

46"Then they will go away to eternal punishment, but the righteous to eternal life."

UNDERSTANDING THE SCRIPTURE

Matthew 25:31. Matthew 23–25 is the fifth of five major sections of Jesus' teaching in the Gospel of Matthew (chapters 5–7, 10, 13, 18, 23–25). Within this section of teaching, Matthew 24–25 is apocalyptic in nature (see 24:3). Thus, although sometimes referred to as a parable, Matthew 25:31-46 can be better described as apocalyptic discourse. Apocalyptic literature is concerned with the end time, the time when God will wrap up all of history. Apocalyptic literature considers the end of this present evil age and the inauguration of the age to come, when God's victory will be demonstrated. Also involved is the conflict between good and evil, which can also be expressed as the struggle between God and evil, with evil often being represented by Satan.

The expression "a son of man" can be traced to Daniel 7:13-14. In that text, God gives this exalted figure "authority, glory and sovereign power; all peoples, nations and men of every language worshiped him. His dominion is an everlasting dominion that will not pass away, and his kingdom is one that will never be destroyed" (7:14 NIV). For verses in Matthew that specifically identify Jesus as the Son of Man, see for example 8:20; 9:6; 11:19; 12:8, 32, 40; 13:37, 41; 16:13; 17:9, 12, 22; 20:18, 28; 26:2, 24, 45. Other verses in Matthew also apply to Jesus as the Son of Man: 10:23; 16:27, 28; 19:28; 24:27, 30, 37, 39, 44; 26:64. When Jesus is called the Son of Man, the title indicates not only Jesus' humanity but also his exalted status.

The coming of the Son of Man "in his glory, and all the angels with him" and with the Son of Man sitting "on the throne of his glory" are all apocalyptic images. The picture emphasizes God's control and magnifies God's coming victory over all opposition.

Matthew 25:32. In Matthew, the expression "all the nations" appears here and in 24:9, 14; 28:19. To whom or what does it refer? One long-standing interpretation is that the expression refers to all the peoples of the world. Interpreting the expression in this manner puts it in line with how it is generally interpreted in 28:19. While this interpretation may well be correct and is the one that Interpreting the Scripture reflects, at least one other possible interpretation should be noted. That interpretation suggests that "all the nations" refers to the Gentiles. That understanding of the Greek words behind the English words would have been common among the Jews of that day, in fact. By this interpretation, the judgment scene is of people beyond the Jewish and Christian communities. An unlikely interpretation sometimes put forward is that "nations" refers to national entities, not individuals. Finding biblical support for this view is difficult, however. In fact, the Greek grammar of this verse militates against it.

In the Palestine of Jesus' day, sheep and goats might be mingled together in one flock. Identifying which were sheep and which were goats was an easy task for the shepherd, though.

Matthew 25:33. "At his right hand" refers to the place of honor. The "left" would indicate the opposite side and thus the place of dishonor.

Matthew 25:34-35. "The Son of Man" in verse 31 has become "the king" in verse 34. The king began the judgment proceedings by inviting those who "are blessed by my Father" to "inherit the kingdom" (25:34). The division is made on the basis of how those gathered before the king treated him when he was in need. Six descriptions of people with needs appear here. The descriptions speak of acts of hospitality and care. Praising such acts would not have been a surprise, for most were spoken of in the Old Testament (see Job 22:6-7; Isaiah 58:7; Ezekiel 18:7). In each case the action met the need.

Matthew 25:37-39. Although the king praised "the righteous" for their acts, they could not recall doing them for the king (compare to 6:1-4). "The righteous" describes those who acted in a just and good manner and thus in accord with God's desires.

Matthew 25:40. The king revealed that "the righteous" had helped him in all the ways described when they had helped "the least of these who are members of my family." Who is referred to as the ones who unknowingly helped the king? Is the reference to all people in need? If those gathered at the judgment scene are all people, the reference here to all people in need would be most appropriate. If those gathered at the judgment scene are the Gentiles, those beyond the Jewish and Christian communities, then additional possibilities have been suggested. Most prominent is the thought that they are Jesus' disciples whom he had sent out on mission. Therefore, to treat Jesus' disciples well was to give the same treatment to Jesus himself (see 10:40-42).

Matthew 25:41-43. The king rendered the opposite judgment to those on his opposite side. He pronounced them "accursed" because of their behavior toward him when he was in need. As indicated in the comments on verse 40, withholding ministry to the needy king had occurred when they had either withheld help from needy people in general or from Jesus' missionaries in particular. The righteous had been blessed by life in the kingdom (25:34). Now the "accursed" were banished from the kingdom and the king's presence "into the eternal fire prepared for the devil and his angels" (25:41). The contrast could not be starker.

Matthew 25:44. Those on the left hand protested that they had never seen the king in need. Their protest implies that was the reason they had failed to respond with kindness and goodness.

Matthew 25:45. As with the righteous in verse 40, the king revealed to those on his left hand why they were being condemned. They were being condemned because they had ignored the needs with which they had been confronted.

Matthew 25:46. "Eternal life" for those who had acted with kindness and goodness contrasts with "eternal punishment" for those who had acted callously.

INTERPRETING THE SCRIPTURE

Final Exam

Students rarely look forward to final examinations. As students enter the room, take their seats, and await the distribution of the tests, some have studied much and yet they are concerned. Some have studied little, but they are confident they will be able to bluff their way through the exam.

Final examinations are about accountability, and that is what Matthew 25:31-46 is about. It is about our accountability for living in ways that honor God.

The emphasis of the passage is not new. Indeed, it is straight out of the prophets. Through the centuries, the prophets had thundered forth God's demand for social reform, joining concern for worship of the true God and concern for human beings' physical needs. For example, Jeremiah had proclaimed to a shocked audience in the Temple, "For if you truly amend your ways and your doings, if you truly act justly one with another, if you do not oppress the alien, the orphan, and the widow, or shed innocent blood in this place, and if you do not go after other gods to your own hurt, then I will dwell with you in this place, in the land that I gave of old to your ancestors forever and ever" (Jeremiah 7:5-8; see Amos 2:6-7).

We see this emphasis on concern for human needs elsewhere in the New Testament also. One of the clearest and most notable is in James 2:15-16: "If a brother or sister is naked and lacks daily food, and one of you says to them, 'Go in peace; keep warm and eat your fill,' and yet you do not supply their bodily needs, what is the good of that?" A similar theme is sounded in James 1:27.

The passages just cited refer, strictly speaking, to extending care and justice to members of the covenant community. Do we dare, though, to limit our concern for people to our fellow church members or even our fellow Christians? The love of the God who "gives to all mortals life and breath," who "is not far from each one of us," and in whom "we live and move and have our being" is not to be so narrowly defined (Acts 17:25-28). It will do us no good to complain to God one day, "We didn't think that was going to be on the test."

God might well respond, "Why didn't you read the Book?"

Questions in Advance

Teachers know that when the first test comes up, and certainly the next, and by all means the final, students often clamor to know this piece of information: "Will that be on the test?" They at least want the teacher to provide questions that will guide their study. In this passage, Jesus, the Son of Man, did even better. He provided the questions in advance. They go like this:

- *When I was hungry, did you give me food?*
- *When I was thirsty, did you give me something to quench my thirst?*
- *When I was a person whom you did not know and who was different from you, your family, and your friends, did you accept and welcome me?*
- *When I was ill-clad because of my poverty, did you give me clothing that would give me dignity again?*
- *When I was sick, did you take care of me?*
- *When I was in prison, did you come to see me and care for my needs?*

Consider these questions another way.

- Did you let my children go hungry? Recent information indicates that 10 percent of the United States population is "food insecure," meaning that they do not have assurance of access to enough food to live healthy lives. This percentage amounts to more than 30 million people, and 12 million of these are children.
- Did you help my children when they were sick? Answering such a question includes visiting those who are ill and finding ways to encourage caregivers. It also includes encouraging research for preventing and curing illness plus providing healthy living conditions so that people are not as susceptible to illnesses.
- Did you find ways to welcome my children from other places and backgrounds into your community and your church? The world is coming to the United States. Hardly any community is so isolated that people of other national backgrounds have not come to it. Will we accept and love them as God does? In the book of Exodus, God instructed that aliens who lived in the midst of God's people be treated rightly. God commanded, "You shall not wrong or oppress a resident alien" (Exodus 22:21; see Leviticus 19:33; 24:22; Deuteronomy 27:19). Indeed, God had instructed, "You shall love the alien as yourself" (Leviticus 19:34; see Leviticus 19:10; 23:22).

- Did you care for those in prison? Religious intolerance around the world can lead to imprisonment. Can we seek ways to promote religious tolerance? What about prisoners here in the United States? Some churches minister to the children of prisoners, who suffer because a parent is in prison.
- Did you let my children be mistreated? Barriers to full acceptance as human beings and children of God are myriad, including such matters as poverty, handicapping conditions, family background, racial background, gender bias, national origin, age, and unusual appearance.

The questions can be multiplied. Leo Tolstoy's classic story, "Where Love Is, There God Is Also," speaks to such questions. The story tells of an old man who is pondering how truly to live the Christian life. He wants assurance that he is being faithful. A voice awakens him from sleep. It is the voice of Christ, telling the man that he will come to him in the coming day. The next day, the old man looks for Christ all day long, but he does not see Christ. He does see, though, an old soldier to whom he offers refreshing hot tea. He also sees a poverty-stricken woman and baby, whom he invites into his home to eat. Then he encourages a merchant to forgive a hungry boy who had stolen an apple from him. The old man then purchases the apple and gives it to the boy. As the day comes to an end, the old man is disappointed that he has not seen Christ. Then a voice whispers to him, "Martuin—ah, Martuin, did you not recognize me?" Then out from the shadows steps each of the people the old man had helped that day.

Tests Graded

The questions on the final examination described in verses 31-46 are not options; they are not for extra credit. They are the basics of real Christianity. Answering them well reveals whether our faith is real or false. They are not means to salvation, but rather they are markers that indicate the genuineness of salvation.

E. Stanley Jones, the great preacher and church leader, writes in his book, *The Reconstruction of the Church—On What Pattern?*, about a group of Christians who were feeding hungry people at the end of World War II. A Polish woman, uncertain of what was happening, asked whether they offered food to everybody who needed it. The group replied that they did. "Poles?" "Yes" was the reply. "Germans?" Again the reply was "Yes." "Russians?" Again, "Yes." "Jews?" "Yes." "Atheists?" "Yes." The woman sighed and said, "I knew there ought to be people like that."

Are you one of them?

SHARING THE SCRIPTURE

PREPARING TO TEACH

Preparing Our Hearts

This week's devotional reading is found in Luke 6:27-31. These verses are part of Jesus' Sermon on the Plain, which Luke records. In these verses we hear Jesus telling us to love and pray for our enemies, to give to those who beg from us, and to do unto others as we would want them to do to us. These are hard words to hear and even harder to enact because they run counter to the way most of us respond. If we give, we want to get in return. No, Jesus says, give without expecting anything. Think about how seriously you take Jesus' teachings. What would he say to you personally concerning this passage?

Pray that you and your students will act in love toward all persons, including those who seem unlovable and those who are in need.

Preparing Our Minds

Study the background and lesson scripture, Matthew 24:31-46.

Write on newsprint:

the first set of questions (in italics) under "Questions in Advance" in the Interpreting the Scripture portion.

list of outreach projects your congregation supports.

information for next week's lesson, found under "Continue the Journey."

Plan to have a list of outreach projects your congregation supports with volunteer time and/or money. You may need to speak with the chairperson of your missions or outreach committee or your pastor to compile this list.

LEADING THE CLASS

(1) Gather to Learn

❖ Welcome the class members and introduce any guests.

❖ Pray that the learners will be open to ways that they can serve God by serving others, just as Jesus taught us to do.

❖ Discuss the following three questions. List the answers for 1 and 2 on newsprint, which will be used later in the session.

(1) **What groups of people in our local community are in need?** (Be sure to list groups, not names of individuals.)

(2) **What church or nonprofit agencies exist to help persons in each group?** (Write the name(s) of the helping organization next to each group. The same organization may be listed more than once.)

(3) **What role do you believe Christians are called to play in assisting people in need?**

❖ Read aloud today's focus statement: **Many people claim there is a tension between religious devotion and involvement in such social concerns as poverty, hunger, and compassion for those who are rejected. How can we best express our devotion and commitment? Christ, to whom we are finally accountable, meets us in our world today through those who are in need.**

(2) Study Jesus' Teaching Regarding the Great Judgment

❖ Note that Jesus has much to say about how persons who pay attention to those in need and how persons who ignore the needy will be treated at the time of the last judgment.

❖ Choose a volunteer to read expressively Matthew 25:31-46, as if Jesus were giving that message. If space permits, ask volunteers to act as sheep and goats, standing at the reader's right and left hands, respectively.

❖ Post the questions that were raised in "Questions in Advance" that you wrote on newsprint prior to the session.

❖ Look at these questions in light of the groups that you identified earlier. How are the two lists similar and different?

❖ Read or retell the bulleted information that follows the sentence "Consider these questions another way" in the "Questions in Advance" section of the Interpreting the

Scripture portion. Invite class members to add any information they know concerning the needs Jesus addresses.

(3) Explore How the Learners' Acts of Service to Others Have Spiritual Implications

❖ Look again at today's focus statement. Encourage the students to discuss their understanding of the relationship between personal piety and action to fill needs and bring social and economic justice.

❖ Read aloud the list of outreach projects you have compiled for your church. Encourage class members to tell brief stories of how they have been involved in this project (either as a helper or recipient).

❖ Distribute paper and pencils. Encourage the students to write a few phrases or sentences about how they feel when they can help to meet the needs of others, or experience the love of Christian brothers and sisters meeting their needs. Volunteers may be willing to share some key words or ideas from their writing.

❖ Indicate that for many people helping activities bring a positive emotional feeling.

❖ Wrap up this part of the lesson by asking the students to go beyond the warm, fuzzy emotions and state aloud whatever spiritual implications they can envision or have experienced as a result of helping someone in need. In other words, what impact does helping others have on one's spiritual life?

(4) Identify and Implement Plans to Serve God Through Helping Others

❖ Direct the students' attention to the sheets of newsprint, which include groups in need and outreach projects, posted around the room.

❖ Challenge the class to accept responsibility for dealing with one or more of these groups. Invite each person in the class to (1) select a group of people he or she would like to help; (2) identify a church or nonprofit agency or project that helps such persons; and (3) make a commitment to get involved as a volunteer, financial backer, or political activist.

❖ Ask each student to write on the back of the paper they already have exactly what he or she would like in the coming week(s) to be able to do to help persons in need.

(5) Continue the Journey

❖ Pray that the learners will each follow through on the commitment they have made to serve someone in need in Jesus' name.

❖ Read aloud this preparation for next week's lesson. You may also want to post it on newsprint for the students to copy. **Prepare for next week's session entitled "What Is My Calling?" by reading the background scripture from Luke 4:14-30, especially verses 16-24 and 28-30. As you study keep this focus in mind: People of all ages question their ultimate goals and purpose. How and where does one find clear direction for one's life? In exploring that question, Christians must also ask, What is my vocation—what is God calling me to do and be? Jesus provided an example when he declared his calling to be a ministry of compassion to those who live in poverty, in bondage, in oppression, and with disabilities.**

❖ Read aloud the following three ideas. Challenge the students to commit themselves to use these activities as a springboard to spiritual growth.

(1) Locate a program through the church or a nonprofit agency where you can volunteer to feed the hungry, work in a shelter for the homeless, or provide assistance in a hospital, hospice, or nursing home.

(2) Be alert for individuals who need help but who are not being cared for. Do whatever you (either alone or with a group) can to assist these persons or families.

(3) Discern groups of people in your community whose needs are not being met. Write to elected officials, lobby, or take other political action to change public policy.

❖ Sing or read aloud "Cuando El Pobre (When the Poor Ones)."

❖ Say these words from 1 Peter one phrase at a time and ask the class to repeat them: **Prepare your minds for action; discipline yourselves; set all your hope on the grace that Jesus Christ will bring you when he is revealed.**

UNIT 3: JESUS' MINISTRY OF COMPASSION
(GOSPEL OF LUKE)
WHAT IS MY CALLING?

PREVIEWING THE LESSON

Lesson Scripture: Luke 4:16-24, 28-30
Background Scripture: Luke 4:14-30
Key Verse: Luke 4:18

Focus of the Lesson:
People of all ages question their ultimate goals and purpose. How and where does one find clear direction for one's life? In exploring that question, Christians must also ask, What is my vocation—what is God calling me to do and be? Jesus provided an example when he declared his calling to be a ministry of compassion to those who live in poverty, in bondage, in oppression, and with disabilities.

Goals for the Learners:
(1) to investigate Jesus' declaration of his call to ministry.
(2) to relate calls of the learners to Jesus' ministry of compassion.
(3) to help learners discern their corporate call and commit themselves to participate in Jesus' ministry of compassion.

Pronunciation Guides:
Buechner   (beek' ner)

Supplies:
Bibles, newsprint and marker, paper and pencils, hymnals

READING THE SCRIPTURE

NRSV
Luke 4:16-24, 28-30

16 When he came to Nazareth, where he had been brought up, he went to the synagogue on the sabbath day, as was his custom. He stood up to read, 17 and the scroll of the prophet Isaiah was given to him. He unrolled the scroll

NIV
Luke 4:16-24, 28-30

[16]He went to Nazareth, where he had been brought up, and on the Sabbath day he went into the synagogue, as was his custom. And he stood up to read. [17]The scroll of the prophet Isaiah was handed to him. Unrolling it, he found the place where it is written:

and found the place where it was written:

18 "The Spirit of the Lord is upon me,
    because he has anointed me
      to bring good news to the poor.
He has sent me to proclaim release to the
    captives
    and recovery of sight to the blind,
      to let the oppressed go free,
19 to proclaim the year of the Lord's favor."

20 And he rolled up the scroll, gave it back to the attendant, and sat down. The eyes of all in the synagogue were fixed on him. 21 Then he began to say to them, "Today this scripture has been fulfilled in your hearing." 22 All spoke well of him and were amazed at the gracious words that came from his mouth. They said, "Is not this Joseph's son?" 23 He said to them, "Doubtless you will quote to me this proverb, 'Doctor, cure yourself!' And you will say, 'Do here also in your hometown the things that we have heard you did at Capernaum.'" 24 And he said, "Truly I tell you, no prophet is accepted in the prophet's hometown."

28 When they heard this, all in the synagogue were filled with rage. 29 They got up, drove him out of the town, and led him to the brow of the hill on which their town was built, so that they might hurl him off the cliff. 30 But he passed through the midst of them and went on his way.

18 "The Spirit of the Lord is on me,
    because he has anointed me
    to preach good news to the poor.
He has sent me to proclaim freedom for
    the prisoners
    and recovery of sight for the blind,
to release the oppressed,
19 to proclaim the year of the Lord's favor."

20 Then he rolled up the scroll, gave it back to the attendant and sat down. The eyes of everyone in the synagogue were fastened on him, 21 and he began by saying to them, "Today this scripture is fulfilled in your hearing."

22 All spoke well of him and were amazed at the gracious words that came from his lips. "Isn't this Joseph's son?" they asked.

23 Jesus said to them, "Surely you will quote this proverb to me: 'Physician, heal yourself! Do here in your hometown what we have heard that you did in Capernaum.'"

24 "I tell you the truth," he continued, "no prophet is accepted in his hometown."

28 All the people in the synagogue were furious when they heard this. 29 They got up, drove him out of the town, and took him to the brow of the hill on which the town was built, in order to throw him down the cliff. 30 But he walked right through the crowd and went on his way.

UNDERSTANDING THE SCRIPTURE

Luke 4:16. In the Gospel of Luke, 4:16-30 serves as an introduction to who Jesus is and what he does. The passage also forecasts what will happen to Jesus. Nazareth was the home of Joseph and Mary (1:26). There, Jesus "had been brought up" (4:16; see 2:39). Jesus would have been quite familiar with the synagogue and the people who attended it. Likewise, the people would have felt that they were quite famil-

iar with Jesus, since they had watched him grow to adulthood in their small village. According to Jesus' custom, he was in the synagogue on the Sabbath day. The statement, "He stood up to read," indicates that Jesus was to read the Scriptures as part of the synagogue service.

Luke 4:17. At that time, a lectionary for the reading of the books of the law in a three-year cycle was used, but definite evidence does not exist for a lectionary cycle for the reading of the books of the prophets. Jesus was given "the scroll of the prophet Isaiah" from which to read. Jesus may have chosen the specific scripture passage from Isaiah himself, however.

Luke 4:18-19. The verses are quoted in Luke from the Greek version of Isaiah 61:1 and 58:6. The quoted verses prophetically describe Jesus' role and the meaning and nature of his ministry. They state that "the Spirit of the Lord" would guide Jesus (4:18). Further, the word "anointed" indicates Jesus' identity as the Messiah. Moreover, the actions to be undertaken are to lift up the downtrodden and marginalized of society. The Messiah would "bring good news to the poor." Ministry to the poor is a theme of Jesus' ministry as described in Luke (see 6:20; 7:22; 14:13, 21; 16:20, 22; 18:22; 19:8; 21:3). The Messiah would "proclaim release to the captives," those who were oppressed. He would provide "recovery of sight to the blind," which Isaiah 35:5 and 42:6-7 also had identified as being the work of the Messiah. Jesus both symbolically and literally enabled the blind to see (see Luke 7:21-22; 18:35). "The year of the Lord's favor" refers to the year of Jubilee. The year of Jubilee was the year after "seven weeks of years" (Leviticus 25:8)—forty-nine years—when land that had been sold would be returned to the family of original ownership. This action was mandated in order to keep the land within the original families and tribes who had settled it when Israel had entered the promised land. This action militated against accumulation of vast landholdings and the oppression of the poor that went with such accumulation. Furthermore, Israelites who had become poor and had had to hire themselves as "hired or bound laborers" (Leviticus 25:39) to pay their debts would be released that year. The year of Jubilee was a way of starting over and preventing the continual impoverishment of people. Likely Jesus was not proclaiming literally the year of Jubilee.

Rather, as Isaiah 61:1-2 used the image of the year of Jubilee to symbolize the Jews' release from Babylonian captivity in 539 B.C., Jesus was using the release from bondage that the year of Jubilee called for to symbolize his proclamation of the kingdom of God.

Luke 4:20. When Jesus "sat down," he took the position, literally and symbolically, of a teacher explaining the scripture he had just read.

Luke 4:21. Jesus' words of comment came as a thunderbolt out of a cloudless sky. He said, "Today this scripture has been fulfilled in your hearing." Note that the first word he said was "today." He was not speaking of an event in the distant future. What Isaiah had prophesied centuries before was now fulfilled.

Luke 4:22. Jesus' statement brought affirmation from the congregation. They expressed their privilege at hearing such gracious words from Jesus. After all, they had known him all his life and his father Joseph, too.

Luke 4:23. Jesus' ministry in Capernaum likely is part of the summary verses in Luke 4:14-15. The proverb, "Doctor, cure yourself," was familiar in that day. The general meaning seems to be that if the scripture Jesus quoted were truly being fulfilled "today," then Jesus should show some evidences of it in Nazareth as he had done in Capernaum.

Luke 4:24. Jesus reminded his hearers of the impossibility of a prophet's gaining acceptance as a prophet "in the prophet's hometown." Those who knew Jesus best and should have received him most readily actually were the most difficult to convince. The people of the little village of Nazareth thus represented not just themselves but all Israel in their reluctance to accept Jesus.

Luke 4:25-26. The story of Elijah referred to in Luke 4 is recorded in 1 Kings 17:8-24. The point of the reference here is the widow's hometown. She was not from the land of Israel, but from Zarephath in Sidon.

She—this foreigner, this non-Israelite—was the one whom Elijah, God's servant, helped.

Luke 4:27. Next Jesus referred to an incident in the ministry of the prophet Elisha (see 2 Kings 5). Naaman, a leper, was not an Israelite but a Syrian. Yet Elisha enabled Naaman to be healed.

Luke 4:28. What is the "this" in "when they heard this" that so upset the synagogue worshipers? It was Jesus' proclamation of God's help for non-Israelites, for Gentiles, that so enraged them. The villagers would have continued to think Jesus had preached a fine sermon had Jesus not suggested that the message and ministry of the Messiah was to people who were not

Jews. They wanted God's blessings for themselves but for no one else. They had missed or rejected God's desire that the Messiah be "a light to the nations" (Isaiah 42:6; 49:6).

Luke 4:29. Those who praised and affirmed Jesus so highly now sought immediately to kill him for the blasphemy they thought they heard from him.

Luke 4:30. Exactly what a video of this verse would show is not certain. What is certain, however, is that the enraged villagers were unable to murder Jesus. Indeed, they were unable even to stop him. Jesus was going on from there on his mission.

INTERPRETING THE SCRIPTURE

Proclaiming God's Call

A visit to one's hometown after having been away for a while can be at once affirming and disturbing. Both elements are at work in Jesus' visit to Nazareth. Think of how Jesus' fellow worshipers at the synagogue viewed him as he entered his boyhood synagogue on the Sabbath. Likely they saw him as the local boy making good who was home on a visit. Perhaps they also viewed him with a bit of uncertainty. They had heard how he had done unusual things, and they likely wondered how that news squared with their knowledge of him as a growing child and teenager and then as a young adult making his way in his profession (4:14-16; also see Mark 6:3).

A synagogue official assigned Jesus the role of reading the Scriptures. The official handed Jesus the scroll of Isaiah from which to read. The passage Jesus chose was Isaiah 61:1-2 and 58:6. The passages Jesus read proclaimed the anointing of God's prophet with "the Spirit of the Lord." Thus inspired by the Spirit, the prophet announced good news to the people of Judah. The news was

that they had been oppressed in the Babylonian captivity but now were to be released to a life of blessing.

Personalizing God's Call

According to synagogue custom, if a qualified teacher were present, the teacher would be offered opportunity to comment on the Scriptures that had been read. When Jesus "sat down," he assumed the role of such a teacher. The statement, "The eyes of all in the synagogue were fixed on him," suggests that the congregation was waiting to hear what he would say. What they heard next indicated that Jesus had personalized the meaning of the Scriptures he read, applying them to himself.

Without attempting to somehow get inside Jesus' inner life from a distance of 2,000 years, what can we learn from this passage that will help us personalize God's call to us? Notice the elements in Jesus' experience.

First, Jesus said that "the Spirit of the Lord is upon me" and "he has anointed me" (4:18). The inspiration to do a certain task can often encourage us to recognize that it is God's call. Call it what you will—inspiration, sense of God's leadership, inner voice, intuition—such a spiritual experience can help us discern what we should do with our lives, including what we should do next. So one question to ask as we attempt to understand God's call is this: *Do I somehow sense God's leadership and inspiration to move my life in a certain direction or act in a certain manner?* Being able to answer *yes* to this question can empower us to move forward, and it can also encourage us when things don't go as smoothly as we had hoped they would.

This passage also suggests a second question we need to ask ourselves: *Is what I feel I am being called to do in line with God's purpose as seen in the Scriptures?* The first question, the question about sensing God's leadership, is rather subjective. People have been led astray and have done great harm to themselves and others because they felt "God told me to do it." This second question enables us to test our interior sense of God's leadership by something more objective. We should test our inward sense of God's call by the way in which God has spoken and acted through the centuries as seen in the Scriptures.

The passage Jesus quoted reveals much about God's purpose. God wants to bring good news, not bad news, to people. God wants to bring release to those who are held captive and freedom to those who are oppressed. God wants to enable people to see and see clearly again. God wants people to have the opportunity to make a fresh start.

What do such matters mean as we seek to discern our own calling? Surely it means that our calling should be in line with God's purposes. Should we not be giving ourselves to the kind of life that lifts people up rather than to the kind of life that oppresses them or simply bypasses them? To bring the meaning further down toward earth, we must ask ourselves how we can live our lives so that we follow God's purpose not just when we are at church or engaged in church activities. We can make a start by seeing that God's call to us encompasses every aspect of our lives. Search the New Testament and you will find that the idea of being called refers simply to being called to follow Christ and to carry out Christ's mission. Within that call, we are to seek to carry out God's purpose and Christ's mission in our work, our community, and our family, as well as in our church.

Furthermore, all of the activities within each area are to be in accord with God's purpose. Does someone in your workplace need the ministry of a kind word or a helping hand? Are actions in your workplace resulting in mistreatment of people because of their race, gender, or other matters? What about in community groups of which you are a part? Perhaps you or someone in your class holds political office. How do you deal with the kinds of needs to which the Scriptures Jesus read refer? What would God's purpose be in the situations you face? What about the activities of your church? Do you just meet, study the Bible, and hold worship services? Those are good things to do, but shouldn't churches actually be doing something about human needs rather than just talking about them or even praying for them? (See James 2:14-17 if further help is needed with this answer.)

Refusing God's Call

When Jesus said, "Today this scripture has been fulfilled in your hearing" (4:21), the townspeople responded with vocal words of approval. The people in the synagogue looked forward to such a time as the Scriptures Jesus read described. When Jesus went further in explaining the meaning of that time and thus the meaning of his call, the townspeople rejected him violently, however.

We must remember that responding to God's call does not mean that our actions will be roundly approved. Far from it. Does the disapproval of others mean that the action we are pursuing is right? Not necessarily. As we seek to discern God's call, we should pay attention to the responses of trusted friends who are also in touch with God. We might be wrong, and they might be able to help us toward the right path. Does the disapproval of others mean that the action we are pursuing is wrong? Again, not necessarily. At the basic, practical level, people generally find dealing with change to be quite difficult. The first response to every proposed change is generally resistance.

Sometimes it is violent resistance, as Jesus experienced.

Responding to God's call may require us to pay a price. A successful young businessperson felt drawn to become a minister. To respond to this call, the individual had to go back to school fulltime to prepare for ministry and give up a rather high level of income. Was responding to God's call worth it? Each person has to answer this question for himself or herself. How much are we willing to back up our Christian profession of faith with action?

SHARING THE SCRIPTURE

PREPARING TO TEACH

Preparing Our Hearts

This week's devotional reading is found in Matthew 13:54-58. Here we see Matthew's account of Jesus' rejection in his hometown of Nazareth. Compare this version with the one in Luke for today's lesson. How are the two accounts similar? How are they different? How do the people of Nazareth respond to Jesus' teachings? How do you respond?

Pray that you and your students will be open to discerning God's call on your lives so that you might live faithfully.

Preparing Our Minds

Study the background scripture from Luke 4:14-30 and lesson scripture from Luke 4:16-24, 28-30.

Write on newsprint:

the sentence stems to be used under "Relate Calls of the Learners to Jesus' Ministry of Compassion."

information for next week's lesson, found under "Continue the Journey."

Plan the lecture suggested under

"Investigate Jesus' Declaration of His Call to Ministry."

LEADING THE CLASS

(1) Gather to Learn

❖ Welcome the class members and introduce any guests.

❖ Pray that the students will be open to discerning God's call on their lives and acting on that call.

❖ Read aloud this definition of "vocation," excerpted from Frederick Buechner's *Wishful Thinking:* **"It [the word "vocation"] comes from the Latin *vocare*, to call, and means the work a person is called to by God. . . . The kind of work God usually calls you to is the kind of work (a) that you need most to do and (b) that the world most needs to have done. . . . The place God calls you to is the place where your deep gladness and the world's deep hunger meet."**

❖ Invite the students to respond to Buechner's definition. If the class is large, suggest they work in small groups.

❖ Provide a few moments for the students to reflect silently on their vocation and how they are fulfilling it.

❖ Read aloud today's focus statement: **People of all ages question their ultimate goals and purpose. How and where does one find clear direction for one's life? In exploring that question, Christians must also ask, What is my vocation—what is God calling me to do and be? Jesus provided an example when he declared his calling to be a ministry of compassion to those who live in poverty, in bondage, in oppression, and with disabilities.**

*(2) Investigate Jesus' Declaration of
His Call to Ministry*

❖ Ask two volunteers, one to play the part of Jesus and one to be the narrator, to read aloud Luke 4:16-24 and 28-30. Invite the rest of the class to read the words in verse 22, "Is this not Joseph's son?"

❖ Encourage the class to identify the elements of Jesus' call, as found in verses 18 and 19. List these elements on newsprint.

❖ Delve into the scene further by using information from the Understanding the Scripture portion (verses 16, 17 and 18-19, 20, and 21) that will help the learners understand why Jesus read in the synagogue and why he chose two passages from Isaiah. Present this information in a brief lecture.

❖ Invite the students to imagine that someone who grew up in your congregation had returned to announce an amazing call from God. Talk about how church members might respond to this individual. (Perhaps their responses would not be very different from the responses to Jesus in Nazareth.)

*(3) Relate Calls of the Learners to Jesus'
Ministry of Compassion*

❖ Direct the students' attention to the newsprint where you have listed the elements of Jesus' call.

❖ Refer back to last week's session when we looked at ways we could meet human need. Briefly discuss how Jesus' call is to fulfill the needs of people.

❖ Distribute paper and pencils. Encourage the students to complete these sentences that you may read aloud and post on newsprint:
- **As I listen, I believe that Jesus is calling me to. . . .**
- **I believe that God would have me to respond to that call by. . . .**

❖ Set up small group discussions so that the class members can share their calls and how they believe their individual calls relate to Jesus' call to minister compassionately to others.

*(4) Help Learners Discern Their Corporate Call
and Commit Themselves to Participate in Jesus'
Ministry of Compassion*

❖ Discuss this question with the entire group: **What would we need to do as a church if we were to live out Jesus' call for social and economic justice in the kingdom of God?** Brainstorm some actions the church as a body could take to bring liberation to the community. Write these ideas on newsprint. If the class has difficulty, here are some ideas that you can use as discussion starters.
- We could become a Micah 6 congregation. (See information about this program, which is sponsored by the National Council of Churches, on www.micah6.org.)
- We could participate in local ministries that help poor people, such as soup kitchens or shelters.
- We could initiate ministries that work toward peace and justice.

❖ Help the students to focus their attention on one or two of the ideas they have brainstormed. Discuss these questions.
   (1) **What steps would we need to take to turn this idea into a reality?**
   (2) **Which groups or committees within the church do we need to approve our idea and help us to implement it?**

(3) **What would have to happen for God to consider this project a success?**

❖ Conclude this portion of the session by asking the students who are willing to help nurture and implement this project to repeat these words that you will read: **With God's help, Jesus' call will be our call. We will work to bring the social and economic justice of his ministry of compassion to fruition in our time and place. Amen.**

(5) Continue the Journey

❖ Pray that the students will be sensitive to God's call on their lives, especially the call to pursue peace and justice by extending God's compassion to the poor.

❖ Read aloud this preparation for next week's lesson. You may also want to post it on newsprint for the students to copy. **Prepare for next week's session entitled "Hope for Healing" by reading Luke 8:40-56. Mull over this focus as you study the lesson: When people desperately seek healing and wholeness they may simultaneously experience both hope and despair. How can people sustain hope and find healing and wholeness? The close relationship between faith and healing can be found in Jesus' response to the faith of a woman who took the risk of reaching out to touch the fringe of his clothing and in Jesus' challenge to Jairus to have and maintain faith in the crisis of a dying daughter.**

❖ Read aloud the following three ideas. Challenge the students to commit themselves to use these activities as a springboard to spiritual growth.

(1) **What do you hear God calling you to do right now? Are you at a transition point, such as your last child leaving home or retirement, where you are more likely to be open to new opportunities? Pray for ears to listen and a heart to respond to this call.**

(2) **Contemplate Jesus' call, as set forth in Luke 14:18-21. As Christians, we are called to follow Jesus. While no one else can be the Messiah, we can all share in his work of compassion and justice. How is his call reflected in what you understand your call to be?**

(3) **Consider steps that you could take to liberate persons in your own community who are marginalized. Who could you work with to achieve your goal? How will you begin?**

❖ Sing or read aloud "Where He Leads Me."

❖ Say these words from 1 Peter one phrase at a time and ask the class to repeat them: **Prepare your minds for action; discipline yourselves; set all your hope on the grace that Jesus Christ will bring you when he is revealed.**

HOPE FOR HEALING

PREVIEWING THE LESSON

Lesson Scripture: Luke 8:40-56
Background Scripture: Luke 8:40-56
Key Verse: Luke 8:48

Focus of the Lesson:
When people desperately seek healing and wholeness they may simultaneously experience both hope and despair. How can people sustain hope and find healing and wholeness? The close relationship between faith and healing can be found in Jesus' response to the faith of a woman who took the risk of reaching out to touch the fringe of his clothing and in Jesus' challenge to Jairus to have and maintain faith in the crisis of a dying daughter.

Goals for the Learners:
(1) to read the stories of the hemorrhaging woman and of Jairus's daughter.
(2) to identify a situation in which they demonstrated faith.
(3) to give thanks for Jesus' ministry of compassion at work in their lives.

Pronunciation Guide:
Jairus　　　　　　　　(jay i' ruhs)

Supplies:
Bibles, newsprint and marker, paper and pencils, hymnals

READING THE SCRIPTURE

NRSV
Luke 8:40-56

40 Now when Jesus returned, the crowd welcomed him, for they were all waiting for him. 41 Just then there came a man named Jairus, a leader of the synagogue. He fell at Jesus' feet and begged him to come to his house, 42 for he had an only daughter, about twelve years old, who was dying.

NIV
Luke 8:40-56

[40]Now when Jesus returned, a crowd welcomed him, for they were all expecting him. [41]Then a man named Jairus, a ruler of the synagogue, came and fell at Jesus' feet, pleading with him to come to his house [42]because his only daughter, a girl of about twelve, was dying.

As he went, the crowds pressed in on him. 43 Now there was a woman who had been suffering from hemorrhages for twelve years; and though she had spent all she had on physicians, no one could cure her. 44 She came up behind him and touched the fringe of his clothes, and immediately her hemorrhage stopped. 45 Then Jesus asked, "Who touched me?" When all denied it, Peter said, "Master, the crowds surround you and press in on you." 46 But Jesus said, "Someone touched me; for I noticed that power had gone out from me." 47 When the woman saw that she could not remain hidden, she came trembling; and falling down before him, she declared in the presence of all the people why she had touched him, and how she had been immediately healed. **48 He said to her, "Daughter, your faith has made you well; go in peace."**

49 While he was still speaking, someone came from the leader's house to say, "Your daughter is dead; do not trouble the teacher any longer." 50 When Jesus heard this, he replied, "Do not fear. Only believe, and she will be saved." 51 When he came to the house, he did not allow anyone to enter with him, except Peter, John, and James, and the child's father and mother. 52 They were all weeping and wailing for her; but he said, "Do not weep; for she is not dead but sleeping." 53 And they laughed at him, knowing that she was dead. 54 But he took her by the hand and called out, "Child, get up!" 55 Her spirit returned, and she got up at once. Then he directed them to give her something to eat. 56 Her parents were astounded; but he ordered them to tell no one what had happened.

As Jesus was on his way, the crowds almost crushed him. [43]And a woman was there who had been subject to bleeding for twelve years, but no one could heal her. [44]She came up behind him and touched the edge of his cloak, and immediately her bleeding stopped.

[45]"Who touched me?" Jesus asked.

When they all denied it, Peter said, "Master, the people are crowding and pressing against you."

[46]But Jesus said, "Someone touched me; I know that power has gone out from me."

[47]Then the woman, seeing that she could not go unnoticed, came trembling and fell at his feet. In the presence of all the people, she told why she had touched him and how she had been instantly healed. **[48]Then he said to her, "Daughter, your faith has healed you. Go in peace."**

[49]While Jesus was still speaking, someone came from the house of Jairus, the synagogue ruler. "Your daughter is dead," he said. "Don't bother the teacher any more."

[50]Hearing this, Jesus said to Jairus, "Don't be afraid; just believe, and she will be healed."

[51]When he arrived at the house of Jairus, he did not let anyone go in with him except Peter, John and James, and the child's father and mother. [52]Meanwhile, all the people were wailing and mourning for her. "Stop wailing," Jesus said. "She is not dead but asleep."

[53]They laughed at him, knowing that she was dead. [54]But he took her by the hand and said, "My child, get up!" [55]Her spirit returned, and at once she stood up. Then Jesus told them to give her something to eat. [56]Her parents were astonished, but he ordered them not to tell anyone what had happened.

UNDERSTANDING THE SCRIPTURE

Luke 8:40. Luke 8:26-39 supplies the context for the statement, "When Jesus returned." Jesus had been in "the country of the Gerasenes, which is opposite Galilee" (8:26). This area was on the eastern side of the Sea of Galilee, and Jesus had now returned to the western side. The crowd "welcomed him," indicating that they knew of him and his previous ministry. Thus the scene is set for two incidents of ministry, with the story of the healing of the woman with the issue of blood sandwiched between a two-part story of Jesus' raising of Jairus's daughter to life. Each incident involved a "daughter" (8:42, 48). Each involved twelve years—a twelve-year-old girl and a condition of ill health that had lasted twelve years (8:42, 43). Furthermore, each involved a significant act of faith (8:48, 50). Moreover, Jewish ceremonial uncleanness was at stake in each. Having an issue of blood made the woman ritually unclean, and her touching Jesus made him unclean (see Leviticus 15:25-30). Too, touching a dead body also rendered one unclean (Numbers 19:11-19).

Luke 8:41-42. In light of the issue of ritual uncleanness in both incidents in 8:40-56, the identification of the concerned father as the ruler of the synagogue surely carries meaning beyond a simple acknowledgment of his vocation. The incidents display the shortcomings of Jewish ritual in solving human problems. The Jewish synagogue leader's falling "at Jesus' feet" and begging Jesus to come to his house show his desperate plight, and by extension the inability of Jewish ritual to solve the problem. The little girl "was dying," and Jesus was her only hope.

Luke 8:43. In the midst of the incident with the distraught father whose twelve-year-old daughter was dying, there came a "daughter" (8:48) who had been ill for twelve years with a continuous flow of blood. As was noted in the comments on 8:40, in addition to the burden of her physical condition was the stigma of being an outcast from Jewish society because her condition made her ritually unclean. Whereas the synagogue ruler would have been considered to be at or near the top of the religious scale, the woman would have been considered to be close to the bottom. One noteworthy difference between the version of this incident in Mark 5:21-43 and this version in Luke is the de-emphasis in Luke on the failure of the physicians. The best Greek manuscripts reflect this de-emphasis, and they are behind the New International Version's translation of this verse.

Luke 8:44. Desperate to be healed, the woman ignored the prohibitions of her religion and took action. Just by being in the crowd, where she might be touched by someone, she had already taken a risky step. Touching Jesus would be even more risky as she purposely broke the prohibition against touching anyone while she was unclean, since doing so would make the person unclean. She was as unobtrusive toward Jesus as possible, though. She came up behind him and touched only the "fringe" or tassel of Jesus' garment. The "fringe" referred to any one of the four tassels on the outer garment of the day. One tassel was at each corner (see Deuteronomy 22:12; Numbers 15:37-39).

Luke 8:45-46. Jesus sensed that the woman's touching the tassel of his garment was more than a mere jostling by the crowd. "Power" had gone out from him through her touch. Four times these verses refer to touching (8:44, 45, 46, 47). Touching an unclean person or thing brought ritual uncleanness, but touching was also the physical means by which the woman received Jesus' healing power.

Luke 8:47. Realizing she could not conceal what she had done, the woman came forward. In a posture that suggests worship, she confessed who she was, what she had done, and what had happened as a result of her touching Jesus' garment.

Luke 8:48. Jesus blessed the woman and affirmed her great faith as the avenue of her healing. The word translated "has made you well" is the word for salvation and could also be translated *has saved you.*

Luke 8:49. Attention again turns to Jairus and his daughter. The girl was no longer at the point of death. She had died. The implication of the message to Jairus is that all hope was gone.

Luke 8:50. Jesus called for faith so that the daughter "will be saved." A form of the same word was used in 8:48 for "has made you well."

Luke 8:51-53. Jesus took with him only Peter, John, and James of his disciples plus the child's mother and father when he went to the room where the young girl lay dead. In the midst of the weeping and wailing, Jesus uttered the shocking words, *stop crying,* "for she is not dead but sleeping." Are we meant to understand that she was in fact dead? In other places in the New Testament, the word translated "sleeping" refers to the sleep of death (see Ephesians 5:14;

1 Thessalonians 5:10). Furthermore, the crowd was certain she was dead. Indeed, they were so certain she was dead that they turned quickly from mourning to laughing at Jesus' statement that she was "sleeping." With Jesus there, the child's "sleeping" the sleep of death was not irrevocable.

Luke 8:54-55. Jesus touched the child, now ritually unclean because her body was dead. Taking her by the hand, Jesus said, "Child, get up!" She did. Why did Jesus call for her to be given something to eat? Perhaps the answer is as simple as that Jesus knew she was hungry. Perhaps the answer is that giving her something to eat would prove she had been restored to life, as when the risen Jesus asked for a piece of fish to eat (see Luke 24:41-43).

Luke 8:56. Could it be that the astounded parents were almost as astounded at Jesus' command that they not tell anyone what had happened? How could they keep quiet when Jesus had restored their beloved daughter to life? In the Gospel of Mark, the command not to tell anyone about Jesus' miraculous acts relates to Jesus' desire not to be known as merely a wonder-working Messiah but as the Messiah who is the Suffering Servant.

INTERPRETING THE SCRIPTURE

Recognizing the Reality of Illness and Death

Denial of reality is not required for being a Christian. Being a Christian does not mean hiding one's head in the sand, keeping a stiff upper lip, looking for the silver lining, or any of a dozen metaphors we might set forth that, when summarized, simply mean denying the reality of the rough parts of life. The fact is that for the Christian as for everyone else, illness is real, and death—of our loved ones and of ourselves—is also real. We live in a real world where people's

bodies really get sick and where people really die.

We have much in common with the synagogue ruler who came to Jesus in desperation because his daughter was dying. Indeed, we are all part of the lowest common denominator of life; we are people who must face death. We have much in common, too, with the woman who came seeking to be healed. If we haven't sought healing yet for ourselves, the chances are overwhelming that at some point we will, if we live long enough. As John Donne discovered, we should not have to ask "for whom the bell tolls." It tolls for us. If it hasn't, it will. Listen.

However people may question Jesus and his identity, they cannot dispute his dealing close-up with the most troubling difficulties of life—sickness and death. Jesus did not deny that they were real, and he did not keep them at arm's length. Indeed, there was something about Jesus that made people want to bring the worst they were experiencing to him for help.

The first step to healing and help is not denial. Denial, in fact, is a barrier to healing and help. Rather, the journey toward healing and help begins with recognition of the reality of illness and death.

Seeking Relief from Illness and Death

We hardly have to demonstrate that we are concerned about getting relief from illness and even from death. After all, that's what we have hospitals for. That's why people are concerned about health insurance. That's why when churches have prayer times, most of the prayer requests have to do with physical illness and with concern for people who are grieving the loss of loved ones.

The jaded words of an advertisement put it this way: "When you've got your health, you've got it all." The opposite of those words suggests that when you've lost your health, you've lost it all. While those words are not necessarily true, only people who are physically well or who are not grieving over the loss of a loved one would dare to suggest that health and life are matters of little importance. People tend to appreciate their health most when they face its loss.

The father of the young girl was desperate that she not die. He was a religious leader, but he found himself no match for death, which was tightening its grip on his daughter. So he called on Jesus, this wandering prophet who was not part of the religious establishment. Indeed, this "leader of the synagogue . . . fell at Jesus' feet and begged him to come to his house" (8:41).

Is there any debate about whether he should have done that? Even though the family of a person who is dying may tell themselves that "it is for the best," there yet exists, even in the most extreme circumstances, the hope that somehow the process can be reversed and their loved one restored to full health. Something in the depth of our being calls us to seek help for people we care about.

The woman, too, was desperate. Only someone who has been fighting a chronic, debilitating illness for many years can come close to appreciating how desperate she was. This concern for her health dominated her life. In addition, the stigma attached to her condition made her have to suffer largely alone. Her situation seemed so hopeless.

The woman sought help from Jesus, though. She felt so unworthy and so much of an outcast that she did not dare to ask for help. She merely moved quietly behind Jesus and touched the tassel of his garment.

Have you faced circumstances that help you identify with the woman and her desperate search for healing? Like her, perhaps you have sought help from physicians. Perhaps unlike her you feel you are receiving help from medical treatment. Indeed, perhaps you hope that the next medical breakthrough will provide help for your condition. Even with your reliance on medical treatment, though, you know that at bottom all healing is from God, and thus you seek God's help.

More than one sophisticated congregation is placing greater emphasis today on offering healing and help to their members and to the community at large. For these congregations, healing services are not merely for what some may consider the fringes of the Christian movement. Services are held in which people and their families bring their concerns for physical healing to God and petition God for help. The very act of engaging in such worship brings healing, regardless of whether physical healing actually takes place.

Being Restored from Illness and Death

In verse 48, Jesus acknowledged what already had occurred in verse 44. The woman was healed. Jesus said that her faith had made her well. The woman's faith had put her literally and figuratively in touch with Jesus. We would do well to take this statement as Jesus' word of affirmation for her faith and not as a word of condemnation of our lack of faith when healing does not come for others and for us. The passage is teaching the need for turning to God for help.

We simply do not know why some are healed physically when they in faith seek God's help and why some are not. It is as cruel and misguided to blame lack of faith for a person's not being healed physically as it was for Job's friends to blame his physical illness and other problems on his sin.

Similar statements can be made about death. While Jairus was still imploring Jesus to help him, word came that Jairus's daughter had died. Jesus did not take that word as final, though. He called for faith on the part of the synagogue leader and set out with him and three of his disciples to break up the funeral plans. Entering the room with them, along with the child's mother and father, Jesus restored her to life.

The event calls us to rejoice. We naturally may wonder, of course, why our loved ones are not restored to life when we pray and seek Jesus' help every bit as fervently as had the synagogue leader. The answer to "why" eludes us.

Everyone dies eventually. As we face this fact, we can be sure of Jesus' concern for us and of his help for us when we grieve. We can also have the certainty of faith as we face God's provision for us beyond death. As Paul wrote, "The last enemy to be destroyed is death" (1 Corinthians 15:26), but death *will* be destroyed. Jesus was flesh and blood like us, "so that through death he might destroy the one who has the power of death, that is, the devil" (Hebrews 2:14). Let us rejoice!

SHARING THE SCRIPTURE

PREPARING TO TEACH

Preparing Our Hearts

This week's devotional reading is found in Matthew 9:18-26. Here we have Matthew's account of Jesus healing Jairus's daughter and the woman who had been hemorrhaging for twelve years. What do these stories say to you about Jesus' ministry of compassion? What do they say about the nature of life in the kingdom of God? Consider how the religious leaders of the day might have thought about Jesus, who allowed a woman who was unclean due to a bloody discharge to touch his garment and who raised a dead girl to life. Jesus knew that both of these actions made him ritually unclean, yet he chose to do them anyway.

Pray that you and your students will be open to the healing touch of Jesus and willing to share your experience with others.

Preparing Our Minds

Study the background and lesson scripture, both of which are found in Luke 8:40-56.

Write on newsprint:

information for next week's lesson, found under "Continue the Journey."

Plan a lecture, as suggested, to conclude the section entitled "Read the Stories of the Hemorrhaging Woman and of Jairus's Daughter."

LEADING THE CLASS

(1) Gather to Learn

❖ Welcome the class members and introduce any guests.

❖ Pray that the participants will live in hope even when threatened by serious illness or impending death.

❖ Invite students to create a prayer list of persons in need of healing in body, mind, spirit, or emotions. To protect the privacy of those in need of healing, the students should just mention an individual's first name without stating any ailment. List these names on newsprint. If any of the students want to add their own names to the list, they may choose to share additional information.

❖ Pray for each one who is listed. If possible, go around in a circle and have each student lift up the next name on the list until all have been prayed for. Close by offering the Lord's Prayer in unison.

❖ Read aloud today's focus statement: **When people desperately seek healing and wholeness they may simultaneously experience both hope and despair. How can people sustain hope and find healing and wholeness? The close relationship between faith and healing can be found in Jesus' response to the faith of a woman who took the risk of reaching out to touch the fringe of his clothing and in Jesus' challenge to Jairus to have and maintain faith in the crisis of a dying daughter.**

(2) Read the Stories of the Hemorrhaging Woman and of Jairus's Daughter

❖ Choose two volunteers, one to read Luke 8:40-42a and 49-56, and the other to read Luke 8:42b-48.

❖ Assign half of the class to review the story of Jairus's daughter and the other half to review the story of the woman with the hemorrhage.

■ Tell the students to read silently their assigned stories. As they read, they are to be aware of words or ideas that "speak" to them, insights concerning Jesus and his ministry, and signs of faith. They are also to note any questions their assigned story raises. Distribute paper and pencils so that the learners can record their thoughts.

■ Ask the students to work in groups of three or four to comment on what the stories have "said" to them. Depending on the size of the class and the room layout, these groups can include persons who studied the same story or both stories.

■ End the group activity by inviting volunteers to share with the entire class some ideas their group discerned.

❖ Conclude the Bible study by sharing a lecture you have prepared, based on information from the Understanding the Scripture portion, that helps the students understand how the characters in the stories, including Jesus, acted on faith rather than follow religious rules.

(3) Identify Situation in Which the Learners Demonstrated Faith

❖ Note that in today's stories faith is a key ingredient in the healing of both Jairus's daughter and the woman.

❖ Share these two stories with the students as a means of encouraging them to tell their own stories of how faith in God brought them through a difficult situation. Although the stories are true, the names have been changed.

■ Roger and Mary are dedicated Christians who are always doing something to serve God and neighbor. Although they were good role models and parents for their children, one son became an alcoholic. They faced many challenges as a family because of Michael's problem, but they never gave up. For nineteen years they prayed until finally Michael recognized his problem and sought help. A decade later, he is a sober family man and contributor to society.

- Alyson was a married young adult with a preschool age daughter when she was diagnosed with brain cancer. Although the situation was extremely serious, she had faith in God's willingness and ability to heal her. Alyson's family and her church surrounded her with love and prayer. The life-threatening cancer was overcome and Alyson is living an active life with her husband and daughter, who is now a teenager.

❖ Invite the students to tell their own stories of faith.

(4) Give Thanks for Jesus' Ministry of Compassion at Work in the Learners' Lives

❖ Lead a short guided-imagery activity that will help the students identify and give thanks for God's healing in their lives.

- **Close your eyes, relax your body, and recall a time when you felt desperately in need of help. Perhaps you or a loved one was ill, or experiencing a crisis, or grieving a loss. Try to call to mind the feelings you were experiencing.** (Pause)
- **Listen as God speaks to you about the faith you exhibited during this crisis.** (Pause)
- **Speak silently to God words of praise and thanksgiving for the comfort and healing you experienced during that difficult time.** (Pause)

❖ Conclude the guided-imagery activity by offering thanks for healings that have already occurred and praying that all who are in need of healing will trust God to care for them.

(5) Continue the Journey

❖ Read aloud this preparation for next week's lesson. You may also want to post it on newsprint for the students to copy. **Prepare for next week's session entitled "Stretching Our Love" by reading Luke 10:25-37. Focus on this idea as you read: One does not have to look far to find instances of human tragedy that could have been prevented if someone had cared enough to help or intervene. Is there any way to counter this trend toward isolation—if not alienation—from one another? Jesus taught that the way of true life is through love of God and neighbor. Through the story of the good Samaritan, Jesus taught that the neighbor is the one who, ignoring all the racial and ethnic barriers, shows mercy to another.**

❖ Read aloud the following three ideas. Challenge the students to commit themselves to use these activities as a springboard to spiritual growth.

(1) **Offer daily prayers for those who are sick.**

(2) **Visit someone who is ill and offer words of hope and encouragement as appropriate in the situation.**

(3) **Write an account of a healing that you or someone you know has experienced. Place this account in your Bible where you can refer to it in the future when you or a loved one are sick.**

❖ Sing or read aloud "Heal Us, Emmanuel, Hear Our Prayer."

❖ Say these words from 1 Peter one phrase at a time and ask the class to repeat them: **Prepare your minds for action; discipline yourselves; set all your hope on the grace that Jesus Christ will bring you when he is revealed.**

STRETCHING OUR LOVE

READING THE SCRIPTURE

NRSV
Luke 10:25-37

25 Just then a lawyer stood up to test Jesus. "Teacher," he said, "what must I do to inherit eternal life?" 26 He said to him, "What is written in the law? What do you read there?" **27 He answered, "You shall love the Lord your God with all your heart, and with all your soul, and with all your strength, and with all your mind; and your neighbor as yourself."** 28 And he said to him, "You have given the right answer; do this, and you will live."

NIV
Luke 10:25-37

25 On one occasion an expert in the law stood up to test Jesus. "Teacher," he asked, "what must I do to inherit eternal life?"

26 "What is written in the Law?" he replied. "How do you read it?"

27 He answered: "'Love the Lord your God with all your heart and with all your soul and with all your strength and with all your mind'; and, 'Love your neighbor as yourself.'"

29 But wanting to justify himself, he asked Jesus, "And who is my neighbor?" 30 Jesus replied, "A man was going down from Jerusalem to Jericho, and fell into the hands of robbers, who stripped him, beat him, and went away, leaving him half dead. 31 Now by chance a priest was going down that road; and when he saw him, he passed by on the other side. 32 So likewise a Levite, when he came to the place and saw him, passed by on the other side. 33 But a Samaritan while traveling came near him; and when he saw him, he was moved with pity. 34 He went to him and bandaged his wounds, having poured oil and wine on them. Then he put him on his own animal, brought him to an inn, and took care of him. 35 The next day he took out two denarii, gave them to the innkeeper, and said, 'Take care of him; and when I come back, I will repay you whatever more you spend.' 36 Which of these three, do you think, was a neighbor to the man who fell into the hands of the robbers?" 37 He said, "The one who showed him mercy." Jesus said to him, "Go and do likewise."

²⁸"You have answered correctly," Jesus replied. "Do this and you will live."

²⁹But he wanted to justify himself, so he asked Jesus, "And who is my neighbor?"

³⁰In reply Jesus said: "A man was going down from Jerusalem to Jericho, when he fell into the hands of robbers. They stripped him of his clothes, beat him and went away, leaving him half dead. ³¹A priest happened to be going down the same road, and when he saw the man, he passed by on the other side. ³²So too, a Levite, when he came to the place and saw him, passed by on the other side. ³³But a Samaritan, as he traveled, came where the man was; and when he saw him, he took pity on him. ³⁴He went to him and bandaged his wounds, pouring on oil and wine. Then he put the man on his own donkey, took him to an inn and took care of him. ³⁵The next day he took out two silver coins and gave them to the innkeeper. 'Look after him,' he said, 'and when I return, I will reimburse you for any extra expense you may have.'

³⁶"Which of these three do you think was a neighbor to the man who fell into the hands of robbers?"

³⁷The expert in the law replied, "The one who had mercy on him."

Jesus told him, "Go and do likewise."

UNDERSTANDING THE SCRIPTURE

Luke 10:25. The question in this verse from the expert in the Jewish law and the response of Jesus in verses 26-28 is somewhat parallel to the accounts in Mark 12:28-34 and Matthew 22:34-40. The expert in the law acknowledged Jesus as an outstanding Jewish teacher. He then asked, "What must I do to inherit eternal life?" The rabbis often sought to arrive at succinct summaries of the law in such a manner. In the similar passages in Matthew and Mark, the question is about the greatest or first commandment. Likely the lawyer's question should be understood to be another way of asking what is greatest or most important, as in Matthew and Mark. The purpose of the question was not to acquire information but to "test" Jesus so as to entrap him.

Luke 10:26. Jesus' response took the expert in the Jewish law back to the law itself. Jesus' questions in this verse thus turned the lawyer's original question back on himself, requiring him to take a stand rather than simply to put Jesus to the test.

Luke 10:27. The lawyer responded with a portion of the *shema* from Deuteronomy 6:5.

The four areas mentioned overlap somewhat and are meant to encompass all of life. Thus one is to love God with all of one's life—heart (inner self); soul (life itself, similar to heart), strength (full resources), and mind (thoughts and intentions). The reference to the *shema* would have been expected, since devout Jews would repeat it twice daily. The unusual part of the lawyer's response is the last part—"and your neighbor as yourself"—which is from Leviticus 19:18. The combination of Deuteronomy 6:5 with Leviticus 19:18 has not been found elsewhere in the literature of the time prior to this passage and its parallels.

Luke 10:28. Jesus accepted the truth of the lawyer's answer. The word translated "right" literally can mean "straight." It is the "ortho" portion of the word "orthodontist," referring to someone who straightens one's teeth. The lawyer's question in verse 25 and Jesus' response in verse 28 turn on the word "do." The Greek word translated "do" in verses 25 and 28 appears twice in verse 37, where once it is translated "showed." Not just knowing the right answer but actually doing it is the source of life. This train of thought is in harmony with other New Testament passages that call for action and not just talk (see, for example, Matthew 7:24; 1 John 4:20-21; James 2:8-26).

Luke 10:29. Since the lawyer had failed in his attempt to trap Jesus, he sought to "justify himself" for approaching Jesus in such a manner. Rather than be trapped himself into actually loving both God and neighbor, he sought to continue the conversation on merely an intellectual level by debating who one's neighbor was. The incident thus fits into the overall purpose of the Gospel of Luke: to show God's acceptance of non-Jews and all sorts of outcasts who were rejected by Judaism. This verse begins a section that has no parallel in the other Gospels. The story of the good Samaritan appears only in Luke.

Luke 10:30. To "go down" from Jerusalem to Jericho was so both geographically and culturally. Jericho was in the Jordan Valley, and so the traveler went "down" to it. Furthermore, since the Temple was in Jerusalem, one spoke of going "up" to Jerusalem regardless of whether one went up or down in elevation to reach it. The serious plight of the man who was left naked, beaten, alone, and "half dead" is obvious. The situation sets up the question of what will happen next.

Luke 10:31-32. The two people who passed by the hurt man without helping him were the most respected people in Judaism. Both the Levite and the priest failed the test set up by the lawyer himself in verse 27. Both failed to practice love of neighbor as themselves. Both "passed by on the other side."

Luke 10:33-35. The identity of the one who truly fulfilled the teaching of verse 27 would have been shocking to the lawyer and indeed to any knowledgeable Jew. In fact, they would have considered that the Samaritan failed the first part of the teaching. According to Judaism, the Samaritans did not love God properly. Jews considered the Samaritans' way of worshiping God to be heretical. Samaritans were half-Jews racially, having come about from the intermarriage of Jews and non-Jews after the conquest of the Northern Kingdom (see 2 Kings 17:24). The thought that a despised Samaritan would be the hero of Jesus' parable would have been both offensive and unbelievable to Jews. Even a despised Samaritan was capable of "pity," though (10:33). Indeed, the Samaritan not only "was moved with pity" (10:33) but he also acted to provide help to the half-dead man. Every action was an action of care. The Samaritan's caring efforts were even lavish and unlimited. He promised the innkeeper he would "repay you whatever more you spend" (10:35).

Luke 10:36. Jesus' question to the lawyer altered the focus of the lawyer's question to Jesus in verse 25. The lawyer had sought to determine who the neighbor was, implying that one's actions of love could be limited to certain people. Jesus questioned who the neighbor was. Was the neighbor the priest, the Levite, or the Samaritan? The irony is that Israel considered itself to be composed of neighbors (Deuteronomy 15:2), but the true neighbor in Jesus' parable was the despised Samaritan. Only the Samaritan actually demonstrated love rather than just talking about it or professing it.

Luke 10:37. The lawyer found himself having to admit that "the one who showed him mercy" was the neighbor. It may or may not be significant, but he avoided saying the word "Samaritan." Obviously the Samaritan was the one who was the neighbor, for the Samaritan was the one who had shown love. As noted earlier, the word translated "showed" is from the same Greek word translated "do" in verses 25, 28, and then in Jesus' final statement in verse 37. Again Jesus emphasized action, saying, "Go and do likewise." Truly loving God and loving one's neighbor requires action in loving service.

INTERPRETING THE SCRIPTURE

What Is the Greatest?

The lawyer asked Jesus, "What must I do to inherit eternal life?" (10:25). This question is sometimes interpreted in a way that emphasizes "what must I do" so as to suggest that the lawyer wanted to bargain his way to salvation. Of course, salvation is by grace through faith, not through our own "doing" (see Ephesians 2:8). A contrast between grace and our "doing" is not the emphasis of this passage in Luke, however. Jesus himself affirmed "doing" (see 10:28, 37). Indeed, in verse 37, Jesus pointedly said, "Go and do likewise." The emphasis of the passage is thus on actually *doing* love. In fact, the emphasis is on *doing* love in a lavish manner to whoever is in need rather than dribbling it out in thimble-sized portions to a select few.

The lawyer was asking, in effect, what the greatest thing in life is. The rabbis often discussed this question by seeking to arrive at a succinct summary of the law. Jesus approved the lawyer's answer that whole-hearted love for God and love of one's neighbor as oneself were most important.

What is the greatest thing in life? Jesus said it is love. Loving God and loving one's neighbor are what life is all about. We must be careful in making such a statement, however. As did the expert in the law, we may seek to define the answer in such a way as to limit our need to do much of anything about it.

Whom Must I Love?

The expert in the Jewish law had intended to trap Jesus. Instead, Jesus put the lawyer on the spot by asking him what he himself read in the law. When the lawyer responded and Jesus affirmed that love for God and neighbor were what was most important, the lawyer sought to untangle himself with another question. If I ought to love my neighbor as myself, then, he asked in verse 29, "Who is my neighbor?"

Do you suppose the lawyer thought loving God "with all your heart, and with all your soul, and with all your strength, and with all your mind" (10:27) was easy? The reality is that love for God can be faked. Just say the right words and avoid the wrong ones; and go to the right places and avoid the wrong ones. The lawyer knew, though, that the hard part, the part that can't be faked, was love for neighbor. So for us and for the expert in the law, it seems important that we be sure to limit this business about loving our neighbor.

Thus the lawyer asked, in effect, *Whom must I love?* Such a question revealed that he was mired deeply in unloving attitudes, however much he knew about religion. He thought that surely there must be a limit to loving one's neighbor. Jesus told a parable to lead him to see otherwise.

Four main characters appear in the parable. The first on the scene is described simply as "a man . . . going down from Jerusalem to Jericho" (10:30). We know nothing more about him. He is really any person of any race, any gender, any group, any occupation, any religion, any social status, or any condition of morality or immorality. Robbers attacked him, "stripped him, beat him, and went away, leaving him half dead" (10:30).

Next came the priest. Since he was "going down" from Jerusalem, he likely was coming from the Temple, having served there in the services of worship. Evidently he had been unaffected by the glories of worship at the Temple, though, for he deliberately "passed by" the half-dead person.

Then came a Levite, another official in the Jewish religious system. He evidently "likewise" was returning from Temple service. He, too, failed to grasp that worship was intended to be more than ceremony but was to affect how one treated other people.

Why did they pass the hurting person by? We can only imagine, but perhaps one excuse could have been that they were too busy. After all, they had been serving in the Temple for a week. Naturally they had things to catch up on at home.

Or perhaps they were afraid. After all, the robbers could still be nearby, ready to attack another traveler.

Or perhaps they were concerned about religious ritual. If the man were dead, touching his body would make them ritually unclean. After all, wouldn't it be a fine fix to spend all week in glorious worship at the Temple and come home ritually unclean? Bummer!

Or perhaps they felt they had discharged their full duty to God by going to the Temple. After all, they'd been to "church." Wasn't that enough?

Or perhaps they simply passed by from force of habit. They'd never helped a hurting person like that, and they couldn't think of a reason to start. They'd never done it that way before!

Or, more likely the basic excuse of the priest and the Levite was connected with the question, "Who is my neighbor?" Was the half-dead person a Jew, *one of our own*? The rigid religionists of Jesus' day had defined neighbor as being only someone like us, a fellow Jew. So, if a person doesn't look like us, act like us, believe like us, or is not kin to us, then we don't have to love that person.

The final traveler was a Samaritan. His religion, his culture, and his race would have marked him as unacceptable to the priest and the Levite as well as to the lawyer who was listening to Jesus' story. The Samaritan did not pass by but instead took extraordinary actions to care for the helpless, hurting person.

Do You Do Love?

When Jesus asked which person was truly a neighbor, only people intent on rationalizing their behavior could miss the answer. The key to the Samaritan's act of extravagant kindness is that he used no excuses. He did not think of all the reasons he couldn't and shouldn't help. He just helped. He did not even know who the victim was, but he gave aid to him.

The lawyer said the right answer, that love is the greatest. The Samaritan *did* the right answer. He acted to show unlimited love.

The lawyer had been concerned with who his neighbor was and thus how he might limit his love. Jesus is concerned with whether we ourselves are neighbors, people who love and help hurting people simply because they need help.

Jesus' command to the lawyer brings into sharp focus what this passage is all about. A literal translation of what Jesus said is, *Go and you yourself do likewise*. The call is for personal action. We are not merely to talk about what a great thing love is or to debate who should be loved. We simply are commanded to *do* love, showing love to all in need of love.

An official of an organization that is known for helping many people was asked the secret of the group's success. She replied that they simply saw a need, prayed about it, and went out and did something. What about the church? Perhaps more often we follow this pattern: We sometimes see a need, and we sometimes pray about it. Next we generally discuss it, maybe even talking about how wonderful it would be if someone would do something about it, and that is the end of that. Jesus' parable, however, reminds us that we are called to do more, to act in love toward everyone, for they are all our neighbors.

SHARING THE SCRIPTURE

PREPARING TO TEACH

Preparing Our Hearts

This week's devotional reading is found in Matthew 22:34-40. Note that verse 37 comes from Deuteronomy 6:5, while verse 39 is taken from Leviticus 19:18. Jesus joins these two crucial statements together to form the greatest commandments. Suppose you had been one of the religious leaders listening to Jesus. How would you have reacted to his summary of the law? Write your thoughts in your spiritual journal.

Pray that you and your students will express your love for God by loving you neighbor.

Preparing Our Minds

Study the background and lesson scripture, both of which are found in Luke 10:25-37.

Write on newsprint:

information for next week's lesson, found under "Continue the Journey."

LEADING THE CLASS

(1) Gather to Learn

❖ Welcome the class members and introduce any guests.

❖ Pray that the students will be open to the message Jesus has for them today and alert for opportunities to care for others.

❖ Retell the story of Catherine "Kitty" Genovese, whose death some of your class members may remember. **Kitty Genovese was killed on March 13, 1964 when returning home to her New York apartment in the wee hours of the morning from her job. Soon after she got out of her car, a man with a knife began to chase her. A woman of slight build, Kitty was unable to outrun her assailant. He stabbed her repeated, holding her to the ground. Responding to Kitty's cries, a neighbor shouted to the attacker from the seventh floor of the apartment building to let Kitty alone. The assailant fled, only to return a few minutes later. As Kitty screamed that she was dying, tenants in her building again tried to see what was happening. The assailant had again fled and returned, this time sexually assaulting her, robbing her of $49, stabbing her again, and finally killing her. She was his third murder victim. During these repeated attacks, no one ventured from the safety of the building, or even called the police. There were no good Samaritans on that fateful night to help Kitty Genovese.**

❖ Encourage the students to ponder this

thought question silently: **Why do many people choose not to help others in need, even when a small gesture, such as calling the police, could make a big difference?**

❖ Read aloud today's focus statement: **One does not have to look far to find instances of human tragedy that could have been prevented if someone had cared enough to help or intervene. Is there any way to counter this trend toward isolation—if not alienation—from one another? Jesus taught that the way of true life is through love of God and neighbor. Through the story of the good Samaritan, Jesus taught that the neighbor is the one who, ignoring all the racial and ethnic barriers, shows mercy to another.**

(2) Examine the Story of the Good Samaritan

❖ Ask someone to read the story of the good Samaritan from Luke 10:25-37. As the story is being read, five students are to pantomime the actions of the priest, Levite, Samaritan, injured man, and innkeeper.

❖ Discuss these questions.

(1) **What reasons might the Levite and priest have given for refusing to stop and offer assistance?** (Use information from both Understanding the Scripture and Interpreting the Scripture to fill in reasons.)

(2) **With which character do you find it most easy to identify? Why?**

(3) **Which character's actions do you find most difficult to understand? Why?**

❖ Encourage the class to imagine what the Samaritan might have been thinking as he assisted the injured man, and what the injured man might have thought as he was being helped. Write these ideas on newsprint.

(3) Explore Learners' Feelings and Experiences Related to Being a Good Samaritan

❖ Distribute paper and pencils. Ask the students to work either independently or

with a partner to rewrite the parable in a contemporary setting. Who comes along to help, and who passes by? What motivates each character's behavior? Here are some scenarios if the class members need some ideas to spark their imaginations.

(1) **A person is lying in an alley in a neighborhood where there is a lot of drug trafficking.**

(2) **An automobile accident has occurred and someone is injured.**

(3) **A person who is clearly disoriented is wandering along a street.**

❖ Encourage volunteers to read or retell their parable to the class. Some students may want to respond to these parables.

❖ Discuss the following questions.

(1) **What would you do if you were to see an injured person by the side of the road?**

(2) **What obstacles exist in your culture and/or community in regard to helping others, especially strangers, as Jesus teaches us to do?**

❖ Invite the students to tell about how good Samaritans have assisted them.

(4) Consider Ways to Act on Jesus' Teaching About Being a Good Neighbor

❖ Invite the students to list contemporary neighbors that many people avoid or refuse to help. Discuss why these neighbors are ostracized and how we can re-envision them as part of the family of God.

❖ Make sure everyone has paper and a pencil. Ask the students to recall a time when they had an opportunity to be a loving neighbor but did not act. Suggest that they write a different scenario in which they do act as a good Samaritan.

❖ Encourage the students to discuss ways in which they can implement Jesus' teachings. Remind them that these ways do not have to be heroic. Had someone called the police, Kitty Genovese might not have been murdered.

❖ Read aloud the following words of

commitment: **I commit myself to respond to those in need by doing whatever I can do to help.** Then ask class members who are willing to commit themselves to action to repeat the sentence as you read it again slowly. Recognize that some class members may not be ready to make such a commitment.

(5) Continue the Journey

❖ Pray that the participants will stretch their love so as to move beyond fears, stereotypes, and prejudices and willingly do good for all who are in need.

❖ Read aloud this preparation for next week's lesson. You may also want to post it on newsprint for the students to copy. **Prepare for next week's session entitled "Building Community" by reading Luke 14:7-24, especially verses 7-11 and 15-24. As you study this lesson, consider these ideas: Our natural tendency is to put ourselves first, but this makes it difficult to form and function as any kind of essential community. How can we recognize the importance of self-esteem while avoiding self-centeredness, and how can we affirm individual worth while maintaining com-** munity? Jesus taught that we need to see things from a new perspective: We need to view ourselves with humility, but graciously accept the recognition and esteem offered by others; not only do we need to graciously receive others into community but we also need gratefully to accept the invitation to become part of the community.

❖ Read aloud the following three ideas. Challenge the students to commit themselves to use these activities as a springboard to spiritual growth.

(1) **Commit yourself to doing a loving act for a stranger.**

(2) **Make a list of people whom you have difficulty accepting as neighbors. Pray over this list daily, asking God to help you see these people as Jesus sees them.**

(3) **Be alert for acts of random kindness that people do for you this week. Thank God for their neighborliness.**

❖ Sing or read aloud "Jesu, Jesu."

❖ Say these words from 1 Peter one phrase at a time and ask the class to repeat them: **Prepare your minds for action; discipline yourselves; set all your hope on the grace that Jesus Christ will bring you when he is revealed.**

BUILDING COMMUNITY

PREVIEWING THE LESSON

Lesson Scripture: Luke 14:7-11, 15-24
Background Scripture: Luke 14:7-24
Key Verse: Luke 14:23

Focus of the Lesson:

Our natural tendency is to put ourselves first, but this makes it difficult to form and function as any kind of essential community. How can we recognize the importance of self-esteem while avoiding self-centeredness, and how can we affirm individual worth while maintaining community? Jesus taught that we need to see things from a new perspective: We need to view ourselves with humility, but graciously accept the recognition and esteem offered by others; not only do we need to graciously receive others into community but we also need gratefully to accept the invitation to become part of the community.

Goals for the Learners:

(1) to examine Jesus' teachings about humility and hospitality.
(2) to identify connections between humility and hospitality in their lives.
(3) to act with humility and hospitality toward others.

Supplies:

Bibles, newsprint and marker, paper and pencils, hymnals

READING THE SCRIPTURE

NRSV
Luke 14:7-11, 15-24

7 When he noticed how the guests chose the places of honor, he told them a parable. 8 "When you are invited by someone to a wedding banquet, do not sit down at the place of honor, in case someone more distinguished than you has been invited by your host; 9 and the host who invited both of you may come and say to you, 'Give this person

NIV
Luke 14:7-11, 15-24

7When he noticed how the guests picked the places of honor at the table, he told them this parable: 8"When someone invites you to a wedding feast, do not take the place of honor, for a person more distinguished than you may have been invited. 9If so, the host who invited both of you will come and say to you, 'Give this man your seat.' Then, humiliated, your place,' and then in disgrace you would start to take the lowest place. 10 But when you are invited, go and sit down at the lowest place, so that when your host comes, he may say to you, 'Friend, move up higher'; then you will be honored in the presence of all who sit at the table with you. 11 For all who exalt themselves will be humbled, and those who humble themselves will be exalted."

15 One of the dinner guests, on hearing this, said to him, "Blessed is anyone who will eat bread in the kingdom of God!" 16 Then Jesus said to him, "Someone gave a great dinner and invited many. 17 At the time for the dinner he sent his slave to say to those who had been invited, 'Come; for everything is ready now.' 18 But they all alike began to make excuses. The first said to him, 'I have bought a piece of land, and I must go out and see it; please accept my regrets.' 19 Another said, 'I have bought five yoke of oxen, and I am going to try them out; please accept my regrets.' 20 Another said, 'I have just been married, and therefore I cannot come.' 21 So the slave returned and reported this to his master. Then the owner of the house became angry and said to his slave, 'Go out at once into the streets and lanes of the town and bring in the poor, the crippled, the blind, and the lame.' 22 And the slave said, 'sir, what you ordered has been done, and there is still room.' **23 Then the master said to the slave, 'Go out into the roads and lanes, and compel people to come in, so that my house may be filled.** 24 For I tell you, none of those who were invited will taste my dinner.'"

you will have to take the least important place. [10]But when you are invited, take the lowest place, so that when your host comes, he will say to you, 'Friend, move up to a better place.' Then you will be honored in the presence of all your fellow guests. [11]For everyone who exalts himself will be humbled, and he who humbles himself will be exalted."

[12]Then Jesus said to his host, "When you give a luncheon or dinner, do not invite your friends, your brothers or relatives, or your rich neighbors; if you do, they may invite you back and so you will be repaid. [13]But when you give a banquet, invite the poor, the crippled, the lame, the blind, [14]and you will be blessed. Although they cannot repay you, you will be repaid at the resurrection of the righteous."

[15]When one of those at the table with him heard this, he said to Jesus, "Blessed is the man who will eat at the feast in the kingdom of God."

[16]Jesus replied: "A certain man was preparing a great banquet and invited many guests. [17]At the time of the banquet he sent his servant to tell those who had been invited, 'Come, for everything is now ready.'

[18]"But they all alike began to make excuses. The first said, 'I have just bought a field, and I must go and see it. Please excuse me.'

[19]"Another said, 'I have just bought five yoke of oxen, and I'm on my way to try them out. Please excuse me.'

[20]"Still another said, 'I just got married, so I can't come.'

[21]"The servant came back and reported this to his master. Then the owner of the house became angry and ordered his servant, 'Go out quickly into the streets and alleys of the town and bring in the poor, the crippled, the blind and the lame.'

[22]" 'Sir,' the servant said, 'what you ordered has been done, but there is still room.'

[23]**"Then the master told his servant, 'Go out to the roads and country lanes and make them come in, so that my house will be full.** [24]I tell you, not one of those men who were invited will get a taste of my banquet.' "

UNDERSTANDING THE SCRIPTURE

Luke 14:7. The Bible student can learn much about the unique thrust of the Gospel of Luke by focusing on the occasions when Jesus ate with people and on the people with whom he ate. In the culture of that day as in ours, eating with someone signifies at least a measure of acceptance and refusing to eat with them signifies rejection. The Gospel of Luke shows Jesus sitting down and eating with all sorts of people, including people who would not eat with one another. For example, in Luke 5:29-32 we find Jesus at a dinner party in the home of the converted tax collector Levi. Also at the dinner party was "a large crowd of tax collectors." The Pharisees were shocked and dismayed that Jesus would eat with such people. On the other hand, the setting for Luke 14:7 is a meal in the home of "a leader of the Pharisees" (14:1). Jesus took this occasion to teach an important lesson about genuine fellowship around the table. The specific thrust of the lesson arose as Jesus "noticed how the guests chose the places of honor" (14:7). Such jockeying for the preeminent position was not limited to the dinner table (see Luke 11:43; 20:46). Jesus told a parable that recognized and provided correction to such prideful behavior.

Luke 14:8-9. In the parable, Jesus instructed his hearers to avoid seeking the place of honor. If "someone more distinguished than you" showed up, the guest who had taken a place of honor would be embarrassed and shamed when the host asked that guest to take a lower place.

Luke 14:10. Jesus gave practical instruction on the wisdom of taking "the lowest place." If one did so and were then invited to a higher place, all would see and recognize that one was receiving an honor. Notice that the invitation to "move up higher" is preceded by the title "Friend." A part of the honor of the invitation was recognition for

being a friend of the host, who presumably was a person of status and power.

Luke 14:11. The parable is not about game playing, though, to receive recognition ultimately. The focus of the parable is on a call to recognize the importance of humility as a characteristic of life in God's kingdom.

Luke 14:12-13. Jesus now turned to offer instruction to the host as he had offered guidance to the guests. Jesus' instruction recognized the tendency to invite to dinner only people who could repay the favor. Such behavior was only a social game based on status. Thus, the host should instead invite the people who lived on the margins of life and would be unable to repay—"the poor, the crippled, the lame, and the blind." All such people were among those to whom the Messiah would bring specific help (see Luke 4:18; 7:22). Mentioning them is a signal, emphasized even more in verse 14, that Jesus' instructions are more than a first-century primer on table etiquette. The instructions are for life in the kingdom of God. People who truly belong to the Kingdom abandon the life of grasping for recognition and favor. Instead they seek ways to minister to people in need, without concern for repayment. Furthermore, the relation between the host and the people in need who are invited is not an over-under relationship. The host participates in the banquet, thus showing acceptance.

Luke 14:14. The blessings of living as citizens of the kingdom of God come later, "at the resurrection of the righteous."

Luke 14:15. The remark of one of the dinner guests serves as a recognition of the blessing of participating in the banquet of the kingdom of God.

Luke 14:16. The parable that begins in this verse focuses on the importance of choosing to participate in the life of the Kingdom and living accordingly. The setting is "a great dinner" to which many were invited.

Luke 14:17. The invitations to the dinner were extended in advance. Then, when everything was ready, the host sent for the guests to come. (See Esther 5:8 and 6:14 for a possible timetable.) Esther issued the invitation on one day for a banquet on the next. Then, when everything was ready, she sent her servants to bring the guests to the banquet.

Luke 14:18-20. Rather than being eager to participate in the banquet, guest after guest offered an excuse. Such behavior would have been insulting to the host in that day as well as in ours. None of the excuses required immediate attention. Seeing the land could have waited, and trying out the oxen could have waited. In the case of the newlyweds, Deuteronomy 24:5 permitted the groom to stay home with his bride for a year rather than go into battle. Staying home with one's new wife did not preclude attendance at a dinner party, however. All of the excuses for refusing the invitation were obviously absurd. No one would buy land or oxen unseen, and no one would think that a recent wedding would prevent one from attending an important banquet.

Luke 14:21. The owner was angry at the refusals, but he was determined that there would be a banquet. Note that the invitation is to the same people mentioned in verse 13.

Luke 14:22-23. The second invitation shows the generous nature of the owner of the house. He was not interested in limiting those in attendance at the banquet but in offering his hospitality as widely as possible. That the servant was instructed to "compel people to come in" may not indicate their unwillingness to come but rather their unbelief that they actually were being included so graciously in such a marvelous banquet.

Luke 14:23-24. The parable serves as a foreboding reminder in the Gospel of Luke that those who think they deserve a place in the Kingdom—likely referring to the Jews, especially the Pharisees—do not have an automatic claim on such a place. Still, the host insisted that the banquet would go on. Thus, those who would not expect to be invited—likely referring in general to people on the margins of Jewish society plus also the Gentiles, as Luke's first readers would have concluded—would be invited to come and enjoy the party.

INTERPRETING THE SCRIPTURE

Up the Down Escalator

Me! Me! Me! The media used to refer to a certain generation as the "me generation." Perhaps certain tendencies do indeed manifest themselves more prominently in one generation than in another. Tom Brokaw's book, *The Greatest Generation*, provides a convincing account of the greatness of the generation who fought and won World War II. That generation's focus was not on "me," but on the need to pull together to achieve a common goal. The focus on "me," though, seems rather widespread among human beings. Some people, especially certain personality types, may manifest it more obviously, but the desire is present in everyone.

Don't we often find it as hard to rejoice with those who rejoice as to weep with those who weep? We may wonder why this cause for rejoicing, this recognition or honor, couldn't have happened to us instead. When someone else is recognized or honored, don't we often wonder at least fleetingly why it didn't happen to us instead or when our turn will come? Or are we so proud of our humility that we can't or won't admit that we have such thoughts?

The parable Jesus told about jockeying for a position of status at a social occasion speaks as pointedly to our day as to the people gathered in the home of a Pharisee in the first century A.D. Many people—including Christians—see their status as being wrapped up in acquiring recognition for themselves. Such behavior manifests itself even in church. God help the pastor who does not bow and scrape properly before a certain pillar of the church, for example, or fails to check signals with an influential family before considering a change of some sort in how things are done. Could it be that we Christians are as out of touch with Jesus' message in this parable as was the Pharisee who first heard it? We may not openly seek the first table at the banquet or the most important chair at the committee meeting and certainly not the front seat of the church, but we may well want everyone to know where we are sitting and that we and our ideas must be reckoned with.

Proverbs 16:18 points out, "Pride goes before destruction, and a haughty spirit before a fall." It is not easy for anyone in our culture, Christians included, to put such a teaching into practice when all the emphasis is on selling ourselves and being sure that the right people notice us and approve of us. How can we, in fact, put this teaching in practice when it runs so counter to our culture? The rest of this parable helps us with this question.

True Upward Mobility

A part of the teaching of this parable is that true humility eventually will be rewarded. What bothers us most about that statement likely is the word "eventually." If we promote ourselves and receive the trappings of recognition and status, we feel that our efforts at self-promotion have been successful. Frankly, there are many indications that the rewards of such self-promotion are real and immediate. In many cases, such folks are indeed the ones who get elected,

get promoted, get recognized, and get rich. What we are afraid of is that if we do not promote ourselves, no one else will and we thus will not "eventually" be rewarded. We are troubled that no one may notice that we have graciously and humbly hung back from claiming the higher position that we really want and deserve and that it is now their job to recognize how successful and worthy of honor we really are. Imagine going to your alumni reunion and trying to explain—subtly, of course—why you're actually more successful than you appear to be and you're just waiting for someone to recognize that reality!

Such thoughts are far from what Jesus is teaching in this parable. He is not teaching a new way to get recognition and status. Hang back and you will eventually be recognized is not the teaching of this parable.

The rest of the parable's teaching clarifies the first part. The emphasis of the parable in the context of this chapter in Luke's Gospel is that true humility characterizes life in God's kingdom and we must leave any thought of exaltation to God.

Perhaps you have been privileged to know someone who seemed to think nothing of recognition, only of service, perhaps even service according to the model of Jesus. Perhaps they received recognition somewhere along the line; perhaps they did not. The message of the parable is that in the life of the Kingdom, such folks will be exalted, and that is absolutely the only life and the only exaltation that matters.

Inexcusable Behavior

Jesus told a second parable in the context of the dinner party. The message of this second parable is related to that of the first in that its setting is also a banquet, but the second parable takes a different tack. This second parable focuses on guests who refused the invitation of the host and on how the host responded to their refusal. The parable teaches the serious consequences of refusing the invitation to life in the Kingdom and the graciousness of God in extending his invitation to all, even the outcasts of society and the Gentiles.

We can see in this parable thus an underlying theme of humility versus self-seeking arrogance, a theme that is prominent in the first parable. To seek to live pridefully on one's own, refusing the invitation to the "great dinner" (14:16), as if the Kingdom does not matter, has serious consequences. All of the refusals were mere flimsy excuses. Those who made these excuses showed that their priorities were greatly misplaced. They and what they were doing was so much more important than life in the Kingdom.

The result was that "the owner of the house became angry" at their refusal (14:21). After he had invited "the poor, the crippled, the blind, and the lame" (14:21) and still others and they had filled his house, he vowed that "none of those who were invited will taste my dinner" (14:24). (See the comments on the nature of parables in general in lesson 7 for July 17 under Understanding the Scripture on Matthew 13:3.)

An Open Invitation

The refusal of the invitations to the dinner did not end the party, though. Even though some refused to come, the party went on. Other guests were invited, and they responded.

The long-ago message of this parable as Jesus told it and as the first readers of Luke's Gospel read it focused on the refusal of the Jews to receive the gospel and on the extension of the gospel to the world at large, the world of the Gentiles. Perhaps for us in addition to this message is the message that we ourselves must beware of presuming arrogantly on our relationship to God.

God loves those beyond the church, including the outcasts of society and people of all other races and nations, every bit as much as God loves us, and God yearns for those in the church to love and accept them in the same way. Now as then, it is not social status or presumption about our "place" in life but life in the Kingdom, offered us through God's grace, that matters.

SHARING THE SCRIPTURE

PREPARING TO TEACH

Preparing Our Hearts

This week's devotional reading is found in 1 Peter 5:3-10. Peter writes about how believers, especially those who have leadership positions, are to exercise humility. Ponder the following questions and write your responses in your spiritual journal. How do you define "humility"? What comes to your mind when you hear the word "humility"? Do you associate the word "humility" with the word "leadership"? How do you see humility practiced among the lay and clergy leaders of your

congregation? How, as a leader of a Sunday school class, do you practice humility? Are there changes you think that God would like you and the other leaders to make?

Pray that you and your students will practice the humble hospitality Jesus taught about and modeled for us.

Preparing Our Minds

Study the background from Luke 14:7-24, and the lesson scripture found in Luke 14:7-11 and 15-24.

Write on newsprint:

information for next week's lesson, found under "Continue the Journey."

Plan an optional lecture to conclude the section entitled "Examine Jesus' Teachings About Humility and Hospitality."

LEADING THE CLASS

(1) Gather to Learn

❖ Welcome the class members and introduce any guests.

❖ Pray that the students will be open to the word that God has for them today concerning humility and hospitality.

❖ Encourage the adults to think of times when they have visited other churches. Ask them to discuss their experiences by answering these questions.

(1) **How did the congregation make them feel welcomed?**

(2) **Were all of the church members treated equally?**

(3) **If the students sensed that some members were treated better than others, how did that make them feel about the church they were visiting? Did they ever return?**

❖ Read aloud today's focus statement: **Our natural tendency is to put ourselves first, but this makes it difficult to form and function as any kind of essential community. How can we recognize the importance of self-esteem while avoiding self-centeredness, and how can we affirm individual worth while maintaining community? Jesus taught that we need to see things from a new perspective: We need to view ourselves with humility, but graciously accept the recognition and esteem offered by others; not only do we need to graciously receive others into community but we also need gratefully to accept the invitation to become part of the community.**

(2) Examine Jesus' Teachings About Humility and Hospitality

❖ Set the stage for today's Bible study by reading or retelling the information for Luke 14:7 in Understanding the Scripture. Be sure to include the idea that Jesus was an invited guest at a Sabbath meal at the home of "a leader of the Pharisees" (14:1).

❖ Choose a volunteer to read Luke 14:7-11 and discuss the following questions.

(1) **What role did social status apparently play in determining who ate together and where they were to sit at the table in Jesus' day?**

(2) **What does Jesus teach about eating together?**

(3) **How do you think the man who was told to "take the lowest place" might have felt?**

(4) **How do you think the "friend" who was asked to move to a more prestigious seat might have felt?**

(5) **How are Jesus' teachings relevant to the church today?**

❖ Choose volunteers to read these parts: narrator (14:15a, 21a), guest at the Pharisee's house (14:15b), Jesus (14:16-17a), first guest (14:18), second guest (14:19), third guest (14:20), owner of the house (14:21b, 23-24), and slave (14:17b, 22).

■ Divide the class into groups of at least three people. In each group at least one person is be the owner; one or more, the invited guests who made excuses; and one or more, the poor, crippled, blind, lame, and all who were invited to come. Encourage the students to "stay in character" as they discuss the motivations for their actions and how they felt about attending or not attending the banquet.

■ Discuss these questions with the class, or answer them yourself and present them as a lecture.

(1) **What does this parable say to you about hospitality?**

(2) **What does this parable teach about humility?**

(3) **What does this parable suggest about the kingdom of God?**

(4) **What does this parable imply about the nature of God?**

(3) Identify Connections Between Humility and Hospitality in Learners' Lives

❖ Note that Jesus teaches that there is a close connection between humility and hospitality. Yet, in our culture, "humility" is almost a negative word, and hospitality is often equated with ostentatious events at high priced restaurants and country clubs.

❖ Distribute paper and pencils. Invite the learners to write their personal definitions of the words "humility" and "hospitality."

❖ Encourage the learners to talk with a partner or small group to compare their ideas.

❖ Conclude this portion of the session by providing quiet time for the students to think about how they do—or do not—live out the definitions of "humility" and "hospitality" they have written.

(4) Act with Humility and Hospitality Toward Others

❖ Ask the students to consider how your congregation welcomes people. List on newsprint everything that is done to offer hospitality to visitors. (Be sure to consider ideas such as adequate signs to help newcomers know where they are to go, easy-to-read room labels, someone in the parking lot to help visitors, current sign board, and so on.)

❖ Discuss ways that the congregation may inadvertently discourage visitors from returning. Encourage the class to suggest solutions to problems they identify.

❖ Provide an opportunity for the students to commit themselves, as individuals and as a class, to show hospitality toward others, especially those who come as visitors to your church.

(5) Continue the Journey

❖ Pray that the students will humbly offer hospitality to all, just as Jesus did.

❖ Read aloud this preparation for next week's lesson. You may also want to post it on newsprint for the students to copy. **Prepare for next week's session entitled "Encountering the Spirit" by reading the background scripture from Acts 2:1-42 and lesson scripture from Acts 2:1-8, 38-42. Focus your attention on these ideas: People search for good news that will transform their lives. How does this life-transforming message come to people today? The story of Pentecost shows that God's Spirit helps people hear the message of the risen Christ.**

❖ Read aloud the following three ideas. Challenge the students to commit themselves to use these activities as a springboard to spiritual growth.

(1) **Make a commitment to welcome newcomers who attend your church and/or class. Invite neighbors, especially new residents, to join you for worship and study.**

(2) **Ponder how your church and/or Sunday school class operates. Is there a hierarchy? If so, what might you do to help people realize that all persons are to be welcomed with respect and equality?**

(3) **Plan to hold a dinner at your home. Include on your guest list persons who may not often be invited out.**

❖ Sing or read aloud "Come, Sinners, to the Gospel Feast."

❖ Say these words from 1 Peter one phrase at a time and ask the class to repeat them: **Prepare your minds for action; discipline yourselves; set all your hope on the grace that Jesus Christ will bring you when he is revealed.**

PREPARING A MEANINGFUL SUNDAY SCHOOL LESSON

Teaching is fun, exciting, challenging, sometimes frustrating, and always an extremely important ministry. At some time, perhaps a month ago or thirty years ago, your pastor or members of the congregation discerned in you the gift of teaching and invited you to lead an adult Sunday school class. Whether you are a seasoned veteran or a novice, God has chosen you to help others delve into the Scriptures and learn who God is and who God would have them become.

So, how do you do this? You have already made a wise decision by selecting a resource that will guide you. Highly respected scholars and pastors write the Understanding the Scripture and Interpreting the Scripture portion of each session, and an experienced educator creates the Sharing the Scripture section of *The New International Lesson Annual*. This resource is based on the work of the Committee on the Uniform Series (CUS) of the National Council of Churches of Christ, an ecumenical group of Christian educators, pastors, and editors who create the framework around which each lesson is developed. This framework includes what you see in each session as the unit heading, lesson title, "Focus of the Lesson" and "Goals for the Learners." It also includes the specific background and lesson scripture passages, as well as the key verse. Our lesson writers shape each session around matrices developed by CUS that link the learner's life experience and faith issues to the biblical passage. Teaching strategies are used to help you, as the teacher, enable the students to explore the biblical passage and relate it to their own lives.

In *The New International Lesson Annual* you have, in essence, all that you need to teach each week's lesson. But, as those of you who have been teaching for years know, a great lesson seems effortless but requires preparation, study, and adaptation to the needs of your class. As you read the Sharing the Scripture portion you will note numerous activities. You have to decide which ones you will use, based on the time you have available, the facilities in which you meet, and the "personality" and "style" of the class. Let me give you an example of what I mean by "personality" and "style." My own adult Sunday school class of men and women, who are mostly retirees including several well into their eighties, loves to discuss everything together. As a group, we represent a wide diversity of opinions and theological understandings, so everyone has something valuable to contribute to the discussion. I encourage this energetic class of "shakers and movers" to share their insights and discern how we can act on them. These brainstorming sessions often result in new mission and outreach projects or other ministries within the church. My class thrives on activities that will challenge them to think about what God wants them to be and do, and then take action so as to be more closely conformed to the image of Christ. What kinds of activities does your class need?

Choosing activities for the class and gathering supplies for those activities are only part of your preparation. You need to immerse yourself in the scripture passage for the week so as to be thoroughly conversant with it. This is important, obviously, if you rely heavily on the lecture method. This scripture immersion is probably even more important if you lead discussions because you have to be able to ask and answer questions, often extemporaneously, rather than work from a script. Here are seven steps you can follow to delve deeply into the Scriptures to be fully prepared to lead others.

Step 1: Read the entire background scripture. When pressed for time, it is tempting just to read the lesson scripture. The problem is that if you skip the background scripture you may miss crucial elements of the context of the story or event you are studying. If the passage is unfamiliar, read it several times to grasp all the points. If the passage is very familiar, read with "fresh eyes" so as to glean new insights. In either case, it is helpful to read the text from more than one Bible translation, noting how the story is enriched by the shades of meaning in the different word choices and sentence structures of each translation.

Step 2: Discover what this scripture means to you. Ask the Holy Spirit to guide you as you read so that you may discern God's word for you. You may want to ask yourself, "What did I hear, see, taste, touch, or smell?" in order to "walk around" with the biblical characters and experience the story with them. Think about what this passage says to you about God, about humanity, and about God's relationship with humanity. Perhaps you will try to rewrite the passage in your own words. Maybe the text will remind you of a hymn that you can sing, or prompt you to draw a picture that illustrates your understanding of it. The point here is to listen to what God is saying to you through this passage before you turn to the "experts."

Step 3: Check Bible reference books. You may find a word or concept that is unfamiliar to you. For example, what does Paul mean when he contrasts being "in the flesh" with being "in the Spirit"? Read the Understanding the Scripture portion of the session. Also check a Bible handbook or dictionary. The article near the end of this volume of *The New International Lesson Annual* entitled "Suggested Reference Books" will point you toward different types of Bible study references and the names of specific books of each type.

Step 4: Discern what the passage may have meant to its original audience. This is perhaps the most difficult step; but as your knowledge of the Bible increases, your ability to envision the original audience will grow as well. It is important to remember that many of the stories of the Old Testament were told around campfires for generations before they were ever written down. Even then, the stories were shaped and edited over many more years. What that means for us is that we are usually looking at the original audience not only through our twenty-first–century eyes, but also through the eyes of the many people who rewrote or retold the story across the centuries.

If you read the Prologue to Luke's Gospel (1:1-4), you can see an example of how this retelling works in the New Testament. We know that Jesus, about whom Luke was writing, was ministering around A.D. 30–33. Many of the eyewitnesses gave oral reports of Jesus' activities (1:2). Likely these reports dated from about A.D. 30–60. Verse 1 gives us a hint that some "orderly" written reports were "set down," perhaps by the "servants of the word" referred to in verse 2. We know, for example, that Paul's first letter to the Thessalonians, reputedly the oldest portion of the New Testament, was written about A.D. 50. Although the precise date is unknown, many scholars agree that Luke wrote his Gospel between A.D. 80 and 85. Luke clearly tells us that his account is based on prior sources "that were handed on to us" (1:2).

In addition to keeping the layers of storytellers in mind, we also need to remember that the original audience would have looked at the "facts" differently than we do. In our era, we want proof of authenticity. We prefer measurable, verifiable facts rather than metaphors and stories. Bible people, however, lived in a pre-scientific age. What to us may seem like contradictions that need reconciling were to them simply different traditions. The story of Noah, which we are studying in the fall, gives us a good example. In Genesis 6:19, God commanded Noah to bring two of every kind of animal, male and female, into the ark. In Genesis 7:2-3, however, God's command is to bring seven pairs of clean animals and one pair of unclean animals. The two versions cannot be harmonized but need to be understood as coming from two different traditions, both of which were considered worthy of preservation. As teachers, we need to appreciate, and help our students appreciate, the variety of rich traditions found in the Bible.

As we consider the original audience, we also need to be aware that the author/editor would have shaped the eyewitness accounts and reports to a particular audience. If we compare the birth narratives in Matthew and Luke, for example, we can discern that Matthew wanted his Jewish readers to see Jesus as the prophet foretold in Deuteronomy 18:15, who was to be raised up after Moses. According to Matthew, for example, Jesus—and in the background, Moses—were both endangered because two evil kings who feared for their power decreed that young boys should be killed. In contrast, Luke is writing for Gentiles and therefore depicts Jesus as a child of humble beginnings who comes for everyone. No mention is made in Luke of Herod or Magi or a flight into Egypt. Conversely, Matthew does not record Mary's *Magnificat* (Luke 1:46-55), which speaks of how God will turn the current world order on its head so that poor, lowly, and hungry will be lifted up. Neither of these accounts can be confirmed as "right" or "wrong" as we understand the concept of facts. Rather, each one helps its respective audience experience how God has drawn near to them in the person of Jesus Christ.

One other point we need to be aware of is that the Old Testament was written for particular people in particular circumstances. From these Scriptures we Christians gain great understandings about the Jewish Jesus, who intimately knew and followed what we call the Old Testament, but we have to be careful about reading passages through our Christian lens without considering what they might have meant for their original Jewish readers. If we think of Jeremiah 31:31-34 in light of its original audience held captive in Babylon, we see that the "new covenant" in which the law will be engraved on people's hearts is also found in the writings of another prophet of the Exile, Ezekiel (see 11:19-20; 18:31; 36:26). While we recognize that "new covenant" has profound meaning for Christians, we cannot overlook or underestimate the meaning it had for God's people in the time the words were written.

Step 5: Consider what the passage meant—and continues to mean—for the church. To continue with our previous example, the "new covenant" is intimately linked with Christian belief and experience. Jesus said, "This cup that is poured out for you is the new covenant in my blood" (Luke 22:20). Paul echoes these words in 1 Corinthians 11:25. In 2 Corinthians 3:6, Paul further writes that God "has made us competent to be ministers of a new covenant, not of letter but of spirit." Thus, for the church, Jeremiah's concept of "new covenant" is clearly linked to Jesus' Last Supper and death, and by extension to us, especially as we partake of Holy Communion. We ponder not only the fact that the "new covenant" is in the blood of Jesus, but also that we have been made ministers of this new covenant. What might that mean for how the church worships and ministers today?

Step 6: Discover how this passage can transform your own life. Let's be clear: although well-grounded information is necessary for understanding the Bible, knowledge is not the ultimate goal. Knowledge helps us only as we allow the Holy Spirit to shape and transform us into the people that God intends us to be. Knowledge, without changes in behavior and attitude that allow us to be more closely conformed to the image of Christ, is essentially useless.

Transformational reading of the scriptures does not focus on the author, audience, literary genre, situation in which a passage was written, or other knowledge-based pursuits. Instead, it is a devotional reading that empowers us to open our hearts and minds to what God is saying to us now, at this time in our lives, at this point in our faith journey. One method for doing this kind of reading is *lectio divina*. This method is suggested for classroom reading in the session for October 10, but was originally designed for personal study. Numerous resources exist to help you master this ancient art, but here are the basics.

- Offer a centering prayer so that you may focus on God and become silent inside.
- Read the passage slowly and listen for a word or phrase that grabs your attention. Concentrate on that word or phrase.
- Repeat the word or phrase, memorizing it if possible, and allowing God to speak to you through it. This is a prayer, in the sense of a conversation with God.
- End the time as you quietly enjoy being in the divine presence.

Step 7: Think about how the class members can relate to this scripture. This step assumes that you know your students and are aware of the joys and challenges of their lives. When you prepare to teach the story of Sarah and Abraham's journey, for example, think of class members whose life situation requires them to take a leap of faith and make a move to an unknown place or situation. Perhaps the Quinton family must move because of a new job. Possibly Mr. and Mrs. Phillips have come to terms with the need to leave their home of forty years and move into a retirement community. Or, as you study the book of Ruth, mentally look around the room. Who are the widows? Who is caring for them? Who are the adult children in the class who are caring for elderly parents? Whatever the story, imagine how various class members will hear and understand the Bible story, based on how their own life experience intersects with the sacred text.

As you think about making the story immediately accessible in the lives of your adult learners, consider any stumbling blocks that the story may set before them. Some barriers will be easy to handle: make a note that you have to explain a certain concept that may be unfamiliar. Other barriers, however, will require clear, compassionate thinking and response. For example, Paul's admonition in Ephesians 5 for wives to be subject to their husbands will create tension in the heart of a woman in your class whose husband has been abusing her. She may wonder if the Bible is telling her to stay and submit to his punishment, even though she has become convinced that her safety and that of her children depend on her leaving this abusive situation. If we take Paul's teaching at face value, the answer is yes, she should stay. But if we consider the nature of a loving God who wants the best for all of us, then obviously God neither requires nor wants anyone to stay in a perilous situation. Think in advance about how you will talk about Paul's teaching in light of domestic violence—even if you are not aware of any students who are abused or the abusers. Such abuse is often hidden.

In closing, remember that as you teach you are acting "as servants of Christ and stewards of God's mysteries" (1 Corinthians 4:1). You "set the table" by selecting activities that will provide a framework in which your class can learn. You study the lesson and allow yourself to be transformed by it. But you are not the host at this feast. You need not know all the answers. This is God's banquet, and the food is already prepared. Jesus invites all to his table. The Holy Spirit leads people to participate. As God's steward-teacher, all you have to do is serve the "meal."

SUGGESTED REFERENCE BOOKS

Are you looking for some reference books that would help you as you prepare your lessons? Do you want some ideas about where to find visual resources to enhance your sessions? If so, consider these suggestions. You may want to talk with your church librarian to see if these references are already on the shelves or could be purchased for the church. Perhaps your pastor has copies of these books that you could borrow. Public libraries are another good place to locate these references. You may want to purchase these books for your personal library, or ask for them as gifts. People know that I love to receive Cokesbury gift certificates, which I use to add books to my collection.

Study Bibles: A study Bible usually includes footnotes, maps, an abridged concordance, articles, and introductions to each book of the Bible. Study Bibles are available in different translations. Carefully examine a study Bible to see if it has the features you want.

The New Interpreter's Study Bible: New Revised Standard Version with the Apocrypha. This Bible, released in 2003, is intended for serious students and teachers of the Bible. Filled with helpful information provided by outstanding scholars, the footnotes are very thorough and yet easy to understand. You may choose to own this Bible in book form or on a CD-ROM.

The New Oxford Annotated Bible: New Revised Standard Version. This Bible is also excellent, though many of the footnotes are not as detailed as those in *The New Interpreter's Study Bible.* For many years, it has been the standard Bible used in numerous theological seminaries.

The NIV Study Bible: 10th Anniversary Edition. This Bible provides introductions and outlines for every Bible book, as well as extensive notes. It includes, maps, charts, diagrams, illustrations, and timelines.

Bible Commentaries: A commentary gives detailed analysis of each passage of the Bible.

The New Interpreter's Bible. This series, available on CD-ROM or as a collection of twelve books, sets the standard for biblical commentary in the twenty-first century. Every church should have a least one copy of this series. Individual books may be purchased from the series, or you may choose to purchase the whole set.

Interpretation: A Bible Commentary for Teaching and Preaching. The books of this set are available individually. Each book contains well-written, in-depth commentary by a well-respected biblical scholar.

Abingdon Old Testament Commentaries. Purchase books of the Bible as you need them in this series. Each volume contains an introduction that addresses key issues; information on the literary genre; the context in which the book was written, theological and ethical significance of the work; analysis of the book; an annotated bibliography; and a brief subject index.

Abingdon New Testament Commentaries. Similar to the Abingdon Old Testament Commentaries, these books provide basic information on the New Testament texts and their meanings.

Bible Concordances: A concordance lists words used in the Bible so that you can locate particular passages in which they are found. Many study Bibles contain abridged concordances. If you prefer a complete listing, *Strong's Concordance* is especially well known. You might also wish to consider software such as Parson's QuickVerse®, which makes finding words very simple. You can even get a QuickVerse® edition for your PDA (personal digital assistant). QuickVerse® has numerous features in addition to its concordance.

Bible Dictionaries. A Bible dictionary provides an alphabetical listing of words, including names, that you find in the Bible. Most of the dictionaries include photographs, line drawings, and maps.

HarperCollins Bible Dictionary: Revised Edition. This popular dictionary, edited by Paul J. Achtemeier, provides concise, easy-to-read information for each entry. It includes a useful pronunciation guide.

Bible Companions. A Bible companion discusses people, places, events, books, religious concepts. Although these items are listed in alphabetical order as in a Bible dictionary, the companion usually offers a broader scope of information.

The Oxford Companion to the Bible. This excellent resource includes over 700 entries written by 250 outstanding scholars. The book is geared to the general lay reader and students of the Bible. You can quickly find very helpful information here.

Teaching Aids. Maps, timelines, charts, videos, and other visual resources can enrich any lesson. You may already have a set of classroom maps, but also consider providing resources that individuals can use.

Bible Student's Map Book. This book contains twelve maps and a timeline. Every student in the class could own one of these very economically priced resources.

Revised Bible Teacher Kit. This invaluable teaching resource includes background articles, reproducible charts, a chronology of the Bible, a glossary, and maps. Many of the pages may be photocopied. This kit also includes a *Bible Lands Video* that for your students can bring Palestine and places that Paul visited to life.

INDEX OF BACKGROUND SCRIPTURES, 2004–2005

EVALUATION OF *THE NEW INTERNATIONAL LESSON ANNUAL*

As you can see from changes in this volume, your comments are extremely important in shaping future editions of *The New International Lesson Annual*. Kindly take a few moments to complete this evaluation and return it to:

Dr. Nan Duerling
Abingdon Press
The United Methodist Publishing House
P.O. Box 801
Nashville, TN 37202

1. I use *The New International Lesson Annual* because:

2. Please check the feature(s) you find most helpful and then write a few words or phrases to tell us why you find it useful.

_____ Previewing the Lesson

_____ Reading the Scripture

_____ Understanding the Scripture

_____ Interpreting the Scripture

_____ Sharing the Scripture

Preparing to Teach

___ Preparing Our Hearts

___ Preparing Our Minds

Leading the Class

___ Gather to Learn

___ Activities based on three goals for the learners

___ Continue the Journey

3. I would like to see the following changes and/or new features in *The New International Lesson Annual:*

4. As I prepare for the Sunday session, I often consult the following references in addition to *The New International Lesson Annual:*

5. Internet Access (Please circle your choice.)
I do/do not have access to the Internet as I prepare the session.

More than half of the class members do/do not have access to the Internet for the purpose of Bible study.

6. I ___would/___ would not be interested in having a CD to accompany *The New International Lesson Annual.* I would like to see the following kinds of data on the CD.

I ___would/___would not be willing to pay more for the CD packaged with the book.

7. In-depth Bible Studies
(a) Have you participated in an in-depth Bible course, such as *Disciple Bible Study?* Circle Yes or No

(b) _____ out of a total number of _____ students in the class have participated in an in-depth Bible course, such as *Disciple Bible Study.*

Thank you very much for taking your valuable time to complete this evaluation!